Warfare in History

THE ART OF WARFARE
IN WESTERN EUROPE
DURING THE MIDDLE AGES

FROM THE EIGHTH CENTURY TO 1340

T0313595

Warfare in History

General Editor: Matthew Bennett

ISSN 1358–779X

The Battle of Hastings: Sources and Interpretations
edited and translated by Stephen Morillo

Infantry Warfare in the Early Fourteenth Century:
Discipline, Tactics, and Technology
Kelly DeVries

The Art of Warfare in Western Europe during the Middle Ages
from the Eighth Century to 1340
J.F. Verbruggen

Knights and Peasants:
The Hundred Years War in the French Countryside
Nicholas Wright

THE ART OF WARFARE
IN WESTERN EUROPE
DURING THE MIDDLE AGES

FROM THE EIGHTH CENTURY TO 1340

J. F. Verbruggen

SECOND EDITION, REVISED AND ENLARGED

Translated by
Colonel Sumner Willard, United States Military Academy
and Mrs R. W. Southern

THE BOYDELL PRESS

First published 1954 as
De Krijgskunst in West-Europa in de Middeleeuwen,
IXe tot begin XIVe eeuw
Koninklijke Academie voor Wetenschappen,
Letteren en Schone Kunsten van België, Brussels

Second, revised and enlarged, edition, in English translation 1997
The Boydell Press, Woodbridge
Reprinted in paperback 1998

Transferred to digital printing

ISBN 978-0-85115-570-8

The Boydell Press is an imprint of Boydell & Brewer Ltd
PO Box 9, Woodbridge, Suffolk IP12 3DF, UK
and of Boydell & Brewer Inc.
668 Mt Hope Avenue, Rochester, NY 14620, USA
website: www.boydellandbrewer.com

A CiP catalogue record for this book is available
from the British Library

This publication is printed on acid-free paper

CONTENTS

ILLUSTRATIONS

Figures and plates appear between pages 182 and 183

GENERAL PREFACE

English-speaking historians probably have none to blame but themselves for, on the whole, not reading and digesting the lessons of *De Krijgskunst in West-Europa in de Middeleeuwen IXe tot begin XIVe eeuw*, when it was first published in 1954. It was unfortunate that the languages of the Low Countries were not widely-enough known, for J.F. Verbruggen was to make a significant contribution to understanding medieval warfare. So it gives me great pleasure to present a newly-translated, expanded and revised edition forty years on. In one sense, at least, his work is now out-of-date. This is clear from the sentences which begin it, in which Verbruggen bemoans the 'unfortunate treatment' which the medieval 'art of war' has received from historians. That this is no longer the case is in a large part due to his influence on a post-war generation of scholars interested in medieval warfare.

I remember with what joy I fell upon the partial translation of his work in the late-1970s when commencing my postgraduate research. Previously, when studying for an MA in Medieval History I had been advised by R. Allen Brown at King's College, London, of the value of the work. Even in the much-reduced translation, I was delighted to find an author who took military historians to task for completely distorting and underestimating the skill with which medieval societies and individual commanders organized war. Delbrück, Delpech and Oman fell alike to his scholarly sword, as he demonstrated the inaccuracy of their assessments which presented the 'Middle Ages' as a primitive period in which the 'Art of War' was lost, not to be regained until the Renaissance. He showed an understanding of strategy, tactics, individual and collective discipline and the management of warfare which stood in stark contrast to their theses. Where they stressed the selfish and disordered behaviour of 'the knights', he was able to point to careful planning of campaigns and battles which emphasized coherent manoeuvre and tactical plans. Flank attacks, ambushes, use of combined arms and rearguards – ignored by the most influential writer in English, Sir Charles Oman – all were discovered by Verbruggen in detailed studies of battles.

For although not entirely about battles, a substantial part of the book is concerned with demonstrating that medieval commanders knew exactly what they were about. That such an approach has borne fruit is evident in Kelly DeVries' companion volume in this *Warfare in History* series, in *Infantry Warfare in the Early Fourteenth Century*. If DeVries does not describe the battles in exactly the same way, this is no disadvantage, for by their very nature, battles are open to a number of interpretations. In effect, J.F. Verbruggen made such a debate possible by identifying the sources and exploring the issues which they raised. He placed an emphasis upon interpreting vernacular materials, especially poetry, which opened my eyes and greatly influenced my own research. His contention that to understand warfare the historian needed to view it through the eyes of practitioners, or at the very least, in the literature through which *they* chose to view it, served to transform our understanding.

It would be unusual in any discipline, for four decades to pass without scholars contributing further to a field of study. J.F. Verbruggen's works, which are wide-ranging and exceed the span of this volume alone, certainly helped to encourage others to write on medieval warfare. Some works are extremely recent indeed and it has not been possible to integrate their approaches into the main body of the work. In such cases reference is made to them in the footnotes (in square brackets).

In some other respects, attitudes have changed over the intervening period as well. It is not perhaps so common today to attribute innate military virtue to the German peoples, an issue which may have influenced the selection of sections for 1977 translation. And if Verbruggen emphasizes the role of the Brabançons, this is not merely pride in the traditions of his native soil, but a recognition that the region's mercenaries dominated the European scene in the twelfth and thirteenth centuries as the English were to do in the fourteenth and fifteenth centuries. If his analysis of infantry tactics favours Flanders rather than Italy, then this displays a praiseworthy attention to his own roots. The lesson remains the same. As to the emphasis on battles, this does indeed contrast with most more recent studies which prefer to play them down for fear of falling into 'decisive battle' approach which can obscure the realities of warfare at a time when sieges dominated the commanders' thinking. However, John France's *Victory in the East: A military history of the First Crusade*, is an example of how battle description, social history, and ideological analysis can be made to sit comfortably together in modern military history.

Finally, if Verbruggen's 'art of war' is principally about battles, that is surely because this is the ground upon which he had to stand and fight the earlier generation of military historians whose views he was challenging. If we read nothing of naval warfare and little of sieges that is not to say that the author considers them unimportant. Chapter I, on strategy, makes clear their significance and illustrates the breadth of vision of medieval military commentators and practitioners. So the reader will find a great deal to open his or her eyes to the realities of warfare on land. Verbruggen also lays bare the ideologies of the combatants in a way which is entirely in tune with modern notions of empathetic history writing. All historians, military or otherwise, will find plenty of value in these pages, especially in the sections now made available for the first time in English. It has been a great privilege to be involved in their republication.

Matthew Bennett

I

HISTORIOGRAPHICAL PROBLEMS

*Weaknesses of Modern Military Historians
in Discussing Medieval Warfare*

Few historical problems have received such unfortunate treatment at the hands of historians as that of the art of war in the Middle Ages. This arises from several causes. In particular, it is not easy to be deeply versed in the military problems of the period and at the same time to possess considerable knowledge of medieval historical writing, with its peculiar problems of historical criticism. This difficulty can be easily highlighted through a brief survey of the literature on the subject of medieval warfare. More than one army officer has devoted his spare time to the study of military life in bygone ages, but this has yielded few tangible results for the history of the Middle Ages. Since their profession has given them no preparation in historical method, most of these military writers have not penetrated to the root of the specialized problem which arises. A notable example is that of H. Delpech, whose voluminous work *La tactique au XIIIe siècle,* published in 1886, was the result of eleven years of research.[1] He tried to show that the armies of the thirteenth century based their operations on carefully thought-out tactics. These tactics were simple, to be sure, like the weapons of the time, but were quite logical and compatible with the means of warfare then available. Delpech amassed an enormous amount of material, for he studied accounts of the battles of the eleventh, twelfth, thirteenth and early fourteenth centuries, but lacked that historical background and critical faculty which are indispensable to a study of the art of medieval warfare. He accepted all estimates of the number of troops at their face value, just as they appear in the sources. He described battles without carefully sifting accounts of them, and texts from the period itself were often neglected in favour of later versions. He saw advances in the art of war, splendid manoeuvres, schools of war, methodical systems. Misled by exaggerated estimates of army strengths, he concluded that tactics were further advanced than they actually were. His work has been completely discredited by historians.

The same mistakes were repeated by the Prussian general Köhler in his work, which is even more voluminous.[2] He developed the theory that the western art of

---

1 Paris, 2 vols.
2 *Die Entwickelung des Kriegswesens und der Kriegführung in der Ritterzeit von Mitte des 11. Jahrhunderts bis zu den Hussitenkriegen,* 3 vols in 5, Breslau, 1886–89, with an *Ergänzungsheft, die Schlachten von Tagliacozzo und Courtrai betreffend,* Breslau, 1893.

war was deeply influenced by that of Byzantium, but he nowhere offered any proof of this hypothesis. He was totally lacking in a critical sense and, like Delpech, was not above inventing manoeuvres. In general he accepted uncritically the data of the sources regarding army strengths, and made no distinction between contemporary and later sources. He visualized triangular knightly formations, the points of which were directed towards the enemy, and three of which were usually placed one behind the other. His work is valuable at times for its collection of useful material, but it must be consulted with due caution. Delpech and Köhler both lacked the indispensable grounding in history and were much too imaginative. Other great works were, however, not written by officers but by trained historians: Sir Charles Oman, Hans Delbrück, Wilhelm Erben, Eugen von Frauenholz and Ferdinand Lot.

Sir Charles Oman, author of many works on general and military history, also wrote a book on the medieval art of war. In 1924 a second edition of this work, revised and enlarged, appeared in two volumes.[3] It is more accurate than the first from a critical standpoint, thanks to the use of Delbrück's work and the studies of Sir James Ramsay. Through these Oman obtained a clearer insight into the strength of the armies without, however, arriving at firm conclusions. His work is interesting, partly on account of his very full descriptions of battles, and also because he discussed English military affairs in great detail. But Oman was too facile. He did not get to the essentials of combat tactics, and his work lacks both synthesis and critical insight. Although the book is useful, it must be carefully checked against source materials.

Perhaps the greatest master in the history of warfare is Hans Delbrück, a Berlin professor whose *Geschichte der Kriegskunst im Rahmen der politischen Geschichte* has been considered definitive.[4] Delbrück studied military problems in the work of Carl von Clausewitz, the best theoretician on the conduct of war. He wrote a biography of Gneisenau, one of the most brilliant adversaries of Napoleon. He discussed military problems with German generals, and carried on a controversy with the best German strategists about Clausewitz's conceptions of the conduct of war. During World War I he was the most competent civilian critic of the conduct of the war in Germany. Endowed with a sharp critical mind, he conducted seminars on the history of the art of war for many years. He personally studied many important campaigns, or had his pupils study them. He divided military history into periods in which there were tactical units, and periods in which these units were replaced by individual fighters. A tactical unit is a battle formation in which such discipline prevails that the individuals obey the orders of their commander as one. This entails sacrifice of the personality of the individual for the sake of the group. According to Delbrück medieval knights did not form tactical units. They were individual fighters, who put their personal honour, fame and reputation above all else. Thus the individual fighter was the basis of tactics at that time; combat formations were of less importance and by no means essential, and the theory of any real 'art of war' was excluded. No discipline in the true sense of the word existed. Delbrück's opinion

3 *A History of the Art of War in the Middle Ages*, London.
4 III, Berlin, 2nd edn, 1923.

was shared by Oman, Erben, von Frauenholz and Lot. The Middle Ages were therefore held to be a period of serious decline in the art of war, the more so because there were no longer any efficient foot-soldiers, nor was there any large-scale strategy.

Delbrück showed that the numbers in medieval armies were small. In this he followed the excellent methods of the first practitioners of historical demography. He applied a healthy critical spirit to the study of the art of war, and pointed out that one should go right through from ancient to modern times in order to outline the evolution of warfare, and that a historian must have the necessary knowledge of military affairs. Delbrück observed that it is not enough to classify texts carefully, according to their date of composition, the place of the author's origin, and his sources of information, nor to have at one's disposal original texts unspoiled by interpolations, but rather that it is absolutely necessary to check the military value of each account. Even the best narratives may include inventions and legends, which can be spotted solely through the comparison of many sources. Delbrück furthermore treated his subject within a broad framework: he continually emphasized the influence that the structure of state and society had both on armies and on the art of war. He rightly prefaced his chapter on knighthood as a military class with a general survey of knighthood as a social class. Yet despite the obvious good qualities of his work and the numerous improvements it shows over other comparable studies, it is difficult to agree with Delbrück in his views on knightly warfare. He had read too few sources personally; his critique of the sources was biased; he depended too much on his students' work for analyses of battles. Moreover, Delbrück's choice of significant battles was arbitrary and he did not succeed in giving a trustworthy picture of knightly tactics. In fact he did not go much beyond providing a general sketch, altogether lacking in life. How incomplete and erroneous Delbrück's ideas were will be shown in the course of this book.

Erben's concise survey published in 1929 was a dispassionate exposition of what was known about medieval military history.[5] The author did not accept all Delbrück's views, and he added little, but his extensive bibliography is very useful. On the same lines is the work of Eugen von Frauenholz, *Das Heerwesen der germanischen Frühzeit, des Frankenreiches und des ritterlichen Zeitalters*,[6] which corrects some details in Delbrück's work, as for example in the use of reserves. In the main, however, von Frauenholz held to the traditional concept of the individual fighter. Quite wrongly, he disputed Delbrück's views on the number of troops in battle. There is also little evidence that he was well-read enough in the source materials.

The French medievalist, Ferdinand Lot, published his very full work on medieval armies and warfare in 1946.[7] From his first-rate knowledge of general history, through his interest in the numerical strength of armies, by virtue of his wide reading, his acutely critical mind and his clear grasp of the correct method of historical research, Lot's study represents a real advance on that of Delbrück. Influenced by

---

[5] *Kriegsgeschichte des Mittelalters, Historische Zeitschrift, Beiheft 16*, Berlin, 1929.
[6] Munich, 1935–37, 2 vols in 3.
[7] *L'art militaire et les armées au moyen âge en Europe et dans le Proche-Orient*, Paris, 2 vols.

the remarkable book of Lefebvre des Noëttes on the history of the saddle (1931),[8] Lot painted a more accurate picture of cavalry tactics, although he might have gone even further than he did. In common with Delbrück he subjected all the data about effective strengths to a merciless scrutiny, sharper even than that of his predecessors. In this respect he achieved results. Yet this fine, carefully written work is not wholly satisfactory. Lot went from general to military history. His synthesis is based largely on secondary sources, and does not go deeply enough into primary sources. In dealing with tactics, where he should have been examining small details, he did not pursue his investigation far enough. Yet it is these very details that illuminate our knowledge of combat technique; if they are carefully sifted and then collected into a coherent system, they give a much more accurate picture. It is from these details that one should proceed to generalities and not the other way around, as Lot did. Lot also believed in the concept of the individual combatant, even though he included a summary of a monograph of 1887 in which O. Heermann questioned this notion,[9] and he accepted Delbrück's conclusions concerning the decline of the art of war through the disappearance of good foot-soldiers and large-scale strategy.

Lefebvre des Noëttes showed that medieval heavy cavalry was technically far more advanced than its ancient counterpart. It made use of certain very important technical inventions: the high saddle with its front and rear supports, provided with stirrups, enabled it to make a very heavy charge, while at the same time horseshoes protected the horses' hooves and made prolonged forays possible. He thought that these technical advances were introduced in the West in the ninth century. Before the work of Lefebvre des Noëttes appeared, Oman, using Byzantine sources, had already established the fact that stirrups were in use there. Indeed, the *Strategikon* (580–582) refers to the stirrup and the horseshoes as a normal part of the equipment, with no indication that it was a recent invention.[10] The saddle arrived in the West as a barbarian innovation in the first century. The heavy horse, ancestor of the medieval destrier, appeared in the same century.

The Romans had been defeated by the Parthian horsemen who destroyed the army of Crassus in 53 BC and were a terrible adversary of the army of Mark Anthony in 36 BC. King Shapur I of the Sassanian dynasty destroyed the army of the emperor Valerian, who was the first Roman emperor to be taken prisoner in battle (260), and the Emperor Julian was killed during his expedition against the Persians in 363. Indeed the heavy cavalry of the Persians inflicted several defeats on the Roman foot-soldiers, and the Roman legions were never able to beat the Parthian and Persian cavalry decisively. In Europe the Romans had to fight against the horsemen of the Goths, the Gepidae, the Vandals, the Alans, and the Huns. In a battle against the Goths the emperor Decius and his son were killed and their army beaten in the

---

8 *L'attelage. Le cheval de selle à travers les âges*, Paris, 2 vols.
9 *Die Gefechtsführung abendländischer Heere im Orient in der Epoche des ersten Kreuzzuges*, Dissertation, Marburg.
10 Oman, *op. cit.*, I, p. 187. *Mauricii Strategicon*, ed. G.T. Dennis, Corpus Fontium Historiae Byzantinae, vol. XVII, Vienna, 1981, I, 2, p. 80. [Translated by G.T. Dennis, *Maurice's Strategikon: Handbook of Military Strategy*, Philadelphia, 1984, p. 13.]

summer of 251 near Abrittus. In 378 the emperor Valens and his army were destroyed by the Goths in the battle of Adrianople.

This superiority of barbarian cavalry led to the introduction of *cataphractarii* into the Roman army, a heavy cavalry which is first mentioned in the work of Vegetius, by the end of the fourth or in the first half of the fifth century, as a very important weapon whose equipment and training left nothing to be desired, in contrast to the foot-soldiers.[11]

From all this we may conclude that the medieval art of war should not be judged on the basis of the capability of the foot-soldiers, as Delbrück did, but rather according to that of the cavalry.

The Strength of Medieval Armies

Thanks to the amount of material which Delbrück and Lot wrote on the strength of medieval armies, we are relatively well informed on this matter. The knightly armies were small because they were raised in relatively small states. They were professional armies, composed of men who were for the most part born into a certain class; their numbers were consequently quite limited. Besides, economic life was underdeveloped, the cities were of recent formation or were still very small, and the limited financial resources of the princes did not at first permit them to field a professional army composed of considerable numbers of mercenaries or of their own subjects. The recruiting of such an army would have taken time, and the logistical support was even more difficult to manage, for transport to bring up supplies was scanty and agriculture was insufficiently developed to support large armies.

For military history the problem of the strength of armies is of crucial importance. It was quite unusual for a numerically weaker army to overcome a more powerful army: it is therefore a matter of critical necessity to establish which was the larger army. Medieval sources, frequently tell us that the numerically weaker force has been successful in conquering a much stronger enemy, primarily through God's help, or through that of a patron saint. The intervention of God or of a saint was often mentioned in the crusades, and the example of the numerically inferior Maccabees was repeatedly quoted. St Bernard of Clairvaux outdoes them all. In a propaganda piece intended to recruit knights for the Order of the Templars, he wrote about the Templars thus: 'They hope to achieve victory through God's strength . . . They have often experienced this already, so that more than once one of them alone pursued a thousand of the enemy, and two Templars put 10,000 enemies to flight.'[12]

On the evidence of some chroniclers, who looked upon the outcome of battles as the judgement of God, men long believed that the Flemings and Swiss overcame their powerful enemies with a numerically inferior army. This notion appealed to the national pride of the victors, and was eagerly accepted. On sober critical enquiry,

---

[11] Vegetius, *De re militari*, III (ed. C. Lang, Stuttgart, 1967) c. 26; I, c. 20.

[12] *S. Bernardi de laude novae militiae*, Patrologiae cursus completus. Series latina, ed. Migne, 182, pp. 926–7. Compare Deut. 32:30; Ps. 90:7; Is. 30:17.

however, the relative numbers of the combatants proved to be exactly the reverse: the foot-soldiers were much more numerous than the knights and this was in large measure responsible for their notable victories. A revolution in the art of war was set in motion, perhaps only for a time – a revolution which was preceded by another in recruitment, and in the social composition of the armies. For the most part this was the consequence of the rise of a new class, which owed its consciousness of power to an improvement in its general welfare.

It is generally accepted that medieval man had no head for figures, and that even the commanders were rarely concerned with accurate statistics. Fantastically exaggerated numbers were accepted and repeated at their face value in the chronicles. The case of the French chronicler Richer is typical: where he followed the *Annales* of Flodoard, he arbitrarily changed the figures, nearly always increasing them.[13] There were nevertheless some clerics who gave accurate figures, thus providing valuable information on the small numbers of cavalry. This was true of the First Crusade and of the period that followed it in the kingdom of Jerusalem. Heermann, through a careful comparison of all the narrative sources, obtained the following results which are worth quoting:

Date	Battle	Nos. of knights	Nos. of foot-soldiers
1098	Battle of the Lake of Antioch	700	–
	Battle of Antioch	(500–600)	–
1099	Ascalon	1,200	9,000
1101	Ramla	260	900
1102	Ramla	200	–
1102	Jaffa	200	–
1105	Ramla	700	2,000
1119	Athareb	700	3,000
1119	Hab	700	–
1125	Hazarth	1,100	2,000[14]

The acceptance of small numbers of troops from a few reliable narrative sources can be justified. Other chroniclers often give a huge figure to show that an army was very powerful, but this is based on a guess, not a count. Figures for a small army may come from a count, certainly where troops were being paid. A chronicler like Gilbert of Mons, chancellor and confidant to the count of Hainault, can be trusted, since he was in a position to know the truth. Sometimes he gives the costs incurred by military expeditions. His information is also free from the above-mentioned evil of giving inflated figures, increased to show the might of the prince. Gilbert's figures run from 80 to 700 knights, and with this last figure he specially mentions two knights

13 Richer, *Historia*, ed. Latouche, I, Paris, 1930, c. 49, 51, 85, pp. 98, 99, 102, 272.
14 Lot, *op. cit.*, I, p. 135.

who were not from Hainault. Since he knew the correct number of men from
Hainault, and considering his position at the court of the count, his guesses at the
number of knights from the other principalities are also of some value. These
estimates deserve to be accepted, not necessarily for each expedition mentioned, but
for the number of knights that each principality could send to the army. The highest
figures which he gives for Flanders (1,000 knights) and for Brabant (700 knights),
which are confirmed not only by other contemporary sources but by general history;
they are indirectly confirmed by the records of the prince-bishop of Liège, which
give a strength of 700 knights for the bishop's army.[15]

In many instances one may be sure that the more reliable sources give correct
figures at least as long as they are small. This is quite logical, for it will be seen in
discussing tactics that knights on the march or before the battle were divided into
units commanded by their lords. Of these small units or *conrois*, from which the
greater units or *batailles* were formed, the strength was naturally known. Moreover
the horses had to be valued as the prince paid for lost horses, and this was another
source of knowledge of army strengths. The troop strengths from Hainault are
valuable in relation to similar figures from other principalities. Just as Gilbert of
Mons did for the counts of Hainault, so other highly placed chroniclers gave similar
information for their principality: Suger for the king of France, Archbishop William
of Tyre for the kings of Jerusalem, Villehardouin and Henry of Valenciennes for the
emperors of Constantinople.

Besides the data of these few well-informed chroniclers, we also have archival
sources. For Brittany we know the number of knights who were called to the duke's
army. For the duchy of Normandy the number is more or less known. In the army of
Philip Augustus we know the number of *sergeants*, the foot-soldiers of the communes, around 1194 and in 1204. In England there is a series of documents for the
thirteenth century, and the archives are particularly rich in fourteenth-century
documents. Careful study of them has shown that the armies of the king of England
seldom exceeded 10,000 men, horse and foot-soldiers. For Flanders there are a few
incomplete figures in feudal rolls and feudal books, and in a couple of documents
concerning the noblemen who served the city of Bruges in 1302. All this information
points to small forces. In Normandy in 1172, only 581 knights had to be raised for
the duke's army from 1,500 fiefs. In fact there were more than 1,500 fiefs, perhaps
2,000, for several barons had not disclosed the number of their vassals. In Brittany
in 1294, 166 knights and sixteen squires were obliged to perform military service in
the army of the duke.[16]

In addition to narrative and documentary sources, there is other evidence to show
that medieval armies were small. A useful indication of this can be found from the
battlefields themselves. Where the front is known, as for example at Courtrai or
Mons-en-Pévèle, it amounts to little over 1,000 yards, which shows that the armies

---

[15] *Chronicon Hanoniense*, c.60, 71, 76, 77, 84, 92, 96, 99, 112, 120. C. Gaier, *Art et organisation
militaires dans la principauté de Liège et dans le comté de Looz au moyen âge*, Brussels, 1968, p. 64.
[16] Lot, *op. cit.*, pp. 14, 219, 220, 236–7, 306–10. *Recueil des historiens de France*, XXIII, c. 434, p.
698.

which fought there were not very large. The size of the terrain does not give so exact a picture as other evidence, but the width of the battlefield does allow us to check information gathered from the narrative sources. For it is evident that on a plain 1,000 yards wide it is extremely difficult to manoeuvre 20,000 men, except in the special case of a frontal attack by troops arranged in battle-order of very great depth, in various formations following each other.

Occasionally, useful indications of numerical strength may be found in the length of the columns during a march. Or conversely, from the fact that an army advances in a single column, it may be deduced that it can never exceed a certain maximum strength. Small calculations make it possible to eliminate exaggerated troop figures, and sometimes cast more light on the causes of victory or defeat. This method does not, however, permit us to settle once and for all whether an army consisted of 10,000, 12,000 or 15,000 men, except in quite unusual cases where we know exactly when the various troop units arrived. Such a check can also be applied when an army marches over a bridge before a battle, or goes out to battle through a city gate. This happened at the battle of Antioch in 1098. Since only a few knights at a time could pass through the gate and over the bridge, it would have taken a very long time indeed for an army of possibly 30,000 horsemen to deploy. For if five knights in a row advanced through the gate and over the bridge, such an army would have had a depth of 6,000 horsemen. Since these horsemen would take up over three yards in a column, we arrive at a depth of over eleven miles, and they would need three or four hours for passing the gate and the bridge, without taking into account the time necessary to form the army up in the field. If only four knights could have ridden abreast, the column would be fourteen miles long. Now for the battle of Antioch we have an estimate of numerical strength in Orderic Vitalis. He says that no fewer than 113,000 soldiers took part in the battle, while 20,000 remained in the city. Yet if five knights rode abreast, this army would have had a depth of 22,600 men. When we consider that it also included foot-soldiers, and if we assume a depth of only six feet for each unit of five men, we arrive at a length of over twenty-eight miles for the whole column. Thus it must have taken at least nine hours to march through the gate and over the bridge, so that the army could only have reached the field in the late afternoon, and it still had to be drawn up in battle array. Clearly, Orderic's figures cannot be accepted.[17]

In the case of ordinary marches, the waggons for equipment and supplies have to be taken into account too. A column of 50,000 men must have been enormously long when the supply waggons are also considered. The area of a camp can also point to an exaggerated army strength. The Roman camps for a legion of 6,000 men occupied an area of sixty acres. On a campaign these camps were possibly smaller, but the classic dimensions are still found in armies as late as the end of the nineteenth century: for 1,000 men a bivouac area of about ten acres was used.

---

[17] Delbrück, *op. cit.*, III, pp. 232–3. R. Grousset, *Histoire des croisades*, 3 vols, Paris, 1934–36, I, pp. 104–5. S. Runciman, in *A History of the Crusades*, 3 vols, Cambridge, 1951–54, I, p. 247. In fact 200 men remained in the city under the count of Toulouse. [See also J. France, *Victory in the East*, Cambridge, 1994, pp. 261–94.]

All these means have already been used in the great works on the art of war: they show just as clearly as the best narrative and archival sources that the armies were small. When we consider that in 1119 at Brémule Louis VI of France and Henry I of England, then duke of Normandy, fought against each other with about 400 and 500 knights respectively, and that in the second battle of Lincoln in 1217 the army of the English king fought with 400 knights and 347 crossbowmen against the rebellious barons, who had perhaps 611 knights and 1,000 foot-soldiers on their side, it is clear that a re-evaluation of the problem is imperative. It is plainly necessary first of all to consider the combat, which was a struggle between relatively small forces, before going on to study the art of war in general.[18]

Combat

Both Delbrück and Lot considered that the study of battles must form the basis of any discussion of the art of war, yet both provided little more than summaries of the most famous battles. They never minutely studied a pitched battle, which is a serious defect in their work. They considered that they did not have sufficient information, or that the information was untrustworthy, and looked upon contradictory details as the result of fantasy, or as insignificant. This is quite wrong. For if our knowledge is not based on the smallest details of fighting and tactics, we run the risk of missing the essentials and a true picture of medieval battles does not emerge. Delbrück's account is incomplete and full of mistakes; Lot studied the battle in broad outline, but only the work of Sir Charles Oman is of any use for a detailed account of pitched battles. R.C. Smail has given a better description of the battles of the crusaders, but his analysis is not complete.[19] We shall attempt to show that a great deal of useful information can be derived from exhaustive analyses of contemporary accounts of battles.

A great deal can be learnt about medieval warfare from the study of battles, for the strength and weakness of a knightly army are revealed in battle. We can enquire why battle was so often avoided, why the pursuit could not be carried very far, and why wars were so seldom decisive. From the study of battles we can then go to other branches of the art of war: the preparation for battle and the exploitation of the enemy's weaknesses, and the avoidance of combat and the manoeuvres that follow such a decision. But many difficulties and dangers beset scholars in this field: for example, fanciful details, and particulars which are peculiar to a single engagement and therefore do not fit into the general pattern. Comparative study is of real assistance, and this shows that certain characteristic features recur in all engagements of the time. An intensive study of battles between small units of armoured horsemen makes one immediately aware of certain special problems associated with them. In

---

[18] Lot, *op. cit.*, I, pp. 123, 295, 317. Oman, *op. cit.*, I, pp. 413–14. *Histoire de Guillaume le Maréchal*, ed. P. Meyer, 3 vols, Paris, 1891–1901, II, vv. 17023–7, p. 251.
[19] *Crusading warfare (1097–1193)*, Cambridge, 1956, pp. 113–15, 123–30. [New edition with an introduction by C.J. Marshall, Cambridge, 1994.]

particular, once such units are committed in hand-to-hand fighting, no one can influence the course of battle, except by throwing in reserves. It is very difficult to withdraw troops from fighting once it has begun. Nevertheless it sometimes happened that the commanders withdrew from battle with tired troops in order to rest and reform. The particular problems of knightly combat remained unchanged in mounted warfare throughout the ages. They are as follows: the helplessness of a small unit which is not thoroughly organized; weakness during the pursuit, when dispersed cavalrymen are on the heels of a fleeing enemy; and the great importance of the reserve corps, which as a compact group falls upon a comparatively disorganized unit of the enemy. We shall consider these problems in the chapter on tactics.

Limitations of the Clerical Sources

The scepticism of Delbrück and Lot about the value of certain details in the sources is fully justified in the case of many descriptions of battles in monastic chronicles. Quite frequently the narrative is incomplete, 'in order not to bore the reader', and as the clergy were sometimes ignorant of military matters, they give fabricated accounts, or add imaginary details. For want of critical insight they often show astonishing gullibility. Clerics also sometimes ascribe a victory to a miracle, the intervention of God, or of a saint or a relic. This leads to the dramatization of the course of a battle, as happens in the account given by Albert of Aix of the battle of Ramla, fought on 7 September 1101. He says that king Baldwin I had over 300 knights and 1,000 foot-soldiers under his command, who were thrown in against 200,000 enemy horsemen and foot-soldiers. An eye-witness, Fulcher of Chartres, sets 260 knights, among whom were a number of newly dubbed knights, and 900 foot-soldiers, against 11,000 cavalrymen and 21,000 foot-soldiers on the enemy's side – a considerable difference in the estimates of the enemy strength! According to Albert, Baldwin drew up his army in five formations. The first three contingents of crusaders were virtually annihilated in their successive attacks. The fourth corps in its turn attacked the enemy, but was driven back, then Baldwin made a successful attack with the fifth contingent, and won the battle. Albert's comment reveals the tendency of his account: 'The heathen fought with pride and might; they beat off the first four contingents, but the entire might of the unbelievers faltered and was brought to nought, and trampled under foot by the fifth corps, in which the wood of the Holy Cross was carried before the king and his companions.'

The next day there remained only 40 knights and 200 foot-soldiers in Baldwin's army, but this did not prevent him from slaying 20,000 of the enemy.[20]

We find a quite different account in Fulcher. In his description the army was composed of six contingents. Two of these were driven back: Baldwin then attacked with his contingent, which he had kept in reserve, and drove the enemy off. But

---

[20] *Liber christianae expeditionis pro ereptione, emundatione, et restitutione sanctae Hierosolymitanae ecclesia*, RHC, Historiens Occidentaux, IV, pp. 549–51. [Trans. S. Edington, forthcoming, Oxford.]

losses were heavy: eighty knights and even more foot-soldiers. Although Fulcher also mentions the help of God and the Holy Cross, his account is not so romanticized and distorted as Albert's. On the next day Baldwin defeated 500 more of the enemy, who the day before had routed a part of his army and had returned as victors up to the moment that they were surprised by the victorious Christian army.[21] Once more we see how credulously Albert accepted the reports of his informants, and how he distorted their accounts in the interest of the miraculous. In his somewhat uncritical work on the crusades Grousset cheerfully borrows part of Albert's account, without eliminating the exaggerations about the destruction of the first three contingents.[22] This is of course not true of all clerical writers. Some of them were very competent and well informed, for example William, the able archbishop of Tyre, whose chronicle is one of the most remarkable historical works of the Middle Ages, containing some excellent descriptions of warfare. Flanders has another very good source of this kind, the Annals of the Ghent Franciscan friar known as the *Annales Gandenses*. Since most of the clerics wrote in Latin, the tendency arose almost automatically to use terms borrowed from classical antiquity, so these sources are apt to use military terminology very inaccurately.

As members of a class which was very often at variance with the knights, the clergy sometimes give a very unfavourable picture of the knights' calling, and are often unjustly critical or extremely partisan, sometimes even descending to the level of caricature. If the contemporary lack of critical spirit is also taken into account, the difficulties of the historian's task can be better appreciated. This is a more serious problem in military history than in other branches of history, because warfare, fighting, and battles easily lend themselves to romanticized accounts full of poetic exaggerations. All these difficulties are aggravated by the fact that we have no theoretical treatises on tactics, except the Rule of the Templars, which is not really a complete treatise on the art of war, though it gives us important information about the knightly system, including various details of military life, the disposition of troops, and the order of the march.

Secular and Other Reliable Sources

We are concerned here with reliable sources in the shape of chronicles or biographies written by knights or their confidants, who were eye-witnesses of certain battles, or actually took part in them. From the Carolingian Renaissance we have the work of Nithard, but we must await the twelfth-century Renaissance, which in fact began in the last decades of the eleventh century, to find similarly good sources in greater numbers. In the First Crusade, both clerks and laymen handled weapons for four years, and had first-hand experience of battles, and in general they described warfare well. The Anonymous (an ordinary knight whose language and style are too simple to be those of a cleric), Raymond of Aguilers, chaplain to Raymond of Toulouse,

---

[21] *Gesta Francorum Hierusalem expugnantium . . ., ibid.*, III, pp. 390–95.
[22] *Histoire des croisades*, I, pp. 225–7.

and Fulcher of Chartres, chaplain to Baldwin of Boulogne, have left us useful descriptions of the conduct of war during a long campaign, even though we might wish for more particulars. Also the work of Ralph of Caen, Tancred's confidant, is important for the art of war, especially for the years that followed the First Crusade. Despite much exaggeration and romanticizing, we can extract some important information from the chronicle of Albert of Aix. His work is very detailed, whereas other eye-witness accounts are frequently too condensed; it is moreover important for the period following the First Crusade for which the sources mentioned above are not entirely adequate. For the later crusades and wars in the Holy Land we have the remarkable chronicle of William of Tyre, and the long account of the Third Crusade by the Norman *jongleur* Ambroise. For the second half of the twelfth century and the early thirteenth the *Histoire de Guillaume le Maréchal* is very useful. The Fourth Crusade is excellently represented by Villehardouin and Robert de Clari, and several campaigns in the Latin Empire of Constantinople are competently described in another good source, the work of Henry of Valenciennes. The memoirs of Jean de Joinville are a most important source for the psychology of the knights on the crusade of Saint Louis in 1250. The Brabançon Jan van Heelu may be classed with the authors of these famous chronicles, because of his detailed description of the battle of Worringen, to which he devoted more than 4,000 lines, one of the most splendid descriptions of a battle in the entire Middle Ages. At the beginning of the fourteenth century a notable work was written by Guillaume Guiart – at least for the period in which he took part in the wars against the Flemings (1304). Later, Jean le Bel of Liège wrote a fascinating description of a campaign in Scotland (1327) and left a good account of the battle of Crécy (1346). In the fourteenth century the sources are generally more detailed and we have many more equally competent accounts of wars. The sources so far mentioned are among the best of their time, but there are other good ones too. The oldest *chansons de geste* could well be included: they are especially useful for their information about the life of the nobles and the solidarity of noble families. Despite the tendency to glorify the personal feats of the great heroes of the epics, these tales offer much interesting information about tactics and other branches of the art of war.

The oldest source mentioned so far is Nithard, whose name seldom appears in general works on medieval military history. Three passages are particularly important for us. The first deals with the cavalry games held by Louis the German and Charles the Bald, which were mock battles intended as military training, carried out in groups, and the example shows that such training of heavy cavalry had taken place under the Carolingians. These cavalry games were the forerunners of the later tournaments. A second passage, concerned with a major problem of knightly warfare, is equally instructive. This concerns the defeat suffered in 834 by Count Wido of Le Mans and his army, who came from the area between the Seine and the Loire, in a battle with the followers of Lothar – Mathfrid, Lantbert, and their men. Although Wido's army was the stronger, it was crushed because of lack of discipline and order. The basic question here is one of discipline within the unit, a problem we shall encounter frequently in the twelfth and thirteenth centuries. A third text of Nithard provides an example of a defensive position according to the soundest principles. In October 841 Charles the Bald tried to prevent Lothar and his army from crossing the Seine between Paris and Melun. He stationed troops in Paris and Melun, and in the places where a crossing could be effected, and held a central reserve at St Cloud, opposite the enemy troops, which were based at St Denis. Charles could move to resist any attempt to cross the river because his units were in communication with each other through a system of sentry-posts, by which signals were exchanged, as among ships. The disposition was only too effective: Lothar resolved the problem in an equally classic manner by outflanking these formations.[23]

Chroniclers sometimes misunderstood a manoeuvre, which makes a critical study of even the more reliable sources essential. This is the case with one of the translations of the *Historia Albigensis* of Pierre des Vaux-de-Cernay, who describes how Simon de Montfort pursued the enemy after his great victory near Muret in 1213, during the crusade against the Albigensians. While two knightly formations out of three pursued the fleeing enemy, Simon remained behind with the third contingent in order to use his men as a support or reserve, in case the enemy should succeed in regrouping his fleeing troops and attempt a new attack. But the translator did not understand the task of this reserve and made it look ridiculous.[24] For a similar use of a reserved corps in a pursuit action, there is another remarkable example of misunderstanding, this time in the *Histoire de Guillaume le Maréchal*.

This excellent source was written by a poet under the guidance of the young marshal, William's son and successor. The writer mostly used detailed notes drawn up in prose, but even this chronicler, despite his excellent vantage point, failed to understand a manoeuvre, and explained it quite wrongly. This was in the famous battle near Fréteval (3 July 1194) when Philip Augustus lost his treasure and archives in a combat with the troops of Richard I. After the victory of the English king, William the Marshal was entrusted by Richard with the command of a reserve unit, which followed after the pursuing victors in perfect order, to protect them, dispersed as they were, in case the defeated French should try an offensive return.[25] The fact that writers should be so mistaken in the interpretation of a relatively simple manoeuvre shows how little some chroniclers knew about the art of war in their time; it also demonstrates that medieval tactics were far more sophisticated than many scholars are willing to believe even today.

The Importance of the Vernacular

Among the best of the most reliable sources are those written in the vernacular and most of those mentioned above were so written. They provide a clear and distinct terminology: we find words like *scaren, scharen, echielles, schieri; bataelgen, batailles, battaglie; conroten, conrois; banieren, bannières.* These vernacular terms

---

[23] Nithard, *Historiarum libri IIII*, 1. I, 5, 1. III, 3, 6, ed. Lauer, Paris, 1926, pp. 20, 94, 110–12.
[24] II, c. 463, p. 155; III, pp. 152–43.
[25] *Histoire de Guillaume le Maréchal*, ed. P. Meyer, 3 vols, SATF, Paris, 1891, 1894, 1901, II, vv. 10,512–676, pp. 17–19; III, p. 140, n. 3, 4. [A translation by David Crouch is forthcoming.]

stem from Germanic words: *eschiele* comes from the Germanic word *scara*, which we meet in the Latin sources of Carolingian times, and which has become *schaar* in Dutch. *Bannière* also stems from a Germanic word, *bandwa*, sign, just like *conroi* and *desroi*, in which *roi* means measure, order. All these Germanic words were taken into the *lingua romana* in the period between the sixth and ninth centuries, which means that these troop divisions were then already in use. In one of the oldest examples of the use of the word *scara*, it means a troop of picked, strong or courageous warriors.[26] Even though chroniclers do not always indicate the difference between these units, the terminology is clear and what is being discussed is unmistakable. Such is not the case with the Latin terms *legiones, cohortes, manipuli, turmae, acies, cunei*. For example, we have two accounts of the battle of Arsuf: the *Itinerarium peregrinorum et gesta Ricardi regis* and the account of Ambroise, *L'estoire de la guerre sainte*. The French text is much clearer than the Latin. For the French word *conroi*, the Latin version uses the words *ordines, turmae, agmina, distinctiones, acies*.[27] The Latin text, the *Itinerarium*, shows that well-organised units were involved, but does not give a clear idea of the battle formations; the French text of Ambroise gives the technical terms. The Latin texts do not allow any study of the evolution of tactical units, because no distinction was made between terms like *batailles, conrois*, or *bannières*, and the Latin names varied from one chronicler to another, so that in Latin we have only an approximate notion of what happened. Only here and there in a detailed Latin source do we know exactly what is meant.

Changes in Tactics Revealed by Lesser-known Sources

It is obvious that too much attention has often been paid to the few great battles which had political consequences, or which formed a turning-point in the art of war, to the neglect of other battles and developments. The most remarkable example of this neglect is the comparatively late discovery by Commandant Lefebvre des Noëttes of the importance of horseshoes, saddle and stirrups, by reason of which medieval cavalry sat so much more firmly astride the horse than the cavalry of antiquity. It has taken time to appreciate fully the significance of this discovery. In fact much can still be achieved through the study of the less important feats of arms between two great battles, or between two turning-points in the history of warfare. Four examples may be mentioned.

Through a close study of several small, apparently insignificant battles, T.F. Tout succeeded in showing that the new English tactics, which brought about the striking victory at Crécy in 1346, in fact existed as early as 1322, and that this new method

26 Fredegar, *Chronicarum libri IV*, ed. B. Krusch, 1888, 1. 4, c. 74, SRM, II, p. 158.
27 Ambroise, *L'estoire de la guerre sainte*, ed. G. Paris, Paris, 1897, vv. 6137–44, 6147–65, 6201–3, 6223–30, 6293–8, 7247, 7308–9. [Translated by M.J. Hubert and J.L. La Monte, *The Crusade of Richard the Lion-Heart by Ambroise*, New York, 1941.] *Itinerarium, peregrinorum et Gesta Ricardi regis*, ed. W. Stubbs, in *Chronicles and Memorials of the Reign of Richard I*, RS 1, 1884, pp. 260–2, 265, 291–3.

of fighting was introduced as an answer to Scottish tactics after the English defeat at Bannockburn in 1314. In another paper he showed that the French knights after Crécy at once set about evolving new tactical methods to offset the fighting technique of the English. He gave examples from the period 1349–1352 to show how the nobility tried to adapt their tactics to those of the enemy.[28] Another English scholar, J.E. Morris, showed that between Bannockburn and the year 1337 the English tried out no less than three different tactical possibilities against the Scots. The classic weapons, archers and heavy cavalry, were strengthened by light cavalry, *hobilars*; occasionally heavily armed foot-soldiers were called upon; finally mounted archers were used in order that they might, with the heavy cavalry, follow the Scots, who moved about on horseback and systematically avoided a pitched battle, and then dismount to fight on foot on the battlefield as useful marksmen.[29] I have shown, on the basis of various references in the *Annales Gandenses*, that the French knights forsook their usual tactics after the battle of Courtrai in order to try out a new method. Later we shall further demonstrate this point on the basis of other chronicles from the period 1302–1304. Subsequent events in Flanders show that at Cassel in 1328 and at Westrozebeke in 1382 the French nobility left the initiative to the Flemish insurgents.[30] This proves that we are again dealing with an important aspect of the art of war of the time, namely, the evolution of new tactics.

These examples show that local changes in combat methods came about and that the nobility modified obsolete methods and even applied new ones. The victories at Courtrai in Flanders and at Bannockburn in Scotland mark the beginning of a period of superiority of foot-soldiers, and at the same time a lack of trust in their own effectiveness among the French and English nobles with the result that some time elapsed before the mounted knights regained the initiative in military operations. Even the narrow victory of the French at Mons-en-Pévèle in 1304 did not restore the confidence of the knights, for they risked no major battles in the campaigns of 1314 and 1315.

Generalizations from Detailed Accounts

If we have a really good description which illuminates all sorts of problems and removes certain question-marks, are we justified in generalizing from these details? It all depends on the nature of the information, as an example will show. The leader of a unit is often mentioned, but we learn only by chance where he was during the advance and in the battle. Frequently he rode at the head of his unit. At other times

---

[28] 'The Tactics of the Battles of Boroughbridge and Morlaix', *English Historical Review*, 19, 1904, pp. 711–15. 'Some neglected Fights between Crécy and Poitiers', *ibid.*, 20, 1905, pp. 726–30.
[29] 'Mounted Infantry in Medieval Warfare', *Transactions of the Royal Historical Society*, Third Series, 8, 1914, pp. 77–102.
[30] 'De Gentse minderbroeder der Annales Gandenses en de krijgskunst in de periode 1302–1304', *Hand. Maatschappij voor Geschiedenis en Oudheidkunde te Gent*, Nieuwe reeks, 4, 1949, pp. 3–19. [See also M. Bennett, 'The development of tactics in the Hundred Years War', in *Arms, Armies and Fortifications in the Hundred Years War*, ed. A. Curry and M. Hughes, Woodbridge, 1994, 1–20.]

it was the standard-bearer who went in front with the standard, and so led the assault. A few explicit texts on this point will serve to clarify the others, since the question of who led was probably a matter of custom. We can be more definite on the density of small units. It is often stated that the units were in close formation when they attacked. Just how close were they in their ranks? We know for certain that the cavalry fought very much jammed up together, and this applies to all cases where it is stated that the units fought in very close ranks: both Ambroise in the *Estoire* and the *Itinerarium* tell us that the men stood so close to their comrades that an apple thrown into the air could not fall without hitting a horse or a man.[31] Guiart says, having seen various combats in 1304, that the ranks of knights were so closely packed that a glove could not fall between them.[32]

Once a battle has thus been visualized down to the last detail, the incomplete accounts become clearer, and one catches many allusions which pass unnoticed until the key to the problem has been found. This is the case with the so-called 'individual encounters'. In many instances we can show that historians, due to a preconceived notion or plain prejudice, have simply not read certain passages in their source carefully. They have kept the name of the prominent nobleman who fought at the head of his unit, but in their account of the engagement they forget the words *cum suis, avec sa gent, cum sua acie*, with the result that the fighting of entire formations is represented as a duel fought out by two champions. Occasionally it happened that a combatant, separated from his unit, was surrounded by an enemy formation. In such a case it is sometimes forgotten that genuine single-combat was involved only on one side. Through a careful comparison of all these little details, often drawn from accounts of insignificant battles which have not been studied before, we have sketched a general picture of medieval battles in which only a relatively few obscure points remain. These we hope to be able to resolve in time.

Accounts of Battles by Eye-witnesses

Although historians prefer to use eye-witness accounts, it is sometimes alleged that the eye-witnesses understood nothing of military actions, or that they were not capable of passing fair judgement on them. Fris, for example, assumes that the combatants themselves could give no account of the movements of the various units on the battlefield and praises the description of this phenomenon by Stendhal in *La Chartreuse de Parme*. Later he assumes that Guiart, in his account of the battle of Courtrai, depended on the assertions of combatants who 'understood nothing of the movements and different attacks'.[33] Here, in common with Funck-Brentano in his *Mémoire sur la bataille de Courtrai*, he quotes an example from Erasmus.[34] Another example of this is Abbot Gilles le Muisit, who explains that every soldier in battle

---

31 Ambroise, *L'estoire* . . ., pp. 164–5. *Itinerarium peregrinorum*, pp. 260–61.
32 *La branche des royaus lingnages*, RHF, 22, vv. 20477–82, p. 291.
33 V. Fris, *De slag bij Kortrijk*, Ghent, 1902, pp. 9, 27.
34 *Mémoire sur la bataille de Courtrai* . . ., p. 259. Erasmus, *Colloquia familiaria*, Basle, 1529, p. 50.

is bound to concentrate his efforts on the fight, so that he can neither see everything at the same time, nor accurately judge events as they take place.[35]

Such assertions are of course exaggerated, to say the least. The young Fabricio del Dongo, whom Stendhal mentions in his novel, was not competent to pass judgement on the movements which he saw because he knew nothing of the units of the French army, because he arrived late on the scene of action, and because the author's conception of his hero makes him stress his naïveté.[36] Erasmus' text consists of a conversation between two people: Hanno and Trasymachus. The latter has taken part in a battle and is being questioned by the former. Trasymachus says that there was so much noise, turmoil, flourishes of trumpets, neighing of horses and people calling out to each other that he could not see what was happening, so that he scarcely knew where he was. Hanno asks how it is possible for some people who had taken part to know all the details – what was said, what happened – just as if they had been omnipresent spectators. Trasymachus thinks that such eye-witnesses 'lie splendidly', and adds that he knew what happened in his tent, but not on the battlefield. Erasmus' criticism is aimed chiefly at those eye-witnesses who purport to tell everything and speak authoritatively about all the deeds of arms in a battle, as if they were acquainted with the leaders' plans and had seen everything that took place. But it cannot be said that the argument of Trasymachus is conclusive. His account of all the noise and hubbub does not stop him from keeping his eyes open. Despite confusion there is always an opportunity to observe something.

These exaggerated representations of the incompetence of eye-witnesses can easily be refuted. Fris in fact considered that Guiart was incomparable for his description of military operations, which flatly contradicts his assertions mentioned earlier. It was precisely because he was an eye-witness that Guiart was able to describe manoeuvres so well. Moreover Gilles le Muisit showed that an eye-witness account is better than a hearsay one by his description of the arrival of the fleeing French soldiers in the evening after the battle of Courtrai. The liveliness and interest of this section contrasts sharply with the rest of his account of the battle of Courtrai. Here is an eye-witness still competent even though he is writing nearly fifty years after the event. Indeed in general it is surely the case that eye-witness accounts are the best, and that all good descriptions of battle come from participants or people who were on the spot. The best account of Bouvines was written by William the Breton who was there, of Worringen by Jan van Heelu, of Arsuf by Ambroise, and of Mansurah by Joinville. We have already seen that Fulcher gives a far better picture of the battle of Ramla than Albert of Aix. The reliability of an eye-witness is limited not so much by his ability to grasp the various operations on the battlefield, as by his opportunities for observation. Gilles le Muisit is right when he states that the man on the spot is witness of only part of the action. This is also evident in Joinville's account of the battle of Mansurah. He particularly describes those actions in which he personally had a part, which provoked unfair criticism from Oman.[37] We, on the

---

[35] Gilles le Muisit, *Chronique et Annales*, ed. H. Lemaître, SHF, Paris, 1905, p. 160.
[36] Jean Norton Cru, *Témoins*, Paris, 1930, pp. 15–16.
[37] *Art of War*, I, p. 350, n. 2; p. 351, n. 1.

other hand, prefer a partial but accurate description of a battle to a complete but over-concise survey which easily becomes a string of generalities.

Jean le Bel's account of his expedition with Edward III's army against the Scots in 1327 is full of information about tactics and strategy. Only an eye-witness could have written this, a masterpiece of its kind. There is a wealth of information on the advance of the units, military discipline on the march, camp customs and usages of leadership and command. It presents a good overall picture of many problems: equipment and supplies, the tactics and armament of the Scots, their choice of troop formations on a suitable terrain, and the value of these formations. Then comes a faithful account of the state of mind of soldiers advancing in unfamiliar surroundings – hunger, thirst and privation, exposure to rain and wind, in a wild region where they had to sleep without shelter; all this is grippingly described. He describes how this privation and misery led them to the point where they all wanted to get the battle over quickly so as to be able to go home. Fear, sense of honour and discipline – the whole psychology of the soldier is described in masterly fashion.[38] Part of the importance of accounts by people who actually took part in a battle thus lies for our purposes not so much in the meticulous description of battles and marches, as in the accurate portrayal of the state of mind, the desire for battle or the fear of it, the general mental outlook of the participant, and the condition of his morale. Such accounts of the feelings of the combatants are found almost exclusively in the writing of eye-witnesses such as Fulcher, Ambroise, Joinville and Jean le Bel, all of whom give us a fair idea of military courage, the fighters' fear, and the tension they feel both before and during the battle. Now the essential element in each battle lies in the attitude of the soldiers during the fighting. The way they handle their weapons, the manner in which they react in the face of danger and behave in a battle for life – this is what counts. Eye-witness accounts are therefore indispensable to the military historian.

---

38 Jean le Bel, *Chronique*, ed. J. Viard and E. Déprez, SHF, 2 vols, Paris, 1904–5, I, pp. 35–77.

II

THE KNIGHTS

The Knight and his Equipment

Medieval warfare was characterised by the dominant role of the heavy cavalry. This preponderance, dating from the barbarian invasions of the fourth century, may be ascribed largely to the excellence of their equipment, which incorporated several technical innovations. The high saddle, with supports behind and before, and stirrups, made it possible for a cavalryman to remain firmly in the saddle during a rapid charge. The hooves of the warhorses were protected by shoes, so that they could travel faster and further. The warriors were encased in long leather cuirasses, and were armed with longish lances, or they were skilled as archers. In addition, these nomads also had the natural advantage of being steppe-dwellers and therefore born horsemen and fighters, whose hard living conditions made them superior to their Roman adversaries. The harsh climate had toughened their bodies, and they had the instinctive strategy which living in wide open space had taught them. The rise of this armoured cavalry put an end to the supremacy of the Roman legions, and brought about a revolution in the art of war. Among the Franks, however, men on foot remained the principal fighting force for a long time, but in the end they too followed the general evolutionary trend towards an army of armoured cavalry. This great change took place between the early eighth century and the middle of the ninth.

In 716 Charles Martel and his Austrasian warriors started a century of aggressive wars and conquest. It was a new strategy because the army attacked one or more enemies every year. Clovis (482–511) had conquered the kingdom of Syagrius in a single battle in 486 and that of the Alamanni ten years later in 496. He defeated the king of the Burgundians in 500 or 501, and conquered the kingdom of the Wisigoths in 507. Charles Martel held a campaign every year, reconquered Neustria, Alamannia, Bavaria, Frisia, Burgundy, Aquitaine, Provence, defeated the Saracens at Poitiers in 732 and on the Berre in 737. He attacked the Saxons in 718, 720, 722, 724, 738, and obliged them to pay tribute. The Austrasians became the masters of the Frankish kingdom, were installed as counts, bishops, abbots, judges and vassals in the regions which submitted, won much booty and enriched themselves. Under Charlemagne the kingdom was vastly enlarged by the conquest of Lombardy, a large part of Italy, the frontier zone of Spain, Saxony and the lands of the Avars and the Slavs. Those conquests were possible because the army of the Franks was better and stronger than that of the enemies. The quality was higher due to the development of the heavily armoured horsemen who had stronger armour and better weapons than the enemy:

the *brunia*, a tunic covered with metal rings or plates, a metal helmet and leg guards, long swords of high quality, lances and bows and arrows. The empire extended from Hamburg to Barcelona and Tortosa, from Rennes to the Ring of the Avars and the Danube. For the foot-soldiers the distances from their home to the land of the enemy became too great and the campaign lasted too many months. The free men owed military service to the king. If a man did not join the army he had to pay the *heribannum*, a heavy fine of 60 *solidi*. It was impossible to send all the free men against the enemy at 1,000 to 1,500 km from their home. The army would be too big for the existing roads and to find food in the country of the enemy. When the king ordered that 'all men should go to the army' in 792/93, that 'all should be ready and fully equipped' in 802, and that 'the count should order every man to join the army' in 803, his counts knew that some of the free men had to go with the army and that the others could stay at home but had to pay for the costs of the expedition to the participants and to the king.[1] The warriors preferred to conquer on horseback and to follow the example of their neighbours and adversaries, the Byzantines, the Goths, the Lombards, the Avars, the Saracens, the Bretons and the Gascons.

In 732 Charles Martel took lands from the Bishop of Orleans and others, part of them for his own uses, part to give to his vassals. In 733 he occupied Burgundy and installed vassals there and at Lyon and Orleans. Under him, Pepin III and Charlemagne the bishops and abbots installed vassals on the properties of the church. Fulrad, abbot of Saint-Quentin, had to come to the army with his horsemen in 806. The abbot of Saint-Riquier had 110 horsemen, his vassals, at his disposal in 831.[2] There were many abbeys in the empire of Charlemagne and they had their vassals. During their wars of conquest Pepin III and Charlemagne realised that they needed permanent troops which they could send to the frontier zone (*marca*) and install as a garrison in a fortress, or send for a raid against an enemy. They kept young vassals at the palace as members of their bodyguard, the *scara*, which replaced the *antrustiones* of the Merovingian kings. Those young royal vassals could be sent against the enemy, while the landed vassals stayed at home on their benefices.

The scara

In 766 Pepin III placed the *scara* of the Franks as a garrison at Bourges in his war against the duke of Aquitaine.[3] In 768 he sent his counts, the warriors of the *scara* and his *leudes* in four directions in the pursuit of the duke of Aquitaine. They were horsemen. In 773 in the campaign against the Lombards, one of the two armies of Charlemagne was held up by the fortifications near Mount Cenis. Charles sent his *scara* by another route to attack the enemy. This *scara* was a group of excellent warriors. After the surrender of the fortified town of Pavia in June 774, Charles returned home. From Ingelheim he sent four *scarae* against the Saxons. Three of

---

1 F.L. Ganshof, *Frankish Institutions under Charlemagne*, Providence, 1968, p. 60.
2 J.F. Verbruggen, *L'art militaire dans l'empire carolingien (714–1000)*, p. 296.
3 J.F. Verbruggen, *op. cit.*, pp. 292–4.

them fought against the enemy. In 776 *scarae* were placed as a garrison in the castles of Eresburg and the Lippe in the conquered region of Saxony. In 778 Charlemagne came back from Spain with his army. From Auxerre he sent the *scara Francisca* against the Saxons, who were plundering the land of the Franks. The *scara* had to march very quickly to chase the enemy. In July 782 Charlemagne held the general assembly at Lippspringe. Peace reigned everywhere, there was no expedition against the enemy, the warriors went home, and the king came back to Gaul. At that moment he received the news that the Sorbs, living between the Elbe and the Saale, were plundering Thuringia and Saxony. He sent his chamberlain, Adalgis, his constable, Geilo and Worad, the count of the palace, with the *scara* against the Sorbs. They had to take with them Eastern Franks and Saxons to punish the Sorbs. When they came to Saxony, they heard that the Saxons had revolted against the Franks. Count Theodoric, a relative of Charlemagne, arrived with Ripuarian troops to fight the Saxons. But the three leaders of the *scara* decided to attack the Saxons with their own forces. They took up their arms not as if they were attacking an enemy in battle order, but as if they were about to pursue a beaten enemy and take the spoils. Every warrior rode as fast as his horse could gallop, at full speed. They came all in disarray on the Saxons, who stood in battle order before their camp and inflicted a serious defeat upon the Franks. Adalgis, Geilo, four counts and about twenty famous and noble men were killed, with other warriors, who followed them and preferred to die with them. In 784 Charles, son of the king, and the *scara* attacked and defeated the Westphalians in a combat of horsemen (*equestri proelio*). During the winter of 785–785 the *scara* stayed with the king in the fortress of Eresburg and units were sent out several times to attack the Saxons. The *scarae* were an *expedita manu*, a quick unit. In 791 the *scara* of Pepin, the son of the king, came from Italy and attacked the Avars before the beginning of the big expedition from Bavaria. In 793 and 803 there was no general campaign against the enemy, but the king sent his *scara* to the places where its presence might be useful. In 806 the son of the emperor, Charles, invaded the territory over the river Saale with the army and sent his *scarae* over the Elbe in the land of the Sorbs. Troops from Bavaria, Alamannia and Burgundy invaded Bohemia. In 812 three *scarae* were sent against the Wilzians and the army attacked the Abodrites. In those two cases the army and the *scarae* invaded different countries on a broad front. In 809 and 810 the *scarae* were sent to the marches on the frontiers of the empire.

In the beginning there was a *scara* of the Franks or *scara francisca*. In 768 and 773 they were *scariti sui* or *scara sua*, the *scara* of the king. In 774 there were four *scarae*, in 776 *scarae* were a garrison in two castles, in 785 *scarae* of the garrison made raids against the Saxons as rapid units. In 806 and 812 the *scarae* invaded the land of an enemy while the big army took the offensive in another country. Several *scarae* were sent out; they became more numerous than in the beginning of the reign. Charlemagne recruited more vassals and got more armoured cavalry. *Scara* became the technical term for a formation of armoured cavalry in the second half of the ninth century.

The Marchfield and the Mayfield

In 692 Pepin II held the muster of the army in March, as was the custom in the kingdom of the Franks under Clovis.[4] Charles Martel and his Austrasians attacked the army of Radbod and his Frisians in March 716, the army of Raganfred at Vinchy on 21 March 717.[5] But in 755 or 756 Pepin III changed the date of the muster of the army from March to May, because in May there was enough grass for the horses to be fed. In 758, the tribute of the Saxons was changed from 500 cows to 300 horses.[6] Pepin held the Field of May in 756, 758, 761, 763, 764 and 766.[7] The army needed so much grass for the horses that a capitulary of 802–803 ordered two-thirds of the grass of some counties to be reserved.[8] In 782 the army could start an expedition in the summer, because there was enough grass, but in April 798 there was not enough grass for the horses when the Saxons rebelled.[9] There was still another reason to start the military operations later. It was better for the horsemen and their horses to invade the country of the enemy at the moment that the crop was ripe in the fields. Charlemagne held a Field of May at most seventeen times during his forty-five years of reign. In 775 and 781 the army went on campaign in July, in 777 in June or July. In 791 the big army on the frontier of Bavaria invaded the country of the Avars on 8 September.[10] In 806 the general assembly was fixed on 17 June, in 807 in August.[11]

When the conquests ended and the yearly campaigns were no longer profitable, the poorer free men wished to stay at home. In 805 the emperor diminished the *heribannum* for the poorer free men. A capitulary of 806 shows a system of regulation: in Frisia a man who joined the army was helped by six men who stayed at home. In Saxony the number was five helpers for the man who participated in a campaign toward Spain or the land of the Avars, two helpers for one man who joined in an expedition towards Bohemia. In 807 the system shows that the poor warriors who had no land received five *solidi* from the five helpers.[12] When Louis the Pious started his campaign against Brittany on 2 March 830, the free men rebelled and followed the sons of the emperor, Pepin and Lothar.[13] During the struggle of Louis the Pious against his sons, and the war between the sons, in the years 840 to 842, the

4 *Annales Mettenses priores*, ed. B.Von Simson, MGH, 1905, p. 14.

5 *Annales S. Amandi, Annales Tiliani, Annales Laubacenses, Annales Petaviani*, ed. G.H. Pertz 1826, MGH, SS, 1, 716, 717, pp. 6–7.

6 J.F. Verbruggen, 'L'armée et la stratégie de Charlemagne', in *Karl der Grosse*, ed. W. Braunfels, I, Dusseldorf 1965, p. 420. *Annales regni Francorum*, ed. F. Kurze, MGH, 1895, 758, p.16.

7 F.L. Ganshof, *Frankish Institutions*, pp. 62, 66.

8 *Capitulare Aquisgranense 802–803*, c. 10, Capit. 1, no. 77, p. 171.

9 *Annales regni Francorum*, 782, 798, pp. 59, 103.

10 *Ibid.*, pp. 62 and 155, n. 22. *Annales regni Francorum* (791), p. 88.

11 *Karoli ad Fulradum abbatem epistola*, Capitularia, I, no. 75, p. 168. *Memoratorium de exercitu in Gallia occidentali praeparando, ibid.* nr 48, c. 3, p. 135.

12 *Memoratorium, loc. cit.*, c. 2, p. 135. F.L. Ganshof, *Frankish Institutions*, p. 114.

13 *Annales Bertiniani*, ed. G. Waitz, MGH, 1883, p. 2.

free men stayed at home and the fighting was done nearly exclusively by the leaders and their vassals, the horsemen.[14]

On 13 May 841 count Adalbert and the leaders of Lothar wanted to fight against the warriors of Louis the German in the Riessgau near the river Wornitz on the left side of the Danube. Before 'arriving at the point of the lances', the terrified vassals of Lothar turned back and fled, losing innumerable men in their flight. This was a combat of horsemen.[15] The evolution was complete: armoured horsemen, vassals, were the principal element of the army, the foot-soldiers the secondary weapon. New and original tactics developed, for this European heavy cavalry used different methods from the Parthian tactics which were still being employed later by the Saracens and other Asiatic peoples. In western Europe the man who fought on horseback was known from the tenth century onwards as a knight. Thereafter, constant evolution took place: his equipment became increasingly heavy and impenetrable up to the end of the fifteenth century as armour was continually being further developed in a race with armour-piercing weapons. This heavy equipment made the cavalry supreme on the battlefield.

It is important to consider the cost of equipping an armoured cavalryman in the middle of the eighth century, at the time when the Frankish heavy cavalry was being developed. The Ripuarian Law gives the price of weapons and equipment as well as the value of horses, oxen and cows.

The helmet	6 *solidi*
The *brunia* or byrny	12 *solidi*
The sword and scabbard	7 *solidi*
The sword alone, without scabbard	3 *solidi*
The leggings	6 *solidi*
The lance and shield	2 *solidi*
The horse	12 *solidi* [16]

A sound ox with horns was then worth two *solidi*, a sound cow with horns anything between one and three *solidi*, a sound mare three *solidi*. The equipment of an armoured cavalryman thus cost as much as fifteen mares or nearly twenty-three oxen, an enormous sum of money. It is not surprising that in 761 a small landowner, Isanhard, sold his inheritance for a horse and a sword.[17] Complete equipment could only be expected of the very rich. The Capitulary of Thionville in 805 required a *brunia* or cuirass only of those who possessed or held as *beneficium* twelve *mansi*,

---

[14] G. Waitz, *Deutsche Verfassungsgeschichte*, IV, p. 543. H. Brunner, *Der Reiterdienst und die Anfänge des Lehnwesens*, p. 9. Oman, I, p. 104. F. Lot, *L'art militaire*, I, p. 104. Nithard, *op. cit.*, 1. II, c. 6, 8, 9, 10, pp. 56, 58, 60, 68, 70.

[15] *Notae historicae Sangallenses*, ed. G.H. Pertz, MGH, SS, I, 1826 p. 70: 'duces Hlotharii cum Hludowico rege pugnam committere volentes, antequam ad punctum lancearum pervenissent timore exterriti refugerunt, ac per hoc innumerabiles in eadem fuga extincti sunt.' *Annales Fuldenses*, ed. F. Kurze, MGH, 1891, p. 32. *Annales Bertiniani*, p. 25. Nithard, *op. cit.*, p. 66.

[16] *Lex Ribuaria*, MGH, Leges, V, tit. 36, 11, p. 231.

[17] H. Wartmann, *Urkundenbuch der Abtei St. Gallen, Zurich*, 1863, I, no. 31, p. 34.

about 300–450 acres:[18] there cannot have been many who were so rich. The emperor of course could provide cuirasses for his men, and bishops, abbots, abbesses and counts were obliged to have certain number to equip their men. A reserve of equipment for poorer vassals was formed from the payments of the fine of the *heriban* by those who did not fulfil their military obligations.[19]

Charlemagne certainly had a stronger army than his adversaries, but he owed his successes primarily to a relatively small number of armoured cavalrymen, whose superiority was largely due to their heavy armament. This small number of well armed men was aided by a considerable number of light cavalrymen, possessing no *brunia*, who formed the mass of the mounted army. The Frankish historiographers often stressed their more efficient equipment. Sometimes indeed, it was too heavy, as in 778, when Charlemagne's army was surprised in a Pyrenean mountain pass by the lightly armed Basques, and suffered the famous defeat which was later described in the *Chanson de Roland*.[20]

The armoured cavalrymen were mostly vassals who could be made knights. Up to the middle of the thirteenth century these knights were the most prominent and usually the most numerous section of the armoured cavalry. They were occasionally reinforced with well-equipped non-vassal cavalrymen serving as mercenaries. A prince's retinue also included warriors who received a mail-shirt from him, but were in no way vassals. Armoured cavalrymen who were not knights are mentioned five times in the army of the count of Hainault, and on four occasions they were equal in numbers to the knights.

In 1172: 340 knights and 340 armoured cavalry
In 1180: 100 knights and 100 armoured cavalry
In 1181: first 100 knights and as many cavalry, then eighty of each

In 1187 there were 110 knights and only eighty armoured cavalry, obviously small numbers. The count of Flanders had on one occasion 500 knights and 1,000 armoured horsemen in his army, at a time when many knights stayed in their own castles;[21] no examples of this occur elsewhere. It is noteworthy that the princes were able to recruit and equip such armoured men.

From the early ninth century to the end of the eleventh there were many vassals who at first had no *brunia*, and later no hauberk, but the social rise of vassals reduced the number of these light cavalrymen. When William the Conqueror introduced feudal organization into England, a knightly fief was a fief for which a vassal with a hauberk had to serve.[22] In 1181 the first clause of the Assize of Arms of Henry II

18 *Capitulare missorum in Theodonisvilla*, 805, c. 6, Capit. 1, no. 44, p. 123.
19 *Capitulare Bononiense*, 811, c. 10. *Capitulare Aquisgranense, 802–803*, c. 9. Capit. 1, nos. 74 and 77, pp. 167 and 171.
20 *Annales regni Francorum*, anno 778, p. 51. Einhard, *Vita Karoli Magni imperatoris*, ed. L. Halphen, CHFMA, 4th edn, Paris, 1967, c. 9, p. 30. *Ermoldus Nigellus, Carmen*, ed. E. Faral, CHFMA, Paris, 1932, 1. III, vv. 1708–9, p. 130.
21 Gilbert of Mons, *Chronicon Hanoniense*, ed. L. Vanderkindere, CRH in 8°, Brussels, 1904, c. 71, p. 111; c. 96, p. 131; c. 99, pp. 136, 138; c. 131, p. 197; c. 114, p. 171.
22 F.M. Stenton, *The First Century of English Feudalism. 1066–1166*, Oxford, 1932, p. 15.

stipulated that every baron who had knights' fees on his demesne should provide hauberks, helmets, shields and lances for them.[23] Horses were also armoured with chain mail after the middle of this century, and about that time a better saddle was introduced, in which the higher pommel and cantle gave more support before and behind. In 1187 the count of Hainault aided King Philip Augustus with a unit of 190 horsemen, of whom more than 109 had barded, or armoured horses.[24] In the thirteenth century squires had to have barded horses to qualify for higher pay: under Edward I in his Welsh wars (1277–1295) squires with armoured horses were paid 1 shilling a day, those with unprotected horses 6d or 8d.[25] Philip IV of France applied the same rule in his wars between 1294–1299: a squire with a good well armoured horse had a wage of 12s 6d *tournois* a day, others only 5s.[26] The use of armoured horses naturally strengthened the cavalry units; the best horses and strongest knights were used in the front rank. From the middle of the thirteenth century onwards the number of squires (i.e. sons of knights who had not yet been knighted) grew continuously, until by the end of that century they were more numerous than the knights. In time of peace they chose to remain squires because the accolade was accompanied by great and expensive festivities. They hoped to be dubbed knights before a battle, as at Mons-en-Pévèle in 1304 and Worringen in 1288. Collectively, the knights and squires were known as *armures de fer*, because they wore mail shirts. This armour was always very expensive, and it was becoming stouter and heavier all the time. The *brunia*, a leather tunic with iron rings or plates, gave way to the hauberk, a mail-shirt, which in turn was replaced in the last third of the twelfth century by the great hauberk, or long mail-shirt. From the middle of the thirteenth century this was reinforced with metal plates. This technical evolution exerted an important influence on the social position of the knight – the completely-equipped horseman *par excellence* – who became increasingly prominent. The number of knights was greatest in the eleventh and early twelfth centuries. At the end of the twelfth, and specially in the thirteenth century, they dwindled rapidly, but those who remained were both more important and far richer than their counterparts of the eleventh century.

As time went on, horses were increasingly used. As early as 1101 every one of the 1,000 knights who were promised by Count Robert II of Flanders to the king of England had three horses.[27] A knight's horses were a great expense. In order to enable the ruler to replace the horses which knights lost during a campaign, the animals had a value placed upon them. The horses of Geraard de Moor, lord of Wessegem, were worth the following sums in 1297, in *livres tournois*:

(1) The best horse, called Mouton   £300
(2) The black horse that he got from Louis, son of Robert of Bethune £250
(3) The horse that he got from the king of France   £125

---

[23] W. Stubbs, *Select Charters*, 9th edn, 1913, p. 153.
[24] Gilbert of Mons, *op. cit.*, c. 131, p. 197.
[25] J.E. Morris, *The Welsh Wars of Edward I*, Oxford, 1901, pp. 52, 53, 83.
[26] P. Contamine, *Guerre, Etat et société à la fin du moyen age*, Paris, 1972, p. 620.
[27] F. Vercauteren, *Actes des comtes de Flandre*, Brussels, 1936, no. 30, c. 2, p. 89.

(4)	A horse he had from the count of Flanders	£225
(5)	Another from William of Dendermonde	£120
(6)	The horse from John of Namur	£140
(7)	A horse for the march (courser)	£ 40
		£1200

Thus an important lord like Geraard had at least seven horses, with a total value of 1,200 *livres tournois*, or 960 *livres parisis*. The chargers of his squires were less expensive: the six squires who were already mounted possessed horses worth £60, £50, £40, £40, £40, and £12 *parisis* respectively, though a £12 horse was not a charger but a horse for the march, and the squire who owned it had, like two of his fellows, to get another charger. Moreover Geraard's retinue included other warriors, among them his brother, who had a horse worth £100 *parisis*, which he had received from the count of Flanders. The others had animals of the following values: £100, £60, £34, £33, £31, £20, £28, £120, £50, £20, £16, £80, £40, £30, £24 and £25 *parisis*.[28] If the squires who still had to buy a charger are left out of account, we find that Geraard's seven horses are worth £960 *parisis* and those of twenty-one men of his retinue were worth £1,046 *parisis*. If we take £12 as the basic value of a horse, we see that Geraard's seven horses cost as much as eighty ordinary horses, while each member of his retinue had on an average a horse worth £48, equal in value to four ordinary horses. The whole company of twenty-two men, including Geraard, had horses worth £2,006 *parisis*, or the value of 167 ordinary horses, and each knight or squire had on average horses worth £91, representing more than seven ordinary horses. This reflects a markedly higher value than in the Ripuarian Law, where a horse cost twelve *solidi*, the same as four mares. The same situation held in 1302. While many people bought horses for £6, £8, £9, £10 or up to £15, the men of Bruges bought chargers for William of Jülich worth £180, £179, £129, £119, £100, and £88 each, and they bought more elsewhere for a total of £349 1/2, not counting the less valuable horses and the chargers of his retinue. The knight Vranken of Zomergem received £100 for his dead horse, while Henry of Lontzen got a charger for £100 and another for £85.[29] In England and France the rich barons and bannerets rode still more expensive war-horses.[30]

Evidently it was not easy for the knights to buy and maintain such expensive war-horses. In addition, they had to be fully equipped themselves, with a mail-shirt reinforced with chest, shoulder and elbow plates, helmet, sword, lance, silken pennon, tent, all sorts of kitchen utensils such as kettles, pots, and pans and of course a beast of burden to carry all this. By the thirteenth century this had become so expensive that the number of knights who could afford it had dwindled considerably. By the end of that century and in the early fourteenth real knights were less numerous:

[28] J. de St-Genois, *Inventaire analytique des chartes des comtes de Flandre*, Ghent, 1843–1846, no. 902, p. 263: error for the sixth horse. The MS gives 140 l.t.
[29] J. Colens, *Le compte communal de la ville de Bruges, mai 1302 à février 1303*, Bruges, 1886, pp. 4–5, 131–4.
[30] Morris, *Welsh Wars*, pp. 49, 82. Contamine, *Guerre, Etat et société*, pp. 655–6. [See also A. Ayton, *Knights and Warhorses*, Woodbridge, 1994.]

in the above-mentioned retinue of Geraard there were only three knights: his brother Philip, Pieter of Uitkerke and Riquart Standaerd. In 1302 Zeger of Ghent and his son had twenty-two squires with them.[31] For nine knights from Zeeland in the same year we find 111 squires.[32] The active strengths of an army of armoured cavalry was limited by the considerable cost of buying expensive arms and equipment. The knights formed a social class living on the work of subordinates who cultivated the land for them, or who helped to assure the welfare of their master in various ways, and the vassals who lived at the court of a prince and were completely supported there cannot have been very numerous. In time knighthood became a hereditary class which had all sorts of privileges and this exclusive class had to recruit its members from its own ranks, which again led to small armies. The armoured fighter had also to be trained as a horseman, and good cavalrymen cannot be turned out quickly.

The Knight's Training

Under the early Carolingians the military training of the supreme fighting man – the armoured cavalryman – began in earliest youth, and later the young men who were destined for a military career were brought up in princes' courts in order to begin their arduous task at an early age. They had to learn to withstand fatigue, to endure hunger and thirst, heat and cold, and to master the technique of the fighting man.[33] The following plan was usually adopted. The young boy, son of a knight, destined for training in the *militia secularis*, was entrusted to another knight, usually a relative or close friend, or sometimes to the monarch, which was naturally a very great honour for him and his parents.[34] There he learned the profession of arms, together with all sorts of court duties. He was trained in riding, javelin-throwing and fencing. These exercises developed his physical strength, for the heavy knight's equipment, which was to be presented to him later, could only be worn by fully-grown adults. As a horseman, he practiced the game of *quintaine*, as Philip of Alsace made his pages do at Arras. He charged on horseback with couched lance towards a shield fixed to a stake: this shield had to be pierced or the boy's lance would break on it.[35] Or he had to charge a dummy for practice in aiming a lance thrust. He spent several years in this way in the castle of his master, where he was a member of the household.

[31] L. Gilliodts-Van Severen, *Inventaire des archives de la ville de Bruges*, Bruges, 1871, I, no. 155, p. 77.

[32] Colens, *op. cit.*, pp. 151–3.

[33] Hrabanus Maurus, *De procinctu romanae militiae*, ed. Dummler, *Zeitschrift für deutsches Altertum*, 15, 1872, p. 444.

[34] Hariulf, *Vita S. Arnulfi episcopi Suessionis*, ed. O. Holder-Egger, MGH, SS, 1888, 15, 2, p. 882. Lambertus Ardensis, *Historia comitum Ghisnensium*, ed. J. Heller, MGH, SS, 24, 1879, pp. 568, 603. Walterus Tervacensis, *Vita Caroli*, MGH, SS, 12, c. 5, p. 541. Walter Map, *De nugis curialium*, ed. R. Pauli, MGH, SS, 1885, 27, p. 70.

[35] Hariulf, *Vita S. Arnulfi*, pp. 879, 888. Giraldus Cambrensis, *De rebus a se gestis*, ed. J.F. Dimock, *Opera*, 5, RS, I, London, 1867, p. 50. *Miracula S. Rictrudis*, AA. SS. Mai 3, p. 104. Galbert of Bruges, *De multro, traditione et occisione gloriosi Karoli comitis Flandriarum*, ed. H. Pirenne, Paris, 1891, c. 30, p. 52; c. 9, pp. 15–16.

What did these young men need to know in their future calling as knights? No one has described this better than Chrétien de Troyes in the *Roman de Perceval*. Perceval learns both how to guide the horse during the charge, and how to stop it in time. He has to put the lance on the felt of the saddle, spur the horse, and couch the lance under his upper arm before the shock. He also learns to handle the shield, to ward off or deflect his adversary's thrust, and he must be well-versed in the art of swordsmanship.[36]

The training of young men for knighthood was taken very seriously, with excellent results. Roger of Hoveden says of the sons of Henry II of England:

> They strove to outdo the others in handling weapons. They realised that without
> practice the art of war did not come naturally when it was needed. No athlete can
> fight tenaciously who has never received any blows: he must see his blood flow
> and hear his teeth crack under the fist of his adversary, and when he is thrown to
> the ground he must fight on with all his might and not lose courage. The oftener
> he falls, the more determinedly he must spring to his feet again. Anyone who can
> do that can engage in battle confidently. Strength gained by practice is invaluable:
> a soul subject to terror has fleeting glory. He who is too weak to bear this burden,
> through no fault of his own, will be overcome by its weight, no matter how eagerly
> he may rush to the task. The price of sweat is well paid where the Temples of
> Victory stand.[37]

The young man who was dubbed knight after several years of learning his duties knew his job thoroughly. This individual training made the young apprentice a good horseman: wearing his mail-shirt, seated firmly in the high saddle with supports before and behind, his feet securely in the stirrups and the couched lance under his upper arm, he was a formidable warrior. From the end of the eleventh century, everything in his training and equipment was geared into a mighty attack on the enemy. This individual training was sometimes supplemented by collective exercises with other young nobles, which were frequently quite realistic. It involved participation in the private wars which raged in the middle of the twelfth century, and brought many an anxious moment for princes and clergy alike, who wanted to put an end to them. In the county of Flanders, the princes managed to stop this kind of fighting in about 1127.

Collective Training: Private Wars

A handful of detailed contemporary sources have brought the violent life of the knights in the eleventh century into sharp focus. Private wars, with vendettas and long feuds, were the order of the day, and families were divided into opposing camps engaged in cruel and savage strife, in which members of the knight's retinue, who were not bound to the families through blood ties, also played their part. There was

---

[36] Chrétien de Troyes, *Perceval*, ed. W. Foerster, Halle (Saale), 1932, 5, vv. 1433–58; 1473–80; 1491–4; 1510–19, pp. 63–7.
[37] R. de Hoveden, *Chronica*, ed. W. Stubbs, RS, 4 vols, London, 1868–71, 2, p. 166.

also savage fighting within the families and retinues of the powerful lords, which often ended fatally. In the tough life of the eleventh and early twelfth centuries violence played so great a part that it could only be put down by the ruthless and uncompromising action of a powerful personality. Sometimes such a man as the saintly future bishop, Arnulf of Soissons, managed to secure peace or limit the bloodshed for a time. In the relatively densely populated county of Flanders there was often no room for all the sons of large noble families, and those who were less well-off were filled with envy of the more fortunate. Sometimes the struggle against an enemy clan drew family bonds closer. There was nothing specially unusual in the case of a well-known knight, Bonifacius, who was driven out of his own castle by his two brothers, who had murdered his young wife and baby son. Undaunted by fate, he killed one of the murderers and put the other to flight.[38] The wild companions (*feroces socii*) of count Robert the Frisian of Flanders helped him to dethrone his nephew, but his ruthless behaviour led some nobles and rich men to plot to replace this cruel count with a gentler prince, count Baldwin II of Hainault.[39] Noble families in the Bruges district set about their private wars so ferociously that the blood money for murders committed amounted to 10,000 marks.[40] Near Furnes the lady Evergerda ignored the conciliatory words of Bishop Arnulf and caused the drawbridge of her castle to be raised, for, on account of the murder of her husband and son, there was a bloody feud in the neighbourhood.[41] A murder among the followers of Hugo of Blaringhem in 1060 nearly caused a pitched battle between the members of the murderer's family and Hugo's retinue.[42]

Solidarity was no empty word in the noble families of that day. The private wars were realistic collective actions for the turbulent and warlike nobility, resulting in heavy casualties whose extent we gather only in chance glimpses. A quarrel between two noble families in Burgundy in the eleventh century dragged on for thirty years; one of the parties lost more than eleven men in one of the first clashes.[43]

Lambert of Wattrelos relates that ten of his father's brothers were killed in a skirmish with their enemies near Tournai.[44] In 1127 the powerful Erembald family all ranged themselves round the murderers of count Charles the Good of Flanders, and with desperate courage sustained a long siege in the castle at Bruges, in the most difficult and nerve-racking conditions. In normal times this family was so influential that even the count did not dare assert his rights openly. The punishment of the defenders is reminiscent of the most epic example of solidarity in a great family: just as the thirty members of the family of Ganelon who had taken an oath on the

---

[38] *Miracula S. Ursmari, in itinere per Flandriam facta*, ed. O. Holder-Egger, MGH, SS, 15, 2, 1888, c. 6, p. 839.

[39] *Chronicon S. Andreae, castri Cameracesii*, ed. L.C. Bethmann, MGH, SS, 7, 1846, pp. 537–8. Hariulf, *Vita S. Arnulfi*, pp. 886–7. Galbert, c. 70, p. 114.

[40] Hariulf, *Vita S. Arnulfi*, p. 890.

[41] *Ibid.*, p. 889.

[42] *Miracula S. Ursmari*, p. 839.

[43] Ralph Glaber, *Historiarum libri V*, ed. M. Prou, Paris, 1886, 1. 2, c. 10. [Translated by J. France, Oxford, 1992.]

[44] *Annales Cameracenses*, ed. G.H. Pertz, MGH, SS, 16, 1859, pp. 511–12.

innocence of the traitor, following the defeat of their champion Pinabel, were hanged together on a tree in the accursed forest, so the last twenty-eight defenders of the castle at Bruges, guilty or not of the murder of Charles the Good, were hurled from the towers. One of them, Robert the Child, who was considered innocent by the men of Bruges, and who had only hastened to stand by his family out of loyalty, was nevertheless beheaded at Cassel by order of the king of France.[45]

The clergy were utterly opposed to these private wars and made strenuous efforts to put an end to them. At the Council of Clermont in 1095 Pope Urban solemnly told the Christian knights that they must stop this useless bloodshed in the West, and apply all their energy against the Moslems. But private wars were deeply rooted in the customs and usages of the time; they were even celebrated in heroic songs, in which knightly passions were exalted to epic proportions, and one of the most beautiful *chansons de geste, Raoul de Cambrai*, is wholly devoted to the conflict between his family and that of Herbert of Vermandois. The efforts of the clergy probably met with very little success, but the princes had every reason to struggle against these everlasting feuds, for their power was threatened whenever order and peace within the country was disturbed. In principalities where the central power had sufficient authority, such as Normandy and Flanders, the rulers succeeded at first in limiting private wars and then in practically stopping them altogether. In Flanders the turning-point was the conflict between count William Clito, supported by the knightly class, and Thierry of Alsace, aided by the cities and some of the knights. From this time onwards private wars in Flanders decreased although the quarrel between the Ingherkins and the Blavotins at the end of the twelfth and in the early thirteenth century is well known. Elsewhere these feuds went on, as is shown by the famous example of the fighting between the Awans and the Waroux in the principality of Liège, but their importance for the art of war disappears. The counts of Flanders and the other princes found a less bloody training ground for their knights in tournaments, where military action also took place in groups.

Collective Training: Tournaments

Even in the Middle Ages it was thought that tournaments were of quite recent origin. Their inventor was said to have been a certain Geoffrey of Preuilly, who died in 1066. Actually they go back to rather primitive collective games, although it is possible that the classic form encountered in the twelfth century had been introduced in the eleventh. Military leaders have always tried to reproduce war conditions as closely as possible in their training exercises. The Romans attempted to do this in their manoeuvres, and the Germans had military games for the whole population. Tacitus speaks of this with reference to the Tencteri: *hic lusus infantium, haec juvenum aemulatio*: 'here lies the diversion of infancy, the rivalry of youth'.[46] They are also

---

[45] Galbert, c. 81, pp. 125–6; c. 84, p. 129. Suger, *Vita Ludovici grossi regis*, ed. H. Waquet, CHFMA, Paris, 1929, c. 30, p. 248.

[46] Tacitus, *Germania*, ed. J. Perret, Paris, 1949, c. 32. [On tournaments in general see R. Barber and J. Barker, *Tournaments*, Woodbridge and New York, 1989.]

mentioned at the court of Theodoric, king of the Ostrogoths,[47] and Isidore of Seville records that the Visigoths liked sham battles and held military games daily.[48] Einhard reports riding exercises and weapon practice, which according to Frankish custom were carried out by Charlemagne's sons, while the emperor himself liked riding and hunting as his ancestors had done, 'for no one matches the Franks in these arts'.[49] During the struggle between the sons of Louis the Pious there were group exercises and military games among the Franks following the celebrated Oaths of Strasbourg of 14 February 842. These cavalry games were often held by the troops of Louis the German and Charles the Bald, probably at Worms: *causa exercitii*, for the training of their own followers. In the presence of spectators ranged on both sides of a place which had been prepared for the spectacle, equal numbers of Saxons, Gascons, Austrasians and Bretons rode at each other at full tilt, as though they were going to join battle. But a moment before they met, one of the parties made a turn and pretended to escape the attacking enemy by flight, while the horsemen protected themselves with their shields. Then it was the turn of the fugitives to attack the pursuers. Finally both young princes sprang on to their horses and with great exuberance took part in the game, encouraged by loud cheers from the crowd. Lance in hand, they charged first one group and then another of those who were fleeing.[50]

This kind of mock battle is not yet like the eleventh – or twelfth – century tournament. The lances were held in the hand and were not used to administer a heavy blow. The attack was devised in the same spirit: there was no clash, it remained just a manoeuvre, in which equal numbers of fighters faced each other. But men from the same region were practising together, attacking and retreating. It is evident from the summary of Vegetius' work on the art of war among the Romans, made by Hrabanus Maurus for King Lothar II, that such exercises were a normal thing among the Franks and he states that the art of horsemanship also flourished among them.[51] Half a century after Nithard, the Council of Tribur mentions heathen games which sometimes had a fatal ending.[52] In the tenth and eleventh centuries the Saxons and Thuringians followed the example of the Franks: foot-soldiers had formerly been their main arm, now they introduced cavalry, which quickly became skilled in the new manner of waging war. The Saxon rulers Henry I and Otto the Great were both praised by their biographer for their military games and their skill on horseback. Henry I surpassed all others in military exercises: *in exercitiis quoque ludi tanta eminentia superabat omnes, ut terrorem caeteris ostentaret*, and Otto practised riding regularly.[53]

In Flanders we find the earliest traces of tournaments in 1095. One was held near

[47] Delbrück, III, p. 264.
[48] Isidore of Seville, *Historia Gothorum, Wandalorum, Sueborum, ad a.DCXXIV*, ed. T. Mommsen, MGH, AA, II. c. 69–70.
[49] Einhard, *Vita Karoli*, c. 19, p. 58; c. 22, p.68.
[50] Nithard, 1. III, c. 6, pp. 110–12.
[51] Hrabanus Maurus, pp. 443–4.
[52] M.Bloch, *Les classes et le gouvernement des hommes*, Paris, 1949, p. 33.
[53] Widukind of Corvey, *Rerum gestarum Saxonicarum libri tres*, ed. H.E. Lohmann and P. Hirsch, MGH, 1935, I, c. 38, 39, pp. 57–8; II, c. 36, p. 97.

Tournai by the burgrave Evrardus, who had a number of gallant knights under him. Henry III, count of Louvain, invited one of his vassals, who was in the opposing camp, to enter the lists against him personally. Jocelyn of Vorst accepted his lord's challenge only after repeated pressure. Finally he couched his lance, spurred his horse savagely, and charged the count with the intent of unhorsing him, but the thrust struck the count in the heart, and he died instantly.[54] The counts of Flanders used tournaments to distract their knights from the private wars which were disturbing the peace in the county, and at the same time to give them a chance to practice. After he had restored peace and order in his county, Baldwin VII went abroad to get practice in the knightly profession of arms.[55] His successor Charles the Good pursued the same policy, and went with 200 knights to tournaments in France, in Normandy and even outside France, to enhance his own fame as well as the might and honour of his land, and being a pious man, he atoned for the sins incurred through these ventures with rich gifts to the Church.[56]

Even after the First Crusade the clergy were just as disturbed about these dangerous games as they had been over private wars, for they thought that both meant needless squandering of strength, and bloodshed, and that knights could test their prowess better against the Moslems in the Holy Land. The Council of Clermont in 1130 forbade tournaments because they entailed loss of human lives: anyone who perished in such a game was not to receive Christian burial.[57] But the knights thought otherwise. For them the tournament was a training-school, a pastime, a source of income and a suitable opportunity for meeting men of their own class, and their best feats could be admired by noble ladies, which was not possible on the battlefield. They let themselves be daunted neither by the criticism of the clergy nor by the prohibitions of the Church.

The ablest clerical figures of the day vigorously attacked tournaments. St Bernard of Clairvaux wrote to Suger: 'Take the sword of the spirit, which is the Word of God, against these accursed gatherings, these *nundinae*, which Robert the king's brother and Henry son of the count of Champagne want to hold after the coming feast of Easter'.[58] These two lords had just returned from the Holy Land and wanted to hold a tournament. One of the biographers of St Bernard wrote that all those who perished in a tournament 'certainly go to Hell'. James of Vitry portrayed the opposing champions in a tournament as follows: 'They are jealous of each other and inflict vicious blows on each other. The victor takes horse and arms from the vanquished. Knights cause considerable damage and destroy whole harvests. The lord burdens his subjects with heavy taxes in order to meet these foolish expenses, and the immorality of the feast follows the slaughter'.[59] The judgement of Humbert des

---

54 Herimannus Tornacensis, *Liber de restauratione S. Martini Tornacensis*, MGH, SS, 14, pp. 282–4.
55 *Ibid.*, c. 24, 26, p. 284.
56 Galbert, c. 4, p. 9.
57 Mansi, *Sacrorum conciliorum . . . collectio*, 21, anno 1130, Venice, 1776–78, c. 9, p. 439. Hefele, *Conciliengeschichte*, Freiburg, 1886, 5, c. 9, p. 410.
58 *Epistolae S. Bernardi*, ed. L. Delisle, *Recueil des historiens de la Gaule et de la France*, 15, 1878, no. 376.
59 A. Lecoy de la Marche, *La chaire française au moyen âge*, Paris, 1868, p. 365.

Romans was less harsh: 'Although tournaments are rightly forbidden because they are so dangerous for body and soul, and fighters often perish in them, yet they also have some advantages; some practices should be condemned and others allowed.' Humbert condemns the dissipation, the gross expenditure, ruinous to the knights and their families, which come from pride and an idle desire for glory because men like to be thought brave and gallant. What was still more serious was that some noblemen seized the opportunity of carrying on personal feuds. Others transgressed the tournament rules and made their opponents a laughing-stock. There were also knights who consorted with women of evil repute after tournaments. So there were three practices to be condemned, 'dissipation through unreasonable expense, desire for vainglory, and malicious intentions in battle'. But if a knight wanted to fight for God, he might take part in reasonable games so that he acquired skill in combat, for without practice one has no knowledge of the art of war. In tournaments the knights encouraged each other, and what they had long been doing for the vainglory of the world, they could also do for God in the worthy fight against the Saracens. In every case, wanton characters, the 'ribauds' and other evil persons were to be removed.[60]

The Church's prohibitions were repeated without much success in an imposing series of Councils: in 1139 at the tenth General Council, at the Councils of Rheims in 1148 and 1157, at the Lateran Councils in 1179[61] and 1215, and at the Council of Lyons in 1245. Tournaments were also forbidden by Pope Nicholas III in 1279.[62] They were, however, permitted twice during the reign of King Philip the Fair of France. The first occasion was after Pope Clement V had forbidden them on 14 September 1313. Pierre Dubois then wrote his treatise *De torneamentis et justis* to please the king and to answer the papal prohibition.[63] The pope permitted them again before Lent in 1314, and later a little known edict of Pope John XXII allowed them again at Philip's request, when their decline had already begun.[64]

In Flanders the reign of Philip of Alsace (1168–1191) saw the full flowering of tournaments and chivalry, which were closely related. About this time Counts Baldwin IV and V of Hainault were busily engaged in fighting in tournaments in the countries bordering their own.[65] A century later duke John I of Brabant reaped as great a success as Philip of Alsace, count of Flanders. Philip used special tactics in tournaments and acted as instructor to foreign princes, such as the young Henry of England.[66] John of Brabant trained his knights so thoroughly in war-games that the victory at Worringen may be said to have been the result of that training.[67] Both

---

[60] H. des Romans, *De eruditione religiosorum praedicatorum*, Maxima bibliotheca veterum patrum, 25, p. 559.

[61] Mansi, 21, c. 14, p. 530 (1139); c. 12, pp. 716–17 (1148); c. 4, p. 844 (1157); 22, c. 20, p. 229 (1179).

[62] *Ibid.*, pp. 681–2.

[63] Ch.V. Langlois, 'Un mémoire inédit de Pierre Du Bois, 1313: De Torneamentis et Justis', *Revue historique*, 41, 1889, pp. 85–6.

[64] N. Denholm-Young, 'The Tournament in the Thirteenth Century', *Studies in Medieval History presented to F.M. Powicke*, Oxford, 1948, p. 243.

[65] Gilbert of Mons, c. 55, 57, 62, 68, 69, 77, 85, 92, 98, 100, 101, 107, 109.

[66] *Histoire de Guillaume le Maréchal*, I, vv. 2723–40. Walter Map, *De nugis curialium*, p. 70.

[67] Jan van Heelu, *Rijmkronijk*, ed. J.F. Willems, CRH in 4º, Brussels, 1836, p. 194.

princes lived the full chivalric life of their day: at the court of Philip of Alsace there were poets such as Chrétien de Troyes, Gautier d'Epinal and the unknown author of *Li proverbe au vilain*. Duke John was a patron of Adenet le Roi, and was praised by Jan van Heelu;[68] he was also an occasional poet himself. Philip took part in two crusades and an expedition against Milan;[69] John twice went on campaigns in Spain and travelled through England to fight in tournaments there. Philip died ingloriously of a common epidemic near Acre, and John of the consequences of a minor wound received in a joust.[70] Both had strong personal military ambitions. Philip's tactics in tournaments seemed lacking in chivalry, although his comtemporaries approved them, and as far as he was concerned anything was permissible in dealing with an enemy. John wanted to settle the battle of Worringen sword in hand, and not with the help of ditches, and he preferred the destruction of robber-citadels to spectacular but useless expeditions to the Holy Land.[71]

Through the influential example of these princes, tournaments flourished in the southern part of the Netherlands and in Lorraine, and Flanders, though they were chiefly held in France. France's renown in this respect was so great that the English chronicler Ralph Diceto called the tournaments *conflictus gallici*, and Ralph of Coggeshall spoke of a conflict *more Francorum*.[72] Tournaments were forbidden in England by various kings, Henry II among them, because they gave rise to endless political troubles. At the time of civil war during the reign of the weak king Stephen tournaments were popular. Later, Richard I, a man skilled in the art of war, saw that the French knights were better trained than his own, so he permitted knightly exercises.[73] Being also an outstanding leader, Richard quickly succeeded in making up lost ground by his own example. This gave his fighting men such confidence that, according to the *Histoire de Guillaume le Maréchal*, from then onwards they risked attacking forty Frenchmen with thirty knights, 'which never used to be the case'.[74] Philip Augustus experienced this English confidence to his shame and sorrow at Fréteval on 13 July 1194, and at Gisors on 28 September 1198. 'In the life of Edward I foreign tournaments were the training ground of a great king' (1260–1262).[75] Tournaments did not differ greatly from real combat on the battlefield; indeed some sources call the clash of knights in full charge a *tornatio* or *tornoiement*.[76] The knights fought with their normal equipment, and there is no mention of the use of other

---

68 H. Pirenne, pp. 161, 209.
69 J. Johnen, *Philipp von Elsass*, BCRH, 79, 1910, pp. 426–33.
70 A. Wauters. *Le duc Jean Ier et le Brabant sous le règne de ce prince (1267–1294)*, Brussels, 1862, pp. 63, 218. Pirenne, *op. cit.*, pp. 147, 161.
71 Jan van Heelu, vv. 4821–5, 4410–12.
72 Denholm-Young, pp. 243–4.
73 William of Newburgh, *Historia rerum anglicarum*, ed. R. Howlett, RS, London, 1884–85, 2, p. 422.
74 *Histoire de Guillaume le Maréchal*, 2, vv. 11,063–8, p. 34.
75 D.M. Stenton, *English Society in the Early Middle Ages (1066–1307)*, Harmondsworth, 1951, p. 86.
76 Galbert, c. 79, 116. Anonyme de Béthune, *Une chronique française des rois de France*, ed. L. Delisle, RHF, 24, 1904, p. 769.

weapons, nor that the point of the lance or the cutting-edge of the sword were dulled.[77] This was anyway not necessary between 1150 and 1250, when the defensive equipment of the knights was strong enough to prevent fatal accidents. Naturally there was a risk of being unhorsed and seriously hurt thereby but the danger was not much greater in the real battles of that time when few men were killed. The main difference between tournaments and real battles lay in the fact that the engagement took place on terrain specially fixed by announcement or agreement. Knights came from far and wide with friends from their own country, or in a group under the command of their lord. Each of these troops took up position on their own 'ground', a piece of land marked out, from which the groups advanced to face each other in the tournament. This area was also a refuge for those who were exhausted and who had to withdraw from the lists. Again this was different from a real battle. Another difference was the custom of laying down arms as soon as one side gave up the battle. But if the enemy did not entirely give up while some of them were fleeing, the pursuit was carried on. An armistice could be brought about by common consent, and lasted until the resumption of the fighting, which was usually on the following day. At the end of the tournament a prize was awarded to the knight who had most distinguished himself by bravery or skill in unhorsing his opponents and taking them prisoner.[78]

The actual engagement in a tournament took place on a flat piece of ground, not marked off. Each side left its own base and rode at the enemy: the knights fought in units, and their numbers varied according to the extent to which the nobility of the region were taking part. Usually knights from the counties of Flanders and Hainault turned out together against the French in France. It was considered a scandal when, during a tournament between Gournay and Ressons, the newly knighted Baldwin of Hainault, later count Baldwin V, who had a grudge against count Philip of Alsace of Flanders, fought on the side of the French knights against the Flemings, instead of following the custom which demanded that the men of Hainault, Flanders and Vermandois fight together against the French.[79] In their own regions, however, Flemings fought against Hainaulters, or the latter against Brabanters.[80] Just as in real wars, tournaments served to foster local pride and increased moral solidarity in military units.

The knights were organised in *conrois* or units of varying strength, according to the power of the lord under whose banner they were fighting, or according to the extent of the participation of the nobility of a certain area. These units were drawn up in very close formation, the horsemen side by side, horse beside horse, and they had to advance and charge in an orderly manner. Such units were so obviously superior to those not drawn up in an orderly way that they were able to turn an unfavourable balance of strength to their own advantage. In a tournament in which

[77] Gilbert of Mons, c. 77, pp. 116–17: *quasi ad bellum ordinatis.*
[78] P. Meyer, in *Histoire de Guillaume le Maréchal*, 3, p. xxxvii, description of the tournaments.
[79] Gilbert of Mons, c. 57, pp. 97–8. *Histoire de Guillaume le Maréchal*, 1, vv. 4465–9, pp. 161–2. J. Bretel, *Le tournoi de Chauvency*, ed. M. Delbouille, BFPLUL, 49, Liège, Paris, 1932, p. X; v. 3949 *et seq.*, p. 127.
[80] Gilbert of Mons, c. 100, pp. 140–1.

the knightly units of prince Henry, son of Henry II of England, fought against the French, the French knights had such confidence in their numerical superiority that out of pride they forgot about unity, and charged, pell-mell, only to suffer a crushing defeat. In the view of contemporaries, one of the greatest stupidities that could be committed was the separate individual charge made by knights who abandoned the protective ranks of the *conroi* in order to rush ahead into battle, for in so doing they destroyed the cohesion of the unit. If on the other hand they attacked in close order, there was no risk of the enemy breaking through.[81]

Philip of Alsace, who was praised in the *Histoire de Guillaume le Maréchal* as being one of the best knights of his time, and as the most courteous count of Flanders, employed sly tactics in tournaments, which shows that he really believed anything was allowable in the face of the enemy. From this it appears that there was a certain continuity in the policy of the counts concerning tournaments, and that the princes' example in knightly exercises directly influenced the art of war. Philip was accustomed to using powerful contingents, some of which comprised very well-equipped foot-soldiers.[82] During the tournament he evidently kept these units skilfully behind the scenes as though he had no intention of their taking part in the game, and patiently waited for an opportune moment while groups of heavy cavalrymen rushed at each other. Then, when the contestants were worn out by the struggle and the units had lost their original cohesion, he gave the signal to charge and fell upon the enemy's flank. This meant victory for him and magnificent booty for his knights. As prince Henry's tutor, he taught him these tactics, first making him pay dearly for the knowledge in an actual tournament.[83] The *Histoire de Guillaume le Maréchal* mentions the dense *conrois* (*seréement*) in which the advance was made without disorder (*disrei*), in which the knights were arranged in close battle order (*serré et bataillé se tindrent*) and could fight in serried ranks (*errèrent sagement et rangié e seréement*) so that no one could get through them (*onques nuls n'en trespassa outre*) contrasting them to the units that advanced in disorder (*a grant disrei*), and in which knights recklessly broke rank in order to fight in front of the unit (*poindre as premiers de la rote*), which for that reason were severely censured (*fols est qui trop tost se desrote*). All this is clear evidence of real tactical units. Philip of Alsace waited until the contestants were no longer fighting in steady ranks (*desrengié*), nor formed a fixed unit (*destassé*). He attacked them on the flank (*lor moveit a la traverse*) and made the foolish knights who had left their units his special prey. When Prince Henry's troops were in disorder (*desrei*) and his men exhausted, the count fell on them. Yet in this text two scholars see only the possibility that Henry's knights were tired when they were attacked by fresh Flemings.[84]

81 *Histoire de Guillaume le Maréchal*, 1, v. 1303 *et seq.*, p. 48; v. 2497 *et seq.*, p. 92; v. 2732 *et seq.*, p. 100; vv. 3527–9, p. 128.
82 *Ibid.*, v. 3243–50, pp. 118–19. Gilbert of Mons, c. 57, p. 97.
83 *Histoire de Guillaume le Maréchal*, 1, vv. 2715–40, pp. 99–100.
84 S. Painter, *French Chivalry*, Baltimore, 1940, p. 48. Denholm-Young, 'The Tournament in the Thirteenth Century', p. 242. Not a word about the fact that they were in disorder and did not fight any longer in serried units.

The Psychology of Knights on the Battlefield

The turbulent chivalry of the eleventh and twelfth centuries had gained the reputation of having a gigantic and insatiable lust for fighting, which led to the innumerable wars of the times. This rather too simple explanation is suggested by the lyrical outpourings of some poets, whose evidence should now be re-examined. No one voiced this warlike attitude more clearly than Bertrand de Born in his well-known poem:

> I love the gay season of Eastertide, which brings forth flowers and leaves, and I love to hear the brave sound of the birds, making their song ring through the thickets, and I love to see tents and pavilions set up in the meadows. And I am overjoyed when I see knights and horses, all in armour, drawn up on the field.

> I love it when the chargers throw everything and everybody into confusion, and I enjoy seeing strong castles besieged, and bastions broken down and shattered, and seeing the army all surrounded by ditches, protected by palisades of stout tree-trunks jammed together.

> And I love just as much to see a lord when he is the first to advance on horseback, armed and fearless, thus encouraging his men to valiant service: then, when the fray has begun, each must be ready to follow him willingly, because no one is held in esteem until he has given and received blows.

> We shall see clubs and swords, gaily-coloured helmets and shields shattered and spoiled, at the beginning of the battle, and many vassals all together receiving great blows, by reason of which many horses will wander riderless, belonging to the killed and wounded. Once he has started fighting, no noble knight thinks of anything but breaking heads and arms – better a dead man than a live one who is useless.

> I tell you, neither in eating, drinking, nor sleeping, do I find what I feel when I hear the shout 'At them!' from both sides, and the neighing of riderless horses in the confusion, or the call 'Help! Help!', or when I see great and small together fall on the grass of the ditches, or when I espy dead men who still have pennoned lances in their ribs.

> Barons, you should rather forfeit castles, towns, and cities, than give up – any of you – going to war.[85]

Bertrand's warlike verses are not unique in their testimony. In the *chanson de geste* called *Girart de Vienne* the aged Garin de Montglane expresses himself in very similar fashion in a family council of war. Peace would make him ill, and he likes nothing better than the neighing of horses, and battle in the open field.[86] In the *Moniage Renoart* a knight would even return from Paradise to fight the Moslems.[87]

---

[85] P. Bec, *Petite anthologie de la lyrique occitane du Moyen Age*, Avignon, 1954, pp. 97–7.

[86] J. Flach, *Les origines de l'ancienne France*, II, p. 453.

[87] L. Gautier, *La chevalerie*, 3rd edn, Paris, 1895, p. 71.

Such lyrical effusions have made scholars think that the knight felt contempt for life and human suffering. Léon Gautier, a great glorifier of chivalry, wrote:

> There were two main elements in chivalrous courage, Germanic and Christian, which were not always properly blended. Too often the knights loved battle for its own sake and not for the cause they were defending. Under their mail shirts the primitive barbarian of the German forests still quivered. In their eyes the sight of red blood flowing on iron armour was a charming spectacle. A fine lance thrust transported them to the heavens. 'I prefer such a blow to eating or drinking!' cries out quite naturally one of the savage heroes of *Raoul de Cambrai*. This naive admiration is most apparent in the oldest epics and, in particular, in the *Chanson de Roland*. In the midst of a horrible battle our Frenchman, more than half dead, still finds time to criticize or admire skilful blows of lance or sword.[88]

We read in Huizinga: 'The psychology of courage in battle has probably never been so simply and strikingly expressed as in these words from *Le Jouvencel*':

> It is a joyous thing, a war ... You love your comrade so much in war. When you see that your quarrel is just, and your blood is fighting well, tears rise to your eyes. A great sweet feeling of loyalty and of pity fills your heart on seeing your friend so valiantly exposing his body to execute and accomplish the command of our Creator. And then you are prepared to go and die or live with him, and for love not to abandon him. And out of that, there arises such a delectation, that he who has not experienced it is not fit to say what delight it is. Do you think that a man who does that fears death? Not at all, for he feels so strengthened, so elated, that he does not know where he is. Truly he is afraid of nothing.[89]

By way of commentary, Huizinga adds that this passage 'shows the emotional ground of pure courage in combat: shuddering withdrawal from narrow egotism to the emotion of life-danger, the deep tenderness about the courage of the comrade, the voluptuousness of fidelity and self-sacrifice'. In discussing the proverbial gallantry of a knight, one scholar was so carried away that he wrote that it was easier for the Knights Templar to stand fast till the end of a battle than to subordinate their will to that of their commander and to fight in units.[90] Without wishing to detract from the courage, daring and self-sacrifice which the knights so freely displayed both in battles and on many other occasions, especially in the East, it is nevertheless necessary to contradict this often-repeated, usually biassed, praise of their warlike spirit and their contempt for death. Despite their great and sometimes wholly admirable gallantry, the knights were still human beings who feared for their lives in the presence of danger, and who behaved as men have always done in battle – in fear of death, mutilation, wounds and captivity. It is better to look for courage in the manner in which they braved danger, for it is important to know how they overcame their fear and what made them fight bravely.

---

88 L. Gautier, *La chevalerie*, p. 67.
89 J. Huizinga, *The waning of the Middle Ages*, London, 1924, pp. 64–5.
90 E. von Frauenholz, *Das Heerwesen der germanischen Frühzeit, des Frankenreiches und des ritterlichen Zeitalters*, I, p. 123.

We shall therefore turn first to the people who were critical of western chivalry or who fought against it as enemies. If we look at the testimony of a competent but critical observer such as Anna Comnena, daughter of the Byzantine emperor Alexius I Comnenus, certain traits in the character of the western knight are represented by the Norman adventurer, a great warrior, tough and brave, rough and sometimes reckless. Count Robert of Flanders would yield to no one when he joined battle with the Saracens with some of his knights in the van of the crusaders' army.[91] However, speaking of the time when she had to make an excuse on her father's behalf for not having hurried to the aid of the western knights after the capture of Antioch in 1098 during the First Crusade, Anna Comnena made this generalization about the tactics and strategy of the crusaders, whom she calls Celts:

> The Celtic race . . . is independent and does not like asking for advice; they have no military discipline nor strategic skill, but as soon as they have to fight and do battle, a raging fury seizes their hearts and they become irresistible, common soldiers and leaders alike. They hurl themselves with invincible impetus into the midst of the enemy ranks as soon as the latter give a little ground. If, however, the enemy goes on laying ambushes with the necessary experience in the art of war, and attacks them according to its rules, then their courage collapses into despair. To put it shortly, the Celts are invincible in the first onslaught, but after that they are easy to overcome because their arms and equipment are very heavy, and they behave recklessly because of their impulsive nature.[92]

Elsewhere she says: 'The Celtic race . . . is indeed very fiery and impetuous; once it has taken the initiative it can no longer be restrained.'[93] This judgement agrees with the contemptuous comment of the emir Ousama ibn Munquidh on the striking force of the crusaders. In his autobiography he wrote: 'Anyone who knows anything about the Franks has looked on them as beasts, outdoing all others in courage and warlike spirit, just as animals are our superiors when it comes to strength and aggression'.[94] But, as is clear from the words of Ousama, such a judgment is purely relative. It is made in comparison with what he saw among his own people, and this is true of the comment of Anna Comnena, who was going by what she knew of the Byzantine warriors of her day, who were not outstanding.[95] These judgments are too general, and do not go to the root of the matter. The essence of this can be seen in the opinion the Bedouin held of the crusaders: *li Frans qui s'arme pour poour de mort*! 'The Franks wear armour because they fear death!' The formidable men in iron were held to be courageous and undaunted thanks to the armour that protected them.[96] In its turn, this does not alter the fact that this contemptuous judgment by the Saracens was largely prompted by jealousy, because they had no such excellent protective

91 Anna Comnena, *Alexiad*, ed. B. Leib, Coll. byzantine, Association G. Budé, Paris, 3 vols, 1937–45 Bk 11: 6, 8. [Trans. E.R.A. Sewter, *The Alexiad of Anna Comnena*, London, 1989, pp. 351, 349, 311.]
92 *Ibid.*, Bk 11: 6, 3, and Bk 10, 5, 10.
93 *Ibid.*, Bk. 10:`5.
94 Ousama, *Autobiography*, p. 172. See Grousset, *Histoire des croisades*, I, p. 35.
95 Lot, *op. cit.*, I, pp. 35 and 73.
96 Joinville, *Histoire de saint Louis*, ed. N. de Wailly, SHF, Paris, 1868, c. 51, p. 89.

armour themselves. The Moslems fled whenever the heavily armoured knights attacked them, in order to save their lives from the long lances. At Arsuf, three successive charges by the crusaders were enough to dissuade the Saracens from making any effort at resistance in the open field for the rest of the campaign.[97]

Fear of death, of mutilation, of wounds – there we have the chief tactical problem, for the art of war is to achieve victory with the smallest possible losses. To defeat the enemy, soldiers have to overcome their inborn fear, and despite all inner anxiety carry out the orders of their superiors. The tactical aim must therefore be to allay fear in one's own army while striving to instil panic into the enemy, if this can be done. This vital aspect of the behaviour of men in knightly combat has not been studied by many scholars. Neglect of such an interesting field of investigation, throwing a new clear light on the psychology of knights, is doubtless due to the excellent repute noble horsemen have for this. The great individual fighter, as the classic representation of him will have it, knew no fear. Undaunted, he continued to fight until his strength was exhausted, even until the last man was driven from the bloody field of battle.

This over-simplified picture of undaunted gallantry is not really a true one. Fear in the fighting man in time of war and on the battlefield is easy to see: if it is not quickly mastered men take to their heels, fleeing in whole units, or becoming panic-stricken. To begin with a well-known example, the defection of some crusaders in the First Crusade, especially at Antioch, may be cited. After a good start, everything went wrong, and matters became so serious that Peter the Hermit and Guillaume le Charpentier, burgrave of Melun, fled. They were overtaken by Tancred, who brought them back to the field. Bohemond publicly denounced Guillaume, whose companions begged mercy for their guilty brother-in-arms: they all understood human weakness, and knew that some men were not strong enough to overcome it.[98] Things became still worse when the crusaders, after taking the city, found themselves encircled by a new enemy army and chose to remain in their houses instead of storming the Turkish citadel, which was still holding out and constituted a terrible danger. The knights were shaking with hunger, and fear.[99] Just before the city fell, Stephen of Blois forsook the crusaders, despite the fact that he had formerly held an important position, possibly that of supreme commander.[100] When he met Alexius Comnenus some time later, naturally the army he had abandoned had been wiped out to the last man, or so the fugitives asserted![101] Fulcher of Chartres frankly recognised what difficulties the crusaders had faced in the first great battle, at Doryleum in 1097, and how afraid the knights were: 'We were all herded together like sheep in a sheepfold, trembling and frightened, and were gradually totally

---

97 See Chapter 4, 'The battle of Arsuf'.
98 Anonymous, *Gesta Francorum et aliorum Hierosolimitanorum*, ed. L. Bréhier, CHFMA, Paris, 1924, c. 15, pp. 76–8. [Ed. & trans. R. Hill, Oxford, 1972, pp. 33–4.]
99 *Ibid.*, c. 26, p. 136. [Trans. R. Hill, p. 61.]
100 *Ibid.*, c. 27, p. 140 [Trans. R. Hill, p. 63]. S. Runciman, *op. cit.*, 1, p. 232, n. 1, thinks that Stephen was only in charge of logistics.
101 Anonymous, *op. cit.*, c. 27, pp. 140–4.

surrounded by the enemy'.[102] Later, when he accompanied Baldwin of Boulogne on the latter's journey to Jerusaiem, where Baldwin was to succeed his deceased brother Godfrey, he admits: 'We feigned bravery but feared death.' On the same journey Baldwin addressed his knights thus: 'Let those who are afraid turn back.' He knew very well that no one would dare acknowledge his fear publicly and lag behind; but during the night a number of men disappeared, both knights and foot-soldiers.[103] Similarly the Norman jongleur Ambroise, whose *Estoire de la guerre sainte* is one of the best sources for the Third Crusade, relates how the majority of the fighting men and pilgrims were so terrified at the beginning of the battle of Arsuf that they all wished the expedition were over.[104]

In a campaign so far from home, escape can be much more dangerous than battle when it comes to saving one's life. Fulcher reports Baldwin as having given this advice at Ramla in 1101: 'Escape is no good since France is too far away.'[105] Robert de Clari says much the same sort of thing of the Fourth Crusade. The new emperor of Byzantium, the usurper Murzuphlus or Alexius V, had ambushed the troops of Henry, brother of Baldwin IX of Flanders. As soon as the crusaders saw this, 'they were terrified', but then they reflected: 'By God! If we flee we'll all be killed! We might just as well die trying to defend ourselves, rather than while trying to escape.'[106] Before Constantinople was captured, many in the army hoped that the ships would be swept away by the current, so that they might be delivered from danger and be able to return home. Henry of Valenciennes also mentions the special circumstances of fighting in a remote theatre of war, in the reign of Henry I of Constantinople: 'You are gathered here in a foreign land, and have neither castle nor any place of refuge where you can seek safety, except your shields, your swords, your horses and the help of God.' The soldiers were then to make their confessions in order to have complete faith in the outcome of the battle; they were to know 'neither fear nor doubt'.[107]

Joinville too confessed quite sincerely what fear he felt, together with other knights, in the army of St Louis in Egypt. This fear was intensified by the enemy's use of Greek fire, which was a great surprise to the French. The king of France was trying to build a dam across one of the tributaries of the Nile. In order to protect the workmen and to guard the dam he had wooden towers built, which the enemy set on fire. The guards in the towers were faced with a dilemma: they could either stay in the towers and be burned to death, or disgrace themselves utterly by evacuating them. They decided that each time the enemy sent over Greek fire they would fall on their knees and beseech God to save them from the terrible holocaust.[108] Another day Joinville was lucky as he honestly admits: the 'cats' or towers were destroyed by

---

[102] Fulcher of Chartres, *Gesta Francorum Hierusalem expugnantium*, RHC, Hist. occ., 3, p. 335.
[103] *Ibid.*, p. 375. R. Grousset, *op. cit.*, 1, p. 209.
[104] Ambroise, vv. 6253–81, pp. 167–8
[105] Fulcher of Chartres, *op. cit.*
[106] Robert de Clari, *La conquête de Constantinople*, ed. Ph. Lauer, CFMA, Paris, 1924, c. 66, p. 66.
[107] Henry of Valencienses, *Histoire de l'empereur Henri de Constantinople*, ed. J. Longnon, Documents relatifs à l'histoire des croisades, Paris, 1948, c. 523, pp. 37–8; c. 516, p. 35.
[108] Joinville, c. 43, p.72

enemy fire just before he had to go on night watch with his knights. 'God did a good turn to my knights', he wrote.[109] In the battle of Mansurah he saw important nobles flee, but did not record their names for the whole family of the fugitive would suffer too much from the great shame.[110] Later on he was still trembling with fright, but also from sickness and fever.[111] Even a nobleman's piety was of no avail when it comes to such a pinch. When Joinville and his servants were on the point of being taken prisoner, one of his cellarers proposed that they should all let themselves be killed so that they might go to heaven as martyrs, 'but we did not believe it' wrote Joinville, who chose to live.[112] During his imprisonment he had some other unpleasant moments. He found himself in a galley with St Louis, when the sultan who was holding them prisoner was put to death by his own rebellious soldiers under their very eyes. Thirty enemy soldiers came for them with drawn swords, their Danish axes round their necks. 'I asked the lord Baldwin of Ibelin, who knew the Saracen tongue well, what the men were saying,' says Joinville.

> He answered that they were talking about cutting off our heads. Many men then made confession to a brother of the Holy Trinity, named John, belonging to the retinue of count William of Flanders. I could not think of a single sin. At the same time I was thinking that the more I defended myself the worse it would be. Then I crossed myself and knelt at the foot of a Saracen who had a Danish axe in his hand, and said 'Thus was St Agnes killed.' Guy d'Ibelin, constable of Cyprus, knelt beside me and made his confession to me. I answered him: 'I grant you absolution by the power which God has given me.' But when I got up, I could not remember what he had said or told me.[113]

The strict rule of the Templars also anticipated that knights might flee *por paor des Sarrasins*, for fear of the Saracens. They were mercilessly expelled from the Order.[114]

These examples from the literature of the crusades and the wars in the East are equally valid for western Europe. There too men fled from the field of battle, and there are many references to panic. There is no need to quote all these. The most beautiful of them all is the ironical mockery which the author of *Le voeu du héron* puts into the mouth of Jean de Beaumont, expressing this wish in the royal palace of Edward III in London in 1337:

> When we are in the tavern drinking strong wines, and the ladies pass and look at us with those white throats, and tight bodices, those sparkling eyes resplendent with smiling beauty; then Nature urges us to have a desiring heart. Then we could overcome Yaumont and Agoulant and the others could conquer Oliver and Roland. But when we are in camp on our trotting chargers, our bucklers round our necks

---

109 *Ibid.*, c. 44, p. 75.
110 *Ibid.*, c. 50, p. 87.
111 *Ibid.*, c. 64, p. 114.
112 *Ibid.*, c. 63, p .112.
113 *Ibid.*, c. 70, pp. 125–6.
114 *La règle du Temple*, ed. H. de Curzon, SHF, Paris, 1886, c. 232, p. 154; c. 419, p. 229; c. 574, p. 298. [Trans. J.M. Upton-Ward, *The Rule of the Templars*, Woodbridge, 1992.]

and our lances lowered, and the great cold is freezing us altogether and our limbs are crushed before and behind, and our enemies are approaching us, then we should wish to be in a cellar so large that we might never be seen by any means.[115]

This realistic confession shows how great the difference was between harsh reality and the embellished accounts of knightly gallantry, or the battle vows taken in the taverns and ladies' chambers of which Joinville wrote.[116] On the battlefield there is no wine to go to the head, and no fair ladies to spur on the knights, but fear strikes to the very marrow of the warriors. Then everyone wishes he were far away from the dreaded battlefield, instead of defeating Eaumons and Agoulant, two Saracen heroes of the *Chanson d'Aspremont*. In this *chanson de geste* the same idea is expressed, not as a Christian knight's confession, but as a sharp reproof to the soldiers of the Saracen camp. Surely the poet was also thinking of the less brave western knights. Eaumons complains bitterly about the lack of courage and bravery among his men, who had taken all sorts of vows about the battle in the presence of beautiful ladies, with the best wine to provide a cheerful atmosphere:

In my great palaces, back in Africa, they were conquering the Christians' land while wooing my fresh-cheeked damsels, giving them loving kisses, drinking my best wines. There, they were splendid conquerors, dividing up the cities and castles of France as spoils. But the French are no cowards – they know how to use the sword and lance. [117]

Lastly, let us look at the account of Jean le Bel, a canon of Liège who went with Jean de Beaumont in the army of the young king Edward III on an expedition to Scotland in 1327. At York, a dispute arose between men of Hainault and English archers over a game. The dispute led to a fight. Knights from Hainault, Flanders, Brabant, and Hesbaye hastened to the help of their men, charged the archers and drove them off. But the English archers in the royal army were very numerous, and they threatened the knights. 'Each day someone came on behalf of the king and of the English knights who bore us no hatred, to warn our leaders that we must be on our guard. They knew that 6,000 Englishmen were gathered in the city, and that they were out to kill or injure us by day or night.'[118] The knights of the Low Countries realized that their fate was in their own hands, and that they must look out for themselves. Their feeling of solidarity increased. They slept at night with their armour on and their arms ready to hand so that they could turn out at the first alarm. During the day they stayed in their lodgings and kept their armour and weapons close at hand. They posted a guard, commanded by the constables, day and night in the fields and on the roads. Half a mile outside the city they set up listening posts to warn the constables, who in turn were to sound the alarm to call the nobles to arms. This would give the heavy

---

[115] J. Huizinga, *The Waning of the Middle Ages*, p. 70, n.1.
[116] Joinville, *op. cit.*, c. 49, p. 86.
[117] *La chanson d'Aspremont*, ed. L. Brandin, CFMA, 19, 25, Paris, 1919–21, 1, c. 200, vv. 3675–84, p. 118.
[118] Jean le Bel, *Chronique*, 1, pp. 44–5.

armoured cavalrymen time to mount their horses and line up at the appointed place under their banners. For three weeks rumours spread daily of an approaching attack by the English archers, but each time they proved false. The noblemen of the Low Countries did not dare go into the city, but stayed together all the time with their armour on, well protected by their foresight and precautions. This example suggests the great influence fear had on the art of war, for it made the knights act cautiously and wisely.

Mass Flight and Panic

Besides considering the ordinary feeling of fear in the individual, we must also look at the question of mass panic in order to see what influence fear had upon the knights' tactics when they fought together against other knights or against foot-soldiers. One of the finest descriptions of panic in an army of knights and foot-soldiers comes from Ralph of Caen.[119] In early May 1104 a battle was fought at Harran, not far from the River Balîkh, by the troops of Baldwin of Bourg, Bohemond, and Tancred, against the Moslems. Baldwin's unit was quickly defeated and he was taken prisoner, but Bohemond and Tancred were victorious, and spent the night on the battlefield, on the enemy side of the river. The banks were very steep, and there was only one fordable place, on which the Norman leaders set a guard during the night, in order to prevent escape and to keep the enemy from gaining control of it. As the night wore on, the men became increasingly uneasy, and the fear of death crept over them. The first little groups of fugitives were easily driven back by the sentinels, but their numbers grew steadily, and finally they overpowered the defenders of the ford. A panic flight began. Bohemond and Tancred were forced to organize a retreat as best they could, and Tancred stayed in the rear guard to cover the retreat and flight.

> While the Turks lay sunk in sleep, the Christian knights fled, casting aside as they went all their costly possessions, their clothes, tents, silver and gold vessels, everything that was heavy and might delay them in their flight, even their weapons, which protect the lives of those who bear them. Rain had made the roads bad and turned the dust into mud; the horses slid about and their tails seemed to drag them down. Archbishop Bernard was fleeing with the others, his mule trotting along covered in mud. No one was chasing them, but it was as if the enemy were at their heels with swords drawn and bowstrings taut. The archbishop's countenance was troubled, and his heart heavy with fear. He called out to his fleeing companions, and begged them: 'Listen to your father, my children, cut off the tail that hangs down behind my mount, which is not just slowing me down, but is bringing me to a standstill. Cut it off, I tell you, for the animal will be lighter, and I shall not blush for riding a mule with no tail. Cut it off, and God forgive you your sins. I grant full absolution to the man who cuts off this tail.' Many crusaders turned a deaf ear and galloped on, so hard of hearing did their terror make them, nor did

---

119 Ralph of Caen, *Gesta Tancredi in expeditione Hierosolymitana*, RHC, Hist. Occ., 3, c. 150, pp. 711–12.

anyone have sympathy to spare for his friends, so much was he taken up with his own fear. The archbishop had grown hoarse when a knight who was fleeing with him at last did what he asked, on condition that he received the promised absolution. Both felt the relief at once, the knight freed from his sins and the animal from his tail. So the knight reaped the double harvest of a mule's tail and absolution by sowing a benediction. The archbishop gave him benediction with heart, mouth and hand, and as soon as the knight had got the benediction as well as the mule's tail he trotted off to Edessa with the archbishop, fleeing with him for whom he had made flight possible.

In a battle under the walls of Acre in 1189, panic broke out in part of the victorious Christian army when some German knights were trying to catch an Arab horse and their pursuit was taken by the others to be flight. This local panic gave Saladin the chance to turn a defeat into victory, though not a decisive one.[120] During the campaigns following the Fourth Crusade and the conquest of the Byzantine Empire, Baldwin I, formerly count of Flanders and Hainault, was taken prisoner close to the walls of Adrianople when he went to the help of the imprudent Louis of Blois. Some of the defeated troops were able to flee, thanks to the intervention of Villehardouin, who provided cover for them with a fresh corps which had been drawn up outside the city walls. But some of the fugitives turned in panic and galloped back into the camp, instead of strengthening the ranks of their friends.[121]

The story of the flight of the French rearguard at the battle of the Golden Spurs near Courtrai on the afternoon and evening of 11 July 1302 is also well-known.

From the towers of the church of Notre Dame of Tournai, of the abbey of St Martin and of the city, they could be seen fleeing along the roads, through hedges and fields, in such numbers that no one who had not seen it would believe it . . . In the outskirts of the city and in the villages there were so many starving knights and foot-soldiers that it was a frightful sight. Those who managed to find food outside the town bartered their equipment for it. All that night and the next day those who came into the city were so terrified that many of them could not even eat.[122]

When the Flemish forces made a surprise attack on the evening of 18 August 1304 near the village of Mons-en-Pévèle, the French knights fled by whole *conrois* and *batailles* beyond their camp. Many of them never came back to the battlefield.[123] 'Then one could see troops defeated without any reason, for no warlike feat was responsible for their defeat.'[124]

Besides these examples in which panic was caused by fear of the enemy, or by a surprise attack, or a growing feeling of unrest and anxiety during the night after a disastrous battle, there were also occasions when mass flight from the camp was in no way due to enemy action. In 1102, the young Louis the Fat was besieging the

[120] Ambroise, *op. cit.*, vv. 2097–3010, pp. 80–1. Oman, *op. cit.*, 1, p. 338.
[121] Villehardouin, *La Conquête de Constantinople*, ed. E. Faral, CHMA, 2 vols, Paris, 1938–39, 2, c. 362–3, pp. 170–2.
[122] G. le Muisit, *Chronique*, pp. 67–8.
[123] *Annales Gandenses*, p. 75.
[124] *Chronique artésienne et chronique tournaisienne*, ed. F. Funck-Brentano, Paris, 1899, p. 86.

stronghold of Chambly, which belonged to Mathieu de Beaumont. During the night there was a violent thunderstorm: torrents of rain and thunderclaps so shook the morale of the troops and their horses that many thought they were going to die. Utterly demoralized by physical suffering, wet clothes and the cold, perhaps also influenced by the fear of the unleashed powers of nature, some of the men got ready to depart early in the morning. When the dawn came, they set several tents on fire, which was usually a signal for retreat, and set off. The whole army did the same. Louis the Fat had difficulty in assembling a small unit to cover the flight even partially, and many fugitives were taken prisoner.[125] In April 1194, Baldwin VIII of Hainault had a similar experience at Arquennes, when he was preparing to storm Nivelles. During the night there was such a violent thunderstorm that horses and men were terrified. At daybreak not only the allies sent by the king of France, but also the knights, horsemen and foot-soldiers of the count all went off without permission, so that scarcely a seventh of the army was left with Baldwin. 'The count was astonished at this, and those who were with him, and the fugitives themselves were also surprised.'[126] The prince was obliged to go home having achieved nothing.

It is a mistake to explain these two examples of panic in terms of lack of discipline. It is clear that the strictest discipline is no use when a whole unit or a great part of an army takes to flight in panic. Even the best troops may be subject to panic as many wars in history have shown. One of the best means of avoiding panic in battle is the use of two or three fighting lines in depth. If the first line wavers, it can be intercepted by the second or third, who are out of danger and whose morale is not affected. The soldiers who are tempted to break ranks in a panic are usually then halted and rounded up not far from the front.

Fear in Knights Facing Foot-soldiers

Another sort of fear is that of knights who find themselves faced by well-disciplined foot-soldiers, who stand waiting for the charge in dense ranks, armed with long weapons. The first example of this comes from the battle of Hastings, in which tightly-packed English foot-soldiers awaited the charge of William the Conqueror's knights on a hilltop. After preliminary action by the archers, the cavalry went into action. But the English put up such a stout resistance that the left flank of William's army, made up of knights and soldiers from Brittany, fled, and the whole attacking army gave way. Knights who managed to penetrate the close formation, including the famous bard Taillefer, who stirred the troops with his martial songs, were killed. The English were armed with fearful battle-axes which 'easily hewed a way through shields and other weapons of defence'. William had to urge on his men, pointing out that general flight could not save them from death.[127]

---

125 Suger, c. 4, pp. 21–2.
126 Gilbert of Mons, c. 204, p. 291.
127 William of Poitiers, *Gesta Guillelmi ducis Normannorum et regis Anglorum* ed. R. Foreville,

At the battle of Bouvines the *Brabanciones* of Renaud de Dammartin were drawn up in double ranks in the form of a crown, and kept the French knights out of their formation with their long lances. These mercenaries were the last of any troops on the battlefield to hold their ground, because the knights, after an initial mishap, did not dare to charge the close formation. 'Our knights were much afraid of these foot-soldiers armed with lances, whom they had to fight with their swords and short weapons. The lances were longer than the swords and daggers and their impenetrable ranks in the form of a crown were as strong as a wall.'[128]

In the survey of the tactics of the foot-soldiers it will be seen how the French knights modified their tactics after the battle of Courtrai. This was also the case with the Anglo-Norman knights after their defeat by the Scots at Bannockburn in 1314. In this battle there was a notable conversation between Henri de Beaumont and Thomas Gray, who had raised an objection to a manoeuvre proposed by de Beaumont. Henri said 'If you're frightened, then flee!' 'Sire,' answered Gray, 'I shall not flee today because I am frightened,' and to show that he was not afraid of the Scottish foot-soldiers he joined the charge, in which his neighbour, Sir William Dayncourt, was killed, while Thomas's horse was killed by the Scottish pikes and he himself was captured.[129]

At Cassel in 1328 the French thought that they were riding to their deaths, or at least that they would lose their horses in a charge against the crown-formation of Zannekin's closely packed troops. They opened up their own encircling formation to let the Flemings get away, and so to kill them more easily.[130]

Not only fear for their own lives, but for their horses too and all that their loss would entail, sometimes made the knights refrain from pressing home a charge against determined and closely-packed foot-soldiers. Jean le Bel gives a remarkable example of this. At Vottem on 18 July 1346, the men of Liège and Huy had taken up their position beyond ditches, where they were attacked by a number of the prince-bishop's dismounted knights. Other knights stayed on horse-back, but did not dare make an attack for fear their horses would be killed. A splendid army of the prince-bishop, reinforced by German allies, fled in panic.[131]

Besides these fears for their horses and themselves, there was another reason why the knights did not like fighting against confident foot-soldiers. The Flemings, Scots, and Swiss did not usually take prisoners, but killed their enemies.[132] It was said that the French lords advised their king, Philip the Fair, to put an end to the war in 1304

CHFMA, Paris, 1952 1. II, c. 17–18, pp. 188–90. Guy of Amiens, *Carmen de Hastingae proelio*, ed. C. Morton and H. Muntz, Oxford, 1972, vv. 409–59, pp. 26–30.

[128] William the Breton, *Chronicon*, in *Oeuvres de Rigord et Guillaume le Breton*, ed. R.F. Delaborde, SHF, 2 vols, Paris, 1882–85 c. 193, pp. 285–6, in the *Philippis* he speaks of three ranks; and *Philippis*, 1. XI, vv. 605–12, pp. 342–3.

[129] Thomas Gray of Heton, *Scalachronica*, ed. J. Stevenson, Maitland Club, 40, Edinburgh, 1836, p. 141.

[130] *Chronicon comitum Flandrensium*, ed. J.J. de Smet, Corpus Chronicorum Flandriae, CRH in 4°, 1, Brussels, 1837, I, pp. 205–6.

[131] Jean le Bel, *Chronique* II, pp. 140–1. C. Gaier, *Art et organisation militaires dans la principauté de Liège*, pp. 294–5.

[132] Verbruggen, *De slag der gulden sporen*, Antwerp, 1952, pp. 261, 284, 299. Delbrück, III, p. 312.

against the Flemings because those cruel people would not take the knights prisoner.[133] The Austrian knights feared the Swiss for the same reason.[134] In time past the Welsh and Irish used similar methods with their enemies. Giraldus Cambrensis describes the difference in the usages of war thus: 'Whereas in France knights are taken prisoner, here they are beheaded: over there they are ransomed, here they are killed.'[135] But in the invasion of Ireland (1166–72) the knights were infinitely better armed than the Irish foot-soldiers, and they had not much to fear from their enemies.[136]

It has been shown that knights as individuals knew fear of death, wounds, and capture, and that individual fear could develop into panic affecting a whole unit, or putting a great part of the army to flight.

Fear exerts great influence on warfare: discipline on the march, tactics and behaviour in battle, all are affected by it. In order to intercept fugitives and get them re-grouped, a second and possibly a third line were formed in drawing the troops up before battle. The second and third line also made it possible to attack the enemy in the flank or the rear, for such attacks had far greater effect than frontal ones on enemy morale. Lastly, the use of standards on the battlefield reflects the human urge to feel attached to a visible unit.

The conviction of many scholars that the knights completely lacked discipline is well-known. They ascribe this to the individualistic behaviour of the nobles and their seeking after personal honour and fame. In reality, knightly armies took insufficient precautions on various occasions, but it is doubtful whether this is to be ascribed to the behaviour of individual knights: it stemmed rather from their optimism and the over-confidence they felt in their numbers. But this over-confidence in military might was not the general rule, for in the cold light of reality it was tempered by the fear of death and the instinct for self-preservation. Jean le Bel's description of the expedition to Scotland in 1327 supports this. At York a dispute between men from Hainault and English archers led to a fight. Knights from Hainault, Flanders, Brabant and Hesbaye hastened to the help of their men, and killed some English archers. The latter tried to take revenge during the expedition, and 'never did men live in such fear, and in so great danger of their lives, without any hope of ever getting home again, as we did then, and this went on day and night as long as we were in England.[137]

Jean le Bel, I, pp. 116–17. W. Schaufelberger, *Der Alte Schweizer und sein Krieg*, Zurich, 1952, pp. 178–9.

133 *Chronique normande du XIVe siècle*, ed. A. and E. Molinier, SHF, Paris, 1886, p. 27. *Istore et Croniques de Flandre*, ed. Kervyn de Lettenhove, CRH in 4°, 2 vols, Brussels, 1879–80, I, p. 289.

134 Delbrück, III, p. 312. Schaufelberger, pp. 178–9.

135 Giraldus Cambrensis, *Expugnatio Hibernica*, ed. J.F. Dimock, *Opera*, 5, RS, London, 1867, p. 395. [Ed. & trans. A.B. Scott and F.X. Martin, Dublin, 1978.] Delbrück, *loc. cit.* [See J. Gillingham, 'Conquering the Barbarians: War and Chivalry in Twelfth-Century Britain', *Haskins Society Journal*, vol. 4, 1992, pp. 67–84. T. Bartlett and K. Jeffrey, *A Military History of Ireland*, Cambridge, 1996. M.T. Flanagan, 'Irish and Anglo-Norman Warfare in Twelfth-Century Ireland' and also the articles by K. Simms and R. Frame.]

136 Lot, I, p. 291.

137 Jean le Bel, I, pp. 44–7.

When the army finally faced the Scots, they had to undergo still more tests of morale, for they were afraid of the enemy as well as the English archers, and above all they feared famine in the camp.[138] Fear made those knights act cautiously and wisely.

Fear and its influence are not the sole causes of all the problems which arise concerning the behaviour of knights in battle. Some attention must also be paid to the ways in which the nobles managed to suppress their fear. Chivalry gave numberless examples of magnificent courage and gallantry, and performed such heroic deeds as belong to the greatest feats of arms. Despite fear of death and wounds, the princes found enough volunteers for their expeditions. What made the knights go on such campaigns? What enabled them to overcome their own fear? What lay behind their martial spirit? Let us first consider a few fundamental factors in this spirit, which may explain why they fought so bravely. First of all the knights were professionals who were fighting for a living. It was possible to become an emperor, a king, a duke, a count, a baron by conquest and a successful military career.

Self-interest and Profits of War

Earlier in this chapter the poem of Bertrand de Born was quoted. It gives a remarkable insight into the true motives which prompted participation in wars. Bertrand wished that rich lords would hate each other, because a rich man is nobler, more generous, and benevolent in time of war than in peace. As soon as hostilities were announced, he said cynically : 'We can laugh, because the barons will love us, . . . but if they want us to stick to them, they will have to pay us well.'[139] But it was not just high pay that made Bertrand anxious to fight. War offered other prospects as well that were far more alluring and entailed less danger. It was a good time for 'taking goods away from usurers', for robbing burghers and merchants on the highways. The riches were there for the taking. The poet belonged to the class of humble vavassors, whose possessions and fiefs were very small. War, and the plundering raids it involved, helped these impoverished knights make ends meet. When Bertrand offered his services to the count of Poitiers he was already wearing his helmet, and had his shield slung round his neck. But then the problem of equipping himself for a campaign, seeing that he had no money, arose. In another expedition, the campaign of Jean de Beaumont in Scotland in 1327 with the army of Edward III – for which more volunteers turned out than had been expected, since all of them were hoping for very high pay – Jean le Bel, who was a member of the expedition, summed up what was necessary for a military campaign: 'Everybody started to buy according to his rank and status: tents, cars, little horses used in the country, and they found enough of them at reasonable price, pots, kettles, and so on, necessary in a campaign.'[140] It cost a great deal of money for a knight to be able to go out completely equipped, especially

---

[138] *Ibid.*, p. 71.
[139] Bloch, *Les classes et le gouvernement des hommes*, pp. 21–2.
[140] Jean le Bel, I, p. 48.

considering his expensive horses. The financial problems of petty vassals are understandable too, but of course this does not excuse their actions as robber-knights.

In the campaign against the Scots just referred to, there is another remarkable example of the knights' attitude to war, namely the case of Hector Vilain. In 1325 this Flemish nobleman fought under John of Namur on the side of the men of Ghent against the men of Bruges and the rebels from the coastal region and the Franc or Liberty of Bruges, and then crushed a rebel unit. In 1327 he went off against the Scots to gain money, and the following year he was in action against men of Bruges. While the king of France was advancing against Cassel, he threatened Bruges, and did his part in weakening the insurgents by compelling them to spread out their forces.[141]

In the romance of *Bauduin de Sebourc*, Bauduin, a very strong but also very poor knight, observed from a hilltop the tents of a camp set up round a beleaguered castle in a plain: like Bertrand de Born he shouted: 'There is going to be fighting here, now I shall get rich!' He went straight off and joined the army.[142] Clearly 'le nerf de la guerre' (the sinews of war) had a great attraction!

Poor knights also managed to carve out a career by taking parts as knights errant in the innumerable wars. William the Marshal is a splendid example: he was the fourth son of a minor baron, and possessed neither land nor fief. He was a knight errant for fifteen years. With a Flemish knight called Roger of Gaugi he managed to capture one hundred and three knights in tournaments in only ten months, not to mention horses and equipment, and the pair of them made huge sums. After that he was put in charge of the military training of prince Henry, son of Henry II of England, Later, when he came into conflict with the king, he left his service, and Philip of Alsace and the duke of Burgundy each offered him an annual rent of £500. Through his physical strength and military qualities he rose to be earl of Pembroke and regent of England, and Roger of Gaugi held an important position under King John.[143]

There were great material advantages to be gained both from booty collected on the battlefield and from captured enemy property. This was especially true of the First Crusade. Before men went into battle, they often thought of the riches that might be theirs as booty: in the battle of Dorylaeum in 1097 the knights encouraged each other in these words: 'Be of one mind in your belief in Christ and in the victory of the Holy Cross, because you will all become rich today, if God wills.'[144] In the *Chanson d'Antioche* we read: 'Out there on the grass, we shall either lose our heads or else become so rich in fine silver and gold, that we shall no longer have to beg from our comrades.'[145] Soldiers of lower rank hoped to improve their social status:

> See how the gold and silver glitter in the meadows!
> The man who gets that will never be poor again.
> So each one of you can improve his status.

---

141 *Ibid.*, p. 40. *Chronicon comitum Flandrensium*, pp. 198–9, 205.
142 Ch. V. Langlois, *Le service militaire en vertu de l'obligation féodale*, Paris, 1899, p. 78.
143 *Histoire de Guillaume le Maréchal*, III, p. XLI; I, pp. 123–5; vv. 6157–62, p. 222. S. Painter, *William Marshal*, Baltimore, 1933. J. Crosland, *William the Marshal*, London, 1962.
144 Anonymous, *Gesta Francorum*, c. 9, p. 48. [Trans. R. Hill, pp. 19–20.]
145 *Chanson d'Antioche*, ed. P. Paris, 2 vols, Paris, 1848, II, c. 31, vv. 927–31, p. 190.

They answered him: 'Lord, as you command!
He who flees on the battlefield shall be counted a heathen.'[146]

Fulcher has described in a famous passage how rich the soldiers became who stayed in the new kingdom of Jerusalem: 'Anyone who was poor there (in Europe) became rich here through God's favour. Anyone who had only a few shillings there has countless bezants here. Anyone who had not even a village there, has a city here thanks to God. Why go back to the west, when we can find all this in the east?'[147]

In the late thirteenth and early fourteenth centuries many princes recruited mercenaries from the Rhineland and Meuse district. In 1297, 1300, and 1302 hundreds appeared in the army of the counts of Flanders.[148] These knights had a bad reputation among the chroniclers. They fought bravely in battle, but otherwise they made a very bad impression with their greed. Louis of Velthem says that they loved wine, good food, and money.[149] Jean le Bel criticised the Germans of his time in the same way: he cited the English nobles as examples and then went on: 'This has not been the custom of the Germans until today; I don't know how they will do from now on, for they show no pity nor mercy for Christian men of war, when they capture them, no more than for dogs.'[150]

Self-interest is an important stimulus to brave conduct in battle. But the search for booty and plunder has more than once hindered the ruthless pursuit of a beaten enemy. Wise leaders therefore forbade the collection of booty, and took effective measures to see that the pursuit was properly carried out. Once the enemy was driven from the battlefield without possibility of return, the booty naturally fell into the hands of the victor,[151] but as long as soldiers were personally responsible for providing their own equipment and horses the inclination persisted to equip themselves as quickly as possible at the enemy's expense, even if this attitude did not coincide with the common interest. The transgressor judged that he was acting for the common good in providing for himself as well as possible with horses and arms.

The Able Commander

An interesting study could be written on the outstanding commanders of knightly armies. In the First Crusade various remarkable personalities stand out, among them Bohemond, Tancred, Baldwin of Boulogne, Godfrey of Bouillon, Raymond of

---

[146] *Ibid.*, II, 1. 8, c. 21, vv. 461–5, p. 222.

[147] Fulcher, p. 468.

[148] Verbruggen, *De slag der gulden sporen*, pp. 25 and 235–56. Idem, 'Het leger en de vloot', AWLSK, Verhandelingen. 38, 1960, pp. 53–4.

[149] Velthem, *Spiegel Historiael (1248–1316)*, ed. H. Vander Linden *et al.*, CRH in 4°, 3 vols, Brussels, 1906–38, II, 1. III, c. 52, vv. 3552–67, pp. 221–2.

[150] Jean le Bel, II p. 238.

[151] For example at Antioch in 1098: Anonymous, *Gesta Francorum*, c. 29, p. 156. [Trans. R. Hill, p. 70.] R. Grousset, I, p. 106. Runciman, p. 248. At Worringen and Courtrai, see Chapters III and IV. At Fréteval: *Histoire de Guillaume le Maréchal*, II, pp. 17–19, III, p. 140, n. 3, p. 141. At Ascalon in 1099: Anonymous, c. 39, p. 218. Fulcher, p. 363 and so on.

Toulouse, Robert II of Flanders and the duke of Normandy. Bohemond was re-nowned as a tactician, and for that reason usually commanded the reserve, as at the two battles of Antioch.[152]

In 1302, John of Renesse, commander of the reserve, enjoyed the reputation of being one of the best field commanders of the day,[153] and indeed it must be said that the strategic and tactical leadership of the Flemings at Courtrai was outstanding. Richard I of England too was praised by his contemporaries as being a very able leader, endowed with the attributes of a skilful tactician. He kept his reserve corps intact after Fréteval[154] in order to protect his troops, and did not rashly try to exploit his success after the great march to Arsuf and the battle there.[155] But he also had, perhaps in too high a degree, the individual qualities of the brave knight, who rushed resolutely at the ranks of the enemy. He was in addition concerned for the personal welfare of his men: he took care to provide for them properly, allowed no unreason-ably long marches, imposed strict discipline to protect the whole column of march, supervised the execution of his orders personally[156] and at the same time was ready for any unforeseen eventuality.

It was as necessary then as now for the commander to be on the danger spot at the critical moment. He had to fight in the front rank if necessary, as John of Brabant did at Worringen, Robert II of Flanders in the first Crusade, William of Jülich and Guy of Namur among the Flemish foot-soldiers at Courtrai, and William again at Mons-en-Pévèle.[157] A well-informed chronicler, William of Poitiers, made an inter-esting comparison between the ways in which Caesar and William the Conqueror commanded their armies. 'In Caesar's case, it was sufficient for his fame and importance simply to issue orders while he was fighting the Britons and Gauls: only rarely did he take part in the fighting. This was the custom in ancient times, as is evident from the *Commentaries*. For William it would have been neither honourable nor effective merely to give orders in his conflict with the English, if he had not at the same time fulfilled his obligations as a knight, as he had always done in other wars. In every battle he fought with his sword, either as the first man or at least among the first.'[158] That medieval concept was inspired by the customs and usages of chivalry, but it was also a natural consequence of the very small size of knightly armies.

Because of this, the commander as a rule stayed very close to his knights. The hierarchy in such matters was not very strict: Tancred's biographer, Ralph of Caen, says that he looked upon his knights as his treasure, and often took over guard-duty from wounded or exhausted men in his retinue, while never letting his own turn go by.[159] On the march the commander always had to be prepared to reach his destination

---

152 Grousset, I, pp. 87 and 105–6. Oman, I, pp. 281 and 284. Lot, I, p. 132.
153 Velthem, *Spiegel Historiael*, II, 1. IV, c. 25, vv. 1745–8, p. 299.
154 *Histoire de Guillaume le Maréchal*, II, pp. 17–19; III, p. 140, n. 3, p. 141.
155 See Chapter IV: The battle of Arsuf.
156 *Ibid.*
157 Other examples are: Worringen, Courtrai, Mons-en-Pévèle.
158 William of Poitiers, 1. II, c. 40, pp. 250–2.
159 Ralph of Caen, *Gesta Tancredi*, c. 51.

with the last knights, and if the enemy laid an ambush, he had to fight with some of his troops. His example always inspired the other knights. In flight or in retreat he had to keep the enemy at bay with the rearguard, as Tancred and the young Louis the Fat did, with the best troops in the army.

> Many of the best knights are taken prisoner.
> Know full well that this is the custom:
> The bravest fight in the rearguard
> If there is a flight.
> The others do not worry about this,
> But try to save themselves
> By fleeing headlong.[160]

The influence of the commander's personal example, marching with his banner at the head of his troops or in the front ranks, was well described by Bertrand de Born:

> I like also when the lord
> Rides to battle at the head of his men,
> Mounted and armed, fearless,
> So he makes his men more courageous
> By his valiant courage;
> And when the assault is given
> Everybody has to be ready
> To follow him with good grace,
> For nobody has valour
> If he has not received nor given many blows.[161]

Two English kings had tremendous influence as leaders: Richard I and Edward III. Edward I might also be mentioned, but he won no victories on the continent. The *Histoire de Guillaume le Maréchal* says of Richard I: 'The bravest were so fearless (under his command) that since that war thirty of our men have dared take on forty Frenchmen, a thing quite unheard of till then. It is plain from this that men who have a good leader are far more courageous and become a better fighting unit.'[162]

It is remarkable that Jean le Bel uses almost the same words about Edward III. 'And you must know that when this noble king Edward first reconquered England in his youth, nothing was thought of the English, and no one spoke of their prowess nor of their boldness, nor in the other *chevauchie*, that took place in Scotland . . . But they have learned so well to use their weapons in the time of the noble king Edward, who has led them often in war, that they are the noblest and strongest warriors that are known.'[163]

Naturally the prince did not only play the part of commander in chief in the field;

---

160 *Histoire de Guillaume le Maréchal*, II, vv. 11024–32, pp. 32–3.
161 P. Bec, *Petite anthologie de la lyrique occitane du moyen âge*, pp. 96–7.
162 T. II, vv. 11063–72, p. 34 (after the victory at Gisors in 1198).
163 Jean le Bel, I, pp. 155–6, anno 1339.

his military measures and preparations for war in accordance with sound military policy were also highly important. The example of a brave and courageous leader had an inspiring effect and helped the knights to overcome their instinctive fear.

Sense of Honour and Duty

A sense of honour is also very important for the psychology of the knight in battle, for the knightly concept of honour forbids flight before the enemy. The ideal knight is of course the hero of the *Chanson de Roland*. Roland accepts a battle against overwhelming odds when he might have avoided the combat, but being a proud and undaunted knight, he chose to fight. He refuses to flee, overcomes his fear, only to die in the end. He offers his life for the cause he is defending, and would never do anything throughout the hard fight which might taint his honour.[164] Young Vivien is another such hero: he fought a battle against a king of Cordova with too few troops, and he too could have fled before it was too late. But when his uncle Guillaume had knighted him, he had solemnly vowed never to flee from the Saracens. He kept his oath and chose to die.[165]

This problem of a knight's sense of honour especially occupied the writers of the *chansons de geste*. They show that the knights feared most of all being denounced as cowards: 'Mieux vauroit estre mors que coars appelés'[166] – Better be dead than be called a coward. One of them wrote that 'a single coward can discourage an army' and 'U nos i garrons tuit, u nos tuit i morron', which may be roughly translated as 'win or die'.[167] Charlemagne is portrayed as the emperor who chooses death rather than escape in the *Chanson de Roland*.[168] Roland and Oliver also die rather than avoid battle: 'Ja pur murir n'eschiverunt bataille.'[169] The solution is clear for the poets in the lines: 'See, the death comes upon us, but as noble men we prefer to die while fighting.'[170] This immutable judgment was given also in the *Chanson d'Antioche*, an epic based largely upon historical fact. 'It would be better for every man to lose his head than to flee even half a foot before the heathen.'[171] The crusaders during the Fourth Crusade considered it better to go down fighting than to be killed in flight.[172]

The mirror that the poets held up to the knights often gives an accurate reflection. Stephen of Blois forsook the Crusaders' army during the siege of Antioch in 1098,

---

164 L.E. Halkin, 'Pour une histoire de l'honneur', *Annales*, IV, 1949, p. 434, P. Rousset, *Les origines et les caractères de la première croisade*, Neuchâtel, 1945, pp. 131–2.
165 L.E. Halkin, *loc. cit.* P. Rousset, p. 313. Gautier, p. 69. J. Bédier, *Les légendes épiques, Recherches sur la formation des chansons de geste*, Paris, 1926–29, I, p. 83.
166 Gautier, p. 66. Halkin, p. 434 (citation from Elie de Saint-Gilles, v. 724).
167 Gautier, p. 66. Halkin, *loc. cit.*
168 C. 196, vv. 2737–8, pp. 226–8.
169 Ibid., c. 87, v. 1096, p. 94.
170 Gautier, p. 70.
171 *Chanson d'Antioche*, II, 1, viij, c. 24, vv. 557–8, p. 227.
172 R. de Clari, c. 66, p. 66.

but three years later he took part in the Lombards' Crusade. He died an honourable death at the taking of Ramla on 19 May 1102, thus restoring his good name. The chroniclers wrote a moving eulogy of him.[173]

It is often difficult to separate the knights' sense of honour and of military duty. The dilemma of Joinville and his retinue during their night watch on the towers in Egypt has been mentioned: they remained at their post for the sake of honour, and did their duty at the same time, for in the Middle Ages, when the conception of duty was rather different from that of our day, knights feared shame more than punishment.

Men were keenly conscious of the shame of cowardice, and for that reason knights usually wrote very carefully about cases known to them personally. Joinville gives no names of the great nobles who fled so wildly at the battle of Mansurah, and who made no effort to redeem themselves even when they were back with their own troops.[174] It was dangerous to describe such acts in full: poets might make up scurrilous songs about them and not only the personal honour of the fugitive or coward would be attacked, but that of his family.[175] If the facts were generally known, the chronicler could not gloss them over, and if he were not a knight himself, he would not do so in any case. In the battle of Arsuf, the count of Dreux was reproached for not having gone to the help of James of Avesnes and his men: 'I heard so many people speak evil of that, that history cannot conceal it.'[176]

But not every knight could be expected to fight as bravely as Roland, Oliver, or Vivien, and human weaknesses had to be taken into account. Nor could it be expected that everyone should let himself be killed as soon as it was clear that the army was beaten. Men knew from experience that a lost battle did not necessarily mean a lost war, which would have been the case if they all let themselves be killed: the absolute concept of honour had to be reconciled with the interests of society and of human safety. It is very hard to decide when this is right. Practice always differed from the ideal, which reminds us of the old German custom which demanded that men should not survive the dead leader of their *comitatus*.[177]

Actually, flight was regarded as a disgrace. Knightly honour demanded a fight to the death, and allowed two possibilities: death in action or capture. In the council of war held before the battle of Bouvines by the emperor Otto, count Ferdinand, Renaud de Dammartin and Hugues de Boves, Renaud is said to have foretold that Hugues would flee as a coward. Renaud would fight to the death or until capture. This happened. He kept up the fight and was taken prisoner after a bitter resistance.[178] William the Breton testified as a spectator that the Flemish knights chose death or

---

173 R. Grousset, I, pp. 232–3, 323.

174 Joinville, c. 50, p. 87.

175 *Chanson de Roland*, v. 1014, p. 86. *Le siège de Barbastre*, ed. J.L. Perrier, CFMA, Paris, 1926, 87, v. 2713, p. 86.

176 Ambroise, vv. 6657–8, p. 178.

177 Tacitus, *Germania*, c. 14, p. 79.

178 William the Breton, *Chronicon*, c. 195, p. 287. Id., *Philippis*, 1. XI, vv. 571–2, p. 341. *Genealogiae comitum Flandriae. Cont. Clar.*, ed. L.C. Bethmann, MGH, SS, IX, 1851, c. 22, p. 333.

capture rather than flight.[179] Count Ferdinand surrendered to the enemy, but his followers fought on till those who would not give in were all killed.[180] In the battle of Worringen, Jan van Heelu tells that the knights from Guelders were also unwilling to leave the battlefield, and preferred to be taken prisoner.[181] The count of Guelders, who wanted to flee with the help of some friends among the allies of duke John, after tearing off his coat-of-arms, was censured by the poet because he could no longer pass for one of the best in the enemy army.[182] The Grand Master of the Templars naturally regarded flight as a terrible scandal: such dishonour would affect not only him personally, but the whole Order. During the Third Crusade, he refused to flee at the battle of Acre while it was still possible, and perished.[183] In the fourteenth century, the knights of the Order of the Star, founded by king John of France, swore that they would not flee further than four 'arpents', otherwise they had to hold out till they were killed, or else surrender.[184]

A distinction must necessarily be made between the escape of an individual in battle when the fight was still going on, and the outcome was still in doubt, and retreat or collective flight when an army was faced with defeat. The Rule of the Templars provided for the case of defeat and its consequences: once the Christians were so near defeat that there were no banners left flying on the battlefield, the Templars might flee where they liked.[185] This was generally accepted practice. It is of course axiomatic that not all defeats were thought dishonourable.

The knights' lofty concept of honour and duty is evident from the records of innumerable councils of war. Many times some nobles advised against a battle, but were overruled by a majority. Those who wanted to postpone the fighting to a more propitious time were frequently mocked because their courage was called into question. But every one of them, even those who did not want to fight, played their part bravely in the attack, and were frequently killed,[186] refusing to survive on the battlefield out of a sense of honour and military duty.[187] At Bannockburn a famous knight, Giles of Argentan, one of the nobles charged with protecting Edward II, led him out of the battle. As soon as he had brought the king into safety, he said he was not accustomed to running away, returned to the battlefield, and was killed.[188]

Public opinion in France could not understand that brave knights sometimes had to flee when they were defeated. In such a case the nobility was considered suspect, or else was openly accused of treason. Such accusations were made after the defeat

---

179 William the Breton, *Philippis*, 1. XI, vv. 229–33, p. 327.
180 *Ibid.*, vv. 240–2, p. 328.
181 Heelu, vv. 6762–8, p. 250.
182 *Ibid.*, vv. 6652–60, p. 246.
183 Ambroise, vv. 3023–33, p. 81.
184 Halkin, p. 437. An 'arpent' was a measure of ground roughly comparable to an acre.
185 *La règle du Temple*, c. 167–8, pp. 126–7; c. 421, p. 230.
186 At Courtrai: Verbruggen, *De slag der gulden sporen*, p. 280. Bouvines: Renaud de Dammartin. See also: Lot, *Art militaire*, II, p. 444.
187 Verbruggen, *op. cit.*, p. 300.
188 Thomas Gray of Heton, *Scalachronica*, pp. 142–3.

at Courtrai.[189] The nobles were said to have behaved treasonably in September 1302 during the retreat of the royal army.[190] They were again accused of treason when the knights fled in panic at Mons-en-Pévèle,[191] but these accusations were very minor compared with those hurled at the nobility after the great defeat at Maupertuis near Poitiers in 1356. This time both clergy and citizens felt that far too many nobles had fled, and had not worried about defending their country, but had plucked the people clean, plundered them and robbed them of their possessions. France had been disgraced. The barons had committed a long-planned treason, as the circumstances of the defeat showed. The writer of the *Complainte de la bataille de Poitiers* advised the king to call up peasants: 'They will not flee to save their lives, as the knights did at Poitiers.'[192] The nobles' shame was all the greater because they misused their military might in time of war, to promote their own interests and to exploit the common people.

Rough Manners and Knightly Customs

The more primitive the soldiers, the rougher their manners, and the less civilised they were, the more bellicose as a general rule. Rough manners were much in evidence in the many private wars of the eleventh and twelfth centuries, and in the first Crusade. Enemies were beheaded and their heads thrown into the beleaguered cities, bodies were dug up in the search for booty, Crusaders impaled the heads of fallen enemies on lances to terrorize the enemy, and so on. The knights met with this later themselves, when they had become more civilised but had to fight against rough and primitive foot-soldiers in Ireland.[193] At the beginning of the fourteenth century they were complaining bitterly about the brutish customs of the Flemish, Swiss and Scottish foot-soldiers.[194]

Obviously in a time of violence such as the tenth and eleventh centuries fighting was particularly reckless, because human life was not then as highly esteemed as later. It is a great pity that we do not know more about the usages of the period, particularly as regards battles and the taking of prisoners. But a passage from Orderic Vitalis is instructive about the behaviour of the knights. In his account of the battle of Brémule in 1119, he says that only three French knights were killed, but 140 were taken prisoner. This was attributable to the fact that their protective equipment was so good, and to the fact that the knights 'spared each other, and tried not so much to kill as to capture the fleeing enemy. Christian warriors had no desire to shed the

---

[189] Verbrugggen, *op. cit.*, pp. 83–4 and 87.

[190] *Ibid.*, p. 61 and note 3.

[191] Verbruggen, 'De slag bij de Pevelenberg', *Bijdragen voor de geschiedenis der Nederlanden* 6, 1952, p. 189. G. Six, 'La bataille de Mons-en-Pévèle', *Annales de l'Est et du Nord*, I, 1905, p. 226.

[192] F. Funck-Brentano, *Féodalité et chevalerie*, Paris, 1946, pp. 139–40. A. Coville, *L'Europe occidentale de 1270 à 1380. II. 1328 à 1380*, in G. Glotz, *Histoire générale. Histoire du moyen âge*, 6, Paris, 1941, pp. 548–9.

[193] Lot, I, p. 289, n. 4.

[194] See Chapter III: The Foot-soldiers.

blood of their brothers.'[195] Orderic's statement reflects the general notion that was part of the knightly code of honour, that the beaten enemy should be spared, since he was a knight and therefore a brother-in-arms. But there was money in it for the victor too; the captured knight could ransom himself for an enormous sum. The text can also be interpreted in another way: the enemy would be less likely to resist when he knows that he would probably be taken prisoner and not killed during pursuit by the victor.

Ferdinand Lot rightly points out that the Anglo-Norman and French knights did not always fight in a humane fashion, so that we must not generalise from Orderic's statement, nor apply it to all fighting.[196] In the battle of Worringen Jan van Heelu laments bitterly that the brave Schavedries family had to leave so many of its members dead on the battlefield.[197] It would have been better to take them prisoner. However, if the knights knew that no quarter would be given, they would fight even more stubbornly:

> Anyone who knows that there will be no prisoners
> Fights stubbornly in such a battle.[198]

Everything here depends upon fortuitous circumstances, and the general attitude of the army. It is possible that the knights fought more bravely to sell their lives more dearly; it is also possible that they fled before it was too late, or to avoid battle against brutal and merciless adversaries.

Rough customs produced the type of knight who endured physical suffering and who probably did not worry much about death. As the knights became more civilised and refined, their manner of waging war was modified. It became more ruthless again as soon as the foot-soldiers were strong enough to stand up to knightly armies. As for being captured, the knights had to solve this dilemma: to save their honour by offering resistance and not fleeing, which increased the danger of being killed, or to leave the battlefield, with the concomitant shame, but without having to ransom themselves for enormous sums and without further danger. So knights had to choose between honour and self-interest.

Faith and Religious Conviction

The art of war in the Middle Ages shows a deep religious strain running through all the customs and usages of the period. Mass was celebrated before practically every battle, with confession and communion beforehand. This happened at Thielt, Courtrai, Mons-en-Pévèle, and most other battlefields. As soon as the English and their mercenaries from Hainault, Liège, Brabant and Flanders found out where the

---

195 Orderic Vitalis, *Historia ecclesiastica*, ed. M. Chibnall, 6 vols, Oxford, 1968–78, VI, p. 241. [See also John Gillingham, '1066 and the Introduction of Chivalry unto England', in *Law and Government in Medieval England and Normandy* (papers presented to Sir James Holt), ed. G. Garnett and J. Hudson, Cambridge, 1994, pp. 31–55.
196 Lot, I, p. 317, n. 5. J. Beeler, *Warfare in England, 1066–1189*, Ithaca, New York, 1966, p. 259.
197 Heelu, vv. 7246–51, p. 267.
198 *Chanson de Roland*, c. 142, vv. 1886–7, p. 158.

Scottish army was, on the expedition which Jean le Bel accompanied, the knights went to confession, attended mass and took communion, and also made their wills, for the coming battle, uppermost in their minds, was a matter of life or death.[199]

The influence of this deep faith is best expressed in accounts of the Crusade, and in *chansons de geste*. While Christian mercy and chivalrous customs, together with a well-understood self-interest, led to the more merciful conduct of war in the west, battles were still conducted in the east with the utmost cruelty. This was partly necessary to protect an army in a far-off land, where a heavy defeat would have meant annihilation and where spreading fear among the enemy troops weakened the Moslem capacity to resist, but this resistance might also be stiffened if they were convinced that no quarter would be given. The Holy War was fought with unheard-of-ferocity and brutality on both sides, which must have spurred on the knights to make extra efforts in battle, lest they should fall into enemy hands.

As for the battle itself, it was of great importance for a knight to know that his sins were forgiven, and that death in battle promised eternal bliss in Paradise. Instead of losing his soul in unholy wars against other Christians, he saved it on a Crusade.[200]

But, as always, human weakness must be taken into account. In a letter to his wife Stephen of Blois wrote: 'Many Christian brothers-in-arms were killed in action: their souls have come to know the joys of Paradise.'[201] Stephen was too weak himself to endure privation and mortal danger during the siege of Antioch, and the deeply devout Joinville preferred life to the death of a martyr.

The service of God was however one of the major reasons for fighting against the Moslems, whose value as fighting men was soon correctly assessed by western knights. This is quite a normal phenomenon in war: the common soldier sees no reason why he should not fraternise with his enemies.[202] In the first Crusade this respect for the enemy was very clearly expressed by an anonymous knight who left us a remarkable account: 'Who can be so wise or learned that he is bold enough to describe the expertise, the martial virtues and the bravery of the Turks? . . . They say that they are descended from the Frankish race, and that no one, except the Franks and they themselves, has the right to call himself a knight. I shall tell the truth and no one can dispute it: if the Turks had held to belief in Christ and in holy Christendom . . . then it would be impossible to find a people surpassing them in might, bravery, and military genius . . . And yet by God's grace they were beaten by our men.'[203]

In the *chanson de geste* it is always the knights' task to spread Christianity.[204] Vivien speaks to his nobles in these words: 'As long as we live, we must not fail to kill Saracens and wipe them out, spreading God's law and putting our souls in the hands of God.'[205] But there is also respect for the good warrior: 'If he would believe

---

[199] Jean le Bel, *Chronique*, I, p. 64.
[200] P. Rousset, p. 82.
[201] P. Rousset, p. 82.
[202] See for the war in Spain in the time of Napoleon: L. Villat, *La révolution et l'empire (1789–1815)*, Paris, 1936, p. 167. 1914–18: J. Norton Cru, *Témoins*, pp. 174, 188, 249, 360, 464, 515.
[203] Anonymous, *Gesta Francorum*, c. 9, pp. 50–2.
[204] Rousset, p. 114. Gautier, pp. 70–1.
[205] Rousset, p. 127.

in Jesus and worship Him, no better knight could be found.' And again: 'If he were to be held over the font and be baptised, no such warrior could be found in the Christian world.'[206] So there are paradoxes here as in other aspects of the knight's life, great cruelty on the one hand, and on the other generosity and respect for the enemy.

The influence of religion on warfare is shown again clearly in the customary war cries: *Diex aie*, the French translation of the earlier Byzantine cry: *Adiuta Deus*;[207] *Saint sépulchre*;[208] *Christus vincit, Christus regnat, Christus imperat.*[209] German knights used to march into battle singing '*Christus qui natus*'.[210] The Holy Lance and the Cross were carried as emblems before the troops. On the Italian *carroccio* a splendid monstrance was borne aloft with the consecrated Host, and priests always went with the waggon.[211] The outcome of the battle was often regarded as a judgment of God, and the belief of many people of that time in the intervention of the Virgin is shown by the number of times it is mentioned.[212]

Religious feeling helped knights to overcome their fear. As soon as they found themselves in trouble, they invoked the help of God, of the Virgin, or of the patron saint of warriors. In all the Crusades, and particularly in the First, faith played a great part in overcoming fear, and the Crusaders thereby brought their expedition to a successful end: once they had started, their greatest hope of salvation lay in their ceaseless striving to accomplish their chosen task. When a monk spoke encouragingly before a battle to Simon de Montfort, leader of the crusaders against the Albigensians, he answered: 'Do you think I am afraid? The cause of Christ is at stake. The whole Church is praying for me, and I know that we cannot be beaten.'[213]

This concludes the brief survey of the fundamentals of the knightly urge for battle. We have discussed the influence of his personal interests, the influence of a brave leader as tactician or strategist, a knight's sense of honour, the rude manners and knightly customs and the role of religious conviction. Actually these motives underlying the attitude of the knights cannot be separated; two or three of them will operate simultaneously. But not all factors are constant: self-interest may yield to the common good, or may function in a broader framework to the common advantage. Leaders may be brave or cowardly, the personal sense of honour may be subordinated to the advantage of the honour of family or country, religion does not always play a great part in every case. These motives thus seem less important than the two essential

---

206 *Ibid.*, p. 116. *Chanson d'Aspremont*, I, c. 311, vv. 6127–9, p. 196.
207 Lot, 'La langue du commandement, dans les armées romaines et le cri de guerre français au moyen âge', in *Mélanges Félix Grat*, I, Paris, 1946, p. 207. Gautier, p. 753.
208 Gautier, p. 753. Rousset, p. 81. Henry of Valenciennes, *Histoire de l'empereur Henri de Constantinople*, ed. J. Longnon, Documents relatifs à l'histoire des croisades, Paris, 1948, c. 539, p. 44.
209 Grousset, I, p. 244.
210 Delbrück, III, p. 357.
211 Rousset, pp. 87–8. Grousset, I, p. 105 and 244. Delbrück, III, p. 375. See also Chapter III: The foot-soldiers in Italy.
212 Rousset, p. 92.
213 P. Belperron, *La croisade contre les Albigeois*, Paris, 1942, p. 184.

factors which will be discussed below, namely the arming of the knights, and the confidence which their armour gave them to overcome fear, the inner cohesiveness of the knightly families and the close ties binding the vassals to their lord.

The Arming of Knights and its Influence

In the Middle Ages emphasis was always laid on the armour, for 'armed' meant wearing a coat of mail. Those without it were unarmed or '*inermes*'. Knights were heavily armed cavalry; in the Crusades they were called 'armed' in contrast to their enemies who were called 'naked'. The knights are 'heavily armed', while the lightly-armed Moslems were 'unarmed' (*desarmée*).

> The Christians are very well armed
> And the Saracens are unarmed
> They have only a bow, a mace or a sword
> Or a well-sharpened stick
> And a cuirass that is not heavy.[214]

The armour and heavy weapons made knights invulnerable to the arrows of the Moslems. They were called the 'iron people' by the Turks. In the Third Crusade Saladin did not dare fight again after his defeat at Arsuf. Against the well-armoured crusaders his troops had no chance of success.[215]

Their armour and heavy weapons were tremendously important to the knights because they made them invulnerable or greatly restricted the numbers of those killed in action. There is ample evidence that a greater sense of security due to their good protective armour spurred the knights on to the utmost bravery on the battlefield.

We know already that Anna Comnena depicted the western knights in the first Crusade as 'unconquerable in a confined area, but easy to capture in open terrain: indomitable on horseback, but powerless when they have to fight on foot, irresistible in the first shock.'[216] She lays great stress on the advantages of heavy armour and equipment, which made it possible for a charge to be so violent that the Moslem cavalry never stood their ground, and generally avoided a hand-to-hand combat. The disadvantages of heavy equipment were not overlooked, however, and she makes the contrast stand out sharply. But it is not true to say that the knights were easy to beat in the open field; on the contrary, the reverse was true, for it enabled them to pursue the enemy effectively. Nor is it true that they were useless on foot. It is quite clear on balance that the armour was invaluable.

When the spoils were divided after the fall of Constantinople in 1204, the clerk Aleaume de Clari asked for a knight's share, since he had fought on horseback,

---

214 Ambroise, vv. 5649–53, p. 151.
215 *Ibid.*, vv. 6368–75, p. 170; vv. 6819–21, p. 182.
216 See the citation of Anna Comnena. Cf. B. Leib, Introduction, in *Anne Comnène, Alexiade*, I, p. LXXXIX.

wearing a coat of mail. The count of St Pol granted his request, because he had borne himself so bravely.[217]

'Li Frans . . . s'arme pour poour de mort!'[218] The knights wear armour for fear of death! The importance of iron armour was great because it eliminated a large part of the danger on the battlefield: anyone who wore it had to fight like a knight, as is clear from the Rule of the Templars.

This Rule contains important information on the knightly art of war, and the distinction is sharply drawn between the armoured aristocrats of the Order and the light *sergeants*, who were not so well armed and did not normally wear full armour. The same tenacity in battle was not expected of them as it was of the knights, and they were allowed to retreat. But if these *sergeants* were given a knight's equipment by their Order, and were therefore similarly armed, this permission was no longer valid. 'The brother *sergeants* who wear an iron cuirass must fight on the battlefield just as is required of the brother knights; and the other brother *sergeants* wearing no armour will have the gratitude of God and of the Order if they fight well. But if they see that they cannot endure the battle or are wounded, they may withdraw without asking permission, and without punishment.'[219] Heavily armoured sergeants could not leave the battlefield without permission or before the Christian army had been routed.[220]

Knights, covered from head to foot in armour, had little to worry about when facing ill-armed foot-soldiers. This is obvious from the swift subjugation of the Irish at the end of the twelfth century by ridiculously small armies. Against those 'unarmoured men, who either won or were beaten in the first charge',[221] such heavy armour was not necessary and this was true wherever the foot-soldiers were not well armed. As long as the common people were too poor to buy heavy arms, and the princes could not buy them any, the situation did not change, until the cities and rural communes solved the problem and at the same time infused greater self-confidence into their men.

The high degree of invulnerability and relatively small number of dead among the knights following a battle encouraged them to fight bravely. The state of the mail-shirt after a battle served as a means of judging the man had fought bravely or not:

> I know full well that you are a coward:
> Your coat of mail is neither pierced nor torn,
> And neither your head nor arms are wounded.[222]

says Bueves de Commarchis to his son Girart.

217 R. de Clari, *La conquête de Constantinople*, p. 96.
218 Joinville, *Histoire de saint Louis*, c. 51, p. 89.
219 *La règle du Temple*, c. 172. p. 129.
220 *Ibid.*, c. 167–8, pp. 126–7; c. 421, p. 230.
221 Douglas Drummond, *op. cit.*, pp. 73–96. Giraldus Cambrensis, *Expugnatio Hibernica*, p. 395.
See also the exact remarks of Lot, *L'art militaire*, I, p. 291. The subjugation was carried out between 1166 and 1172 with about 100 knights.
222 *Le siège de Barbastre*, c. 77, vv. 2287–9, p. 72.

The excellent protection of the armour also impressed the Moslems after the defeat of the army from the kingdom of Jerusalem at Hattin near Lake Tiberias in 1187. The knights of king Guy of Lusignan had struggled vainly to break out of the encirclement of their army. Totally exhausted by thirst and fatigue after a full day's fighting in the scorching heat, and a night without food or drink, following sporadic attacks, they were forced the next day to cease fighting and capitulate. Their horses were dead tired and covered with wounds. 'It was an extraordinary and wonderful thing that the French knights kept on fighting as long as their horses were all right. They were armed from head to foot in a sort of armour made of a fabric of iron rings. They seemed to be an iron mass, off which blows simply glanced.' . . . 'These Christians were lions at the start of the battle; by the end they looked more like scattered sheep.' Their might had been feared at first, but the Moslems mocked the miserable aspect of their disarmed and exhausted prisoners.[223]

Contemporary western observers were also conscious that in combat between knights there were fewer casualties than in battles of classical antiquity. 'Formerly, many thousands perished in battle, but now, because of increasing calamities the means of protection have also been improved, and new defence has been found against new weapons.'[224]

It is true that there was no difference in equipment when knights in western Europe were fighting against their equals. In such case they knew they could give themselves up if the odds seemed hopeless, and they could count on their comrades in battle. We must now consider the units in which the knights fought, and discuss the inner cohesiveness of these formations.

Solidarity in the Knightly Families and Clans, and in a Lord's Retinue

It is common knowledge that the old Germans in their mighty *Geschlechter* (clans) united in solid formations in time of war, thanks to the natural cohesiveness or solidarity which had developed among them from living close together in time of peace. The same men were leaders of society in peace and in war. There was firm mutual trust, for the warriors were fighting by the side of companions whom they had known for years. Strict discipline, as imposed by the Romans to counteract fear, was not necessary, for anyone who fled from the field of battle was expelled from society, and had to live as an outlaw. Besides, if a people is warlike by nature, such characteristics of daily life may compensate for many other qualities which in an army of more civilised folk would have to be artificially fostered by long drilling under strict discipline, as in the case of the Romans.

The head of a family was also a military leader, so that if he was in command of a unit of men bound by ties of blood, he did so as the leader of a clan or tribe. 'Neither chance nor a haphazard grouping makes up the unit of cavalry or foot-soldiers, but

---

[223] See the text in H. Delpech, *La tactique au XIIIe siècle*, I, p. 374, n. 1 and 3. Oman, I, p. 331. Grousset, II, pp. 795–7.

[224] William the Breton, *Philippis*, 1. XI, vv. 129–32, p. 323.

families or clans.'[225] The men so grouped from one family advanced under a sign or banner, the *fano, gundfano,* or *bandwa*.[226]

After the Franks had settled in Gaul, this family organisation and its concomitant military qualities disappeared. The warriors became farmers, and it has been thought that there was no question of the influence of the clans upon the art of war in the new military class which then arose, and later evolved towards chivalry. This however is a widely held misconception, sharply contradicted by trustworthy sources well into the thirteenth century.

The role of knightly clans in private wars has already been mentioned. In these conflicts between noble families there appear not only the actual family members, but also men of the retinue, the vassals who were maintained by the lord and lived with the family proper.

In comparison with the old *Geschlechter,* the medieval aristocratic clan or *lignage* did not perhaps have the same solidarity, but this is hard to decide, and other characteristics which the old Germans certainly did not possess compensated for what was lost. The knightly clan was smaller, making for greater solidarity. It was provided with better weapons and had much more efficient equipment. As warriors, the knights had greater individual dexterity, and better training in tournaments, which were held more often than the old Germans' war games. The knights were also conscious of belonging to the ruling class: for in their eyes they naturally occupied a lofty position far above the common people and even above the clergy.[227] Many texts show this:

> 'That is well done', says the archbishop,
> That is how a knight should behave,
> Who is armed and well mounted:
> He must be strong and proud in battle,
> Otherwise he is not worth a groat,
> And should go into a monastery and become a monk
> And pray for our sins every day.[228]

And elsewhere:

> The archbishop . . .
> Likes buying horses and fine weapons
> For dubbing squires knights better
> Than heaping up riches. . . .
> He explains this to the pope:
> 'Reverend Father, do not worry too much about this:
> We ought to think well of knights,
> When we are sitting down to dine,
> Or are at matins,

225 Tacitus, *Germania,* c. 7, p. 75.
226 J. Flach, *Les origines de l'ancienne France, II,* Paris, 1886–1917, p. 435–7.
227 Bloch, *La société féodale. Les classes et le gouvernement des hommes,* p. 15.
228 *Chanson de Roland,* vv. 1876–82, p. 158.

They are fighting for the defence of our land.
You and I and our abbot Fromer
Ought to empty the treasure chest for them.
Each of us should give them so much
So that they will come and serve and honour us.'[229]

The same sense of superiority comes out in a military form in mounted combat – the cavalryman always feels superior to the foot-soldier.

There are many texts which show the value of the ties binding the clan to the lord. The best known of these dates from the end of the thirteenth century, proving that these conditions lasted for a very long time. Joinville tells us that at the time of the battle of Mansurah in Egypt in 1250, during the first Crusade of St Louis, the *bataille* of Guy de Mauvoisin achieved splendid results: he adds that this should cause no surprise, for this formation consisted entirely of members of this clan and vassals of this lord.[230] This was not of course true of all lords, since they were accompanied on Crusades by volunteers only.

To Ambroise the knightly clans and closely serried units were synonymous:

The clans advanced together
And regrouped themselves together
This made the army so tightly packed
That it could scarcely be harmed.[231]

In the battle of Arsuf the great hero of the day was James of Avesnes, who fought with his clan and perished with three members of his family.[232] During one of the battles of the Third Crusade, the Knights Templar were surprised by the enemy. Since they had had plenty of experience of fighting in the East, and were used to fighting in units, they dismounted and drew themselves up in crown formation, in which the men stood back to back to repel the enemy attack. They fought then, not as we should expect of a professional army, in very close units, but rather 'as if they all sprang from one father'.[233] The poet shows that he considers that units formed from family members were much more closely united than those which the Templars could form as a military order, with their own rules for the conduct of war. The Schavedries clan began the battle of Worringen, and remained on the battlefield until the end.[234] Jan van Heelu wrote in the same vein about the men of Brabant, who fought as brothers under the leadership of their father, duke John I.[235]

These facts are born out in epic poems. In the German *Heldenlieder* there are constant references to *magen und mannen*, the family members and the vassals. The

---

[229] *Chanson d'Aspremont*, I, c. 5, vv. 108–11; vv. 116–25, pp. 4–5.
[230] Joinville, c. 50, p. 88. See also the relevant pages of M. Bloch, *La formation des liens de dépendance*, pp. 191–5.
[231] Ambroise, vv. 6187–90, p. 165.
[232] *Ibid.*, vv. 6440–1, p. 172 and v. 6651, p. 177.
[233] *Ibid.*, vv. 7261–2, p. 194.
[234] Heelu, vv. 7163–69, pp. 264–5.
[235] *Ibid.*, vv. 5173–8, p. 194.

thousand liegemen of duke Bègue in *Garin le Lorrain* all belonged to a single clan.[236] They were the best warriors, and formed one of the most solid bases of a lord's power, together with his liegemen, his castles and his revenues.[237] In the epics the clans had many members:

> And there were more than a thousand comrades together
> All of one lineage and one nation.[238]

The whole group of *chansons de geste* about Aymeri de Narbonne and his sons is devoted to his clan. 'There is neither rivalry nor jealousy among the members, as soon as one of them is threatened they all rush to help. No one esteems himself more highly than his brothers: they make no boast of their own feats of arms, but about those of their clan, and each one is proud to be able to behold his own image in others, many times reflected as in mirrors. As the clan grows, the braver they feel.'[239] This is well expressed in another poem *Le siège de Barbastre*:

> '. . .
> And I tell you, Sire, by fine truth
> That the heroic deeds of Aymeri are kept in heredity.
> Not one will die in a castle or a city,
> but in hard battle against infidel heathen.
> That fee will I keep as my best inheritance.
>
> Well, let us go to strike the infidel heathen
> So that nobody can sing a bad song about it,
> So that Aimeri's family will not be criticised,
> So that no cowardice will be done in his age.
> Let us go to fight so that nothing can be changed.'
> At these words they have pricked their horses
> All together once, with good will.[240]

The text shows that the clan cannot be permitted to be dishonoured by the cowardice of one of his sons. Even when other members of the clan were not on the battlefield, the thought of the family has its effect, and helps to overcome fear in terrible danger. 'Come and help me, that I may not be guilty of cowardice, which would be a reproach to my family!' Thus Guillaume d'Orange invoked the help of the Holy Virgin in order to be saved in extremity.[241] And why did not Roland summon the aid of Charlemagne's army by sounding the Oliphant?

> 'Now Roland, my companion, sound your horn,
> If Charlemagne hears it, he will send the army back,
> The king will save us with his great power.'

236 Bloch, *op. cit.*, p. 193.
237 *Ibid.*, *loc. cit.* Gilbert of Mons, c. 180, p. 266.
238 *Le siège de Barbastre*, vv. 6211–12, p. 194. Cf. *Chanson d'Aspremont*, II, c. 448, vv. 9128–30, p. 97.
239 J. Bédier, *Les légendes épiques*, I, p. 57.
240 *Le siège de Barbastre*, vv. 2706–18, pp. 85–6.
241 *Le couronnement de Louis*, ed. E. Langlois, CHMA, 22, Paris, 1920, vv. 787–9, p. 25.

Roland answers: 'May it please God
Never to let me bring disgrace on my family,
Nor bring sweet France into disrepute.'[242]

The honour of the clan would thereby be jeopardised, even the honour of the country; the shame would be general because the poets would make mockery in a song.

But the clan system alone did not bring cohesion in the knightly units. As we saw in the case of private wars, feudal bonds between the lord and his vassals must also be taken into account, and particularly those with the liegemen, who lived at court or in the castle of a lord, and who constituted part of the family itself. The maintenance of a retinue or band of warriors by a powerful lord followed a very old custom dating from the time of the Teutons.

In those days prominent leaders surrounded themselves with brave young men and tried to keep the greatest possible number of close companions in their following. In time of peace these warriors increased their prestige, their social position and their power, in time of war they formed their lord's bodyguard. On the battlefield it was a disgrace for the leader to be outdone by his companions in courage or bravery, and for them it was a disgrace not to equal their lord in these qualities. They were dishonoured for life if they survived their commander after his death in battle. As members of his bodyguard they had to protect him, rescue him and even ascribe their own heroic deeds to him. This was their most important duty. The commander fought for victory, his men fought for their leader. He maintained them out of the booty and the profits that flowed in from war, and he provided them with their costly charger, their arms and their board at his table instead of paying them a fixed salary.[243] Centuries later the same custom is found in *Beowulf* and in the Norse sagas.[244] In the tenth century the Normans knew such old German customs which they had doubtless brought with them from their northern fatherland. Three hundred men were ready to fight and die at the side of William Longsword. With one accord they came to him, swore their oath of fealty and promised to be true and faithful. In accordance with Danish custom they all touched lances together, this was called *wapentake*, and served to strengthen comradeship in arms ceremoniously in a special circumstances. In the eleventh century it appears again among the Anglo-Saxons and Normans.[245]

Among the Franks private retinues also existed up to the sixth and seventh centuries. The royal *trustis* corresponds to the *comitatus* described by Tacitus. The bodyguard was a sort of permanent little army which had to protect the king, but which could also be set to other tasks. Its members were called *antrustiones* and enjoyed a special protection. When a member was killed, the murderer had to pay his family three times the normal *wergeld*. The member of a royal retinue was thus a person of considerable importance in society, even if he had risen from the lower

---

[242] *Chanson de Roland*, vv. 1059–64, pp. 91–2.
[243] Tacitus, *Germania*, c. 13–14, pp. 78–9.
[244] Bloch, *La formation des liens de dépendance*, p. 238.
[245] Dudo of St.-Quentin, *De moribus et actis primorum Normanniae ducum*, ed. J. Lair, Caen, 1865, I, c. 45, p. 190. Flach, *Les origines de l'ancienne France*, II, p. 438. Stenton, *Anglo-Saxon England*, 2nd edn, Oxford, 1947, p. 497.

classes. He enjoyed this special status because of the oath of fealty, sworn with his hand in the king's, and because he lived in the royal entourage. The chief lords of the Merovingians also had their personal retinues, which formed the cadre of professional soldiers. They were fed, clothed and protected in exchange for services rendered.[246]

The Carolingians had the *scara*, a corps of young and strong warriors, living at the court, who could be sent where they were needed. Young squires were trained for the profession of arms and were maintained at the court.[247] There are many examples of young squires and knights who were given bed and board by their lord in his court or castle. These were the *tirones*, the *milites de sua familia, de sua domo*, the *domestici milites*, the *commilitones*, the knights of the *mesnie* or the *hus*.[248] In 1108 Louis the Fat was thus able to raise a small army made up exclusively of knights belonging to his household.[249] In the Third Crusade Richard I had a personal retinue, which formed one of the main units in the battle with his bodyguard.[250] During the war in Wales Edward I's household consisted sometimes of more than a hundred bannerets and knights, and thirty or more sergeants-at-arms.[251] During his campaign in Flanders in 1297 his household consisted first of 475 and later of 550 armoured cavalrymen. Some of these men were only temporarily incorporated into the royal retinue, which numbered at least 400–420 permanent members at that time, i.e. between August and 1 November 1297.[252] The hostel of the king of France in 1317 included 235 armoured cavalrymen.[253] The prince-bishop of Liège had a *familia episcopalis* which among other duties was charged with the defence of the castles.[254] Sometimes he recruited a special retinue to deal with rebellious liege-men.[255]

Rulers always wanted to surround themselves with specially brave liegemen who would protect them in battle as faithful bodyguards. Young Henry of England sought out the most courageous knights and tried to recruit them for high pay and lavish maintenance.[256] Philip of Alsace made a similar offer to William the Marshal.[257] Baldwin IV and Baldwin V of Hainault chose the most courageous knights of the

---

[246] Ganshof, *Qu'est-ce que la féodalité?* Brussels, 1947, p. 18. Bloch, *La formation des liens de dépendance*, pp. 238–41.

[247] See Chapter II. Rabanus Maurus, *De procinctu romanae militiae*, ed. Dummler, *Zeitschrift für deutsches Altertum*, 15, 1872, p. 444.

[248] Guilhiermoz, *Essai sur les origines de la noblesse en France au moyen âge*, Paris, 1902, pp. 244–7.

[249] Suger, c. 12, p. 78; c. 15, p. 90.

[250] Oman, I, pp. 307 and 318.

[251] M. Prestwich, *War, politics and finance under Edward I*, London, 1972, pp. 40–66. Morris, *Welsh Wars*, pp. 84–7. Oman, II, p. 65.

[252] N.B. Lewis, 'The English forces in Flanders', in *Studies in medieval history presented to F.M. Powicke*, Oxford, 1948, p. 314.

[253] Lot, I, p. 270.

[254] *Cantatorium sive Chronicon Sancti Huberti*, ed. K. Hanquet, CRH in 4°, Brussels 1906, c. 93, p. 241. Ganshof, 'Etude sur les ministeriales en Flandre et en Lotharingie', Ac. Belg., Cl. Lettres, Mém, in 8°, xx, I, Brussels, 1926, p. 139.

[255] Ganshof, *op. cit.*, pp. 242–3.

[256] Gilbert of Mons, c. 48, p. 83; c. 104, p. 146.

[257] *Histoire de Guillaume le Maréchal*, I, vv. 6157–62, p. 222.

county as *commilitones*. There were about forty noblemen in the entourage of Baldwin V, who like vassals completely supported by a prince, received horses, arms, clothes and money, and the fiefs of several of them were increased.[258] All the members of the court of the count, the socially prominent knights as well as the lower servants, had to protect the count in the army, and in return their expenses were borne by him. If one of them became needy through sickness or age, he had a right to some assistance with food and clothing.[259] Jan van Heelu described how solid the bonds were between such humble servants and their prince. The *sergeants* who had received clothing from the duke fought particularly well in the battle of Worringen in John I's unit:

> There were from Brabant
> Many courageous *sergeants*,
> Certainly the equals of knights,
> That seemed so in the unit
> Of the duke, their master,
> Where they, with the most honour,
> Did the best acts of fighting,
> That anyone saw in the army.
> And most of all those
> Who received from the duke
> Clothes, and were his servants,
> They showed always, without stinting,
> That they preferred to die
> Than to abandon their master.[260]

The harsh reality of the battlefield provides plenty of examples. Although the old German custom that members of a retinue should not survive their dead master no longer applied, it seems that this sort of thing did actually happen. It was the case at Courtrai in 1302.[261] At Mons-en-Pévèle the members of the royal retinue unhesitatingly offered themselves to rescue Philip the Fair, and many sacrificed their lives.[262] At Bouvines, both commanders, Otto and Philip Augustus, were rescued from certain death by the devotion of their followers.[263] At Steppes in 1213 Henry of Huldenberg wore the armorial devices of his master, duke Henry I of Brabant, and perished on that account.[264] It was one of the primary obligations of a vassal to defend and protect his lord. In an assembly of peers at the castle of Lille the lord spoke thus to his liegeman: 'You shall protect and defend my body, my honour, my estate and my possessions, as befits a vassal for his lord. I promise to protect you and the fief for

---

[258] Gilbert of Mons, c. 46, p. 80; c. 56, p. 97 and specially c. 252, pp. 327–8. See also c. 155, p. 241 for the *mansores* or men of the 'mesnie'.

[259] *Ministeria Curie Hanoniensis*, in Gilbert of Mons, p. 343.

[260] Heelu, vv. 8647–60, pp. 316–17.

[261] Verbruggen, *De slag der gulden sporen*, p. 300.

[262] Verbruggen, *De slag bij de Pevelenberg*, pp. 190–2.

[263] See Chapter IV: Bouvines.

[264] Reinerus, *Annales S. Jacobi Leodiensis*, ed. G.H. Pertz, MGH, SS, XVI, 1859, p. 668.

which you do me homage, to give you counsel and support you as a lord must do for his liegeman.'[265]

As time went on, feudal obligations assumed priority, although the influence of families was still felt. This can be seen in family relations themselves: the father was regarded as the lord, the sons as his vassals. Family bonds had to give way to obligations to the liege lord, for example in the punishment of the Erembalds after the murder of Charles the Good, and their resistance in the castle at Bruges, clan solidarity could not prevail against the lord. Anyone who fought with his family in such a case was mercilessly punished.[266]

In the *chanson de geste Raoul de Cambrai*, the writer deals with this conflict between family bonds and feudal obligations. Raoul made war on the sons of Herbert de Vermandois. One of his squires, Bernier, who had belonged to Raoul's retinue from the age of fifteen, was descended through his father from the same clan as Herbert. Bernier's mother was a nun in the abbey of Origni. She implored her son to forsake Raoul, but Bernier refused, because his lord had given him horses and clothes, and the boy wanted to serve him until he had the right to leave him.

> Lord Raoul is more felonious than Judas.
> He is my lord; he gives me horses and cloth,
> And garment and rich cloth of Baudas.
> I will not abandon him for the honour of Damas,
> Till the moment that everybody says: 'Bernier, you are right.'

His mother admits that he is right:

> 'Son,' said the mother, 'by my faith, you are right.
> Work for your master, God will win by it.'[267]

But Raoul ordered an attack on Origni. The nunnery was set on fire, and Bernier's mother was burnt to death before the eyes of her son. After this attack Raoul returned to his camp. Under the influence of drink he insulted Bernier and even struck him in the face with the shaft of his lance. Other knights of the retinue came between the two men: now Bernier had the right to avenge himself if Raoul made no reparation. Raoul proposed that he should go on foot from Origni to Nesle (27 miles) with Bernier's saddle on his back as a punishment. The latter refused, and left Raoul's army with his men, despite the fact that the other knights considered that his lord had made him a fair proposal.[268] Bernier was absolutely loyal, although he had good grounds to abandon his lord, and when he finally left his master, he had right on his

---

[265] R. Monier, *Les lois, enquêtes et jugements des Pairs du Castel de Lille*, Bibl. Soc. hist. droit 3, Lille, 1937, c. 129, pp. 84–5.

[266] Bloch, *La formation des liens de dépendance*, pp. 356–9.

[267] Raoul de Cambrai, *Chanson de geste*, ed. P. Meyer and A. Longnon, SATF, Paris, 1882, c. 67, vv. 1381–7, pp. 45–6.

[268] *Ibid.*, c. 84–8, pp. 56–61.

side. If the lord struck the vassal with a stick, the vassal could break the agreement; this had been laid down in a capitulary of Charlemagne.[269]

Other writers of *chansons de geste* described what close bonds existed between the lord and his retinue. In *Doon de Mayence* the attachment of the liegeman was well described: 'If my lord is killed, I shall die too. If he is hanged? Then I shall hang with him. If he is cast into the fire? I too shall be burned. And if he is drowned, let them throw me in too!'[270] The vassal had to endure a great deal for his lord:

> A man must bear much hardship for his lord
> And endure great heat and great cold
> And lose both hair and hide for him if need be.[271]

In the *Chanson d'Aspremont* Charlemagne entrusted the standard to the seneschal Fagon, who had guarded it for thirty-three years and had never been driven from the field of battle. He belonged to the royal house and guarded the banner with his personal retinue of a thousand liegemen.

> A thousand knights elected from the country,
> His liegemen, of his private retinue,
> Everybody has his head well armed,
> All wish to come in the fight.
> He leads them that day so close together
> That an apple thrown in the air
> Would not touch the ground during half a mile.[272]

When Joinville wrote of the famous *bataille* of Guy de Mauvoisin, he praised not only the clan, but also the liegemen who gave assistance to their lord: as vassals most closely bound to their lord, their obligations were absolute,[273] in contrast with those of many ordinary vassals who had different lords. The system existed from the middle of the eleventh century, and contributed a great deal to the tightening of personal bonds between the overlord and his vassals, as is evident from the narrative sources and the *chansons de geste*. The thirteenth and fourteenth centuries saw a relaxation of the obligations of the liegemen, but in the same period it became usual for soldiers practically everywhere to be paid. The knights and squires were then very well paid for their military service, so that their devotion generally left nothing to be desired.[274]

In the thirteenth and fourteenth centuries there were fewer knights and more squires, and by the end of the thirteenth century squires were in fact more numerous than knights. Did this weaken the solidarity between the lord and his vassals? There

[269] Bloch, *La formation des liens de dépendance*, p. 352. Ganshof, *Qu'est-ce que la féodalité?*, p. 46.

[270] Bloch, *op. cit.*, p. 355.

[271] *Chanson de Roland*, vv. 1010–13, p. 86.

[272] *Chanson d'Aspremont*, II, 491, vv. 10106–18, pp. 127–8. Citation: vv. 10112–18, p. 128.

[273] Bloch, *op. cit.*, pp. 331–3. N. Didier, *Le droit des fiefs dans la coutume de Hainaut au moyen âge*, Lille, 1945, pp. 31–32.

[274] Lot, II, p. 424. M. Sczaniecki, *Essai sur les fiefs-rente*, Bib. Hist. Droit 6, Paris, 1946, p. 31.

is insufficient evidence for this despite the defection of the Flemish knights and squires in 1297. These nobles were divided into two factions, that of the count of Flanders and that of the king of France; the incident is too isolated to permit any conclusions to be drawn.

The professional military class was made up of knights and squires who were more than ever the social elite. The solidarity seems not to have been weakened among the French noblemen who perished in such numbers at Courtrai, some of them had not wanted to survive their lord and returned to the battlefield instead of fleeing after the defeat. The Anglo-Norman nobles too suffered heavy losses at Bannockburn. In both battles knights and squires were ready to sacrifice themselves, nor is there any reason to doubt the devotion and solidarity of the men who fought at Mons-en-Pévèle.

Yet these great defeats were, after all, concrete examples of the weakening of the noble caste. From the middle of the twelfth century the knights had gradually formed a caste which was closed by the mid-thirteenth century: this contained the germ of the decline. The great knightly defeats which came after the beginning of the fourteenth century were a sign of inner weakening, not yet clearly visible, but becoming clearer by the middle of the fourteenth century.

In short, the units which were formed from a knightly clan, or from the retinue of a lord, or from his liegemen, showed exceptional cohesiveness in this period. In most cases the formations in the West were composed of these elements, or at least had a solid core of such men. Of course there were also bad vassals, and cowards, but they were mercilessly abused by the chroniclers, if their flight was too obviously prompted by a lack of courage. Heelu praised the lord of Borne thus for his heroic deeds:

> . . . the good knight of Borne
> who was the finest of the Dutch tongue
> among old or young
> to be found at that time
> in the Roman empire, far and wide . . .[275]

and above all because, having been wounded, he had to be removed by force, and wanted

> . . . rather to die with honour
> than dishonour the name of Borne.[276]

The lord of Keppel, on the other hand, was severely censured for having abandoned his overlord, the count of Guelders:

> Another followed, fleeing
> with untattered banners,
> and after him a great band

---

275 Heelu, vv. 6524–8, pp. 241–2.
276 *Ibid.*, vv. 6507–8, p. 241.

of knights and squires, without need:
he was called the lord of Keppel.
May God condemn him
for fleeing so shamefully
and leaving his overlord in the lurch.[277]

The example of the lord of Keppel, who fled with his whole unit, and 'without need', is instructive. The evidence of various writers is contradictory; it seems clear that despite the bonds of clans, personal retinues of lords, lofty conceptions of individual and collective honour, there was still not always sufficient solidarity and spirit of sacrifice to stand up to the ordeal of battle. Sometimes still more was needed. Together with the individual and collective training, the tightly knit social structure, noble conceptions of honour and duty, there was still another means of reducing danger, overcoming fear, preventing capture, and increasing the effectiveness of fighting units – this was to go into battle in small tactical units, *conrois*, which in turn formed larger units, *batailles* or 'battles', in order to be able to give more effective support.

Tactical Units in Knightly Warfare

In order to lessen the danger for the individual, to give him confidence in battle, to carry out an effective charge, but also to go into action in tactical units, the formations of knights were in closely serried ranks. It has already been shown how Ambroise and Guillaume Guiart, the one late in the twelfth century and the other early in the fourteenth, described the advance of the knightly units. Both chroniclers were eyewitnesses, and had a sound knowledge of methods of warfare of their time. Ambroise gave us several fine examples, and it is hard to resist the temptation to quote another good extract:

There were many units,
The most beautiful Christian warriors
That ever saw the people of the earth.
They were serried in ranks
As if they were people forged in iron.
The battle line was wide and strong
And could well sustain fierce attacks;
And the rearguard was so full
Of good knights that it was difficult
To see their heads,
If one was not higher up;
It was not possible to throw a prune
Except on mailed and armoured men.[278]

---

[277] *Ibid.*, vv. 6540–3, 6549–52, p. 242.
[278] Ambroise, vv. 3974–86, pp. 106–7.

And in the *Chanson d'Antioche* we read:

> And the other units of the Frankish family
> March serried and in step.
> The princes lead them on their lively chargers,
> There is no space open where a glove can fall to earth.[279]

Even the *chansons de geste* which are naturally inclined to relate the individual heroic deeds of the great lords, are here close to the accounts of eyewitnesses. The same image of the apple or glove thrown in the air is used over and over again:

> Their units advance towards them in serried ranks;
> If you throw a glove over their helmets
> It would not land within a mile.[280]

And:

> The barons are so closely packed as they advance
> That if you throw a glove on their helmets
> It would not fall to ground within a mile.[281]

Even between the formations of knights, advancing beside each other on the same front, there were sometimes only small spaces. When a formation is especially well drawn up, in order to make a surprise attack on the enemy, it advanced like the detachment of duke Girart de Fraite in the *Chanson d' Aspremont*:

> They advanced secretly through a valley.
> He had seventeen hundred men with him.
> He led them in such close formation
> That the wind could not blow between their lances.[282]

Allowing for poetic exaggeration, the fact remains that the units were so closely packed that the horses were touching each other in formation.

An excellent narrative source explains why the cavalrymen were formed up so closely. In 1180 king Amalric wanted to relieve the fortress of Darum in the kingdom of Jerusalem, which was being besieged by Saladin. It describes how the king acted in order to break the enemy lines: 'Our army observed the enemy camp. Terrified because they were so powerful, our men began to draw closer together, as they had been trained to do, indeed so closely that they could scarcely carry out an attack because of the mass. The enemy fell upon them at once, and tried to force them apart . . . but our men . . . were too tightly packed. They fought off the enemy attack and continued their advance deliberately.'[283] By means of this dense formation, which

---

279 *Chanson d'Antioche*, II, viii, 32, vv. 856–9, p. 238.
280 *Chanson d'Aspremont*, I, c. 174, vv. 3241–3, p. 104, see also: II, c. 428, vv. 8645–9, p. 81; c. 491, vv. 10116–19, p. 128; c. 502, vv. 10397–400, p. 137. Gautier, *La chevalerie*, p. 749: it was the general rule in the epic poems.
281 *Raoul de Cambrai*, c. 119, vv. 2412–14, p. 82.
282 *Chanson d'Aspremont*, II, c. 451, vv. 9201–6, p. 99; c. 468, vv. 9621–4, p. 112, a similar example.
283 William of Tyre, I, pp. 975–6. Delpech, II, p. 213 and n. 3. Grousset, II, pp. 560–1.

made a charge very difficult, king Amalric broke through the besieging army and liberated the beleaguered fortress. Here it is explicitly stated that the very dense formation was used for fear of the enemy, and this shows that our analysis of the psychology of the knight is borne out by the statements of contemporaries. But at the same time the chronicler points out that in this case the formation was too dense, and made the charge more difficult: nevertheless, this density enabled the army to make stouter resistance to the attacks of the enemy, who tried vainly to break it up.

The importance of such descriptions of battle-order can scarcely be over-emphasised. If an advance in very close order is the ideal to be aimed at, and is indeed achieved as far as possible, then it follows that duels and individual combats are out of the question. They became, in fact, increasingly difficult as the ranks were more tightly packed. These formations are a complete negation of the so-called duels, of which a battle between two knightly armies was supposed to have consisted.

Closely drawn-up units are encountered in the tournaments as they were described in the *Histoire de Guillaume le Maréchal*. They are also found in the battles at Acre and Arsuf during the Third Crusade, in the battles of Bouvines, Worringen and Mons-en-Pévèle, and in most of the narrative sources. It has been shown elsewhere that the chronicles are clear on this point.[284] All the sources written in the vernacular and quoted above – Ambroise, the *Histoire de Guillaume le Maréchal*, Villehardouin, Robert de Clari, Joinville, Guiart, and many other chroniclers – mention *conrois*, banners, *batailles* and *échelles*. Knights in *conrois*, *échelles* or *batailles* fight on nearly every battlefield. The close similarity of the technical terms – *bataille, battaglia, bataelge; eschiele, scara, scare, schiere; conrois* and *conroten* – shows that they have a common origin and that they were widely spread over western Europe. The Germanic origin of the words indicates that tactical units had been used for a long time.

In small units the vassals wore the insignia of their lord, if he was rich and powerful enough to maintain them in his retinue. When William the Marshal belonged to the retinue of the chamberlain of Tancarville, he wore a shield with the device of his lord: 'Sis escuz est de Tankarvile'.[285] In 1176 Raymond le Gros had a retinue of some thirty kinsmen with shields of one pattern in Ireland.[286] A while later the coat of arms was introduced.

> His horse was covered with iron
> On it was placed a cloth of blue silk
> With golden flowers of the arms of the king
> Of France, the whole unit bore the same.[287]

In the thirteenth century English barons and knights had the right to let their squires

---

[284] Verbruggen, 'La tactique militaire des armées de chevaliers', *Revue du Nord* 29, 1947, p. 163.
[285] *Histoire de Guillaume le Maréchal*, I, v. 1478, p. 54.
[286] Giraldus Cambrensis, *Expugnatio Hibernica*, p. 335.
[287] Ph. Mousket, *Chronique rimée*, ed. de Reiffenberg, CRH in 4°, 2 vols, Brussels, 1836–38, II, vv. 17406–9, p. 194.

and knights wear a badge or uniform.[288] It was considered a scandalous thing when a robber captain gave his men a uniform, just as if he were a baron! In the fourteenth century a man had to be a banneret at least for his knights and squires to deck themselves out in such a fashion.[289] In the *Scalacronica*, Sir Thomas Gray of Heton wrote that the followers of the English barons who rose against Edward II wore identical clothes.[290] At Bouvines the emperor Otto was recognised by the device of his *conroi*.[291]

The strength of these units varied according to the power of the liege lord, but at Worringen several small banners were grouped together.[292] The second half of the twelfth century sees the appearance of the bannerets, commanders of a unit of twenty knights.[293] In the Welsh wars of Edward I some bannerets have 20 knights and squires, but others have less warriors in their unit.[294] Since Guiart described these *conrois* as square units, it may be assumed that formations with 12 to 24 cavalrymen placed 6 or 8 of them in the front rank, the others lined up in a second or third rank. The great *bataille* was formed of a series of *conrois* drawn up next to each other. This gave rectangular formations two or three men deep, with a front of fifty, sixty or more knights and squires.

The best example of the complete deployment of an army in 'battles' and banners was that of the royal French army which advanced to Cassel in 1328 to crush the rebels from coastal Flanders. It was made up of ten 'battles' with 177 banners when it reached its destination, and with some reinforcements finally totalled 196 banners.[295]

It is useful to trace what later happened to these small units: in 1351 king John the Good of France wanted to draw up his troops effectively, and gave the order to form larger units, *routes* of at least twenty-five cavalry, better still thirty to eighty.[296] It is perfectly possible and logical that as far as the strength of small units was concerned, there was a return to the conditions that had prevailed in the twelfth century, when

288 N.B. Lewis, 'The Organisation of indentured Retinues in fourteenth-century England', TRHS, 4th series, 27, 1945, pp. 29–30.
289 *Ibid., loc. cit.*
290 *Scalachronica*, pp. 147–8.
291 Ph. Mousket, vv. 22025–30, p. 369.
292 See Chapter IV: Worringen.
293 William the Marshal was a banneret by 1180 (S. Painter, *William Marshal*, Baltimore, 1933, pp. 33 and 45). A knight could become a banneret and receive a double pay when he commanded 20 knights and squires in the 13th century, but that custom seems to date from the second half of the twelfth century. See an example from 1282 in Verbruggen, 'Het leger en de vloot', p. 65, from Lille, Archives départementales, Cartulaire de Namur, pièce 29, fo 17 bis, v°. More examples in the French army in Flanders in 1300: Paris, Archives nationales, J 543, no. 17. *Journaux du trésor de Philippe IV le Bel*, ed. J. Viard, Collection de documents inédits sur l'histoire de France, Paris, 1940, in 4°, c. 3633–6, pp. 540–1; c. 3675, p. 545; c. 3727, p. 552; c. 3802, p. 560. Verbruggen, *De slag der gulden sporen*, p. 239.
294 Morris, *Welsh Wars*, p. 163: 5 bannerets and 96 lances, and p. 314, John de Segrave. But in most cases the units of the bannerets in the Welsh wars are a bit under strength. Morris takes 18 as an average for the unpaid cavalry at Falkirk: *Welsh Wars*, p. 314. In 1297, the average was 17: N.B. Lewis, 'The English Forces in Flanders', pp. 310–18.
295 *Istore et Croniques*, I, pp. 343–4. Lot, I, p. 223, n. 2.
296 *Ordonnances des rois de France*, IV, Paris, 1734, p. 67, c. 2.

these formations apparently had more horsemen than in the early fourteenth century. This would certainly be in accordance with the decrease in the number of knights. According to the *Histoire de Guillaume le Maréchal*, the chamberlain of Tancarville actually had forty knights or more in his banner, while William the Marshal himself had fifty and more in his *conestablie* when he was in the service of Henry II.[297]

One of the best indications that such small formations made up tactical units comes from the East, in the kingdom founded by Baldwin IX. His brother and successor, Henry of Constantinople, divided his army into fifteen 'battles', each of which consisted of twenty knights and armoured cavalry, except the fifteenth, made up of fifty men and commanded by the emperor himself. There were also three similar units made up of Greeks in this army.[298] The units are notably small for the times, simply because the army was very small altogether. This little army made its attack in four lines staggered in depth, in units of forty men each, that is, two small units joined. 'And Pieres de Braiscuel and Nicholes de Mailli were put in the vanguard with Joffroi the marshal, and they said that they would charge in front, between him and Milon le Brabant, and then Guillaumes dou Parçoi and Lyenars de Helemes; and the emperor covered the chargers.'[299] In 1211, there was another example of this sort in the battle by the river Espiga. Henry I had again formed fifteen units, each consisting of fifteen knights, except that of the emperor, which had fifty. Henry ordered twelve units to begin the attack, lest the balance of numbers turned out too much to the disadvantage of his troops. A detachment remained in camp to guard the tents. The emperor was victorious, and pursued the enemy from midday till sunset. He said that he lost no men.[300]

Here we are clearly dealing with tactical units. What would be the point of carrying out their charges in the manner described if there were no tactical units executing the commands of the leader as one man? Why else were the formations so small, instead of forming a large detachment, and keeping another as a reserve as soon as the propitious moment comes. At the same time it must be pointed out how Henry was motivated in the second instance: this time the ratio of numbers was so much to his disadvantage that he only dared put a small part of his army in the second and possibly the third line.

Discipline in Camp and on the March

We need to examine the questions of discipline on the march and in camp: we are particularly well informed about these matters as regards the Knights Templar, and their Rule contains many interesting details. Since they had to fight constantly against

---

[297] *Histoire de Guillaume le Maréchal*, I, vv. 1314–15, p. 48; vv. 8918–19, p. 322 and vv. 8893–8, p. 321.
[298] Henry of Valenciennes, c. 543, pp. 46–7, c. 533, pp. 41–2.
[299] *Ibid., loc. cit.*
[300] Letter of emperor Henry I: RHF, XVIII, p. 533. Delpech, II, p. 60, notes 1, 2, 3 and p. 61, notes 1 and 2. Ch. Verlinden, *Les empereurs belges de Constantinople*, Brussels, 1945, p. 129.

the Moslems, they drew up strict regulations as to how to prepare for battle, and how everything had to be done with the greatest circumspection.

On arrival in camp, after a march, the Templars provisionally chose a place round the chapel, which, with tents for the Master and the local commander, formed the nucleus of the camp, and were therefore the first to be put up. While the owners of these tents moved in, the other knights awaited the order that would allow them to take their place within the ropes marking out the camp boundaries. The marshal of the Order had the provisional right to each place until the order was given to set up the tents.[301]

No knight could send members of his retinue to forage or fetch wood without permission. One squire out of two might search for necessities close to the camp, but only close enough to be recalled by shouting. In an emergency each unit leader had to have all his men on call. The herald always had to lodge near the standard-bearer, and his orders had to be strictly carried out, just as strictly as those of the leader in whose name he announced them. The attention of the soldiers was first called by a shout or the tolling of a bell – this in contrast to knightly armies, in which orders were also proclaimed by a herald, but in which trumpets were mostly used.

Food had to be fetched in close ranks, by each man personally. Two knights received the same rations as three turcopoles: two turcopoles got the same as three junior brothers of the Order or sergeants. The Master and the sick men enjoyed a special diet.[302]

Probably the horses and equipment were inside the circle formed by the knights' tents: this was prescribed in the Rule of the Teutonic Order, which derived from that of the Templars. The regulations for the march emphasize that the same rules were valid for the Templars.[303]

If an alarm were sounded in the camp, it had to be dealt with in an orderly and disciplined manner. The high command did not want everyone to rush at once to the danger spot, and sought above all to avoid panic. On an alarm, the knights who were nearest had to go at once, armed with lance and shield. The others had to report to the chapel and wait for orders there. If the alarm sounded outside the camp, no one was to go without permission, even if a lion or other ferocious beast paused in its tracks.[304] In such a case, and also when the Templars were in quarters, the commander of the turcopoles, or native mounted troops, was ordered by the marshal to send one or two men on reconnaissance, in order to decide what ought to be done.[305] When the Templars were in permanent camp, or in quarters in time of war, the standard had to be brought out first and then the knights came as quickly as possible.[306]

As in modern armies, a distinction was made in the Rule between a march in peacetime and one in war. In the latter case the regulations were stricter, in that

301 *La règle du Temple*, c. 148, pp. 115–16.
302 *Ibid.*, c. 152–3, pp. 118–19.
303 E. von Frauenholz, *Das Heerwesen*, p. 126.
304 *La règle du Temple*, c. 155, p. 120 and c. 380, but with an error in that chapter. See Frauenholz, *op. cit.*, p. 127, n. 2.
305 *La règle du Temple*, c. 169, 127.
306 *Ibid.*, c. 160. p. 123.

everyone had to act more quickly. Strict discipline was imposed from the moment camp was broken until the units were on the move, undoubtedly because these minutes were critical for a cavalry army.[307] When camp was broken, horses could not be saddled, harnessed, mounted, or fetched from their places until the marshal gave the order. The Templars could then attach a few articles to their horses: tentstakes, empty flasks, ropes, a pail and so on. If a Templar wanted to ask a question of the Marshal before the march off, he had to go to him on foot, and then return to his place. He could not leave his place in camp for any other reason, but meanwhile he had his tent struck and folded, and awaited the order to move.[308]

As soon as the marshal gave the order to move, the brothers would take a quick look round to see that no equipment had been left behind. Then they moved off, well grouped together, in step, followed by their squires. Each man took his place in the column. Once they were all moving, the squire with the equipment and baggage was stationed in front of the knight. At night they marched in complete silence.[309]

Each man had to stay behind his armour, and ride calmly in his unit. By day a knight might carry on a conversation with his companion. If he rode alongside a column to do this, while his squire accompanied him with the equipment, this always had to take place on the leeward side, in order not to throw dust or sand into the faces of other men. He then took a place temporarily in the unit of his companion, for it was forbidden to ride separately abreast of the column with two, three, four or more men. If a knight or a squire lost his place in his unit during the night, he had to stay with the other unit till the morning.[310]

No one might leave his unit without permission to water animals, or for any reason, but if the line of march passed through flowing water in a peaceful region, the beasts might be allowed to drink if it did not slow up the advance. In a danger area the march had to go on at all costs, but if the standard-bearer let his horse drink, all the others could do so too.

If the alarm was sounded on the march, the knights closest to the source of the alarm had to mount their chargers and take their lance and shield, and then wait quietly for the marshal's orders, while all the other Templars gathered round the marshal to hear his orders too.[311]

When the Templars were lying in ambush, or were protecting foraging squires, were travelling from one place to another or found themselves in a dangerous place, they could not unbridle or unsaddle their horses, or feed them, without permission from their commander.[312] On the march the standard-bearer rode at the head of the whole column of march, under the marshal's orders and followed by the banner borne by a squire. In time of war, when the knights were advancing in their *eschieles* at the

---

[307] Frauenholz, p. 128.
[308] *La règle du Temple*, c. 156, pp. 120–1.
[309] *Ibid.*, c. 157, pp. 121–2.
[310] *Ibid.*, c. 158, p. 122.
[311] *Ibid.*, c. 159, pp. 122–3.
[312] *Ibid.*, c. 160, p. 123.

ready, the banner of the Order was borne by a turcopole, and the standard-bearer was in command of the Templars' squires.[313]

When battle was imminent, the Templars were divided into *eschieles*. Once a knight had taken his place in the unit, he was not allowed to leave it again: he was also forbidden to mount or take up his shield and lance without permission. When the Templars were fully armed and were moving off, their squires had to ride in front of them with the lances, while the other squires came behind with spare horses. All this was done on the orders of the Marshal, or his deputy. As the knights rode out in their formation they were not allowed to turn their horses aside to fight or to answer an alarm.[314]

At that point the Templars were permitted to ride their horses, in order to find out whether the saddle was secure and the coverings were properly attached. After this short ride they returned quietly to their unit. If they wanted to take shield and lance with them on this test ride they had to ask permission: if they wanted to put on the mail cap worn under the helmet, it might be put on, but not taken off again. Above all, it was strictly forbidden to dash on ahead and leave the ranks without permission.[315] If it nevertheless happened that a Christian recklessly went on and was set upon by a Turk, so that his life was in danger, then a Templar might leave the ranks to help him, if conscience prompted him to do so. Afterwards he had to return quietly to his unit. But if a knight of the Order undertook an attack on his own in other circumstances, or left the ranks, his infringement of the regulations was investigated, and he was punished: he might for example have to return to camp on foot, but he was not deprived of the dress of the Order for such a breach.[316]

This summary of the Rules of the Order of the Templars pertaining to discipline in camp and during the march to battle makes it clear that all eventualities were provided for, plainly as the result of long experience. The German historian von Frauenholz, who could boast of twenty years' experience as a cavalry officer, wrote on this subject: 'The regulations for the march, as well as those for the camp, show that those moments of danger in which confusion may easily arise, were clearly anticipated, and that every effort was made to avoid possible defeat. In purely cavalry formations nothing has been altered to this very day that deals with these regulations or the moments of danger. It cannot be assumed that the knights of the religious Orders alone acquired this war experience: secular knights too knew and feared such moments'.[317]

Naturally there were not nearly so many regulations to hedge round the march of an ordinary knightly army. On the march, the marshals rode ahead with their banners, as happened in the royal French army in 1304 and 1328, and in the English army in 1327.[318] Edward III strictly forbade anyone to leave the unit. Each knight remained

---

313 *Ibid.*, c. 179, p. 133.
314 *Ibid.*, c. 161, pp. 123–4.
315 *Ibid.*, c. 162, p. 124.
316 *Ibid.*, c. 163, p. 124; c. 243, p. 158; c. 613, p. 316. An example of punishment of a Hospitaller in Ambroise, vv. 9907–43, pp. 265–6.
317 Frauenholz, pp. 130 and 116, n. 2.
318 1304: G. Guiart, *La branche des royaus lingnages*, ed. N. de Wailly and L. Delisle, RHF, 22, vv.

in his lord's formation and might not leave the ranks nor ride in front of the banner, though exceptions were made for attending to natural necessities, or for adjusting girths or other parts of the harness. At the sound of the alarm, or whenever the vanguard was thought to have made contact with the enemy, each unit hastened forward to help.[319] The march of Edward III's army went on briskly over the rough terrain and was very exhausting. Yet knights and squires were manifestly capable of great physical exertion on very little food, and with nothing to drink but water from streams and rivers.

The French royal army in 1328 provided a good example of the march and arrival in camp of a knightly army. When it reached Cassel, the units advanced in the following order: the first *bataille* was led by the two marshals and the master of the crossbowmen, it consisted of six banners. All the foot-soldiers and baggage followed these units. As soon as the marshals had reached the camp site, they showed the quartermaster-sergeants (*fouriers*) the place for their masters. Then came the second 'battle', under the count of Alençon, made up of twenty-one banners: these took up a position facing the city of Cassel, in order to make it possible to set up camp and to afford protection for the troops against a possible attack by the insurgents. The third formation was made up of thirteen banners, and was led by the master of the Knights Hospitaller from overseas, and by lord Guichard de Beaujeu. This unit also included all the troops from the region of Languedoc. The constable Gautier de Châtillon led the fourth 'battle', consisting of eight banners; the fifth was the royal formation, in which the king commanded thirty-nine banners; it included the king of Navarre, the duke of Lorraine, and the count of Bar, and was protected by a wing under Miles de Noyers, standard-bearer of the *oriflamme*, that was made up of six banners. The duke of Burgundy commanded the sixth formation, eighteen banners strong. The seventh was led by the dauphin of Vienne, who commanded twelve banners. The eighth formation, of seventeen banners, was led by the count of Hainault. There was also a wing under John, brother of the count, with the troops of the king of Bohemia. The ninth unit, of fifteen banners, was under the duke of Brittany.

All these units took their places in the camp under the direction of the two marshals. Then, when everyone was in place, the rear-guard arrived. This was the tenth 'battle' under Robert d'Artois, consisting of twenty-one banners. It advanced towards the hill on which Cassel stands, and went on right through the camp, past the king's tent, in the direction of an abbey, where it encamped. The next day the duke of Bourbon came with reinforcements, consisting of an additional 'battle' of fourteen banners. Finally the royal army was further strengthened by five banners commanded by Robert of Cassel. In all the army consisted of 196 banners.[320]

According to this eyewitness description, the various camp-sites were occupied in accordance with the directions of the marshals, who marched in with their

---

19551–2, p. 282; vv. 19600–3, p. 282. In 1328: *Istore et Croniques*, I, p. 343. In 1327: Jean le Bel, I, p. 54.
[319] Jean le Bel, I, pp. 54, 56, 58.
[320] *Istore et Croniques*, I, pp. 343–4.

standards in the first formation. The second formation protected them while the camp sites were being allocated.

Of course camps were guarded at night, but on some occasions the guard was inadequate: Edward III's army in 1327 was surprised by a night raid carried out by the Scots. After that incident the night guard was never relaxed, and appears to have been effective.[321] Guard was also carefully mounted in the camp of St Louis at Mansurah in Egypt.[322] Before and after the battle of Mons-en-Pévèle, the king of France had his camp carefully guarded by armoured cavalry.[323] After a victorious battle it sometimes happened that the camp was not guarded that night, because of a general feeling that the enemy had been utterly crushed. Jan van Heelu mentions this after the battle of Worringen, and it happened elsewhere too.[324]

Some commanders fortified their camp during the siege of a fortress, as Raymond of Toulouse did several times during his struggle against Simon de Montfort in the crusade against the Albigensians, and Simon copied him.[325] During the siege of Acre, king Guy of Lusignan fortified the crusaders' camp to protect it against Saladin and his relief army. The crusaders did the same thing at Constantinople in 1203 and at Damietta in 1218.[326] During the siege of Lille in 1304 Philip the Fair had ditches dug to protect his men against sorties from the garrison, while the river Marcq later served to protect his camp in the direction from which the Flemish relief force appeared.[327]

Though we do not know much about camp regulations of medieval armies, we have some good examples of their marches. One of the best is from the Holy Land of the march of the Crusaders from Acre to Jaffa under Richard I. There is another one of a well-disciplined march before the battle of Bouvines by the army of Philip Augustus, while on the other hand the army of Otto set about the pursuit far too hastily, with the result that it was defeated. The author of the *Histoire de Guillaume le Maréchal* praised the French in this respect:

> The army departed serried and in formations
> The French are very wise in those matters.
> When they see that they are inferior
> And they depart from some place,
> They go in good order and wisely.[328]

There is another good example in the difficult journey of the army of young Baldwin III from the kingdom of Jerusalem to Bosra in 1147. The army was carefully protected: it was alert and well-disciplined, and it was forbidden to make sorties. But

321 Jean le Bel, I. pp. 70–2.
322 Joinville, c. 42. p. 71.
323 Verbruggen, 'De slag bij de Pevelenberg', pp. 176 and 194.
324 Heelu, vv. 8856–75, p. 323; vv. 8893–7, p. 234. *Chanson de Roland*, v. 2495, p. 208.
325 P. Belperron, *La croisade contre les Albigeois*, pp. 231, 233, 272, 318, 332.
326 Oman, I, p. 340. *Chronica regia Coloniensis cum continuationibus*, ed. G. Waitz, MGH, SS, 1880. p. 206. Ernoul, *Chronique, d' Ernoul et de Bernard le Trésorier*, ed. L. de Mas Latrie, SHF, Paris, 1871, p. 420. Grousset, III, p. 209.
327 *Chronique artésienne*, pp. 89–90.
328 II, vv. 12251–6, p. 70.

at a certain moment the king's strict rule about attacking the enemy was broken by a Saracen cavalryman in his army.[329] It is puzzling why this rule was broken, and why the cavalryman was apparently not punished. We must now examine this question of discipline on the march and during battle.

Battle Discipline

Trouble about leaving units in battle and during the march occurred chiefly in the East, in the struggle against the Saracen light cavalry who harassed the western knights at a distance. The best example of this again comes from the Templars' Rule, where it was forbidden to undertake individual attacks or to attack with a single unit before the order was given. But one exception was foreseen: it was permitted to go to the help of a Christian in danger.[330] Herein lies the whole drama of discipline in the knightly armies. Should a knight let an imprudent comrade die, or should he rush to help him? Both chroniclers and knights saw the importance of this problem clearly. They condemned reckless attacks and individual feats of arms of a knight who left his formation to make an attack. King Louis IX had strictly forbidden this during his Crusade in Egypt. When Gautier d'Autrèche despite everything attacked and was so gravely wounded that he died, the king had no sympathy whatever for him.[331] In an army of 2,000 or more heavy cavalry, the loss of a leader was not too serious a matter: it was different in a little army of 500 or even only 300 horsemen, like that of Henry of Constantinople or his brother Baldwin. Baldwin was seriously wounded and taken prisoner as he assisted the count of Blois during the latter's reckless pursuit of the enemy cavalry.[332]His brother Henry hurried to help one of his knights, Leonard de Hélesmes, when the latter had attacked despite the prohibition. Henry succeeded in rescuing his vassal, but his action was severely censured by Peter of Douai. The emperor's answer was characteristic: the loss of a brave warrior such as Leonard de Hélesmes would be too great for a small army, and would have brought shame to each man. Comradeship, which forged such strong bonds between the knights and which gave their little units such strength, prevailed over strict and inflexible discipline.[333]

Is it right to punish excessive bravery? Examples from medieval sources need to be considered with care. Perhaps the chronicler is realistic and keeps to the facts in his account. One would certainly be astonished to read the full truth about present-day battles: acts of imprudence, errors, exaggerated recklessness, together with lack of initiative, with fear and cowardice – anyone reading the accounts of men who

---

[329] William of Tyre, *Historia rerum in partibus transmarinis gestarum*, RHC, Hist. occ., 1, pp. 719–23. Smail, *Crusading Warfare*, pp. 158–9.
[330] *La règle du Temple*, c. 162–3, 243, 613.
[331] Joinville, c. 37, pp. 61–2.
[332] Villehardouin, II, c. 358–60, pp. 167–70.
[333] Henry of Valenciennes, c. 508–13, pp. 31–3.

fought in the two world wars would say that barrack discipline is entirely different from discipline on the battlefield.[334]

This is true of the Middle Ages as well. The representatives of the only really permanent army, such as the Templars and the Hospitallers, broke their own strict rules quite as often as the secular knights. The battle of Arsuf began on the initiative of the Hospitallers against the orders of Richard I;[335] during the Crusade of St. Louis in Egypt the Templars attacked the enemy under the command of their marshal contrary to the king's orders,[336] and during the battle of Mansurah they followed the count of Artois in the reckless attack which led to their destruction.[337] The reason for such neglect of discipline is not hard to find: as soon as the Turks, who preferred to keep their distance in battle, noticed that the knights tended to stay in formation, they became bolder, attacking at increasingly close range. As the result, the knights lost their horses and were hard pressed in the face of growing danger. Besides they knew that a single vigorous charge was usually enough to put the enemy to flight, and gain a short respite. The strain became so intense that they chose to go into action and put up a determined defence, rather than to wait for the enemy attack passively. All that was needed was for one knight to charge to make the whole army follow, as happened at Arsuf and on St Louis' expedition into Egypt.[338]

The question then arises how orders were given for an attack. It has been seen elsewhere that provision was made, as for example at Arsuf, to give the signal by trumpets. Was this a common practice?

Orders signalled by Trumpets and Banners

Signalling with trumpets has been noted as early as their use by the Merovingian armies.[339] Their use in the ninth century is briefly mentioned: Louis the Pious ordered a trumpet signal for breaking camp.[340] These were also used elsewhere, for example in the Middle East, where orders were given as follows: at the first trumpet blast each man had to arm himself, at the second blast the banners or units had to be formed, and at the third blast the whole army had to be assembled.[341] At Worringen the trumpets sounded the calls 'to arms' and 'take arms' before the battle. They sounded again to start the attack, as in tournaments. When the duke's standard was brought down however, the trumpeters were so distraught over the outcome of the struggle that they stopped blowing the trumpets, which shook the soldiers' morale. As soon

---

334 See J. Norton Cru, *Témoins*, and *Du Témoignage*, Paris, 1930. Cf. A. Ducasse, *La guerre racontée par les combattants*, Paris, 1932.
335 Ambroise, vv. 6391–6402, pp. 171–2.
336 Joinville, c. 39, pp. 65–6.
337 *Ibid.*, c. 45, pp. 77–8.
338 Cf. Arsuf, in Chapter IV. Joinville, c. 39, pp. 65–6.
339 Lot, 'Les destinées de l'empire en occident de 395 à 888', in G. Glotz, *Histoire générale. Histoire du Moyen Age*, Paris, 1940, I, pp. 256–7.
340 Ermoldus Nigellus, 1. III, v. 1589, p. 122.
341 Grousset, I, p. 555.

as the banner was raised again, the trumpets sounded once more, and after the victory they were used to summon the men for supper.[342] In the battles of Arsuf, Bouvines, Courtrai and Mons-en-Pévèle, trumpets were frequently mentioned, but the use of them was so general that the chroniclers thought it superfluous to speak of them, or to explain for what purpose the instruments were used. During the retreat of the Flemings at Mons-en-Pévèle they were used to re-assemble the troops, a use that may be frequently noted in the *chansons de geste*.[343] In the *Chanson de Roland* camp was broken at the sound of the trumpets; they were also used to herald the assault and to give the soldiers the order to take arms.[344] During the battle the scattered troops were collected again at the sound of the trumpet or horn.[345] Jean le Bel described the same custom in the English army of Edward III: at the first blast the horses had to be saddled, at the second the troops had to put on their arms, and at the third they had to mount and get into formation.[346] The same usage was codified by Charles the Bold in the *Grande Ordonnance* of 1473.[347] It was thus a general usage which was also common in the Flemish cities, where trumpeters are found in every expedition.

Banners were also used to give orders. To take a banner forward was the sign to begin the attack, and it was also used to halt it, and to direct the setting up of camp. Men rallied round the banner in hand-to-hand fighting to re-form a compact unit.

Commands and Evolutions: a Comparison with Byzantium

In order to form a clear idea of the training of knightly units it is very important to know what movements the knights could perform, with or without orders. Fortunately excellent material is available for comparison in the cavalry orders as they existed in Byzantium, where the classical tradition lingered on for a long time in the army. These orders were derived from the *Strategikon*.[348] They are the exercises of the *tagma*, the basic tactical unit, consisting of about 300 horsemen.

In this unit the standard was placed in front of the first rank or in it, which coincided with knightly custom, for the banners were brought forward before the attack,[349] and the attack was started with the standard in the front rank by the Templars, among others.[350] The *mandator*, one of the commanders, then called out: '*Silentium! Nemo demittat, nemo antecedat*', which agrees with the prohibition against leaving the

---

[342] See Chapter IV. Worringen.

[343] See Chapters III and IV. Gautier, *La chevalerie*, pp. 748–9.

[344] *Chanson de Roland*, vv. 700–3, p. 60; vv. 1454–5, p. 122; v. 1796, p. 150 and so on.

[345] Gautier, *loc. cit.*

[346] Jean le Bel, I, p. 55.

[347] E. Hardy, *Origines de la tactique française*, 2 vols, Paris, 1879, II, p. 34.

[348] Lot, 'La langue du commandement dans les armées romaines et le cri de guerre français au moyen âge', pp. 203–9. *Mauricii Strategicon*, ed. G.T. Dennis, l. III, c. 5, pp. 152–8; c. 9, p. 172; l. XII, B, 16, p. 442; B, 24, p. 484.

[349] G. Villani, *Historie Fiorentine*, ed. L.A. Muratori, Rerum Italicarum Scriptores, 13, p. 387. *Chronographia regum Francorum*, ed. H. Moranvillé, SHF, 3 vols, Paris, 1891–97, I, pp. 107–8.

[350] *La règle du Temple*, c. 164, p. 125.

ranks during a charge, which we have also seen in the tournaments.[351] 'And he gave strict orders that no one should move in front of the banners, nor move at all until commanded to do so', said Jean le Bel of the order given by Edward III in 1327.[352]

The march was begun at the sound of the *buccina* or *boukinon* – a trumpet-like instrument that was also used among the knights –, or at the command of a leader who shouted: 'Move'. This order, 'Mouvez', was given at Courtrai by Artois.[353] Sometimes the signal was given by the banner, as in the case of the Templars.[354]

The signal to halt was given by striking a shield, by a hand sign, by a trumpet-signal on the *tuba*, as in many cases in knightly armies, or by the order 'Stop' (*Sta*). In the *Chanson de Roland* Roland halts the column by a banner signal.[355]

In order to march off properly lined up, the leader gave the order 'Aequaliter ambula', which is the same thing as 'ordinata aequaliter acies', in which Henry I's men marched against the Hungarians in 933.[356] It was the general rule to march in perfectly aligned formations: 'nobody dared, by the fear of losing his head, to ride before the banners, except the marshals'.[357]

In order to draw up the cavalry units in thinner lines and thus to encompass a broader front, the command was given '*Largiter ambula*'. This is immediately reminiscent of the advice given by Raas of Liedekerke to the men of Brabant at Worringen:

> 'I look at their line and see
> That it is broad and long;
> They could against our will
> Encircle us before we knew it:
> So make our ranks long and thin,
> Before they attack us.'

To get the men into closely packed ranks Liebrecht of Dormael shouted:

> 'Thick and tight! thick and tight!
> Let every man bravely press as
> Close as he can to his comrade.'

And then they all shouted:

> 'Stick together, thick! thick!'[358]

Two commands used by the Byzantine armies were not common among the knights. They were primarily intended for units in deep formation: '*ad latus stringe*',

---

351 Lot, 'La langue du commandement', p. 204. See higher, the text of the *Histoire de Guillaume le Maréchal* about the tournaments.
352 Jean le Bel, I, p. 65.
353 G. Guiart, v. 15119, p. 239.
354 *La règle du Temple*, c. 164–5, pp. 125–6.
355 *Chanson de Roland*, vv. 707–9, pp. 60–2; vv. 2949–52, p. 244.
356 Liudprand, *Antapodosis*, in *Opera*, ed. J. Becker, MGH, SS, 1915, 1. II, c. 31, pp. 51–2.
357 Jean le Bel, I, p. 54.
358 Heelu, vv. 4918–49, pp. 185–6.

close in on the flank, and '*iunge*', to close ranks from back to front, so that the last lines came closer to the first. It is quite possible that this is what is meant by the 'thick and tight' of the Brabançons at Worringen, however. In order to speed up the cavalry advance, the order was given: '*cursu mina*', which might be translated as 'Spur your horses'. It is obvious that such an order was also used among the knights: in the struggle for the capture of Constantinople during the Fourth Crusade, Robert de Clari explains it in these words: 'Two of the bravest and wisest men were selected from each *bataille*, and whatever they commanded was done. If the command '*Poingniés*' (spur!) was given, we spurred our horses; if the order '*Alés le pas*' (go on step), we stepped slowly.'[359] The knights' formation advanced slowly at first, and then charged when they reached a suitable distance from the enemy.

Another command was used in the Byzantine armies: '*cum ordine seque*', given as soon as the skirmishing cavalry came within a mile of the enemy. To lead them back the order '*cede*' was given, to make them attack again: '*torna mina*'. Other orders, such as '*depone sinistra, depone dextra*' meant that the cavalry had to move left or right. In case of an attack on the rear, the order was given to make a new front in that direction, but without making the original front move its position. There is no reference to these orders in the chronicles, but the knights were able to execute them. This was indispensable for fighting and manoeuvring with foot-soldiers on the battlefield, in close co-operation.

Finally, it was foreseen that the front line of cavalry might give ground and move back to the second line or the reserve. Then the standard-bearer (*bandophoros*) of the formation shouted: '*Suscipe*', 'take them up'. It was thus that Villehardouin hastened to give help after the defeat of Baldwin I at Adrianople. At Arsuf the reserve twice let attacking units withdraw in order to regroup. This was another reason why a reserve unit was held back during a pursuit. At the end of the battle of Hastings, during the pursuit of the defeated enemy, Count Eustace, at the head of fifty knights, wished to sound the retreat: *receptui signa canere*. Duke William arrived there and ordered the pursuit to be continued.[360]

Finally, the Byzantine army had yet another custom: a bowshot from the enemy a soldier cried out '*Parati!*' Another answered '*Adiuta*' and then they all shouted '*Deus*'. It was taken over very early by the French knights, and we find it in the *Chanson de Roland* as '*diex aie*'.[361] It was also used by the Crusaders before Jerusalem:[362] it was especially used by the Normans.[363]

The *cantator* was an important figure in both the Byzantine and knightly armies. It was his duty to urge on the troops by harangues and especially by martial songs. This was the role of Taillefer in the battle of Hastings.

---

[359] R. de Clari, c. 47, p. 47.
[360] William of Poitiers, 2, c. 24, p. 202.
[361] *Chanson de Roland*, v. 3358, p. 278.
[362] Lot, 'La langue du commandement', p. 207.
[363] *Ibid., loc. cit.* Gautier, p. 753.

> A *jongleur*, whose courageous heart made him noble,
> rides before the innumerable formations of the duke.
> He encourages the French by his words and terrifies the English,
> He plays at casting his sword in the air.[364]

This evidence of Guy de Ponthieu, bishop of Amiens, was slightly modified by later chroniclers or poets:

> Taillefer the great singer
> Rode on a swiftly trotting horse
> Before the great duke, singing
> Of Charlemagne and Roland
> And of Oliver and the vassals
> Who were slain at Roncevaux.[365]

The chronicler William of Malmesbury said: 'Then they sang the *Chanson de Roland*, so that the example of the military hero might inspire the men, and after calling on God's help, the battle began.'[366]

There was a similar singer in the early *Chançun de Willame*.

> Lord William had a jongleur
> There was no finer singer in all France
> Nor bolder swordsman in battle
> And he could recite songs from the epics
> About Clovis, the first emperor
> Who in sweet France believed in God, our Lord,
> And about his son, Flovent the bold,
> And about all kings who became famous
> Up to Pipin, the brave little fighter,
> And Charlemagne and Roland, his nephew.[367]

Lastly there is another historical text of about 1100, in which a *jongleur* who sang about the heroic deeds of their ancestors accompanied a band of robbers from Burgundy in a local war.[368] But with him the *cantator* disappears from our sources; at least we can find no further trace of him. It is worth noting that the *cantator* appeared both in the West and in Byzantium and it seems that this was a common custom, of Germanic origin but very early taken up elsewhere, apparently from the time when the Germans entered the Roman army in large numbers as mercenaries.

---

364 *Carmen de Hastingae proelio*, vv. 391–4, p. 26. R. Fawtier, *La chanson de Roland*, Paris, 1933, p. 78, n. 3. Oman, I, p. 160 and n.5.

365 *Maistre Wace's Roman de Rou et des Ducs de Normandie*, ed. Hugo Andresen, 2 vols, Heilbronn, 1878–79, vv. 8035–40, p. 348. R. Fawtier, *op. cit.*, p. 77.

366 *De gestis regum Anglorum, libri V, Historiae novellae libri III*, ed. W. Stubbs, Rolls Series, London, 1887–1889, II, p. 302. Fawtier, p. 77.

367 *La chançun de Willame*, ed. E. Stearns Tyler, New York, 1919, in 12°, vv. 1259–70. J. Bédier, *Les légendes épiques*, I, p. 349.

368 Bloch, *La formation des liens de dépendance*, p. 158.

The use of standards in battle leads us to consideration of a further point: how long did the knights continue in combat, up to the last man, or until the last individual combatants had fallen?

The Tactical Significance of the Standard

Saladin's son is a valuable witness for the tactical significance of the standard. He described the annihilation of the royal army of the kingdom of Jerusalem by the lake of Tiberias at Hattin in 1187: 'I found myself next to my father in battle . . . When king Guy de Lusignan was on the hill with his knights, they made a tremendous charge against our troops and drove them back to my father. I looked at him and noticed that he had become sad and pale, and was holding his beard in his hand. Suddenly he ran forward shouting "Show that the devil is a liar!" The Moslems then charged the Franks, who retreated and rode back up the hill. As soon as I noticed that the Franks were withdrawing and the Moslems were pursuing them, I shouted joyfully, "We have put them to flight!" But the Franks returned and made a second charge, and drove our troops back to where my father was. He did as he had done before, and again our men drove the enemy down the hill. I cried out again "We have driven them off!" But my father turned and said to me, "Be quiet, and do not say that they are beaten until you see the king's banner is down." A little later we saw the banner go down: then my father sprang off his horse and threw himself on the ground to thank God, and wept with joy.'[369]

This account by a soldier who was actually on the battlefield is confirmed by the Rule of the Templars. The flag was not just a useful and practical assembly-point round which the troops re-grouped themselves, but also the symbol of resistance, for the troops fought on as long as the banner was flying. The Rule of the Templars stated explicitly that a knight who was cut off from returning to his own banner in battle had to continue the fight under the first Christian banner he came to. If the Christian army were defeated, no Templar might leave the field as long as a Christian banner was still flying. When no banners were left flying, he could then seek refuge.[370]

But if the banner served as a sign of successful attack or stout resistance, and the troops knew that if the banner was down it marked the beginning of defeat and was a signal for flight, then it was naturally necessary to protect the banners with the utmost vigilance. This was the Templars' practice: the marshal and the commander of any unit could detail ten knights to guard the flag, and every deputy commander had a spare banner which was unfurled when the first had been brought down.[371] The banner was thus not a unique symbol, but a sign of authority for the execution of orders, and ensuring that the fight went on to ultimate victory.

---

[369] Ibn al-Athir, *Kamel-Altevarykl* (extract), RHC, Historiens Orientaux, Paris, 1872, I, pp. 658–86. Oman, I, p. 331, Delpech, I, p. 374. Grousset, II, pp. 795–6.
[370] *La règle du Temple*, c. 167–8, pp. 126–7; c. 421, p. 230.
[371] *Ibid.*, c. 164, 166, 242, 612.

An excellent account of the battle of Worringen survives, which shows that all this is not true only of a well-organised army like that of the Templars. In that battle the flag was guarded, and served as a sign for the stern continuance of the struggle. As soon as it came down the trumpets stopped sounding: the flag rose again above the ranks of fighting men and the trumpets sounded again.[372] This also happened in the enemy army. When the lord of Valkenburg lost his banner, he unfurled a new one, and a new company rallied round it.[373] The resistance of the knights and cavalry from Guelders collapsed as soon as the count's standard was brought down. In the *chansons de geste* too the *oriflamme* was well protected by a strong guard which had to fight with no thought of themselves if need arose.[374]

Besides ensuring that the banner was guarded, the Templars had other rules. It was strictly forbidden to attack with the lance to which the banner was attached, and even the lance itself, round which the reserve banner was rolled, might not be used against the enemy. Violation of this rule meant risking the loss of the Templar's habit. If any damage resulted from his action, he was dismissed from the Order, and might even be put in irons and thrown into prison. He could never act as a commander of the knights again. It was dangerous for the course of the battle to let the flag fall, and the Rule of the Templars emphasised this: 'If the banner comes down, the men on the edge of the battle do not know why this is, and may think the Turks have cut it down. Besides, the enemy can more easily lay hands on the banner if it is used as a lance than if it is waving freely in the air. If the troops lose their banner, they are shocked, and this can lead to terrible defeat. For this reason it is most strictly forbidden to strike with the lance of the standard.'[375]

We have already seen that Saladin's son knew that the loss of the standard signified the end of the battle, and so did Jan van Heelu. The writer of the *Chanson d'Antioche* also mentions the custom:

> Corbaran sees his men take to their heels
> And the Franks kill them with their swords or cut off their limbs.
> When he sees his standard fall to the ground
> He begins to call on Mohammed with a loud voice.[376]

And in the *Chanson d'Aspremont* we find:

> The Africans see their standard falling:
> They start to flee at once.[377]

and

> These two traitors . . .
> Hope to conceal their treachery

372 Heelu, vv. 5668–740, pp. 211–14.
373 *Ibid.*, vv. 6760–75, pp. 249–50.
374 Gautier, pp. 753–4, n. 3.
375 *La règle du Temple*, c. 611, pp. 315–16 and c. 164–5.
376 *Chanson d'Antioche*, II, viij, c. 52, vv. 1306–9, p. 265.
377 *Chanson d'Aspremont*, I, c. 179, vv. 3333–4, p. 107.

They have betrayed their lawful lord
Who had entrusted his banner to them
Round which all the others should have gathered.[378]

The poem on the siege of Barbastro gives these two characteristic passages:

Corsout our standard-bearer has betrayed us:
He mistook five barons for five thousand men
When he heard 'Montjoie' shouted out on both sides.
Because of this our men are killed and wounded,
He threw down the dragon with which he should have rallied us.[379]

Bruiant has mounted his horse again and raised his banner
The heathen are re-grouping round him
The Saracens return there, ready to give battle.[380]

John Chandos reported the victory of his master, Edward, the prince of Wales, at the battle of Poitiers with these words: 'I see neither banners nor pennons left among the French, nor any company among them which could rally'.[381]

Once the standard was down, the men no longer had a rallying-point, and they could not form new units out of widely scattered men, as the lord of Valkenburg was able to do at Worringen, for the organic connection between the formations was lost, and since this betokened defeat, they fled. This should effectively dispel the notion that the fighting took place in the form of duels. If it was not done in units, it would not have mattered whether the flag was flying or not, since each man had to choose only one opponent in order to go on fighting. Besides, it would have been unnecessary to draw units up in formation before the battle.

The Re-Grouping of Units and the Manoeuvre of Feigned Flight

Cavalry regulations at the end of the nineteenth century emphasised that the cavalry was at no time more vulnerable than just after a charge. Order had to be restored forthwith, and the units had to be formed up again. 'In an army of knights, the unit round the banner serves the same purpose in some measure, but there is no question whatever of grouping, of signals and commands during a battle, any more than there is of an outflanking movement during an attack, or of protection against an outflanking movement of the enemy, of a second wave, or of reserves, for the deciding factor lies in the hand-to-hand fighting. Then there is no more leadership, the fighting is left entirely to the knight himself, to do whatever damage he can to the enemy, where and how he can.'[382]

---

[378] *Ibid.*, II, c. 325, vv. 6540–4, p. 12.
[379] *Le siège de Barbastre*, c. 84, vv. 2660–4, p. 84.
[380] *Ibid.*, c. 170, vv. 6308–10, p. 197.
[381] J.M. Tourneur-Aumont, *La bataille de Poitiers (1356) et la construction de la France*, Poitiers, 1940, p. 274.
[382] Delbrück, III, p. 314.

We shall soon prove that this categorical assertion of Hans Delbrück is entirely erroneous. First of all, we have the evidence of the *chansons de geste*, and rather than draw a general conclusion from those which we have studied, we will let a scholar who has studied them very closely speak about this. L. Gautier, in his book *La chevalerie*, says: 'In general, from the eleventh to thirteenth centuries, there is no true strategy (for this read tactics) employed in large encounters or small skirmishes. The commander of the *ost* (host, or army) invariably splits his knights into a certain number of units, called *batailles* or *échelles*. He groups them, so far as possible, according to their nationality or regional origin . . . In front of all his units, which he deployes in a single line stretched across the field, he places his vanguard, his attack force. Behind his *échelles*, he places his rearguard, a true reserve[383] which must not take part in the battle until towards the end of the day or in case of desperate need, to precipitate the resolution or hasten the victory . . .'

After that followed an account of the battle: first the advance guards, then the battle line, finally the reserve. But according to Gautier it was a question of a series of duels, ending with the supreme duel between the two commanders.[384] A pursuit ended the battle.

'Certain of our heroes, like Girart de Rousillon, devise genuine battle plans which they explain to their commanders, in some corner of their castle, and as secretly as possible. The most popular method is the ambush (*agait*).'[385]

Gautier describes the battle thus: 'drums (*tabors*) and trumpets (*buisines*), horns and bugles (*araines*) sound simultaneously and call the "*menée*", the charge. During the fighting they repeatedly sound the rally (*aünée*) . . . The ranks of the combatants are closely packed, so that if one were to throw a glove on to them, "it would not fall to ground for half-a-league".'[386]

This shows that the epic poets were well acquainted with the re-grouping of units (*le ralliement*), in view of the frequency with which this usage is described. This is also true of the reserve, and from the very close marching of the knights it is obvious that Gautier's notion of individual fights has little to support it. Let us take an example from the *Chanson de Roland*: 'He sounds a trumpet to rally his men'.[387]

In another passage we read:

> At the head rides a Saracen, Abisme . . .
> He carries the dragon (banner) round which his men assembled.[388]

And again:

> The Emir . . .
> Puts a bright trumpet to his mouth,

---

383 Gautier, *La chevalerie*, p. 739. E. von Frauenholz, *op. cit.*, p. 110, has corrected Delbrück for the use of the reserve.
384 Gautier, *op. cit.*, p. 740.
385 *Ibid., loc. cit.*
386 *Ibid.*, pp. 748–9.
387 *Chanson de Roland*, v. 1319, p. 112.
388 *Ibid.*, vv. 1470 and 1480, p. 124.

He blows it hard, so that the heathen hear it:
The comrades unite on the whole battlefield.[389]

We also come on an indirect example, which indicates the importance of the standard for the regrouping:

> Ogier the Dane . . .
> Spurs his horse, lets it run full tilt,
> He is going to strike the man who bears the dragon.
> He sinks down both the dragon,
> And the king's ensign.
> Baligant sees his standard fall
> And Mohammed's standard remain.
> The Emir sees too
> That he is wrong and Charlemagne is right.
> The heathen of Araby flee . . .[390]

Another extract shows that re-grouping normally took place after a charge, for five charges followed each other:

> Everything went well in four charges,
> But the fifth was most terrible and difficult for them.
> All the French knights were killed
> Except sixty, whom God spared.[391]

Other *chansons de geste* provide some useful passages, for example in the *Chanson d'Aspremont* we find:

> Then a unit of knights
> Made an attack on this heathen people:
> They attacked the enemy so ferociously
> That the heathen fell back a bowshot.
> Then Balans, their leader,
> Blew a horn, encouraged them and re-grouped them.[392]

And:

> He made the fugitives turn back
> When they heard the oliphant sounding again.[393]

In the *Siege of Barbastro*: 'He blew a horn to re-assemble his men'.[394]

---

[389] *Ibid.*, vv. 3520–5, p. 292.
[390] *Ibid.*, vv. 3546–55. p. 294.
[391] *Ibid.*, vv. 1686–9, p. 142.
[392] *Chanson d'Aspremont*, I, c. 247, vv. 4478–86, p. 144. Cf. c. 288, vv. 5459–64, p. 175; c. 291, vv. 5599–600, p. 179; II, c. 438, pp. 88–9; c. 455, vv. 9321–2, p. 103; c. 475, vv. 9775–6, p. 117.
[393] *Ibid.*, I, c. 287, vv. 5453–4, p. 174.
[394] *Le siège de Barbastre*, c. 126, v. 4335, p. 136.

Aymeris also blew a horn and everyone re-grouped round the lord of Narbonne.[395]
In the *Chanson d'Antioche*:

> Corbaran was so cast down that he was almost beside himself.
> He called for his banner to assemble his men.[396]

The *chansons de geste* leave the reader in no doubt about what happened. As soon as was judged necessary, the men were regrouped and close units were formed again.

These poems are good sources for our knowledge of the art of war of the knightly armies. They describe the military life of their time, but in order to please their knightly readers, they embellish the narrative, giving it colour and life, and magnifying the heroic deeds of the lords. This led to a tendency to make the battle end with a duel between the great heroes.

But what is the case in the narrative sources? There is an excellent example in the battle of Babain in the Middle East in 1167. King Amalric of Jerusalem broke through the enemy centre, but his own wings came under attack. Amalric returned with his triumphant men. 'He had taken a high hill, and set his standard up on top, to re-assemble his scattered troops.' He regrouped his horsemen in order to draw off the enemy: 'in close formation they marched slowly through the enemy lines to right and left of them. They advanced against them so resolutely that the enemy did not have the courage to attack: in close formation, with the bravest and best-armed men in the outer ranks, they came to a stream and passed over it unscathed.[397] Here we have the assembly of the troops after hand-to-hand fighting, the densely packed formation, and the retreat of a tactical unit drawn up in such close order that the enemy cannot inflict any damage.

Another extract may be quoted, from the battle of Arsuf in 1191. A general charge was made on the Moslems, but the reserve stayed behind and followed at a distance. But a mounted attack is exhausting for the men who make it, and cannot be kept up for long:

> The Christian attackers
> Halted after their assault,
> But as soon as they stopped their attack
> The Saracens started again.[398]

Once the enemy had re-grouped, they in their turn advanced to attack, and then the crusaders had to fall back to their reserve. During this pause they also re-grouped their units and went on to make a fresh charge:

> And the brave warriors recovered
> When they had got their breath back;

---

[395] *Ibid.*, c. 185, vv. 6734–5, p. 210.
[396] *Chanson d'Antioche*, II, viij, c. 44, vv. 1078–9, p. 251.
[397] William of Tyre, *Hist. Occ.*, I, p. 927. Delpech, II, p. 212, n. 1 and 2. Lot, *Art Militaire*, I, p. 144. Grousset, II, p. 492.
[398] Ambroise, vv. 6539–42, p. 174.

> They attacked with great energy
> And struck at their companies
> And broke them like nets.[399]

The second charge met with stout resistance on the part of the enemy:

> There are people who so charged
> That they could not advance further than a bowshot
> And their units had to halt
> Or to pay a high price.[400]

They did not get further than a bowshot, i.e. over a hundred meters, and the enemy attacked again while the Christians were returning to their banner.[401]

The third and decisive charge was then carried out by the units of Guillaume des Barres and Richard I, while the other detachments were regrouped under the royal standard:

> Then the brave Guillaume des Barres
> Made an attack that everybody praised
> He and his men threw themselves
> Between our men and the mass
> Of the envious and bad people
> And they struck them so hard
> That I don't know how many Turks fell
> Who since that moment have not seen war again . . .
>
> And Richard the king of England
> Attacked towards the mountains
> He and his stout company . . .
> He and his men attacked the enemy
> And threw them back and contained them
> While our other men came to the standard
> And regrouped there immediately.[402]

Besides this splendid and apparently accurate example, another may be quoted. During the same crusade, the count of St Pol proposed to the earl of Leicester that he should carry out an attack with his formation while Leicester remained behind with his knights as a reserve. Or, vice versa, Leicester would charge, and St Pol would cover this attack by standing ready to come to his help at once or to let the attacking troops return after their charge in order to re-group under the protection of St Pol's men.[403]

In the example previously given of the battle of Philippopoli fought by Henry I

---

[399] *Ibid.*, vv. 6552–6, p. 175.
[400] *Ibid.*, vv. 6559–62, p. 175.
[401] *Ibid.*, vv. 6580–1, p. 176.
[402] *Ibid.*, vv. 6594–614, p. 176.
[403] *Ibid.*, vv. 7311–25, pp. 195–6.

of Constantinople in 1208, the emperor remained behind with the reserve. He had to let the attacking troops re-form after the charge: 'the emperor would protect the attackers'. The *oriflamme* was borne before the emperor. 'And his brothers-in-arms rode round him, most ardently longing to charge and ready to spur on their horses they followed the pursuers who rode on ahead of them. No one could reproach them at all, for they were all brave men and showed it. Those who had been ordered to do so charged first, and the others protected them as necessary.'[404] Here the reserve stayed to fulfil its usual duty during the pursuit, as it did in the above-mentioned examples of Fréteval and Muret. This was later prescribed in the cavalry regulations at the end of the nineteenth century,[405] which is another proof that the knights' tactics were carefully thought out.

At Bouvines the count of St Pol and his men rested, and later came back with them to the fighting. At Worringen the lord of Valkenburg formed a new unit, and Duke John returned also to the battle with a small formation.[406]

Closely connected with the regrouping of troops and the formation of new units was the manoeuvre of the feigned flight, and the real flight followed by a return to the attack, both of which are possible if scattered troops can be re-assembled at all. Delbrück thought there was too little discipline in the knightly armies to feign a flight and then attack again. He chose an unfortunate example for this, namely the battle of Hastings, where Norman knights and their allies carried out these manoeuvres against Harold's foot-soldiers. Such a manoeuvre is so easily employed against foot-soldiers who cannot quickly pursue cavalrymen that no one accepted Delbrück's assertions.[407] Why should the knights not have been able to regroup once they were out of reach of the more slowly advancing foot-soldiers?

---

[404] Henry of Valenciennes, c. 533, pp. 41–2; c. 542, p. 46.

[405] J. Meckel, *Les éléments de la tactique*, translated by H. Monet, 2nd edn, Paris, 1887, p. 157.

[406] See Chapter IV. Worringen, and Bouvines.

[407] The feigned retreat at Hastings has been criticised by W. Spatz, *Die Schlacht von Hastings*, Berlin, 1896, pp. 60–2. Spatz was a student of Delbrück, and he was so misled by the concept of the individual fighter that he admits no tactics at all, a view that Delbrück himself had to correct (Delbrück, III, p. 163.). Spatz's views were criticised by J.H. Round, *Revue historique*, 1897, pp. 61–77. Cf. Oman, I, p. 62, n. 4. Lot, *Art militaire*, I, p. 284. Colonel C.H. Lemmon, *The Field of Hastings*, St Leonards on Sea, 4th edn, 1970, and 'The Battle of Hastings, 1966', in D. Whitelock, D.C. Douglas, C.H. Lemmon, F. Barlow, *The Norman Conquest, Its Setting and Impact*, London, 1966, completely rejected the feigned retreat and replaced it by a forced retreat. His views are accepted and praised by J. Beeler, *Warfare in England*, pp. 21–2. We cannot accept the views of Colonel Lemmon for the following reasons:

1. Most sources, and the best sources, attest the feigned retreat.

2. In the battle of Hastings, writes Lemmon, 'the Normans were put to flight locally three times' (*The Battle of Hastings*, p. 114). The troops of William executed thus a more difficult manoeuvre than the feigned retreat; they retreated while they were followed by the enemy, or were under counterattack by the enemy. If they were able to execute the flight under a counterattack of the Anglo-Saxons, why where they not capable of doing it by their own will, before they penetrated into the ranks of the enemy?

3. The cavalry of William knew the tactics of a feigned retreat, they had applied them already at St Aubin in a combat against the king of France (W. Spatz, *Die Schlacht von Hastings*, pp. 61–2). We have seen that the Frankish cavalry was often trained for such an attack: Saxons, Gascons, Austrasians and Bretons participated in such wargames in 842 (Nithard). The Normans were also trained for combat.

The history of Flanders gives two very important examples of this. First, the battle of Thielt in 1128, where William Clito pretended to flee, then re-grouped his troops, and after that defeated his enemies with these units and the reserve. There is also the example of Mons-en-Pévèle, where the French knights fled in panic. but their rapid flight soon brought them out of range of the Flemish foot-soldiers, and they could quietly re-form their units at a safe distance. This actually happened to part of king Philip's army of knights. But the rest were too panic-stricken, and in such a case it was often impossible to rally them again close to the battlefield.

The simulated flight, in which retreating troops were helped by a reserve force, was possible because the knights, just like later cavalry, were especially vulnerable as soon as their close formation broke. The importance of order within the formation must be investigated.

The Importance of Order Within the Formation

As the conclusion of his work on the art of war in the First Crusade, Heermann wrote that a charge executed in a disorderly fashion meant defeat.[408] Delbrück cited three examples of defeats which were attributed to lack of order, two of them from the period studied by Heermann.[409]

The defeat of king Louis VI of France at Brémule in 1119 was ascribed by both Suger and Orderic to lack of order in the formation of the French king. Suger explained the defeat thus: 'The king attacked . . . rashly yet courageously . . . the French who wanted to follow were in disorder, and fell upon the extremely well ordered and smartly formed (enemy) troops. As happens in such a case, they could

---

4. At every moment of the battle of Hastings, William's forces were more than one battle line in depth. In the beginning of the battle, three lines advanced to the enemy: 1. archers, 2. heavy foot-soldiers, 3. cavalry. After the unsuccessful first attack and the partial flight, William could counterattack with a reserve. Later, he always had at least two lines at his disposal: one of cavalry, one of foot-soldiers. That disposition allowed him to manoeuvre and to regroup under the protection of the second line, a fact that Lemmon and Beeler have not noticed. There was also the possibility of attacking with one formation of cavalry, while the other formations of cavalry contained the enemy by the menace of their charge, and the line of foot-soldiers backed them.

5. Lemmon invokes considerations like 'troops committed to the attack cannot be made to change their direction'. But the troops of William attacked and came back many times during the battle. Lemmon speaks of 'the impossibility of passing orders to hundreds if not thousands of individuals, all engaged in separate hand-to-hand combats' (*Field of Hastings*, p. 44). William did not have to give orders to hundreds or thousands. His warriors fought in units. Lemmon himself speaks of pauses in the conflict, and a long interlude (*The Battle*, pp. 106–7). During these pauses it was possible to tell the leaders what should be done after the miscarriage of the first attack, or the second attack.

6. Lemmon says that the chroniclers dared not record that the Norman cavalry ran away. But William of Poitiers writes about the flight of the Normans: *non . . . pudenda fuga*; . . . *vero dolenda* (c. 17, p. 190); *fuga, effugiendum* (c. 19, p. 190), and *cedit fere cuncta ducis acies* (c. 17, p. 190). Other sources speak also of the flight of the Normans. In the First Crusade we also have testimony by the Anonymous and Ralph of Caen about the flight of Normans (see above).

[408] See the conclusions in Lot, *Art militaire*, I, p. 133. Smail, pp. 127–8.

[409] Delbrück, III, p. 293.

not withstand the controlled pressure of the enemy, and beat a hasty retreat.[410] Orderic wrote: 'At the beginning the French rushed into the attack bravely, but it was a disorderly advance and they were beaten.'[411]

Just as king Amalric of Jerusalem rescued the main body of his army in 1167 by forming a very close mass of troops for the retreat, so he prevented his army once more in 1170 from being shattered by the enemy.[412] Nor could Saladin achieve much against the royal army in 1183 when it was drawn up in especially close ranks.[413] On the other hand, when the army was dispersed after the victory over Saladin's vanguard in 1179, it was severely defeated.[414] The victory at Arsuf was entirely due to the excellent orderliness of the formations.

There is a parallel example in the victory of Simon de Montfort in the battle of Muret in 1213, which was remarkable for several reasons. The commander gave the order to make a mass attack right through the enemy units: 'Do not stop to fight with the front line of the enemy, but press on, like Christian knights, into the enemy formations'. When they went into battle, 'they all charged as they were ordered, and penetrated right through to the king of Aragon.'[415] While two units were thus forcing their way into the enemy ranks, Montfort attacked the flank with the reserve, and during the pursuit this corps resumed its role of reserve to be able to stand by the pursuing knights.

At Bouvines, too, victory went to the better-ordered French units, who defeated Ferdinand's and Otto's army, which had advanced too quickly.

Many reliable sources show the importance of good order. Nithard attributes the defeat of count Wido to it in 834. The *Histoire de Guillaume le Maréchal* demonstrates its importance in tournaments. Villehardouin gives it as the reason for the defeat of the emperor Baldwin I and for the deliverance of the remnants of his army, and we have quoted descriptions of close and smartly ordered formations in the *chansons de geste*. There are other equally remarkable examples.

King Henry gave his Saxons the following advice before their battle against the Hungarian light cavalry on 15 March 933. 'Let no one ride past his companion on a faster horse when we are beginning the battle. Rather protect yourselves with your shields in such a way that you receive the first enemy arrow with it. Then rush at them with all your might, so that they cannot shoot a second arrow at you before they are wounded by your weapons.' The Saxons faithfully followed this sound advice, and rode at the enemy in good battle order, so that no one with a quicker charger overtook another with a slower horse, and they parried the first arrows with

410 Suger, c. 26, p. 196.

411 *Historia ecclesiastica*, IV, 1. xii, c. 18, p. 359. Lot, I, p. 317 and n. 3. J. Douglas Drummond, 'Studien zur Kriegsgeschichte Englands im 12. Jahrhundert', Berliner Dissertation 1905, pp. 45–8, says nothing about the problem of order and disorder at Brémule. The examples of W. Spatz and J. Douglas Drummond show how badly Delbrück was informed by the works of his students.

412 William of Tyre, I, pp. 927 and 975–6. Delpech, II, p. 212, n. 1 and 2., p. 213, n. 3. Grousset, II, pp. 492–3 and 560–1.

413 Lot, I, pp. 148–9. Grousset, II, pp. 725–75.

414 Lot, I, pp. 147–8. See further for that example.

415 Delpech, I, p. 220, note. Lot, I, p. 212.

their shields and prevented them from shooting a second time, and put them to flight.[416]

We have already mentioned in passing another striking example, but it deserves to be examined more closely. Again it is from the *Histoire de Guillaume le Maréchal*. At the beginning of July 1194 Philip Augustus was defeated at Fréteval by Richard I. The king of France lost his treasure and his archives. After the battle, Richard gave William the Marshal command of the reserve corps, which had to support the pursuing troops if the French were to turn and make another attack. The Marshal and his knights put aside all thoughts of booty, and concerned themselves only with covering their victorious army against surprise attack. On his return from the pursuit, Richard advised William to turn back with him, for, he said, 'I can see quite well that those who are now fleeing show no sign of coming back!' But the Marshal answered that he was quite willing to wait, because many knights were still searching for booty, and the French who did not like them might possibly attack them. When each of them that evening spoke about his booty and told about his feats of arms, the king said that no one had been as useful as William, for he would have gone to the help of anyone who had needed it, and added: 'If you have a good reserve, you have no fear of the enemy.'[417]

A letter from the count of St Pol to the duke of Brabant shows a similar fear of falling into an enemy ambush with not very well ordered troops. He gave an excellent account of the fighting outside the walls of Constantinople, where he and count Baldwin IX had marched out to meet Alexis III who was marching out of the city with his army on 17 July 1203. Their formations were well-ordered and closely packed. When their opponent saw the courage and tenacity of the Crusaders, and realised that their orderly formation could neither be easily defeated nor scattered in disorder, he took to flight in panic, and no longer ventured to fight the knights from the West. 'And note,' said St Pol, 'that in the whole of our army there were no more than 500 knights and an equal number of horsemen, with only 2,000 foot-soldiers, most of whom were looking after our siege-engines. But when we saw them fleeing and retreating we had no desire to chase them, lest through their ruses and ambushes, harm might come to our army, our gear, and the towers which the Venetians had captured.'[418] After their triumph at Carcano in 1160 the Milanese knights did not dare pursue the troops of Frederick Barbarossa at once, because they were afraid that the emperor was only pretending to flee, and had laid ambushes.[419]

If knights who had broken formation were attacked by enemy troops, they were lost. This fact leads us to emphasise once more the great importance of orderliness in formation. We have already quoted an example of this, in which Baldwin IV's troops drove off the vanguard of Saladin's army. William of Tyre relates what happened next: 'Our men were helping themselves to booty found on the slain,

---

[416] Liudprand, *Antapodosis*, 1. II, c. 31, pp. 51–2.
[417] *Histoire de Guillaume le Maréchal*, II, pp. 17–19, and III, p. 140, n. 3, p. 141.
[418] *Chronica regia Coloniensis cum continuationibus*, p. 207.
[419] *Gesta Federici I. imperatoris in Lombardia (Annales Mediolanenses majores)*, ed. O. Holder-Egger, MGH, SS, 1892, pp. 45–6.

thinking that victory was secure. They were sitting peaceably on the river bank.' The knights had chased the enemy, but did not know that Saladin was coming with the main mass of his army. 'When the knights saw the enemy, whom they had considered defeated, streaming in their direction with renewed strength, they had neither time nor opportunity to form up their units and get into position according to military discipline. They fought in disorder, offered resistance for a time and withstood the onslaught bravely. But in the end the odds were too much against them, because they had to fight spread out and in disorder, and could not help each other. They were shamefully put to flight.'

The knights were an easy prey for the enemy when they were no longer closely drawn up. William's evidence shows that fighting in close formations was more effective than individual combat. If a battle consisted merely of duels, dispersal would have been of no importance in a fight with the Turks, who fought in looser formation.

Events after this defeat emphasize the value of an organised unit. The fugitives met Renaud de Sidon, who was coming to the king's help with his retinue, and forced him to turn back because they considered the battle was lost. William of Tyre added this observation: 'By this action they did great damage to our men, for if he had reached his fortress, which was close by, the Turks would not have dared to seek out our forces, who had hidden themselves after the battle. Renaud could have sent out horsemen and foot-soldiers to rescue the men who had gone to ground in rocks, caves and bushes, whereas now the Turks were free to seek out the fugitives and take them prisoner.'[420] William points out here the great importance of small but orderly units, who would have inspired sufficient fear into the scattered and pursuing Turks to permit the rescue of the hidden fugitives.

The same thing happened as at Thielt: the scattered army of Thierry of Alsace, in full pursuit, had an identical experience to that of Baldwin's men in 1179. Again Richard I at Fréteval, Simon de Montfort at Muret, and Henry I of Constantinople at Philippopoli avoided similar mishap through helping the pursuing troops by means of a well-ordered unit, which could support the dispersed knights as a reserve if the enemy should make an offensive come-back. We have also learned how the defeated troops of Baldwin I of Constantinople and Louis of Blois were saved in their flight by the troops of Villehardouin and Manassier de Lille, who were posted before the gates of Adrianople while the others were fighting.[421]

All these complex examples illustrate both feigned flight and the regrouping of troops. They emphasize the paramount importance of order in formations, which was all the more necessary because medieval armies, and particularly armies of knights, were normally small, even ludicrously so.

The importance of a solid line-up of units which advance in orderly fashion, being forbidden to overtake ranks in front of them who had slower horses, is stressed in the advice of Henry I to the Saxons, in the orders of Edward III in 1327, and in the Rule of the Templars.

---

420 William of Tyre, pp. 1056–7. Grousset, II, pp. 675–5. Delpech, II, p. 217.
421 Villehardouin, II, c. 362–3, pp. 170–2.

When the Templars were going to attack, the Marshal of the Order took the banner from the deputy marshal. Then he picked five, six, or even ten knights to defend him and the standard.[422] These had to fight any of the enemy who approached the banner, so they were always to stay close to it, in order to give assistance at a moment's notice. The other knights from this company could attack in front and behind, to left and to right, wherever they could engage the enemy, but always so close to the standard that the guard could come to their rescue, and they in turn could support the standard-bearer and his guard.[423]

The commander of the knights, around whose lance the second banner was rolled, was among the ten knights set to guard the standard. He always had to stay close to the marshal, for if the leader's banner fell, or was torn, or met with any other mishap, he had to unfurl his reserve banner. At any rate, he had to station himself somewhere where the knights could range themselves round his flag if necessary.[424] If the marshal were wounded, or for some reason were unable to lead the attack, the commander gave the order and attacked. He was then supported by the guard of the standard. The marshal was not allowed to thrust with the lance from which the standard flew, nor might he let it fall. The same prohibition applied to soldiers carrying a furled banner round their lances.[425]

The leaders of other units of Templars were not allowed to engage in an attack, nor leave their ranks without the Master's permission, if he were present, or that of his deputy. If it was impossible to ask permission because of the size of the army, or in a narrow pass, they might advance to attack to get their units out of danger. But if this happened in any other circumstances, an investigation was ordered, and the disobedient knight risked losing his right to the Templar's habit. Every troop commander might take a reserve banner with him, and choose up to ten knights to defend him and the standard. All these rules affected the subordinate commanders as well.[426] A knight might not leave his unit without permission, even if he was wounded. If he were so seriously wounded that he could not ask in person, he had to send another brother to do so.[427] We have already seen that a Templar who had become separated from his banner in battle was permitted to leave the battle field only after the last flag had been brought down.

While the marshal was attacking with the knights, squires followed with one of their master's horses at their right side. Other squires took away the mules which had been ridden on the march, and drew themselves up in their units under the command of the standard-bearer, who handed over the Templars' standard to the marshal, keeping another banner still furled round his lance. Once the cavalry were formed up with the squires, the standard-bearer unfurled this banner and followed

---

[422] *La règle du Temple*, c. 164, p. 125.
[423] *Ibid., loc. cit.*
[424] *Ibid.*, c. 165, p. 125.
[425] *Ibid., loc. cit.*
[426] *Ibid.*, c. 166, p. 126.
[427] *Ibid.*, c. 166, p. 126; c. 242, p. 157; c. 612, p. 316.

the attacking troops, as quickly as he could, with his men, either in step or at whatever pace suited him.[428]

Thus the Templars made their opening attack, probably in a single line. Before they began their attack, a single file, consisting of squires carrying the lances of their masters, rode out before the battle order while another file of squires followed with the mules or horses which had been ridden on the march. The knights could have been drawn up in two ranks at the most, the men in the second rank in the spaces between the first. This made it possible to take the lances and shields from the squires, and to change horses so as to mount a charger before the fighting began. Once the Templars were mounted and fully armed, the squires in front of the unit moved away, while others followed at a distance with spare horses.[429] The light cavalry or *sergeants* of the Templars followed the attacking knights in tightly packed units, close enough to come to the help of the knights if necessary. They also had a banner, and could, if need be, have the support of small units of Templars.[430] Lastly, yet another formation could follow, who had earlier been carrying the knights' shields and lances, and then were drawn up under their own banner.

All these arrangements show that great importance was attached to order and discipline in the Rule of the Templars, and that they went into battle in perfect array, very close together, with their commander and the banner in front. However, since they knew that the attack might possibly fail, and that units had to be regrouped after a charge, they kept other formations in the second line: this was especially necessary in case of panic. It is important to note that the discipline of the Templars did not differ from that of secular knights, since the vital regulations were identical, and particularly since no narrative source depicts the Templars' units as stronger formations than the usual knightly units. Investigation suggests that the actual discipline on the field was the same for Templars and other knights from the West.

The knightly formations were as much concerned in making a firm close line as was the cavalry in later periods. Tactics of the medieval knights and those of the seventeenth, eighteenth, and nineteenth century cavalry were not essentially different: there was merely a higher degree of automatic discipline in the later cavalry, the consequence of the new resources of modern states, but it would in any case have been necessary since the average fighter no longer had the natural qualities for war, nor his unit the social cohesiveness proper to chivalry. The high conception of honour of the individual and of the clan no longer existed, so that an artificial sense of military honour had to be cultivated. Where this was not possible, drill had to replace the lost innate characteristics.

---

428 *Ibid.*, c. 179, p. 133.
429 *Ibid.*, c. 161, pp. 123–4.
430 *Ibid.*, c. 171, p. 129.

Tactical Aims

To break through the enemy line was without doubt the chief aim in knightly tactics, and this was the result of increasingly heavy equipment. Carolingian cavalry already had heavier equipment than their opponents, and were proud of it. Heavy equipment helped the confidence of the fighting-man, and contributed considerably to overcoming fear of death or wounds.

Delbrück wrote of the break-through as follows: 'The natural urge of the knightly class, in which everything was founded on the cult of personality – personal honour, personal fame, personal courage – is not conducive to order and equalization, but to individual sorties and attacks. Therefore quite contrary to King Henry's recommendations, it often happens in epics that one particular hero rushed out to attack the enemy, and his men after him. But what is good in poetry does not necessarily mean good tactics, and historical accounts sometimes have to stress that, contrary to what the poets say, the fight was started in a proper and orderly fashion; often also they attribute a defeat to the fact that the ranks were thrown into disorder.'[431]

A careful reading of the *chansons de geste* and the narrative sources reveals however that we are dealing with two different phases: first the charge in closely serried formation, and then the penetration into the enemy units. During this penetration the bravest men assumed the leadership: this, quite simply, is a common human trait; after all, someone had to take the initiative and set the example.

Breaking through an enemy formation could however result in the annihilation of the small units who were carrying out this manoeuvre. This was especially true if the unit that broke through was too small, and it clashed with troops from the second enemy battle line, as the example of Berthout of Malines at Worringen shows.[432] Therefore the knights preferred to turn back immediately after the break-through. In other cases they attacked the enemy from the rear, to break through again, as at Bouvines. There are descriptions of this in many of the epic poems. 'Strike, kill, turn everything upside down in the mêlée until you have pushed through the enemy ranks and then attack them again all together', is the advice in *Girart de Roussillon*.[433]

But a flank attack was well thought of too. The crusaders' enemy in the East systematically sought to encircle the opposing army, and the soldiers in the First Crusade took appropriate counter-measures. They always tried to protect their own flanks while attacking the enemy in the rear or flank. The first important battle in this crusade, at Dorylaeum in 1097, was decided by a flank attack.[434] This also happened in the battle of Legnano in northern Italy in 1176,[435] and in the battles of

---

[431] Delbrück, III, p. 293.
[432] See Chapter IV. Worringen.
[433] Gautier, *La chevalerie*, p. 740, n. 1.
[434] Grousset, I, p. 34.
[435] P. Pieri, 'Alcune questioni sopra la fanteria in Italia nel periodo comunale', *Rivista storica Italiana*, series 4, 4, 1933, p. 19. Delbrück, III, p. 363. Oman, I, pp. 448–9. Lot, II, pp. 165–6.

Muret in 1213 and Worringen in 1288. These were the tactics commonly used against the foot-soldiers, who usually reacted by making every effort to cover their flanks carefully by choosing a favourable position or by drawing themselves up in a crown formation.

Protection of the Flanks

Delbrück gives the impression in the passage just quoted that no units in the knightly armies were used to protect the flanks, or to attack the enemy on the flank. Closer investigation shows that this was not the case. In fact, medieval commanders went to great lengths to protect their flanks by various means, through careful selection of terrain, by expanding the front, by depth in formation, or by the use of special units charged with the task of covering the flanks. Delbrück was forced to concede, however, that precautionary measures were taken during the crusades. It was repeatedly stated that crusaders advanced in three columns, side by side, so as to be able to give battle in any direction.[436]

In the battle near the lake of Antioch the flanks of the knightly units were protected by the terrain, which made a broad front impossible.[437] During the sortie from Antioch the crusaders tried to prevent a flanking movement along one side by spreading out their front, while the other flank was protected by the river Orontes.[438] In this they were unsuccessful, but then they used a quickly formed unit to protect their flank and back and won the battle.[439] At Bouvines, the French bishop Guérin warded off a threat from the flank by spreading out his front.[440]

The flanks of knightly armies could also be protected by a special formation. There are two quite remarkable examples of this – the battle of Ascalon in 1099 saw the crusaders advancing in nine units: three in the vanguard, three in the middle, and three in the rearguard. From whichever side the enemy appeared, three formations were always ready to hold them in check, while the centre units could always rush in where help was needed, and the back units covered the rear.[441] The battle of Hab in 1119 gave an even more remarkable example.[442] But in both instances units of foot-soldiers were also taking part in the battle, so these examples will be more closely examined in our exposition of general tactics. On the march from Acre to Arsuf the flanks of Richard I's army were well protected, so as to be ready to fight.

There is one further more important example from the late Middle Ages. Since Delbrück rightly pointed out that tactics remained practically unchanged up to the end of the fifteenth century, it seems permissible to give a very late but striking example. Jean de Bueil gives this advice in *Le Jouvencel*: 'If you are riding in enemy

---

436 Delbrück, III, pp. 317–18.
437 Raymond of Aguilers, *Historia Francorum qui ceperunt Jherusalem*, RHC Hist. Occ., III, p. 247.
438 *Ibid.*, p. 260.
439 Anonymous, *Gesta Francorum*, pp. 154–6.
440 See Chapter IV. 'Bouvines'.
441 Raymond of Aguilers, pp. 303–4.
442 Oman, I, p. 298.

territory with one hundred, five hundred or one thousand men, whether in the hope of encountering him or of being challenged, without knowing what you expect to find, you must have men in front, behind and on the flanks to ensure that you are not surprised.' He proposes the following battle order: skirmishers were to go first, followed by a small body as vanguard. Then came the main body of the army, an efficient and powerful unit, flanked on each side by a wing, whose duty it was to attack the enemy flanks. A rearguard could come quickly to the help of the main army, and could if necessary be protected in the rear by detached knights, who could give the alarm if the enemy came from that direction.[443] So there were quite substantial flanking units for the battle. In the column of march of the French royal army at Cassel in 1328, there were two wings, one with the fifth or royal detachment, the other with the eighth.

The deep formation which was used at Ascalon, Hab, Arsuf, Philippopoli, Worringen and in Jean de Bueil's advice, formed a stout protection against enemy attack on the flank. This was also true of the reserve, and it will be profitable to consider the use of this unit and the place of the unit commanders in battle.

The Place of the Commanders in Battle

In considering the place of leaders in battle, it is of course necessary to distinguish between the commander of a tactical unit and the supreme commander. Occasionally the leaders personally carried the standard or banner of their detachment, and the standard-bearers normally rode at the head of their detachment. Many texts show this:

> Before them all rode Fagon the seneschal:
> Who was a duke and Charles' kinsman,
>
> And in battle bore his standard.[444]

During the first Crusade, according to the *Chanson d'Antioche*, the Holy Lance was borne before the troops:

> You will go in front, armed and mounted on your destrier
> You will carry the Lance with which Christ was wounded.[445]

And again:

> Each squadron led by a silk dragon standard.[446]

And:

> Anyone who wishes to lead his army must carry his standard.[447]

443 Delbrück, III, p. 278. Jean de Bueil, *Le Jouvencel*, I, pp. 158–9.
444 *Chanson d'Aspremont*, II, c. 493, vv. 10166–9, p. 129.
445 *Chanson d'Antioche*, II, 1. VIII, viii, vv. 131–2, p. 205.
446 *Ibid.*, xiii, v. 266, p. 211.
447 *Ibid.*, 1. VII, xxviii, v. 764, p. 181.

Bertrand de Born praised the good leader who rode into battle at the head of his troops. With the Templars, the standard was brought forward to start the attack, and this was done elsewhere, for example by the French nobles at Courtrai.

It is difficult to determine how far ahead these leaders rode. The fact that they frequently fought at the head of their units explains why the poets of the epics allowed their descriptions of battles to end with the ultimate struggle between the two supreme commanders, which naturally makes a fine dramatic ending. The custom of minor leaders fighting out in front naturally strengthened the mistaken impression of individual fights, and this idea provided several supposed examples to prove the theory. When scholars then read that a lord went out to attack, they often thought that this meant a kind of duel between two combatants. A particularly striking example of this comes from the battle of Bouvines, which owing to a superficial reading of the sources was wrongly imagined to have been a series of duels, because it had not been noticed that the barons did not go out alone, but with their whole formation.[448]

Similarly, an erroneous generalisation from the preliminary skirmish, in which knights sometimes acted individually, led to this notion. In the *Chanson d'Aspremont* Girart de Fraite expressly forbade duels:

'I forbid all of you, whether nephew, son, peer and comrade, to start a single combat. He who starts one will never get my pardon; he will not be allowed to come back in my house.'[449]

The order was carefully carried out in his specially closely serried formation.[450]

Contrary to what is commonly supposed, the supreme commander or tactical leader of the army very often took no part in the hand-to-hand fighting. He remained outside the hurly-burly, in order to keep a better watch on the situation, and to throw in the reserve at the right moment. This problem will be considered in the chapter on tactics, where a couple more examples will be given of a feigned flight and the placing of a reserve corps in ambush.

The Knights Fighting on Foot

The knights were the complete warriors of western society; they could fight mounted and on foot. When it was necessary or preferable, they dismounted for combat.

At Louvain in 891, when king Arnulf could not attack the Viking camp with his cavalry, most of his men made a successful assault on foot.[451]

During the following centuries, the knights were often obliged to attack a fortress

---

448 Verbruggen, 'Le problème des effectifs et de la tactique à la bataille de Bouvines en 1214', *Revue du Nord* 31, 1949, pp. 192–3.
449 *Chanson d'Aspremont*, II, 479, vv. 9877–81, p. 120.
450 *Ibid.*, 480, vv. 9899–900, p. 121.
451 *Annales Fuldenses*, anno 891, pp. 119–20. On the dismounted cavalry, see: Delbrück, III, pp.

as foot-soldiers. In 1112, Louis the Fat and his knights attacked on foot the castle of Le Puiset.[452] In May 1197, the knights of king Richard I stormed the castle of Milli, near Beauvais. William the Marshal was directing a part of the attack and climbed a ladder to take the wall.[453] In most wars the knights defended their castles fighting on foot.

The knights also fought on foot in the naval battles of the middle ages. They were ready to fight dismounted during a landing operation at Constantinople on 6 July 1203.[454] On 12 April 1204 during the attack on Constantinople by the fleet, knights fought also on foot.[455] In the army of St Louis near Damietta (5 June 1249) Joinville and many other knights landed on foot and established a beachhead.[456] The Flemish army of Guy and John of Dampierre, reinforced by French knights, tried to land at Westkapelle in Walcheren on 4 July 1253. It became a disastrous defeat.[457]

The knights dismounted also to stiffen the ranks of the foot-soldiers and to encourage them. The dismounted knights would not flee on horseback and would stay with the foot-soldiers till the bitter end or the victory. Robert Guiscard used knights for such missions. At Tinchebray (1106), king Henry I dismounted with his retinue and took up a position in the middle of the foot-soldiers. His opponent, Robert of Normandy, did the same. At Brémule (1119) Henry I ordered knights to dismount and fight on foot. At Bourg Théroulde (1124), Norman knights increased the effectiveness of their archers by dismounting and fighting in the ranks of the foot-soldiers. At Northallerton (1138) many Anglo-Norman knights dismounted and took up positions among the foot-soldiers. At Lincoln (1141), the second line of king Stephen's army consisted of foot-soldiers reinforced by dismounted knights.[458]

The knights fought also on foot when the terrain was too difficult for combat on horseback, or when there were too many obstacles. Sometimes they preferred to defend a small passage on foot.

As leaders of the foot-soldiers, the knights fought on foot in the defence of fortified towns and castles. On a battlefield they gave strength to the formation, by taking place in the first rank of the foot-soldiers. They gave moral support, for they could not abandon the foot. In Flanders some hundreds of knights fought with the foot-soldiers at Courtrai, Arques, and Mons-en-Pévèle.

At Boroughbridge (1322), English knights and men-at-arms dismounted. Together with pikemen they defended the northern end of the bridge. They placed other pikemen in the form of a schiltron, as the Scots did, to defend a ford. They used archers to ward off the enemy's attack. Their adversaries attacked the defenders of

318–21. Gaier, *Art et organisation militaires dans la principauté de Liège*, pp. 190–4. Lot, I, pp. 315–19; II, p. 148.
[452] Suger, c. 21, pp. 158–60.
[453] Painter, *William Marshal*, pp. 110–11.
[454] Villehardouin, I, c. 156–7, p. 156.
[455] *Ibid.*, II, c. 243, p. 44.
[456] Joinville, c. 33, p. 55.
[457] Verbruggen, 'Het leger en de vloot', pp. 145–6.
[458] See chapter IV: 'Co-operation of cavalry and foot-soldiers in battle'.

the bridge with dismounted knights, and their cavalry attempted to cross the ford, but they were defeated.[459] Ten years later these tactics were perfected at the battle of Dupplin Moor. In 1333, at Halidon Hill, the skilful combination of English archers with armoured nobility on foot and on horseback enabled Edward III to defeat the Scots completely, and to establish the military superiority of the English armies firmly.[460]

During the Hundred Years War, the French knights adopted the English fashion of fighting on foot in 1351. They dismounted at Maupertuis (1356), Cocherel (1364), Auray (1364), Najera (1367) and so on.[461]

The Course of a Battle

The leader formed one, two or three lines behind each other, according to the terrain and the formation of the enemy. The first line started the approach on the command 'Forward' (mouvez), or 'March' (allez le pas). The approach was done cautiously, 'as if the men were carrying a bride before them in the saddle'.[462] The lances were carried upright, but as soon as they were within the appointed distance from the enemy they were levelled, and the charge began at the command 'Spur on' (poigniez), at a signal with the standard, or at the sound of a trumpet. Trumpets sounded the charge as at a tournament. The soldiers shouted their war-cry to frighten the enemy and to bolster up their own courage. The speed of the advance was increased to a quick trot or even a gallop, being governed by the weight of the man and his equipment, and was naturally bound to be a compromise between speed and the maintenance of good order. All men attacked together, in a compact unit, for it was strictly forbidden to break ranks or to charge ahead on a faster horse. Until the end of the eleventh century the lance was used to thrust and strike as well, but when later it was held under the arm, the charge was more forceful. A good initial shock could be quickly decisive in a battle. The army which fought under the best discipline won the battle. If the charge did not bring immediate victory, a mêlée developed. Even in that phase of the battle they still fought in little units: since the charge was made in closed units and more slowly than was the case with later cavalry, the battle-order suffered less from the shock of the attack. The battles of Bouvines and Worringen were in this respect typical. Exhausted units were withdrawn for a time and re-grouped, then they returned to the mêlée. Sometimes a leader even rallied widely scattered knights round a new banner. Fighting went on until the formations were shattered: once the troops were scattered, facing a better organised opponent, the standard easily fell into enemy hands. If the standard was brought down or lost, there was little chance of re-assembling the troops, and they fled. For that reason the

---

459 Tout, The Tactics of Boroughbridge and Morlaix, pp. 222–3.
460 Oman, II, pp. 103–7, Lot, I, pp. 328–9. Morris, Mounted Infantry, pp. 91–2.
461 Verbruggen, 'La tactique de la chevalerie française de 1340 à 1415', Publications de l'Université de l'Etat à Elisabethville, I, 1961 pp. 45–7.
462 Heelu, vv. 4900–4, p. 184.

standard was often kept in the rear on a cart, with the reserve unit round it, so that the rallying point was well out of danger; this was frequently done in the Middle East, where often only part of the army went into action while the rest stayed in the rear to help the attacking troops in their return from a charge. The Moslems did all they could to avoid the knights' charge, and on the whole there was usually no hand-to-hand combat, or if there was, it lasted only a very little while. An attack was exhausting, and the formations had to be systematically regrouped. A series of charges was made in order to hurl the deep Turkish formations on top of each other in confusion, and to shatter this mass of men in a decisive charge. If this was not successful, attacks were continued until the enemy realised that the Western knights were not vulnerable in their close units, and fled.

But armies of knights had some major weaknesses in battle. Like later cavalry, they had to take the offensive, and it was their best method of defence as well. If they wanted to fight a defensive action, some of the knights had to fight on foot. A pursuit was a difficult business owing to the small number of troops, and to the continual necessity of regrouping; also a reserve corps had to be maintained. If there were none, the victors, pursuing the enemy in scattered formation, ran the risk of being beaten by a fresh enemy unit or by troops in ambush, as happened at Thielt in 1128, at Tagliacozzo in 1260[463] and at Bäsweiler in 1371.[464]

General Conclusion

After thorough individual training, the knight received collective training too, in the feuds between families, and in tournaments, and gained experience in war. Although it is a mistake to imagine him as a man who lusted after war, yet the life of a soldier, being his profession, had a powerful attraction for him. Human nature, however, asserted itself in battle and when his life was at stake: fear of death exercised its terrifying influence, but this is sometimes overlooked because the psychological problems are not often described, and because literature which was often intended for knightly readers and was devoted to their praise cast a mantle of silence over these delicate and private matters. Honest witnesses nevertheless testify that these feelings existed then just as much as later in the history of war. This makes us suspicious of many deeds of arms which have been described with poetic licence, and of the so-called individual actions of the knight. If these are examined with a critical eye, the truth becomes plain that, on the contrary, the behaviour of the knightly units shows how anxiously they pressed together in order to give each individual the protection of mass action.

The formation of units was governed by the nature of the armies themselves: members of the same family, men from the standing retinue, vassals of the same lord fought together, joined in the larger formation under the head of a principality or the lord of a region. In a time when the state did not have complete authority, the family,

---

[463] Lot, II, pp. 177–81. Delbrück, III, pp. 376–81.
[464] Delbrück, III, p. 566.

in the wider sense including a retinue, took the place of public authority. The bonds between lord and vassal were just as important as those within the family, and the personal relationship between leader and led represents a very important factor in an army. Out of all this, from the late eleventh and early twelfth centuries, came a very strong sense of honour, – personal honour, the honour of one's clan, of the leader, of the country. Although precept and reality did not always coincide, there was sufficient sense of honour to incite the great mass of a knightly army to make the necessary sacrifices on the field of battle. Not everyone would choose to fight to the death rather than escape, as the *Chanson de Roland* would have it, but what actually happened – fighting till death or capture – was often the expression of a high degree of courage and self-sacrifice, and could lead to a very stubbornly fought battle.

Strongly conscious of their position as lords, forming a privileged social class at that time, and thanks to a thorough collective training, the knights had the ability to execute whatever manoeuvres were necessary on the battlefield. Since they were by nature excellent fighters, they compensated for scanty artificial expertise by considerable moral cohesiveness. They used sound military tactics which were within the capability of their troop strength and the special requirements of cavalry warfare. They adapted their fighting technique at once to the tactics of the enemy in the Middle East, just as they had done against the foot-soldiers in Western Europe: they could not have done better with the means at their disposal, and in comparison with armies of similar size, they were without doubt the finest military force of their day. Their consciousness of social rank and military efficiency, despite the size of their armies, may sometimes have led them to recklessness, but this happens in all successful armies in every age.

The knightly armies, then, deserve a favourable verdict. They were the product of their time, in which they played a great part socially, politically, and militarily. They brought about the expansion of Western Europe; sword in hand, they opened up new markets, they made a new part of the world better known, and their conduct and protection enabled the culture of their day to flourish. While they braved death, hunger, thirst, mental and physical suffering in the Middle East and on the battlefields of Eastern Europe, the merchants, craftsmen, scholars and artists of the West enjoyed the fruits of peace, in which they could practise their *métier* and develop a new power which was ultimately to displace the knightly class.

III

THE FOOT-SOLDIERS

The Foot-soldiers and their Remarkable Development in the Fourteenth Century

The splendid victory of the Flemish foot-soldiers in the battle of Courtrai, 11 July 1302, won them a place in history as the first to defeat a great knightly army since Roman times. But these foot-soldiers already had a considerable past history by 1302, and it is worth taking the trouble of looking into their evolution and their place in contemporary military history.

The battle of Courtrai was followed in 1314 by Bannockburn, the signal triumph of the Scottish foot-soldiers over the Anglo-Norman knights of Edward II of England, in 1315 by Morgarten, the first great victory of the Swiss over the Austrian knights, and in 1319 by the victory of the peasants of Dithmarschen over the knights of Holstein. How did these great victories of foot-soldiers, in widely separated theatres of war, come about at the beginning of the fourteenth century? Why should such a remarkable thing have happened just then? This is an important question which we should consider closely, at least in those areas in which there is factual evidence. Something is known about the communal armies of Flemish cities from the year 1127, and these cities played a vital role in the county from then onwards under the control of their *Poorters*, the rich burghers: yet the foot-soldiers remained scarcely more than a secondary arm, an auxiliary weapon at best, often put to no use at all because the count and his nobles underrated their possibilities. Then suddenly these same foot-soldiers scored a brilliant victory, and became conscious of their own strength. The same phenomenon occurred in Scotland, Switzerland and Dithmarschen – so this is no isolated instance. More than a hundred years earlier it had happened in the Lombard cities, particularly Milan.

Medieval foot-soldiers were apt to suffer from an inferiority complex and to lack confidence in their own ability, which was to be blamed on their relatively lowly social status. They also lacked that inner cohesiveness so characteristic of the knights, whose social position and military training were far superior. Fighting men had to be comparatively numerous, and sufficiently well-to-do to equip themselves well, which in turn depended on demographic and economic development, and they needed capable leaders, who for the most part would not be found among farmers or townspeople. It is not surprising that the Flemings, Scots, Swiss and Dithmarschen fought for freedom and independence. They all had a keen national feeling, permeating wide social strata; the struggle for a better life in the Flemish cities increased their sense of fellow-feeling and made them stubborn and tenacious in war. After several centuries of social and economic development these main factors matured simultaneously, and the situation of the foot-soldiers was helped by the fact that their chief rivals, the knights, had then passed their peak as a social class.

This whole question will be considered broadly in the light of what is known about certain principalities, since the study is necessarily limited by a lack of knowledge for many areas.

Historical Survey

1. *Peasant Foot-soldiers*

By the middle of the ninth century wars were fought almost exclusively by cavalry. It was then that the vassals developed as a class through the rise of the feudal system: they were the principal free men, hence the common people held an inferior position. This state of affairs greatly influenced the military characteristics of ordinary people: nearly everywhere in western Europe the foot-soldiers declined in military importance. The vassals were in fact living on the labour of the rural population, and the more powerful they became, the less chance there was of making useful foot-soldiers out of the peasants.

But there were a few exceptions. The most conspicuous were the foot-soldiers of the Anglo-Saxons. Their *huscarls* and *thegns* moved about on horseback, but fought on foot. They had the necessary sense of unity and the means to arm themselves properly, in contrast to poor peasants on the continent. When, however, they had been defeated at Hastings by William the Conqueror in 1066, good foot-soldiers also disappeared. Other exceptions on the continent make this matter and the problem of medieval foot-soldiers still clearer. Peasant communities which had been the ancestral organization of the Old Germans, or autonomous peasant republics remained in existence in the Frisian lands on the North Sea coast, in the Dithmarschen and among the Stedinger on the Weser. The last were however defeated in 1234 at Altenesch, and completely subjugated by the archbishop of Bremen and his allies. The most famous example of peasant foot-soldiers comes from Switzerland.

The foot-soldiers in Switzerland

Three cantons played the greatest part in the formation of late medieval Switzerland: Schwyz, Uri, and Unterwalden. In Schwyz the valley was inhabited in the time of the Franks by communities of a hundred families. Up to the beginning of the thirteenth century they were under the leadership of a *hunno*, who by ancient custom was also the judge. There were also serfs living side by side with the free peasants, dependent on the abbeys, for example Einsiedeln. Both the free and the not-free together formed the 'Mark-association' or free community, which controlled the use of the *allmende*, or common meadow-land, and the economic policy. The free peasants made up approximately two-thirds of the population, which around 1281 was perhaps 1,530 families strong. For an expedition to Besançon in 1289 another

1,500 men were called up.[1] In the second half of the thirteenth century the inhabitants of these valleys had become rich enough to buy their freedom from bondage, which was followed by a quick fusion with the original free inhabitants. The principal economic activity in this region was cattle raising, practised chiefly in the *allmende*, which was 'ten hours long and five hours wide'. In these mountain valleys with little fertile soil the common meadow formed a strong bond among the inhabitants. In such a small area the able-bodied men could be assembled in a few hours.

In Uri the evolution was peculiar. From a legal point of view, this land had for a long time no more free men than Schwyz. Uri was a possession of the Fraumünster-stift at Zürich, and was therefore under the rule of the protector. The original free people of the region were subject to the same legal authority as the serfs, and together formed a judicial community, which meant that the free and non-free became integrated here more quickly than elsewhere. Just as in Schwyz, the mark-association played an important part locally, free and non-free using the *allmende* jointly. The economic community exercised more influence on their daily lives than the judicial: it was the basis for political freedom. As in the case of Schwyz, the rural community of Uri was also eager to expand: pasture lands in other valleys were taken by force of arms to help supply the growing population. In time the inhabitants of Uri acquired a legal status that differed in no way from the complete freedom of Schwyz. It is true that *seignories* arose, but they did not exercise any important influence.

In the twelfth century the route over the St Gotthard pass was opened, running straight across Uri, bringing with it new duties and new rights for the 'land-community', the *universitas hominum vallis Uraniae*.[2] The inhabitants had to perform 'all manner of services for the merchants in the transport of goods over the pass roads, giving shelter, furnishing provisions and fodder, supplying horses and mules, and finally, and most important of all, keeping the roads in a passable state, and being responsible for all roads and bridges. Freight traffic over the passes was an organized undertaking, practised by the valley inhabitants, who held the monopoly'.[3] As the result of this, the welfare of the inhabitants improved greatly. On 26 May 1231 Uri came directly under the power of king Henry, son of the emperor Frederick II, who bought the suzerainty over Uri from the count of Habsburg in order to bring the strategic road to his confederates in Italy under his own rule, and therefore not to have to depend on powerful lords. For Uri this meant political freedom, for the imperial power crumbled shortly afterwards. It is true that the prince now and then sent a representative for the administration of justice, and for taxes, but the community really enjoyed self-rule. An *amman* governed the land-community, called the *land-amman* after 1291. By 1243 the community had its own seal, a symbol of autonomy later preserved in the fortress at Attinghausen.[4]

At first there was no community for the whole region in Unterwalden, though

---

[1] R. Durrer, 'Premiers combats de la Suisse primitive pour la liberté', in *Histoire militaire de la Suisse*, eds M. Feldmann and H.G. Wirz, 1er Cahier (Berne, 1915), pp. 35–8.
[2] *Ibid.*, p. 45.
[3] B.H. Slicher van Bath, *Boerenvrijheid* (Groningen, 1948), p. 18.
[4] Durrer, *op. cit.*, pp. 45–7. H. Nabholz, *Geschichte der Schweiz*, I (Zürich, 1932), pp. 111–12.

there were communal parcels of land for each parish. The free peasants formed barely a third of the population, whose chief occupation was cattle-raising. A *communitas* developed in Nidwalden, part of Unterwalden, during the interregnum, and certainly existed before 1261 (*communitas hominum intramontanorum vallis inferioris*). Like Uri and Schwyz, it soon had its own seal.[5]

Following the example of Uri, Schwyz also wanted independence. In 1240 the region tried to escape from the rule of count Rudolf the Younger of Habsburg, who had cast in his lot with the pope against Frederick II, and on 20 December of that year Schwyz became free of the hereditary overlordship of the Habsburg. Together with Unterwalden, Uri and Lucerne it revolted against Rudolf, who was however victorious in 1244. A new uprising from 1245 to 1252 was equally unsuccessful.[6]

Thereafter a great part of what was later Switzerland came under the rule of Rudolf the Elder of Habsburg, a nephew of the former count: these petty counts of Habsburg later became the powerful Austrian dukes, and Rudolf the Elder became king of the Romans. He wanted to collect heavy tolls on the trade through the St Gotthard pass, and the pressure of taxes in Uri, Schwyz and Unterwalden became greater than before, so that the old urge for independence also became stronger than ever. The three cantons waited for an opportune moment to strike and to obtain self-rule again. Scarcely two weeks after the death of Rudolf (15 July 1291) Uri, Schwyz, and Unterwalden – first only Nidwalden, then Obwalden as well – formed in August the 'Everlasting League', by which they accepted only the judicial authority of a person native to the valleys.[7] This provided the basis for the political freedom of the *Waldstätte*, just a few days after the death of Rudolf had been confirmed. Once again a Habsburg, Albert, succeeded in bringing the three cantons under his rule from 1298 to 1308. After his death the long-drawn-out conflict began in which the *Waldstätte* won their independence by magnificent military victories, and established the state of Switzerland.

The freight traffic over the St Gotthard pass to Italy and France brought the peasants not only extra profits, but through their contact with the merchants new ideas about farming. They were also in constant touch with the north Italian cities, and well understood the struggle of those communities for freedom and independence. There was too little fertile soil in the *Waldstätte* to support a rapidly expanding population. This not only led to the seizure of other valleys from the monasteries in the surrounding area, but also to military service as mercenaries in Italy, and in the neighbouring districts. Soldiers from Schwyz and Uri fought for the abbot of St Gallen in 1252, and ten years later for the baron of Vatz.[8] In Italy they learned tactics from the foot-soldiers from the communal armies. The men-at-arms from the *Waldstätte* enjoyed fighting just as their forefathers did in the days of the old Germans. Their remarkable talents in this direction were put to work in their

---

5 Durrer, pp. 58 and 39.
6 *Ibid.*, pp. 51 ff. Nabholz, pp. 112–14.
7 Durrer, pp. 62–3. Nabholz, p. 120. Delbrück, III, pp. 572–4.
8 Durrer, pp. 80–1.

powerful drive for independence. Basic wildness and lust for gain made them very aggressive warriors with an indomitable offensive spirit.[9]

Friesland

In Friesland, just as in the Swiss cantons, there was a *universitas* or defensive community, which was upheld by a solemn oath taken by the peasants.[10] These free peasants were occupied in cattle-raising, trade and shipping, and in Friesland just as in Switzerland they had always had the right to bear arms. Through the general rise in the standard of living in the eleventh, twelfth, and thirteenth centuries they had considerably improved their armament. The Frisians also liked fighting, and the virtual political independence of these countries, with the unhindered development of the social and economic life of the free communities, had greatly contributed to the population's fighting potential. The terrain was not favourable to knightly armies on account of the mountains and damp valleys in the Swiss cantons, and the marshes in Friesland. Because of their peculiar geographical situation neither had powerful neighbours to fear. The crumbling of the imperial might, and the favourable political situation in the Holy Roman Empire helped them towards autonomy: in Friesland and Switzerland the power of the central authority never became strong. A true knightly class never existed, at least, what there was of such a class never gained much strength. Dithmarschen was in a similar position.

The foot-soldiers in Dithmarschen

Dithmarschen was one of the three districts north of the Elbe in Saxony, at the frontier of Denmark. The country was protected by the North Sea in the west, the Elbe in the south, the Eider and marshes in the north. The eastern frontier, towards Holstein, was less well protected. But there were difficult regions and marshes, which protected a part of that frontier. Only one road had been built on the watershed between the river Gieselau and the river Holstenau. The sea, the rivers and the marshes made nearly an island of Dithmarschen, and a dike was the only approach. The direction of an invasion by the enemy was always known. The country itself consisted of a higher region, the *Geest*, near Holstein, and the *Marsch*, along the sea, cut by ditches, water-courses and marshes. The humid *Marsch* could be inundated by opening the sluices. The country was very favourable for the defenders, and extremely difficult for armies of knights.

The Saxon district probably became a county under Charlemagne. In the twelfth century Dithmarschen was part of a county situated on both banks of the Elbe under the counts of Stade. The last count of the house of Stade, Rudolf, was killed by the people of Dithmarschen in 1144 on the Böcklenburg. Henry the Lion, aided by Adolf II of Schauenburg, count of Holstein, held in 1147 a punitive expedition against Dithmarschen to avenge the death of count Rudolf, and installed a new count. After the fall of Henry the Lion, Dithmarschen became a fief of the archbishop of Bremen.

---

[9] W. Schaufelberger, *Der Alte Schweizer und sein Krieg*, p. 23.
[10] Slicher van Bath, *Boerenvrijheid*, pp. 8 and 12.

From then until the battle of Bornhöved in 1227, the history of Dithmarschen was influenced by the foreign powers: the county of Holstein, the bishopric of Schleswig, and Denmark. As a result of the battle of Bornhöved, the Danish influence was eliminated for a long time.

Dithmarschen had always defended itself against foreign powers. The house of Schauenburg obtained the comital power in Holstein and extended its lordship in the twelfth century. It was the principal enemy of Dithmarschen. The population preferred the archbishop of Bremen as feudal lord, because he was too far away to exert a strong influence. A guardian represented the archbishop in Dithmarschen. He summoned the army, administered the high justice, and presided over the assembly of the district. Later there was a guardian in each of the five areas, in which the land was divided. In the thirteenth century, there were knights in Dithmarschen; they constituted a 'nobility by service'. But these nobles were obliged to give up their rights, or to leave the country. Those who stayed constituted the *Geschlecht* of the guardians.

The *Geschlechter* of Dithmarschen arose from the fusion of agnate *Sippen*. The *Geschlechter* reclaimed land from the sea, in the *Marsch*, and cultivated it. Like the old *Sippen*, the *Geschlechter* played an important role in the daily life of the people. They protected their members, preserved peace, and assured the vendetta. The vendetta was one of the principal duties of the *Geschlechter* till the middle of the sixteenth century. The big families acquired also land in the *Geest*. At the end, all the peasants were grouped in *Geschlechter*. But the country was not simply a land of *Geschlechter*.

New institutions were introduced in the thirteenth century, in the further development of self-government. The parishes obtained more influence. The representatives of the parishes were the advisers and the jurors (*consules et iurati*). In the same period there was a general development in Germany of leagues to preserve the peace, and urban communities with sworn groups. In the coastal regions of Friesland and Saxony, there were everywhere *iurati* and *consules* as representatives of the parishes. They were opposed to the authority of the representatives of the overlord. At the head of the *universitas* of Dithmarschen were the *advocati et milites*.

At the end of the thirteenth century, an equilibrium existed between the rival powers in the country: the guardians, the parishes and the big families. Each group had his foreign ally: the archbishop of Bremen aided his guardians, the city of Hamburg supported the parishes, the count of Holstein the *Geschlechter*. About 1300 the peasant republic had a society without classes. There were no big landowners in the country. The parishes had a nearly complete political autonomy. In the fourteenth century Dithmarschen was a federal republic of parishes.

The cities of Lübeck and Hamburg were allies of the republic. Hamburg had special interests there, because of the navigation on the Elbe. The navigation was made unsafe by the *Geschlechter*, and Hamburg intervened in favour of the parishes against the *Geschlechter*.

Dithmarschen was an old and prosperous country of peasants. In the sixteenth century there were 35,000 inhabitants. The principal characteristic was the general liberty. The peasants were strong, bold and lithe men, in general of big size, and without much flesh. They were ready to offer their life for the liberty of their country. They preferred to die rather than to live in bondage. Through their knowledge of the difficult country, their experience in the use of weapons, their good equipment, their cohesion, fruit of a long tradition and strong family bonds, the peasants constituted an excellent army that numbered 6,000 men in the middle of the fifteenth century. The rich *Geschlechter* procured the leaders. The peasants assured their national independence till 1559, with the aid of the favourable terrain, and the special circumstances in the foreign countries. Three times they destroyed or chased out an invading army: in 1319 and 1404 the army of the count of Holstein, in 1500 the army of the king of Denmark.[11]

The foot-soldiers in Wales

Like the Swiss, the Celtic tribes in Wales had a valuable ally in their own land, criss-crossed by high and rugged mountain ranges whither the inhabitants could flee, or whence they could defy the enemy. If the worst came to the worst, their leaders could also flee to Ireland, to await a propitious moment to return. Wales was always a hard nut to crack for the English kings, but it was also difficult for this region to develop any kind of political unity. The mountain ranges divided the country up into areas which remained isolated from each other for lack of means of communication. Wales never knew lasting national unity, and possessed no national political institutions.[12]

This was also true of the armed forces. Soldiers in South Wales were armed with bows, in North Wales with pikes. The Celtic tribes in the area were rude and warlike, and put up stubborn resistance to any expedition which threatened their independence. The lightly-armed fighters from South Wales were probably the most famous: Giraldus Cambrensis extolled their speed and flexibility, and the accuracy of their bows. Their uncivilized ways meant that enemy knights could expect no quarter, so that it was better to be killed in battle than to be taken prisoner, and probably killed anyway.[13] This warlike nation provided mercenaries for the kings of England. In the first battle of Lincoln in 1141 they fought against King Stephen, and were then described as 'daring rather than skilled in the handling of weapons'.[14] The barons of the Welsh Marches collected enough troops in their area and among the Celtic tribes to conquer Ireland.[15] Henry II went out against the Scots with lightly armed soldiers from Wales;[16] he also used them on the continent in the struggle against his rebellious sons,[17] and in 1188 against Philip Augustus.[18] Richard I used

---

[11] W. Lammers, *Die Schlacht bei Hemmingstedt. Freies Bauerntum und Fürstemacht im Nordseeraum*, pp. 46–56, 110–17, 121–3. *Quellen und Forschungen zur Geschichte Schleswig-Holsteins*, 28, Neumünster (Heide in Holstein, 1954).

[12] A.L. Poole, *From Domesday Book to Magna Carta*, The Oxford History of England (Oxford, 1951), pp. 283–4.

[13] Giraldus Cambrensis, *Expugnatio Hibernica*, Opera V, p. 395.

[14] Oman, I, p. 398, n. 2. Poole, *op. cit.*, pp. 141–2.

[15] Poole, p. 305. Giraldus Cambrensis, pp. 395–6.

[16] Poole, p. 278, n. 2.

[17] *Ibid.*, p. 337.

[18] *Ibid.*, p. 344.

them in his campaign in France;[19] king John raised armies in his Welsh possessions, and they even remained faithful when the rest of Wales revolted.[20] In the revolt of the barons against Henry III Simon de Montfort used many auxiliaries sent to him by Llewellyn of Wales,[21] and Celtic archers, after the conquest of their land by Edward I (1277–1295), often formed the backbone of the English foot-soldiers.

South Wales was the cradle of the famous longbowmen. Giraldus Cambrensis refers several times to this weapon in his picturesque description of his journey through Wales in the reign of Henry II.[22] The men of Gwent and Morganwg (Monmouthshire and Glamorgan) excelled as archers. During the siege of Abergavenny in 1182, their arrows pierced an oak door four inches thick. The arrows were left sticking in the door and Giraldus saw them six years later when he passed the castle, the tips of the arrows being just visible on the inner side of the door. One knight was nailed fast to his horse by an arrow which went through the flap of his mail shirt, pierced his mail breeches, his thigh, and the wooden saddle, and went on into the flank of his horse. Giraldus asked whether an arrow from a crossbow could do more than that. The bows from Gwent were not made of horn, ash, or yew, but of unpolished elm which looked very rough. They were stiff, broad, and powerful, good at long or short range.[23] Giraldus strongly recommended that archers should always be made to co-operate with knights in expeditions into Wales and Ireland,[24] where the terrain was so difficult for knights that lightly armed men were particularly useful.

These bows were not introduced at once into English armies. Richard I and John used mercenaries armed with the crossbow, as well as Welsh men-at-arms. In the Assize of Arms of 1181, no mention was made of the bow. On the other hand, the Assize for 1252 imposed the use of the weapon on those who had less than a hundred shillings in land, and on city-dwellers who had between nine and twenty marks worth of furniture.[25] In the civil wars under Henry III hardly any bowmen were used, and all the evidence points to the fact that at that time the old-fashioned small bow was still used. But after the conquest of Wales there was a double change. Welsh archers made up the greater part of the English foot-soldiers, and through their overwhelming effect brought about the great victory over the Scottish pikemen at Falkirk in 1298. There their action in a great campaign was described for the first time, so that presumably the introduction of the longbow dates from that time.

Historians of the art of war have long been preoccupied with the problem as to why the longbow superseded the crossbow in England, while the latter was still used for a long time on the continent, and was further developed there. The longbow was a remarkable technical improvement on the short one, formerly used in England.

[19] *Ibid.*, p. 373.
[20] *Ibid.*, pp. 297–8 and 300, n. 1.
[21] Oman, II, p. 59.
[22] *Itinerarium Kambriae*, ed. J.F. Dimock, *Opera* 6, Rolls Series, London, pp. 54, 123, 127.
[23] Oman, II, p. 59. [See J. Bradbury, *The Medieval Archer*, pp. 15–16, 18, 75, 83–85.]
[24] *Expugnatio Hibernica*, pp. 395–6. Delbrück, III, pp. 284–5.
[25] Oman, II, p. 60. Lot, *Art militaire*, I, p. 313.

Some scholars think that the improvement lay in the fact that the string of the longbow was drawn to the archer's right ear, whereas the string of the short one was drawn merely to the chest.[26] This would give the longbow greater power, and the arrows would penetrate more deeply. But drawing the bow to the ear was not a completely new idea, for it had already been done by the mounted archers of Justinian in the Byzantine empire.[27] It is possible of course that this method had never been employed in the West, or that it had been lost. In any case the longbow was stronger than the short one, but we do not know whether it was more powerful than the crossbow. It may be that in the late thirteenth and early fourteenth centuries it surpassed the models of crossbows then existing, till the latter in their turn were improved and were as strong or stronger than the longbow. However this may be, the longbow in any case could shoot faster, sending ten to twelve arrows a minute as against the crossbow's two, with an effective range of up to two hundred yards.[28] Made out of locally grown wood, the bow was also much cheaper than the crossbow, and poorer people could equip themselves much more easily.

It has not been sufficiently emphasized by historians in the past that Edward I used his bowmen *en masse*, thousands at a time, whereas previously in England, and for a long time to come on the continent, units of crossbowmen were only a few hundred strong. There were only a few hundred crossbowmen in the armies of Philip the Fair and his followers. The tactical effectiveness of such weapons increases as they are used on a massive scale: such use resulted in a technical as well as a tactical surprise as these archers were used in more important tasks on the battlefield. The Scots experienced this at Falkirk, at Dupplin Moor, and at Halidon Hill, and the French were taken by surprise at Crécy in 1346.

The evolution of the short bow and its tactical use may be summarized as follows. Although men with small bows played a prominent part at Hastings in William the Conqueror's army,[29] these bows afterwards fell into disuse in England, except in forested areas, where archers now and then proved effective. This happened in Sussex in 1216, when the rebel army under Louis, son of Philip Augustus, was attacked by about a thousand archers in the Weald, and in 1266 Henry III raised an army of bowmen in the same area to put down a rebellion.[30] Edward I saw the usefulness of the archers during the war in Wales, and perhaps also on his crusade. Since he was methodical in his conquest of Wales it is logical to suppose that he had reached the same conclusion as Giraldus nearly a century earlier. At that time he naturally used soldiers from the border counties and South Wales, who were skilled in the use of these weapons. There were 5,297 archers from Wales out of a total of 7,810 foot-soldiers in the royal army that was sent to Flanders in 1297.[31] The following year he had a very large number of them at Falkirk, and used them *en*

[26] Morris, *Welsh Wars*, p. 34. Lot, *op. cit.*, I, p. 314.
[27] Delbrück, III, p. 405. Oman, I, p. 26. Lot, *loc. cit.*, n. 4, also has some objections.
[28] Lot, I, p. 314. [The range is much debated, see R. Hardy, *The Longbow*, 2nd edn, 1986, p. 60.]
[29] Oman, p. 160. Delbrück, III, p. 403.
[30] Oman, II, pp. 60–1.
[31] Lewis, *English Forces in Flanders*, p. 311. [See Bradbury, *The Medieval Archer*, pp. 85–86, 90; Bennett, 'Tactics', pp. 4–5, for the impact of massed archery.]

masse.[32] Edward I was rich enough to use and support them in large numbers. It seems plain that the weapon was much more effective when used in this way than it had been in the very small armies of the Welsh princes, who were too weak to engage great armies in the open field. In time of peace archers could practise more effectively than pikemen or other heavy foot-soldiers could. As the king came to rely more and more on archers for his army, the example of Wales and the Marches was followed in the rest of England, and the technique was continually improved.

It is likely that Edward I preferred the longbow to the crossbow chiefly because he could recruit these longbow men in large numbers in his own country. As we have seen, an archer could shoot faster with the longbow than with the crossbow, and it may have been as strong or even stronger than the contemporary models of crossbows. It is hard to believe that Edward I preferred the longbow simply because he was fighting the Welsh who had no armour, while Richard I in his day had chosen crossbowmen because he was fighting knightly armies.[33] It is quite possible that Richard was principally influenced by the third Crusade, in which he used crossbowmen, and was not familiar with the skill of Welsh archers. It is also quite probable that the twelfth century bowmen from South Wales were neither so experienced nor so numerous as their counterparts in the next century, and their effectiveness not so apparent, because they were unable to win sensational victories with their small armies.

Why did other countries not follow England's example? For one thing, knights were still pre-eminent on the battlefield. So long as there was some lingering doubt whether archers could defeat knights, armoured cavalry continued to be the mainstay of the army. If a prince wanted to train his subjects to be archers, he had first to be sure that he could pay them well in time of war, and such a change was necessarily slow, since it remained to be seen whether they were suitable for this type of training. In England itself there were many expeditions between 1297 and 1333 before the English archers in the royal army outnumbered the Welsh.[34] The arming and training of a particular social group involved some risks, for it meant the rise of a new power which might take matters into its own hands, or limit the authority of the king and that of the other groups.

Such development was not always continuous where it was under the ruler's control; for example, after Bannockburn Edward I's son and successor Edward II tried another way, reverting to older techniques. In that battle the archers had been badly deployed from a tactical point of view, and as the result the king had made an unwise decision and concluded that a change was necessary. In the wars against the Scots it had been very difficult to force them to fight a pitched battle, because the Scottish warriors moved about on horseback and could easily get away. The English armoured cavalry were helped for the first time in these wars by *hobilars*, a kind of light cavalry who fought equally well on foot. Only once did the king have recourse to heavy foot-soldiers, and then unsuccessfully, against the Scottish pikemen. During

---

[32] Morris, *Welsh Wars*, p. 287. Morris, *Mounted Infantry*, p. 93.
[33] This is the explanation of Delbrück, III, p. 412.
[34] Morris, *Mounted Infantry*, p. 93.

the reign of Edward III mounted archers were used, who could move up quickly and then dismount before the battle.[35] These English bowmen showed during the Hundred Years War that they were the best foot-soldiers of the day, and contributed not only to the conquest of the Scots, but also scored resounding victories over French knights.

The foot-soldiers in Scotland

As in Wales, the population of Scotland was predominantly Celtic. There were strong Norse elements in the west; Lothian in the south-east came quickly under English influence, with the result that the Lowlands were anglicized while the Highlands remained Celtic. The kings of England tried to impose their rule on the Scottish nobles, and make them vassals of the crown, which they naturally resisted vigorously, and they even laid counter-claim to the northern counties of England.

The Scots, particularly the Highlanders, were barbaric fighters. Their invasion of England in 1138 was notorious for its acts of cruelty, and the English chroniclers were unanimous in their protests against the barbaric behaviour of the enemy. The Picts from Galloway were the most notorious of all, and were singled out as 'bestial people'.[36] The wild Highlanders and the men from Galloway murdered even women and children, or bound them and drove them into slavery.[37] They were mostly lightly armed soldiers, who wore short kilts and carried spear and shield or a broad sword.[38] Their ferocity showed itself very clearly in the battle of Northallerton (1138), when they successfully demanded the right to attack first. With the cry 'Albanach! Albanach!' they thrice stormed the 'iron wall' of the English battle order but were repulsed.[39]

At first no feudal system existed in Scotland, with the possible exception of the south, where English influence was strong. In the first half of the twelfth century King David was largely responsible for replacing the Celtic clan system by a feudal system in which the king would be the source of all landed property.[40] But the king of Scotland never had a powerful knightly army at his disposal, and in this respect was much weaker than the king of England. During the reign of Henry II, one of his armies captured the king of Scotland, William the Lion, and in the ensuing peace treaty at Falaise, William had to acknowledge the king of England as liege lord.[41] During the reign of Richard I the Scottish king bought himself free of this obligation, at the moment when Richard was setting out on a Crusade.[42] The good relations between these princes ended with Richard's death in 1199. King John forced his

---

[35] *Ibid.*, pp. 80–4, 87–8, 93–5. Oman, II, p. 119.
[36] Poole, pp. 270–1.
[37] *Ibid.*, p. 270.
[38] *Ibid.*, p. 272. Oman, I, p. 392.
[39] Oman, I, pp. 392–3. Beeler, *Warfare in England*, p. 91. D. Drummond, p. 61, writes that the Picts constituted no tactical units, and were not able to attack three times. But we have very good sources who attest the three assaults. For that reason we cannot accept the hypercritical attitudes of Drummond.
[40] Poole, p. 273. [See also J. Gillingham, 'Imagining the Barbarians'.]
[41] *Ibid.*, pp. 277–8.
[42] *Ibid.*, pp. 279–80.

adversary to conclude a humiliating peace in 1209.[43] William's successor, Alexander, continued the struggle, but without success, and in 1237 the kings of Scotland finally had to give up their claim to the northern counties of England.[44]

In 1296 Edward I made a successful invasion, and passed through the Highlands. At Scone he removed the sacred stone on which the kings of Scotland had been crowned for centuries, and sent it to Westminster, where it still remains. Scotland was annexed to England.[45]

To subdue Scotland was one thing, to keep it in subjection was quite another. As early as July 1297 the whole region rose under one knight, William Wallace, who defeated the weak English garrison on 11 September near Stirling Bridge.[46] Wallace had taken up his position on a steep wooded height, a couple of hundred yards behind a stream over which there was a narrow bridge. The English commander, John, earl of Warrenne, advanced over the bridge and marched upon the enemy, even though Sir Richard Lundy had advised him to cross the river at some shallow spot. When the English vanguard and part of the foot-soldiers had crossed the stream, Wallace suddenly launched a counterattack with the Scottish pikemen. One unit gained control of the bridge, another attacked the English vanguard, who were either trampled underfoot or flung into the river. It was a resounding victory for the Scots: after this they even made raids into Cumberland and Northumberland.[47]

In the following year Edward I came back from Flanders, and marched out against the rebels with a large army; he won a great victory at Falkirk on 22 July 1298. Once again Wallace had chosen a favourable site on a hilltop, with a wood close behind his army. His pikemen were drawn up in four *schiltrons*, circular formations which were supported by reserve armoured cavalry, while a swamp protected the front of his army and each flank was covered by archers, drawn up between the *schiltrons*.[48] Edward had split his army into three divisions, each consisting of thirty to thirty-five 'banners'. The two divisions which advanced on the flanks found that the swamp was uncrossable, and at once outflanked the Scottish position. They scattered the archers protecting the Scottish flanks, and the reserve as well. When the English cavalry charged the *schiltrons* the Scottish pikemen in their tightly packed formation offered very stiff resistance: the men in the front rank were kneeling, with the butt end of their pikes planted in the ground, while the next rows held their weapons above the heads of their comrades.[49] Many English riders lost their horses during the charge against the dense enemy mass. The attack was repulsed with heavy losses, and the nobles had to withdraw and regroup.

Then King Edward came on the scene with the third division of his army and realised what the situation demanded. At his command the cavalry made ready for the charge, but before he sent them into action he ordered a great band of English

[43] *Ibid.*, p. 282.
[44] *Ibid.*, p. 283.
[45] Lot, I, p. 321.
[46] *Ibid., loc. cit.*
[47] Oman, II, pp. 76–7.
[48] Oman, II, pp. 78–9. Lot, I, p. 323.
[49] Oman, II, p. 80.

and Welsh archers to advance. They began to shoot at very close range, and concentrated their arrows on certain points in the Scottish *schiltrons*; the pikemen did not dare undertake any counter-offensive because the English cavalry stood ready to charge, so they had to remain in their close ranks since the Scottish archers and armoured cavalrymen had been put to flight, and this exposed them to the extremely accurate flights of arrows of the English archers. When this softening-up phase had lasted long enough, Edward ordered his horsemen to charge. They penetrated into the Scottish formations at those points which had suffered most from the rain of arrows, and scattered them. The Scots had to leave nearly a third of their army behind on the battlefield, and the rest fled into the woods. But this costly defeat did not end the Scottish resistance to the king of England. Several campaigns followed: one in 1300, another from June 1301 to January 1302, a third in May 1303 and a fourth in 1304.[50]

In 1306 a new uprising broke out under Robert Bruce, who allowed himself to be crowned king of Scotland at Scone on 25 March. Bruce's weak fighting units were defeated in June 1306, but he escaped, and had some successes in 1307. Edward I died on 7 July 1307, and his son Edward II inherited the difficult task of conquering Scotland. Before he could put a strong force into the field, Bruce had almost completely cleared the English out of Scotland. By 1314 only the fortresses of Stirling, Dunbar and Berwick were holding out. Then Edward led his troops to the relief of the beleaguered castle of Stirling before the garrison were forced to surrender,[51] but Bruce commanded a powerful and battle-seasoned army which had full confidence in its leader. He chose to fight, in a carefully picked position that was very favourable to him. The position was so strong that the English vanguard after its arrival on 23 June made only one attack and withdrew immediately. But Stirling Castle was surrendered on 24 June, and this spurred Edward on to outflank the Scottish position during the night. In this advance the English formations crossed the Bannockburn and continued through the marshes along its banks. They were not yet fully deployed when the Scots advanced against them in the morning.

The English vanguard resolutely charged one of the Scottish *schiltrons* but was checked. On the English right flank the archers attacked the Scots. Bruce's cavalry mounted a quick assault against them and drove them back. A considerable part of the English cavalry could not deploy its ranks, and became involved in a bloody mêlée with the Scots, all the while having the Bannockburn and the marshes at its back. The English foot-soldiers, especially the archers, could do nothing effective, because they were drawn up behind the formations of knights. When Bruce ordered a *schiltron*, which he had been holding in reserve, to attack the flank of the English cavalry, panic broke out, resulting in 'the most lamentable defeat which an English army ever suffered'.[52]

But Bruce was aware that his victory was largely due to the defective leadership and tactics of king Edward. During the succeeding campaigns and raids which both

---

[50] Oman, II, pp. 82–3. Lot, I, pp. 323–5.
[51] Oman, II, p. 84.
[52] Oman, II, p. 98.

sides undertook against each other, he carefully avoided a pitched battle. He ordered his foot-soldiers to move on horseback during the march so that their mobility should make them more elusive. Although the Scots then had the initiative and dominated the English armies, Bruce did not exploit that superiority in a purely tactical way, but prudently took offensive action merely to carry out raids, and to surprise the enemy by ambushes and night attacks. In 1322 he scored yet another great victory at Byland, where he fell upon the English camp at daybreak, and surprised both the front and the flank. During the attack the English only managed to hold out long enough to allow the king to escape.[53]

During this period of Scottish military predominance the Liège canon Jean le Bel wrote a very good description of the Scots. They were stout and courageous warriors who had no fear of their English adversaries. They marched very quickly, he said, and could cover anything from twenty to thirty-two miles in a night. The Scottish army was mounted, with the exception of the *ribaudaille*, or poor men. The knights and squires had good horses, the bulk of the foot-soldiers only small hacks. The Scots had practically no baggage, which helped them greatly in their rapid marches through the mountains. They took neither bread nor wine, and were very abstemious, living mostly on half-roasted meat, which they ate without bread and washed down with the clear water of the streams. The meat was roasted in the animals' hides, so that they did not need to carry pots and pans or kettles. They found cattle in abundance in their enemies' land, and took the animals they needed. Each man carried a flat stone under his saddle, which was cast into the fire, then he sprinkled some meal on the hot stone and made a sort of cake which took the place of bread.[54] They were always ferocious and merciless towards their enemies, whom they preferred to kill rather than take prisoner.[55] During the campaign of 1327 they managed to surprise the English in a night attack.[56] But Scottish tactics could not stand up to the new English methods.

2. *The Foot-soldiers in the First Crusade*

At a time when no foot-soldiers in western Europe were attracting the attention of the chroniclers, they evolved in the First Crusade, and made progress in the Middle East. Their importance grew with their developing role as a support to the knights on the battlefield. A brief survey of the exploits of those foot-soldiers during this crusade will serve to clarify this point.

As contemporary chroniclers often stated, the foot-soldiers who accompanied Peter the Hermit and Walter the Penniless were virtually useless. Lacking discipline, able leaders, and suitable arms, this disorderly and reckless rabble was soon cut to ribbons by the mounted marksmen of the Moslems. But the foot-soldiers who

53 *Ibid.*, p. 100.
54 Jean le Bel, I, pp. 50–2.
55 *Ibid.*, I, p. 117.
56 *Ibid.*, p. 70.

accompanied the more important leaders soon showed that they were made of sterner stuff.

At first these men-at-arms performed a humble task. When the first great battle began at Dorylaeum in 1097, Bohemond ordered part of the foot-soldiers to pitch camp, while the knights went off to fight the enemy.[57] During this battle that unit did not manage to protect the camp satisfactorily. Enemy cavalrymen broke in and killed many half-armed men, as well as women and children.[58] Another unit of foot-soldiers, however, was drawn up behind the knights. When the knights were driven back, they rode over some of their foot-soldiers, but were then checked by the thick forest of lances of the remaining foot-soldiers, so that the flight of the knights was stopped, and they took cover behind the foot-soldiers.[59]

The foot-soldiers played only a small part in the siege of Antioch. While Bohemond and Robert II of Flanders had gone off foraging, the count of Toulouse was keeping watch over the camp with his troops. His knights had driven off an enemy unit which was making a sally, and the foot-soldiers moved up after them, then drew themselves up beside a bridge close to the city. The Moslems attacked this formation of foot-soldiers: they marched straight over the bridge, and outflanked the Provençal men-at-arms at a ford. At that moment the western knights were chasing an enemy horse, and trying to catch it. The foot-soldiers, who had left their banners behind during the approach march, thought that the knights were fleeing, and fled too in sudden panic. When the knights of the count of Toulouse came to the rescue and counter-attacked, the frightened foot-soldiers clung to the manes and tails of the horses, and to the weapons of the knights. This prevented the knights attacking, and they had to retreat, while the Moslems pursued them. They all fled towards the camp: the count of Toulouse lost at least fifteen knights and about twenty foot-soldiers.[60] This unfortunate incident was the reason why the foot-soldiers were not allowed to take part in the battle by the Lake of Antioch, 'because there were too many people who had no experience and were afraid'.[61] But while this battle was going on, the foot-soldiers fought very bravely against the garrison of Antioch, and successfully repulsed all sorties.[62]

In the crusaders' sortie from the beleaguered city of Antioch the foot-soldiers played a useful part in the fighting. Before the battle started, a council was held which decided the battle order in which the crusaders were to advance, 'who should go first and who should follow in the second line; where the pikemen or spearmen should be drawn up and where the bowmen should be placed; whether the knights or the foot-soldiers should attack, and who should remain in a defensive position'.[63] At first the foot-soldiers moved forward, then came the units of knights, who had to protect

---

[57] Anonymous, *Gesta Francorum*, p. 44. [Hill, pp. 18–19.]

[58] C.D.J. Brandt, *Kruisvaarders naar Jeruzalem*, Utrecht, 1950, p. 128. [J. France, *Victory in the East*, pp. 175–83.]

[59] Ralph of Caen, *Gesta Tancredi*, c. 22, p. 622 A.

[60] Raymond of Aguilers, c. 5, p. 244.

[61] *Ibid.*, p. 246.

[62] *Ibid.*, p. 247. Anonymous, *Gesta Francorum*, p. 86. [Hill, p. 70]

[63] Ralph of Caen, c. 83, p. 655 C.

the rear of the foot-soldiers. The units were to advance or halt at the command of the princes.[64] At first the foot-soldiers protected the knights in front, so that the rain of Moslem arrows should not hit the mailed cavalrymen and their horses, and at the right moment the knights overtook the foot-soldiers, who moved up behind the cavalry, then the foot-soldiers in turn could cover the rear of the formation of knights. When the Moslems had outflanked the left wing of the crusaders, they fell upon a unit of foot-soldiers at the rear. These immediately made a front in the new direction and bravely resisted the enemy attack.[65] They were then relieved by a newly formed group of knights, which was intended to assist the reserve corps and the foot-soldiers, and to throw back the outflanking enemy.[66] This new reserve drove off the Moslems.

In the battle of Ascalon in 1099 the archers and the rest of the foot-soldiers again advanced to the front at the beginning of the fighting, in order to let the formations of knights then come forward and pass them: the foot-soldiers then followed up the knights in order to kill or capture those of the enemy who had fallen or been ridden down.[67]

Poorer knights, who had no horse left, naturally fought by side with the foot-soldiers in these battles of the First Crusade, and helped to stiffen their morale, and it is plain that the foot-soldiers became increasingly important in the long campaign, with its many battles and sieges. The knights however remained the chief military power in the new kingdom, though foot-soldiers were regularly used. During the first battle of Ramla, on 7 September 1101, they were seriously tested.[68] During the second battle there, in 1102, the king suffered a defeat, which according to Fulcher was to be blamed on the fact that all the troops had not arrived, that the formations were not well ordered, and that the king had not waited for his foot-soldiers, and had attacked imprudently.[69] Contemporary eyewitnesses like Fulcher viewed the failure to use the foot-soldiers as a grave mistake. The battles of Jaffa in 1102 and Hazarth in 1125 showed how important they were:[70] in the battle of Merdj-Sefer in 1126 it was explicitly stated that knights and foot-soldiers co-operated and gave mutual support.[71] Foot-soldiers followed the knights into battle and killed those Moslems who fell from their saddles, and helped their own fallen knights to remount or carried them away if they were wounded. Some units even killed the Moslems' horses, so that their fallen enemies could be dispatched by their comrades who were following.[72]

These tactics were also used in the battle of Arsuf,[73] and in western Europe, but the First Crusade and the years immediately following give the earliest examples. It

---

64 Raymond of Aguilers, p. 259 E.
65 *Ibid.*, p. 260 G.
66 Anonymous, *Gesta Francorum*, c. 29, p. 154. [Hill, p. 169.]
67 *Ibid.*, c. 39, p. 212. [Hill, p. 96; France, *Victory in the East*, p. 364.]
68 Oman, I, p. 293.
69 Fulcher, p. 400 C D.
70 Oman, I, pp. 295 and 302. For Jaffa, see Fulcher, p. 405 A.
71 Fulcher, p. 477 G.
72 William of Tyre, p. 584.
73 Chapter IV, 'The battle of Arsuf'.

is generally agreed that the foot-soldiers played a more important part in the First Crusade and in the kingdom of Jerusalem than in the West. This was partly due to the shortage of horses among the knights. In the face of the fast mounted Moslem archers, the crusaders had to be more careful to protect the rear of their knightly formations with foot-soldiers in battle, and to cover the front till the moment when the armoured cavalry had come close up to attack the enemy with full force. After the First Crusade there were so few knights left in the kingdom that they had to make the greatest possible use of foot-soldiers. We have already seen that between 1102 and 1125 their strength fluctuated between 200 and 1,100 mailed horsemen,[74] who had to be reinforced with foot-soldiers, who consequently saw action frequently, and thus acquired battle experience and cohesion. In the three instances in which it is known, the numerical strength of the foot-soldiers amounted to 900, 2,000 and 3,000 men.[75] Strict discipline could be maintained in such small units, and the knights would not have taken these formations into battle if they had not been certain that the foot-soldiers were battle-seasoned. Although the foot-soldiers were more useful in the kingdom of Jerusalem than in western Europe at the beginning of the twelfth century, it was nevertheless an auxiliary arm which had to assist the knights. Better foot-soldiers were to appear in the West in the second half of the twelfth century, made up of mercenaries and of the communal armies of northern Italy.

3. *Mercenaries*

Although the feudal economy was largely agricultural in character, with little money circulating, feudal armies nevertheless included mercenaries at an early period. These mercenaries were important because they performed remarkable feats when there were as yet few good foot-soldiers in Europe. Little is known of the tactics of armoured cavalrymen who fought as mercenaries, and their tactics were probably much the same as those of the knights.[76]

---

[74] Cf. Lot, I, p. 135. Smail, *Crusading Warfare*, p. 119, writes: 'All their feats would have been possible at any time in history to a body of resolute men armed with bow and spear.' Resolute men also need battle experience, and the foot-soldiers of the First Crusade had fought for four years. After four years they were not 'temporary' soldiers and not 'amateurs' (Smail, p. 123).

[75] Lot, I, p. 135.

[76] H. Géraud, *Les routiers au XIIe siècle*. Id., *Mercadier. Les routiers au XIIIe siècle*. E. Boutaric, *Institutions militaires de la France avant les armées permanentes*, Paris, 1863, pp. 240–5. Köhler, III, 2, pp. 146–54. Delbrück, III, pp. 329–37. Oman, I, pp. 368–9. J.J. De Smet, *Notice sur Guillaume d'Ypres ou de Loo, et les compagnies franches du Brabant et de la Flandre au moyen âge*. Nouv. Mémoires ac.roy. Belg., 1842, xv. P. Henrard, 'Les mercenaires dits Brabançons au moyen âge', *Annales de l'Académie d'Archéologie de Belgique*, 22, 1866. A. Mens, *De 'Brabanciones' of bloeddorstige en plunderzieke avonturiers* (Brussels, 1946) [Miscellanea A. de Meyer, 1, Louvain]. J. Boussard, 'Les mercenaires au XIIe siècle. Henri II Plantagenet et les origines de l'armée de métier', *Bibl. Ec. Chartes*, 106, 1946. H. Grundmann, 'Rotten und Brabanzonen. Söldner-Heere im 12. Jahrhundert', *Deutsches Archiv für Geschichte des Mittelalters* 5: the best study on the subject. J.O. Prestwich, 'War and Finance in the Anglo-Norman State', *TRHS*, 5th ser., 4 (1954), pp. 19–43. C.W. Hollister, *Anglo-Saxon military Institutions*, pp. 9–24 (Oxford, 1962). *The Military Organization of Norman England* (Oxford, 1965), pp. 167–90. Beeler, *Warfare in England*, pp. 298–307. [M. Chibnall, 'Mercenaries and the *Familia Regis* under Henry I', *History*, lxii (1977), pp. 15–23.]

Mercenaries in Venice were mentioned as early as the tenth century.[77] In 991, Fulk Nerra, count of Anjou, employed such soldiers in his war against count Conan of Brittany,[78] and the earliest *chansons de geste* speak about them.[79] Pope Leo IX raised an army of mercenaries in Germany to fight against the Normans in southern Italy, and these hired fighters were depicted as adventurers, rogues and bandits.[80] The Norman knights in southern Italy were themselves mercenaries in the employment of local lords at first. It is known that countess Richildis of Hainault recruited mercenaries to carry on the war against count Robert the Frisian of Flanders after his victory at Cassel in 1071.[81] Other territorial princes also strengthened their knightly armies with such fighters, but they were apparently always very small bands. William the Conqueror, on the other hand, had many knights and many rapacious adventurers recruited in the neighbouring principalities of France, when he undertook the conquest of England in 1066. When Canute IV of Denmark and Robert the Frisian were preparing an invasion of England in 1085, William the Conqueror raised thousands of mercenaries, including archers, in France. The terms used, '*solidariis, pedonibus, et sagittariis multis millibus conductis*',[82] show clearly that they consisted of foot-soldiers, but another source speaks also of cavalry.[83]

The successors of William the Conqueror, William Rufus and Henry I recruited also mercenaries, mostly cavalry. Henry had many Bretons in his service.[84] The kings of England also paid money fiefs to the count of Flanders in 1101, 1110, 1163 and 1180 in order to raise a contingent of 500 to 1,000 Flemish knights.[85] These money fiefs had both military and political aims. The Flemish knights, and others thus recruited, may be considered as mercenaries. But in the examples given here the men were mercenaries only during a limited campaign, and were neither self-contained units nor professional hired soldiers as we meet them later.

This was perhaps the case of the soldiers mentioned in 1106: during the siege of Cologne by king Henry V, duke Henry of Limbourg sent 'a kind of men called *gelduni*' to the help of the beleaguered inhabitants. 'They were pugnacious, brave, experienced in battle'.[86] More information about the origin of these troops comes from Flanders in 1127. When the communal army of Ghent advanced on Bruges after the murder of Charles the Good, a crowd of people who displayed many of the characteristics of the later professional mercenaries flocked to it. From the neighbourhood of Ghent came bold freebooters; besides the archers and workmen came robbers, murderers, bandits and all kinds of people wanting to take advantage of the

77 Delbrück, III, p. 329.
78 *Ibid.*, pp. 329–30. Richer, II, pp. 282–3. Boussard, p. 192. Lot, I, p. 221. Boutaric, p. 240.
79 Lot, *loc. cit.*
80 Delbrück, III, pp. 330 and 335.
81 Gilbert of Mons, c. 10, p. 15.
82 1066: William of Poitiers, II, c. 2, p. 150. 1085 Florence of Worcester, *Chronicon ex Chronicis*, ed. B. Thorpe, 2 vols (London, 1848–9), II, p. 18. Henry of Huntingdon, p. 207.
83 *Anglo-Saxon Chronicle*, anno 1085.
84 Prestwich, *War and Finance*, pp. 26–32. Hollister, pp. 180–1.
85 Verbruggen, *Le problème des effectifs et de la tactique à la bataille de Bouvines*, pp. 185–6.
86 *Annales Hildesheimenses*, ed. G. Waitz, MGH, SS, 1878, anno 1106, p. 56.

opportunities afforded by a siege. But the men of Bruges refused to allow this motley rabble into their city.[87] Among Bertulf's partisans in the castle of Bruges was a mercenary (*coterellus*) called Benkin, a skilled archer whose arrows inflicted deadly wounds, and caused great damage among the armoured men.[88] Again, we are told that Count William Clito gathered knights and *coterelli*, who were the professional mercenaries of the day, at Ypres.[89]

In England the use of mercenaries was important in the wars of King Stephen against Empress Matilda. Stephen employed the first mercenary commander recorded in medieval warfare, the Flemish nobleman William of Ypres, son of Philip of Ypres and grandson of Robert the Frisian. William had assembled mercenaries to help in his struggle for the comital throne, and when Stephen became king of England in December 1135, William entered his service with a band of Flemish mercenaries. It is quite possible that at first they merely wanted to fight temporarily as mercenaries, but as the civil war in England dragged on, they really became professional. William had knights and foot-soldiers under his command, and acted as their leader and overlord.[90] His men were looters and wild ruffians who did not hesitate to desecrate cemeteries, rob churches, and carry off priests as prisoners.[91] They lived on their pay and their plunder. William also used Bretons.[92]

William became the king's principal adviser. He fought with Stephen in Normandy in 1137, but the Norman barons were not enthusiastic about working with Flemings.[93] In the following year he tried to restore the king's authority: at the battle of Lincoln in 1141 William and the count of Aumâle jointly commanded part of the royal army, and when it was beaten, William fled. 'He was a very able commander, but when he saw that he could no longer help the king, he postponed his help until a more propitious moment'.[94] Stephen was taken prisoner in the battle. William went to the queen in Kent and raised new troops, with whose help he fought on and turned the tide. After an important battle near Winchester, he and his Flemings captured Robert of Gloucester, the powerful half-brother of the empress, and Stephen was exchanged for this prisoner.[95] Stephen rewarded the commander of his troops with an annual income of £450 from the royal revenues in Kent. William's mercenaries were the strongest support Stephen had in the whole course of the war: although they included a sizeable contingent of foot-soldiers, these were in no way outstanding. When Henry

---

[87] Galbert, c. 33, p. 55.

[88] *Ibid.*, c. 36, p. 59.

[89] *Ibid.*, c. 95, p. 140.

[90] *Ibid.*, c. 49, p. 79, c. 79, p. 123. Gervase of Canterbury, *The Chronicle of the Reigns of Stephen, Henry II and Richard I*, ed. W. Stubbs, RS, 2 vols, London 1879–80, I, p. 105. William of Malmesbury, *De gestis regum Anglorum, libri V: Historiae novellae libri III*, ed. W. Stubbs, RS, 2 vols, London 1887–89, I, p. 540.

[91] William of Malmesbury, *loc. cit.*

[92] *Ibid.*, p. 561.

[93] Poole, *From Domesday Book to Magna Carta*, p. 135. K. Norgate, 'William of Ypres', in *The Dictionary of National Biography*, 21, London 1937–38, p. 358. Beeler, *Warfare in England*, pp. 300–1.

[94] Henry of Huntingdon, pp. 273–4.

[95] Poole, pp. 143–5. Beeler, pp. 128–9.

II became king in 1154 he banished William's troops, but William was allowed to remain for a time in England, and drew the income of his lands in Kent until 1157.[96]

On the continent Henry II sometimes preferred a mercenary army to the usual knightly one, and he replaced then the military service owed by the knights by a scutage levied on each fief. The revenue from this and the ample royal exchequer enabled him to recruit mercenaries regularly, and to support them through a long campaign. The king was able to keep the hired knights under arms for an indefinite length of time, and at the same time develop his own foot-soldiers, who consisted chiefly of professional mercenaries. With these troops he could carry on extensive campaigns in his great Angevin realm and protect it effectively as long as he had the means to do so.

Henry II and his son Richard, at the head of their mercenaries, put down the rebellious lords of Aquitaine: they captured their strongholds and repulsed their attack in the open field with great success.[97] Henry II had a corps of foot-soldiers who received regular pay of a penny a day,[98] which was doubled under Richard, and he standardized the arms of his troops.[99] The foot-soldiers fought with sufficient cohesion to deal effectively with enemy knights on the battlefield, but they were of greater importance in besieging fortresses, especially at that time, when few battles were fought. The king had enough money to keep these men under arms for a long time, and thus force the enemy strongholds to surrender.

In 1159 Henry made an expedition to Toulouse against count Raimond de St-Gilles. He considered the great distance and difficulties of the expedition, and did not want to call up the rural knights, peasants and countrymen, but exacted sixty shillings of Angevin money for each knightly fief in Normandy, and two marks in England. This levy brought in the considerable sum of £8,000, which enabled him to raise a strong mercenary army,[100] whose strength however is not known. The chief barons of England, Normandy, Anjou, Aquitaine, and Gascony, and the king of Scotland marched with it. During the campaign the king forbade anything to be taken forcibly from the local inhabitants: every soldier had to buy what he needed honestly,[101] for Henry certainly knew that in this matter the mercenaries were not to be trusted. His army advanced triumphantly through Aquitaine, and had some success in Quercy, but the fortress of Toulouse put up a stiff resistance. King Louis VII had hastened to the help of the count of St-Gilles. Henry proved unsuccessful because he had stretched his supply lines too far: his nearest base was in fact at Cahors, more than 100 km from Toulouse, so that supply and maintenance were extremely difficult.[102]

Henry recruited foot-soldiers for his expedition to Wales in 1165. Each soldier

---

96 Poole, pp. 321–2 and 140. Norgate, p. 358. Gervase of Canterbury, p. 161. Grundmann, p. 440.
97 Boussard, 'Les mercenaires au XIIe siècle', p. 193.
98 Ibid., loc. cit.
99 Ibid., loc. cit. Poole, p. 372.
100 Boussard, p. 197.
101 Grundmann, p. 442.
102 Boussard, pp. 198–9. Poole, p. 326.

received fifteen shillings and threepence, which was six months' pay, and arms and clothing – probably uniforms – from the king. Three hundred targes or great shields were also provided,[103] which suggests that the contingent was not large, though it included Flemish mercenaries.[104] Though the operation was unsuccessful, Henry also recruited mercenaries from Wales from then onwards,[105] and he used whole squads of Brabançons when his sons rebelled in 1173, which is the first time Brabançons are explicitly mentioned in English sources.

Similar mercenaries had been used some years before in Italy by Emperor Frederick Barbarossa, when he marched over the Alps for the third time to settle the papal question by force of arms in October 1166. He had little support from the German princes, who were fighting against Henry the Lion. Just as king Stephen had done in England, he resorted to mercenaries, and recruited a body of Brabançons, estimates of whose strength vary greatly. The *Chronica regia Coloniensis*, which was unusually well informed because of the participation of Rainald von Dassel, archbishop of Cologne, and some Cologne knights,[106] gives 500 men; Otto of St Blasien gives 800;[107] Vincent of Prague, who took part in the expedition, says 1,500, and the latter and Rainald von Dassel called them men of Brabant,[108] as did Otto Morena.[109] The *Annales* of Magdeburg speak of Flemings and Brabançons.[110] In the *Chronica regia Coloniensis*, which made use of a letter from Rainald von Dassel, and in Otto of St Blasien's chronicle, they were simply called *sergeants*, but in the sense of mercenaries.[111]

In a battle near Tusculum on 29 May 1167 a little band of Brabançon mercenaries distinguished itself by its brave conduct. Archbishop Rainald, with over 100 knights from Cologne, was surrounded in Tusculum. Frederick Barbarossa was besieging Ancona at the time, and sent archbishop Christian of Mainz with knights and a detachment of Brabançons to his help. After a long and exhausting march they reached Tusculum on 29 May at about 3 p.m., and were at once attacked by the enemy, who were much greater in number, and drove off the Brabançons and some of the knights. Then Rainald made a sortie with the Cologne knights, and turned the tide. The Brabançons and the knights of the archbishop of Mainz again advanced, and they all pursued the fleeing enemy up to the very gates of Rome.[112] Eyewitnesses told the Italian chronicler Otto Morena that the Brabançons fought especially bravely and inflicted the greatest losses on the Roman forces.[113] Otto of St Blasien says they were skilful fighters.[114] According to Rainald von Dassel all the booty that was

---

[103] Boussard, pp. 199–200.
[104] Poole, p. 293.
[105] Boussard, pp. 200–1.
[106] Chronica regia Coloniensis, p. 117.
[107] Otto of St Blasien, *Chronica*, ed. A. Hofmeister, MGH, SS, 1912, p. 23.
[108] MGH, SS, XVII, p. 683. Grundmann, pp. 442–3.
[109] Grundmann, *loc. cit.*
[110] *Ibid.*, p. 442, n. 3. MGH, SS, XVI, p. 192.
[111] *Chronica regia Coloniensis*, p. 117. Otto of St Blasien, *Chronica*, p. 23.
[112] *Chronica regia Coloniensis, loc. cit.* Grundmann, p. 443.
[113] Grundmann, *loc. cit.*

collected was given to the Brabançons and the servants, while the knights contented themselves with the honour of victory.[115]

After this, the Brabançons are not mentioned again. It is possible that in August 1167 the little band was struck by plague, which practically decimated the Imperial army. But ten years later a detachment of Brabançons was defeated at Malemort in Limousin: the leader of this unit was a former clerk, William, who was a native of the Cambrai region and had taken part in the capture of Rome with these same mercenaries under Frederick Barbarossa in July 1167.[116] There is a possibility that the Brabançons had established themselves here in France.

The Brabançons had apparently been guilty of all sorts of debauchery on their way to join Frederick's army in 1166. In the summer of that year the abbot of Cluny sent two letters to king Louis VII asking for help. Besides internal strife, he wrote, an even greater evil had broken out. Germans, who were called *Brabantiones*, roamed through the region like wild bloodthirsty animals so that no one could feel safe; they were to be dreaded like the plague.[117] In his second letter he wrote: 'A very great plague is breaking out here. Men more like beasts than human beings, small in number – about 400 of them – but terrifying in their savagery, came not long ago out of the Empire into our land. No one offered resistance. They spared no one, and respected neither sex, age, nor social status, but attacked churches, fortresses and villages. What would a great number do, when so small a band had done so much damage?'[118]

Louis then advanced against the count of Chalon. The latter was accused of having used freebooters, popularly called Brabançons, against Cluny. These terrible brigands had removed the vestments of the abbey clergy and slaughtered hundreds of burghers like cattle. The news of this crime spread far and wide, and impelled Louis to undertake an expedition.[119] The Brabançons whom he found during the expedition were hanged: one of them tried to ransom himself with an enormous sum of money, but he was also executed.[120]

These new mercenaries were soon notorious. After one attack in Champagne, an abbot asserted that he had got into debt in order to buy back the possessions of his monastery after it had been partly occupied by the mercenaries. In 1171 Pope Alexander III ordered an enquiry to be made into this allegation.[121] The count of Champagne was excommunicated by the Church because he had let his vassals and *coterelli* despoil the church of Rheims. The count however appealed to the Pope and said that the raid had taken place without his knowledge or consent. The Pope then

114 *Chronica*, p. 23.
115 Grundmann, *loc. cit.*
116 *Ibid.*, pp. 443–4. Godfrey of Bruil, *Chronica*, RHF, XII, p. 446.
117 RHF, XVI, p. 130. Grundmann, p. 445.
118 RHF, XVI, p. 130. Grundmann, p. 446.
119 Suger, *Historia gloriosi regis Ludovici*, ed. A. Molinier, Coll. Picard, Paris, 1887, c. 23, pp. 172–3.
120 *Ibid.*, p. 174.
121 Grundmann, p. 448.

wrote to the king of France, asking him to settle this dispute peacefully; he no longer attributed the plundering to mercenaries.[122]

Plundering mercenaries certainly harassed eastern France in those years, for on 14 February 1171 Frederick Barbarossa and Louis VII met for a discussion at the frontier of the Empire between Toul and Vaucouleurs. It was agreed that the malefactors called *Brabantiones* or *coterelli*, who fought on horseback and on foot, should no longer be employed or tolerated in the area bounded by the Rhine, the Alps, and Paris. Their vassals also were not to support them or permit them to stay, unless the mercenaries had married locally and settled there permanently. Anyone violating this agreement was to be excommunicated, and was to make good the damage. They were to be forcibly restrained by other lords and prelates, or else these latter in their turn would be liable to punishment. Should the transgressor be too powerful, the emperor and the king themselves were to come out against him.[123] This pact left the emperor free to use mercenaries east of the Rhine and beyond the Alps. The savage bands were feared in France above all, and Louis hoped to keep them out of his territory between Paris and the border of the Empire. Then the Brabançons suddenly turned up in the west.

In 1173 Henry II of England had to quell the rebellion of his sons. They had the support of the king of France, the count of Flanders, and the majority of the Anglo-Norman barons. Philip of Alsace conquered Aumale and Neuchâtel-en-Bray with the Flemish army, Louis besieged Verneuil, and the king of Scotland invaded England. The count of Flanders also fitted out a fleet for the invasion of England.[124] The situation seemed hopeless for Henry. But he drew heavily on his exchequer and raised a great mercenary army. Companies of Brabançons were assembled, and formed an army of 10,000.[125] The strength is clearly exaggerated, but it is quite possible that Henry raised several thousand such men in the south of France, where it was said that he offered the royal sword which he had worn at his coronation to the mercenaries as security.[126] These troops were concentrated at Conches, in Normandy. Henry struck at once: he marched to Verneuil, where the king of France at once ordered the signal to retreat. Meanwhile the Flemings had already withdrawn after the death of Matthew of Boulogne, brother of Philip of Alsace. Then Henry sent his Brabançons from Rouen into Brittany, because 'he trusted these troops more than the others'. They advanced with unusual speed, and covered the 132 miles between Rouen and St James-de-Beuvron in under seven days.[127] Then the king went on with them to Anjou, took Vendôme, and returned to Normandy.

In England, Robert, earl of Leicester, was defeated and captured with his Flemish

---

[122] *Ibid.*, pp. 448–9.

[123] *Ibid.*, pp. 449–50.

[124] *Ibid.*, p. 452. Poole, pp. 334–5. Boussard, pp. 204 ff.

[125] *Gesta regis Henrici II Benedicti Abbatis*, ed. W. Stubbs, RS, 2 vols, 1867, I, p. 51. Roger of Hoveden, *Chronica*, ed. W. Stubbs, RS, 4 vols, London 1868–71, II, p. 47, gives 20,000. Grundmann, p. 452.

[126] *Ibid.*, pp. 452–3.

[127] *Gesta regis Henrici II*, I, p. 56. Boussard, p. 206.

mercenaries at Fornham. Earl Hugh Bigod had to promise to send the rest of the Flemish soldiers back to their country.[128]

In 1174 Henry set out for England with Brabançons: he did not however have to fight, since the king of Scotland, who had recruited Flemish mercenaries, was taken prisoner. The count of Flanders, who had already sent an advance guard to England, no longer dared set out with the fleet. Exactly a month after his arrival in England Henry returned to the continent, with a contingent of 1,000 men from Wales as well as his Brabançons. He relieved Rouen, then under siege by the king of France and the count of Flanders, and after his arrival there on 11 August Brabançons are not mentioned again in his army.[129]

They next reappeared in the army of Frederick Barbarossa on his fourth Italian expedition. They apparently fought under the command of the archbishop of Mainz, who conquered Bologna with them and kept them with him in Italy to the end of 1175.[130]

About Eastertide, 1176, the count of Angoulême invaded Poitou with a band of Brabançons. The count of Poitou (later Richard I) was with his father in England at the time, but the bishop of Poitiers and the leader of Richard's knights defeated the mercenaries at Barbezieux, near Angoulême. When Richard returned to his county, he attacked the count of Angoulême with a powerful army of knights, for he paid them well and the noblemen flocked to him. He defeated his adversary's mercenaries and took the count prisoner.[131]

Mercenaries continued to make trouble in the area. On Palm Sunday, 1177, the abbot of St-Martial at Limoges summoned the people to arms against them. The local nobles advanced with the bishop and the count of Limoges against the band, and on 21 April the decisive battle was fought between Brive and Malemort. After five hours of fighting the Brabançons left 2,000 dead, both men and women, and the rest fled. The leader, William of Cambrai, who had laid waste Rome with these very Brabançons, fell in the battle.[132]

After the defeat at Malemort the mercenaries did not disappear, but continued to fight under a new leader, Lobar or Lupacius, also called Lupatus. His successor was Mercadier, who later became famous and dreaded as the faithful follower of Richard I. In the winter of 1176–77 Basques also appeared as mercenaries in southern France. Some years later, Godfrey of Breuil, whose chronicle is the best source for this subject, listed the mercenaries in Aquitaine as follows: *Brabançons, Hannuyers, Asperes, Pailler, Navar, Turlannales, Roma, Cotarel, Catalans, Aragones.*[133] Meanwhile the three kings of the west kept the bands out of their lands. Louis did this through active intervention and by the treaty of 1171; Henry II prevented them from

128 Boussard, pp. 208–9. Poole, pp. 335–6.
129 *Gesta regis Henrici II*, I, p. 74. Roger of Hoveden, II, p. 65. Grundmann, p. 454. Boussard, *loc. cit.*
130 Grundmann, pp. 455–7.
131 *Ibid.*, pp. 457–8.
132 Godfrey of Bruil, RHF, XII, p. 446. Grundmann, pp. 458–9.
133 Godfrey of Bruil, pp. 446–7 (*excerpta*, ed. O. Holder-Egger, 1882, MGH, SS, XXVI, c.73, p. 203). Grundmann, p. 460.

gaining a foothold in his domains, but used them during the uprising in 1173–74; Barbarossa employed them in Italy but kept them out of Germany, where they seem to have appeared only once, in 1179.

At the third Lateran Council, held in 1179, the use of *Brabantiones, Aragonenses, Navarii, Bascoli, Coterelli* and *Triaverdini*, was forbidden, since these infamous bands had no respect for churches or monasteries, widows or orphans, old men or children, age or sex. Like the heathen they smashed and laid waste everything.[134] The Church always considered war for the sake of looting a sin,[135] but it was easier to proscribe these troops and threaten transgressors with excommunication than to enforce the prohibition.

This interdict of the council was speedily defied by the archbishop of Cologne, Philip von Heinsberg, who then employed professional mercenaries for the first time in Germany. He marched on the fortress of Haldensleben, the strongest bastion of Henry the Lion, duke of Saxony. It was being besieged at the time by the bishop of Halberstadt. Philip von Heinsberg had only a few knights, but a good many foot-soldiers. The strength of these mercenaries was estimated at 4,000 men. They devastated Saxony with unprecedented brutality: not only were the fortresses and cities destroyed and burned, but these ferocious savages also set fire to churches and monasteries. Nuns were violated and removed by force.[136] The archbishop's 'companies' put the populace in fear for their lives. At Steterburg near Wolfenbüttel the nuns were removed to safer places, even though the mercenaries did not actually appear in the region.[137]

On 28 April 1181 the young count of Bar appeared before Henry II and asked for support for an expedition to Spain. The Pope had imposed this campaign on him, and had allegedly raised a mercenary army of 20,000 men, who were to march under the Count's leadership. Henry II had just taken a vow to set out on a Crusade and wanted to use the mercenaries for that. The count of Bar had first to consult his *Brabanciones* before he could comply with this proposal. But Henry II did not go on the Crusade, and the mercenaries stayed in southern France.[138]

In the autumn of 1181 the young king Philip Augustus of France was the next to employ mercenaries. He sent them into the domain of the count of Sancerre, where they seized great booty. In 1184 he used such troops again against Philip of Alsace.[139]

In 1183 the mercenary bands were in action again in the fighting between the sons of Henry II. The young Henry and Geoffrey attacked their brother Richard, who was supported by his father. Geoffrey allowed his hirelings to plunder Richard's domain and that of his father. 'The perfidious band of Brabançons', who were excommunicated by the Church, now looted the lands of the king who in 1173 'trusted them

134 Mansi, *op. cit.*, XXII, p. 232, c. 37. Grundmann, pp. 436–7.
135 Grundmann, p. 438.
136 'Annales S. Petri Erphesfurtenses maiores', ed. O. Holder-Egger, in *Monumenta Erphesfurtensia*, MGH, SS in usum scholarum, anno 1179, p. 63.
137 Grundmann, p. 422.
138 *Ibid.*, p. 463.
139 *Ibid.*, pp. 464–5.

more than his other troops'.[140] Prince Henry paid his Brabançons very punctually for fear they might desert to his father for better pay. As soon as he fell into financial difficulties he exacted huge sums from the burghers of his cities, and took the treasures of St Martial at Limoges, and of other churches and monasteries round about at a cheap price to pay his men. The count of Turenne brought a band of Basques from Gascony as reinforcement, recruited by Sancho of Savagnac and Curban or Curbaran. Philip Augustus sent a contingent of mixed origins, called *Palearii* or *Pailler*. All these made up a evil crew of mercenaries.[141]

But young Henry died suddenly on 11 June 1183. The rebellion against Henry collapsed: the mercenaries no longer had anything to do and plundered south-western France savagely. They were soon employed again in the wars between Richard I and Philip Augustus. Richard raised a standing army for the defence of his kingdom and for the protracted wars he had to fight. His knights were usually paid a shilling a day. In Wales he recruited foot-soldiers who were paid twopence a day, and cavalry who got fourpence a day if they had a horse, or sixpence if they had two.[142] He took on Genoese crossbowmen as mercenaries, and used them in Normandy about 1180, and after his crusade he also used Saracens in this duchy: both nationalities were chosen for their professional skill.[143] The greater part of the mercenaries were *Brabantiones*, who were recruited by the famous leader Mercadier, and came from all parts of western Europe.

Mercadier, a Provençal like his predecessor Lupacius, appeared in the autumn of 1183 as a mercenary leader in southern France. In October 1183 he besieged Pompadour and laid waste the surrounding country. Constant de Born, brother of the poet Bertrand de Born, took part in these operations.[144] Mercadier, however, retreated with his troops as soon as he heard that the brotherhood from Auvergne planned to attack him. In 1184 he was in the service of Richard, then duke of Aquitaine. In that year, 'in the shadow of the duke' he attacked and laid waste the land of the count Adhémar of Limoges.[145] Four years later Richard fought with Brabançons against the count of Toulouse and took seventeen castles in the neighbourhood of Toulouse. Mercadier probably took charge of these castles for the king: it appears from a document that he faithfully defended them and was in command of Richard's army.[146] After that he set out with the king on the Third Crusade, but Richard sent him back when Philip Augustus sailed from Acre for France. It was certainly Mercadier's task to defend the king's lands with his mercenaries. From May 1194 to Richard's death nearly five years later Mercadier was more than ever the king's right hand. Together they gained a great victory at Fréteval in 1194, and early in the following year Mercadier took Issoudun and placed a garrison in the

140 *Gesta regis Henrici II*, I, pp. 292, 295, 297 and p. 56.
141 Grundmann, pp. 466–8.
142 Poole, p. 372.
143 *Ibid., loc. cit.*
144 Godfrey of Bruil, RHF, XVIII, p. 220. Grundmann, p. 472.
145 Godfrey of Bruil, p. 223. Grundmann, p. 473.
146 Grundmann, p. 474.

fortress.[147] He also fought in Brittany, and carried out a raid on Abbeville, where he robbed the French merchants and took much booty.[148] In 1197 he ambushed the martial bishop of Beauvais and took him prisoner.[149] In the following year Richard and Mercadier cut off the retreat of the French at Vernon, and drove the defeated troops into the Epte. After that they took the castle at Courcelles, and intercepted the army of Philip Augustus, who had hastened to help. They won another victory and chased the fleeing troops to the castle of Gisors. There was so great a crush before the castle gate that Philip Augustus fell into the moat when the bridge collapsed under his knights.[150] When Richard was mortally wounded on 26 March 1199 during the siege of the castle at Chalus, belonging to count Adhémar of Limoges, Mercadier's physician cared for him. Mercadier then stormed the castle and avenged the death of his master.[151] While he was in the service of John he punished the renegade city of Angers, and was afterwards killed at Bordeaux on 10 April 1200.[152]

Just as William of Ypres did for Stephen, so Mercadier fought constantly for Richard, yet he was never ennobled, but remained a commoner, who held and kept the full confidence of his master. In the great castle of Château-Gaillard, designed by Richard himself, one of the bridges was named after Mercadier.[153]

John was obliged to use mercenaries, since he could not count on the help of the English nobility. As commanders of his mercenaries in south-western France there was a Gascon, Arnold, and a Provençal, Lupescair. Another commander, Martin Algais, was at that time seneschal of Gascony and Périgord. Later he fought in the crusading army against the Albigensians, entered the service of the count of Toulouse, but was taken prisoner by Simon de Montfort in 1212 and hanged.[154] When John left Normandy, they went off to England, where they were greatly hated for their rapacity. *Magna Carta* in 1215 forced the king to send away 'all foreign knights and crossbowmen and mercenaries, who had crossed over with their arms and horses to harm the land', and to banish their leaders.[155] Hugues de Boves, who in the year before had recruited mercenaries before the battle of Bouvines and had fled precipitately there, was then ordered to send the foreign troops out of Dover and back to the continent.[156]

But the struggle against the barons broke out afresh, and John had mercenaries recruited 'in the regions of Louvain, Brabant, and Flanders', and marched against his enemies with these robbers, plunderers and fire-raisers.[157] The mercenary leader

---

[147] Rigord, *Gesta Philippi Augusti*, ed. H.F. Delaborde, SHF, I, Paris, 1882, c. 104, p. 132. Grundmann, p. 475.

[148] Grundmann, *loc. cit.*

[149] *Ibid., loc. cit.* Rigord, *Gesta Philippi Augusti*, c. 123, pp. 142–3.

[150] Poole, p. 377.

[151] Grundmann, pp. 475–6.

[152] *Ibid.*, p. 476.

[153] William the Breton, *Chronicon*, c. 111, p. 208 and n. 4.

[154] Grundmann, pp. 476–7. Belperron, *op. cit.*, pp. 232, 240.

[155] Oman, I, p. 370. Poole, pp. 471 and 477.

[156] Poole, *loc. cit.*

[157] Grundmann, p. 481, n. 3.

Gerard d'Athée remained in England. Other leaders were active under Henry III, and Falkes de Bréauté, the famous captain of the crossbowmen, was honourably mentioned with his troops at the second battle of Lincoln in 1217.[158] When he was banished in 1225, people in England felt that he had served the king and his father well for many years, and braved innumerable dangers, and he was therefore exiled rather than executed.[159] But the great days of mercenaries in the service of the English kings were over, and king Edward used troops from his own lands, and later archers from Wales.

In France young Philip Augustus quickly realised what Suger had already observed during the struggle of Louis VI against William Rufus, namely that the English kings, because of their great revenue, could pay or hire many more knights than the French king.[160] Philip's biographer, Rigord, relates that the king imposed heavy taxes on the clergy, and collected great treasure in various places, while he lived very frugally himself. Philip declared that his predecessors had been poor, and had therefore not been able to recruit paid knights in time of need, so that the kingdom had shrunk through war. He gathered treasure in order to be able to defend his land readily, and perhaps to enlarge it as well, and not primarily, as Rigord says, to retake the Holy Land.[161] Some of the French reproached the king with being over-ambitious and grasping.[162]

At first Philip Augustus only took on bands of mercenaries for a particular campaign, as in 1181 against the count of Sancerre, and in 1184 against Philip of Alsace. In 1187 while he was at Châteauroux he sent away his mercenaries on a pious pretext. The following year he sent a band of Germans whom he no longer needed to Bourges to be paid there, but when they got there he had them disarmed, their horses and money were taken away from them, and they were driven out.[163]

Later, when his revenues increased considerably, (by the end of his reign they were valued at about 1,200 pounds *parisis* a day, but this sum is probably exaggerated),[164] in the decisive struggle with Richard I, Philip also had a mercenary leader, Cadoc, who remained permanently in the royal service and became as famous as Mercadier.[165] He defended the castle of Gaillon against Richard in 1196, with 300 foot-soldiers.[166] His men were the first to penetrate the strong castle of Château-Gaillard, which Richard had built outside Les Andelys near Rouen, and which Philip took in 1204 after a six months' siege.[167] After that Cadoc took the city of Angers.[168] He enjoyed the favour of king Philip, who entrusted the conquered city of Les

---

158 Poole, *loc. cit.* Oman, *loc. cit.*
159 Grundmann, p. 477 and n. 3.
160 Suger, *Vita Ludovici grossi regis*, Paris, 1929, c. 1, p. 8. [*The Deeds of Louis the Fat*, ed. & tr. R. Casimano and J. Moorhead, Washington, 1992, p. 26.]
161 Rigord, *Gesta Philippi Augusti*, c. 99, p. 129.
162 *Ibid., loc. cit.*
163 Grundmann, pp. 473, 478–9.
164 Bloch, *Les classes et le gouvernement des hommes*, p. 215 and n. 1.
165 Anonyme de Béthune, *Chronique*, p. 758F.
166 Grundmann, p. 479.
167 William the Breton, *Chronicon*, cc. 122–9, pp. 213–19. Boutaric, p. 242. Lot, I, pp. 220–1.
168 William the Breton, *Chronicon*, c. 133, p. 222. Boutaric, *loc. cit.* Grundmann, p. 480.

Andelys to him in 1204. As a reward for his services, he was made burgrave of Gaillon and bailiff of Pont-Audemer.[169] About 1210 he was sent to Auvergne, to fight its count, who had attacked the clergy and was plundering the churches.[170] In 1213 he took part in the invasion of Flanders. Six years later, on account of all sorts of misdeeds, Cadoc was thrown into prison and not released until 1227. He lost everything he had received from Philip Augustus. In an expedition of Louis VIII against Avignon he reappeared as a leader, but this time had no mercenary band with him.[171] The upkeep of Cadoc and his men was very expensive, although there were not many of them: William the Breton asserts, with great exaggeration, that Cadoc had £1,000 per day for himself and his band. Certainly on one occasion the huge sum of £4,400 was paid out to him.[172] Under the successors of Philip Augustus these mercenaries disappeared, as they did in England and Germany.

In the south of France they were regularly employed by the rulers, although popes vainly intervened to put an end to this practice. This was naturally impossible in the region where so many mercenaries had taken refuge. Pope Celestinus III wrote about this to the archbishop of Arles: 'I know that your province has fallen prey to the Aragonese, *Brabanciones*, and other foreigners. Strike back at them, and do not fail to punish those who hire these bandits and take them into their castles and cities'.[173] Innocent III upbraided the archbishop of Bordeaux for letting mercenary leaders come into his lands and plunder, but in his reply the archbishop contended that he had permission to do so from the pope.[174] In 1204 the archbishop of Narbonne was accused of having let a leader and his band store away their treasure, stolen from churches and monasteries.[175] Innocent III excommunicated Raymond VI of Toulouse partly for having kept mercenaries and using them in his wars. But he used them again during the Crusade against the Albigensians in considerable numbers, and they played an important part in his counter-offensive against Simon de Montfort,[176] who also had to use mercenaries because he had too few troops of his own. At one time when Simon was in financial difficulties, he wrote to Innocent III: 'The great lords have all deserted me, leaving me alone with very few knights . . . now I shall have to take on mercenaries, who will only stay with me for a higher price than in other wars: I can scarcely keep them unless I pay them double.'[177] The burghers of Toulouse indignantly told the king of Aragon: 'We cannot keep silence about the unjust severity with which the clergy persecute us. We are detested and excommunicated for the bands and cavalry by whom our lives are defended, while they subvert these hirelings for a certain price. These terrible men shed our blood, but their sins are forgiven them.'[178]

---

[169] Boutaric, p. 242. Grundmann, pp. 479–80.
[170] William the Breton, *Chronicon*, c. 156, p. 235, n. 4.
[171] Grundmann, *loc. cit.*
[172] Boutaric, p. 243. Lot, I, p. 221, n. 1. Grundmann, p. 479 and n. 4.
[173] Belperron, p. 24.
[174] Grundmann, p. 439.
[175] *Ibid.*, p. 439.
[176] Belperron, pp. 135–6, 319, 332.
[177] *Ibid.*, pp. 190–1, 321 and 24, n. 2. Grundmann, p. 439.
[178] Grundmann, p. 440.

Raymond VI raised his *coterelli* in Navarre and Catalonia.[179] When the treaty of Paris put an end to the long war in 1229, it fell to his son Raymond VII to drive the mercenaries out of the land, and to punish where it was necessary. They disappeared in France during the rest of the thirteenth century, and reappeared in the Hundred Years War.

Although information about the mercenaries is incomplete, it is plain that their leaders were real *condottieri*.[180] Men like Mercadier, Sancho of Savagnac, and Curbaran, already had a band under their command when they took service with the ruler. The leaders naturally sought the best opportunities for gaining money and booty. For that reason they moved about from one theatre of war to another: in 1167 in Italy, in 1173 and 1174 in the Angevin kingdom with Henry II, then straight back to Italy with Frederick Barbarossa in 1174 to 1175. After that they returned to southern France to take service with princes or live on plunder.

These marauders and adventurers could ensure their existence only by warfare. As soon as peace was signed, there was nothing left for them to do, and they pined for the good old days when they used to tread conquered lands as lords and masters, and live a gay life at the expense of the inhabitants. They settled chiefly where they could go on robbing and plundering by seizing a castle, which could serve as a base for extortions and plundering forays. In a society bitterly opposed to them, they had to keep strict discipline in their bands so that they could face their adversaries. The terrible things they had done together, and fear of frightful punishment, increased the solidarity which campaigns and battles had already fostered in them. The men looked up to their leaders, as is evident from the fame of William of Cambrai and his Brabançons, who took Rome, and lived and fought together for ten years.

The bands were highly organized, and were sharply differentiated by leadership and possibly also origin. The best informed chronicler, Godfrey of Bruil, described separately the bands of William of Cambrai, Curbaran, Sancho de Savagnac, and the Palearii.[181] The brotherhood of the White Hood, founded by Durand, defeated first the *Palearii* and then Curbaran. The brotherhood from Auvergne crushed a band of Brabançons.[182] In order of nationality there appeared first Brabançons, then Aragonese, Basques, Navarrese, Catalonians, and Germans, Flemings and Hainaulters. All these professional mercenaries were commonly described as *coterelli*. This is the oldest term, and is obviously derived from the French *cote*. Later the name *rotten* appeared, likewise also found first in Old French sources such as the work of the poet Chrétien de Troyes. The *rotten* were bands or detachments, and this name was first used in connection with events in 1179 in Germany. The *Annales Pegavienses* in which these happenings were recorded at the latest two years afterwards, called the foot-soldiers of the archibishop of Cologne *roten*.[183] Shortly afterwards

---

179 Belperron, p. 332.
180 Grundmann's study shows very well that the old ideas about the mercenaries of the twelfth and thirteenth centuries have to be corrected.
181 RHF, XVIII, p. 215. Grundmann, p. 468.
182 Grundmann, pp. 469–70.
183 MGH, SS XVI, p. 262. Grundmann, p. 422

the word *ruta* occurs in Anglo-Norman sources, such as the work of Walter Map, who wrote the first book of his *De nugis curialium* about 1180. At the same time he gives a most detailed description of the bands which Henry II took such pains to keep out of his kingdom. 'A new and particularly noxious sect of heretics arose. The fighters of these *rotten* were protected from head to foot by a leather jerkin, and were armed with steel, staves and iron. They went about in bands of thousands and reduced monasteries, villages and cities to ashes. With violence, yet thinking it no sin, they committed adultery, saying "There is no God". This movement arose in Brabant, hence the name Brabançons. From the start these marauders drew up for themselves a curious law, which properly speaking was based on no concept of right. Fugitive rebels, false clerks, renegade monks and all who had forsaken God for any reason, joined them. Their number has already risen so sharply . . . that they can with impunity stay where they are or wander about all over the land, greatly hated by God and man.'[184]

William of Newburgh, writing about 1196–98, relates that Henry II had recruited detachments of mercenaries in 1173, Brabançons who were called *rotten*.[185] In the *Gesta regis Henrici II* a German *rotte* of *Brabançons* was mentioned in the year 1188, in a part of the chronicle written about 1191–93.[186] Thus the word *rotte* is first mentioned in the chronicles around 1170–80, after the bands of professional mercenaries had already been on the scene for at least thirteen years. From the word *rutta* came *ruttarii* or *rutarii*, while the French *rote* gave *roters* and *rotiers*. Around the year 1200 the word *rupta* began to be used, and enjoyed wide success because of its frequent use by the papal chancery.[187]

The term *rotte* shows that emphasis was laid on the formation or unit, not on the individual fighters. They formed a closely-knit society with a strong *esprit de corps*. This fact is important not only for the foot-soldiers, but also for the cavalry who fought as mercenaries in similar detachments. They were frequently accompanied by their wives or other women. Clerics were among the band, having fled from their order or their monastery out of lust for adventure; they could act as chaplains to the mercenaries, who although they were usually regarded as heretics, remained faithful in word if not in deed to the Church. The presence of priests among them was particularly noted by their contemporaries, and was often mentioned.[188] The Church took counter-measures: the ban of the Third Lateran Council, in which heretics and mercenaries were spoken of together, was confirmed by Celestinus in 1181 in his letter to the archbishop of Arles, but it was not repeated in the fourth Lateran Council in 1215. At that time the struggle against the Albigensians was raging, and Simon de Montfort used mercenaries himself against them. But the Council forbade clerics to act as leaders of professional mercenaries, crossbowmen, or bloodthirsty bands.[189]

---

[184] Walter Map, *De nugis curialium*, I, c. 29, p. 56. Grundmann, p. 427, n. 1 and 428.

[185] *Historia rerum Anglicarum*, I, p. 172. Grundmann, p. 428.

[186] *Gesta regis Henrici II*, II, p. 49. Grundmann, pp. 428–9.

[187] Grundmann, pp. 429–32.

[188] *Ibid.*, pp. 485–6.

[189] *Ibid.*, p. 485.

The mercenary bands were not usually very large. As has been said, they contributed 500, 800, or at the most 1,500 men in 1167, 4,000 men to the troops of the archbishop of Cologne in 1179, 400 or 700 men at the end of the battle of Bouvines. Cadoc's band was 300 men strong. Henry II gave 300 shields to his *coterelli* in 1165. 10,000 Brabançons are mentioned in 1173, but from the calculations of J. Boussard it appears that Henry II took 3,000–6,000 mercenaries to England in 1174, and that earl Hugh Bigod had collected 1,000–1,500 Flemings there. Boussard considers 6,000 professional mercenaries the maximum figure.[190]

They fought mostly on foot. Henry II's Brabançons in 1173 were foot-soldiers, so were the *rotten* under the archbishop of Cologne in 1173 and the Brabançons at Bouvines: it is also apparent from the description of the *rotten* by Walter Map. Elsewhere everything points to the greater part of the mercenaries having fought on foot, though there were occasionally horsemen too.

The value of the mercenaries as foot-soldiers became evident in the battle of Bouvines in 1214. The Brabançons who fought there were probably from Brabant and the Low Countries. Under the able leadership of Reginald of Boulogne they distinguished themselves so greatly that they are mentioned by all the chroniclers. They put up a splendid defence, and were the last troops to make a stand on the allied side. The mercenaries were drawn up in a circle only two ranks deep, and the knights' attack was smashed on their grounded pikes. The Brabançons were not numerous, for by the end of the battle there were only 400, or at the most 700 of them left.[191] But they were an example to any foot-soldiers of the time, since they fought as bravely as the knights, or even more so, as true 'preudomes'.[192] Such excellence was of course the result of long experience in the practice of their profession on battlefields and in sieges, and of the *esprit de corps* which they had developed. To a lesser degree, the same phenomenon was seen in the foot-soldiers of the First Crusade, who became increasingly useful as the expedition went on. In both instances the commanders had enough time to foster and maintain a military *esprit de corps* among these troops.

During the late twelfth and early thirteenth centuries professional mercenaries played a prominent part, but did not fully replace knightly armies, and they never became the more important arm. Professional mercenaries came from principalities such as Brabant, Flanders and Hainault, which really took no direct part in the conflict between the French and English kings, or between the emperor and the Lombard cities.

When considering the appearance of the mercenaries from Brabant one's mind turns to the Grimberg war between Godfrey III and Walter Berthout, which raged for twenty years. The peasants who had lost everything abandoned the devastated region. But the war ended in 1160, and Brabant mercenaries appeared for the first

---

190 Boussard, p. 220.
191 *Genealogiae comitum Fl. Cont, Clarom.*, c. 22, p. 333. William the Breton, *Chronicon*, c. 197, p. 289. [G. Duby, *Le dimanche de Bouvines*, Paris, 1973.]
192 Ph. Mousket, *Chronique rimée*, II, vv. 22127–9, pp. 372–3.

time in 1166.[193] A war lasting twenty years in a small duchy gives little incentive for mercenaries to leave: Brabant was also struck by famine, and this disaster took a heavy toll. Still, between this famine and the year 1166 there is a gap of four years. It is possible that the deteriorating economic situation made them leave. In Brabant, men who did not want to work went off as mercenaries in foreign armies. In this case the mercenaries came from comparatively rich districts, but elsewhere, as in Gascony, Navarre, and Aragon, poor and even marginal lands provided the new armies. Other rather unproductive areas were soon over-populated in proportion to the arable land.

The use of these mercenary bands brought advantages and disadvantages. Their upkeep was extremely expensive, and the troops caused considerable damage. Since even the richest princes had limited means, the units were never very large, at the most of few thousand men strong. It is striking that the powerfully centralized Anglo-Norman kingdom of William the Conqueror, William Rufus, Henry I, Stephen, and Henry II made the greatest use of them, and Henry II and Richard I were consequently independent of their vassals. But a reaction, which had important political consequences, set in under king John.

Germany was still an agricultural state, but Frederick Barbarossa got the necessary income to pay his mercenaries from the taxes which he levied on the Lombard cities. While he waged war without the help of the foremost German princes, and made no use of the service owed him by these landed nobles and their vassals – in contrast to England, where the great barons took part in the wars while the lesser vassals stayed at home under Henry II and Richard I – these German princes grew more powerful during the absence of the emperor. In order to subjugate Henry the Lion, Frederick allowed the barons who remained loyal to him to attack. On that occasion the archbishop of Cologne used mercenaries just once in Germany. Otto IV lacked the means to recruit such an army, but his enemy Philip of Swabia called in auxiliary troops from Bohemia and Moravia, who plundered just as badly as the mercenaries. They had been used before only in Italy, again by Philip of Swabia, in 1198. But in 1203 they fought for Otto, and in 1213 changed sides again, to the advantage of Otto's new opponent, Frederick II. Not only were these troops appalling plunderers, but the king also had to grant important concessions to their prince in order to get them at all. Duke Przemysl-Otakar received the title of king from Philip of Swabia, and when he later supported Otto IV, he was recognized as king by the pope and crowned by a papal legate. Later Frederick also recognized him as king, and limited his obligations to the Empire to a minimum.[194] Frederick II was able to count on a vast income from his kingdom of Sicily: in a letter to the Sicilian cities in 1236 he wrote: 'Germany gives us many soldiers, so that we can spare you . . . but so great an undertaking cannot be launched without very great expense'. So he asked for their financial help.[195] He also used Saracens, whom he had settled in southern Italy round

---

[193] *Sigeberti Gemblacensis Chronographiae Auctarium Affligemense*, ed. P. Gorissen, AWLSK, Verhandelingen, 15, 1952, pp. 141–2.
[194] Grundmann, pp. 490–2.
[195] *Ibid.*, p. 489, n. 1.

Lucera and Nocera.[196] In Germany he made such far-reaching concessions that after his reign the Holy Roman Empire was helpless.

In France, Philip Augustus had to recruit mercenaries in order to fight Henry II and Richard I on level terms, but he succeeded in destroying the Angevin kingdom and winning great victories. By this means he so increased the royal power that from then onwards the prince could summon a mighty army of knights, and let the mercenaries go again. By 1214 he had no further need of mercenaries, but used foot-soldiers from the cities, which meant that larger and cheaper armies were raised, who in time made excellent fighting troops.

4. The Foot-soldiers from the Cities

On the whole, peasant armies in France, in the greater part of the Holy Roman Empire, the Netherlands, in northern Italy, Spain, and most of England, were nothing but a mass of men without cohesion and without good armament, and everybody knew it. When Giles of Rome wrote for his pupil, then crown prince Philip the Fair, on the art of war in the De regimine principum, he used the sole surviving treatise from Roman antiquity, that of Vegetius. But when he read that the rustica plebs furnished the best soldiers to the Roman emperors, he improved upon his model after a thorough discussion, because in his own time the nobiles[197] made the best soldiers, and to a lesser degree, the urbani or city-dwellers.

The Italian communal armies

The cities which developed earliest, those in northern Italy, produced the first good foot-soldiers in the second half of the twelfth century. These city-armies, of which Milan's was the best known, consisted of armoured cavalry and foot-soldiers. The titled aristocracy, who lived in the country in other states, in Italy lived in the cities too, and with the richer citizens formed the cavalry. The mass of the citizens formed the foot-soldiers.

The communal armies were grouped by the city districts, which were named after the nearest city gates. Usually only part of the army was called up, while the rest guarded the city. Frequently horse and foot-soldiers were sent out from two city 'gates', and after some time these were relieved by men from two other districts. A great city such as Milan was divided into six city gates, and could send three of them off on an expedition, and later the other three relieved the first or reinforced them. When a battle was imminent, the whole communal army could be called up.[198]

The Lombard foot-soldiers went out to battle in closely packed formations, behind which came a great waggon, the carroccio, with a banner on a tall pole. On this flagstaff was often also a monstrance, with the consecrated Host, and there were priests on the cart, around which troops who were driven back, or were fleeing, could

---

196 Lot, II, p. 168. Köhler, I, p. 206.
197 Delbrück, III, p. 671. Cf. Egidio Colonna, Li livres du gouvernement des rois, ed. S.P. Molenaer, New York, 1899, pp. 379–81.
198 Köhler, I, p. 184. Gesta Federici I. imperatoris in Lombardia, ed. O. Holder-Eggar, MGH, SS in usum scholarum, 1892, pp. 18, 19, 20, 21, 22, 23 and ff.

be re-formed in battle order, and to which the wounded were brought. This means of regrouping troops on the battlefield was mentioned for the first time in 1039 at Milan.[199] It was quickly adopted in the rest of Europe: in the twelfth century it was used in the Netherlands, including Flanders, in England at Northallerton in 1138, in the third Crusade, at Bouvines in 1214, and at Worringen in 1288.[200]

The Italian cities had their own administrative systems and were really city-republics, in which local patriotism was strongly developed. The cities were also rich, thanks to flourishing trade and industry, and the foot-soldiers could thus be well armed.

The feeling of unity within each city provided the necessary solidarity among the soldiers: a man who left his comrades in the lurch was abandoning his fellow-citizens, and made himself liable to punishment by the city council. Strict laws maintained discipline with heavy penalties, for example soldiers who did not answer the call-up of troops were subject to heavy fines, deserters were rigorously pursued and houses in which they took refuge were set on fire, and their names were read out in Church on the first Sunday of the month.[201]

The foot-soldiers of the Italian cities were the forerunners of all good medieval foot-soldiers. Their methods of warfare differed very little from those used elsewhere, since they were supported on the battlefield by armoured cavalry from the city, the chief difference lay in the better co-operation between more efficient foot-soldiers than were found elsewhere and heavy cavalry, who actually were not so good as the German counterparts against whom they were fighting. The Italians won the most notable victory of their hundred years of fighting against the Germans at Legnano in 1176.

The political situation forced Frederick Barbarossa to stay in Italy. The archbishops of Cologne and Magdeburg had raised an army for him in Germany, and came with these reinforcements over the St Gotthard to Bellinzona, and on to Como. The emperor was waiting for them there with a relatively small army, probably about 1,000 horsemen, 500 of them knights. The archbishops brought about 2,000 knights. With this great army, and a contingent from Como, the emperor went on to meet his allies at Pavia.[202]

The Lombards went out to meet the emperor's army to prevent him from meeting the reinforcements at Pavia. Milan had the help of contingents from other cities, 50 knights from Lodi, about 300 from Novara and Vercelli, about 200 from Piacenza, and the knights from Brescia, Verona, and the Marches. The foot-soldiers from Verona and Brescia stayed in Milan, the other foot-soldiers went out with the Lombard army.[203] Both armies were preceded by advance guards, 700 knights from the Lombard army and 300 from the German. The clash between them came by

---

[199] Delbrück, III, p. 375. Köhler, I, p. 185.

[200] Delbrück, *loc. cit. Sigeberti Gemblacensis, Chronica, cum continuationibus; Auctarium Afflige-mense; Auctarium Hasnoniense*, ed. L.C. Bethmann, MGH, SS, VI, 1844, p. 422, anno 1184.

[201] Köhler, I, pp. 184–5. *Gesta Federici I. imperatoris*, p. 20.

[202] *Gesta Federici I. imperatoris*, p. 63. P. Pieri, *Alcune quistioni sopra la Fanteria in Italia*, pp. 18–19. Delbrück, III, p. 363. Oman, I, pp. 448–9. Lot, II, pp. 165–6. Köhler, I, pp. 69–82.

[203] *Gesta Federici I. imperatoris*, p. 63.

surprise, when the Lombards suddenly appeared out of a thicket. As soon as the Lombard vanguard came into contact with the imperial army, it was driven back.

When the emperor learned the strength of the enemy force from his spies and advance guard, he was advised to avoid a battle. Frederick 'considered it unworthy of his imperial majesty to flee', and ordered a general attack.[204] The German knights put several Lombard cavalry formations to flight. Nearly all the knights from Brescia, a great number of other Lombard knights and a good number of the knights and rich burghers of Milan were chased off the battlefield. The rest of the knights turned back to join the Milanese foot-soldiers.[205]

Frederick felt confident of victory. Only the Milanese foot-soldiers and a small number of knights who had already been defeated still opposed his victorious army: victory seemed almost too easy.[206] Everything shows that the fleeing Lombard armies were not pursued, and the emperor was able to prepare for the *coup de grâce* with all his forces well concentrated. The Milanese foot-soldiers seemed to be in a hopeless position, faced with total destruction. 'But the Lombards were ready for death or victory', testified a follower of the archbishop of Cologne, who took part in the battle with many knights.[207] The foot-soldiers were fully aware of the serious position. There may be two diametrically opposed reactions to such a situation: the soldiers may flee panic-stricken, or may by superhuman courage, generated by the appallingly dangerous situation in which flight meant certain annihilation, suddenly put up a stubborn resistance displaying extraordinary qualities. This is what happened at Legnano.

The Milanese grouped themselves shoulder to shoulder round the *carroccio*. When the Germans made a fierce charge, they hurled themselves against a wall of shields and grounded lances. The Milanese held their ground determinedly, and the repeated attacks of the German knights were shattered on the thick hedge of long pikes. The imperial standard-bearer was wounded in the first charge, fell from his horse and was trampled underfoot. The emperor's horse was killed: Frederick fell, and disappeared from his men's view.

But the fleeing Milanese knights were by no means defeated. They met reinforcements from Brescia who were moving up to the battle, and they turned back together to Legnano. There they attacked the flank of the exhausted German army at the very moment that Barbarossa fell from his horse. The Milanese foot-soldiers made a counter-attack, which decided the battle, which had lasted from 9 a.m. to 3 p.m. The German knights suffered a great defeat and many were taken prisoner. Their allies from Pavia were cut to pieces. The pursuit was carried on as far as the Ticino, nine miles from the battlefield, and many fugitives were drowned in the river.[208] The emperor's shield and lance, the imperial battle-standard and the imperial treasure fell into the hands of the victors. Barbarossa was not able to flee with his knights, and it

---

204 *Chronica regia Coloniensis*, p. 128.
205 *Gesta Federici I. imperatoris*, p. 63.
206 Romuald of Salerno, *Annales*, MGH, SS, XIX, p. 441.
207 *Chronica regia Coloniensis*, p. 128.
208 Romuald, MGH, SS, XIX, p. 442. *Gesta Federici I. imperatoris*, p. 63.

was supposed that he had been killed until he turned up three days later safely in Pavia, after numerous adventures.

About fifty years later, on 27 November 1237, the Milanese foot-soldiers again successfully tackled a knightly army, this time led by the emperor Frederick II. He had feigned a retreat in order to make the citizens return to their cities. When the Lombard army crossed the river Oglio on 27 November, the emperor was informed by smoke signals, and advanced to the attack immediately. The Lombard army scarcely had time to send out an advance guard, which would delay the imperial army to some extent. These Milanese knights, with the help of knights from Piacenza, managed to hold off the German knights for an hour, but they were then routed. Panic broke out and many men fled from the battlefield, but some of the knights and the foot-soldiers from Milan and Alessandria bravely gathered round the *carroccio*. Their backs were protected by the village of Cortenuova, and their formation stood behind a small ditch. The Germans made repeated attacks, some penetrating as far as the *carroccio*, but without success. The emperor was obliged to halt the attacks and wait for his Saracen bowmen. During the night, however, the Lombard foot-soldiers abandoned the battlefield and went home.[209]

The Italian foot-soldiers did not undergo the continuous evolution which made the foot-soldiers the most important arm on the field of battle. This was not really their fault: their enemies, the mighty German emperors with their great knightly armies, were responsible. The great days of the foot-soldiers had not yet arrived, which is easily understood if one remembers that the knights were still at their peak.[210]

It was only at the beginning of the fourteenth century that really important victories were won by foot-soldiers, who had by then become the chief, or in some cases the only fighting arm. The first was at Courtrai in 1302. Then in 1314 the Scottish foot-soldiers achieved a brilliant victory over the Anglo-Norman nobles at Bannockburn, a victory which was compared by three chroniclers with that of Courtrai.[211] The following year at Morgarten the Swiss scored their first important victory over the knights of the duke of Austria. In 1319 the peasants of Dithmarschen defeated the knights of Holstein. In 1346 the men of Liège achieved their great triumph over the knights and mercenaries of their prince-bishop at Vottem.

Of the four victories of the early fourteenth century Courtrai was undoubtedly the most important, in that Europe's most powerful army was defeated with heavy casualties. The fact that victory was totally unexpected had far wider repercussions than the earlier successes, since it came at the moment when the armies of the king of France seemed invincible. France was the land of the flower of chivalry, and her cavalrymen were famed throughout western Europe. The weak English king Edward II failed in his conduct of the battle at Bannockburn, and the Anglo-Norman knights

---

[209] P. Pieri, pp. 25–8. Delbrück, III, pp. 367–9. Oman, I, pp. 494–6. Lot, II, pp. 168–9. Köhler, I, pp. 220–3.

[210] P. Pieri, pp. 25–8. Delbrück, III, pp. 373–4. Oman, I, pp. 494–6. Lot, II, pp. 168–9.

[211] Verbruggen, *De slag der gulden sporen*, p. 2.

seem not to have been very impressive: their losses were also smaller than those of the French at Courtrai.[212]

The Swiss victory at Morgarten owed more to the terrain than the two already described. In the mountainous country of the narrow pass beside the Aegerisee, the column of Austrian knights could not deploy their formations, and the Swiss hurled big stones, pieces of rock and treetrunks down on them from the mountains. Then the nobles were attacked in the flank and could not fight a proper battle.[213] The great importance of the Swiss victory at Morgarten lay precisely in the fact that it was the starting point of a long and unbroken evolution, accomplished without significant setbacks. This evolution lasted from 1315 to the end of the fifteenth century, and culminated in the famous victories over Charles the Bold at Grandson and Mürten in 1476, and at Nancy in 1477. But by then a revolution in the art of war had taken place: as in ancient times, the foot-soldiers stood out as the foremost arm in European armies.

At the beginning of the fourteenth century the renaissance of the foot-soldiers was just beginning, and at that moment the Flemish communal armies were particularly important in the evolutionary process, because they could raise more powerful units than the Scots or Swiss – Switzerland then consisting only of the three autonomous cantons, Schwyz, Uri, and Unterwalden. They were also pre-eminent in their outstanding equipment, which they owed to greater prosperity. The Flemish organization was also very efficient, and they had had considerable experience during the second half of the thirteenth century, especially after 1297. But the Flemish citizens lived by working in trades in the city, and could not therefore sustain the same martial spirit as the Scots or Swiss. The Flemings were also constantly menaced by a very powerful France, and just like the Scots in their wars against England, they had on many occasions to accept defeat. After a hard-won victory the French and English nobility immediately changed their tactics, making it much harder for the Flemings and Scots to win next time. The Swiss on the other hand were continually expanding their dominion: more and more cantons concluded mutual alliances and were helped in their development by the weakness of their neighbours, who were involved elsewhere in serious wars.

The Flemings, Scots, and English, with their combination of bowmen and well-armoured noblemen on foot, supported by a reserve of heavy cavalry, did not reach as high a level of excellence as the Swiss. Their foot-soldiers performed wonderful feats of arms, but made no special innovation in the art of war.

---

212 *Ibid.*, p. 248: 1,000 knights and squires at Courtrai and perhaps 1,100; more than 60 important nobles and barons. At Bannockburn: 43 important nobles and 200 knights and 700 squires: Oman, II, p. 98. These numbers from Bannockburn are given in a late source and it is possible that they are exaggerated.

213 R. Durrer, *op. cit.*, pp. 83–91. The best source is John of Winterthur, *Chronica*, ed. F. Baethgen, MGH, in 8°, nova series, 3, 1924. But we have fewer sources and no 'control' as for Courtrai and Bannockburn.

The Flemish foot-soldiers

By the time they became famous in 1302, the Flemish foot-soldiers already had a long history behind them, and it is worth considering why they had not become more important earlier as a factor in the Flemish army.

Foot-soldiers helped the knights – the mainstay of the comital army – on the battlefield and in defending fortresses, very early in Flanders. They are not mentioned at first in the narrative sources of the eleventh century, and only indirect evidence shows that they existed. Through exemptions from army service, granted by the counts, it is clear that Flemish foot-soldiers were then employed at a time when they were not used, or only occasionally used, by other principalities. The Flemish communal armies were first explicitly mentioned in 1127, and some even had their own traditions, indicating that they had by then been in existence for several years or even decades. Their origin dates in any case from the period between 1071–1127.[214]

In 1127 these communal armies appeared as a *communio*, a brotherhood bound by a mutual oath. The *communio* did not however appear to be based on such an oath everywhere. A brotherhood of citizens was called a *communio* at Ghent and St Omer, but *amicitia* at Aire. These three brotherhoods were recognized by the count at least by 1127.[215]

In this early period the communal army of Ghent was outstanding. The soldiers were well armed, and had at their disposal a baggage train and siege equipment: they were battle-seasoned, and enjoyed the reputation for being specialists in besieging fortresses. As well as heavy foot-soldiers, armed with lances, pikes, swords and shields, there were also archers. The men of Ghent had ladders which took ten men to carry them, and a sort of tower equipped with ladders, which were intended for besieging and storming strongholds. They also had iron hammers, and implements for boring through walls, and siege engines to shatter them. Their baggage was carried on waggons, of which they brought thirty to Bruges to besiege the murderers of count Charles the Good. They also had a corps of experienced workmen who could set up or take down the siege engines, and rebuild the wooden towers to make a battering-ram.[216]

Ghent was then the leading city in Flanders, and count Philip was obliged to build the counts' castle 'in order to subdue the excessive pride of the people of Ghent'.[217] After his death they exacted a most advantageous charter from his widow, by which they severely limited their military service in the comital army, and gained the right to fortify their city as they saw fit. The new count, Baldwin, also had trouble with the city. The French chronicler William the Breton wrote with a great deal of bombast and exaggeration that Ghent was capable of sending up to 20,000 men into the army at her own expense. In 1211, the city refused to receive Ferdinand of Portugal within her walls. The husband of countess Johanna was forced to assemble an army to

---

[214] Verbruggen, *Het leger en de vloot van de graven van Vlaanderen*, pp. 87–9, 99.

[215] *Ibid.*, p. 100.

[216] *Ibid.*, p. 101.

[217] Gilbert of Mons, *Chronicon*, c. 180, p. 266.

subdue Ghent, and two years later it was the only Flemish city able to offer resistance to Philip Augustus, who was helped by duke Henry I of Brabant in the siege of Ghent. After the defeat at Bouvines, the emperor Otto was advised to continue the struggle with the communal army of Ghent.[218]

In the reigns of the counts of Flanders Thierry and Philip, Baldwin and Ferdinand of Portugal, the communal armies were regularly integrated into the comital army. At the same time many Flemish mercenaries were fighting in England and Scotland. During the reign of king Stephen foot-soldiers followed the mercenary leader William of Ypres. They fought for Henry II in an unsuccessful expedition to Wales in 1165. After that, Flemish mercenaries fought against Henry with the troops of William the Lion, king of Scotland, and with the insurgent earl of Leicester, who had recruited many Flemish weavers, who had mostly crossed over to England in search of wool or work. They used to sing in chorus, blithe and mightily pleased with themselves:

> Hoppe, hoppe, Wilekin, hoppe, Wilekin,
> Engelond is min and tin.

lines which are among the oldest surviving in Dutch literature. But these weavers suffered a heavy defeat at Fornham in Suffolk on 17 October 1173. A group of them then settled in Britain, where a Flemish colony existed in Pembrokeshire, and there were many Flemings in the army of king John. The princes greatly valued these 'Flemish wolves', but the English people who suffered from plundering by the mercenary armies hated them, and after each war they made every effort to expel them as quickly as possible. The Flemish foot-soldiers had a considerable reputation at that time, and foreign chroniclers were full of praise for them. One of them mentioned the power of Philip Augustus' knights, but acknowledged that Philip of Alsace excelled with his hand-picked stoutly armed foot-soldiers, who were equipped with a waggon with a banner on it, in other words a kind of *carroccio*. Speaking of the powerful army with which Baldwin IX was able to re-conquer part of the territories that had been lost under Philip of Alsace, or after his death, the *Histoire de Guillaume le Maréchal* mentioned the proud and spirited *communes* with their numerous army waggons.[219]

William Marshal, who was at the time ambassador of Richard I at the court of Baldwin IX, witnessed the siege of one of the lost cities, which he does not name. When a French relief army arrived, the Flemish nobles and the count decided to build a fortification with a number of waggons from the communal armies, and the foot-soldiers had to man the defences, while the knights were to fight the royal army. William Marshal thought otherwise. No rampart should be thrown up, since this would show that they were afraid, or had too few men. He proposed instead that they should advance with the whole army and seek battle, thinking neither of retreat nor fortifications. The waggons should be placed outside the city to block the exit, and

---

218 William the Breton, *Philippis*, p. 44, vv. 89–90. *Idem, Chronicon*, c. 199, p. 291.
219 Verbruggen, *Het leger en de vloot*, pp. 248–50. *Histoire de Guilllaume le Maréchal*, II, pp. 23–7.

to prevent an attack on the rear of the Flemish burghers. The count and his barons agreed to this suggestion, and when on the following day the Flemish troops marched out of their camp in good order to do battle, the king, whose spies had been active in the meantime, chose to retreat.

In general the Flemish foot-soldiers still played a minor role, and the army of knights were the chief power, but by the late twelfth and early thirteenth century they had become much weaker than the royal army, so that after the reign of Philip of Alsace the counts of Flanders were no longer capable of offering resistance to the king of France on their own, and had to seek the support of powerful allies. As the knightly class in Flanders grew weaker in proportion to the foot-soldiers, it was increasingly possible that the communal armies would become the principal element in the comital forces. This evolution occurred in the thirteenth century: the nobility was becoming poorer and the number of knights gradually dwindled, for the majority of the aristocracy remained squires, while the population was greatly increasing in the cities and in the country, probably even doubling in number. The general standard of welfare also rose in other classes, in contrast to the impoverishment of the aristocracy. The count constantly had to consider the political and military power of his cities.

In the thirteenth century the quality of the communal armies steadily improved. Perhaps as early as the end of the twelfth century and certainly by the beginning of the thirteenth, it was prescribed that every man must possess arms and equipment according to his means, both in the country and in the city. Of the cities, the earliest information we have is for Douai in the middle of the thirteenth century, when the richest burghers had to do military service on horseback, the others on foot. They were divided in constabularies, territorial groupings according to city districts, and these units were led by constables, appointed by the 'echevins' or aldermen. In 1276 the communal army of Ypres was also divided according to the districts and streets of the city. Most likely this was the general rule, for the same was done at Lille, and it was still done at Bruges for the burghers in the fourteenth century.[220]

In the second half of the thirteenth century the artisans strove for autonomy for their guilds, and to draw up the communal army on the basis of these units. At the same time they were taking part in many expeditions, so that they gained experience and self-confidence. This increased the workers' importance in the social conflicts of the day, and they hoped to increase their influence still further by means of their arms. We are best informed about conditions in this period in Bruges, whose communal army was the most important in Flanders at the end of the thirteenth century and the beginning of the fourteenth. It owed this in large measure to the fact that the city was the richest in the country.[221]

Certainly from 1280, and perhaps earlier, the initiation fees for new apprentices, artisans, and masters entering the guilds of the wool industry had to be used to buy and maintain tents and banners. This measure allowed the guilds to procure the

---

[220] Verbruggen, *op. cit.*, p. 251.
[221] *Ibid., loc. cit.*

materials collectively. In 1292 a citizen cavalry was inaugurated. All who possessed more than £300 were burghers, and these citizens were divided by wealth into five classes. According to the class to which they belonged, they had to have a horse of specified value in order to do military service as cavalrymen. The two highest classes, with horses of £40 and £30, had to have metal protection on their horses. The other citizens were grouped according to their guilds, whose internal organization is not however known. From later documents that can be compared with precise texts from the period 1297–1304, it appears that the whole communal army was efficiently organized.[222]

Bruges applied a clever system to send its warriors on expedition. According to the importance of the army that was sent against the enemy, the city summoned a small or a large part of its troops: one or two *vouden* for small expeditions, up to five or six *vouden* for big armies. A *voud* consisted of 96 burghers and 511 artisans of the guilds. If a force proved too small for its task, reinforcements could be sent, perhaps as many as three or four *vouden*. The whole communal army of Bruges was 8,280 men, or 13.333 *vouden* strong.[223]

The basis of the communal armies was at that time the guild, or group of workers in the same occupation. After 11 July 1302 these became independent, chose their own leaders, acquired political power, made their own legal system, and controlled their own finances. The guild had a banner, the rallying point of the unit, which was an important symbol fiercely striven for in those cities where the guilds were not yet independent, such as Tournai.[224] The guild formed a brotherhood, with its own privileges. It was like a great family for its members: through trade, periodic meeting, processions, social festivities and funerals the members were bound to each other through thick and thin, which fostered mutual trust. In all conditions the honour of the guild and the city had to be upheld. Moral solidarity was strengthened in military units by uniform; the tunics for a guild were all made out of the same cloth.[225] A man who fled from the battlefield laid himself open not only to the scorn of fellow-craftsmen, but also to punishment meted out by the authorities. In neighbouring Tournai, which had much in common with the Flemish cities, some citizens were banished after the battle of Cassel in 1328, because they had fled during the fighting.[226] Anyone who was killed in action knew that his next-of-kin would be cared for.

For years the artisans had striven for the recognition of their trade-groups. As soon as they won their victory, they hoped to be able to control their own destiny, and that

---

222 Verbruggen, 'De organisatie van de militie te Brugge in de XIVe eeuw', *Hand. Soc. Emul.*, LXXXVII, 1950, pp. 163–70.
223 Verbruggen, *Het Gemeenteleger van Brugge van 1338 tot 1340 en de Namen van de weerbare Mannen*, CRH in 8°, Brussels, 1962, pp. 13, 80.
224 C. Wyffels, 'De oorsprong der ambachten in Vlaanderen en Brabant', *AWLSKB, Verhandelingen* 17, 1951, pp. 113, 115.
225 See the frescoes of the Leugemeete: F. de Vigne, *Recherches historiques sur les costumes civils et militaires des gildes et des corporations de métiers*, Ghent, 1847, plates. A. Van Werveke, *Het Godshuis van Sint Jan en Sint Pauwel te Gent bijgenaamd de Leugemeete*, Maatschappij der Vlaamse Bibliophilen, 4th series, 15, Ghent, 1909, plates. H. Koechlin, *Chapelle de la Leugemeete à Gand. Peintures murales. Restitution*, Ghent, 1936, pp. 12–20.
226 G. le Muisit, *Chronique et Annales*, p. 100.

social exploitation would be a thing of the past. They took part in the direction of city affairs, and their leaders were able to influence the administration of the county. Throughout the fourteenth century the influence of the craftsmen's social and political struggle was felt. Their idealism and self-interest in social matters explain the tenacity with which they fought on the battlefields, and in wars against the French king this was further strengthened by a lively national spirit which had received enormous stimulus from 1302 to 1304 from military successes, and which was thereafter fostered by their opposition to the treaty of Athis-sur-Orge of 1305.

The artisans' military potential is clearly evident from their heavy armament and equipment, as will be shown later. In order to be able to procure such weapons, citizens had to be relatively well off, as indeed they were. Some of them were crossbowmen, who formed famous guilds such as that of St George in the fourteenth century. They practised regularly, and their effectiveness was not to be despised, as the battles of the period showed. But there were too few of them to perform really outstanding feats of arms. In 1350 a contest took place at Tournai between the crossbowmen of thirty-six cities, and the two prizes offered for the best archers were won by men from Bruges and Ypres.[227] The innumerable battles in which these archers had taken part in the first half of the fourteenth century contributed greatly to their success in this contest.

The Flemish citizens also found many recruits among the peasants of the county. Especially in coastal Flanders, a peasantry had developed which was notorious for its rough way of life, and its turbulent, pugnacious behaviour. In this thickly populated region the free peasants had acquired a high degree of self-government, while the nobility had suffered greatly during the crises of the first half of the thirteenth century. After fighting continuously from 1302 to 1304 against the French, and having become conscious of their own strength, they played an important part in the uprising from 1323 to 1328, and fought very bravely at Cassel, as was evident from the thousands of dead who remained on the field of battle.

On the other side of the Southern Netherlands too, the foot-soldiers became powerful and famous. This brings us to a study of the communal armies of the cities of the Meuse in the prince-bishopric of Liège.

The communal armies of Liège

Just like those of Italy and Flanders, the cities of the Meuse valley enjoyed an early development and great prosperity. Some of these grew earlier than those in Flanders, and the communal armies developed sooner. The citizens of Liège appeared as early as 1047 during the rebellion of duke Godfrey the Bearded against the emperor and his faithful subject prince-bishop Wazo, who organized the defence of the city of Liège. He set up a guard on the citadel, and had the city gates closed day and night. He had weapons issued to the home of clerics and laymen, and gave orders from time to time to the citizens to take up arms.[228]

---

[227] *Ibid.*, pp. 272–3.
[228] Anselmus, *Gesta pontificum Trajectensium et Leodiensium*, ed. R. Koepke, MGH, SS, VII, 1846, c. 54, pp. 221–2. F. Rousseau, 'La Meuse et le Pays mosan en Belgique. Leur importance historique

The early existence of militia in the prince-bishopric is shown by the charter granted in 1066 to the men of Huy giving them the privilege of only being obliged to participate in a campaign when the men of Liège had been called up, and had joined the army. 'They were not to join the army until eight days after the men of Liège had set out on the day appointed for an expedition.'[229]

The evolution of the communal armies in the prince-bishopric was very similar to that of the communal troops in Flanders; they too played an increasingly active part and became more important, until finally they became the most prominent element in the army. But in the prince-bishopric the foot-soldiers were important earlier than in Flanders, because the knights were frequently at variance with the prince-bishop, and therefore would not join the army. If the nobles revolted against their prince, the latter had to call upon the cities to besiege and destroy the knights' castles.[230] The bishops were never able to impose their authority so firmly on their vassals as the counts of Flanders, and for this reason they lacked such powerful armies of knights. At first the prelates had very little power over the great lords of their dioceses: it is said of prince-bishop Notger that he was obliged to spend a third of the income of his diocese on the formation of an army of mailed cavalrymen, who consisted largely of *ministeriales* who were not, at first, so well armed as the knights, and were not so useful on the battlefield. For lack of a good knightly army the bishops were obliged to employ communal armies much earlier and to a greater extent than was the case elsewhere. This can be seen in the survey that follows.

As early as 1106, the communal army of Liège accompanied duke Henry of Limbourg and Godfrey of Namur with their troops, when they met and defeated three hundred German knights near the bridge at Visé on 22 March. These Germans had been sent by Henry V against his father the emperor Henry IV, who had at that time fled to Liège.[231] In 1129, the men of Liège took part in the battle near Wilderen, where bishop Alexander I defeated the duke of Brabant.[232] In the same year the knights of Liège with their prince had besieged the fortified castle at Duras, and defeated the men of Godfrey of Brabant and Thierry of Alsace, and put them to flight. But the fortress could not be taken, for the impecunious knights who were supporting the bishop were obliged to go home when it was time to harvest the crops.[233] This example shows that the prince had no great number of rich vassals. In 1141 the

---

avant le XIIIe siècle', *Annales de la société archéologique de Namur*, 39, Namur, 1930, p. 132. G. Kurth, *La cité de Liège au moyen âge*, Liège, Brussels, 1910, I, pp. 46–7.

[229] S. Balau and E. Fairon, *Chroniques liégeoises*, II, CRH, Brussels, 1931, p. 13. A. Joris, 'Remarques sur les clauses militaires des privilèges urbains liégeois', *RBPH*, 37 (1959), pp. 297–316.

[230] For the foot-soldiers of the principality of Liège and the county of Looz, see C. Gaier, *Art et organisation militaires dans la principauté de Liège et dans le comté de Looz au Moyen Age*, Ac. Roy. Belg., Cl. Lettres, Mém., in 8°, 59, Brussels, 1968, pp. 145–76.

[231] *Cantatorium sive chronicon Sancti Huberti*, pp. 252–3. *Vita Heinrici IV imperatoris*, ed. W. Eberhard, MGH, SS in usum scholarum, 1899, pp. 38–9. *Annales Hildesheimenses*, p. 56. *Chronica regia Coloniensis*, pp. 43–4. Kurth, *op. cit.*, I, p. 43. F. Rousseau, *op. cit.*, p. 133. Gaier, *op. cit.*, pp. 231–4 and p. 146.

[232] Gaier, pp. 146, 237–40. Kurth, I, p. 80.

[233] Rousseau, *op. cit.*, p. 135.

communal armies of Liège and Huy marched on the castle of Bouillon with bishop Albero II and took it.[234] Both armies came to the aid of their prince again in 1151, when prince-bishop Henry of Leez, who had already been very active in the siege of Bouillon, crushed the small army of knights from the county of Namur at Andenne. The count of Namur had more knights at his disposal than his opponent, who was relying chiefly on his citizen-soldiers.[235]

The armies of the Meuse cities were at that time more active than the Flemish armies, and played a more important role on the battlefield. Unlike the Flemings, they were not yet organized as sworn societies, such as already existed in Flanders in 1127. But when Henry of Leez left his principality in order to take part in an imperial expedition in Italy, he wanted peace and order to reign in his land. He permitted the burghers of the cities – or perhaps was forced to permit them – to enter into alliances for the maintenance of peace and justice, so that they might act *en bloc* and with one accord against any disturber of the peace.[236] Of course it is possible that this was the first official recognition of communes already in existence. In any case, the commune of Liège employed its force in 1184 against the knights of the Dommartin family, to make war on them.[237]

In the charter which prince-bishop Albert of Cuyck granted to Liège between 1196 and 1200, the military obligations of the inhabitants were set out. 'If a fortress in the principality is occupied or besieged, the bishop must fight the enemy for the first fifteen days with his own army. Once this time has elapsed, the men of Liège must turn out under the leadership of the *avoué* of Hesbaye, who must lead them to the prince's army where they must take their part in the operations until the end of the campaign.'[238] So it appears that the prince generally relied on his armoured cavalry-men as the spearhead of his army, while the service of the communal army was a useful reinforcement of a purely defensive nature. In any case he could call on the help of a powerful vassal, the count of Looz, who regularly helped him in the wars against the duke of Brabant.

In 1212, a serious conflict broke out between Liège and duke Henry I of Brabant. He had collected a strong army as if to attack Moha. The prince-bishop, Hugh of Pierrepont, called out his men and set off for Huy, from where he could more easily ward off the threat against Moha. An ordinary knight, Rase, whose surname is not known, had taken the place of the *avoué* of Hesbaye, who had died in 1207. As commander of the army he allowed himself to be armed by the canons of the cathedral, and took the great standard of St Lambert from the altar on the first of May. He also took an oath never to abandon the standard until he was killed or captured. He rode on a white horse at the head of the communal army to Horion, where the troops had to camp a couple of miles from the city.[239] But Rase had only

[234] Gaier, pp. 146, 240–51. Rousseau, pp. 136–7. Kurth, I, p. 81.
[235] Gaier, pp. 147, 251–4. Rousseau, p. 138. Kurth, I, *loc. cit.*
[236] Rousseau, p. 139. Kurth, I, p. 81.
[237] Kurth, I, p. 93.
[238] *Ibid.*, pp. 106–7.
[239] *Ibid.*, pp. 118–19.

about ten knights with him, and was forced to retreat toward the city on 2 May, when he was threatened by the advancing Brabant army. Back in Liège he decided that at least three hundred knights would be needed to defend the city. The prince-bishop, who was still in Huy, had evidently been taken completely by surprise, and had called up his army too late. Panic broke out in Liège as the Brabant army neared the city in the afternoon, and burghers and clerks alike fled. On 3 May the bishop quickly turned back to Liège and faced the first attacks of the duke of Brabant, whose army had been reinforced by the troops of Walram of Limbourg. The city was insufficiently reinforced, and was taken by the Brabant army, which looted it for four whole days.[240] On 7 May the duke abandoned Liège and on the 8th appeared outside Moha, which he besieged in vain. He went home on the 10th.

The prince-bishop then carefully prepared his revenge. At Liège the whole populace worked on the improvement of the fortresses and the building of new works. At the beginning of July Hugh of Pierrepont had a powerful army of knights, said to be 2,500 strong, though this is certainly exaggerated. As allies he had Ferdinand of Portugal, husband of the countess of Flanders, and Philip of Namur. He could also count on the help of the count of Looz. But in order to collect so great an army of knights, the bishop needed to have the vassals from his own principality with him. Faced with this superior force, duke Henry I of Brabant gave in. He chose to negotiate, and among other points renounced his claim to Moha, but he did not keep the promises he made.[241]

The war started again in 1213 with an invasion of Brabant by Ferdinand of Portugal. In October of that year the bishop and the prince had made a plan to invade Brabant from two sides.[242] But the count of Flanders could only temporarily advance with his troops to the west of Brabant close to Brussels, and then quickly had to pit his troops against the king of France.[243] Henry I took advantage of this to take the offensive himself in the Liège sector, but this time the bishop was on his guard. It is true that more than 150 of his knights were serving as mercenaries under Ferdinand, but he could still rely on the count of Looz, and called up his remaining vassals.

Henry advanced through Waleffe and Borgworm to Tongres, where he failed to take the fortress. Then he marched on Liège, but the city was now better fortified than it had been the year before. Even so, the frightened citizens of Liège wanted to flee on 11 October, and only the personal intervention of the count of Looz, who promised them help, persuaded them to remain in the city. The bishop hurried personally to Huy to fetch the communal army and the men of Dinant, who had not yet arrived. On the morning of the 12th he returned with these troops, and the communal armies then pressed for an immediate attack on the men of Brabant. But it was decided to wait for the forces of the count of Looz, who was collecting his men near the castle of Brustem. Except for the knights who were under Ferdinand, the greater part of the Dommartin clan was absent, as they had concluded an

---

240 G. Smets, *Henri Ier, duc de Brabant (1190–1235)*, Brussels, 1908, pp. 133–4. Gaier, p. 255.
241 Smets, pp. 137–8. Gaier, p. 256.
242 *Vita Odiliae (De triumpho S. Lamberti in Steppes)*, ed. J. Heller, MGH, SS, XXV, 1880, p. 181.
243 Reinerus, p. 667.

agreement with the duke of Brabant. Thierry de Walcourt, Hugues de Florennes and Arnoul de Morialmé had however arrived, and took command. The Liège forces were collected at Lens, and the men from Looz were ready at Brustem. At midnight both armies moved off, and joined up at Montenaken, near Steppes.[244] The decisive battle took place there on 13 October. The knights played the greatest part in the battle: the foot-soldiers from Liège and the other cities, Huy, Dinant, and Fosses, did however give effective help to the knights and gave an excellent account of themselves, but the men from Looz panicked. The armies of the Meuse cities felt a justifiable pride in their national victory, which completely effaced the humiliation of the preceding year. At Liège new banners were made for the communal army, the citizens repaired their damaged equipment, and the whole city put itself in a state of readiness for war. The following year the episcopal army was again called up, this time against Otto, for whom Ferdinand was waiting in the decisive campaign against France. Once more Hugh of Pierrepont had assembled a splendid army of knights: Reiner says he had 700 knights, the *Vita Odiliae* 1,000, probably an exaggeration.[245]

The cities of the prince-bishopric wanted in any case to exploit their military power politically. Following the death of Hugh of Pierrepont, Liège, Huy, Dinant, Fosses, St Trond, Maastricht and Tongres concluded an alliance and formed a confederacy. But the new prince-bishop, John of Eppes, was able to get what he wanted without making concessions. In 1230 the communal armies under his leadership besieged the fortress of Poilvache, which belonged to Walram of Valkenburg. When the bishop died during the siege, the discouraged besiegers retreated after a successful sortie by the enemy garrison. A levy was raised to cover the cost of this expedition.[246]

An important step in the evolution of the Liège communal armies took place under the rule of Henry of Dinant. In 1253, he refused to let the army march on Hainault, where it was to support the prince-bishop's vassal, John of Avesnes. The emperor vainly intervened in an edict of 8 January 1254. He declared that the communal armies must march with the army of the bishop Henry of Guelders. But Henry of Dinant ignored the edict, and organized the Liège army better for the coming conflict. For this purpose he introduced territorial divisions according to the city districts, a system which was also used in Flanders. The six districts of Liège were each allotted a commander, who in his turn had under him a fixed number of leaders, in charge of twenty soldiers. In this way it was easier to assemble the troops. He also effected an alliance with Huy and St Trond, and later with Dinant. In each of these cities similar organisations of the militia were set up. Armed conflict with the bishop followed, who made an alliance with the duke of Brabant and the counts of Looz, Guelders and Jülich. The knights did not attack the fortified cities at once, but began by blockading them from a distance and cutting their lines of communication. They tried to lure the communal armies into the open country, so that they might finish them off there. The communal armies on the other hand directed their attacks against the lords' castles. The people of Huy set fire to Borgworm, and made a vain effort

[244] Reinerus, pp. 667–8. *Vita Odiliae*, pp. 181–3.
[245] Reinerus, p. 671. *Vita Odiliae*, p. 187. Gaier, pp. 259–62.
[246] Kurth, I, pp. 142–3. Gaier, p. 205.

to take Moha. But on their return from Moha they were ambushed by the knights of the count of Jülich and suffered very heavy losses. Dinant was completely cut off and gave up the fight, Huy followed suit; Liège was then besieged and in the end had to capitulate. Each of the rebellious cities was obliged to give up a city gate to the prince, so that he could control the city with a garrison. At Liège, after a renewed rising, during which the exiled Henry of Dinant returned, he built a new fortress at the St Walburgis gate.[247] The reforms which had been introduced were abolished. But in 1269 the men of Liège captured the citadel during an absence of the prince-bishop: a new rebellion broke out, in which Liège again took the lead, with Huy, St Trond, and Dinant. The Liégeois this time appealed to the duke of Brabant and offered him the protectorship of their city. In 1271 a peace treaty was made, which gave the St Walburgis fortress back to the city.[248]

At the end of the thirteenth century the famous private war broke out between the Awans and the Waroux. Many burghers of the city of Liège were involved in the conflict between their families and friends, and this led to a serious weakening of the nobility and the burghers. The city of Huy sided with the Waroux, Liège with the Awans, who afterwards regularly provided mercenaries and commanders for the communal army of this city. But the cities carefully remained neutral in the armed conflict proper. The result of this private war, which raged on into the early fourteenth century, according to the chronicler Hemricourt, was: 'All chivalric honour of men at arms has declined, and the strength of the free towns has grown.'[249] The communal armies stood ready to exploit this favourable opportunity and to take over the role of the knights as the chief power in the principality.

As in Flanders, there followed a period of social conflict in the large cities. Huy, the city that had evolved most in the principality both socially and politically, had an important dispute between the weavers and the cloth merchants. An armed struggle ended favourably for the workers, and the city councillors had to flee to Liège. The prince-bishop Hugo of Châlons supported the guilds of Huy, especially because a rebellion had broken out in Liège against his monetary reforms. Although the workers of Liège profited by this devaluation, they let themselves be swayed by the burghers, who still held complete power. Liège again made an alliance with Dinant, St Trond, Tongres, Maastricht, Fosses, Couvin and Thuin. The bishop asked the count of Looz and the duke of Brabant for help, and since he had almost no troops he was forced to recruit mercenaries. He employed *bidauts* or javelin-men, who attacked the merchants who supplied Liège. The Liégeois reacted with raids on the merchants who brought supplies to Huy. On 9 March 1300 the men of Huy captured the stronghold at Clermont. When they returned to the city after their victory, they were surprised by cavalry and the communal army of Liège, and suffered some losses. But together with the bishop's troops they took their revenge at Bléret and

---

247 John of Hocsem, *Chronicon*, ed. G. Kurth, CRH in 8°, Brussels, 1927, c. 5, pp. 21–3. Kurth, I, pp. 190–212. F. Vercauteren, *Luttes sociales à Liège*, Brussels, 1943, pp. 51–4.
248 Hocsem, c. 7, p. 45. Kurth, I, pp. 218–20.
249 Jacques de Hemricourt, *Le Miroir des Nobles de la Hesbaye*, ed. C. de Borman, and A. Bayot, *Oeuvres de Jacques de Hemricourt*, CRH in 4°, Brussels, 1836, I, c. 1, p. 2.

Pousset. The trouble ended when pope Boniface VIII transferred the bishop of Liège to Besançon.[250]

The new prince-bishop, Adolf of Waldeck, made peace with his subjects. He took away from Huy the privilege with regard to military service, and the inhabitants from then onwards had to do army service, even if the troops of the other free cities of the prince-bishopric did not allow military service to the bishop.[251]

At Huy the prince had already recognized the guilds. At Liège the power of the guilds became obvious in 1303. The burghers then wanted to levy a tax on consumer goods, and the rich citizens' sons assumed a most defiant attitude. They called themselves 'enfants de France', and wore a white hood as a badge. Their choice of name was clearly a reaction against the victory of the Flemish artisans in 1302. An alliance between the clergy, under the leadership of the chapter of St Lambert, and the leaders of the guilds of Liège, gave the representatives a favourable opportunity to fulfil their plans. The guilds at once began military preparations and made their claims. They wanted, besides abolition of taxes and subsidies, to be consulted whenever the communal army had to be called out by the prince.[252] At the end of the meeting at which they set out their demands, they also extorted the concession of representation in the municipal government. Once the guilds had control of half the seats, they wanted still more power, and trouble broke out. In 1307 the two armies faced each other at Vottem, but the citizens seemed so powerful that the prince-bishop chose to negotiate and as the result the guilds kept their representation on the city council. When the burghers and nobility tried to recover their power in 1312, they suffered a terrible defeat called the Mal St Martin.[253] Once they had power in the city council, the guilds appeared in the cities of Liège as military units, exactly as in Flanders, and from then on they formed the basis of the communal armies.

The foot-soldiers in France

Within the general peace movement in France – started and led by the bishops – there developed many 'brotherhoods' of peasants, with priests at their head. In 1038 archbishop Aimon of Bourges formed a confederation in which all men of the diocese over fifteen years old took an oath before their pastors, who unfurled the sacred banners of the Church, and marched at the head of the parish militia. This folk-army destroyed castles and fortresses until its ill-equipped troops, among whom some rode donkeys, were crushed by the lord of Déols on the banks of the Cher.[254] These brotherhoods very often came to a fatal collision with the seignorial or comital law: they were always looking out for their rights, and as they met with success and became conscious of their power, they formulated and presented political and social demands designed to modify society as it then existed. Their lords were naturally

---

[250] Hocsem, c. 24, pp. 100–3. Kurth, I, pp. 251–9.
[251] Hocsem, c. 25, p. 104.
[252] *Ibid.*, c. 26, pp. 106–8. Kurth, I, pp. 268–72. Vercauteren, pp. 66–9.
[253] Hocsem, c. 33, pp. 134–6. Kurth, I, pp. 277–83. Vercauteren, pp. 73–7.
[254] Bloch, *Les classes et le gouvernement des hommes*, p. 206. Boutaric, p. 171.

disturbed to see that the peasants were arming, and were ready to use violence against their masters.

Clearly these examples influenced the communal movement in France. In 1070, the French communal movement started at Le Mans, arising out of punitive expeditions undertaken under the banners of the Church against fortresses of rapacious overlords. The *communio* included in its aims not only the securing of order in the city, but also the struggle against brigands, plunderers and thieves who were causing damage to the community. Just as the peace movement had been founded among the peasants, the sworn brotherhood was established in the cities on the basis of the equality of its members. The commune was limited to inhabitants of the same town or village, whose solidarity and class-consciousness gave them considerable power.

In the reign of Philip I, the inhabitants of Corbie, led by their abbot, took part in several wars at the end of the eleventh century.[255] Under Louis VI and Louis VII these parish and diocesan militia were still active. Led by their priests, the peasants strengthened the royal army in its action against the castles of the greedy lords: the troops were of small value, but they seem to have been useful in sieges. When Louis VI besieged the castle of Le Puiset in 1111, the parish 'communes' took part. The pastor of Guilleville distinguished himself by specially brave conduct, managed to approach the palisade of the castle, and began to demolish it on his own initiative, while the defenders' attention was elsewhere. He called his troops to help, and they made a breach in the wooden fortification, through which the royal army penetrated into the fortress and took it.[256]

Louis VI and his son saw that the establishment of 'communes' was very useful in raising the military standard of the ordinary foot-soldiers, whose purpose however was primarily defensive. Thus Louis VII granted the right to form a 'commune' to Mantes in 1158–59 because the inhabitants, who lived on the border of the royal domain, had always been active in the royal service during his reign and that of his father, and had fortified their city at their own expense.[257] At the end of his reign, Louis VII used the communal armies against one of his vassals for the first time, and in 1177 the citizens of Laon and the communes of Soissons and Vailly helped the royal provost of Laon against bishop Roger of Rozoy.[258]

After the reign of Louis VII the parish and diocesan militia were to all intents and purposes never called out again. Philip Augustus called out the communal armies with increasing frequency after he had granted the status of 'commune' to many places. In so doing, he followed the example of Henry II of England, who had set up similar communes in French cities which were particularly threatened by the enemy. By granting a measure of autonomy he encouraged the administrators of the town to erect fortifications and to arm the commune of those capable of bearing arms

255 A. Luchaire, *Les communes françaises à l'époque des Capétiens directs*, Paris, 1890, p. 178.
256 Suger, *Vita Ludovici grossi*, c. 19, pp. 138–40. Boutaric, p. 200. [*Deeds of Louis the Fat*, pp. 87–90.]
257 Ch. Petit-Dutaillis, 'Les communes françaises. Caractères et évolution des origines au XVIIIe siècle', in *L'évolution de l'humanité* 44, Paris, 1947, p. 116.
258 *Ibid., loc. cit.* A. Luchaire, *op. cit.*, p. 185.

so that they could defend their city properly. Henry II granted a charter to the city of La Rochelle between 1172 and 1178, which had been founded not long before. He permitted the city to form a 'commune' for the defence and safety of the city and the property of the citizens, in return for a promise that they would serve him and his son faithfully. This privilege was granted for as long as the citizens made reasonable use of it. La Rochelle was inhabited by people of every description, who had come streaming in from France and elsewhere, attracted by the privileges that had been granted. The commune had to forge some bond which would unite this mixed population, and give it the necessary cohesion, so that they might collectively defend the honour of the city. Queen Eleanor confirmed this charter in 1199, and asked the community to defend its rights with its arms and the power she had given them. In 1208, king John of England requested those burghers who could afford it to buy a horse, in order to do their military service and assume the responsibility of defending the city. Henry II had given these rights to La Rochelle so that it should not again fall into the hands of the turbulent nobility. King John tried to keep the castle when it was threatened by Philip Augustus. During the captivity of Richard I the seneschal of Normandy also ordered the inhabitants of Evreux to set up a commune when they feared an attack by Philip Augustus. In 1199, queen Eleanor granted the status of a commune to Poitiers, 'in order that the city should better be able to defend our rights and her own, and to preserve it more fully'; she used the same expression in her charter for the commune of the island of Oléron. When Philip Augustus began the conquest of Normandy in 1202, king John granted the status of commune to Fécamp, Harfleur, and Montivilliers. He demanded that they should be prepared to defend the land with arms and anything else that was asked of them.[259]

From a purely military point of view, these communes were useful for the defence of their fortresses, but they were of less importance in the army in the field. Under Richard I and John they were particularly important in a political sense, but their military usefulness was limited to the defence of their cities.

Philip Augustus however took these communes into his army, and under him they were more important than they had been in the armies of Richard and John. He set up new communes in the region of Vexin, in the region of Paris, and later in his newly conquered territories such as Artois, the city of Tournai, and the Vermandois, for the better protection of these places.[260] The charter granted to Tournai in 1188, and confirmed in 1211, specified that the city had to send 300 well-armed men whenever other royal communes sent their contingents.[261] When the king came with his army to the Arouaise region, close to Bapaume, or the same distance from Tournai, the whole commune had to march out with him, if they could get there without hindrance. Following the conquest of Poitou, he exacted unconditional service from Niort: 'all the men of the commune must come at once whenever the king may so desire.'[262]

---

[259] Petit-Dutaillis, pp. 117–21. Poole, *From Domesday Book to Magna Carta*, p. 370, n. 2.
[260] Petit-Dutaillis, p. 120.
[261] *Ibid., loc. cit.* P. Rolland, *Tournai 'Noble Cité'*, Brussels, 1944, p. 28. A. Cartellieri, *Philipp II August, König von Frankreich*, 5 vols, Leipzig, 1899–1922, I, p. 268, n. 6.
[262] Petit-Dutaillis, pp. 120–1.

Two communes deserve special mention because of the defence of their city under enemy attack. In 1185, the commune of Corbie offered stout resistance to Philip of Alsace, and by doing so gave Philip Augustus the chance to come to the rescue.[263] Three years later the commune of Mantes played an important role in the defence of the city during the attack by Henry II.[264]

About 1194, Philip Augustus had more than 5,435 foot-soldiers under his command, and after his great conquests he had between 7,695 and 8,054 men in the royal domain in 1204. The total in 1202 was 8,069 men. Out of these his thirty communes had produced 5,410 men.[265] He made this militia march to the battlefield at Bouvines in 1214, and here it was obvious that they were properly more useful in the defence of the city fortifications. The men of the communes were placed in the centre of the French battle order, but they were driven back by the enemy and played no vital part in the battle. In time, perhaps, they might have acquired greater competence, but in France the kings had so many knights that there was no need to pay attention to the foot-soldiers.

The French communes were in action again in 1233, when nineteen of them were called up during the reign of Louis IX to put down a rising in Beauvais. They were called up again in 1253, and in 1272 they marched in an expedition against the count of Foix.[266] In the wars against the county of Flanders the French communes took part in certain campaigns, notably in 1303 and 1304, but they never distinguished themselves.

In the south of France the communal army of the city of Toulouse deserves notice. This fortress played a great part during the crusade against the Albigensians, and the citizens particularly distinguished themselves in the defence of their city against Simon de Montfort.[267]

It is worth pausing to look at one rural commune, formed in France against the mercenaries who, after the war with Henry II, could no longer find work. A simple carpenter named Durand founded a 'brotherhood' for the restoration of peace and order, asserting that the Holy Virgin had entrusted this mission to him in a vision. He found many supporters among the despairing peasants, and he is said to have gathered 5,000 men. A canon from Le Puy drew up the necessary rules for the brotherhood, and provided it with a piece of uniform – a white hood, made of linen for the summer and wool for winter. On a scarf, or on a white cloak, they wore a leaden image of Our Lady of Le Puy, and inscribed on it as a motto: 'Lamb of God that taketh away the sins of the world, grant us thy peace.' This brotherhood of the *caputiati* followed a strict rule, in which a vendetta was forbidden. The members promised not to swear, not to wear luxurious clothes, never to set foot in taverns, and to come at once at the first summons of their leaders. Each year at Whitsuntide

---

263 Luchaire, p. 187.
264 William the Breton, *Philippis*, I, III, v. 327 ff., p. 77; *Chronicon*, c. 45, p. 189. Petit-Dutaillis, p. 123. Luchaire, p. 187.
265 Lot, I, pp. 219–20, 227. Boutaric, p. 203, n., 204.
266 Boutaric, p. 209, n. 1, 3. Petit-Dutaillis, p. 123. Luchaire, p. 188.
267 Belperron, pp. 330 ff.

they contributed ten pennies. The brotherhood spread all over the regions of Langue-doc, and in Berry and Auxerrois.[268]

They succeeded in defeating a band of mercenaries called the *Palearii* at Dun-le-Roi on 20 July 1183. Philip Augustus' biographer, Rigord, says that the brotherhood was helped by an auxiliary corps sent by the king.[269] This is possible, but not certain, since other sources do not mention this help.

Less than twenty days later, the brotherhood crushed the band of the mercenary leader Curbaran near Milhau in Rouergue.[270] The peace brotherhood from Auvergne defeated a gang of *Brabançiones* in this region, who had made the land unsafe for years.[271]

These victories made the peace brotherhoods realize their own power, and they began to want to use it for political and social ends, and to seek a better lot for the peasants. They threatened the counts and barons if they would not treat their subjects better. The lords of the surrounding countryside became uneasy, and defenders of established authority quickly came to regard these simple folk as disturbers of the peace who threatened the very peace that they had themselves established a short time before. 'They had no respect and no fear of authority, but only wanted to regain the freedom which they claimed to possess as an inheritance from their first ancestors, from the creation of the world. They did not know that bondage was the penalty for original sin. There no longer existed any difference between the great and the humble, but rather a dangerous confusion carrying in its wake the destruction of institutions which now, in accordance with God's will, were ordained by the wisdom and authority of the great. The madness of the rebels went so far that they united in order to seek their freedom.'[272] Robert of Auxerre, a monk who had greatly praised the brotherhood in 1183, also condemned this disobedient sect in 1184.[273]

Bishop Hugh of Auxerre then marched against the brotherhood of the White Hood, and defeated it. Elsewhere the brotherhood was beaten by the notorious mercenary leader Lupatius, and the nobles used mercenaries for the same purpose. In 1184 the brotherhood ceased to exist.[274]

The short life of these White Hoods shows what possibilities there were through the formation of sworn brotherhoods. But at the same time it is obvious that the foot-soldiers could not develop their full potential in a land where the knights unquestionably had the upper hand.

---

[268] Boutaric, p. 172. Bloch, *Les classes et le gouvernement des hommes*, pp. 207–8; A. Mens, *De 'Brabanciones'* . . ., pp. 566–7. Grundmann, Rotten und Brabanzonen, p. 469.

[269] Grundmann, p. 469. Boutaric, p. 172. Mens, pp. 566–7. Rigord, *Gesta Philippi Augusti*, c. 23, p. 36; c. 24, p. 37.

[270] Godfrey of Bruil, RHF, XII, p. 219. Grundmann, p. 470.

[271] Robert of Auxerre, *Chronicon cum continuationibus*, ed. O. Holder-Egger, MGH, SS, XXVI, 1882, p. 247. Grundmann, p. 470.

[272] *Historia episcoporum Autissiodorensium*, RHF, XVIII, p. 729. Grundmann, p. 471. Boutaric, p. 173. Bloch, p. 200.

[273] Robert of Auxerre, *Chronicon*, p. 247. Bloch, p. 208.

[274] Boutaric, p. 174. Grundmann, p. 471. Bloch, *loc. cit.*

The Numerical Strength of the Foot-soldiers

There is almost no reliable information on the numerical strength of the foot-soldiers in medieval armies up to the beginning of the fourteenth century. In general, the earliest reasonably accurate figures were recorded as soon as the foot-soldiers became an important element in the army, but as is well known, most chroniclers exaggerate army strengths. Occasionally however more accurate figures may be obtained. This is the case with the chronicler of Hainault, Gilbert of Mons, who has given accurate troop strengths for the knightly armies of the south Netherlands. Usually Gilbert gives the exaggerated numbers which occur in almost all the sources of his time. In 1170, the duke of Brabant is said to have set out with 30,000 foot-soldiers against the future Baldwin V of Hainault, who had gone to a tourney with 3,000 men in his train. In 1178, Baldwin is said to have sent 60,000 men against the king of France, and as many again in 1181. In 1184, the duke of Brabant is supposed to have used 60,000 men against the count of Hainault, and in 1185 the king of France was said to have 2,000 knights and 140,000 cavalry and foot-soldiers in his army, as opposed to 400 knights and 40,000 horsemen and foot-soldiers under Philip of Alsace. In the same year Baldwin V entered Namur with 30,000 foot-soldiers. In 1188, he is said to have besieged the count of Namur with 300 knights and 30,000 horsemen and foot-soldiers to the 240 knights and 20,000 foot-soldiers of the count of Namur.[275]

Obviously these figures are worthless. On the other hand, the figures Gilbert gives elsewhere are interesting. In 1172, the count of Hainault went to the help of the count of Namur with 1,500 picked foot-soldiers, and they besieged Arlon. Three years later Baldwin V went off to a tourney with 200 knights and 1,200 picked foot-soldiers, and in 1180 he dispatched 3,000 foot-soldiers to the king of France, who had asked for good fighters.[276] In these instances it is clear that Gilbert's figures are trustworthy: since it was a question of hand-picked foot-soldiers, it is quite possible that a count was made, and that the number of troops is accurate.

The same tendency to exaggerate is found among the chroniclers of the First Crusade. Fulcher of Chartres and Albert of Aix both mention 600,000 combatants. Ekkehard put them at 300,000 and Raymond of Aguilers at 100,000 men. Anna Comnena gave the strength of the army of Godfrey of Bouillon as no less than 10,000 knights and 70,000 foot-soldiers.[277] But Raymond did not exaggerate so seriously during the siege of Jerusalem, when he estimated the strength of the crusaders' army at 12,000 men of whom 1,200 to 1,300 were knights.[278] As has already been stated in the first chapter, their strength at the battle of Ascalon in 1099 reached 1,200

---

275 Gilbert of Mons, *Chronicon Hanoniense*, c. 62, p. 101; c. 84, p. 123; c. 99, p. 134; c. 114, p. 172; c. 118, p. 181; c. 120, p. 186; c. 143, p. 219.
276 *Ibid.*, c. 71, p. 111; c. 77, p. 117; c. 95, p. 131.
277 S. Runciman, *The First Crusade*, p. 396.
278 Raymond of Aguilers, p. 298. Runciman, p. 337.

knights and 9,000 foot-soldiers.[279] Fulcher, who so greatly over-estimated the initial size of the crusaders' forces, later gave very small figures for the armies of the kings of Jerusalem: Baldwin went off to Jerusalem to succeed his brother with 200 knights and 700 foot-soldiers. During the first battle of Ramla in 1101 he had 260 knights and 900 foot-soldiers; the second battle of Ramla was fought without foot-soldiers and only 200 knights. In the third battle there, in 1105, Baldwin's army included 500 knights, with some lighter cavalry and 200 foot-soldiers.[280]

Luckily there are some isolated reliable documents from the archives which give us a better insight. This is true of the French foot-soldiers during the reign of Philip Augustus, who had stipulated what numbers the communes and the ecclesiastical institutions had to send to the army. In the *Prisia servientium* it was specified how many men had to be sent by each provostdom, monastery, and commune. About 1194, the king had over 5,435 *sergeants* under his control by this method, but when several great conquests had enlarged his territories there were 7,695 to 8,054 men, if he called them all up. In 1202, the count totalled 8,069 men.[281] These were mostly foot-soldiers from the communes: the thirty communes gave a total of 5,140 men. Several communes fought in the battle of Bouvines with a strength of 3,160 foot-soldiers. In 1202–3, Philip Augustus maintained 257 knights, 267 mounted *sergeants*, 80 mounted crossbowmen, 133 unmounted crossbowmen and about 2,000 *sergeants* on foot on the Norman border, not counting the 300 mercenaries under Cadoc.[282] The king was able to maintain these men for quite a long time, and then disband them later, as soon as Normandy was conquered. This little permanent army did good service in the defence of the border.

Louis IX called on the foot-soldiers to reinforce his army of knights. In an expedition against the count of Brittany in 1231, he employed 1,600 foot-soldiers, and two years later the forces from nineteen communes came out under command of the king in order to restore order at Beauvais between rich and poor.[283] There are some isolated figures for the year 1253 for some communes in the north of France, when they sent 3,700 men.[284]

These examples clearly show that the kings of France did not call up very large units of foot-soldiers; they could however make greater demands on their communes when military operations were taking place close to these towns. We have already seen that this was expressly provided for in the charter granted to Tournai. In 1242, Tournai sent the required 300 soldiers to the royal army, which routed Henry III of England at Taillebourg. In 1298, 300 men from Tournai again took part in a royal expedition in Flanders. But at Cassel in 1328 this number was raised to 200 crossbowmen and 400 pikemen, and in 1339 the city sent 1,000 men to Buironfosse. The following year Tournai provided the king with 250 crossbowmen and bowmen,

[279] Lot, I, p. 135.
[280] Fulcher, p. 373 AB, 391 C, 400–1, 413 C.
[281] Lot, I, pp. 219–20, and 227, n. 2.
[282] Lot, I, pp. 227 and 220.
[283] Lot, I, p. 236. Boutaric, p. 209, n. 2.
[284] Boutaric, p. 209, n. 1.

750 pikemen and 16 cavalrymen.[285] Corbie was supposed to send 200 men according to the *Prisia*, but sent 400 in 1253. The contingent from Noyon fluctuated between 150 and 500 men.[286]

There are scarcely any trustworthy figures for foot-soldiers in most of the principalities. It is not until 1302 that we get a relatively exact idea of the number of troops in the county of Flanders. In the battle of Courtrai we have definite figures for part of the Bruges contingent, and can calculate the approximate strength of the other part. The Flemish army may be reckoned to have consisted of at least 8,000 fighting-men and about 500 auxiliaries, with a maximum of 10,500 heavily-armed fighters and 500 lightly-armed auxiliaries.[287] In 1303 and 1304 we can closely determine the strength of the Bruges communal armies in Zeeland and Holland, and we get the first indisputable numbers for a part of the communal foot-soldiers.

In 1303 the first contingent of the city of Bruges consisted of:

	Soldiers	Servants
Aldermen with their retinue	33	10
Physician	1	
Crossbowmen	200	
Shieldbearers		100
Sergeants	183	
English mercenaries	7	
Guildsmen	830	
	1,254	110

The total sent by the city of Bruges is 1,364 men, but this included a certain number of foreigners, e.g. the English and some of the *sergeants*.

After some weeks, this communal army was relieved by new troops from Bruges and returned home.[288]

For the expedition in Zeeland and Holland starting on 18 March 1304, the totals are as follows:

Ships	Masters	Sailors	Total	Number of soldiers transported
10	10	34	44	300
29	30	98	128	930

These 1,230 men were commanded by three aldermen or councillors.[289]

---

285 Delpech, II, p. 83. Rolland, Tournai, p. 29. G. le Muisit, pp. 53, 99, 119–20, 125. In 1365 the total strength of the communal army of Tournai was 3,991 men: L. Verriest, *Les luttes sociales et le contrat d'apprentissage à Tournai jusqu'en 1424*, Brussels, 1912, p. 16, note.
286 Luchaire, p. 180.
287 Verbruggen, *De slag der gulden sporen*, pp. 202–5, 211.
288 J.F. Verbruggen, *Vlaanderen na de Guldensporenslag. De vrijheidsstrijd van het graafschap Vlaanderen, 1303–1305*, Bruges, 1991, p. 42.
289 *Ibid.*, p. 85.

In the important expedition to Zierikzee which started on 11 May 1304 there were 2,400 men.[290]

In the same year Bruges had 144 ships in service, which in theory enabled them to transport 144 x 30, or 4,320 men. But actually they could not always count on so many ships, and usually had to make do with less. We can calculate the maximum number of troops who could be transported by the fleet: it amounts to 9,600 men, a figure which was probably never reached. The Flemings at this time also had to fight the king of France along their southern border. He was their chief enemy, and they would certainly use the main body of troops against him. It is therefore possible that in 1304 they had at least 20,000 or 24,000 men under arms in Zeeland and along the French border.[291]

In the later fourteenth century the Flemish communal armies were even stronger than around the early years of the century. At Ghent, the entourage of the count of Namur sought to raise 4,120 men in 1325, but had to be content with 3,200. At that time the weavers were not allowed to do military service, and for this reason at least 2,192 weavers were not included.[292] The Transport of Flanders, introduced in the years 1321–25, fixed the number of foot-soldiers to be sent by every town and village. It was based on the system of taxation and the financial possibilities. An army of 10,000 foot-soldiers consisted of 1,520 men from Bruges, 1,384 from Ghent, 1,333 from the Franc of Bruges, 1,072 from Ypres, etc.[293] In 1340 James van Artevelde and the towns of Bruges and Ghent made a big effort and sent large armies in the service of King Edward III, who was giving subsidies. The total strength of the communal army of Bruges was 8,280 men and 6,547 of them participated at the siege of Tournai. Ghent sent also a big army, 5,455 men. The count of Flanders, Louis of Crécy, was with 929 knights and squires in the army of the king of France.[294] In the battle of Cassel in 1328 at least 3,185 Flemings from the Westhoek were killed in action,[295] so that this army must have had between 6,500 and 8,000 men, perhaps even more. The Flemings had three such armies at that time.

The Flemish counts had very powerful armies for those days. Their foot-soldiers were perhaps the most numerous of the time: only the kings of England, who similarly managed to maintain large units of foot-soldiers for a very short time, had such large armies.

In July 1277, Edward I had 2,576 foot-soldiers in the first Welsh war, and at the end of August 15,640, of whom 9,000 were Welsh. In September there were only 2,125 foot. In 1282, on June 15, the foot numbered 7,000. The total was not kept up. The combat strength fluctuated from week to week. In the army of Edward I there

---

[290] *Ibid.*, p. 85.

[291] *Ibid.*, pp. 91, 118.

[292] Verbruggen, *Un projet d'ordonnance comtale sur la conduite de la guerre pendant le soulèvement de la Flandre*, BCRH 118, 1953, pp. 124–5, 122.

[293] W. Buntinx, *Het Transport van Vlaanderen, 1305–1517*, unpublished dissertation, University of Ghent, 1965.

[294] Verbruggen, *Het Gemeenteleger van Brugge van 1338 tot 1340*, p. 16.

[295] H. Pirenne, *Le soulèvement de la Flandre maritime de 1323–1328*, Brussels, 1906, in 8°, pp. xxix and lv–lvi.

were between 3,000 and 4,000 foot-soldiers; other forces had perhaps the same strength. In 1287 the royal army at one moment numbered 11,000 foot, among whom were only 3,710 Englishmen, and the rest came from south Wales. In November 1294 the king had probably more than 31,000 foot in pay in various armies in Wales, and 16,000 assembled at Chester early in December. The army of Warwick had some 14,500 foot-soldiers early in January 1295, but only 2,400 at the battle of Maes Moydog in March.[296] In 1297 Edward's foot-soldiers reached their peak figure of 7,810 men in Flanders.[297] The following year the king called up many foot-soldiers, and at the start of the campaign against Scotland their number totalled 12,500, of whom 10,000 were Welshmen. At Falkirk he had 25,700 foot. In 1300 the maximum strength was 9,000, but that level was not maintained. In 1301, the maximum was just over 7,500, in 1303 almost 7,500.[298] Edward also had armoured cavalry. In general his armies were more powerful than those of the Scots, for which we have no reliable information. At Bannockburn the number of Scots was reckoned at a maximum of 6,900, and according to one chronicler there were 900 cavalry and 6,600 foot-soldiers at Halidon Hill in 1333.[299]

There is practically no information about the strength of the Swiss armies up to the beginning of the fourteenth century. At Morgarten the Confederate troops were reckoned at only 3,000 to 4,000 men in 1315. At the battle of Laupen in 1339 the city of Bern had 6,000 men, of whom 1,000 had been sent by the Waldstätte, the victors at Morgarten, who had been hired by Bern.[300]

From this survey it is clear that the Scottish and Swiss armies were still comparatively small at this time. The king of France commanded so powerful a knightly army that he used a bare minimum of foot-soldiers. A strength of 10,000 was thus especially large. It was perhaps quite exceptional for the foot-soldiers to number 15,000: such numbers were only rarely exceeded, and for limited periods. The kings of England succeeded in raising armies of 10,000 or more men for a few days or a couple of weeks, but as we have said before, such great numbers could not be maintained for a month or more. In Flanders it was also possible to raise armies of 10,000 to 15,000 or even more foot-soldiers, but this seldom happened in practice. In France as well as in England and Flanders troops were normally called up in areas under threat of attack or in border areas, where military operations were taking place. In England it was the counties bordering Wales and Scotland which principally provided the ordinary foot-soldiers for the royal expeditions in those areas. Following the subjugation of Wales, the majority of soldiers for the royal army were recruited in this district, and then reinforced with foot-soldiers from the counties close to the theatre of war. In 1322 Edward II, perhaps for the first time in the military history of his kingdom, raised foot-soldiers from every county of England.[301] In

296 Morris, *Welsh Wars*, pp. 128, 131–2, 160, 162. M. Prestwich, *War, Politics and Finance under Edward I*, pp. 92–3.
297 Lewis, *The English Forces in Flanders*, p. 311.
298 M. Prestwich, *War, Politics and Finance under Edward I*, pp. 94–7.
299 Lot, I, pp. 327–8.
300 Delbrück, III, pp. 580 and 509.
301 Morris, *Mounted Infantry*, p. 91.

Flanders this was also the case in all the major campaigns. At Courtrai in 1302, only troops from part of the county were present. In 1303, the Westhoek alone furnished the foot-soldiers who fought at Arques. The following year there was fighting almost simultaneously at Zierikzee and Mons-en-Pévèle, so that all the forces of the principality could not go into action at the same time on one field of battle. In 1328 three armies were formed, but only one of them, again the troops from the Westhoek, fought at Cassel.[302] In the case of 'landweer', defence of the land, as for example in September 1302, foot-soldiers were called up in the entire county, but we do not know their numbers. It is possible that at that time there were more than 15,000 soldiers in the army, but this is not certain. The city of Bruges, which occupied a leading position and from a financial point of view was the most affluent, did not send a particularly large contingent to this campaign. We know the expenditure for the expedition to Douai and Pont-à-Raches, which lasted forty-one days from 30 August to 9 October: a calculation made according to the same method as that used for determining the strength of the Bruges militia on 11 July 1302 shows that at least 1,605, possibly as many as 2,258 men were sent by Bruges.[303]

If the foot-soldiers were 8,000 to 10,000 men strong, their numbers were three to four times greater than those of the knightly army against which they were pitted. Knightly armies of 2,500 to 3,000 armoured cavalry were among the most powerful of the time. In such a case the foot-soldiers could successfully fight and defeat the enemy, if their morale was good, and they were suitably armed.

The Equipment of the Foot-soldiers

At the end of the thirteenth century and in the early fourteenth century, the Flemings, the Scots and the Swiss had equipment well suited to fighting against armoured cavalry. Each of these armies had its archers, crossbowmen among the Flemings and Swiss, and archers armed with the longbow among the Scots, who were far less numerous, and therefore could not have so great an effect as their enemies the archers from South Wales and England. But the archers were only an auxiliary branch in the Scottish, Swiss and Flemish armies. The strength of the army lay in the heavily-armed foot-soldiers, the pikemen and those with other heavy weapons.

The foot-soldiers used weapons serving both offensive and defensive purposes. With these weapons they could strike as well as pierce, and the pikes of the foot-soldiers were longer than the lances of the noble cavalry. At Courtrai the Flemings combined the use of the pike with that of the 'goedendag', or mace. The pike is a long and heavy weapon, the butt-end of which was planted in the ground, or pressed against the ground with the foot, and was used thus to stop a cavalry assault and to break up the enemy battle order. They had to inflict such losses that the knights who had penetrated into the ranks were too few to continue the fight successfully, and to break through the battle order. The Swiss and the Scots also used

---

[302] *Istore et Croniques*, I, pp. 342 and 534. Verbruggen, *De slag der gulden sporen*, p. 272.
[303] J. Colens, *Le compte communal de la ville de Bruges*, pp. 160 ff.

pikes in the same way. Flemings also used *goedendags*, the Swiss halberds, and the Scots great battle-axes. These weapons, it is true, were shorter than a knight's lance, but longer than the nobles' swords. They were wielded with both hands, just like the pikes, which meant that the men could not have a shield, but wore short mail shirts, and iron plates, or they had a habergeon under their helmet, so that head and neck were protected: they also had iron gloves and a doublet. Because they were not so well protected as the armoured cavalryman, and had to avoid being ridden down by the horses, the foot-soldiers needed the long pikes to halt the charges, but as soon as they had done this, the long weapons were a nuisance in hand-to-hand fighting. Then the men with the *goedendags*, the halberds and the axes came into their own. For this reason they were placed between the pikemen, or in the second rank, so that with their shorter, very heavy weapons they could put the horses out of action, for a heavy blow, according to eyewitnesses, could knock down a horse or kill it, or make it rear up and throw its rider.[304] The weapons had to be heavy and fairly long to shatter or pierce the knights' protective mail, and particularly to break through the iron cuirasses and helmets. On the *goedendag* there was a stout steel pin which was fastened to the thick wooden handle with an iron ring, so as to form an enormous club with a heavy head. A skilful fighter could strike with this and then pierce.[305] The Swiss halberds also had points projecting above a very wide battle-axe:[306] these were as greatly feared by their Austrian enemies as the Flemish *goedendags* were by the French.[307] It is possible that the halberd had a hook on the back of the axe, so that it could be used to pull the knights out of the saddle, for which the Flemings used their hooked pikes. The Scots' battle-axes were made on the same principle. Behind the pikemen, the warriors with the *goedendags*, halberds, or battle-axes, were placed the foot-soldiers with shorter weapons: swords, axes, curved falchions and fist-shields, and so on. They could attack the knights in the hand-to-hand fighting and surround them.

Soldiers had to be quite well off to be able to provide themselves with such weapons. A Franciscan friar of Ghent put this into words proudly when he wrote: 'Here and in the following battles I make no mention of the strength of the French foot, because the Flemings, brave and well-fed, are exceptionally well-armed fellows who are not much worried by the French foot'.[308] This may be exaggerated, but it has some foundation. We know, in fact, the equipment of some citizens of Bruges and its value, and this is worth a glance.

A few unpublished fragments from the time just after the defeat of the Flemings at Zierikzee in 1304 give us the following information: among the citizens of Bruges, Joris Voet, Gillis Voet and Michiel die Coelnare lost equipment respectively worth

---

304 *Annales Gandenses*, p. 76.
305 G. Guiart, vv. 14415–23, p. 233. H. van Duyse, 'Le Goedendag, arme flamande: sa légende et son histoire', *Bull. de la Société d'histoire de Gand*, 1896, pp. 38–43.
306 Good reproductions in: H. Schneider, 'Die Neugestaltung der Waffenhalle im Schweizerischen Landesmuseum in Zürich', *RIHM*, no. 9, 1950, p. 352.
307 John of Winterthur, *Chronica*, p. 80.
308 *Annales Gandenses*, p. 22.

£28 10s, £34 and £35.[309] Their arms consisted of a short mail tunic worth £10 to £15, a staff or *goedendag* worth ten shillings, a habergeon, a buckler or shield (£1), iron plates that served as body-armour, gloves with small iron plates, a pair of armoured hose, sleeves with plates, and possibly a doublet if the man had no mail tunic. Rich burghers from Ypres had equipment worth at least £100; others had mail tunics worth £20.[310]

Although every soldier did not possess such heavy equipment, it is clear that an outfit costing for example £21 was a considerable matter in the life of an artisan then earning three shillings a day.[311] In order to buy himself such equipment he had to set aside 140 days' wages, which is more than half a year's wages in a time when the total working year was reckoned at 240 days – a very heavy expense for an individual. Besides, there was collective equipment such as tents, banners, etc. The artisans and city authorities had made some provisions for this by purchasing collective necessities at the expense of the community, either the city or the guild. The city was responsible for the arms of the crossbowmen, and they were always indemnified for lost bows. Each member of a guild had to be responsible, however, for his own arms, according to his status. It testifies to the extraordinary military spirit of the city council and the population that the Flemish cities succeeded in enforcing such regulations so meticulously, and it does them great credit. For the members of the guilds, their arms were a sign of their dignity as free citizens, and represented a highly valued privilege. As free members of a guild they were proud of their power, and their arms and organization were obviously very useful in the social and political conflicts with the burghers.

The heavily-armed soldiers formed the backbone of the Flemish foot-soldiers, and of the Scots and Swiss, but in England the archers were of paramount importance, and the utmost reliance was placed on this weapon. In the English royal army they were able to compete on equal terms with the mailed cavalry, which was partly employed on foot to support the efforts of the bowmen.

It has already been seen that the longbow represented a technical improvement in range and especially in rapidity of shooting. But what use is a weapon except in the hands of brave and capable soldiers? Skill in the use of the bow and the tactical employment of the archers also played a most important part. Each soldier had to have a bow perfectly suited to his physical strength, for too light a bow could be easily broken by a strong man, and a weak man could not draw one that was too stiff and heavy. 'The maximum efficiency was reached when an archer, facing sideways, giving his full attention to the task in hand, used the full strength of his left arm, which drew the bow forward while his right hand pulled the string up to his eye. His back, shoulders, and arms contributed to the effort, together with his weight and physical strength. The adaptation of the archer to his weapon was essential to successful shooting: every limb, every joint, the muscles as well as the weight,

---

[309] Ghent, Archives of the State (Rijksarchief), Fonds St. Genois, no. 1098. Supplement Verbaere, no. 33 bis.

[310] F. Funck-Brentano, 'Additions au Codex diplomaticus Flandriae', *Bibl. Ec. Chartes* 57, 1896, p. 43.

[311] Bruges, Account of the city, 1304, 2, fo. 47. It is the daily pay of a soldier.

endless practice and inborn skill, all these things had to be brought to the cultivation of the delicate art of archery.'[312] The training of one generation after another ensured for the English archers at the time of the Hundred Years War incomparable skill.

Yet the individual proficiency of an archer was not enough. The tactical use of the weapon was also of the utmost importance if it was to have its maximum effect, and it was the wholesale use of archers by the thousand which turned the scale, making it possible to kill vast numbers of enemy troops, or at least put them out of action. Even if the shots came from too great a distance to be fatal, or if the enemy were too heavily protected by armour, these great bands of bowmen could blind their opponents under a hail of arrows, or wound their horses making them rear up and throw the riders. At Dupplin Moor in 1332 the Scottish soldiers were pressed closely up together by the accurate showers of English arrows, and were thrown into disorder, blinded or wounded, and the press was so thick that many died without having been wounded.[313]

The archers were placed along the flanks of the battle order, or interspersed between the various units of the front line, or occupied the first ranks with the dismounted knights behind them. Both small formations and the battle order as a whole were thus protected, so that the archers could also outflank the enemy and shoot directly into their flanks in the first two cases. In the other case they inflicted heavy casualties on the enemy while protecting the whole battle order. In 1333, the English knights and mailed cavalrymen dismounted and fought on foot at Halidon Hill: bands of archers were placed among their three formations, and a reserve stood behind the battle order.[314]

The excellent arms of the Flemings, Scots, Swiss and English were not however enough to bring victory by themselves. Cohesion in the formations of the foot-soldiers also played a very important part, and this is the next problem which we must examine, making use of the examples given above in the brief historical surveys of the development of the foot-soldiers in various lands.

Solidarity or Cohesion of the Foot-soldiers

From this historical survey it is clear that in the Middle Ages there were wide differences in the foot-soldiers according to the society from which they came. In lands where the feudal system prevailed, and the mailed cavalry were lords of society, it was difficult for the foot-soldiers to shake off their inferiority complex. In areas where the feudal system was less strongly in force, or not at all, there were always foot-soldiers, who were sometimes the only branch of the army and therefore naturally important. Their value, however, depended on their numerical strength, armament, and the close co-operation or solidarity of their formations. This

---

312 Lot, I, p. 315. Morris, *Welsh Wars*, p. 101.
313 Oman, II, pp. 104–5.
314 Morris, *Mounted Infantry*, p. 92.

cohesiveness was necessary for the creation of the indispensable trust between the fighting men and their leaders, and also mutual trust within the units.

In order to stress the value of the Flemish foot-soldiers in comparison with those of Hainault, the Franciscan friar of Ghent, whom we have already quoted, pointed out the fact that the latter were far smaller in numbers, possessed practically no defensive equipment, and lacked the courage of the Flemings. In his account of the siege of Lessines in 1303, he wrote disdainfully: 'The count of Hainault with all his serfs – even though he ruled two counties at the time and could also count on the help of the French, – never once dared do battle with the Flemings.'[315] The personal liberty of the soldiers, citizens, craftsmen or peasants, who bore the heavy burden of military service, was a powerful incentive to strict fulfilment of the task laid on them. It was also a great honour to be able to bear arms in defence of one's country.

Personal liberty was one of the important elements in holding the foot-soldiers together, and in all the countries already mentioned the foot-soldiers were free men, who fought with a certain cohesion. Serfs were rarely used as soldiers in medieval armies, and when they were, they were of no great value. The example of the brotherhood established by the carpenter Durand in France for the struggle against the plundering mercenaries shows unmistakably that the lords made their authority over these poor peasants very quickly felt, and made them recognize their status as serfs by force of arms.

But the mere collection of free men was not enough to create disciplined units. We have already seen that a widespread custom, namely the establishment of a commune on the old German lines, encouraged *esprit de corps* within its free society. Such communes continued to exist among the Frisians, in the Dithmarschen, and among the Swiss. In Anglo-Saxon England the nucleus of king Harold's army in 1066 still consisted of *huscarls*, who formed a military 'guild' under king Canute. The *huscarls* lived in the entourage of the king, and were under strict discipline, as professional soldiers. They had their own code of honour, which obliged them to respect the honour of their master and their comrades, and to protect their interests.[316] Elsewhere new communes were set up; in the case of Italy, Flanders, Liège and France this took place in the cities. In principle, the inhabitants who formed these communes were all free and equal, and their group felt a class-consciousness which brought solidarity. The commune defended the interests of its members against outsiders, at first chiefly against robbers and bandits from the surrounding country. It was quickly isolated from the neighbouring districts by fortifications, and was favoured with privileges, so that it could do as it liked. As the cities grew more powerful, the communal armies played an important part in military affairs. In the municipal troops from Lombardy, Flanders and the prince-bishopric of Liège solidarity was fostered by the grouping of the army according to districts and streets. A further subdivision was introduced in the cities of Flanders and Liège when the guilds formed military units. The commune then rested on a solid framework, in which

---

[315] *Annales Gandenses*, pp. 42, 100.
[316] C.W. Hollister, *Anglo-Saxon Military Institutions*, pp. 12–15.

solidarity and cohesion could be easily developed and maintained, since they supported the professional interests of the members. Municipal patriotism inspired the general formation of the commune, but the guilds were motivated by political and social aspirations. The development of the spirit of solidarity made the smallest units of the communal armies stronger than before.

Among mercenaries the formation of a brotherhood appeared to be indispensable for the exercise of their profession. Strict discipline was absolutely necessary for them and they had to move in units on the march and on the battlefield. Since society was hostile to these plunderers and robbers, the gang was forced to maintain its close cohesiveness for the protection of its members. We have seen how the French peasants in some districts seized upon the same expedient in their action against the lawless mercenaries. As soon as this particular enemy had been overcome, the brotherhood turned against the political and social enemy – the selfish nobility.

The units of foot-soldiers had their own insignia or banners, like the knights, both in the cities and the rural communes. While the Lombard armies used a large banner-waggon or *carroccio*, the Flemish cities had their own banners, and later the guilds also had their own small banners. The beautiful Oxford chest bears witness eloquently for the Flemings of 1302: the unknown artist has splendidly depicted a whole series of guild banners with the standards of the cities and the county, and the princely coat of arms.[317] In the frescoes of the Leugemeete, or chapel of St John and St Paul in Ghent, the communal army is portrayed in the same military spirit.[318]

The communal armies also wore a uniform, as is evident from the Oxford chest, the Leugemeete frescoes, and innumerable entries in the city records. The wearing of the same clothes by the crossbowmen and fighters of the same guild was an important evolutionary step toward the subdivisions of the municipal army. In the French cities the communal soldiers also wore a uniform, and two examples show that those uniforms were conceived on similar lines. The soldiers of Orléans, in 1304, wore black tunics with a heraldic device on the chest and back, so that they could readily recognize each other in battle.[319] In the fourteenth century the men of Tournai wore red tunics with a silver castle, the arms of Tournai, on the chest and back.[320]

Social conditions played a large part in fostering solidarity in the communes, but common experience in battle was just as important, as the example of the mercenaries shows. Professional soldiers could acquire skill in battle more quickly than the communal armies, some of which had been developing for nearly two hundred years before they became the chief fighting unit of their principality, as in the county of Flanders. The crossbowmen could practise in time of peace, as the English bowmen did, and thus became extremely proficient, but for the pikemen and heavy foot-soldiers this was more difficult. Real systematic training of their formations was non-existent for lack of money. But the foot-soldiers acquired experience in the daily

---

317 Courtrai Chest at New College, Oxford. Verbruggen, *De slag der gulden sporen*, p. 258 and plates IV and V.
318 A. Van Werveke, *Het Godshuis van Sint-Jan en Sint-Pauwel te Gent*, plates.
319 G. Guiart, vv. 566–72, p. 261.
320 G. le Muisit, pp. 99, 119–20, 125.

life of the city, even in times of peace. This was the case when a whole communal army marched against a local lord who had done some wrong to the city of the citizens, as often happened. In 1274 the commune of Tournai captured the knight Watier de Le Plagne in the neighbouring territory of Mortagne.[321] At Lille the commune went on such an expedition under several banners, carried in front and behind to ensure an orderly and disciplined march.[322] At Valenciennes a similar custom was mentioned in the *charta pacis*, the peace charter of 1114. The members of the brotherhood had to follow their banners, and no one might march in front of these banners, nor straggle behind them. Each man had to march under the standard of his unit.[323] Most cities had customs of this kind, and communal armies learned in that way how to march properly in good order.

As well as preserving order and keeping an eye on the aristocracy outside the towns, the communal armies also gained experience by marching out against neighbouring towns with whom they were not on good terms, such as Lille and Douai in 1284.[324]

When there was a ceremonial entry into a city, or if a prince made a state visit to a city, units of the communal army usually went out to bear him company. On 17 April 1127, young men marched out of St Omer to join William Clito. They were drawn up in formation under their banners, carrying bows and arrows, and carried out mock attacks as though offering resistance to the new count. Their units were followed at some distance by bands of citizens.[325] When the victors of the battle of Courtrai made their ceremonial entry into Ghent on 14 July 1302, anyone who could carry a bow went out to meet them.[326]

Communal soldiers also gained experience in political and social conflicts in the cities, and this emphasises the importance of their banners. When the commune of Tournai rebelled on 10 April 1307 against the city council, which had imposed a very unpopular tax, the guilds appointed leaders in their units and fetched the city banners from the houses of the constables.[327] When the duke of Brabant gave permission for each of the twenty-five guilds to have a banner at Louvain in 1267, he stipulated that they should not sound the 'banclock', nor could they go and fetch either the city banner or their own banners, or march off with them without the permission of the mayor, the aldermen and the councillors.[328] Following an uprising in Cambrai, bishop Pierre de Lévis, count of Cambrésis, ordered the knight Ferri de Pickigny to pronounce sentence against the insurgents. His judgement ran thus: since they marched out in battle order, as though in an army, with banners flying, both within and without Cambrai, the banners must be handed over. Ferri shall do what

---

[321] *Ibid.*, p. 34.
[322] *Le livre Roisin*, ed. R. Monier, Bibl. Soc. hist. droit, 2, Paris, Lille, 1932, pp. 7–9.
[323] MGH, SS, XXI, pp. 608–9.
[324] G. Espinas, *Une guerre sociale interurbaine dans la Flandre wallonne au XIIIe siècle, Douai et Lille, 1284–1285*, Bibl. Soc. hist. droit, Lille, 1930.
[325] Galbert, c. 66, pp. 106–7.
[326] Lodewijk van Velthem, II, 1. IV, c. 43, vv. 3086–7, p. 353.
[327] G. le Muisit, pp. 40–1.
[328] C. Wyffels, *De Oorsprong der Ambachten in Vlaanderen en Brabant*, p. 111.

he will with them. Only one banner may remain in the county, that is the one bearing the arms of the bishop. It shall be given into the charge of the prince's men. If a citizen should unfurl another banner without the bishop's permission, he will be summarily judged, will forfeit all his goods, and will be banished from the city and county.[329] The political and social conflicts between 1280 and 1302 gave the men much military experience particularly in the Flemish cities, as the risings in Bruges and Ghent in 1301 and 1302 show, and this continued into the fourteenth century.

There was more important experience to be gained on the battlefield itself. In Italy, foot-soldiers took part in innumerable expeditions in the second half of the twelfth century, and in the thirteenth. Out of the fifty years between 1155 and 1205, the communal army of Milan was fighting in about twenty, and this was the case with most of the Lombard cities.[330] Although the French communes were not called up for war service as often as the Italians and Flemings, the French historian A. Luchaire rightly observes that the discharge of their military obligations took up a great deal of the townsmen's time and energy.[331] In their studies and criticism of medieval warfare scholars have not taken sufficient account of the great number of wars, and of the experience which both knights and foot-soldiers gained in them.

In the thirteenth century the foot-soldiers had more opportunity than before to fit themselves for military operations. In England this was so during the campaigns for the subjection of Wales, which took place in 1277, 1282–3, 1287–8, 1294–5. Foot-soldiers from the borders, and their Welsh adversaries, remained under arms for months at a time, and thus gained priceless experience. When Wales was subdued, the campaigns against Scotland began, and followed each other in 1296, 1298, 1300 and then from June 1301 to January 1302, in May 1303, and there was another campaign in Flanders in 1297 lasting till he beginning of 1298. In view of the fact that the royal armies largely consisted of Welsh foot-soldiers, who had already taken part in fighting in that region, we may assume that these foot-soldiers understood their business. This was of course also true of the men from Scotland. Although the strength of the English armies continually fluctuated, we may be certain that the best elements were those who had been longest on campaigns, and that only those men deserted who were called up in an emergency. The Flemish foot-soldiers also took part in many expeditions in the second half of the thirteenth century; at some periods there were military campaigns almost every year. In the last ten years of the century the citizens were perpetually in campaign against the count of Hainault or against the count of Holland, until the struggle against the king of France began in 1297. There were campaigns and sieges in 1297 and 1300, followed by the revolts of 1301 and 1302. Military operations in June 1302, leading up to the battle of Mons-en-

---

329 Abbé Dehaisnes, J. Finot, Inventaire sommaire des archives départementales Nord. Archives civiles. Série B, I, 2, Lille, 1906, p. 138.
330 *Gesta Federici I. Imperatoris in Lombardia (Annales Mediolanenses maiores)* and *Continuatio*, under the years: 1155, 1156, 1157, 1158, 1159, 1160, 1161, 1162, 1168, 1175, 1176, 1202. Johannes Codagnellus, *Annales Placentini*, ed. O. Holder-Egger, MGH, SS, 1901, years 1172, 1185, 1186, 1193, 1199, 1200, 1201.
331 *Les communes françaises*, pp. 183–4.

Pévèle in 1304, show that practical experience made a great difference to the skill of the foot-soldiers, as the men of Bruges demonstrated. Their crossbowmen did not throw down their bows after the preliminary skirmishing, and the heavily armed citizens of Bruges distinguished themselves in their determined sortie. In the same year the army adopted a marching order in which the men of Bruges marched at the head of the column, while the men of Ghent argued with them over the place of honour.[332] It would appear from this that the communal army of Ghent had normally marched in front before 1302.

Excellently equipped, imbued with high morale and spurred on by their own ideals, the sturdy and powerful units of foot-soldiers had to face testing situations on the battlefield. How did they conduct themselves in the face of danger? Were their nerves sufficiently steeled to face the enemy in the open field? We shall now investigate this in an analysis of the battle psychology of the foot-soldiers.

The Battle Psychology of the Foot-soldiers

Foot-soldiers are only of value when they are employed in strong formations, because operating as a large body breeds confidence. Usually the foot-soldiers far outnumberered the knights, which had an influence on their psychology. The communes were proud of their might: this is expressly stated of the Flemish,[333] and Thomas Gray of Heton said it of the English 'communes'.[334] This pride in their power, their equipment and their formations often led to recklessness, characteristic of young troops who are not yet battle-seasoned. At the time when the communal armies of Brabant are mentioned for the first time in the history of the duchy, the youthful rashness is obvious. At Gulpen in 1284 their enthusiasm overcame them and they wanted to give battle at once. Duke John I had to intervene to curb their desire for battle.[335] The inhabitants of Maastricht allowed themselves to be captured by Walram of Valkenburg. He lured them out of their city by appearing outside the gates. The men of the guilds sprang at once to arms, and sallied forth recklessly. The bailiff John of Mille accompanied them with a small band of cavalry, but he was defeated by Walram's forces, and then the citizens fell an easy prey to this lord, who made many prisoners.[336] In 1128, the men of Bruges marched out against Oostkamp, to rescue one of their allies who was being besieged by count William Clito. But no sooner did the citizens see the enemy knights than they turned and fled precipitately. Many of them were taken prisoner. In July 1128 the men of Bruges again went to Oostkamp, to make another attempt to rescue the fortified manor of a knight who was besieged by William Clito. When William made a heavy attack on the sixth day of the siege, the men of Bruges fled back to their city terror-stricken, and panic broke

---

332 *Annales Gandenses*, p. 58.
333 *Histoire de Guillaume le Maréchal*, II, vv. 10775–6, pp. 23–4.
334 *Scalachronica*, p. 149.
335 Jan van Heelu, vv. 1749–56, p. 69.
336 *Ibid.*, vv. 1868–1909, pp. 73–5.

out among the people living outside the city. They also fled and hastened towards the city with their cattle and household belongings: the population of Bruges was so terrified that no one slept that night. No one dared tell the truth about what had happened, and why the citizens had fled, for anyone who gave a pessimistic explanation was accused of treason, and was denounced as a partisan of William Clito.[337] When the commune of Cambrai rebelled against the bishop and the burgrave in 1138, these latter begged aid of the count of Flanders, Thierry of Alsace, who sent his constable Michael of Harnes to subdue the insurgents. One day the communal army advanced with a flourish of trumpets and waving banners, to storm the fortress of Crèvecoeur. The burgrave sent a message to Michael of Harnes, who hurried up from L'Ecluse with a small band of Flemish knights. They charged the citizens in well-formed units, and put them to flight at once, leaving about 90 dead and 300 prisoners.[338]

So long as the foot-soldiers lacked experience they were not much use against knights, for they could be terrified by the charges of the heavily armoured nobles. At Courtrai the Flemings were 'sore afraid in the face of the terrible encounter. There was no chance of retreat, and the enemy was advancing. Each made his confession on the spot, and then they crowded together, one against another. Thus they formed as it were a stone wall in order to endure the frightful ordeal.'[339] In the first charge some of the men from the Franc of Bruges, thoroughly frightened, took to flight. During the attack by the count of Artois, just as the French rearguard were advancing, local panic broke out in the ranks of the troops of Guy of Namur. At the end of the battle, the French foot in its turn fled in panic from the battlefield.[340] Two years later this happened near the village of Mons-en-Pévèle, at the end of the battle.[341] In 1213 the foot-soldiers of the count of Looz fled a short distance from the battle of Steppes, because they thought that the count had perished and the battle was lost.[342] In the night of 20–21 March 1304, Zeelanders and Flemings from the army of Guy of Namur made a surprise attack on the camp of the Frisians and Hollanders on the island of Duiveland. A great panic then broke out in the army of William of Avesnes: such confusion arose that Frisians and Hollanders fought each other in the darkness, while others fled to the ships, or sought refuge in Zierikzee. As the result, William of Avesnes suffered so heavy a defeat that he lost the greater part of Holland and the bishopric of Utrecht.[343] Later, in the night of 25–26 July 1340, the Flemings who were encamped south of Cassel under Robert of Artois, also fell into a terrible panic, although they were not attacked. Only at a considerable distance from the camp could

---

[337] Galbert, c. 111, p. 158; c. 116, p. 167.
[338] Lambertus de Wattrelos, *Annales Cameracenses*, pp. 514–15.
[339] Velthem, II, 1. IV, c. 26, vv. 1844–54, p. 303.
[340] *Ibid.*, c. 37, pp. 334–7. G. le Muisit, pp. 67–8.
[341] See the story of this battle, pp. 000–00 below.
[342] Reinerus, p. 669. *Vita Odiliae*, p. 184.
[343] J. Sabbe, 'De Vijandelijkheden tussen de Avesnes en de Dampierres in Zeeland, Holland en Utrecht van 1303 tot 1305', *Handelingen der Maatschappij voor Geschiedenis en Oudheidkunde te Gent*, Nieuwe reeks, V, 1957, p. 268.

order and discipline be restored.[344] In the First Crusade too, the foot-soldiers fled in panic under the walls of Antioch and hindered the knights so seriously that the crusaders were defeated.[345] At Laupen in Switzerland in 1339 nearly 2,000 men out of a contingent of 5,000 from Bern fled at the beginning of the battle.[345a]

The foot-soldiers were always liable to panic, just like the best knightly units. But there is a tremendous difference to be seen in the tenacity with which they defended themselves once they had gained the necessary experience. So long as they did not show complete cohesion, they nearly always fled during the initial charge. Later the foot-soldiers learned how to deal with these attacks, and when they managed to score a great victory over the nobility, their self-confidence soared, for there is no better stimulus to morale than success on the battlefield. This is a common phenomenon, and it occurred after Courtrai, after Bannockburn in Scotland, and after the victory of the men of Liège at Vottem in 1346.[346]

Once the knights realized the skill of their opponents on the battlefield, they saw that fighting would have to be done on new lines. They knew that the foot-soldiers not only remained at their posts during a charge, but that the choice of position was nearly always to the disadvantage of the knights.

In Flanders this is very clear during the period between 1302 and 1304. 'So proud and undaunted were the Flemings after their victory at Courtrai that one Fleming with his *goedendag* was not afraid to take on two mounted French knights'.[347] In September 1302 the Flemish communal army wanted to take the offensive and attack the royal army in the open field. Enthusiasm when preparations were being made for battle was tremendous. The men of Ghent were particularly cheerful, and did a round-dance.[348] On 17 and 22 September the Flemings once more made ready for battle, with the greatest enthusiasm. That most popular and skilful leader, William of Jülich, was an ardent advocate of an attack on the royal army.[349] But Philip the Fair carefully avoided battle. His knights did not dare to make a frontal attack, and risk a fierce hand-to-hand fight. They resorted to a feigned attack in front and a real attack on the flanks and in the rear, when they found themselves facing a powerful Flemish army. Like the Scots and Swiss, the Flemings then drew themselves up in a crown-like formation, protected on all sides by the hedge of pikes, lances, and *goedendags*. In face of this, the French knights could only make small feints, which on the whole were unsuccessful. When they were facing the large Flemish army, the knights tried to exhaust the foot-soldiers by forcing them to stay for a whole day in battle order in their heavy equipment without food or drink. This was clearly thought out before the battle of Courtrai, since the plan was expounded to some extent by

---

[344] Jean le Bel, I, pp. 189–90. *Istore et Croniques*, I, p. 391.

[345] Raymond of Aguilers, c. 5, p. 244.

[345a] Oman, *op. cit.*, 2, p. 244, n. 1. Delbrück, *op. cit.*, 3, pp. 594–5.

[346] Verbruggen, *De slag der gulden sporen*, pp. 58–9. Thomas Gray of Heton, *Scalachronica*, p. 145. Jean le Bel, II, p. 141.

[347] Villani, *Historie Fiorentine*, p. 388.

[348] Velthem, II, 1. IV, c. 49, vv. 3604–10, p. 373.

[349] *Ibid.*, pp. 379 and 381–2. *Annales Gandenses*, p. 40.

two writers, the Brabanter Louis of Velthem and the Florentine Giovanni Villani.[350] The same tactics were used by the French after their defeat. At Mons-en-Pévèle this new method, together with a plan of fighting in very small units, brought success to the French knights. But the victory was so questionable that it is risky to draw a definite conclusion, all the more so because the knights never fought another pitched battle in subsequent campaigns. The Flemish foot-soldiers, on the other hand, kept their self-confidence, and never avoided a battle. They even advanced to attack at Cassel in 1328, but then were heavily defeated.[351]

In Scotland also the morale of the foot-soldiers was very high following the great victory of Bannockburn in 1314. 'The Scots had become so courageous and spirited that they conquered the Border counties, and the English did not dare wait for them', writes Thomas Gray of Heton. 'Such was their superiority that they scarcely gave the enemy a thought'.[352] In 1327 they still kept the initiative in operations, and their warlike spirit was praised by Jean le Bel.[353] But the Scottish military hegemony was then brought low by the new tactics of the English armies. As has been said, the charges of the Anglo-Norman nobility at Falkirk against the stubborn resistance of the Scottish foot-soldiers failed in 1298, but the Welsh archers shot so fiercely that the dense *schiltrons* suffered terrible losses. At Bannockburn these bowmen were not used to the best advantage, and the English suffered a crushing defeat. After much trial and error the new tactics brought about the victories at Dupplin Moor in 1332 and Halidon Hill in 1333. In these battles the English bowmen acquired the tremendous self-assurance that enabled them to defeat the French nobility at the beginning of the Hundred Years' War.

The men of Liège won a great victory at Vottem in 1346. 'After this battle they became so haughty that they did not wish for peace that year, and refused to discuss any reasonable proposal. All good cities and the surrounding country became their allies, and they carried on the war for the whole year. Everything went so well for them that they could not have wished anything better.'[354] They took the castles of Clermont and Hamal, but were defeated the following year at Waleffe by the troops of the prince-bishop and the count of Looz.[355]

The Flemings, the Scots and the Liégeois did not however let their defeats demoralize them, and still relied absolutely on their foot-soldiers to re-open hostilities later. The memory of their earlier successes remained vivid, and they did not forget that for a time at least they had had a considerable advantage over their enemies. The battles of Courtrai, Bannockburn and Morgarten were regularly commemorated, and to this day are looked upon as great events in national history.

Good foot-soldiers always showed strong discipline in battle, and the fight against enemy knights had to be carried on to the bitter end. This was the secret of their

---

350 Villani, p. 386. Velthem, c. 25, pp. 298–9.
351 Pirenne, *Le soulèvement de la Flandre maritime*, p. xxviii ff. Lot, I, pp. 276–7.
352 *Scalachronica*, p. 145.
353 *Chronique*, I, p. 47. Thomas Gray, p. 155.
354 Jean le Bel, II, p. 141. Gaier, pp. 289–97.
355 Jean le Bel, II, pp. 142–4. Gaier, pp. 298–306.

success. No booty was to be gathered during the battle: this command was given to the Flemings at Courtrai and to the Swiss after the battle of Sempach.[356] Knights were preferably not taken prisoner, but were killed during the battle. For this reason the Flemings, as well as the Scots and Swiss, were notorious among their enemies, and the Irish and Welsh foot-soldiers behaved equally ferociously in battle. They were well aware that they could expect no mercy from the enemy, and that in battle or during the pursuit they would be mercilessly ridden down by the heavy warhorses. The ferocious determination of the foot-soldiers naturally had its effect on the knights and armoured cavalry, who hated and feared them for their practices.

The foot-soldiers were not just military opponents of knighthood, but frequently political and social adversaries as well. We have seen how the French knights took action against Durand the carpenter and his brotherhood. In Flanders this enmity was evident during the rebellion in the coastal region, between 1323 and 1328. The peasants would no longer tolerate the strongholds of the nobles in their villages, and destroyed them. The attitude of the knights towards the peasants and the inhabitants of the communes was well expressed in the famous *Kerelslied*, which dates from this time. The *kerels* (churls) had so much self-confidence that they had altogether too good an opinion of themselves, and too much trust in their own powers. At *kermesses*, or fairs, these free men behaved as though they were lords, and did not hesitate to use their arms:

> To the fair he will go
> He thinks himself a count,
> There he will destroy everything
> With his rusty staff.
> Then he goes a-drinking wine
> At once he is drunk
> Then all the world is his,
> Both town and country.

The knights would have been glad to curtail the personal freedom and autonomy of the peasants. These churls hoped to restrict the might of chivalry:

> They think of nothing but evil.
> I know a good fate for them:
> They should be dragged off and hanged,
> Their beards are too long;
> They cannot escape,
> They are good for nothing except under restraint.[357]

This opinion of the Flemish nobility of their peasants and townsmen was shared by their equals in every country where the military power of the foot-soldiers involved improvement of the common man's lot, and the acquisition of new political and social rights, at the expense of the aristocracy and the rich burghers in the cities.

---

[356] Delbrück, III, pp. 620 and 688. Schaufelberger, pp. 184 and 178–9. John of Winterthur, *Chronica*, p. 80.
[357] Kervyn de Lettenhove, *Histoire de Flandre*, II, Brussels, 1847, pp. 538–9.

On the Flemish battlefields the cavalrymen were able to gain the upper hand again after several defeats, although their supremacy was never unquestioned as of old. But in political and social spheres the able-bodied men who fought on foot in many countries continually increased in power.

The excellent Swiss foot-soldiers went on developing steadily without any serious defeats. Their confidence in their own power grew constantly and was never shaken. At the same time their territory was continually expanding, so that their armies became increasingly powerful. The Swiss army went on developing in this way for nearly two hundred years, and in all its fighting it never met an opponent of the magnitude of the kings of France and England. When they did come into conflict with the king of France in 1444, a tiny Swiss army of between two and three thousand men was completely annihilated by the French cavalry, and the rest of the Swiss retreated, so that the French achieved their objectives in a single day's fighting.[358] The Swiss were able to practise their tactics under the protection of their mountainous land, on a terrain very favourable to foot-soldiers, and in the framework of a continually expanding state.

Tactics of the Foot-soldiers

1. Formations and Positions of the Foot-soldiers on the Battlefields

Although the Flemings, Scots and Swiss were more or less similarly armed, their tactics were not the same. The Flemings liked to fight on a broad front, in the manner of the phalanx of antiquity. The Scots used circular formations or *schiltrons*, while the Swiss were famous for their deep formations.

Before the battle began, the front of the battle-order was protected from a short distance away by crossbowmen or ordinary archers. These men had to cover the deployment of the main battle order and then start the fighting by skirmishing. They established contact with the enemy and no decisive action was expected of them, since the part they played had normally no effect on the course of the battle. The archers could also be used to protect the flanks of the battle order, in which case the protection was merely temporary, since they could be driven off by the enemy. For this reason the foot-soldiers usually sought to cover their flanks by natural obstacles, such as ditches, rivers, hills, woods, and so on. If a defensive battle was being fought, the foot also tried to protect its front: at Courtrai the front and flanks of the Flemings were protected by ditches. At Mons-en-Pévèle one wing was supported by the village hedge, and the other was up against a brook. At Falkirk the Scots had a marsh in front of their battle order, and archers on the wings were stationed to cover the flanks. At Bannockburn their front was protected by artificial pits, and the main battle order was drawn up in a wood.[359] The Swiss also made good use of the terrain as a protection for their flanks in battle.

---

358 Lot, II, pp. 73–4.
359 Oman, II, pp. 86–7. [See G. Barrow, *Robert the Bruce and the community of the realm of Scotland*, Edinburgh, 1968, for a more detailed account of the likely disposition.]

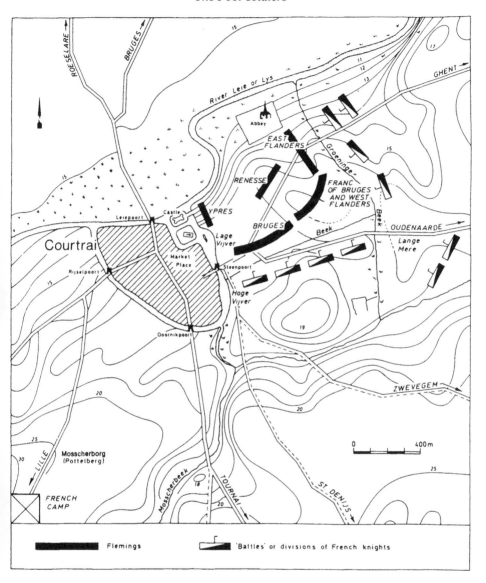

Fig. 1. Plan of the battle of Courtrai

Courtrai

Fig. 1. Plan of the battle of Courtrai

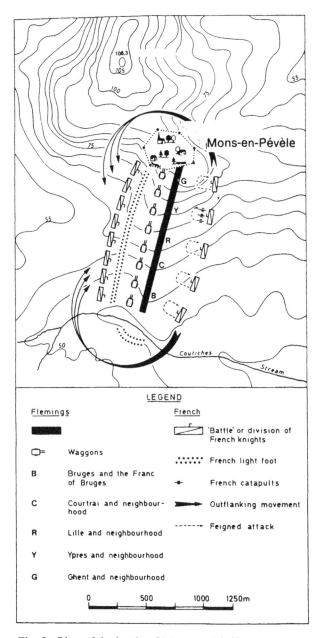

Fig. 2. Plan of the battle of Mons-en-Pévèle

Fig. 2 Plan of the battle of Mons-en-Pévèle

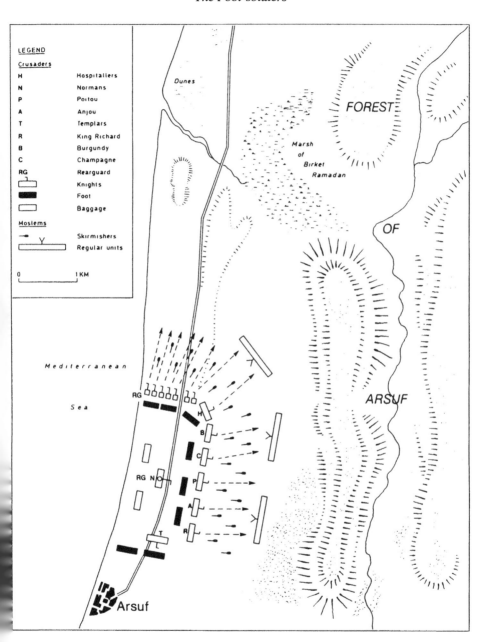

Fig. 3. Plan of the battle of Arsuf

Fig. 7. Plan of the battle of Arsūf

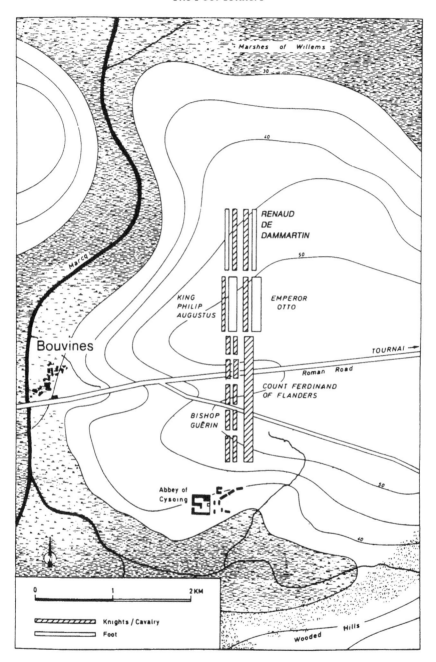

Fig. 4. Plan of the battle of Bouvines

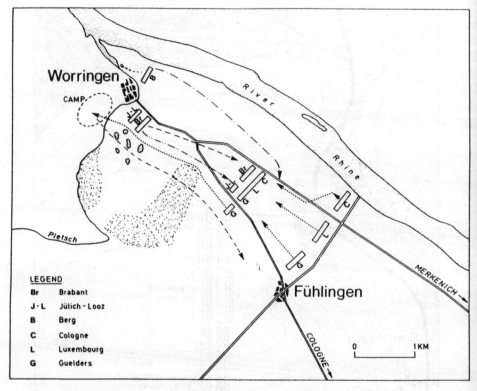

Fig. 5. Plan of the battle of Worringen

1. The communal army of Ghent on the march. Illustration from the chapel of SS John and Paul at Ghent called the Leugemeete. c.1346.

Above left, the White Hoods (Witte Kaproenen). The second group, above right, is the guild of St George, the crossbowmen. Under them, one of the guilds of the towns people, armed with pikes and *goedendags*.

2. The Book of Maccabees. Siege of a fortress, attack on a tower with cavalry and archers shooting arrows, c.925. (Leiden, University Library, MS Periz, F.17, f. 9a)

3. Book of Maccabees. Formations of heavy cavalry in serried ranks, similar to the formations described by Nithard in the cavalry games at Worms in 842, c.925. (Leiden, University Library, MS Periz, F.17, f. 22a)

ET SYRIAM SOBAL · ET CONVERTIT
IOAB · ET PERCVSSIT EDOM INVAL
LE SALINARVM · XII MILIA

4. The Golden Psalter, second half of the 9th century. Right, the bearer of the dragon standard. On the foreground the cavalryman wears a nice *brunia* and carries his long lance under his arm: one of the oldest examples of the couched lance for the attack. (St Gallen, Stiftsbibliothek Codex 22, p. 141)

5. The Golden Psalter, second half of the 9th century. Siege of a tower by cavalry
and foot-soldiers. The cavalrymen are shown under a banner carrying lances; one
is armed with a bow. (St Gallen, Stiftsbibliothek Codex 22, p. 140)

6. Battle of Mons-en-Pévèle, 18 August 1304. On the left, king Philip the Fair
wearing his crown, on the right Flemings with *goedendags*. 14th century.
(Royal Library, Brussels, *Grandes Chroniques*, MS 5, f. 333)

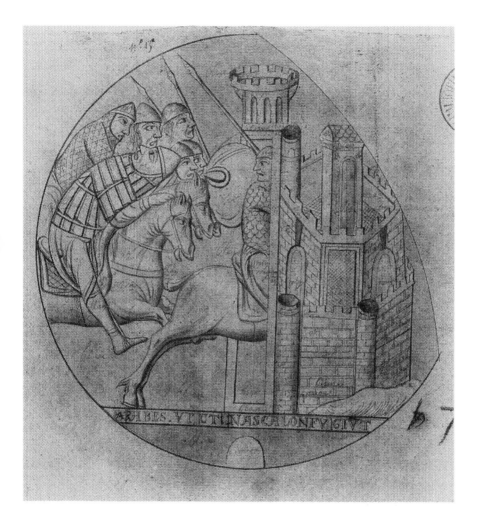

7. Flight of the defeated Arabs at Ascalon. Illustration on a window in the church of the abbey of St Denis. 12th century. (Bibliothèque Nationale, Paris)

8. Duke Robert of Normandy unhorses an enemy on the First Crusade. Window of the church of the abbey of St Denis. (Bibliothèque Nationale, Paris)

9. The Courtrai Chest, New College, Oxford. The events of 1302 in Flanders and the battle of Courtrai. The Flemish battle formation shows lowered pikes, crossbowmen, men with *goedendags*, under the command of Guy of Namur and William of Jülich, with the banners of the crafts of Bruges and the banner of Pieter de Coninc. The men of Ypres are fighting at the gate of the castle of Courtrai.

10. The emperor Henry VI prepares a fleet and army for the invasion of Sicily: foot-soldiers, Bohemian archers and Bavarian crossbowmen. (Bürgerbibliotek, Bern, MS 120.III, f. 131)

11. Cavalry encounter, first half of the 12th century. Three 'battles' of cavalry, consisting of a single line, are shown charging the enemy with couched lances. (Pierpont Morgan Library, New York, MS 736, f. 71)

12. Two Welsh archers, from the margin of a Welsh plea roll.
(Public Record Office, London)

The formations of the foot-soldiers became increasingly closely packed, so that enemy knights could not penetrate them. If the terrain and the army's size permitted, a reserve corps was placed behind the front. Whereas in general knights could not break through the solid units of the foot-soldiers, it was occasionally thought unnecessary to keep the troops in reserve behind the strong main force. Thus the Flemings had no unit in reserve at Mons-en-Pévèle, but their rear was protected by the army waggons, and foot-soldiers were posted on top of these.

Among the Flemings, Scots and Swiss the battle order consisted of two, three, or more large units which could operate independently if necessary, but in a defensive action they could merge into a single tightly closed formation. Among the Flemings each of these units had its own large banner, usually that of an important city. The whole army was drawn up under the standard of the principality. The little formations of the guilds each had their own banner, which served as a rallying point on the march and in battle. This banner could of course be used to convey orders, and to maintain direction both in attack and retreat. The Flemish foot-soldiers also used trumpets, the Scots horns and other instruments, and the Swiss used drums, whose beat helped the marching men.[360] Certain orders, such as assembly, march, and so on, could be sounded with these instruments. Among the Swiss each village and city had its banner or standard, but these were usually collected together in the middle of one large formation, thus they were no use to indicate direction. By virtue of the fact, however, that the Swiss usually operated on narrow fronts, it was much easier for them to maintain direction during the advance than it was in units which, like those of the Flemings, marched on a broad front. Later in the fourteenth century the Swiss used a rectangular formation in which there was an equal number of men abreast in each rank, packed shoulder to shoulder, and at a greater distance apart in depth.[361]

The Germanic peoples had used this type of narrow and deep column, and it is possible that the Swiss had retained it from the early Middle Ages. For fighting in the narrow Alpine valleys such formations were particularly useful, in that they moved on so narrow a front. They were also better able to withstand the charges of the mailed cavalry against the flanks. In such a case the foot-soldiers always had to halt, and make a front in the direction of the threat, but the Swiss could offer resistance along a broad front since their flank, turned to make this front, had great width. Later the Swiss usually fought in three large units, each supporting the other, the second and third not marching level with the first, but following at a certain distance. The first unit, for example, would form the left wing, the second unit rather further back would be the centre, and the third even further back was the right wing. Thus it was possible for the second formation to protect a flank of the first, while its own flank was covered by the third. Sometimes the leading formation, serving as the centre, pushed forward, while the second and third advanced to the left and right of it. In that case both flanks of the first unit were protected by the second and third. It was enough for the Swiss to choose the battlefield so that one of their flanks was naturally protected, the other could then be protected by the units marching further

---

360 Delbrück, III, p. 619.
361 *Ibid.*, p. 686.

behind. The third formation in the meantime kept its freedom of operation, and if need arose, could outflank the enemy and attack him both in the flank and rear.[362] If the knights charged two units in the flank, the third formation could carry out its own attack and break through the front of the enemy knights. Once this was accomplished, the victorious unit rescued the two formations which had been checked, and defeated the enemy. It was understandably very difficult for the knights to attack one of these Swiss units in the flank, since they always had to remember the other units coming up behind.

The more powerful the units of the foot-soldiers were, the greater their chance of beating a mounted enemy army. However in order to keep the requisite flexibility it was necessary to split the army into three or four units. If one of these units was threatened by the enemy on all sides, they assumed a circular formation, like a crown, in order to be able to resist the charges of the armoured cavalry from all directions. The Swiss used these crown-formations for defence, as for example the men of Bern in 1271, who were drawn up in closely serried ranks, with grounded pikes. The Habsburg knights hesitated, for the foot-soldiers seemed very stubborn and resolute. No one thought it wise to charge. Then one brave knight boldly made up his mind to attack. He was caught by the Swiss pikes and killed.[363] In 1289 the army of a son of king Rudolf of Habsburg surprised the men of Bern on the Schlosshalde. Count Louis of Homberg-Rapperswyl managed to penetrate into the formation, which was defeated. The same thing was done in 1332 by the Austrian knight Stülinger of Regensburg, in a battle against the men of Bern and Solothurn. He penetrated the formation of the foot-soldiers and was killed, but had done enough to bring victory for his comrades.[364]

We have already seen that the Scots used these crown-formations regularly. Between 1302 and 1304, and during the battle of Cassel in 1328, the Flemings also often formed a crown, even during the actual battle, so as to be able to fight off attacks from any direction. Small corps of Flemish foot-soldiers were annihilated in such battles, or heavily defeated, as happened for example to two units at Arques in 1303. This was partly due to the fact that owing to their small numbers they did not have their normal confidence in a successful defence, for the proportionate strengths were greatly in the enemy's favour. There was an interesting battle in 1325 in which 800 rebels of the Franc of Bruges fought against the men of Ghent, who were on the side of count Louis of Nevers. The men of Ghent were led by the knights Zeger of Courtrai and Hector Vilain, who also commanded a small unit of heavy cavalry. The rebels drew themselves up in crown formation, with the bravest and best-equipped men in the outer ranks, and the rest of the soldiers behind them. The leaders of the men of Ghent first rode round the crown with their cavalry, seeking a weak spot, and making a few attacks for this purpose, but they were beaten off. Then Hector Vilain made a great charge with forty picked cavalrymen, specially devoted to him. He rushed at the rebels with loud war-cries, while his own foot-soldiers apparently attacked as

362 *Ibid.*, *loc. cit.*
363 *Ibid.*, pp. 604–5.
364 *Ibid.*, p. 605.

well. His charge carried him right through the formation, and the little body of rebels was destroyed.[365]

When the surprise attack on the French camp at Cassel in 1328 was unsuccessful, Zannekin drew up his largest unit in the shape of a crown, which was violently attacked by the French king and his knights, both sides suffering heavy losses. The Flemings were completely surrounded and defended themselves with the courage of despair. Many French nobles lost their horses in the tremendous charges. The Flemish formation stood firm however, and drove off the attacks, and the French barons saw that they could not destroy this unit by force. They retreated, leaving the road to Cassel open to the Flemings, and the latter were captured by a trick. Perhaps they thought that the French armoured cavalry were being obliged to retreat, or perhaps they hoped to retreat in good order with their whole unit, but it was a desperate flight, during which the French cavalry pursued them relentlessly. In this battle the peasants from the Westhoek abandoned the traditional Flemish tactics, and marched resolutely to attack the enemy instead of waiting in motionless defence. They chose the courageous solution to the great problem of the foot-soldiers of that time – to offer a defensive or to give an offensive battle.[366]

2. *Defence or Attack in Battle?*

We have already seen that the foot-soldiers usually operated defensively. This was absolutely necessary as long as they were inexperienced, and could not produce flexible formations which would remain in good order during an attack. Even as late as the fifteenth century the outstanding authority on tactics of the day, Jean de Bueil, prescribed defensive tactics for the foot-soldiers. This French nobleman was the real victor over the Swiss in 1444 at the battle of St Jacob-en-Birs.[367] He was convinced that the Swiss defeat was due to their taking the offensive in the battle.

Up to the beginning of the fourteenth century it was rare for the foot-soldiers to dare to attack enemy knightly formations. Great battles like Falkirk, Courtrai, Mons-en-Pévèle and Bannockburn were started with foot-soldiers playing a motionless defensive role. But it was possible to exploit the exhaustion of the knights after the failure of their charges. As soon as the armoured cavalry were worn out by the stubborn defence of the foot-soldiers, the latter went over to the offensive with a strong counter-attack. Those cautious tactics brought the Flemings victory at Courtrai, and might have helped them to win at Mons-en-Pévèle, where their counterattack was almost successful. During the second day of the battle of Bannockburn the Scots forced the English to attack at once, when they were not yet ready for battle. It is possible that the Scots then attacked in their turn, but this is not quite certain. In any case, Robert Bruce systematically avoided major battles after his victory, and had evidently not come to the conclusion that his foot-soldiers could attack and defeat mailed cavalry in the open field. He made surprise attacks in favourable circum-

---

[365] *Chronicon comitum Flandrensium*, I, pp. 198–9.
[366] *Ibid.*, pp. 205–6.
[367] Lot, II, pp. 73–5.

stances, and in these he was always successful. In 1327, the Scots acted defensively, and chose such favourable positions that the English knights could not attack them.[368] At Dupplin Moor in 1332, and the following year at Halidon Hill, the Scots took the offensive, and in both cases they were heavily defeated.[369] They also had to reckon with excellent English defensive tactics.

After the victory at Courtrai in 1302 there was a growing demand among the Flemish communal armies to abandon the defensive in battle and go over to the attack. Although William of Jülich was a strong advocate of attack in the open field, the more cautious commanders succeeded in having his plans rejected.[370] The powerful counter-attack on the battlefield at Mons-en-Pévèle, and offensive operations in small groups during the battle, like the successful sortie of the men of Ypres against the French missiles, encouraged the communal armies to adopt new methods. They wanted in future to attack by night, by the light of the full moon. If this was not possible, they thought of attacking by day immediately the battle was joined, in order to make the French knights fight hand-to-hand at once,[371] for in such close fighting larger armies enjoyed great advantages, as we shall soon see from our account of the battle of Courtrai, and from the general picture of battles of foot-soldiers. Against a very powerful royal army, and in far less favourable circumstances, the peasants from the Westhoek came to attack at Cassel in 1328. They hoped to surprise the enemy at nightfall, but the raid failed and ended in frightful disaster for the Flemish insurgents. When the men of Ghent and their allies attacked another mighty royal army just as bravely at Westrozebeke in 1382, they in their turn were crushingly defeated. The offensive tactics of the Flemings miscarried just as miserably as those of the Scots. In both cases the foot-soldiers were attacked by heavy cavalry on the flank and in the rear, and could not break out of the encirclement. The Flemish formations were unwieldy, and not flexible enough. They seemed capable of transforming their phalanx quickly into a crown-formation, but this was a defensive position and made further attack impossible. In the beginning of the fourteenth century the Flemings lacked the indispensable experience to give offensive battle successfully.

The Swiss had considerable luck in the development of their foot-soldiers. They not only acquired the necessary experience, but their armies grew stronger as well, owing to the expansion of their confederation. Their formations were also better adapted to attack than the broad formations of the Flemings, who were forced to fight on their open plains against the armies of the French knights. The Swiss military system was to attain a very high standard by the end of the Middle Ages, and to revolutionize the art of war, but in the period just covered, their tactics were in an early stage of development and were as yet no better than the Flemish and Scottish tactics.

Following this general survey of the evolution of the foot-soldiers and a study of

---

368 Jean le Bel, I, pp. 65, 68–9.
369 Oman, II, pp. 104, 106–7. [Bennett, 'Tactics', pp. 4–5.]
370 *Annales Gandenses*, p. 40.
371 *Ibid.*, p. 82.

the principal problems of their tactics, the moment has come to give a general picture of a battle as it was fought by the foot-soldiers against their enemies, the knights. After that we shall examine a few battles which are characteristic of the tactics of the foot-soldiers, who were fighting alone against the formations of armoured cavalry.

3. *Foot-soldiers versus Knights in Battle*

It is not easy nowadays to piece together an accurate picture of medieval warfare, and to re-create the atmosphere of battle, but this must be done if we are to form an idea of the value of the foot-soldiers in battle.

Early in the morning, about 6 a.m., the men were called to arms, usually by trumpet. Sometimes the tents were first struck, huts were pulled down, and camp broken. The men armed themselves, then attended mass or went to confession and took Holy Communion, for they never omitted spiritual preparation. Franciscan friars usually served as chaplains in the Flemish communal armies.[372] The men were restless and nervous, thinking of the forthcoming battle: many of them had no appetite and ate almost no breakfast, often just bread dipped in wine.

The preparation of the troops, and getting them ready in battle order took a long time. By 8 or 9 o'clock they would be ready for battle, drawn up in closely packed ranks, practically shoulder to shoulder, though the men with the *goedendags* had to have plenty of room to move so that they could strike and stab. The pikemen with their pikes or long lances got ready to halt the cavalry attack.

A pikeman was stationed next to each man armed with a *goedendag*, or the pikemen formed the first rank, the men with the *goedendags* the second.

It is very rare to find a reliable description of the mental state of soldiers before a battle. Nervousness, tension, fear and dread all create a psychological condition which may just as likely lead to a heroic and stubborn defence as to disgraceful and cowardly flight. The feeling that defeat meant total ruin was often decisive in successful defence. At Legnano in 1176, at Cortenuova in 1237, as at Courtrai in 1302, the foot-soldiers knew that they must win or die. In each of these apparently hopeless situations they conquered their fear and beat off the attack of the armoured cavalrymen successfully. Once this was done, they had the self-confidence to offer further resistance.

It is difficult for us to imagine how hard the foot-soldiers of those days were tested. To stand up to the medieval heavy cavalry charge was no child's play, for in the thirteenth century cavalry could approach the foot-soldiers with impunity to within a hundred meters, and it was sufficiently well-protected to stand up to the defenders' rain of arrows while covering that distance as quickly as possible. The iron-clad horsemen attacked in close formations, their horses flank to flank, which increased mutual confidence and swept the less brave along irresistibly. In flat open country they came on at 250 meters a minute at a trot, and almost twice that speed at a gallop. The defending crossbowmen thus had only 15–24 seconds in which to shoot, as the

---

[372] *Ibid.*, pp. 60, 79. *Chronicon comitum Flandrensium*, I, pp. 196–9.

cavalry approached, and they were possibly so nervous that they shot too high or too low. The cavalry came on in such force, with heavy horses and armoured riders, that the shock could easily break the wooden shafts of the pikes. It has been calculated that ten riders were mechanically equal to a hundred foot-soldiers, and that a galloping rider was equal to ten foot-soldiers on the defensive.[373] This theoretical calculation is valid only in those cases where the knights carried the charge through to the final terrible clash.

If the ranks of the foot-soldiers wavered a bit, the cavalrymen could drive their horses between the pikes into any little gap, instead of riding up on them. The physical strength of the foot-soldiers was not great enough to withstand the assault if it was carried through quickly and relentlessly, but the absolute immobility of the foot-soldiers made their front into a kind of hedgehog, and the cavalry only ventured between the pikes with the terrifying prospect of death. Instead of breaking the pikes in the shock of attack, it often happened that the horses were killed by the stout steel points of the long weapons. The fall or death of the horse threw the knight hard to the ground, right in front of the foot-soldiers or even in their ranks. Worse still, the rider was often pinned under his horse, or had to reckon with the long weapons of the foot-soldiers. Nothing but the strength of the foot-soldiers' morale could stand up to the attackers' brute force.

Such a charge took place amid deafening noise. The enemy blew trumpets to herald the attack and to encourage the troops. The horses became excited and whinnied. The shrill notes of the trumpets demoralized the foot-soldiers: many of them felt their heart beat faster, and almost everyone at such a moment would have preferred to be anywhere but on that terrible field of battle. Only the most experienced could remain unmoved by the hellish din. In the words of the French foot-soldier Guiart: 'Drums and trumpets boom, if you are not used to these things, you would soon be frightened.'[374] The enemy knights shouted their battle cry to terrify their opponents and to bolster up their own courage, hoping up to the very last moment that the foot-soldiers would abandon their position and take to their heels in panic. The horses were naturally not at all willing to break into the ranks of the foot-soldiers and ride them down. But out of a sense of duty, from courage, a high concept of personal or corporate honour, or simply because the others were doing it and one had to behave like a brave man, the cavalry forced their warhorses to charge. This was best done in a group at a quick trot, or rather more slowly if there was any hesitation, and the horses, who immediately sensed it, had slackened their pace.

In any case, even if some of the knights did not carry on the charge to the utmost, a terrible shock followed. This came with a hellish din when the armoured formations charged a wall of foot-soldiers, exactly as when two knightly armies met each other. 'Four hundred carpenters would not have made so much noise.' 'They closed in with

---

[373] M. de Maere d'Aertrycke, *De la Colme au Boulenrieu*, Namur, 1935, p. 33, n. 1. [More recent commentators stress the relatively slow spread of a knightly cavalry charge. See M. Bennett, 'The *Règle du Temple* as a Cavalry Manual', pp. 15–17.]
[374] Guiart, vv. 15760–2, pp. 245–6. *Chronicon comitum Flandrensium*, p. 169 for the battle of Courtrai.

such force that the clash of weapons and the din of blows made the air ring, just as though trees in the forest were being cut down with innumerable axes.' 'The fighters were like woodcutters, chopping down the trees of a forest.' 'The din was so frightful that one could not have heard even God's thunder.' 'It was as if all the smiths in Brussels and Bruges were striking their anvils.'[375]

Yet the frightful noise of the battle was merely a minor part of the atmosphere. Far more terrible was the fact that men saw their comrades fall, trampled by enemy warhorses, or felled by the lances of the knights. Some men fell dying, others were more or less seriously wounded and their blood stained the ground or the grass on which they fought. Fighting with heavy weapons was extremely fatiguing. The men wore very heavy clothing or some kind of protective equipment, and had to lift the pike or *goedendag* with both hands in order to bring the iron head down on the warhorses, aiming at the legs, head, or belly of the animals. The tremendous blows resounded fiercely on the helmets or metal plates of the knights. Every man was put through a terrible trial.

In the most favourable situation – that is when the foot-soldiers were greater in number than the cavalry, and in the mêlée two or three foot-soldiers could tackle each knight – the knights who had broken into the ranks were mercilessly slaughtered. Horses were brought down, the riders fell, and before they could get up again, or could scramble free from under their chargers, it was often too late. In such a case the fighting might go on for a long time, but the knights' fate was sealed: they were doomed.

This was not always the case however. Sometimes the knights entrusted the task of holding the enemy in check in front to their own foot-soldiers, perhaps reinforced by dismounted noblemen, as happened at Westrozebeke in 1382.[376] Then heavy cavalry units attacked the enemy foot-soldiers on the flanks and in the rear, so that the flanks of the foot-soldiers were hurled back, and they lost a great deal of their room to manoeuvre. The men who were attacked on their unprotected flank had to form a new front hastily, which was not always an easy thing to do. If the cavalry were successful in keeping up the attacks, they pressed the men on the flanks up against those in the centre. They then had too little room to move, and could not easily use their weapons. The more successful the cavalry were, the more they went on charging, and the more tightly they crushed the foot-soldiers together. After the battle of Westrozebeke the body of Philip van Artevelde was found, and it showed no wound. He had been crushed in the tightly packed mass of the men of Ghent. The same thing occurred in the Scottish army at the battle of Dupplin Moor in 1332, when their foot-soldiers had gone out to attack, but were held in check in front and then were attacked on both flanks by English archers. The Scots on the flanks were driven in toward the centre to such an extent that more men perished by being crushed to death than were killed by arms.[377]

---

[375] *Le siège de Barbastre*, c. 6, vv. 220–2, p. 8. Delpech, I, p. 227, n. 1. Gautier, *La chevalerie*, p. 751 and note. *Chanson d'Aspremont*, I, c. 244, vv. 4415–7, p. 142; c. 245, vv. 4431–3, p. 142. Henry of Valenciennes, c. 526, p. 39.
[376] Lot, I, pp. 451–2. Delbrück, III, pp. 456–7.
[377] Oman, II, pp. 104–5.

This general picture of a fight between foot-soldiers and armoured cavalry would naturally show different features from battle to battle. As remarkable examples of pure tactics of foot-soldiers, let us now turn to a brief discussion of the two important battles of Courtrai and Mons-en-Pévèle, and a less important but nevertheless interesting battle of Arques. They give an excellent picture of the possibilities and limitations of the tactics of the Flemish foot-soldiers.

THE BATTLE OF COURTRAI, 11 JULY 1302

Guy of Namur assembled the Flemish army at Courtrai. With shrewd strategical and tactical insight the Flemish leaders had chosen the best site: the road to Ghent, a city which was not co-operating with the insurgents, as well as the one to Bruges, was blocked by them and that to Ypres was protected. The French garrison was ill-supplied and could not hold out for any length of time. The royal army appeared outside the walls of Courtrai on 8 July. On the 9th, the French commander ordered an attack on the Tournai Gate, and on the 10th on the Lille Gate, but neither was successful; on the 11th he decided to advance against the Groeningekouter, where the Flemish leaders had taken up a favourable position.[378]

About 6 a.m. the call to arms was sounded in the French camp. Ten big units of knights and squires were formed, and contained about 2,500 nobles, supported by foot-soldiers, crossbowmen and *bidauts*, light foot-soldiers armed with javelins. The Flemish army was rather larger. It consisted of 8,000 well-armed foot-soldiers, perhaps even 10,500, including several hundred knights and squires. But the royal army included the flower of the French nobility, and 100 such cavalrymen were considered the equal of 1,000 foot-soldiers, so that qualitatively speaking the count of Artois had a very considerable advantage. But the Flemings had selected a very good position which enabled them to protect their flanks. At their back flowed the Lys, and in front of their left wing was the Groeningebeek, while the Grote Beek, or Great Brook, protected their right wing. Both brooks severely hampered the knights' charge. The site which had been so well chosen from a tactical point of view showed also serious drawbacks: flight was impossible, defeat risked total annihilation. But the determination of the rebels drew new strength from the situation; they had to win or die.

When the French marshals had completed their reconnaissance, they must have appreciated this situation. Artois decided to hold a council of war to discuss the tactical problem of an attack on that terrain. Raoul de Nesle pointed out the grave dangers which threatened the knights once they were fighting on the far side of the brooks. If the French nobles then had to give way, those brooks could prove disastrous, since it would be impossible to recross them. He suggested luring the Flemings out of their good position. Jean de Burlats, Grand Master of the crossbow-men, wanted to harass the Flemings with his light foot-soldiers, hoping to inflict such great losses on them that they would have to give way. Then the moment would come

---

[378] Verbruggen, *De slag der gulden sporen*, pp. 276–303. Lot, I, pp. 252–64.

for the knights to deliver the *coup de grâce*. Godfrey of Brabant thought it was wiser not to attack at all, but rather to wear the Flemings down by making them stand all day in battle order with their heavy equipment on, without food or drink on a hot July day, so that they would not dare to fight on the following day. But the majority of the council thought that the battle should be fought at once.[379]

William of Jülich, Guy of Namur and John of Renesse placed their heavy foot-soldiers far enough away from the brooks to minimize the effect of the French crossbowmen's attack, at the same time leaving only a small space in which the French knights could develop their assaults on the Flemish side of the brooks. The Flemings had to await their opponents in a motionless defensive position. On the Flemish right wing the men of Bruges stood behind the Grote Beek under the command of William of Jülich, in the centre were the men from the Franc of Bruges and West-Flanders, partly behind the Grote Beek and partly behind the Groeninge Beek, and on the left wing Guy of Namur commanded the men of the region of Alost, Oudenaarde and Courtrai, and the men of Ghent. The right flank was protected by the Lage Vijver, or Lower Moat, the left flank by the monastery of Groeninge. John of Renesse waited with a reserve corps behind the centre. The communal army from Ypres had to keep the castle garrison in check, and guard the rear of the Flemish formation.[380]

They waited a long time for the enemy. The Flemings were nervous, restless, and apprehensive, for they knew that the royal army had the reputation of being the best in Western Europe. But as soon as the French moved, it was impossible to leave the battle-field. The insurgents were encouraged by their noble leaders, who had sent away their horses and were fighting on foot to share the lot of the common man. All the nobles were volunteers, and still had an account to settle with their enemies. The peasants too had a grudge against their opponents, and the men of Bruges were fighting for their lives. William of Jülich and Guy of Namur encouraged their men, and together with the nobles and the heads of the guilds they drew up their men in battle array.[381]

At last Guy of Namur and William of Jülich addressed the troops, and John of Renesse, commander of the reserve, explaining how he was to rush to the help of the long battle formation, gave excellent advice: 'Do not allow the enemy to break through your ranks. Do not be afraid. Kill both man and horse. The "Lion of Flanders" is our battle cry. When the enemy attacks the corps of Lord Guy, we shall come to your help from behind. Anyone who breaks into your ranks, or gets through them, will be killed.' It was given out that no one should collect booty, and that anyone who did so, or who surrendered or fled, would be killed at once. No prisoners were to be taken.[382]

---

[379] *Anciennes Chroniques de Flandre*, ed. N. de Wailly and L. Delisle, RHF, XXII, p. 377. Velthem, pp. 297–8. Guiart, pp. 238–9. Villani, p. 386. [See K. DeVries, *Infantry Warfare in the Fourteenth Century*, Woodbridge, 1996, pp. 9–22 for a more detailed interpretation of Courtrai.]

[380] Velthem, II, pp. 310, 313, 317. *Annales Gandenses*, p. 31.

[381] *Chronicon comitum Flandrensium*, I, pp. 168–9. Villani, p. 385. *Annales Gandenses*, p. 32. G. le Muisit, p. 66. *Chronique artésienne*, p. 51. Velthem, II, p. 311.

[382] Velthem, II, pp. 303–6. *Annales Gandenses*, p. 33. *Chronicon comitum Flandrensium*, I, p. 168.

Guy of Namur knighted Pieter de Coninc and his two sons in front of the Flemish army, together with about thirty of the leading citizens of Bruges. Then the two princes sent their horses away, and armed like the rebels, with the visorless helmet of the communal soldiers, they took their place in the front rank, grasping a pike or *goedendag*.

Fighting broke out between crossbowmen a little before noon. The Flemish archers slowly gave way under pressure from the numerically superior enemy, who were followed at some distance by the units of knights. The French foot-soldiers advanced, and their arrows reached the front ranks of the main Flemish lines, but without serious effect. As soon as they reached the Groeninge and Grote brooks, they were called back by Artois, who was afraid that they would be overwhelmed on the far side by the Flemish heavy foot-soldiers, while the French knights could not support their own soldiers. In this case the Flemings would advance right up to the brooks, which would make an attack by the French knights practically impossible. Besides, the French foot-soldiers would get in the way of the armoured cavalry on the far side of the brooks. By beginning the assault quickly with the nobles, they would at the same time profit by the preparatory shooting of the crossbowmen.

Artois then gave the order: 'Foot-soldiers, come back', while the banners were moved to the front of the knights. Then came the word 'Forward!' and seven French cavalry units rode to the brooks with the banners unfurled. The left wing, commanded by Raoul de Nesle, attacked across the Grote brook. It consisted of four bands of knights. The right wing had three bands of knights and advanced to the Groeninge. The foot-soldiers managed to get out of the way of the cavalry, but some men had not heard the order, or else stumbled in their haste; others were trampled by the armoured knights, but most of them were able to retreat through the spaces between the knights' units, or along the flanks. The knights quickly began to cross the ditches. They made haste, so as not to be surprised by the counter-attack by the Flemish heavy foot-soldiers. Some horses missed their jump or stumbled, others refused, and had to be forced to jump. Knights fell from their saddles into both brooks, but on the whole the crossing was successful. The left wing was the first unit ready for attack on the opposite side of the Grote Beek. After quickly reorganizing the formations, the constable charged the right wing and part of the Flemish centre with his four units of knights. The Flemish archers flung their bows away and hurriedly took refuge behind the main battle line. Under Jean de Burlats, Godfrey of Brabant, Raoul de Nesle and the two marshals, the French knights rode at a quick trot with couched lances toward the Flemings. This awe-inspiring and terrible drama was accompanied by a most fearful din. Never in their lives had the Flemings experienced anything like it: never had they known such critical and nerve-racking moments. They pressed closer and closer together, their hearts pounding. They held their pikes firmly planted in the ground, and the men with the *goedendags* raised their weapons, ready to strike. There was a bitter surprise in store for the French. The living wall of pikes, lances, and *goedendags* did not flinch. The French nobles had never seen anything like it in their long and glorious career. The weavers and fullers, the artisans and peasants, did not flee but stayed courageously at their posts. Then the bravest knights had to ride their horses at the Flemish lines. Some hesitated and slackened their pace, but the majority were swept along in their close formations, or bravely carried on the attack. Then came the frightful impact against the heavy pikes, with earsplitting noise, but on the Flemish right the men of Bruges withstood the charge, and inflicted heavy losses on the French nobles. Godfrey of Brabant knocked down William of Jülich and hurled the prince's banner to the ground. But after breaking into the Brugeois ranks he was brought down and killed. Raoul de Nesle also fell in the initial charge. A stubborn hand-to-hand mêlée ensued, and the fearful *goedendags* crashed down heavily on men and horses.[383]

In the centre, the French knights drove deep into the ranks of the men from the Franc of Bruges. Some of these yielded, but others manfully stood their ground. The heavy cavalry carried on their attack and penetrated deeper into the Flemish lines, where a breakthrough seemed likely. A number of foot-soldiers took to their heels.[384]

Meanwhile the French right wing charged across the Groeninge Beek. The charge was made in dense units, and with less commotion than on the French left wing. With tremendous force the formations of knights hurled themselves against the East Flemings, but the Flemings resisted stoutly and the cavalry were checked. This in turn was followed by violent hand-to-hand fighting.[385]

While heavy fighting now developed along the whole front, Jean de Lens made a sortie from Courtrai castle to attack the Flemings from the rear. First he sought to divert the attention of the men of Ypres by setting fire to a fine house on the market square. But they remained on the alert near the castle gate, and successfully beat off the attack.[386]

Meanwhile the mêlée continued along the entire front. Most of the royal army was involved in the fighting. At one point the situation looked critical for the Flemings, especially in the centre where the men of the Franc of Bruges fought bravely but ran into difficulties. John of Renesse hastened to help with the reserve. The French knights were driven back in the centre. This success encouraged the Flemish centre to go over to the attack, followed by both wings, and a general Flemish counter-attack developed, in which the rebels were at a considerable advantage. Three or four thousand Flemings were attacking 1,600 heavy cavalry with weapons that were longer than those of the nobles. The French knights were forced to give ground, and were driven back towards the two brooks. Robert of Artois, who had not taken part in the general charge, realized at once that his army would be defeated if it were thrown back into either of the brooks. He ordered the rearguard to advance and personally went into action with his knights.[387]

Artois and his men, with a flourish of trumpets, charged the troops of Guy of Namur. The ranks of the East Flemings had become much less compact in the

---

[383] Guiart, vv. 15119–20, p. 239. Geoffrey de Paris, *Chronique rimée*, ed. N. de Wailly and L. Delisle, RHF 22, vv. 1206–7, p. 100. *Anciennes Chroniques de Flandre*, p. 378. Villani, p. 387. Velthem, II, pp. 312–16.
[384] Velthem, c. 29, vv. 2085–95, p. 313. *Chronicon comitum Flandrensium*, I, p. 169.
[385] Velthem, c. 31–2, pp. 317–19.
[386] *Annales Gandenses*, p. 31. Guiart, vv. 15144–60, p. 240. *Chronicon comitum Flandrensium*, I, p. 169. Chest of Oxford, scene VI: Verbruggen, *De slag der gulden sporen*, pp. 259–60.
[387] Velthem, pp. 313–14.

counter-attack. Artois drove deep into their ranks and reached the standard, where he tore off part of the banner. His charge, coupled with the approach of the French rearguard, started panic in the ranks of Guy's troops, some of whom fled. In the meantime Artois was being fiercely attacked by other Flemings. He defended himself splendidly, but Willem van Saaftinge, a lay brother of Ter Doest, felled the horse of the commander-in-chief. Artois was dragged off in the fall, and perished, covered with wounds. On the banks of the brooks the knights and squires defended themselves with desperate courage, and a horrible slaughter ensued. Many of them fell into the water and were drowned, nor were the horses spared. The French losses were appalling: only one leader of all the cavalry units who had taken part was captured, all the rest were killed.[388]

As soon as they had defeated the enemy on the banks of the brooks, the Flemings crossed over themselves, to attack the rearguard of the French. These two cavalry units acted as though they intended to make an attack in their turn, but made no move; they were trying to gain time for the retreat of the baggage. But no sooner did the Flemings advance, than the heavy cavalry fled in panic, and headed hell-for-leather towards Lille and Tournai, while the French foot-soldiers also took to their heels. The Flemings chased them as far as Zwevegem, St Denijs, and Dottenijs, eleven kilometers from the battlefield. By evening the fleeing Frenchmen reached Tournai exhausted, where they bartered their equipment for bread, though some of them were still too shocked to eat.[389]

Between noon and three o'clock in the afternoon the Flemings had achieved a great victory, which cost the lives of more than a thousand French noblemen. Half of the attacking knights had perished – an appallingly high proportion. The victors amassed enormously valuable booty, and at least five hundred golden spurs and many banners were picked up on the battlefield; these were preserved in the church of Our Lady in Courtrai, whence the French removed them eighty years later, after the battle of Westrozebeke. The victors lost only a few hundred dead.[390]

THE BATTLE OF ARQUES, 4 APRIL 1303

The war between the Flemish insurgents and the French continued after the French defeat at Courtrai. In March 1303 William of Jülich had raised an army in the Westhoek of Flanders, and assembled the troops at Cassel. On 3 April, he advanced to a point close to the border near Arques, not far from St Omer. The Flemish offensive against St Omer began on Maundy Thursday, 4 April. The Flemings marched in five divisions: first came the men from Ypres, dressed all in red, then two units from St Winoksbergen and its neighbourhood, finally two corps under William of Jülich, consisting of contingents from the Cassel and Furnes district. There was a considerable space between each of these units. The Ypres men crossed the Neuf-fossé and the river Aa and immediately stormed the village of Arques. The

388 *Ibid.*, pp. 329–30, 326–9, 333.
389 *Ibid.*, pp. 334–7. G. le Muisit, pp. 67–8.
390 Verbruggen, *De slag der gulden sporen*, p. 302.

French garrison, which consisted of only sixty *bidauts*, could not stand up for long against the assault, and was killed, and the fortress set on fire. The French commander at St Omer, Jacques de Bayonne, summoned his heavy cavalry with a trumpet signal, which started a panic in the fortress. The French nobles were afraid of the Flemings, and hastened to confession before the fight. Priests at the crossroads granted absolution to all who would fight against the Flemings. Jacques de Bayonne commanded more than 1,300 heavy cavalry, accompanied by foot-soldiers. The dense units of cavalry left the market-square, their banners flying, and advanced against the Flemings. When the French leaders came outside the city, they saw that the men of Ypres were already very close, so they summoned the rest of their foot-soldiers out of the city and drew them up in front of the hospital outside the city walls.[391]

In the French garrison of St Omer there were many *leliaarts*, Flemish partisans of the king, who knew the district where they formerly lived very well. They knew all about the marching order of the five Flemish detachments. While part of their foot-soldiers had to hold off the men of Ypres in front of the hospital, and could retreat into the city if they had to, the knights of Jacques de Bayonne and the rest of the foot-soldiers left this Flemish unit on their left, and advanced towards Blendecques. There they turned northwards, crossed the watercourses, and prepared themselves for an attack on the two St Winoksbergen detachments. At the same time, they noticed a whole column of Flemish army waggons. The two Flemish corps thought themselves securely protected by the Ypres men, and had taken no precautions against a French raid. While the French nobles were preparing their formations for an attack, a good number of their foot-soldiers went off to attack the column of Flemish waggons. These were unprotected, and the men in charge were usually not combatant troops. These poorly equipped men were soon put to flight or killed, and the rapacious French foot-soldiers went straight back to St Omer, with the booty they had seized. The French nobles meanwhile formed up in five units. They were reinforced by 300 heavy cavalry under the burgrave Jean de Lens and Jean de Vervins, so that the total of the French nobles was 1,600.[392]

The French nobles deployed their units opposite the second of the corps from St Winoksbergen, which they hoped to take by surprise. When these French 'battles' appeared out of the wood where they had been hiding, the Flemings drew themselves up at once in battle order. Jacques de Bayonne had briefed his cavalry about his plan: he meant to destroy the men from St Winoksbergen before the other Flemish corps, which were on both sides of him, could rush to their aid. With his 1,600 heavy cavalry he could risk attacking a rather weak detachment of the Flemish army. At a trumpet-signal two 'battles' made a frontal attack on the Flemings, while another 'battle' charged the left and the fourth 'battle' the right.[393] Oudart de Maubuisson

---

[391] *Istore et Croniques*, I, pp. 261–2. *Chronique artésienne*, p. 60. *Annales Gandenses*, pp. 43–4. G. Guiart, pp. 242–3.
[392] Guiart, pp. 243–4. *Annales Gandenses*, pp. 43–4. *Istore et Croniques*, I, p. 263. *Chronique artésienne*, p. 60.
[393] Guiart, vv. 15726–36, 15742–74, pp. 245–6. *Annales Gandenses*, p. 44.

stayed in reserve, ready to check or delay the Flemish units that might come to help. The men of St Winoksbergen were thus attacked by nearly 1,300 heavy cavalry. They defended themselves bravely, so stoutly that one of the French sources says that they fought as if they were all Rolands from the *chanson de geste*.[394] They laid about them with their pikes and *goedendags* and wounded many horses. But the French cavalry pressed home their attack with overwhelming force, and thanks to their attacks on both the Flemish flanks they succeeded in more or less surrounding the little detachment. They rode their heavy chargers into the ranks of the foot-soldiers, and made them gradually give way. The Flemings hoped help would come quickly.[395]

The second detachment from St Winoksbergen came to their aid at once. Oudart de Maubuisson was afraid that this corps might surround the French nobles, and he decided to attack forthwith. With their standard-bearer in front, the 300 heavy cavalry turned to the left and charged the Flemings. The cavalry on the heavy chargers rode down the Flemish soldiers, and French foot followed and killed the trampled Flemings or took them prisoner. This Flemish detachment was thrown back, but they managed to take refuge in a garden and there to re-form their ranks. Maubuisson, however, got reinforcements, for the lord of Pickigny rushed to his side from the other band of French knights with about sixty heavy cavalry.[396] The two units from St Winoksbergen emerged with heavy casualties. According to the Franciscan friar from Ghent whom we have quoted before, they lost 1,000 men, of whom the majority were servants and waggoners:[397] luckily for them the French heavy cavalry were unable to pursue them, for William of Jülich hastened up with two powerful corps. Since the prince had only a few knights with him, he gave the order for every man to fight on foot. He made his two groups into a single strong formation, which he drew up in the form of a crown. On the outer edge he stationed his bravest and best-equipped men. Meanwhile the French nobles had regrouped, and were advancing against new opponents. They succeeded in capturing William of Jülich's horse, which was led away too late, but they did not manage to press home their attack to the point of hand-to-hand fighting. They realized that there was no hope of success against the powerful and tightly packed units of William. Then they tried to lure the Flemings out of their formation in order to ride down individual men, and they sought at the same time to find a weak spot in the crown-formation. But those cavalrymen who came too close to the Flemings were knocked down and killed, and those stout-hearted Flemings who attacked them in small groups were also killed. The opponents stood their ground, facing each other for nearly two hours.[398] Then the French leaders decided to retreat, for their horses were tired, and many of them had been wounded in the first fighting. They carried out an orderly and methodical retreat, one formation of knights moving out behind another, each under the protection of part of the army, standing ready to charge. But when William saw this, he

394 *Istore et Croniques*, I, p. 262.
395 Guiart, vv. 15775–81, p. 246.
396 Guiart, vv. 15926–38, 15957–61, 15974–16000, pp. 247–8.
397 *Ibid.*, vv. 16011–12, p. 248. *Annales Gandenses*, pp. 43–4. *Istore et Croniques*, I, pp. 263–4.

advanced to attack the enemy. Then the French troops halted, and made ready for a general charge. As soon as the Flemings halted, the French advanced once more: in this way William forced the enemy to halt five or six times.[399]

The French nobility had some uncomfortable moments as they approached the Neuf-fossé. They hoped to cross this obstacle at Arques, and then the river Aa, in order to return to St Omer by the shortest way, but their retreat was cut off by the men of Ypres, who blocked the crossing of both watercourses. The men of Ypres had drawn themselves up in crown formation, and seemed unassailable. The French cavalry therefore quickly went to Blendecques, and from there back to St Omer, where the inhabitants were awaiting the outcome of the fighting with fearful apprehension. The French foot-soldiers who had plundered the waggons, were intercepted by the men of Ypres on their way back to St Omer, and suffered heavy losses.[400]

William continued his advance up to the city walls of St Omer, remained till the next day, but the French cavalry did not appear outside the city till the Flemings had gone away again.

Arques is a very interesting example of warfare in the period 1302–1304 in that we can assess the strength and weaknesses of the French heavy cavalry in one and the same battle. These armoured noblemen were able to encircle average or comparatively weak Flemish units and destroy them, but they dared not make heavy charges against powerful and densely packed troops. They had the great advantage of mobility, and could therefore fight the battle whenever and wherever they chose. The Flemish foot on the other hand had to fight defensive battle continually and their success depended on whether the French cavalry dared make a big attack, followed by a violent mêlée. Guiart gives a loss of 300 men in the French army for the battle of Arques,[401] we do not know how many heavy cavalry were involved, but we can assume that it was probably a large number. According to the Franciscan friar of Ghent, the Flemings probably lost 1,000 men, of whom the majority were servants and waggoners.[402]

The battle of Arques was a Flemish victory in that William of Jülich remained in charge of the battlefield, and this counted as a victory in the Middle Ages. He managed to drive off the enemy, but at enormous cost to the Flemish army, and the victory thus gained yielded little result. William was criticized in Flanders in view of the fact that the losses were so enormous: the Franciscan friar reproached him for having left too much space between the corps of his army, and because he came too late to help the men from St Winoksbergen, who advanced without due care.

---

[398] *Annales Gandenses*, p. 44. Guiart, vv. 16036–80, p. 248. *Chronique artésienne*, p. 60.
[399] *Istore et Croniques*, I, p. 263.
[400] *Ibid., loc. cit.*
[401] Guiart, vv. 16148–50, p. 249.
[402] *Annales Gandenses*, pp. 43–4.

THE BATTLE AT MONS-EN-PÉVÈLE, 18 AUGUST 1304

In 1304 king Philip the Fair of France raised a mighty army and advanced against the southern border of Flanders. This border was well defended by the Flemings, and Philip was forced to make a long detour by way of Tournai in order to invade Flanders. On 13 August, the Flemings proposed to do battle in so favourable a position that the king did not dare attack them. Negotiations followed, on the 14, 15 and 16 August, but without result. On 17 August, the Flemings advanced again and pitched camp at Mons-en-Pévèle, so close to the royal army that Philip had to stay where he was. On the morning of the 18th the Flemings again advanced toward the royal army and this time forced a battle to the south of the village of Mons-en-Pévèle.[403]

About six in the morning the Flemings armed themselves, after a meagre breakfast and attending Mass. They took down their tents and left them behind in the camp on the hill. The nobles and rich citizens left their horses there, for every man was to fight on foot. The communal soldiers then advanced, and chose a site south of the village, sloping north to south. They protected the back of their long battle array with their waggons. The carts were securely fastened together, and one wheel of each was removed. There were narrow passages left between the ranks of waggons, and soldiers guarded the waggons. The troops stood shoulder to shoulder in dense battle array, making a front of 1,000 to 1,200 metres. The left wing stretched out to the village hedge. The right wing stretched out to a brook, the 'courant de Coutiches', and was partly protected by a ditch.[404] The Flemish army was probably between 12,500 and 15,000 men strong. The dense battle array was protected by big shields, such as the crossbowmen used. The leaders told them to keep their ranks closed, so that no knight could break through. The men of Bruges and from the Franc of Bruges formed the right wing, commanded by Philip of Chieti, the men of Ghent and their local comrades were on the left wing, under John of Namur; William of Jülich with the men of Ypres, the men of Courtrai, the troops from Lille and its neighbourhood under Robert of Nevers were placed between the men of Ghent and those of Bruges.[405]

In the French army a watch was kept during the night, and early the next morning they observed the Flemings' preparations and sounded the alarm in the royal camp. Each man took up his arms, and put on a white scarf as a distinctive mark.[406] The Grand Master of the crossbowmen, Thibault de Chepoix, assembled his troops and advanced right up to the Flemings, with the crossbowmen and *bidauts* in front. The knights also formed up in the meantime, making with 3,000 heavy cavalry a front which was broader but less deep than the Flemings. The king had first knighted three hundred squires.[406]

---

403 Verbruggen, *De slag bij de Pevelenberg*, pp. 169–98. G. Six, *La bataille de Mons-en-Pévèle*, pp. 210–33. [See also K. DeVries, *Infantry Warfare*, pp. 32–48.]

404 *Annales Gandenses*, p. 69. *Chronique artésienne*, p. 84. Guiart, vv. 20090–135, p. 287; vv. 20538–41, p. 291.

405 *Annales Gandenses*, pp. 69–70. Guiart, vv. 20170–200, p. 288, but not correct.

406 *Chronique artésienne*, p. 84. Guiart, vv. 20055–85, pp. 286–7; vv. 20224–86, pp. 288–9; vv. 20300–422, pp. 289–90; vv. 20540–41, p. 291; v. 20668, p. 292. *Annales Gandenses*, p. 70.

Fighting between the crossbowmen started just after nine o'clock. On the left wing, Thibault realized that he had little chance of breaking through the powerful Flemish battle formation, and began an outflanking movement. Both the count of St Pol and the two marshals did the same. On the French right wing, Gaucher de Châtillon began a similar manoeuvre, in which the 'battles' of Charles of Valois, Louis of France and the dukes of Brittany and Burgundy took part. Six knightly 'battles' began the outflanking movement, as well as the foot of the Grand Master of the crossbowmen, and there were still six 'battles' in front of the Flemings, while the king followed in the second line with the rearguard. Five catapults were set up under the protection of the count of Boulogne's men to bombard the Flemings.[407]

Philip's knights were firmly resolved to fight this time with finesse. The main attack was to fall on the back and flanks of the Flemish army. There was to be no frontal attack, for this could too easily go disastrously wrong. On the Flemish side the battle was fought, as usual, defensively, but in contrast with Courtrai no reserve waited behind the phalanx: the famous commander John of Renesse had in fact been killed two days earlier in Holland. But there were soldiers on the waggons to defend them.

The skirmishing of the crossbowmen along the entire front did not last long, for the French commanders recalled their light foot-soldiers and the cavalry units which were in front of the Flemings attacked them at a trot. All the Flemish archers, except those from the Franc of Bruges and Bruges itself, cut their bowstrings and threw their weapons on the ground, and quickly moved off toward the main body. There the communal soldiers confidently awaited the charge, which they hoped to withstand with their long pikes and lances, while the men with the *goedendags* stood at the ready. But the French nobles did not press their charge home to hand-to-hand fighting, and just before they reached the wall of pikes they drew rein and sat motionless. It was simply a feigned charge, made to frighten the Flemings and to put their archers out of action. But the Brugeois archers shot several volleys which drove the knights back beyond range of the bows. The French archers and *bidauts* were sent forward again.[408]

At the same time the French began shooting at the Flemings with the five catapults. But the men of Ypres made a sortie with a strong corps. The French light foot-soldiers tried vainly to halt them. The men of Ypres suffered but marched bravely on and captured the catapults, which they put out of action. Then they turned back to the main formation, still in good order.[409]

Meanwhile the men of Ghent and those of Ypres took part in a series of small engagements, such as often took place in the years 1302–1304. Only small parties of both sides were involved. The French knights tried to lure these Flemings out of

---

[407] Guiart, vv. 20530–49, p. 291. *Chronique artésienne*, p. 85. *Annales Gandenses*, p. 70. *Chronicon comitum Flandrensium*, I, p. 174.
[408] *Annales Gandenses*, pp. 70–1, confirmed by *Chronique artésienne*, p. 86. Guiart, vv. 20666–78, pp. 292–3, is wrong.
[409] Guiart, vv. 20666–78, pp. 292–3. *Annales Gandenses*, pp. 72–3. *Chronique artésienne*, p. 86, places this sortie too late. *Chronicon comitum Flandrensium*, I, p. 174.

their battle-order and then to ride them down. The Flemings hoped to inflict heavy
losses on their adversaries without moving too far away from the protecting line of
waggons, since they feared attacks on the flank and rear.[410]

While there was not very much going on along the Flemish front, there was very
heavy fighting in progress behind the main battle-order round the protecting carts.
Eight French units out of fourteen attempted a strong attack. The French foot-soldiers
stormed the barricade and tried to haul away the waggons, in order to clear the way
for the nobles. A few French knights managed to get among the three rows of
waggons, but there was too little space, and they were killed. On the right wing about
thirty to forty heavy French cavalry got in between the carts and the Brugeois, but
were killed also. The attack by the French foot-soldiers, supported by the knights,
was a complete failure, and they were driven back by the Flemings.[411]

The French foot-soldiers noticed the Flemish camp at Mons-en-Pévèle, shortly
after noon, and advanced towards it at once. The Flemish waggoners and the servants
and grooms who looked after the horses of the nobles and rich burghers, and the
carts, were not well enough armed to defend the camp. They fled with the animals
in the direction of Lille. The tents and a large quantity of booty thus fell into the
hands of the French, who carried off the goods at once to their own camp. When
Thibault de Chepoix's foot-soldiers saw this, they left their Grand Master in the lurch
and also set off to the camp. The plunderers sold their booty at once in the French
camp, and went on a drinking spree. Only a few of them took any further part in the
battle.[412]

In the meantime the situation in both armies was terrible. It was stiflingly hot, and
everyone was suffering from fearful thirst. The men of Ghent and Ypres exhausted
themselves in small fights, which caused them heavy casualties and rather less to the
French. In both armies warriors died of sunstroke. The situation was even worse in
the Flemish army, since they were surrounded. Only the men of Bruges, who were
near the Coutiches brook, could now and then go to the watercourse to let the soldiers
drink, but first they had to drive off Chepoix's soldiers, until the latter went off to
plunder the camp. Troops of both armies suffered agonies of thirst the whole
afternoon.[413]

There was talk of an armistice, and the negotiations were favourably received in
both armies. While negotiators went over to the Flemish army, the French knights
went to drink and refresh themselves. Opposite the Flemings they posted a unit of
bidauts, the best French foot of the day. Even king Philip dismounted and relaxed.
He called the count of St Pol's men back from behind the waggons, and posted them
in front of the Flemish front line.[414] But while the French enjoyed such freedom of

410 *Annales Gandenses*, pp. 71–2.
411 Guiart, vv. 20703–802, pp. 293–4; vv. 20605–33, p. 292; vv. 20999–21101, p. 296. *Annales
Gandenses*, p. 74.
412 Guiart, vv. 20998–21005, pp. 295–6, gives the exact time. *Chronique artésienne*, p. 85, places it
too early. *Annales Gandenses*, pp. 73–4, puts it too late.
413 Guiart, vv. 20812–84, p. 294. *Annales Gandenses*, p. 74. *Chronicon comitum Flandrensium*, I, p.
174.
414 Guiart, vv. 21093–130, pp. 296–7.

action, things were not so comfortable for the Flemings. They could not so easily refresh themselves, since they could not leave their position. The negotiations came to nothing. Just before sunset the Flemish leaders held a council. John of Namur pointed out that the men of Ghent were exhausted. Philip of Chieti, William of Jülich and Robert of Nevers decided on a general attack. The whole army was to advance, leave the waggons and storm the enemy lines. Hand-to-hand fighting, which the French had been so anxious to avoid, was to be the answer.[415]

William of Jülich attacked first. The *bidauts* tried to block this advance, but were thrown back, and driven from the battlefield. The French army was taken completely by surprise: many of the nobles were not ready for battle, and mounting their horses took to flight, which degenerated into panic.[416] William's corps was followed by a strong formation under Philip of Chieti and Robert of Nevers. The Flemings advanced with banners unfurled, shouting their war-cries. The French knights fled in whole companies, and the Flemings slaughtered anyone they could catch. This panic created a stir throughout the kingdom, and Geoffrey of Paris even accused the nobility of treason.[417]

While the right wing, with William at their head, drove off the French, the left wing took no part in the attack. John of Namur, who was not physically a strong man, left the battlefield with the exhausted men from Ghent, Ypres and Courtrai, and marched off towards Lille.[418] William of Jülich, Philip of Chieti, and Robert of Nevers pursued the French with the men from Bruges and the neighbourhood, strengthened with the bravest Flemings from other corps. Many knights whose horses were tired fell into the pits and ditches which dotted the battlefield and the neighbourhood of the French camp. Some Flemings fell into them too, but not so many.[419]

The Flemish attack took Philip the Fair by surprise. He was sitting on the ground, and his first attempt to remount failed, but he was more successful the second time. He had only a small following with him, but even though he saw his troops fleeing, he resumed the unequal battle. He was scarcely in the saddle when William's men came up. The king's horse was killed, his faithful knights perished, but Philip defended himself stoutly. At one moment he lost his weapon, but a butcher gave him a gigantic battle-axe, with which the king felled several of the enemy. Luckily for him he was not recognized, for his knights had ripped off the royal lilies. The *oriflamme* lay on the ground in shreds. William went on with his men towards the French camp.[420]

---

[415] *Annales Gandenses*, p. 74.
[416] Guiart, vv. 21139–63, p. 297. *Chronicon comitum Flandrensium*, I, p. 174. *Annales Gandenses*, p. 75.
[417] *Annales Gandenses*, p. 75. Geoffrey de Paris, *Chronique rimée*, vv. 2815–24, 2867–9, *Chronicon comitum Flandrensium*, I, p. 174.
[418] *Annales Gandenses*, p. 75. Guiart, vv. 21433–6, p. 298, puts this retreat later.
[419] *Annales Gandenses*, p. 75.
[420] *Ibid.*, pp. 75–7. *Ex anonymo regum Franciae chronico*, RHF, XXII, p. 18. Guiart, vv. 21316–30, pp. 298–9. *Chronique de Jean Desnouelles*, RHF, XXI, p. 194. *Chronique artésienne*, pp. 86–7, but with errors.

Philip of Chieti and Robert of Nevers followed with their strong formation. Meanwhile Philip the Fair was trying to mount another horse, but because of his weight, and after his heavy fall, this was even more difficult than before. Then one of his knights dismounted, and kneeling, offered the king his back as a mounting block. Philip had scarcely mounted when the other Flemings attacked. The French knight who had sacrificed himself was killed instantly, and his head rolled in front of the hooves of the horse he had given up to his sovereign. A Flemish knight then sprang upon the king and dealt the horse such a blow with his *goedendag* that the animal bolted, and thus brought the king in safety to a group of nobles who had been watching the result of the encounter anxiously. The knights who had helped the king to remount were killed. Some knights hastened to the king's help: his brother Charles of Valois came up first with Gautier de Brienne, Louis of France and Louis de Clermont followed with their knights. The Bretons and Picards re-grouped their units.[421]

These bands of knights had been re-formed out of reach of the Flemings, and together with those of the constable, the two marshals and the Burgundian nobles they had just attacked William's little band. William had only a few men with him – perhaps 700 when he set out but their numbers had been weakened during the attack – and he tried in vain to ward off this counterattack. The French knights were more numerous and charged from all directions: William tried once more to organize a crown-shaped defensive formation, but it was too late. His companions on all si s were overwhelmed, and they died to the last man.[422]

Then this band of knights rushed to the help of the king, and heavy fighting followed between these nobles and the large formation of men under Philip of Chieti. According to the French chronicler Guiart, the French broke up the Flemish formations, but he had to concede that the Brugeois triumphantly pushed through the French camp.[323] The victorious Flemings found some wine and food in the royal tent and elsewhere. They saw that the rest of the army had not followed, but that the French knights were still about: it had grown completely dark, the moon had risen, and they feared attacks from all directions in the moonlight. They took council and decided to move off. They returned in smart formation along the Coutiches brook to the camp on the hill at Pévèle, their banners flying. They picked up their scattered comrades on the way. The French debated whether to attack them, but decided not to risk it because of the darkness, and the retreat went on without incident to the camp. There the Flemings sounded victorious trumpets, and looked on themselves as the winners. They were joined on the hill by more men who had got scattered, but they found neither food, drink, nor tents, and returned out of sheer necessity to Lille,[424] leaving the battlefield in the hands of the king, who rightly proclaimed

---

421 *Ex anonymo regum Franciae chronico*, p. 18. *Annales Gandenses*, p. 76. Guiart, vv. 21316–30, pp. 298–9. *Chronique de Jean Desnouelles*, p. 194. *Chronique artésienne*, pp. 86–7, again with errors.
422 Guiart, vv. 21163, 21197–203, p. 297, but too early in the battle. See *Annales Gandenses*, p. 78, and *Chronicon comitum Flandrensium*, I, p. 174.
423 Guiart, vv. 21366–81, 21396–402, p. 299. *Annales Gandenses*, p. 77, do not mention an attack by the French knights at that moment.
424 *Annales Gandenses*, p. 77. Guiart, v. 21445, p. 299; vv. 21457–65, p. 300.

himself the victor. But the engagement had been so hotly contested, and so indecisive, that the men from the triumphant Flemish army still felt they had won. The losses on both sides were heavy, about 300 nobles in the French army, and perhaps 1,500 to 2,000 foot-soldiers. The Flemings had lost as many men, or very nearly so, but they had many wounded as well, and had lost their waggons and tents.[425]

---

[425] For the losses: *Annales Gandenses*, p. 79. *Chronique artésienne*, pp. 87–8, but the numbers are too high. Verbruggen, *De slag bij de Pevelenberg*, p. 195. In Bruges the 'victory' was commemorated every year in the Procession of Our Lady of the Blind, the fulfilment of a promise of the women of Bruges if their men won the battle. [DeVries, *Infantry Warfare*, puts a different complexion on the outcome, p. 47.]

IV

GENERAL TACTICS

So far, cavalry and foot-soldiers and their tactics have been studied separately in some detail. But there are many problems which concern them both, before and during battle in the disposition of troops, at the end in flight or retreat, and the place of the commander and of reserve troops. The battles chosen as examples here are those for which particularly detailed accounts exist, or which are interesting for the tactics used in them.

Choice and exploitation of terrain

Choosing the most suitable terrain for a battle was naturally an important matter for a medieval commander. He had to consider the lie of the land and the composition of his army, since a place might be ideal for cavalry but quite unsuitable for foot-soldiers, or vice versa.

Giraldus Cambrensis discussed this very sensibly in describing the differences between tactics in France, Wales and Ireland. 'Although the French cavalry are excellent', he says, 'and well versed in the arts of war, they used methods very different from those employed in Wales or Ireland. In France they choose fields or flat country, in Wales or Ireland difficult or rugged places and forests. Fighting is an honourable occupation in France, but here it is a heavy burden: sheer strength triumphs there, but agility here. Over there they take prisoners, here they are beheaded: there they are ransomed, but here they are killed. Where military formations are fighting in open country, knights are both protected and decorated by heavy and complicated armour, made of iron and linen. But if they have to fight in a confined space, or in wooded or marshy country, where foot-soldiers can fight better than cavalry, light armour is much more suitable. Against these unprotected men (from Ireland) who almost invariably win or lose in the first assault, much lighter weapons suffice. Where a highly mobile army is fighting in a confined or rugged area, it is only necessary to have a few heavy and medium-weight troops make a flexible attack in order to get the enemy confused. Complicated armour and high curved saddles make it difficult to dismount, and it is even harder to remount. Also, it is much more exhausting to fight on foot if one has to.'[1] Several centuries earlier,

---

[1] Giraldus Cambrensis, *Expugnatio Hibernica*, p. 395 [trs. Scott and Martin, pp. 246–7]. Drummond,

the author of the *Strategikon* had already noticed this in the Frankish cavalry. Since they were used to charging with their lances in their hands, they needed flat ground, and could not fight so well in a small space or on uneven ground. Of his own army, he wrote that his cavalry was best on flat ground in open country, his foot-soldiers in wooded country.[2] The crusaders also chose spacious and open country for their battles. Twelve battles which Heermann was able to study took place in flat open country. The Turks also needed this sort of country to let their mounted archers manoeuvre and encircle the Western cavalry. The crusaders had to solve the important problem of protecting their flanks. In the battle of the Lake of Antioch they chose a confined space in which both flanks were supported by impassable obstacles.[3] During the great sortie from Antioch itself they protected their left flank by placing it against the hills. The deployment of these forces was not yet complete when the Turks outflanked this formation, and a hastily collected force was able to put the enemy to flight.[4]

Baldwin of Boulogne set out for Jerusalem in 1100 to follow in the footsteps of his dead brother, Godfrey of Bouillon, with a little force of 160 knights and 500 foot-soldiers. Originally his army had consisted of 200 knights and 700 foot-soldiers, but when these soldiers heard that the enemy was likely to intercept them, many of them went no further. The coast road from Tripoli to Beirut was constricted at the river Nahr al-Kalb into a narrow pass between the sea and the mountains where a hundred men were enough to hold the pass against a larger force, by the forces of Duqaq, ruler of Damascus, and his ally the emir of Homs. An enemy squadron was ready at sea to hinder Baldwin's retreat. When Baldwin's scouts approached the bottleneck, they espied Turkish scouts and realized that a stronger force lay in ambush further on. They sent a message to their commander who at once got his troops into battle-order and ordered the first section to advance. This formation attacked the enemy, but soon found that it was impossible to break through their lines. Baldwin stopped the fight at nightfall, pitching his tents as close as possible to the enemy. 'We pretended to be brave, but were in fear of death. It was hard to stay there, but even worse to retreat: we were besieged on all sides by the enemy. They were threatening us from the sea, and from the hills they were pressing down on us. We had neither food nor rest that day, nor any drink for our beasts. How much rather would I have been in Chartres or Orléans!' says Fulcher, who was there as Baldwin's chaplain. They spent the night outside their tents, wide awake.[5]

In the morning Baldwin decided to lure the enemy from their position in order to attack them in a place where the cavalry would have the advantage. The little army set off with the baggage animals, the knights forming the rearguard to protect the baggage and the foot-soldiers. He withdrew to a small plain, where he hoped to be

---

'Studien zur Kriegsgeschichte Englands im 12. Jahrhundert', dissertation, Berlin, 1905, pp. 95–6. Delbrück, III, pp. 284–5.
2   Maurikios, *Strategikon*, VIII, 2, 20, 21; XI, 3 (ed. G.T. Dennis, pp. 281–3, 369–71) [tr. *Maurice's Strategikon*, pp. 83–4, 96–100].
3   Delbrück, III, p. 315, n. 1. [See France, *Victory*, pp. 170–181 for a new interpretation of the battle.]
4   See below, the story of the battle.
5   Fulcher, pp. 373–5. Albert of Aix, pp. 527–9.

able to deal with the enemy decisively. His enemies had wanted to attack him first by night but this plan had not worked. Then they thought of surrounding the Christian army completely by occupying a pass in its rear. They harassed the flanks of the Christians along the sea, and attacked Baldwin's troops from the mountains and the road. Nevertheless, the crusaders managed to reach the little plain. There the knights suddenly faced about, couched their lances and charged in close formation. The shock was so tremendous that the enemy was halted and thrown back to the narrow pass. There was the utmost confusion in the Turkish ranks: some made for the ships, others fled to the mountains, the rest poured through the pass in full retreat. They made no further effort to stop the crusaders.[6]

It was his clever use of terrain which secured this victory. Tancred provides us with a similar example at Tizin on 20 April, 1105. There was a battle between the Norman armies and Ridwan, ruler of Aleppo. Between the two armies lay a rocky plain, on which horses could not move faster than a walking-pace, and even so, many were injured and fell. Tancred knew this and waited on the far side of the plain in order to induce the enemy to attack. Ridwan advanced over this difficult country and fell into the trap. Tancred opened the battle with his first formation, which checked the enemy and brought him to a standstill. Then the Norman commander led a counter-attack himself. The enemy withdrew a little in the hope of being able to employ his favourite tactics. But it was too late: the Turks were overtaken and crushed. Their foot-soldiers had already advanced further and had reached the crusaders' camp, but after the flight of the cavalry they were mercilessly cut to pieces by Tancred's men.[7]

There are other examples of this clever exploitation of terrain. At Thielt William Clito made use of a hill to defeat his enemy with a hidden reserve.[8] At Arsuf, Saladin's armies attacked the crusaders' armies under Richard I in a wide plain which admirably suited his encircling tactics. They advanced out of a great wood, which allowed them to surprise the enemy and which made pursuit exceedingly difficult for their opponents in the case of retreat.[9]

In each of these battles it can be seen how the commanders tried to get an advantage from the nature of the terrain in order to force the enemy into an awkward position. Again, King Philip Augustus of France left Tournai in 1214 to seek a suitable battle-ground where he could better deploy his knightly formations, at Bouvines.[10] While the knights sought wide open country for fighting, the foot-soldiers naturally chose country in which armoured cavalry could not charge. Giraldus Cambrensis has already been quoted on this subject, describing how the Welsh and Irish fought against this sort of cavalry. At Hastings the English took up a position on a ridge

---

6 Fulcher, pp. 375–6. Albert of Aix, pp. 529–30.
7 Albert of Aix, p. 620. Ralph of Caen, pp. 714–15. Grousset, I, pp. 420–1.
8 See below, the story of the battle.
9 See below, the story of the battle.
10 See below, the story of the battle.

which was very favourable for the foot-soldiers against the cavalry and archers of William the Conqueror; the forest behind their position would facilitate a retreat.[11]

Every victory of the foot-soldiers in the early fourteenth century was won on ground that was very difficult for knights, such as Courtrai, Bannockburn, Morgarten, and Vottem. At Cortenuova the Lombard foot-soldiers were placed behind a ditch, with their rear protected by the village.

Jean le Bel, who gave such an excellent account of the campaign of 1327, also gives very interesting examples of the use of terrain. The Scots had chosen a position on the slope of a hill behind a brook, at such a distance from the water that the English could get part of their troops across but could not properly manoeuvre on the far side.[12] The rocky nature of the ground was extremely unfavourable to the knights, who dared not risk an attack. Four days later, the Scots chose another position, once more on a hill and behind a river, but better than the first one. Their troops camped in a wood so that they could move off unseen when the command came.[13]

The Welsh selected similar sites. At Orewin Bridge, in 1282, they took up position on a steep hill behind the bank of the river Yrfon, accessible only by a bridge which was blocked by their pikemen, who were nevertheless out of range of arrows from the further bank.[14] In 1295, at Maes Moydog near Conway they stood on the slope of a hill, above the road between two woods into which they could withdraw if an enemy attack were successful.[15] During the conquest of Ireland, at the Dinin in 1169, the knights lured the Irish foot-soldiers out of a secure position by a feigned flight and then defeated them soundly in open country.[16]

In general, the Flemings could not reckon on terrain as favourable as the Welsh, Scots and Swiss, but they exploited the advantages of brooks and ditches with considerable cunning. In September 1302, at Flines, they did as they had done at Courtrai, and again in 1304 a few days before the battle of Mons-en-Pévèle. In each case the French king had the sense to delay his attack.[17] At Falkirk and at Bannockburn the Scots derived great advantage from the lie of the land, as we have seen.

If the position of the foot-soldiers was far enough behind the water, and the enemy knights were allowed to cross this obstacle, then the foot-soldiers could fall on the enemy when only part of their forces had crossed. In that case, a large proportion of the enemy cavalry could be annihilated while the obstacle was behind them and the rest were powerless to help. This is just what happened at Stirling Bridge in Scotland in 1297, and demonstrates the great importance of the choice and exploitation of terrain for a battle.

---

[11] Guy of Amiens, *Carmen de Hastingae Proelio*, p. 24. William of Poitiers, p. 186, H. Delbrück, III, p. 157. Oman, I, p. 165. [S. Morillo, *The Battle of Hastings*, Woodbridge, 1995.]
[12] Jean le Bel, I, p. 65.
[13] *Ibid.*, pp. 65–6, 68–9. Thomas Gray of Heton, p. 154.
[14] Oman, II, p. 69.
[15] M. Powicke, *The Thirteenth Century*, Oxford, 1953, pp. 442–3. Morris, *Welsh Wars*, p. 256. Oman, II, p. 70.
[16] Oman, I, pp. 405–6.
[17] *Annales Gandenses*, p. 40. *Chronique artésienne*, pp. 55, 80.

The March into Battle

Very often we have to be content with meagre information about the march towards the enemy when battle was intended. Only the best and most detailed accounts give us any indication that the knights' tactics and their co-operation with the foot-soldiers were more highly developed than has been thought hitherto. Even in the First Crusade there are usually no descriptions of the formations used by the crusaders when close to the enemy, but fortunately there is an interesting description of what happened before the battle of Ascalon in 1099. Raymond of Aguilers, who was present at the battle, relates how the crusaders made their approach. Two hundred knights went first as scouts. The main army followed, split up into nine divisions of knights which were equally divided into centre, advance and rear-guards. They were thus able to face the enemy on whichever side they might come. Three sections were always ready to meet them, and the three units of the centre were always ready to dash to the rescue. Delpech and Heermann have pictured these sections as line formations, riding on a broad front. Delbrück does not agree with this conclusion and thinks they were columns with a narrow front and considerable depth, because otherwise the flanks of marching units would have been insufficiently protected.[18] It seems to me that Delpech and Heermann are probably right. The nine formations anyway advanced in three lines, each consisting of three units adjoining each other. When one flank was threatened, the formation advancing there had to swing round in order to make a new front facing in the direction which was most threatened. This was not difficult, and had the advantage that the formations of knights were always ready to attack the approaching enemy at any moment. They were already very close to the Egyptian army and advancing towards them. They also knew more or less where they were. The greatest danger was therefore threatening the front of the formations, where the battle would have to begin. If the crusaders were marching in deep narrow columns they would first have to deploy before they could fight. Also, they would first have to deploy the rear-guard sections if the enemy attacked in the rear. The battle order which Delbrück imagined would not be very practical, since it offered some advantages only on the flanks. But the safety of the flanks is secondary to that of the front, where the battle might well be decided. This suggests that the nine formations were deployed in line and did not march in columns.

We find a similar situation in 1328, when the army of king Philip VI of France advanced to Cassel, and immediately had to get ready to ward off an attack by Flemish rebels. The first division was commanded by the two marshals, who usually reconnoitred the enemy positions. They were followed by foot-soldiers, who could be sent forward very quickly. While the camp was being pitched, the second division took up a position to repel any possible Flemish attack. This section could act as advance guard, delay the enemy, and give the other formations a chance to attack in their turn. But the Flemings stayed in their strong positions on the hill.[19]

18 Raymond of Aguilers, pp. 303–4. Delbrück, III, p. 424.
19 *Istore et Croniques*, I, p. 343.

In the battles of Legnano and Cortenuova the foot-soldiers were preceded by an advance guard consisting of armoured knights, who started the battle. Although the Lombard cavalry were put to flight in each case, their resistance to the enemy gave the foot-soldiers the necessary time to get into proper position and then to fight off the charges of the enemy knights successfully.

A most remarkable example of an army's approach towards the enemy, and of preparation for the battle is found in the battle of Arsuf, which we shall examine later.

Battle Order

The battle of Hab, in 1119, gives an interesting example of battle order, fully described by a contemporary writer.

King Baldwin II of Jerusalem formed his armies as follows: the front line consisted of three detachments, each made up of a body of knights and a body of foot-soldiers, for mutual protection. In the second line was the count of Tripoli with his vassals, but these troops were drawn up further to the right than the first line, thus broadening the front. Robert Fulcoy, lord of Zerdana, was on the extreme left, with the knights from Antioch in several smaller formations. These formations also made up part of the second line, and extended the front leftwards. In the third line came King Baldwin, with three detachments, which were drawn up behind the front line units.

```
------- ------    ------- ------    ------------     (Knights)
==== ====    ==== ====    ==== ====                  (Foot)

-- -- -- -- -- --                          -- -- -- -- --

(Robert Fulcoy)                            (Pons of Tripoli)

        ------------    ------------    ------------
                    (Baldwin II)
```

Thus the troops of Robert Fulcoy and Pons of Tripoli were able to perform a double task, first to broaden the front and to attack the enemy frontally or in the flank, and secondly to protect the flank of their own army. Baldwin's battle order was just such as Leo the Wise of Byzantium had praised centuries earlier in his *Taktika*.[20] As in the advance of Ascalon, Delbrück would like to suppose that these troops were marching in narrow columns, which were first deployed at the start of the battle. But the source says nothing about this, and we have already shown that there is no advantage in it if the enemy's position is known and fighting can start at once.

Attacks were also sometimes made by echelons rather similarly disposed. The first line charges first, then those formations move which are to the right and left of the front line, but form a second line. These units can react to the enemy's manoeuvres, and either protect the two flanks of the front lines, or else attack at each

---

[20] Oman, I, pp. 298, 198. Smail, p. 181. Delbrück, III, p. 426.

end of it in order to relieve their own men or outflank the enemy. Thus in attacking with formations in echelon the battle is enlarged along the flanks. They can either check the enemy's encircling tactics, or else outflank him in his turn, instead of supporting the rear of the formation in front.[21] The crusaders used these tactics several times so that they could fight on a broader front than if the formations of the second and third line were placed immediately behind the first. At the same time, they enjoyed the advantage of having a deep formation, with three lines of troops. Sarmin (14 September 1115), Athareb (28 June 1119) and the battle of Hab discussed above are all good examples of this.[22]

From the chronicle of Henry of Valenciennes we gather that the troops of the emperor Henry I of Constantinople used this sort of battle-order in the battle of Philippopoli. 'Piers de Braiesceul and N. de Mailli were in the advance guard with Geoffrey the Marshal, and they said they would push ahead between him and Milon le Braibant with Guillaume dou Parçoi and Lyenars de Hyelemes behind them, and the emperor would guard the attackers.'[23] This gives us the following battle order, in which we have made the necessary allowance for the arrangement right and left of the forces listed. Villehardouin (Geoffrey the Marshal) might of course have been on the left and Milon le Braibant on the right, and this applies to the other formations too.

(P. de Br.)	(Mailli)
(Milon)	(Villehardouin)
(Guillaume)	(Liénard)
(the emperor Henry I)	

Of course, it is possible that the formations of Villehardouin and Milon le Braibant were originally as far forward as those of Piers de Braiescuel and Nicoles de Mailli. But, in any case, these two units of the advance guard moved off before Milon and Villehardouin charged. During the attack, the position was as shown, and it is a pity that we do not know the positions of the three units of Greek troops who took part in the battle.

The dispositions of Louis VI in 1124, for the battle at Rheims, are also interesting. Louis VI had come up quickly with his followers to the threatened position, calling up his vassals as he came, and his powerful liegemen crowded to his banner.

As the forces came up the following tactical units were formed:

---

21 Delpech, II, p. 5 and n. 4, p. 319, has not found examples of attacks by echelons. Heermann and Köhler have shown that this method was employed several times. Cf. Smail, pp. 200–1.
22 Delbrück, III, p. 426.
23 *Histoire de l'empereur Henri de Constantinople*, c. 533, pp. 41–2.

1. A contingent of soldiers from Rheims and Châlons, both cavalry and foot.
2. A contingent from Laon and Soissons.
3. A contingent from Orléans, Etampes, Paris and St Denis. The king himself was to fight with this group, because they knew him best and were his loyal subjects.
4. A division of the troops of Theobald of Blois and count Hugh of Troyes. Theobald IV, count of Chartres, Blois and Brie was at war with Louis VI at that time, but he stopped fighting in order to be with the levies for the defence of the country.
5. The fifth division was to act as advance guard and consisted of the men of the duke of Burgundy and the count of Nevers.
6. The sixth division formed the right wing and consisted of the men of the count of Vermandois, the men from St Quentin and other places in the county.
7. Troops from Ponthieu, Amiens and Beauvais made up the left wing.
8. Count Charles the Good of Flanders and his men formed the rearguard.

The duke of Aquitaine, the count of Brittany and the count of Anjou also brought men, but reached the collecting area too late.[24]

Before the battle it was decided to put the battle waggons with wine and water behind the troops in a circle where the ground made this possible. Inside the circle of waggons wounded and exhausted soldiers could quench their thirst and rest, and return (if possible) bandaged or refreshed. But Emperor Henry V drew off before there was any fighting.

Co-operation of Cavalry and Foot-soldiers in Battle

Where knights and foot-soldiers appeared together in any co-ordinated battle-order the knights were usually the main force and the foot-soldiers the supporting troops. This was the result of the hegemony of armoured cavalry. Already in the time of Vegetius the foot-soldiers were playing a passive part. The heavily armed legionaries had to stand still in close formation while the lightly armed troops started the fighting. If the latter were successful, they pursued the enemy, but if they failed they retreated behind the heavier troops as behind an iron wall. Then, if the enemy were beaten off, the light foot and cavalry took up the chase together, but the heavy foot-soldiers stayed put, for fear of their ranks being broken up by a renewed enemy attack. According to Vegetius, a legion of his time could neither easily pursue nor flee themselves. The foot-soldiers were already playing a comparatively passive part at the end of the fourth century. Vegetius then thought of putting the cavalry on the flanks of the legion.[25] The author of the *Strategikon* claims that the foot-soldiers had been neglected for a long time, or even no longer existed. He drew up a new code for their use. In order to secure co-operation between the two branches he proposed

---

[24] Suger, c. 28, pp. 22–6. Lot, I, pp. 121–2.
[25] Vegetius, 1. II, c. 17. Delbrück, III, p. 289.

an initial attack by foot-soldiers followed up by cavalry, who were then to move up through the ranks of the foot-soldiers in order to charge. In case of failure, the cavalry were to take up their position behind the foot-soldiers.[26] Emperor Leo VI 'the Wise' gave the following case in his *Taktika*. If the enemy had a strong army of knights and the Byzantines only a weak force of foot, the foot-soldiers were to be stationed one or two bow-shots behind the Byzantine cavalry, so that the latter could withdraw behind them if a charge failed. But their retreat was to be along the foot-soldiers' flanks, not through their ranks.[27]

The foot-soldier's passive role is very old. According to whether it had kept a satisfactory standard, or had improved or increased with time, it could support knights in battle in different ways. A differentiation should be made between those armies in which the knights remained the more important section and the foot played the humble role of supporting troops, and those countries where the foot had early reached some degree of excellence and were helped by the knights.

Preparation for Battle by Archers

Just as the heavy foot could be used to prepare for cavalry charges, and protect the rear of the knights' ranks, follow in the mêlée and deal with those of the enemy who were unhorsed, so crossbowmen and ordinary archers could play a most useful part in co-operating with the other branches of the army.

One of the oldest and most famous examples of archers preparing for a cavalry battle is found in William the Conqueror's great victory at Hastings. His archers advanced first of all against the dense English formation. They were followed by heavy foot-soldiers. But when they were within reach of the enemy on the hill, they were met by a rain of missiles, arrows, lances, small axes and stones tied to heavy sticks. They were driven back, but were able to avenge themselves later in the day. Then the archers advanced between two cavalry charges. While the armoured cavalry were re-forming after the charge, the archers harassed the solid blocks of English foot-soldiers. This caused heavy losses among Harold's soldiers. The king himself was hit in the eye by an arrow. In the splendid representation in the Bayeux tapestry the great shields of the English are stuck full of arrows. There is no doubt that William's archers made a very useful contribution in this battle.[28]

In the First Crusade the western knights met with mounted archers, a form of fighting hitherto unknown to them. They protected their formations by foot-soldiers, especially crossbowmen, who had to keep the enemy cavalry at a distance, and so to protect the knights' horses from the enemy arrows. While the Turkish horsemen were trying to put the crusaders' archers out of action, the knights were able to come closer and prepare a powerful charge. Once the knights were in the battle, the foot-soldiers withdrew to protect the rear of the armoured cavalry. In case of need

---

[26] *Strategikon*, 1. XII, c. VIII, p. 416. Lot, I, pp. 52, 54.
[27] *Taktika*, c. XIV, 20.
[28] Oman, I, pp. 160, 164. *The Bayeux Tapestry*, ed. D.M. Wilson, London, 1985, plates 60, 68–70.

they could be sent forward again to keep the enemy at a distance. The arrows of the crossbowmen caused severe wounds among the Turks.

During the First Crusade the foot-soldiers put these tactics into practice in the break-out from Antioch and in the battle of Ascalon. In the Third Crusade the crossbowmen played a very important part before the knights started charging at Arsuf. Saladin's biographer speaks very highly of the quality of the foot-soldiers and mentions the devastating effect of their arrows.[29]

The battle of Jaffa in 1192 is another very interesting case in this crusade. Richard I placed foot-soldiers armed with spears in the first rank, They knelt down, and held the shafts of their spears embedded in the ground. Their shields were held in the left hand, point downwards and embedded likewise in the ground. Between every two spearmen the king placed a crossbowman, with another man as loader next to each of them. These crossbowmen were Genoese and Pisans, already well known for their skill in handling their weapons. The formation of foot-soldiers made a circle, within which Richard stayed with a very small group of knights. Saladin's warriors advanced towards this formation but soon swerved aside when they saw that the foot-soldiers were drawn up in dense formation. As they rode by the circle, they were greeted with arrows from the crossbowmen. No Moslem troops dared make a charge against this circular formation of Christians. Finally Richard himself counter-attacked, charging through with his little retinue.[30]

We have already seen that Richard had made use of Genoese crossbowmen in Normandy. After his crusade he had some Moslems in his army as well.[31] In the thirteenth century the Emperor Frederick II had Moslem bowmen in his army but could not use them soon enough at the battle of Cortenuova.[32] In the battle of Mansurah in the first crusade of St Louis in Egypt, the crossbowmen were only able to take part in the final stages of the battle, but when they were placed in front of the knights and shot off their rain of arrows, the enemy withdrew.[33]

Large numbers of crossbowmen were seldom used before Crécy (1346). When Edward I of England used his longbowmen in large numbers he had a much more efficient weapon for preparation for charges by his knights. This happened at Falkirk with astounding success, after the knights' attack had been beaten off by the Scottish *schiltrons*. These Welsh and English bowmen became later the best troops in the army of the English king, and we have already noticed in passing what splendid success they had at Dupplin Moor and Halidon Hill. But very often the number of archers in medieval armies was too small, or else they were checked by the enemy's crossbowmen. Army leaders could, of course, use other foot-soldiers, armed with pikes and lances, but these were mostly used for defensive purposes.

[29] See below, 'The Battle of Arsuf'.
[30] Ambroise, pp. 307–8. Lot, I, p. 164.
[31] Poole, p. 372.
[32] Pieri, pp. 25–8. Delbrück, III, pp. 367–8.
[33] Joinville, c. 49, p. 86.

Foot-soldiers as Supporting Troops for Cavalry

We have seen that the Emperor Leo VI of Byzantium posted foot-soldiers as supporting troops behind his armoured cavalry in certain cases. We meet the same use of foot-soldiers elsewhere. Armed foot-soldiers were stationed to right and left, and single cavalrymen were posted among them so that they should hold their positions. The foot-soldiers had to let in the armoured cavalry, should some of them be driven back.[34] Part of the foot played a similar role while the rest were striking camp at the battle of Doryleum, during the first crusade. This served to check the flight of the cavalry: or gave them the chance to re-form their ranks, while the close-packed foot kept the enemy at a distance.[35]

A strong body of foot-soldiers placed behind the formations of knights could be a great help while the latter were regrouping after a charge. Under the protection of the pikes or lances of the foot, the knights could get their breath again after their exhausting charges. In some cases, small companies of knights even took refuge in the circle of foot-soldiers, as Renaud de Dammartin did at Bouvines.[36]

In general, the foot played a passive part until the cavalry had started fighting. That was the moment for the foot to move up to help the knights. There are many examples of this. At Steppes, Thierry de Walcourt told the civic levies of the Meuse towns to stay in close formation, with pikes and lances stuck into the ground. These foot-soldiers had to turn back their own knights, if these tried to flee through their own ranks. As in the treatise of Leo VI, the knights had thus to withdraw along the flanks of the foot-soldiers in case of need, in order to regroup. The civic levies from Liège, Huy, Dinant and Fosses, however, moved up behind their knights as soon as the latter had attacked the enemy. They killed those of their opponents who had been unhorsed, or took them prisoner, and followed the knights during the pursuit.[37]

Mutual Support of Knights and Foot-soldiers

The mutual support of formations of knights and foot can best be seen in the First Crusade and in the subsequent war fought by the armies of the Kingdom of Jerusalem against the Moslems. In the early stage of the battle the foot-soldiers advanced in front of the knights, protecting them frontally, their own rear being covered by the cavalry. These archers shot at the enemy cavalry and tried to keep them at a distance. At the vital moment the knights rode past them, followed by the foot-soldiers. While the knights bore the brunt of the frontal attack, the foot in turn protected their rear. The Turkish archers naturally outflanked the Christian archers and often preferred to attack the foot in the hope of putting them out of action at once, then being able to attack the knights from the rear. When this happened, the cavalry had no supporting troops behind which they could withdraw between charges, if their first

---

[34] Guillaume de Pouille, *La geste de Robert Guiscard*, ed. M. Mathieu, Istituto Siciliano di Studi Bizantini e Neoellenici. Testi e Monumenti. Testi 4, Palermo, 1961, bk I, vv. 260–4, p. 112.
[35] Ralph of Caen, c. 22, p. 622 A.
[36] See below, the study of the battle.
[37] *Vita Odiliae*, pp. 183–4. Gaier, p. 261.

attack should fail, or if they were exhausted. As soon as the knights had made their highly mobile enemy join battle, then had ridden down the enemy formations by their tremendous charges, the foot could rush up. Any Turks who had been unhorsed were killed or captured and bound by the foot-soldiers, who also helped the fallen knights of their own side to remount, and carried off wounded knights. If the foot got the chance, they also took part in close-range fighting, and attacked the horses of the Turks and Arabs.

The foot eased the task of the cavalry also by taking on a part of the enemy forces which might otherwise have been fighting against the cavalry. The knights realized that the foot-soldiers were necessary to increase the strength of their forces and put out of action any of the enemy who were unhorsed. The foot-soldiers were also useful in protecting their flanks. The knights then had to take care not to leave them too far behind, so as to be able to hurry to their help in good time if need arose.

Already by 1102 a defeat of the knights of king Baldwin I of Jerusalem was attributed, among other things, to the fact that they had fought without foot-soldiers. In the crusaders' great march to Arsuf under Richard I in 1191, the knights protected the main body of the foot while the crossbowmen of the rearguard protected the knights in their turn. Once the battle of Arsuf had begun, the foot-soldiers quickly finished off the unhorsed enemy before the knights had to come back to regroup after the charge.

These tactics were also applied in western Europe, but the knights had less reason to fear an attack from the rear than they did in the Middle East. Indeed, the great armies of knights had large enough forces to fight their own battles in most cases. It was not always so necessary to use foot-soldiers and there were many battles in which knights alone were involved.

In the West, army leaders tried to make their foot-soldiers more effective on several occasions by stiffening their ranks with knights fighting on foot. Robert Guiscard did this, and at Tinchebray in 1106, King Henry I dismounted with his retinue and took up a position in the middle of the foot, who did not actually have to fight in this battle. His opponent, Robert of Normandy, did the same and also stayed in the middle of his foot-soldiers. These soldiers were beaten after the knights had been defeated.[38] At Brémule Henry I ordered knights to dismount and fight on foot, while another party of knights made up the mounted reserve. He defeated king Louis VI who attacked with insufficiently ordered formations of knights.[39] At Bourg-Théroulde Norman knights increased the effectiveness of their archers against rebellious noblemen, by dismounting and fighting on foot with the foot-soldiers,[40] and at Northallerton in 1138 the Anglo-Norman riders dismounted and took up positions among the foot.[41]

[38] Lot, I, pp. 316–17.
[39] *Ibid.*, p. 317.
[40] *Ibid.*, pp. 318–19.
[41] Oman, I, pp. 391–2, 395. Beeler, p. 89. [C.W. Hollister, *The Military Organization of Norman England*, p. 128; J. Bradbury, 'Battles in England and Normandy, 1066–1154', *Anglo-Norman Studies* 6, pp. 1–12.]

Independent Action of Foot-soldiers in Co-operation with Cavalry

While duke John I of Brabant was making a frontal attack with his allies at Worringen in 1288, the peasants from the county of Berg and the communal army from Cologne marched towards the flank of the army of the princebishop of Cologne and attacked it. Their action against this flank and the enemy's rear decided the outcome. But we do not know whether the initiative for this came from the count of Berg or from the tactical leader of the battle, the count of Virneburg.[42]

Foot-soldiers in the army of the Scottish kings naturally provided various examples of independent action, since they had only a few knights, in comparison with English kings. The co-operation of these two branches depended chiefly on the strength of the foot. The knights protected the flanks or were used as a reserve. The foot-soldiers played the chief part and the mounted knights acted as supporting troops.

In the armies of the English kings, the archers also had independent tasks against the enemy's flanks, and in these armies the foot-soldiers became more important. In the middle of the fourteenth century, however, Edward III succeeded in also raising large armies of knights, so that there was a balance between foot-soldiers and cavalry. A genuine interacting tactical system was evolved between the two branches in which the archers were the more effective force. But this joint action was only possible if these archers could rely on the support of knights fighting on foot, and on a mounted reserve.

The battle of Hausbergen is an interesting case in which foot-soldiers fought successfully on their own. In 1262 the bishop of Strasbourg, Walter of Geroldseck, had an argument with the commune of the city. He collected an army consisting of 300 knights and a good body of foot-soldiers. But before the foot-soldiers arrived, he advanced on the communal army of Strasbourg and their allies. The Strasbourgers were led by two knights, the lords of Ohsenstein and Hohenstein, who had also brought their armoured cavalry with them. The citizens had sworn to obey all their orders implicitly. Both commanders decided to join battle with the bishop's mounted army before his foot-soldiers arrived. They therefore placed 300 crossbowmen on the road which the bishop's foot-soldiers would have to use, in order to prevent them, if possible, from taking part in the fighting. Half of these crossbowmen were to shoot as continuously as possible, while the other half loaded for their companions. Thus they could reckon on an effective rain of arrows. While the bishop's foot-soldiers were thus kept out of the battle and a good deal of time was wasted, both commanders, with their knights, began the battle with the bishop's cavalry. The communal army from Strasbourg had to join in the mêlée. While the battle was raging, the Strasbourg soldiers came up quickly and outflanked the bishop's mounted knights. With their pikes they stabbed and cut down the horses of the Alsatian knights, so that the knights were dragged down with their horses. Thus the communal army on foot supported the attack of their allies and thanks to superiority of numbers, they won the battle.[43]

---

[42] See below, 'The Battle of Worringen'.
[43] See the account of Ellenhardus Argentinensis, in Delpech, I, pp. 308–9, notes. Köhler, III, 3, pp. 298–300. Delbrück, III, pp. 389–93.

The Position of the Supreme Commander and the Reserve Corps

Up till now, historians of the art of war have maintained that the supreme commander of a medieval army almost always, like ordinary soldiers, fought man to man in battle. But this view is wrong. Delbrück even went so far as to deny the use of tactical reserves.[44] This view was later refuted. But it is well to be cautious about this. The sovereign does not always appear as supreme commander, but often entrusted tactical command to a proficient and well-known general. At Bouvines, a former Hospitaller, Bishop Guérin, was in command, while King Philip Augustus started by taking part in the battle, but was later kept further back by his own guard. At Worringen John I was fighting but the count of Virneburg was in command. At Fréteval Richard I took part in battle, but kept a good reserve; at Arsuf he led the reserve in the battle. In a minor battle at Jaffa in 1192, he also led the reserve, which consisted of knights and was positioned behind the foot-soldiers.[45]

In order to deal with this problem thoroughly, I have examined all the battles discussed or mentioned in the works of Oman and Delbrück, and added some more examples.

One of the earlier examples is the strategic disposition of the army of Louis the Pious which besieged Barcelona in 800 A.D. One corps surrounded the city under the command of Rotstagnus. A second corps stood by, close to the town, and protected the besiegers against attack. Louis the Pious led the third corps which could come from Roussillon to the help of the others.[46] There is another interesting example in the first chapter of this book, namely the defence of the Seine between Paris and Melun by Charles the Bald in 841. The king stayed with the central reserve corps at St Cloud. In 940, Sarilo, margrave of Camerino and Spoleto, divided his army into six parts. Three formations began the fight and were then supported by two others. Sarilo kept the sixth formation in reserve and won the battle.[47] At Noit, in 1044, Geoffrey Martel of Anjou made six formations, and himself commanded the sixth formation, which acted as reserve corps.[48] The Emperor Henry IV led the reserve in the battle by the river Unstrut in 1075 and did not have to attack with this body.[49] In the First Crusade, Bohemond was often in command, and yet in important battles he often led the reserve: once during a foraging expedition,[50] again at the battle of the

---

[44] Delbrück, III, pp. 307–8. Beeler, *Warfare in England*, p. 91: 'unusual for the period (1138) was a tactical reserve'. We have given 21 examples of a tactical reserve between 940 and 1138 in this chapter. Beeler himself provides two other examples: Civitate (1053) and Nocera (1132). Beeler, *Warfare in feudal Europe*, pp. 78, 81–2.

[45] Ambroise, vv. 11455ff., pp. 307–11. Oman, I, pp. 318–19. Lot, I, p. 164.

[46] Astronomus, *Vita Hludovici imperatoris*, ed. G.H. Pertz, MGH, SS, II, 1829, p. 612.

[47] Liudprand, *Antapodosis*, 1. V, 7, pp. 133–4.

[48] *Chronique des comtes d'Anjou et des seigneurs d'Amboise*, eds L. Halphen and R. Poupardin, Paris, 1913, pp. 56–7.

[49] Köhler, III, 3, pp. 99–100.

[50] Raymond of Aguilers, pp. 244–5. Grousset, I, p. 77. Runciman, p. 221. Smail, pp. 170–1.

Lake of Antioch,[51] and in the break-out from that city.[52] Thus he was outside the hurly-burly of the battle. King Baldwin I also appeared as commander of the reserve in the first battle of Ramla in 1101 and in the third battle of this name in 1105.[53] King Henry I of England at Tinchebray in 1106[54] and at Brémule in 1119[55] stayed on foot in the second line, which formed the reserve. In 1118 he moved up with the rearmost detachment of his army towards Alençon, intending to seize the town from count Fulk of Anjou. In that battle, Fulk attacked at the head of his reserve corps and won the battle.[56] It is not known where king Henry was during the battle. In the battle of Hab in 1119 the supreme commander was also with the reserve.[57] The king of Jerusalem at Hazarth in 1125 brought up the rear with the reserve,[58] and in 1137 king Fulk was in the rear-guard.[59] At Northallerton in 1138 the commander of the English army kept a reserve round the standard-bearing waggons and led this detachment; his adversary, king David of Scotland, also led his reserve.[60] At Lincoln in 1141 both commanders fought on foot with their reserves.[61] During his march across Asia Minor, in the winter of 1147–8, king Louis VII of France led the reserve.[62] During the advance on Constantinople in 1203 the marquis of Montferrat led the rear-guard and this happened again in the attack of 17 July, 1203.[63] In 1204, Henry, future emperor of Constantinople, led the rear-guard during a plundering expedition.[64] At Philippopoli and at the Espiga, when he was emperor, he led the reserve.[65] Simon de Montfort did the same at Muret in 1213.[66] His son, in his turn, led the reserve at the battle of Lewes in 1264.[67] At Benevento in 1266, Manfred fought with his reserves, while his opponent Charles of Anjou led the second corps of the opposing side, but had placed the reserve corps under the command of his son-in-law Robert of Béthune.[68] At Tagliacozzo in 1268 both leaders, Conradin and Charles of Anjou,

51 Oman, I, p. 281. Smail, p. 171.
52 Oman, I, p. 284. Smail, pp. 173–4.
53 Oman, I, p. 293. Fulcher, p. 414. Albert of Aix, pp. 622–3.
54 Oman, I, p. 382. Lot, I, p. 317.
55 Oman, I, pp. 386–7.
56 *Chroniques des comtes d'Anjou*, pp. 156, 159.
57 Oman, I, p. 299.
58 Delbrück, III, p. 308, note. He says: 'Ganz selten finden wir einmal, dasz ein König hinter der Front bleibt', and quotes two examples: 1125 and Tannenberg 1410. Beeler, *Warfare in Feudal Europe*, p. 144, n. 6: 'It can be fairly well established that the medieval general usually put all his troops in line or in column of divisions and fought in the front rank himself.'
59 Grousset, II, pp. 72–3.
60 Oman, I, p. 393. Beeler, *Warfare in England*, p. 91.
61 Oman, I, pp. 397–8.
62 Odo of Deuil, *De via Sancti Sepulchri a Ludovico Francorum rege inita*, ed. H. Waquet, Documents relatifs à l'histoire des croisades, Paris, 1949, pp. 71–2.
63 Villehardouin, I, pp. 152–3. R. de Clari, p. 46. Lot, I, pp. 171–2.
64 Villehardouin, II, c. 227, p. 26.
65 Henry of Valenciennes, c. 543, pp. 46–7; c. 533, pp. 41–2. RHF, XVIII, p. 533. Delpech, II, p. 60, n. 1–3, p. 61, n. 1–2.
66 Oman, I, p. 460; Lot, I, p. 213.
67 Oman, I, p. 425.
68 *Ibid.*, pp. 500–1. Lot, II, p. 175.

were each with their reserves, in the third corps.[69] In the battle of the Marchfeld of 1278, the king of the Romans, Rudolf of Habsburg, was in his third corps, which was the reserve, while his opponent, King Ottokar, fought with the sixth corps and one of his nobles led the reserve.[70] At Falkirk, king Edward led his reserve, the third division,[71] and at Bannockburn in 1314 both leaders fought with their reserves.[72] In 1303 the defence of St Omer was thus arranged: the Boulogne gate was defended by Theobald de Chepoix, the Thérouanne gate by the lord of Pene, the Aire gate by a knight from Auvergne, Pons de Bisac, the watergate on the Gravelines side by John of Haveskerke, lord of Watten. Each of these bannerets commanded a troop of the communal army. The towers of the town defences were occupied by look-out men, the lords of Fiennes and Mercoeur, with the leading citizen, were in charge of the defence and apparently led the reserve.[73] At Mons-en-Pévèle Philip the Fair was also in charge of the reserve at the beginning of the battle.[74]

Other examples are neither so clear nor so explicit. At Hastings, in 1066, William the Conqueror was in the centre of the third line, which was made up of knights, while the first two lines consisted of foot-soldiers; he counter-attacked with a reserve.[75] In other battles the commander was fighting, but had a reserve ready in the second or third line. At Bourg-Théroulde in 1124, Eudes Borleng, the commander-in-chief, was bound to fight in the front line for reasons of morale, but kept a mounted reserve.[76] At the battle of Thielt, in 1128, William Clito took part in the battle, but had a reserve in ambush.[77] At Acre in 1189 king Guy of Lusignan fought in the front line while his brother and James of Avesnes led the reserve.[78] At Courtrai the count of Artois kept the rear-guard as reserve, but he rode to the attack himself with his men who were in the second line. Guy of Namur and William of Jülich were in the first formation but they had entrusted the reserve to the efficient leadership of John of Renesse.

We are badly informed about the position of the commander in many battles, because the account is not sufficiently detailed and therefore no survey can be complete. In any case we know about more than thirty major battles and smaller battles or defensive formations in which the commander stayed with the reserve and thus was able to direct or influence the battle from a distance. There are plenty more examples which could well be added to ours, which have escaped examination because they have not been studied in the classic works.

We also know about ten battles in which the commander or sovereign took part

[69] Oman, I, p. 509. Delbrück, III, p. 377. Lot, II, p. 178.
[70] Lot, II, p. 150. Oman, I, pp. 519, 521.
[71] Oman, II, p. 79.
[72] *Ibid.*, pp. 94, 97.
[73] *Istore et Croniques*, I, p. 272.
[74] See the study of the battle.
[75] Oman, I, p. 159.
[76] Orderic Vitalis, *Historia ecclesiastica*, c. 39. Delpech, II, p. 287.
[77] See below, the story of the battle.
[78] Oman, I, p. 335.

personally in the fighting, but had entrusted the leadership of the reserve to a competent nobleman. If we examine only those battles for which we have detailed and trustworthy accounts, we see that a general custom was to keep a reserve in order to force a decision. It appears also from our sources that the commander of the army usually led his reserve himself. Heermann reached these two conclusions in his work on the battles of the First Crusade and the early years of the kings of Jerusalem.[79] This discovery is very important because it completely contradicts one of the most often expressed and principal objections to medieval warfare as an art.

In addition, it must never be forgotten that medieval armies were very small. The commanders could not allow themselves the luxury of staying out of the fighting with an efficient bodyguard during the whole of the battle, for this would have meant a serious weakening of the forces involved. The commander was thus bound to take an active part, at least during the decisive attack of the reserve. William of Poitiers says in his comparison of William the Conqueror and Julius Caesar: 'For William it would have been neither honourable nor efficient merely to give orders, if he had not at the same time fulfilled his knightly obligations, as he was accustomed to do in other wars.'[80] From the great diversity of examples which have been quoted here, it seems clear that we cannot generalize from this view. As a knight, a medieval commander had to set an example in battle, but that is a general custom which still holds good today for the subordinate commander. Supreme commanders usually trod a little more carefully. The fighting men often made their generals act sensibly. In this we have also to reckon with the tendency of a biographer who wants to glorify his commander, which was certainly the case with William of Poitiers.

The use of the reserve was naturally not always necessary, indeed its use depended on the terrain, the enemy's dispositions, and on all sorts of circumstances which often escape us since in many cases the sources do not tell us why a certain plan was adopted for the battle. If there was an overwhelming superiority of numbers over the enemy, it was not necessary to have a reserve. It could also be superfluous in a surprise attack. There is an interesting example of this in the battle of Ascalon in 1099. The crusaders advanced in perfect order before the battle. They made nine formations which marched up in three lines. As we already have seen, three units made up the advance guard, three the rear-guard, and there were three in the middle so that these troops could very quickly form a front in any direction. The centre could always act as reserve while the other two lines protected their front and rear. This excellent plan for the march was not, however, used for the battle. Then six of the units advanced close to each other. Now it is quite possible that some formations stayed rather behind in relation to the others, and made a second line extending the length of the front. In this case it was an attack in echelon, of which examples have already been cited. But this explanation is not necessary, in that we find a better one in the course of the battle itself. According to Ibn al-Athir, the Egyptians were

79 Lot, I, p. 134.
80 William of Poitiers, 1. II, c. 40, pp. 250–2.

surprised by the quick attack of the crusaders.[81] In their account of the battle the chroniclers confirm that the combat was very short. Duke Robert of Normandy cut down the enemy standard-bearer immediately. Tancred at once pressed through, right into the enemy's camp. Although Christian sources relate that the enemy was ready for battle, it is quite possible that the crusaders partly surprised the Egyptians. In that case Godfrey of Bouillon seems to have decided that it was best to carry out the attack with all the knights at his command on a broad front. Whatever the truth may be, the attack was amazingly successful in a very short time.

The enemy's dispositions and the type of terrain could also be decisive. When fighting took place on a broad front and flank and rear attacks were to be feared, it was sometimes impossible to hold a reserve – e.g. at Bouvines in 1214.

The attack of a hidden reserve which took the enemy by surprise could also be decisive. The intervention of such troops might be preceded by a feigned flight, such as has been mentioned above. At Visé in 1106 foot-soldiers of the communal army of Liège were placed in ambush, while the knights of duke Henry of Limbourg and count Godfrey of Namur attacked the German knights and feigned a flight. The knights of king Henry V were defeated.[82] In 1112, king Louis VI was beaten in storming the fortress of Le Puiset because the enemy had concealed a reserve in ambush.[83] During the siege of Thouars in 1129 Geoffrey V, count of Anjou and Maine and duke of Normandy, hid 500 knights in ambush in a wood. When the besieged forces made one of their usual sorties, Geoffrey withdrew past his reserve, which immediately fell on the enemy from behind. The garrison was overcome, and fled back in disorder to the town, but the besiegers managed to follow them in and capture the fortress.[84]

Retreat and Flight from the Field of Battle

Withdrawal from the battlefield was a very tricky problem, especially if the enemy was still in contact. Highly mobile bands of knights could mount a tremendous attack on the troops who were withdrawing, and turn an orderly retreat into flight. Withdrawal was a very serious problem for an army of foot-soldiers faced by an army of knights. It was less difficult for knights faced by foot-soldiers, or for an army consisting of knights and foot-soldiers. The most difficult type of withdrawal of all was that of a wholly or partly beaten army when scattered remnants were taking to their heels.

If the commanders had decided to retreat, they first sent away supplies with the provision waggons, then the foot-soldiers, while the knights followed on to hold up

---

[81] Grousset, I, p. 175. Runciman, p. 296. Delbrück, III, p. 484. According to Fulcher, Godfrey of Bouillon, commander of the army, was at the head of the reserve. But Fulcher was not present at Ascalon. Cf. Smail, p. 175, n. 2. Beeler, *Warfare in Feudal Europe*, p. 144, takes the order of march for the battle order!

[82] Gaier, p. 233.

[83] Suger, pp. 159–60.

[84] *Chroniques des comtes d'Anjou*, pp. 202–3.

the enemy in case of need, for a strong rearguard was absolutely necessary. The precise moment for the start of the retreat depended on the tactical situation, or on the alertness of the garrison if the besiegers were attacking a fortress.

We have already seen that the army of Baldwin of Boulogne stayed awake all night while it was in contact with the enemy, and started to retreat at dawn. The baggage train and foot-soldiers were protected by a strong rearguard of knights.[85]

In the crusades and in the kingdom of Jerusalem the rearguard was often reinforced by crossbowmen, who were intended to keep enemy archers at a distance. This was so at Arsuf, where the crusaders under Richard I were in contact with the enemy during the march. There the baggage train and the main force of the foot-soldiers were protected by the rear-guard, which was made up of bands of knights and crossbowmen on foot, and by a flank-guard.[86] Louis VII had also flank-guards and a rear-guard, which was reinforced by archers, during his march across Asia Minor in 1147–48.[87] The last part of the march of the French army which moved out of Tournai to Bouvines in 1214 was done in contact with the enemy's advance guard. Philip Augustus had formed a strong rear-guard, and placed it under the command of Bishop Guérin, the tactical commander. This corps was made up of knights, light cavalry, and crossbowmen. It had to halt five times, and fall back, still fighting, on the main force of the French army, but it succeeded in making enough delay to deploy the royal army completely.[88]

When Villehardouin and Manassier de Lisle had saved the remains of the emperor Baldwin's bands of knights on 4 April 1205, it was decided to give up the siege of Adrianople and to withdraw. But this was bound to be dangerous, because their enemy, the king of Bulgaria, had great numbers of light cavalry. Villehardouin and his corps stayed in battle array outside their camp until nightfall. Then the Doge of Venice moved off with the main army, leaving Villehardouin to follow with the rear-guard. The Doge left many torches burning in the camp, to give the impression that it was still occupied, but they took everyone, even the wounded. The enemy noticed nothing at all in the dark.

By noon of the following day the retreating troops had marched so quickly that they were 46 miles away. Their strategic retreat towards Rodosto was also most remarkable: they covered more than 83 miles in less than 48 hours.[89]

Between 1302 and 1304 the French armies retreated several times in face of the Flemings. Twice the withdrawal almost turned into flight, namely on 29 September 1302 and 10 July 1303. In September 1302 the armies were separated by the Scarpe. The royal army was able to move off unhindered by the Flemings, but morale was at a very low ebb in the French camp, where the battle of Courtrai was not forgotten, and the withdrawal was so panic-stricken that it resembled flight.[90]

---

85 Fulcher, pp. 375–6.
86 See below, 'The Battle of Arsuf'.
87 Odo of Deuil, pp. 71–2.
88 See below, 'The Battle of Bouvines'.
89 Villehardouin, II, cc. 362–73, pp. 170–82.
90 Verbruggen, *De slag der gulden sporen*, p. 59.

On 10 July the two armies were facing each other again, close to St Omer. The constable of France had six companies of knights, and French and Lombard foot-soldiers. A council of war was held, and most of the nobles were in favour of fighting, but the constable refused in view of the great losses the royal army had suffered the year before at Courtrai, and he gave the order to retreat. The nobles had to return to the towns which they had to defend against the Flemings. Each soldier was to follow the banner to which he belonged. First the waggons were driven off, then the foot set out. The knights stayed facing the Flemings in battle order. There was a watercourse, probably the Aa, between them. When the Flemings noticed the enemy's retreat, they first thought they were going to encircle the Flemish army. So the French army was able to march off unhindered, even though the withdrawal was disorderly.[91]

On the battlefield of Arques on 4 April 1303, however, the French knights manoeuvred methodically and in good order. One company after another moved off, covered by the rest of the army. When William of Jülich noticed this, he moved up with the Flemish foot-soldiers to attack. Then the knights halted, and made as though they would attack, and this threat made the Flemings re-arrange themselves for a defensive battle. As soon as they stood still, the French began to retreat again. William moved again, and again the knights came to a standstill. While withdrawing to St Omer they had to re-deploy their battle-array five or six times in order to keep the Flemings at a distance.[92]

On 13 August 1304 the royal army was again in retreat under the command of king Philip the Fair. The Flemings had advanced towards the French camp as far as Mons-en-Pévèle. They had taken up a strong position with marshes before and behind them. The king divided the French troops into 15 divisions and advanced to give battle, after knighting many squires. Crossbowmen of both armies were ready for preliminary skirmishing, when several over-eager Flemings started to shoot. But closer inspection showed that the Flemish position was too strong, so the king decided to withdraw to his camp. He himself led the rearguard which was to cover the withdrawal, and the retreat was carried out without mishap.[93]

The Flemings also took special precautions when they retreated after the siege of a fortified town. After the retreat of the French army on 10 July 1303 part of the French army stayed at St Omer. However the town was well defended, and nine days later the Flemings moved off. They set out at night, leaving a strong rear-guard behind them on a hill until the baggage train was safely away.[94] The same year the Flemings besieged Tournai during a 47 day campaign. When they raised the siege, the soldiers set fire to the huts which they had built out of branches and straw. Thick smoke prevented the enemy from seeing that the Flemings had left a strong rear-guard behind. The Flemish foot-soldiers moved off covered by a band of

---

[91] *Annales Gandenses*, pp. 52–3. *Chronique artésienne*, pp. 66–8. *Istore et Croniques*, I, pp. 270–1.
[92] See 'The Battle of Arques'.
[93] *Chronique artésienne*, p. 83. G. Guiart, vv. 19959–66, p. 286. *Annales Gandenses*, p. 67.
[94] *Istore et Croniques*, I, p. 272.

cavalry. When the French knights made an attack they crashed into the Flemish rearguard and suffered heavy losses.[95]

When an army took to flight, commanders tried to protect their fleeing troops with a hastily formed rearguard, or with the reserve corps if that were not already involved in the fighting. When the army of Bohemond and Tancred suddenly took to flight on the banks of the Balîkh in May 1104, both leaders collected a corps, which later had to hold the enemy in check under Tancred.[96] When Louis VI fled at the siege of Chambly in 1102, he managed to regroup a small body of men and use them as a rearguard.[97] In general a commander could reckon on his bravest men sacrificing themselves or using their vast experience to save the terrified fugitives. In such a case, the prince's own faithful followers made his own escape possible: Otto's followers saved him at Bouvines, Edward II was brought to safety at Bannockburn by the knight Giles of Argentan, who was no coward and returned to meet his death on the battlefield.[98]

Stout resistance by some troops, who were overwhelmed where they made their stand, often made possible the flight of demoralized units, who would throw away weapons and equipment so as to get out of the reach of the heavily armed pursuers. The victors often moved cautiously for fear of falling into an ambush.

At Courtrai the French rearguard let the baggage train move off while the knights stood by in case of attack, and in the end the foot-soldiers got away as well. But when the Flemings went over to the attack, the rearguard in their turn panicked and fled. For the foot-soldiers such a flight often meant disaster. Quick-moving knights could ride down the fugitives with heavy horses, and kill them. After the unsuccessful attack on the French camp at Cassel in 1328 the main body of Flemings was surrounded by knights but they took up a circular formation and defended themselves so stoutly that many knights were unhorsed. It seemed virtually impossible to destroy the Flemings by force of arms, but then a section of French knights withdrew, leaving a way through. The Flemings tried to escape, but could not get away in good order: they fled but were fiercely chased, and many of them were killed.[99]

Detailed examination of a few actual battles, beginning with two from the First Crusade will help to throw light on the practical solutions to some of the tactical problems of the day.

THE BATTLE OF THE LAKE OF ANTIOCH, 9 FEBRUARY 1098

On 8 February, during the siege of Antioch, the crusaders were warned of the approach of enemy relief troops. Thereupon Bohemond held a council of war in the tent of the bishop of Le Puy. He proposed that the foot-soldiers should be left in the camp to guard it and to deal with any sortie of the garrison of Antioch, and this was

---

95 *Annales Gandenses*, pp. 54–5. Account of the city of Bruges, 1303, fo. 47 vo.
96 Ralph of Caen, c. 150, pp. 711–12.
97 Suger, c. 4, pp. 21–2.
98 *Scalachronica*, pp. 142–3.
99 *Chronicon comitum Flandrensium*, I, p. 205.

agreed. The enemy was then near the castle of Harenc, beyond the bridge over the Orontes.[100]

As soon as night fell, Bohemond moved off in the dark with the knights, to prevent the garrison noticing anything and warning the approaching relief troops. Bohemond's army was made up of about 700 knights. He wanted to fight between the lake of Antioch and the Orontes, where the restricted front prevented the Turks from attacking the crusaders' flank, or from surrounding them, and he kept his men concealed until daybreak.[101] Early in the morning he sent out scouts to reconnoitre the enemy formations, and find out their exact positions and probable intentions. They saw the Turks moving up along the river in two large divisions, the stronger in the second line. The scouts hurried back to report. The other leaders entrusted the conduct of the battle to Bohemond. He ordered them to take up battle positions, making each prince responsible for the command and good order of his men. They were drawn up in six formations, five advancing together towards the enemy, while Bohemond followed with the sixth.[102]

Fighting broke out against the enemy's front line, which was thrown back. Then came the most powerful body of the Turks, who attacked and drove back the crusaders. This had the effect of packing the Turkish formations more tightly, the second line had assimilated the first and both had attacked again. Bohemond then ordered his constable, Robert fitzGerard, to attack with part of the reserve. The whole force of the enemy was forced to fight the heavily armoured western knights in the narrow space between the lake and the river. The attack by the reserve was decisive. With banners flying, the constable dashed at the Turkish formations and drove them off. The other formations of crusaders, relieved by the counter-attack, re-formed their ranks and attacked again. The enemy was put to flight and fiercely pursued for ten miles.[103]

This battle is interesting for the following reasons:

1. Through choosing to fight in a confined space the crusaders prevented an outflanking movement by their enemies, as their flanks were well protected.
2. The knights made their main attack only at the moment when the Turks were forming a dense mass, just after their advance guard had withdrawn to the main body, and both had attacked the Christians. They had thrown in all their strength and could not collect their troops again after they had been thrown back: they were nevertheless fiercely pursued.
3. Part of the reserve was thrown in at exactly the right moment, and this proved decisive. The rest of the reserve was there still under the commander, who could use it for support during the pursuit.

---

[100] Raymond of Aguilers, p. 246. *Gesta Francorum*, c. 17, p. 82 [Hill, p. 35].

[101] Raymond of Aguilers, pp. 246–7. *Epistulae et Chartae ad historiam primi belli sacri spectantes*, ed. Hagenmeyer, Die Kreuzzugsbriefe aus den Jahren 1088–1100, Innsbrück, 1901, pp. 150, 158. *Gesta Francorum*, p. 83, n. 3 [Hill, p. 36]. Albert of Aix, p. 381.

[102] *Gesta Francorum*, p. 84. Raymond of Aguilers, p. 246.

[103] Raymond of Aguilers, p. 247. *Gesta Francorum*, p. 84. Grousset, I, pp. 86–7. Brandt, pp. 161–2. Oman, I, pp. 280–1. Delpech, II, pp. 161–4. Smail, p. 171.

THE SORTIE AND THE BATTLE OF ANTIOCH, 28 JUNE 1098

After the crusaders had taken Antioch they were besieged in the city by an enemy force under Kerbogha, Atabeg of Mosul, and the citadel of Antioch was still occupied and fiercely defended by an enemy garrison. The crusaders were extremely hard pressed and suffered severely from hunger: the crisis was so extreme that some nobles even deserted. In this desperate situation came the discovery of the Holy Lance. Although there was some doubt about the authenticity of the find it gave tremendously valuable moral uplift to the besieged Christians, who gained fresh courage. Bohemond wanted to make use of this revival of morale to fight a decisive battle. An embassy was sent to Kerbogha. Peter the Hermit and Herluin, who knew the Seldjuk language, were entrusted with the task. Peter the Hermit delivered an ultimatum to the Seldjuk commander requiring him to raise the siege, but he came back without having succeeded. The preparations for battle lasted three days. In view of the coming battle the horses were fed with such grain as the knights still had. Godfrey of Bouillon himself had no charger left, but received one from Raymond of St Gilles, who was ill. During these three days the army fasted, prayed, and did penance. Masses were offered and alms distributed, and finally they all received communion. The morale of the crusaders was at one of its highest peaks. They preferred a quick death on the field of battle to a slow death by starvation.[104]

28 June was the decisive day. Four grand divisions were formed within the city. Each division was composed of two corps: one of cavalry and one of foot-soldiers. The knights and their followers were to fight under the command of their prince, and group themselves under his banner. Hugh of Vermandois, count Robert II of Flanders and Robert of Normandy were to march at the head of the army with their troops, in the first division. Godfrey of Bouillon with his men and the Burgundians constituted the second division. Bishop Adhémar of Le Puy commanded the third division which consisted of the warriors from Aquitaine and Provence. Raymond of Aguilers went with them bearing the Holy Lance. Bohemond led the fourth division, the reserve. Raymond of Toulouse stayed in the city with 200 men to pin down the garrison in the citadel, stationed on the wall opposite this citadel. A detachment of foot-soldiers who marched in front of the knights was to advance or stop at the order of the commanders. The knights were to follow the foot-soldiers and protect their rear.[105]

The excitement among the crusaders was intense, as they felt the hour of battle drawing near. Each knight had prepared his charger and his equipment to the highest degree: they had been too busy to think much about death, and this short-lived tension gave expression to their deepest feelings. They wanted to fight quickly in order to shake off the feeling of the oppressive waiting. Bishops, priests, clerks and monks went with them, wearing vestments, carrying crucifixes, praying and encouraging the fighting-men. Others stood on the city walls and blessed the troops.[106]

---

104 Delpech, II, pp. 155–61. Brandt, pp. 181–2. Runciman, pp. 247–8. Grousset, I, pp. 105–6. Delbrück, III, pp. 422–3. Smail, pp. 172–4.
105 Raymond of Aguilers, p. 259 E. *Gesta Francorum*, pp. 150–2 [Hill, p. 68].
106 Raymond of Aguilers, p. 260. *Gesta Francorum*, p. 153 [Hill, p. 68].

When the first division of crusaders had gone out of the city gate and crossed the bridge over the Orontes, Watthab-ibn-Mahmud, one of Kerbogha's commanders, advised him to attack the Christians at once. Kerbogha refused, since a hasty attack could put only part of the Christian forces out of action. Those who have made a study of the battle have wondered why he let the whole army of western knights come out of Antioch unhindered. It may be that he was well content to fight in the open since his efforts to take the city had failed. Considering the state of the crusaders' army, their behaviour during the siege and the desertions from their ranks, he must have thought that victory over this little army was assured. Probably he was surprised not only by the knights' courageous sortie, but also by their speed in making it. But Kerbogha had first of all to collect his army and deploy it, and certainly thought he would be able to kill a reasonable number of Christians. In February the crusaders' army consisted of 700 knights with horses fit for battle, or anyway well under 1,000, but the siege had reduced their numbers considerably, and by that time it was very small. Ralph of Caen speaks of about 600 knights in this battle.[107] It is more difficult to fix the numbers of foot-soldiers, but there were possibly only about 3,000. In this case, the advancing army would have no great depth, and if they came out four or five abreast through the gate and over the bridge, the line would have been about 120 to 150 riders long, and about 600 ranks of foot. By taking great care in packing the formations tightly, it is possible that a cavalry column measured only 420 to 525 metres for the horsemen, and 900 metres for the foot, say 1,320 to 1,425 metres in all.

They must of course have realized that there was a strong chance of the Turks making a lightning attack, and would have taken the necessary precautions. In a normal advance at a pace of about 5 km an hour this army would have covered a kilometre in 12 minutes, so that the whole column could have got out of the gate in 18 minutes. Actually, the far end of the column could have been stationed about 1.5 km from the gate, and closer in the side streets. Of course the troops were moved out rather quickly, but even if we suppose that the movement was not perfectly ordered, we can still assume that the whole army was out within 30 minutes, and they could afford to be crowded for so short a distance. Indeed, even if there were far more foot-soldiers than has been supposed, the whole garrison could have been out within an hour, in other words, so quickly that Kerbogha could only have taken counter-action if his army had been assembled and ready, which of course is rarely the case.

Raymond of Aguilers, speaking of what Kerbogha did, says that at first the Seldjuk could have hindered the crusaders' breakout. According to him, and to Fulcher of Chartres, the Emir was playing chess in his tent at the time. The *Gesta Tancredi*[108] tells the same story, so it appears that the element of surprise was on the side of the crusaders.

Other sources speak of Kerbogha hoping to be able to destroy the whole army of the Franks in the open field. The Anonymous has this version, and Moslem accounts

---

[107] *Gesta Tancredi*, pp. 665–6. Runciman, p. 248. Grousset, I, p. 105.
[108] Raymond of Aguilers, pp. 259–60. Fulcher, pp. 348–50. Ralph of Caen, pp. 665–6.

confirm this, adding that their army felt certain of victory, because Kerbogha would annihilate all the crusaders' army in the battle.[109] Now that he had the chance to win a single decisive victory over the besieged Christians he wanted to exploit it fully. The speed of the crusaders' advance in fact left him no other choice.

The Christian knights formed up behind their leaders' banners. The first division deployed in line with its right flank on the Orontes. The second division marched behind the first, and deployed in line on the left of the first; so did the third. A wide front of about two miles was occupied towards the mountains. There the left flank would be protected by these obstacles.[110] The Turks intended to use their customary tactics: they withdrew before the advancing crusaders, and sent one formation round to the rear of their opponents. But this manoeuvre was observed in time, and Bohemond had the sense not to throw in his reserve at once. A band of knights was quickly formed under Rainald, who advanced towards those Turks who were attacking the left flank of the crusaders. The knights meanwhile had pushed through their foot-soldiers in order to be able to charge the enemy's light cavalry more easily. The Turks first attacked the foot-soldiers protecting the rear of the Christian left flank. But the men of the crusaders' army quickly turned round and formed a circle so that they could beat off the attacks from the threatening quarter. The arrival of Rainald's band of knights proved decisive. The Turks were thrown back and began to flee, setting fire to the dry grass to hinder the Christians and to signal to their own side as they went.[111]

The units of the first division under Hugh of Vermandois, Robert of Flanders and Robert of Normandy had made the first attack along the front, followed by the division of Godfrey of Bouillon, and the division of Adhémar of Le Puy. They fought against the main strength of the enemy. After the failure of the outflanking movement the Turks gave way under incessant pressure. They fled incontinently, hotly pursued by the Christian knights, who chose immediate pursuit rather than booty, and chased them a long way from the battlefield. Afterwards they found immensely rich spoils in Kerbogha's camp.[112]

From this brief account it is again apparent that the small size of knightly armies must not be forgotten. It made it possible for an army to move very quickly, and to deploy in open country. In this case they were able to render Kerbogha's counter-attacks ineffectual, and even to surprise him in some measure. While the Turks used their normal tactics, the crusaders were clever enough to keep a reserve and not to throw it in at once, and to make a new formation to deal with an unforeseen threat. It is also worth noting that the foot-soldiers marched in front of the knights in the beginning of the battle and that they offered very good resistance to the enemy's cavalry.

109 *Gesta Francorum*, p. 152. Grousset, I, p. 105. Runciman, p. 248.
110 *Gesta Francorum*, p. 154 [Hill, pp. 68–9]. Raymond of Aguilers, pp. 259–60.
111 *Gesta Francorum*, p. 156 [Hill, p. 69]. Raymond of Aguilers, p. 260.
112 *Gesta Francorum*, p. 156 [Hill, p. 70]. J. France, *Victory in the East*, provides a radically new interpretation of the battle, emphasising its character as an infantry battle, pp. 286–96.

THE BATTLE OF THIELT, 21 JUNE 1128

The battle of Thielt, or Axpoel, although it had no great effect on the general course of the struggle between two claimants for the title of count in Flanders, is, however, remarkable for its tactics. It shows clearly that small armies of knights were sometimes able to solve tactical problems which, at a first glance, seem insoluble. But a thorough study shows that such situations might arise in many battles.

The general circumstances are well known. In February 1128 a rebellion broke out against count William Clito. On 30 March the communes of Ghent and Bruges chose Thierry of Alsace as count and two important barons, Daniel of Termonde and Iwain of Alost, did homage to him. These powerful nobles brought him the support of some of the Flemish knights, and in addition the rebels could soon count on the help of Lille and then of the men of Ypres, who supported the new count secretly at first, but later openly. Armed conflict broke out between William Clito, supported by most of the knights, and Thierry, the candidate supported by the towns, who was helped by a minority of vassals. Although the citizens, 'the power of the future' as Pirenne has called them, were on Thierry's side, it was by no means certain that he would win, as the story of the battle of Thielt shows.[113]

On June 18 and 19, 1128, Thierry of Alsace gathered a strong army at Ghent, in the Four 'Ambachten' (Axel, Hulst, Assenede and Boekhoute) and the Land of Waas. Armed with material for siege, he went to Axpoel, near Thielt, to besiege the fortified manor of the knight Fulk, a follower of William Clito. The men of Bruges came on 20 June, led by their burgrave, Gervase of Praat, whose army was also reinforced by men from the coastal region.[114]

But William Clito had observed these troop movements and went out at once to spy out the terrain and enemy army. The next day he collected his knights at dawn. They made their confession together to the abbot of Oudenburg and the count and his men made a vow to protect the Church and the poor from henceforward. The knights had their hair cut, threw aside their ordinary clothes and put on their armour. They quickly advanced towards Thielt to relieve Fulk's castle.

The exact strength of the armies is not known. But there are useful indications in the story as told by Galbert of Bruges. William Clito appears once with more than 400 knights and had 400 with him at the siege of Alost. He certainly had more than 400 here, let us say 450. In any case Thierry had fewer, possibly about 300. But he had part of the communal armies of Bruges and Ghent under his command and foot-soldiers from the Four 'Ambachten', the Land of Waas and the coastal strip. In view of the small role they played, we can set the figure low, and say 1,500. Thierry had to make sure that the siege of the fortress of Fulk was thoroughly maintained,

---

[113] Ganshof, *La Flandre sous les premiers comtes*, 3rd edn, Brussels, 1949, pp. 122–3. H. Pirenne, *Histoire de Belgique*, I, Brussels, 1948, ill. edn, p. 136.
[114] Galbert, c. 114, pp. 162–4. *Genealogiae comitum Flandriae Lamberti continuatio*, p. 313. Simon, *Gesta abbatum S. Bertini Sithiensium (1021–1145)*, ed. O. Holder-Egger, MGH, SS, XIII, 1881, p. 659. *Annales Elmarenses*, in *Les Annales de Saint-Pierre de Gand et de Saint-Amand*, ed. P. Grierson, CRH in 8°, Brussels, 1937, p. 103. *Annales Elnonenses, ibid.*, p. 164. Verbruggen, *La tactique militaire des armées de chevaliers*, pp. 168–73.

and that his siege material was safely guarded. If we allow 500 men for this, then he must have had 1,000 left for battle. Together with his knights, who were inferior in number, these men could offer battle to the enemy with some hope of victory.[115]

It seems that William arrived at the field of battle with a plan in mind. The previous day's reconnaissance had given him some idea of the strength of the enemy army. He knew that they had to fight in difficult tactical circumstances of the siege. His plan was clear: he placed one of his three bands of knights in ambush behind the hill he had reconnoitred on 20 June. The attack was to come from the other two, one led by William himself, the other apparently by the standard-bearer Riquart of Woumen.[116] They were to withdraw in due course to the third company of knights, who were only to join in after the first and second, pursued by the enemy, reappeared over the top of the hill. In this way Thierry's knights would be separated from his foot-soldiers and they could be separately beaten. The foot-soldiers could not, of course, follow the cavalry during a speedy pursuit and Thierry's knights would become scattered during the chase. As the plan was explained to them in advance, William's knights could be quickly re-grouped while the reserve, in close ranks, rushed out of its ambush to attack the scattered or at least somewhat disordered pursuers. If the plan had not been made and explained beforehand and the third body had been an ordinary reserve, William Clito would have had much greater difficulty in collecting up his scattered knights again and in their plight they might easily have taken the reserve with them.

William Clito appeared on the hill with two troops out of three. As soon as Thierry observed the enemy he also made two formations, the first under his own command with Gervase of Praat, the second under count Frederick. The knights were to fight in front followed by the foot, who were to capture or kill those of the enemy who were unhorsed. Daniel of Termonde was in command of Thierry's knights during the pursuit. We have thus the following dispositions:[117]

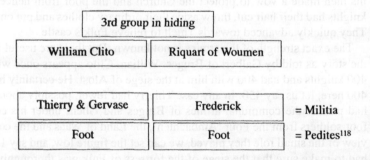

3rd group in hiding		
William Clito	Riquart of Woumen	
Thierry & Gervase	Frederick	= Militia
Foot	Foot	= Pedites[118]

115 Galbert, c. 116, p. 117; c. 118, p. 168; c. 116, p. 167.

116 Lambertus de Wattrelos, *Annales Cameracenses*, p. 512.

117 Delpech, I, pp. 427–8. Köhler, III, 3, pp. 123–4. Oman, I, pp. 443–4. H. Van Houtte, *Essai sur la civilisation flamande au commencement du XIIe siècle d'après Galbert de Bruges*, Louvain, 1898, pp. 147–8. Galbert, c. 14, p. 163. Beeler, *Warfare in Feudal Europe*, pp. 50–1, follows Oman, without reading the sources and the critical studies, and adds some errors to Oman's.

118 The foot-soldiers are the warriors from Ghent, Bruges, Four 'Ambachten', Land van Waas, and so on.

Once the troops were in battle positions both armies rode at each other with lances couched. Daniel hoped to penetrate directly into the enemy line in order to make a real breakthrough, but count Frederick was unhorsed in the first shock. On the other side Riquart of Woumen shared the same fate, was taken prisoner and fettered. Both counts took part in the fight, just like their ordinary knights.[119] Once a lance was broken, or became useless in hand-to-hand fighting, swords were drawn. However, William Clito realized that he must not let his troops be mauled too much and that if he got too close he would have to deal with the enemy foot, who might turn things to the advantage of his opponent. He therefore gave the signal to retreat. Daniel started the pursuit with Thierry's knights, and advanced to the top of the hill. There an unpleasant surprise awaited him: he was attacked by a fresh, well-ordered company of about 150 knights.

William Clito collected his retreating troops again. A powerful charge by the reserve found Daniel's knights defenceless. In a few seconds the pursuit was changed into a disorderly flight and William's knights then appeared as victors on the hilltop and rushed down to the plain where Thierry, with the foot-soldiers, was amazed to see the enemy coming back. Panic broke out among the inexperienced troops. Thierry himself fled with his followers, throwing down their weapons as they went. He reached Bruges with only ten knights.

But when William saw that the enemy troops were throwing away their weapons and fleeing in panic, he was ready to run further risks to turn this tactical victory into a great success. He made his knights take off their coats of mail so that they could ride faster and take more prisoners. The pursuit was a calamity for the Brugeois. Galbert describes it as something unique: 'such fierce pursuit and the taking of so many prisoners had never been known in this part of the world before this war.'[120]

We must not allow ourselves to be misled by the small forces involved, for many medieval battles were fought with armies just as small. The battle of Thielt is remarkable for the way in which William Clito put one company of knights out of three in ambush, after making a reconnaissance of the terrain. This Norman, who had several times previously misled the enemy, was perfectly aware of the weakness of a victorious army during a pursuit, had exploited it very cleverly in ordering the reserve to attack at the psychological moment and in rallying his knights behind the reserve. His own audacious pursuit shows very well what dangers were involved in such an exploitation of a tactical success. It shows most clearly that in such a case it was necessary to have a rearguard or reserve in order to protect the knights who became scattered while chasing the beaten enemy. A fresh reserve of this kind was used after the victory at Fréteval (1194) in the army of Richard I, after the victory at Muret (1213) by Simon de Montfort and after the victory at Philippopoli (1208) by Henry I of Constantinople.

[119] Galbert, c. 114, p. 164.
[120] Galbert, *loc. cit.*

THE BATTLE OF ARSUF, 7 SEPTEMBER 1191

The march from Acre to Jaffa, and the battle of Arsuf (22 August – 7 September 1191) are outstanding feats of the crusades. They were also the last great triumph of the Christians in the Near East, and deserve special mention because at the time the Christians were fighting Saladin, a most formidable foe. He had united the various Moslem states under his rule into a powerful empire, able to produce greater armies than those which the crusaders had fought against in the First Crusade. In his earlier battles Saladin had annihilated the troops of king Guy of Lusignan near the lake of Tiberias, at Hattîn (4 July 1187) and then captured Jerusalem (2 October 1187). We have excellent accounts of the battle of Arsuf by witnesses from both sides, giving details of every stage of the march and the battle. The terrain is known, and the site of the battle can be identified unhesitatingly.[121]

The commander of the crusaders, king Richard I of England, was a soldier of very high quality. As far as strategy is concerned, he seems to have been a man of excellent judgement, prudent and wise. He took good care of his troops, did not ask too much of them on the march and kept a close watch on their material needs. In the sphere of tactics he showed prudence and insight. He reacted quickly to his opponent's tactics by excellent ordering of his troops and the imposition of strict discipline on the march. He was not the man to be surprised by a quick-moving enemy, but always kept a good reserve, as a study of his French campaigns also shows. He waited calmly for the moment to strike from a favourable position, and was never incautious in the use of his troops, even in the moment of success. But although he won victories as a tactician and strategist, and cared for his men, his personal courage bordered on recklessness. He was, without doubt, one of the bravest men involved in the Third Crusade, and this has made him a legendary figure, not only in the West but also to the enemy in the East. After the Crusade, during his campaigns in France, he repeatedly defeated Philip Augustus.

After the siege of Acre, Richard decided with typical determination to press on to Jerusalem. The most direct route from Acre to Jerusalem lay through the mountains of Ephraim, and was ill-suited to military operations. Another road followed the coast to Jaffa and thence to Jerusalem: this was preferable because the crusaders would have the use of alternative ports, which would greatly facilitate the movement of supplies brought up by merchants. During a march along the coast, the fleet would be able to provision them and cover their flank on the sea side. For the subsequent march to Jerusalem, which meant penetrating deeply into the interior, the Christians would have a suitable base on the coast. The port of Jaffa lay closest to their objective. The road along the coast was very good, probably an old Roman road through Haifa, Athlit, Caesarea and Arsuf.

This plan was doubtless the best, but it involved all sorts of difficulties. In a long

---

[121] Ambroise, *Ricardus S Trinitatis, Itinerarium peregrinorum et Gesta Ricardi regis*, ed. W. Stubbs, in *Chronicles and Memorials of the Reign of Richard I*, RSI, 1884. Beha ed-Din, in *Recueil des Historiens des Croisades. Historiens orientaux*, III, pp. 251–8. Grousset, III, pp. 18–44, 48 ff. Lot, I, pp. 153–64. Oman, I, pp. 248–50, 305–18. Smail, pp. 162–5.

flanking march along the coast, the crusaders had to advance through a region offering very little food and still less water in exceedingly hot weather. They were perpetually menaced by Saladin's army, which was naturally hoping to surprise the long column of crusaders. In order to protect themselves from such a threat, a large part of the crusaders' army was bound to leave the road, which made the march even more exhausting. Saladin could attack behind and before as well as on the flank.

The March[122]

On 22 August the army left Acre, but not without difficulty. After the numberless privations they had suffered during the siege, the crusaders had not only taken a well-earned rest, but had led a merry life in the conquered city. Many were extremely unwilling to leave that pleasant place where they had amused themselves so well. But Richard laid down detailed regulations for the long march. The female camp-followers were to stay behind at the port, and an eyewitness states that only a few washerwomen were allowed to go with the army 'to keep the crusaders' linen clean, to wash their hair and de-louse them, at which task they were as skilful as monkeys.' As much baggage as possible, and food for ten days, biscuits, wine, meat, and flour, were loaded on to the transport fleet, and were to follow the army by sea to provision them.[123]

Their marching order was very good. The army moved off in large formations, or divisions sub-divided into companies. These formations were well organized. Advance and rear-guards covered the troops, the former led on the first day by the king himself. Another day he commanded the rear-guard. Usually the two great military orders of the Holy Land, the Templars and the Hospitallers, carried out this dangerous task.[124] The baggage train marched along the coast. The provision waggons were protected by a detachment of foot-soldiers, which was also laden with personal baggage and tents. They were protected on their right flank by the fleet. Alongside this column of baggage and foot-soldiers came the main part of the army, the knights, arranged in their divisions. These two columns were also protected on the left flank, the more dangerous side, where Saladin might try an attack at any moment. There was a flank guard, a special band of knights who were sometimes supported by the retinue of king Richard or of the duke of Burgundy. In case of an attack in front, behind, or on the flank, the commander always had three formations, closely following each other, at his disposal, to meet and repulse the enemy. The body of Norman and English nobles who made up the reserve marched right in the middle. They were guarding the royal standard, which flew from a tall mast mounted on a waggon. This standard served as the rallying point for the whole army and the reserve was the hard core round which the other units were to reform in order to attack again. In the rear and advance guards and on the knights' flank there were also crossbowmen. They were to keep the Turkish cavalry at a distance, and prevent them from killing the knights' horses.

---

[122] Oman, I, pp. 305–18. Köhler, III, 3, pp. 234 ff. Delpech, I, pp. 375–91. Smail, pp. 162–3.
[123] Ambroise, vv. 5691–8, p. 152; vv. 5550–3, p. 148.
[124] *Ibid.*, v. 5701, p. 152.

Turkish tactics differed essentially from knightly fighting technique. The Christians wore heavy armour, protecting them from top to toe, which had earned them the nickname of 'iron men' among the Moslems, who were more lightly equipped with bows and arrows, clubs, spears, and light armour. They had very fast horses, 'as swift as swallows', which made it possible for them to escape the crusader knights when they were attacked, and practically impossible for the heavy cavalry to catch them up at all. But as soon as the Turks realized that they were no longer being pursued, they turned round quickly to attack the scattered Christian knights in their turn. 'They set about them like flies: as soon as they were chased off, they fled, as soon as the knights turned, they followed'.[125] So the Turkish horsemen had to be surprised in a lightning attack by the western knights before they could escape the weighty charge.

Because of all these safety measures and since there was very little transport to be had and part of the foot-soldiers were carrying stores and tents, the army moved on very slowly. This is apparent from the distances covered.

Thursday 22 August: from Acre to the river Belus, 2 miles
Friday 23 August: crossed the river Belus, 2 miles
Saturday 24: rest and preparation for continuing the march
Sunday 25: march to Haifa, 11 miles
Monday 26: rest at Haifa
Tuesday 27: march from Haifa to Athlit, with a diversion round Mount Carmel, 12 miles
Wednesday 28: rest in camp
Thursday 29: rest in camp while the fleet unloaded stores and reinforcements
Friday 30: march from Athlit to Merla, 13 miles
Saturday 31: march to Caesarea, 3 miles. The fleet brought more stores and reinforcements
Sunday 1 September: from Caesarea to the Dead River, Nahr-al-Khudeira, 3 miles
Monday 2: rest in camp
Tuesday 3, from the Dead River to the Salt River, Nahr Iskanderuna, 7 miles
Wednesday 4: rest in camp
Thursday 5: from the Salt River through the Forest of Arsuf to the River Rochetaille, Nahr-al-Falik, 10 miles
Friday 6: rest in camp
Saturday 7, from the River Rochetaille to Arsuf, and the battle of Arsuf, 6 miles
Sunday 8: rest in camp at Arsuf
Monday 9: from Arsuf to Nahr-el-Aujeh, 6 miles
Tuesday 10: over 5 miles to Jaffa, where the fleet unloaded stores[126]

At this slow pace it took 19 days to travel about 81 miles from Acre to Jaffa. They marched in the morning only, and were perpetually harassed by attacks by the Turks, who were trying to separate the elements of the column from each other, in order to

125 *Ibid.*, vv. 5647–62, p. 151.
126 *Ibid.*, pp. 153–63, 184–6. Oman, I, p. 307.

be able to finish them off in one great battle. Even on the first day the Turks came out from the hills in little bands of twenty or thirty to harass the crusaders, but without effect. On 25 August they succeeded in causing some loss among the waggoners of the baggage train as the army was going through a pass. But after this the crusaders marched in better order than before. At Haifa the foot-soldiers threw away their surplus equipment, as they were too heavily loaded with food and weapons. Some men died of heat and thirst during the march. On 30 August and 1 September the army was again troubled all day by minor attacks. On 3 September the count of St Pol and his knights lost many horses, and so did the Templars who formed the rearguard.[127]

Between the 26 and 29 August the crusaders were left in peace, since they were going round Mount Carmel and Saladin was forced to follow them by a detour which lay further inland. But from 30 August to 7 September the enemy was so close to the Christians that they expected a general attack at any moment.

Beha ed-Din, Saladin's biographer, has given an interesting description of this march by Richard's army. 'The enemy moved in battle order, the foot-soldiers in front of the cavalry, and packed together solidly like a wall. Each foot-soldier wore armour made of very heavy felt, and so stout a coat of mail that our arrows did no harm. But they shot at us with their great crossbows and wounded both horses and riders. I saw foot-soldiers with as many as ten arrows in their backs, who marched on just as usual without breaking rank. The foot-soldiers were divided into two groups, one half protected the riders, while the other half was not supposed to fight and took it easy while they were marching along the coast. If one section became exhausted, or had many wounded, they were relieved by the other, and rested in their turn. The knights marched between two bodies of foot-soldiers, and only emerged to charge. The cavalry were divided into three main corps. In the middle of the army there was a waggon with a turret built on it, as high as one of our minarets, from which they flew the royal standard. The Franks marched in this order, always fighting steadily. The Moslems shot arrows at them from all directions to harass the riders and to make them leave the protecting wall formed by the foot-soldiers. But it was all in vain: they remained unmoved, and went on marching without undue haste, while their fleet sailed along the coast till they reached the camping place. They never made very long marches, because they did not want to overburden the foot-soldiers, half of whom were carrying baggage and tents because there were not enough transport animals. One could not help admiring the patience of these people: they bore the most extreme hardships although they had no good military organization of their own, and derived no personal advantage.'[128]

Saladin had not been able to carry out his plans during the first stage of the march. However he found ideal terrain near Arsuf, between the river Rochetaille and the deserted town. The forest of Arsuf made it possible for the Turks to concentrate

---

[127] Ambroise, vv. 5705–7, p. 152; vv. 5770–1, p. 154; v. 5829, vv. 5851–60, p. 156; vv. 6047–54, pp. 161–2; vv. 6059–64, p. 162.

[128] Beha ed-Din, *Anecdotes et beaux traits de la vie du Sultan Youssof (Salah ed-Din)*, RHC, Hist. or., 3, pp. 251–2.

unobserved, close to their enemy, and to force them to fight in a broad open plain which was excellently suited to the swift evolutions of their own light cavalry. In some places the forest was less than two miles from the sea, and Richard had to march between the forest and the sea for two days. Nothing happened on 5 September, the crusaders rested on the 6th and went on on the 7th. This time the king was certain that the enemy would attack, and spoke to the troops about the serious danger threatening them. He himself indicated who was to be entrusted with the advance and rearguards. He formed 12 divisions, each divided into companies. The Templars were in the advance guard, the Hospitallers in the rear-guard. Bretons and Angevins followed in the second division. Men from Poitou and the troops of Guy of Lusignan made up the third formation. Normans and English with the standard formed the fourth division. The Hospitallers brought up the rear, reinforced with the barons' men. 'The "conrois" led by these nobles "were placed side by side, so closely packed that you could not throw an apple without hitting either a horse or a man".' There were at least eleven of these nobles with their followers, including the earl of Leicester, James of Avesnes, count Robert of Dreux, the bishop of Beauvais, and other French barons. These nobles kept close together, ready to support each other. 'The battle order was so sound that it could not be broken without great difficulty'. Count Henry of Champagne covered the left flank on the side of the forest of Arsuf. King Richard and the duke of Burgundy rode up and down the columns all the time to keep an eye on the order of the march.[129]

The Battle

As soon as the crusaders had left their camp and the column was on the march, Saladin launched a full-scale attack. Hordes of the enemy rushed suddenly out of the forest towards the plain. In front were light cavalry meant as skirmishers. They were followed by well-ordered formations to which the first troops withdrew after their initial attack. Sudanese archers, Bedouins and Turkish light horsebowmen rushed up on the left flank and the rear-guard of the crusaders. The whole plain was covered in a few minutes with combatants, and a cloud of dust rose in the air. Trumpeters, drummers and men with cymbals rode in front of the emirs, and the troops urged each other on with tremendous whoops.[130]

The weight of the attack fell chiefly on the Christian crossbowmen of the rear-guard. They put up a stout defence and inflicted considerable losses on their attackers with their arrows. But the enemy attack was so determined that some of the foot-soldiers took to flight at once, throwing away their bows and arrows, and sought protection among the various columns. The bravest of them stuck to their positions and went on at a walking pace, still facing the enemy and shooting as they went. Our eyewitness, the Norman jongleur Ambroise, freely admits that at this moment even the bravest would gladly have been anywhere else but on the crusade. The army was so hard pressed that many knights lost their horses and went on fighting

---

129 Ambroise, vv. 6128–44, vv. 6147–6209, pp. 164–6. Beha ed-Din, p. 258.
130 Beha ed-Din, *loc. cit.* Ambroise, vv. 6211–51, pp. 166–7.

on foot as crossbowmen.[131] The Hospitallers also got into difficulties and asked the King's permission to attack. But Richard refused and ordered them to stay as they were and go on marching. They went on slowly towards Arsuf.[132]

After the failure of his skirmishers, who lost many horses to the well-aimed arrows of the crossbowmen, Saladin decided to throw other units into the attack, who had to push on to the enemy. Instead of crossbowmen he sent in cavalry, armed with clubs. There was another heavy attack on the rearguard. The Hospitallers were in despair, because their horses were being wounded while they had to face the enemy attacks without replying. The Grand Master, Garnier of Napes, rode to the king himself to ask permission to attack. The king considered that it was still not time to attack and asked the knights to continue to stay on the defensive for a bit longer.[133] He soon decided to give the signal for a general attack because the head of the column, the foot-soldiers of the advance guard, had almost reached the outskirts of Arsuf. He gave the necessary orders for everyone to charge simultaneously. Six trumpeters were sent to their posts: two in front of the army, two behind and two in the middle.[134] The king of England waited for the moment at which the greatest part of Saladin's army was engaged to strike with his heavy cavalry. Up till then only the rearguard and part of the flanking column had been subjected to the enemy's attacks.

The Hospitallers were grumbling among themselves and grew very impatient. 'They had never lived through anything so shameful, never had they been forced to remain passive like that during attacks of the unbelievers'. Enemy pressure grew too strong and the tensions among the attacked crusaders too great. Suddenly the marshal of the Hospitallers and Baldwin Caron could bear it no longer, and charged. They felled two of the enemy at once. All the Hospitallers turned and made their attack in tightly packed formation. The barons followed with their men on hearing the war cry 'St George'. The count of Champagne and James of Avesnes with their men, count Robert of Dreux, the bishop of Beauvais and the earl of Leicester, who attacked along the coast, in fact the entire rear-guard let fly at the enemy and was followed by the Angevins, the Bretons, the men of Poitou and the other companies.[135]

Despite the fact that the attack started prematurely, it was carried out in a perfectly orderly fashion and came as a complete surprise to the enemy. Beha ed-Din, who was present at the battle, admits this freely. He says that the Moslems pressed the Christians on every side and thought they would be able to finish them off quite easily. But when the crusaders' foot-soldiers reached the outskirts of Arsuf, the cavalry suddenly formed up in a solid mass and since they thought that only a tremendous effort could save the Christians they decided to charge. 'I myself saw all the knights collected within a great wall formed by the foot-soldiers. They gripped their lances, shouting their battle cries, and the line of foot-soldiers opened up to let

[131] Ambroise, vv. 6253–81, pp. 167–8.
[132] *Ibid.*, vv. 6293–6302, p. 168.
[133] *Ibid.*, vv. 6315–20, p. 169; vv. 6368–6402, pp. 170–1.
[134] *Ibid.*, vv. 6409–18, p. 171.
[135] *Ibid.*, vv. 6391–6402, pp. 171–2.

them through. Then they attacked our troops in all directions. One of their formations hurled itself at our right wing, another at the left wing, and a third at the centre.'[136]

The crusaders certainly put everything they had into the attack. Most of the enemy who had been rash enough to dismount in order to shoot straighter, were ridden down. Their cavalry were also utterly surprised and thrown into confusion so that it could only escape with fearful losses. The crusaders' foot-soldiers who followed the knights quickly finished off the unhorsed cavalry. King Richard, in his turn, charged straight to the right. The crusaders saw their enemy fleeing all over the plain for two miles. Some Moslems even jumped into the sea to escape their pursuers. During this attack by the rearguard and the flank-guard the Normans were following the charging knights at a distance with the standard, in order to rally them if they were thrown back after an unsuccessful attack.[137]

The charge was not carried on too far, for an attack like that demanded tremendous effort from the knights and their horses. As soon as the knights stopped to regroup, the fleeing Moslems returned to the attack. The enemy rushed back to rescue their friends before the Christians could kill them. But they did not press this counterattack very far, for as soon as the knights had got their breath back and the companies had been regrouped, they organized another attack and scattered the enemy again. But apparently the enemy had now thrown in all his troops. The knights got no further than a bowshot, and then had to withdraw again to the reserve to re-group their formations. Then William des Barres and king Richard, with his bodyguard, attacked too. This charge threw the Turks back and allowed the Christian troops to collect and reform.[138]

A fourth charge was unnecessary. The enemy was so demoralized that another counter-attack was impossible, as Beha's description shows. At the beginning of the battle he was in the centre of Saladin's army. He relates his adventures thus: 'Every formation was put to flight. When the centre was scattered, I wanted to take refuge with the left wing, which was nearest to me. But they were fleeing there even faster than in the centre so I went to the right wing. There I found the situation worse than on the left wing and went to join the sultan's own formation, since this was to be the general rallying point. But I found only seventeen men there, though the banners were still flying and the drums were still beating. When the sultan saw what a terrible blow his army had suffered, he came to his own squadron and found only this tiny handful of men. He stopped there and when he saw that the whole place was overrun with fleeing soldiers, he ordered the drummers to go on drumming without stopping, and made all the fleeing soldiers come up to where he was'.[139] Saladin managed to get his men more or less re-grouped, but they were thoroughly demoralized. The Moslems were beaten.

Richard ordered no pursuit, in which they might have fallen into an ambush, or might have had to leave their foot-soldiers. Among the dead was the famous baron,

---

136 Beha ed-Din, p. 258.
137 Ambroise, vv. 6454–81, pp. 172–3; vv. 6523–38, p. 174.
138 *Ibid.*, vv. 6539–62, pp. 174–5, vv. 6594–6614, p. 176.
139 Beha ed-Din, p. 258.

James of Avesnes. This knight from Hainault, who was also a vassal of the count of Flanders, and whose family had provided brave sons for each crusade, seems to have gone through too far into the enemy lines. His horse fell, but the baron fought stoutly on foot. Round his body, Ambroise tells us, were found those of three other members of his family and fifteen of the enemy. In the ranks of the crusaders' army it was freely said that the count of Dreux with his followers had not rushed quickly enough to his help. James was compared to such heroes as Alexander, Hector and Achilles.[140]

Richard's victory was complete, although the premature attack of the Hospitallers and Baldwin Caron was generally regretted. Saladin realized that further fighting would be of no advantage to him. His troops were completely demoralized. He decided to offer no further resistance in the numerous fortresses and gave orders that all towns and castles were to be demolished except Jerusalem and two important castles, Darum and Krak des Chevaliers. When Richard later attacked Darum the garrison surrendered the fortress after only four days' siege by the king's own followers who were certainly not very numerous.

Jerusalem was not conquered. The city was not besieged on the advice of the military Orders and the knights of the former kingdom of the Holy Land. They were convinced that the operation would be very costly, since supplies would have to be brought from the coast and might be intercepted on the way. They knew also that it would be very difficult to hold the city after the withdrawal of the crusaders who would be returning to the west. The unhappy crusaders who had borne so many privations and were ready to bear still more in order to reach their objective, were not convinced by these arguments and were bitterly disillusioned.

THE BATTLE OF BOUVINES, 27 JULY 1214

King John of England had landed on 15 February 1214 at La Rochelle in Aquitaine. He was accompanied only by mercenaries, since the Anglo-Norman nobility would not follow him, and he managed to collect quite a number of followers in Poitou, and some nobles in Anjou and Maine. This expedition in the south-west was of course connected with the attack on the French in the north and would weaken his enemy, since it removed a certain number of knights from the army of Philip Augustus, who was facing the forces of the emperor Otto, count Ferdinand of Flanders, and Renaud de Dammartin, in the north.

Otto reached Nivelles about 12 July. Count Ferdinand had gone towards him, to the Meuse, with 200 knights, to persuade the prince-bishop of Liège, an ally of Ferdinand in the campaign against Henry I of Brabant but a violent opponent of the emperor Otto, to allow the emperor free passage through the prince-bishopric.[141] The Bishop of Liège was on the side of the Pope who had excommunicated Otto and was allied to the king of France.

---

[140] Ambroise, vv. 6634–7, 6640–58, pp. 177–8. [See J. Gillingham, *Richard the Lionheart*, London, 1978, for a detailed survey of the strategic problems faced by the crusaders: pp. 169–70, 194, 198–200, 210–16.]

[141] *Vita Odiliae*, p. 187. Reinerus, *Annales S. Jacobi Leodiensis*, p. 671.

From Nivelles the emperor and his followers went to Valenciennes, where the main army had been collected.[142] He was still there on 23 July. On that date Philip Augustus advanced from Péronne to Douai, reached the Boulenrieu on 24 July, and crossed the bridge over the river Marcq at Bouvines on the 25th. On the 26th he reached Tournai, the invasion gateway to Flanders and Hainault.[143]

Otto's army had meanwhile made a raid into the Cambrai district, and had marched on to Mortagne. Thus on 26 July the French were at Tournai, the emperor and his allies at Mortagne. The armies had unwittingly marched past each other. The French held a council of war. Philip Augustus seemed prepared to launch an attack on Mortagne, but his advisers were definitely against this since the entrance to the fortress, which lay between the Scarpe and the Scheldt, was through a very narrow and difficult passage, where the ground was marshy and unsuitable for cavalry. They decided not to plan an attack for Monday 28 July, but to start back on the 27th by an easier route, in order to attack the country held by count Ferdinand and find a convenient flat piece of ground for a possible battle, in which the French knights could deploy their strength fully.[144]

On Sunday, 27 July, the French army set out early. The king intended to go to Lille and stay there overnight. They marched off in excellent order, first the waggons of the communal armies followed by foot-soldiers, who loaded their weapons on to the waggons during the march, to conserve their strength, after them the riders and the knights in their formations. To avoid being surprised by the enemy, they sent out a rearguard in the direction of Mortagne. These troops were led by the burgrave of Melun and the duke of Burgundy, and included the contingent from Champagne. They were accompanied by the supreme tactical commander, bishop Guérin, who had previously been in the Holy Land and had been a member of the Order of Hospitallers.[145] Guérin was to be in charge of all military operations first with the rearguard and then during the battle, where he was not to take any active part himself.

The rearguard marched three miles in the direction of Mortagne, about halfway between Tournai and Otto's camp, the distance given in the same source as six miles between the two. The commanders posted observers on a hill having a good open view, to watch for any enemy movement towards the royal army.[146]

Meanwhile the French marched in perfect order over an old Roman road to the bridge at Bouvines. They moved very quickly: a reliable chronicler says that so large an army had never ridden so fast.[147]

142 Anonyme de Béthune, *Chronique*, p. 767 H. *Genealogiae comitum Flandriae. Continuatio Clarismariscensis*, MGH, SS, IX, c. 20, p. 332. Ph. Mousket, *Chronique rimée*, II, vv. 21473–8, p. 348.
143 William the Breton, *Chronicon*, c. 181, p. 266. Mousket, II, vv. 21514–9, p. 349. Lot, I, p. 231. Oman, I, pp. 474–5. Delpech, I, pp. 73–4.
144 William the Breton, *Chronicon*, c. 181, p. 267. *Idem, Philippis*, 1. X, vv. 687–9, p. 310. Mousket, II, vv. 21553–6, 21567–80, pp. 351–2. Anonyme de Béthune, p. 768 D. *Genealogiae com. Fl. Cont. Clar.*, MGH, SS, IX, c. 20, p. 332.
145 William the Breton, *Chronicon*, c. 182, pp. 267–8. *Philippis*, 1. X, vv. 819–20, p. 315. Mousket, II, vv. 21591–2, p. 352. Anonyme de Béthune, p. 768.
146 William the Breton, *Chronicon*, c. 181, p. 267; c. 182, p. 268. Anonyme de Béthune, p. 768.
147 Anonyme de Béthune, *loc. cit.*

As soon as the allies in Mortagne realized that the French had moved out of Tournai in the direction of Lille, they also held a council of war. The emperor did not wish to fight on a Sunday. Renaud de Dammartin thought the moment not yet ripe, and that the French would suffer losses and their morale would be shaken by retreating, while the allies had nothing to lose thereby. But Hugues de Boves was still anxious to fight and insisted that the French were fleeing. Several other knights in the allied camp agreed with him.

Now was the time to advance, said Hugues, so as not to waste the English king's money on a long-drawn out campaign, when it could all be finished off in a single battle. They decided to follow the French in the hope of meeting part of the French army still on the right bank of the Marcq, east of the only bridge at Bouvines, and of destroying them.[148]

In fact there was another Roman road, called the Chaussée Brunehaut in the Middle Ages. It connected Mortagne directly with the Tournai–Bouvines road, joining it north of Cysoing. This Roman road was discovered in 1879 by Delpech, by making borings in the ground. He was able to trace its course northwards from Cysoing nearly to Rumes.[149] Since like all Roman roads it is absolutely straight, its line can be traced further, showing that it came out somewhere to the north of Mortagne and Maulde, on the Mortagne–Tournai road, which is also a Roman military road. The distance between Mortagne and the Tournai–Bouvines road, along which Philip Augustus went, is about 12½ miles on the map, which is less than the other way which goes towards Tournai and then follows the Tournai–Bouvines road. According to Delpech's plan this would be a little over 14 miles.[150]

Now the allies clearly knew this road, and used it in the hope of catching up the rear-guard or even a good part of Philip Augustus' army. If they took the other way, as Delpech unreasonably supposes, they would have had very little chance of catching up the enemy. The French had very little more than 9 miles to go from Tournai to Bouvines. They moved off before the allies, and thus had a good start. If the allies, despite this, still hoped to catch up the enemy before the whole army had got across the river Marcq, it was because they knew the ground, and thought that quick marching along the direct Mortagne–Bouvines road would make up lost time.

Much of this road ran through forest, and the allies would have had no chance to spread out into fields to get their cavalry along more quickly. This is important for calculating the length of their column during the march northwards.

The allies collected their army in haste to make up for lost time. 'They mounted fully armed and went after them at full speed, as if anxious to reach their prey'.[151] It was soon said of the Flemish nobles that they 'began to break ranks, as if they had never been in formation'.[152] This extended the column dangerously.

---

[148] *Genealogia com. Fl.*, c. 22, p. 333. Mousket, II, vv. 21611–35, p. 353. William the Breton, *Chronicon*, c. 195, p. 287; c. 183, p. 269. *Philippis*, l. XI, vv. 564–72, p. 341.
[149] Delpech, II, pp. 341–5.
[150] See the map in Delpech, I, plate II, p. 71.
[151] Anonyme de Béthune, p. 768.
[152] Mousket, II, vv. 21650–1, p. 354.

The French Forces

As usual, the chroniclers disagree about the numbers of the two armies. The only eyewitness of the battle, William the Breton, gives no figures for his own side, but is content to say that the enemy was three times as strong. Information about the strength of the army of Philip Augustus must be pieced together from various other accounts.[153]

In September 1214 the French army invaded Poitou. It included over 2,000 knights.[154] But at the time of the battle of Bouvines, Louis, the king's son, was fighting King John with 800 knights,[155] presumably leaving Philip Augustus with 1,200 at Bouvines. The *Servitia Feodorum* of 1211–12 gives the contingents which the vassals from the royal domain and the region north of the Seine had to send to the royal army, and we also have accounts of 1300 and 1317 in which the French nobles' contingents are listed.[156] In the narrative accounts, and especially in William the Breton, the names of the nobles appear, and from the dated sources listed above we know how many men they usually had to send. This makes it possible to decide within reasonable limits how the army was composed.

William the Breton gives the name of the following knights who fought in the French right wing. We know the contingents of some of these knights in 1211–12 and 1317. Figures in brackets are guesses.

	In 1211–12	In 1317[157]
Knights from Champagne and followers	180	
Duke of Burgundy	(180)	
Gaucher de Châtillon, count of St Pol	30	50
Seigneur de Montmorency	20	30
Count of Beaumont	20	
Count of Sancerre	10	30
Burgrave of Melun	(25)	25
Hugues de Malaunay	(5)	
Hugues de Mareuil	(5)	
Jean de Mareuil	(5)	
Gilles d'Aci	5	
Michel d'Aci	(5)	
	490	**540**

---

153 The numbers given by the chroniclers were collected and discussed by A. Cartellieri, *Philipp II. August*, IV, 2, pp. 608–20. Lot, I, pp. 224–5. William the Breton, *Philippis*, 1. X, vv. 646–7, p. 308, vv. 206–7, p. 289.

154 William the Breton, *Chronicon*, c. 204, p. 298.

155 *Idem, Philippis*, 1. X, vv. 131–4, p. 286. *Chronicon*, c. 181, p. 266.

156 *Servitia Feodorum*, RHF, XXIII, p. 693, cc. 415–16, pp. 807–8. *Les journaux du trésor de Philippe IV le Bel*, pp. 518–622. Verbruggen, *De slag der gulden sporen*, pp. 239–43. Lot, I, pp. 270–1.

157 William the Breton, *Chronicon*, c. 186, p. 276. *Philippis*, 1. X, vv. 466–7, p. 301. Champagne had to send 180 knights: see for 1317: RHF, XXIII, p. 807. Lot, I, p. 266, n. 4, p. 270.

On the right wing there were also 150 light cavalry sent from Soissons by the abbey of St Medard. Perhaps we may add as many light cavalry from Champagne?[158]
The following knights were in the centre:

Gales de Montigny	(5)	
Guillaume des Barres	(5)	
Barthélemy de Roye	(5)	
Gauthier de Nemours	(5)	
Pierre Mauvoisin	5	
Gérard la Truie	(5)	
Etienne de Longchamp	5	
with 70 Norman knights	70[159]	
Guillaume de Montemer	(5)	
Jean de Rouvrai	10	
Guillaume de Garlande	20	
Henri count of Bar	(30)	
Pierre Tristan	(5)	
	175	

The following knights were on the left wing:

Thomas de St Valery with his followers	20	50[160]
Jean de Nesle and his knights	40	
Count of Dreux	(40)	
Bishop of Beauvais	20	
Bishop of Laon	10	
Guillaume count of Ponthieu	–	
Ponthieu	60	
Vimeu	(30)	
Count of Auxerre, Nevers and Namur	(30)	
Pierre de la Tournelle	(5)	
Hugues de Fontaines	5	
Gautier de Fontaines	5	
Jean de Coudun	(5)	
Quesnes de Coudun	(5)	
	275	**305** knights

---

[158] William the Breton, *Chronicon*, c. 186, p. 277. *Philippis*, 1. XI, vv. 77–90, p. 321, gives 300 horsemen, but the figures of the *Philippis* are unreliable when they differ from those in the *Chronicon*. Light cavalry is mentioned in the rear-guard, as light cavalry from Champagne: *Chronicon*, c. 183, p. 270.
[159] William the Breton, *Philippis*, 1. X, vv. 497–8, p. 302. The normal contingent from Normandy was 180.
[160] *Idem*, *Chronicon*, c. 192, p. 285; c. 197, pp. 289–90. *Philippis*, 1. X, vv. 490–5, p, 302; 1. XI, vv. 509–11, p. 339: 60 knights, 'decies sex' for the needs of the verse.

Knights mentioned in the narrative sources, or whose position is unknown:

Count of Guines (right wing?)	(20)
Count of Soissons	(30)
Roger de Rozoy	10
Enguerrand de Couci	(30)
Raoul Flamens	(5)
Giles de Marque	(5)
Guy de la Roche	10
Thomas de Mongumbert	(5)
Amiens[161]	20
	135

William the Breton says explicitly that his list is not complete, especially for the centre, the royal division.[162] It is also probable that some of the knights at Bouvines had more fighting men under them than is stated in the *Servitia Feodorum* of about 1211. We know this to be true of Thomas de St Valery, and it may also have been true of other knights, since William does not mention some districts, and some nobles will have added these troops to their own. Mousket mentions the men of Hurepoix from beyond the Seine, and the men from the Amiens district.[163] William the Breton never mentions the counts of Guines or Soissons, who are named by the Anonymous of Béthune.[164]

We therefore have a total of 490+175+275+135 = 1,075 knights, or 1,155 according to the highest count, which is very near the 1,200 we have already accepted. If Normandy sent the usual 180 knights instead of the 70 under the command of Etienne de Longchamp,[165] we arrive at the 1,200 knights that we get from William the Breton.

We can also calculate the respective strengths in another way. We have given above the list of levies raised from part of the royal domain and from small districts north of the Seine according to the *Servitia Feodorum* of 1211–12. We already know that several of them were mentioned in the battle of Bouvines. If we now assume that they all took part in the battle, and disregard the knights whose contingents are not mentioned in the list – which is anyway incomplete and therefore will not lead to exaggerated figures – we get a total of 765 knights. To this must be added the knights sent by other districts, which gives the following results.

Districts north of the Seine	765
Champagne	180
Burgundy	(180)
Burgrave of Melun	(25)
Count of Guines	(20)

161 Anonyme de Béthune, pp. 768–9. Mousket, II, v. 21663, p. 355; v. 21996, p. 368; v. 21973, p. 367. William the Breton, *Philippis*, 1. X, v. 462, p. 300.
162 *Chronicon*, c. 184, p. 272.
163 Mousket, II, vv. 21969–73. p. 367.
164 Anonyme de Béthune, p. 768.
165 Lot, I, p. 226, n. 6.

Count of Soissons	(30)
Normandy	(70)
Count of Bar	(30)
Count of Auxerre	(30)
Couci	(30)
	1,360

This total is higher than the 1,200 knights we derived from William the Breton but elsewhere he mentions that there were 'more than 2,000 knights' in the royal army in 1214, which does make the 1,300 knights at Bouvines seem possible. We can be certain that the king of France had 1,200 or possibly even 1,300 knights at Bouvines.

These knights were supported by the 150 light cavalry sent by the abbey of St. Medard at Soissons, and perhaps as many from Champagne.

The *Catalogus Captivorum* (166) helps us to get some idea of the strength of the French foot-soldiers. It gives the numbers of prisoners given to each of the French communes who took part. From this we can deduce which towns were represented. They normally contributed the following numbers:

Noyon	150
Montdidier	80
Montreuil-sur-Mer	150
Soissons	160
Bruyères	120
Hesdin	80
Cerny and Crépy-en-Laonnais	80
Crandelain	40
Vailly	50
Corbie	200
Roye	100
Compiègne	200
Amiens	250
Beauvais	500
	2,160
Arras	1,000
	3,160 soldiers

Of these, the following were in the French centre:[167]

Corbie	200
Amiens	250
Beauvais	500
Compiègne	200
Arras	1,000
	2,150 foot-soldiers

---

[166] *De pugna Boviniensi. Catalogus Captivorum*, ed. A. Molinier, MGH, SS, XXVI, pp. 391–7. Lot, I, p. 227.

[167] Lot, I, pp. 219–20. Boutaric, pp. 203–4. William the Breton, *Chronicon*, c. 191, p. 282.

We cannot tell whether the other communes took part in the battle. They totalled 1980 foot-soldiers.[168]

If only part of the contingents of the abbeys and the places not having the status of commune were called up, or if some of them had been sent to the army of Louis the king's son, we get a strength of four to five thousand men for the French foot at Bouvines, out of a total of 8,069.[169] Considering the extremely limited role played by these troops, this part of the army was relatively unimportant. But since – with considerable exaggeration – 2,000 foot-soldiers are credited to Thomas de St Valery alone, the total may perhaps be raised to 5–6,000 foot-soldiers.[170] Actually we only see his troops, perhaps a thousand men, and the foot-soldiers in the centre, involved in a very brief phase of the battle.

The Strength of the Allies

There are two interesting sets of figures for the number of the knights in the army of the allies: two sources give 1,500 knights, and a third 1300, but since all three chroniclers are French their evidence is suspect.[171] Yet, in view of the fact that there are sufficient reasons to explain the defeat of the emperor and Ferdinand of Portugal, and considering the earlier figures for the number of knights in Flanders and Hainault, these figures may be taken as reliable. A strength of 1,500 knights seems most probable, but since little is actually known about the circumstances in which the army was raised, the smaller number should not be rejected out of hand. In the first of these calculations we estimate the Flemish contingent at 650, the Hainaulters at 500, and only 350 with Otto, Renaud de Dammartin, the earl of Salisbury and Hugues de Boves. The following breakdown seems most probable in the second calculation: 600, 425, 275.

This is how the figures are justified. Otto had so few men with him that Ferdinand had to go towards Liège with 200 knights to meet him. A reliable source says that the emperor had only a few men with him.[172] He found few allies in Lorraine, and in the prince-bishopric of Liège he came up against the enmity of the prince-bishop, who forced many knights to stay at home by gifts or threats.[173] The duke of Brabant only joined them out of necessity, as his two sons were held hostage by Ferdinand.[174] The contingents of Otto and Renaud contained so few knights that the foot-soldiers

168 Lot, I, p. 227.

169 *Ibid.*, p. 227, n. 2.

170 William the Breton, *Chronicon*, c. 192, p. 285; c. 197, pp. 289–90. *Philippis*, 1. X, vv. 490–1, p. 302; 1. XI, vv. 509–11, p. 339.

171 *Chronicon S. Martini Turonensis (excerpta)*, ed. O. Holder-Egger, MGH, SS, XXVI, 1882, p. 465. Andreas Marchianensis, *Historia regum Francorum. Continuatio (excerpta)*, ed. G. Waitz, MGH, SS, XXVI, 1882, p. 213. Lot, I, p. 230. Delpech, I, p. 4.

172 *Historia ducum Normanniae et regum Angliae*, ed. O. Holder-Egger, MGH, SS, XXVI, 1882, p. 713: 'Poi amena li empereres de gent; mais nonpourquant grant fieste fist li cuens de lui'. Cartellieri, *Philipp II August*, IV, 2, pp. 433, 437, 443. W. Kienast, *Die deutschen Fürsten im Dienste der Westmächte*, Bijdragen van het Instituut voor middeleeuwse Geschiedenis der Rijksuniversiteit te Utrecht, 2 vols, I, Utrecht 1924–31, p. 213.

173 *Vita Odiliae*, p. 187.

174 Balduinus Ninovensis, *Chronicon*, ed. O. Holder-Egger, MGH, SS, XXV, 1880, p. 539.

were more important, especially the excellent mercenaries. The total of 350 (or 275 in case the number included only 1,300 knights) is too high rather than too low.

We have no information at all about the strength of the foot-soldiers. In all probability they were stronger than the French. Arras sent the greatest contribution, but the French king made no great demands on his communes, so that the Flemish towns could easily send a similar number (1,000). The largest towns, Ghent and Bruges, possibly sent more than 1,000 men. In addition there were troops from Ypres, Lille, Douai and Valenciennes, from similar cities and towns, from the country, and the mercenaries of Renaud de Dammartin, Hugues de Boves and the earl of Salisbury. We would put the total at 7,500, since we hear so little about the number of foot-soldiers on the battlefield in the early thirteenth century that it cannot have been very large.

Out of this number we have credited Otto's corps with 3,500, in the centre, since this contingent with the German knights defeated the French foot of the centre, at least 2,150 strong. Since the mercenaries of Renaud de Dammartin were still in position at the end of the battle with 400 or 700 men we assume that the whole allied right wing, led by the earl of Salisbury and the count of Boulogne, contained about 1,500 foot-soldiers in the beginning of the battle.

All these numbers are estimates, but these estimates are founded upon the story of the battle.

The March of the Allies from Mortagne to Bouvines

If we calculate the length of the column of Otto's army on the march, we find that the hasty march of his troops was in large part the cause of their defeat. The advance guard was constituted by the knights of Ferdinand, about 1,200 knights and their squires who led the warhorse of their master. Then came the formation of Otto, about 175 knights, their squires, and 3,500 foot-soldiers. Renaud de Dammartin had as many knights as Otto and 1,500 foot-soldiers. The rest of the army followed: a corps of 2,500 foot.

If the knights and squires marched four abreast on the old road in the forest, their column had a length of 2,100 metres.[175] The knights and the foot of Otto formed a column of 1,600 metres. The troops of Renaud de Dammartin needed 850 metres and the last corps 950 metres. If we take a distance of 100 metres between two corps, we may add at least 300 metres, and probably more, 500 or 600 metres. In total it was a column of 6,000 metres, without taking account of the waggons of the foot-soldiers. In a case like this, the normal place of the waggons was between the main corps and the rearguard. These waggons made the column much longer. There is a remarkable example on the same road between Tournai and Bouvines: the army of Philip the Fair in 1304 occupied the whole distance between Tournai and Bouvines.[176] A total length of almost 10 kilometres is reasonable for the army of Otto.

---

[175] For the calculation we took as length of a horse, 2.5 m, a horse following a horse at 1 m. For the foot: 1.5 m for a rank of four soldiers.

[176] *Chronique artésienne*, p. 82: 'li roy . . . se loga là u li Flamens furent logiet quant il assirent Tournay. Et estoit près du Pont-de-Bouvines li bous de l'ost, qui bien duroit .ij. liues'.

The French army advanced at a good speed. The cavalry of Ferdinand had to move faster. They rode perhaps at 7 kilometres an hour, and the foot marched at 5 kilometres an hour. So the foot-soldiers lost an hour during the march of 20 kilometres between Mortagne and the north of Cysoing. The column of the foot had a length of 5 kilometres, for we may assume that they, like their French opposite numbers, put their weapons on to the army waggons during the march in order to advance more quickly. But a column of foot of that length would need two hours to get the whole of itself to the battlefield and to deploy on arrival.

The accuracy of this calculation is largely borne out by the account of the battle itself. By the time Philip Augustus realized that the allies were advancing towards Bouvines to fight, Ferdinand was already very close to the battlefield with his foremost troops. The French cavalry were mustered at once, and already partly deployed, and the king had only to deploy his knights a little more when the allied army arrived. But the French foot was already over the Marcq and were close to the *Hôtellerie*, about 2½ miles beyond the battlefield. Philip Augustus had enough time between Ferdinand's arrival and Otto's troops being ready to call back the levies and place them in front of his knights in the centre and on the left wing.[177]

From their observation post the French rearguard had spotted the allied advance. Since the enemy were ordered and ready for combat, Bishop Guérin was convinced that they intended to force a battle.The position of the French rearguard can be accurately fixed: it was on high ground, close to a wood, which suggests Longue Saule, on the 74 metre contour line, the highest point south of Tournai, in the direction of Mortagne and very close to the wood.[178]

Bishop Guérin left the burgrave of Melun on the spot, and went to report to the king, but could not easily convince him. The order to halt was given, and the leaders summoned. Most of them thought that the march should go on. They were supported in their view by the movements of the allied troops, who were crossing a stream. In order to find fording-places they had to slow down and turn in the direction of Tournai. These who supported the advance therefore concluded that Otto was moving to Tournai. The king gave the order to continue, despite Guérin's opposition.[179]

The French advanced to the bridge at Bouvines, and part of the army crossed it, with the communal foot-soldiers. The king took off his armour, and rested in the shadow of an ash-tree by the church at Bouvines. His rest and meal were disturbed by a messenger from the rearguard. Gérard la Truie rushed up with the news that Ferdinand's troops were advancing, and were already in contact with the rear-guard. The duke of Burgundy was having great difficulty in holding off the advancing Flemings with crossbowmen, light cavalry and knights.[180] Then the king was at last

177 William the Breton, *Chronicon*, c. 191, pp. 281–2.
178 *Ibid.*, c. 182, p. 268. *Philippis*, 1. X, v. 739, p. 312. Anonyme de Béthune, p. 768. Delpech, I, map II, pp. 70–1. See also the map of Cassini.
179 William the Breton, *Chronicon*, c. 182–3, pp. 268–9. *Philippis*, 1. X, vv. 741–90, pp. 312–14.
180 *Idem, Chronicon*, c. 183, pp. 269–71. *Philippis*, pp. 315–16. Mousket, II, pp. 354–8. Anonyme de Béthune, p. 768.

convinced that there was to be a battle, and that the enemy set no store by a Sunday rest. He prayed briefly in the church, then put on his armour, mounted, and ordered the troops to form up. Everywhere the shout went up, 'To arms! to arms!' Trumpets sounded and passed on the order. The communal armies were called back with their colours, the Oriflamme from the Abbey of St Denis, but the companies of knights were formed up at once without waiting for the standard to be set up, and the king took his position in the centre of his troops.

The bands of French knights stood there partly in position and ready to arrange their formation to match the deployment of the allies. Certainly the latter were unpleasantly surprised to find the enemy knights facing them in proper formation. This is emphasized in each of the accounts. Instead of being able to take part of the French army by surprise and break it up east of the bridge at Bouvines, Ferdinand and Otto came upon an army already prepared for battle. It would take hours to turn their long column into proper battle order. Renaud de Dammartin had foreseen this, but now it was too late.[181] They would have to fight, and the allies deployed their troops at once as they reached the plain north of Cysoing. The enemy copied them and spread out their front proportionately as the allies avanced northwards. Bishop Guérin took care not to be attacked in the flank, nor to be surrounded. Once he was sure of this, it was time to take the initiative in the battle.

The Disposition of the Armies

Count Ferdinand took up position with his troops facing the French rear guard, who from then on formed the right wing of the royal army in the south. The scene of the battle was a broad open plain stretching from Cysoing in the south to Gruson in the north. Left of the plain, in the west, flowed the Marcq, whose banks were very marshy. In spreading out the cavalry formations northwards the allied left wing, containing the knights from Flanders and Hainault, crossed the Tournai-Bouvines road. This meant that Otto had to leave the road on which he was going westwards, and turn right, towards the north. There he gradually got his troops into position on a piece of high ground, and halted.[182]

While the allies were deploying their troops, Philip Augustus was also broadening the front of his formations of knights. After the arrival of Renaud de Dammartin with his troops this made a front of 2,000 paces. The allies were facing west, the French east. It was a hot day and the sun was shining into the eyes of the allies and on the backs of the French. It was a little after noon.[183]

The whole front was 2,000 paces broad, of which the left wing of the allies and the right wing of the French took up 1,040 paces.[184] The allies' left wing was made

---

[181] *Genealogiae com. Fl.*, c. 22, p. 333. William the Breton, *Chronicon*, c. 184, p. 271. *Philippis*, 1. XI, vv. 8–11, pp. 317–18. Anonyme de Béthune, p. 768: 'Mais sachiés qu'il ne se venoient pas si bien ni si ordenéement com li François aloient vers els, et ce lor parut'.

[182] Sir James Ramsay and F. Lot (I, p. 230, n. 9) have given the accurate position of the troops.

[183] William the Breton, *Chronicon*, c. 184, pp. 271–2. *Philippis*, 1. XI, vv. 15–16, p. 318; 1. X, v. 816, p. 315.

[184] *Idem, Philippis*, 1. XI, vv. 15–16, p. 318. *Chronicon*, c. 186, pp. 274–5. In the *Chronicon*, William

up of mounted men from Flanders and Hainault under Ferdinand. The emperor placed himself, with his knights and foot in the centre. He had brought a waggon with him, resplendent with the imperial eagle over a dragon. This waggon with the huge banner served as a rallying point during the battle.

Four German nobles were with the emperor, Bernard von Horstmar, Otto von Tecklenburg, Conrad von Dortmund and Gerard von Randerath.[185] It is not easy to make out whether mounted men or foot-soldiers were in front in Otto's formation; the most logical thing would have been for the knights to be in front, and the sources do not contradict this. Since the emperor had very little cavalry, these knights would be followed in an attack by footmen.

Renaud de Dammartin and the earl of Salisbury were with the right wing of the allies. Renaud seems to have used special tactics here. He put his foot-soldiers into a crown or circle formation, two ranks deep, and launched his attack through an opening in this formation, in order to be able to withdraw under cover of the foot's pikes.[186] Such a manoeuvre can naturally only be carried out by a small cavalry force.

The French put the following units in their right wing: 150 light cavalry sent by the abbey of St Médard at Soissons, the contingent from the county of Champagne, consisting of 180 knights led by Pierre de Remi, Gaucher de St Pol and his men, Mathieu de Montmorency and his men, count Jean de Beaumont and his men, Eudes duke of Burgundy, the burgrave of Melun and his knights, Etienne de Sancerre and his men, Hugues de Malaunay, Hugues and Jean de Mareuil, Michel de Harnes, and Gilles d'Aci.[187]

Philip Augustus had taken up his position in the centre, with the royal fleur-de-lys standard borne by Gales de Montigny. With the king were Guillaume des Barres, Barthélemy de Roye, Gautier de Nemours, Pierre Mauvoisin, Gérard la Truie, Etienne de Longchamps, Guillaume de Montemer, Jean de Rouvrai, Guillaume de Garlande, count Henry of Bar, and Pierre Tristan.[188] On the left wing of the royal army were Robert count of Dreux and his men, his brother Philip, bishop of Beauvais, the bishop of Laon, Pierre de Courtenai, count of Auxerre, Nevers and Namur, Jean de Nesle viscount of Bruges and his knights, Thomas de St Valery, seigneur de Gamaches with knights and foot, Guillaume count of Ponthieu with the troops from his county and those from Vimeu. With them were also Pierre de la Tournelle, Hugues and Gautier de Fontaines, Jean and Quesnes de Coudun.[189]

The French attached most importance to their right wing, which was the first to

speaks of the front of the French right wing (1,040 paces), in the Philippis of the whole front (2,000 paces).

185 *Idem, Chronicon,* c. 184, p. 272; c. 193, p. 285. *Philippis,* 1. XI, vv. 20–31, pp. 318–19; vv. 391–5, pp. 334–5; vv. 516–17, p. 339.

186 *Idem, Chronicon,* c. 193, p. 285. *Philippis,* 1. XI, vv. 251–2, p. 328; vv. 605–12, pp. 342–3.

187 *Idem, Chronicon,* c. 186, p. 276; c. 190, p. 281. *Philippis,* 1. X, vv. 465–75, p. 301; 1. XI, vv. 111–14, p. 322; v. 235, p. 327.

188 *Idem, Chronicon,* c. 184, p. 272; c. 191, pp. 281–2; *Philippis,* 1. X. vv. 458–64, pp. 300–1; 1. XI, v. 41, p. 319.

189 *Idem, Chronicon,* c. 194, p. 286; c. 196–7, pp. 287–9. *Philippis,* 1. XI, vv. 337–46, pp. 332–3; v. 538, p. 340; vv. 647–8, p. 344; vv. 677–84, pp. 345–6.

be deployed. The commander in chief, bishop Guérin, was there, anxious to join battle as quickly as possible. Since the battlefield was so wide, he took care first to ensure that the enemy could not outflank him, and ordered his knights to spread out their formation, to prevent any threat to the flank and the rear. He put the most skilful and courageous knights in front, as was the custom. Some nobles put themselves into this front rank out of knightly pride, to show that they were not afraid, though in fact they were no heroes. The bishop moved them to the back row. The really brave knights were to fight in front, not using each other as a shield. He arranged his knights so neatly that they could all fight on one front, and yet stay close together in their formations.[190] For this reason Guérin made them into a fairly thin line. Having made this sensible disposition, which was carefully planned to suit the terrain and the enemy's troop formation, the bishop gave the signal to attack, on the advice of St Pol.

The Battle

The detachment of 150 light cavalry from the abbey of St Médard started the battle, with the aim of putting the ranks of the allied left wing in disorder. The Flemish knights despised these horsemen, and no one came out against them. Since the horses of these light cavalry were not protected by any armour, they were killed by the knights from Hainault and Flanders, and the cavalry were soon forced either to fight on foot or to retreat. Then a few of the Flemish knights left the ranks of their division to join battle with the enemy knights. Walter of Gistel and Baldwin Buridan unhorsed a few of the light cavalrymen and then went on. Buridan cheered on the others by shouting to them to think of their lady-loves and of the tournament.[191] Arnulf, burgrave of Raisse, Eustace of Machelen, Rase of Gaver and others distinguished themselves. But it was still only preparation for the general charge:

> ... no one was in order,
> Everyone charged as they wished.[192]

The battle proper began with the attack of the division from Champagne whose knights put the imprudent Flemish nobles out of action or took them prisoner. Then the count of Flanders attacked with his whole formation and flung back the knights of Pierre de Remi. The count of St Pol took up the attack with his splendid knights, who had been carefully handpicked. 'Quick as an eagle' he swooped on the enemy. He was followed by the count of Beaumont, Mathieu de Montmorency, the duke of Burgundy, the burgrave of Melun and the count of Sancerre, all with their men.[193] 'This battle halted the pursuit, and there was such a good fight that the valiant men

---

[190] *Idem, Chronicon*, c. 186, p. 276. *Philippis*, 1. XI, vv. 62–3, p. 320. Lot, I, p. 229 and n. 2, and Delbrück, III, p. 296 and n. 1, thought that only one rank of knights was formed. This is wrong because the less courageous knights were put behind the others.

[191] William the Breton, *Chronicon*, c. 186–7, p. 277. *Philippis*, 1. XI, vv. 77–99, p. 321; vv. 142–3, p. 323. Anonyme de Béthune, p. 768. Mousket, vv. 21782–90, pp. 359–60.

[192] Mousket, vv. 21791–2, p. 360.

[193] William the Breton, *Chronicon*, c. 187–8, pp. 277–9. *Philippis*, 1. XI, vv. 112–15, p. 322. Anonyme de Béthune, p. 768.

who were there bore witness that they had never seen such good tourneying as this battle achieved.' For William the Breton it was an admirable combat for the knights of both armies.[194]

Then the attackers brought their classic tactics to bear. Gaucher de Châtillon and his men broke through the ranks of Flemish knights, then attacked them from the rear only to break through again elsewhere. The burgrave of Melun and his men copied them. While this was going on, the count of St Pol and his men were busy killing horses as well as men, or throwing their enemies out of the saddle, but taking no prisoners. In this tremendous charge many knights were unhorsed on both sides. The duke of Burgundy's horse was killed, and the duke fell. Immediately he was ringed in by a group of his knights, who closed their ranks and beat off the enemy so that others could go to the help of the duke and fetch him a new horse.[195]

But such charges, bringing down men and horses, are most exhausting. After his breakthrough and return through the thin ranks of Hainault and Flemish knights, the count of St Pol and his men had to recover their breath. Then he saw that one of his knights had not been able to keep up, and was surrounded by the enemy, so he immediately dashed to his aid. Bent low over his horse's neck, he forced his way through the enemy ranks to get his man out and bring him back. After a short rest, he returned to the fight with his company.[196]

The better ordered formations of French knights carried out a devastating attack on Ferdinand's more loosely packed formation. They let them feel the weight of their close formation, and it had a great effect. The ranks of Flanders and Hainault grew thinner and thinner, but no one thought of fleeing. Knightly honour kept them on the battlefield, where they defended themselves stoutly.[197]

After the battle had gone on for about three hours, Hugues and Jean de Mareuil cut their way through to the wounded count of Flanders, whose horse had been killed. Ferdinand had to give himself up, and this was the death-blow to his formation.[198]

Meanwhile the troops of the French communes had arrived on the battlefield, having advanced almost to the Hôtellerie, 2½ miles away. These levies marched under the banner of St Denis, the renowned Oriflamme, and they made for the formation of Philip Augustus, where they could see the standard of the fleur-de-lys. The men of Corbie, Amiens, Beauvais, Compiègne and Arras drew themselves up in front of the king's knights.[199] But they had only just taken up their positions when Otto and the allied centre made their attack. The levies were thrown back, and Otto's knights broke through towards the French king. The French knights left him a little

194 Anonyme de Béthune, pp. 768–9; William the Breton, *Chronicon*, c. 188, p. 279.

195 William the Breton, *Chronicon*, c. 188, pp. 278–9. *Philippis*, 1. XI, vv. 155–77, pp. 324–5; vv. 200–13, p. 326, but with much exaggeration in the poem.

196 *Idem, Chronicon*, c. 189, pp. 280–1. *Philippis*, 1. XI, vv. 218–26, p. 327.

197 *Idem, Philippis*, 1. XI, vv. 228–34, p. 327.

198 *Idem, Chronicon*, c. 190, p. 281. According to the *Relatio Marchianensis*, in *De pugna Boviniensi*, ed. G. Waitz, MGH, SS, XXVI, p. 391, this struggle lasted only one hour. Anonyme de Béthune, p. 769. Mousket, vv. 21795–9, p. 360.

199 William the Breton, *Chronicon*, c. 191, pp. 281–2. The story in the *Philippis*, pp. 328–9, has no value. Mousket, v. 22165 ff, pp. 373–4. *Chronicon S. Martini Turonensis*, p. 465.

behind, for the sake of protection, and charged the emperor's knights. But during this battle of knights, Otto's foot-soldiers broke through further, which certainly shows that mounted men were scarce on both sides. The allied foot were armed with useful pikes, some of which had hooks which they used to pull the riders off their horses. Philip Augustus was thrown from his horse, with very few of his men near him, and narrowly escaped death. Gales de Montigny called for help at once, and signalled to the other knights with the royal standard. Pierre Tristan dismounted and offered the king his horse, so he was saved partly by the devotion of his followers and his stout armour, and partly by his own physical fitness, which enabled him to leap quickly into the saddle.[199]

Both sides suffered heavy losses. Etienne de Longchamp was killed in the royal division, wounded through the eye-slit in his helmet. The enemy used fine three-edged daggers, with which they could stab through the weak spots in the Frenchmen's armour. But the French counter-attack was successful. The few foot-soldiers who got through to the king were thrown back or killed. Otto's whole division had to fall back.[200]

Pierre Mauvoisin even reached the bridle of the emperor's horse, but he could not get Otto out of the close formation which hedged him in. Gérard la Truie tried to kill the emperor with a dagger, but the blade glanced off his coat of mail, and struck Otto's horse in the eye. The wounded beast sprang away and bolted, only to fall a little way off. Otto then mounted the horse of one of his faithful knights, but before he could get away there were some nasty moments. Guillaume des Barres rushed up behind him, caught up with him and seized him. But he could not get Otto out of the saddle, and was soon attacked by the emperor's bodyguard. Guillaume was thrown from his horse, but fought on bravely on foot, hemmed in by German knights. Just as he was about to collapse, Thomas de St Valery rushed to his help with his following of 50 knights from the French left wing.[201]

Meanwhile, Philip Augustus stayed back a little, with Gautier de Nemours, Barthélemy de Roye, and Guillaume de Garlande, who thought it wiser to keep the king well behind the front line.[202]

Under cover of the followers of four German lords, Bernard von Horstmar, Otto von Tecklenburg, Conrad von Dortmund and Gerard von Randerath, Otto managed to get off the battlefield. His followers fought bravely and in the end sacrificed themselves, all being taken prisoner. The French had meanwhile captured the waggon with the eagle and dragon, and had brought it to the king.[203]

Although resistance had collapsed in the centre, after the allied left wing had been shattered, there was still a man of great character fighting on the right wing, Renaud de Dammartin, using his own special tactics, founded on the superb efficiency and equipment of his mercenaries, fighting on foot. He used these foot as a solid base

---

[200] William the Breton, *Chronicon*, c. 192, p. 283.
[201] *Ibid.*, c. 192, pp. 283–5. *Philippis*, 1. XI, vv. 445–512, pp. 336–9. Mousket, vv. 22083–95, pp. 371–2.
[202] William the Breton, *Chronicon*, c. 192, pp. 204–5.
[203] *Ibid.*, c. 193, p. 285.

from which he made sorties with his heavy cavalry. After charging the enemy, he and his men withdrew to rest a little under the protection of the solid wall of the Brabançons' long pikes. The mercenaries stood in a circular or possibly semi-circular formation, only two ranks deep. An opening in the formation, doubtless in the rear, let the count and his men inside the living palisade.[204]

Beside Renaud was the earl of Salisbury with some mercenaries. Both attacked very late, probably at the moment when the battle in the centre was already turning to the French advantage. Hugues de Boves, who was supposed to be fighting in the allied right wing is never mentioned as being involved in the battle. As soon as he, with the duke of Brabant and the duke of Limbourg realized that Ferdinand was beaten, and that the centre under Otto was also going to collapse, they took to their heels with their men 'in groups, in hundreds, in fifties', says William the Breton, certainly with some exaggeration.[205]

The Flemish foot-soldiers who had only just arrived, and pass equally without mention in the battle, saw that all was lost. The men of Bruges, who were closest, turned at once and gave the signal for a general retreat on the left wing and in the allied centre.[206]

While the centre and left of the allied army were defeated, Renaud and the earl of Salisbury were involved in heavy fighting with knights of the French left wing, including the count of Dreux, Thomas de St Valery, the bishop of Beauvais, the count of Ponthieu, and the men of Ponthieu and Vimeu. The bishop of Beauvais saw the men of his brother, the count of Dreux, weakening under the pressure of the earl of Salisbury's men. Since as a cleric he was not permitted to shed blood, he rushed up to the earl with a bludgeon, and hit him such a tremendous blow on the helmet that he fell and was taken prisoner.[207] But Renaud went on pursuing his own tactics on the right wing. The French knights, with their short weapons, did not dare attack the foot circle with their long pikes. Their horses were much too vulnerable. In the end there were only about six knights fighting with Renaud. During one of his sorties the count's horse had been wounded by Pierre de la Tournelle, whose own charger had been killed, and who was fighting on foot. One of Renaud's knights took his lord's horse by the bridle and tried to lead it away. He was hewn down by the brothers Jean and Quesnes de Coudun, and the count's horse fell too, dragging his rider down with him so that he lay with his right shoulder under his horse's neck. Hugues and Gautier de Fontaine hastened up with Jean de Rouvrai, and while they were still arguing as to whom the noble prisoner really belonged, Jean de Nesle and his knights came up. Although he had done no great feats that day, and had not even taken part in the battle, de Nesle wanted the glory for this capture, and thanks to his followers he would have succeeded. But at that moment Guérin arrived, now free of

---

204 *Ibid.*, pp. 285–6. *Philippis*, 1. XI, vv. 251–2, p. 328, speaks of three ranks.
205 *Chronicon*, c. 196, p. 287. According to the Anonyme de Béthune, p. 769, Henry of Brabant fled at the moment of the breakthrough of the count of St Pol: 'Et quant ce vit Henris, li dus de Louvaign, qui encor n'ert asemblés, il se mist à la fuie et commencha la desconfiture'.
206 *Genealogiae comitum Flandriae*, c. 22, p. 333. This happens after the capture of Ferdinand.
207 William the Breton, *Philippis*, 1. XI, vv. 337–46, pp. 332–3; vv. 538–58, pp. 340–1.

responsibility for the rest of the battlefield, and Renaud surrendered to him, but let himself fall again as he saw that Arnulf of Oudenaarde was coming to help. But Arnulf and his men could not save him and were taken prisoner themselves. Renaud was led away to the king.[208]

In the end, a few hundred allied foot-soldiers were left on the scene of this great battle of knights, who had been fighting for the leadership of western Europe. Renaud's mercenaries, reduced to 400, or at the most 700, had been able to fight off all attacks with their pikes. After one early and unsuccessful attack against the wall of pikes, the knights never tried again. Now the king ordered Thomas de St Valery to finish off the mercenaries. He attacked them with his 50 knights and his own foot-soldiers, and managed to break their solid formation, probably after completely surrounding them with foot-soldiers.[209] This ended the battle of Bouvines. Philip Augustus gave the order not to prolong the pursuit further than a mile as night was falling, and because he was afraid that during the chase some of the important prisoners might manage to escape. He ordered the trumpeters to recall the divisions.[210]

No less than 131 knights had fallen into French hands, including 5 counts and 25 knights banneret.[211] We have little reliable data for the number of dead, but according to an inscription in the church of St Nicolas at Arras, 300 knights were captured or killed, which would bring the number of dead to 169.[212]

Conclusion

The battle of Bouvines provides excellent examples for the study of early thirteenth century tactics, and even for the tactics of the Middle Ages as a whole. There is something interesting in every phase of the engagement: a purely knightly battle between the French right wing and Ferdinand's knights, an example of an attack by knights with the support of foot-soldiers in the centre, and a similar example on the defensive with close co-operation between knights and foot under Renaud de Dammartin.

Although at first glance the battle does not seem to have had a very different result militarily from other battles of the day, its political effect was of the utmost importance. For the county of Flanders, it meant the destruction of centuries of effort by the counts; for nearly a century after it the kings of France held undisputed sway over the principality. Moreover king John's attempt to re-establish the lost Angevin kingdom was abruptly terminated.

---

[208] *Ibid.*, vv. 605–12, pp. 342–3; vv. 647–60, pp. 344–5; vv. 677–718, pp. 345–7. *Chronicon*, c. 196, pp. 287–9. *Genealogiae comitum Flandriae*, p. 333. Mousket, vv. 21815–28, p. 361; vv. 22125–45, pp. 372–3.

[209] *Genealogiae comitum Flandriae*, c. 22, p. 333. William the Breton, *Chronicon*, c. 197, pp. 289–90. *Philippis*, 1. XI, vv. 614–29, p. 343; Philip Augustus orders him to use 'ter mille clientes, hastis armatos in equis' against the mercenaries. The text is in opposition to the story of the *Chronicon* and the exaggerated number of light horse is worthless. Mousket, vv. 22127–9, pp. 372–3.

[210] William the Breton, *Chronicon*, c. 197, p. 290.

[211] *Genealogiae comitum Flandriae*, p. 333. *De pugna Boviniensi*, pp. 391–7. William the Breton, *Chronicon*, c. 198, p. 290.

[212] Delpech, I, p. 169. Lot, I, p. 233, thinks that it is the number of the prisoners.

Tactically, Bouvines is often spoken of as a typical example of a knightly battle, consisting of a series of single combats between individual knights, who, like the champions in the epics, cut the enemy to pieces by astounding deeds of personal valour. 'Brilliant although the battle of Bouvines was from the point of view of great deeds of opposing individuals, it provides little idea of the military skills of the age. On neither side is it possible to see any kind of tactical manoeuvre or any kind of central direction', says Ferdinand Lot.[213] 'An infinite number of combats took place, with which we need not concern ourselves, though they form a large part of William the Breton's tale of the battle. The whole encounter must have borne a great resemblance to a vast tourney – individual knights fought till they were tired, fell back a while to take breath, and then returned to the mêlée', says Oman, and elsewhere, 'How could individual knights like St Pol and Melun have cut their way through the Flemish front line?'[214]

The course of the battle will answer the question whether it was made up of single combats or was fought in tactical units. We are not concerned with a trial and ultimate condemnation of knightly tactics, but with condemning those who read their sources over-hastily. Taking William the Breton's *Chronicon* as a basis, we shall in passing also cast an eye at the poetical digressions in the epic *Philippis*. This summary can be very brief, as we have almost invariably followed the *Chronicon* as the most reliable source.

Individual feats of arms	*Fighting as units*
1. The prelude to the battle.	1. Attack of 150 light cavalry.
2. St Pol rescues one of his knights, fighting against a group.	2. Attack of the division from Champagne.
	3. Attack of St Pol and his men, the burgrave of Melun and his men, the duke of Burgundy and his men, the count of Beaumont and his men, Montmorency and his men.
	4. St Pol rests with his unit.
	5. The duke of Burgundy loses his horse: some of his knights keep the enemy off, others help him re-mount.
	6. Attack by Otto and his men. Counter-attack by the French knights. The French king in peril, but surrounded by some knights who fight off the enemy foot.
	7. The whole of Otto's company is driven
3. Pierre Mauvoisin and Gérard la Truie cannot get Otto away from his followers.	back.
4. Guillaume des Barres cannot kill Otto, 'his knights are densely grouped in front of him'. He is surrounded by the enemy.	

213 *L'art militaire*, I, p. 235.
214 *History of the Art of War*, I, pp. 483, 482, n. 1.

8. Thomas de St Valery with his men saves Guillaume des Barres.
9. Defence by Otto's bodyguard.
10. The tactics of Renaud de Dammartin.
11. Mass flight, 'in hundreds, in fifties', etc.
12. Finally Renaud is fighting alone with 6 knights.

5. The two Coudun brothers cut down one of Renaud's knights during a pursuit.

13. Arnulf of Oudenaarde dashes to the rescue with other knights.
14. Thomas de St Valery attacks the Brabançons with his men.
15. The pursuing units were recalled by trumpet-signal.

The *Philippis* has a different account of certain feats of arms: Michel de Harnes, who the chronicler says was overthrown horse and all in the first charge, was thrown in the preliminary skirmish in the version in verse, which says he avenged himself on his vanquisher.[215] This is the only addition of a single combat, and even then it is in the prelude, and is of course a poetic embroidery of the original story. Also, in the *Philippis* the final fighting is not against the foot but against Renaud de Dammartin, which would be more to the taste of knightly readers.

Next, we should consider closely such individual combat as we have found. Naturally the preliminaries were of the nature of individual fights, but even then it should be noticed that Eustace of Machelen was surrounded by several Frenchmen.[216]

Other examples lend little weight to the theory that the battle was just a series of duels. St Pol's knight and Guillaume des Barres, who were surrounded by the enemy, are men whose fellows could not follow them in the breakthrough and the return, or else who made so quick a breach that their followers never got through at all. The example of Pierre Mauvoisin, Gérard la Truie and the brothers Coudun is after all quite a usual thing in battle. Pierre Mauvoisin and Gérard la Truie failed in the face of a considerable number of the enemy. The Couduns were chasing two knights who were fleeing from the battlefield.

Thus we can safely conclude that the duels between individual knights are purely incidental as must inevitably happen in a battle of limited forces, and were of not great importance. The essence of knightly battle is found in fighting between tactical units. There is a striking example in the *Philippis*: the poet would really like to make the king fight the emperor, but cannot stretch the facts too far, the formations were dense and closed and there was no opportunity for the two champions to fight a duel.[217]

In contrast to the quotations from Lot and Oman given above, the description of the battle of Bouvines gives the opportunity of collecting a considerable list of data

---

[215] L. XI, vv. 105–9, p. 322; vv. 144–8, pp. 323–4.
[216] William the Breton, *Chronicon*, c. 187, p. 278.
[217] L. XI, vv. 376–83, p. 334.

on fighting technique, manoeuvres of small units in battle, the position of knights in their companies, and so on.

In the battlefield, despite the broadening of the front by bishop Guérin, they managed to keep their formations well closed with the units in close contact with each other: 'They stood in an unbroken line: their formations were closely packed by the commanders so that when the trumpets sounded they could dash out quickly to the attack.'[218]

Bishop Guérin gives a good example of the arrangement of the knights in their units – the bravest are put in the front rank, the rest follow behind. The first attack, with light cavalry, was a preparation for the attack by the knights, not aiming at any great slaughter, but so that the latter might find the enemy a bit moved and disturbed. When the duke of Burgundy was thrown to the ground, 'The Burgundian ranks closed round him and surrounded him'. During the close fighting units like St Pol's were able to withdraw from the fighting and rest a little in order to return and fight again. When the Flemish knights gave up, they broke up their fighting unit, 'dum se laxant acies . . .' But Otto was saved by his bodyguard, and by a considerable body of Saxons who gave him the chance to get away in safety.[219]

When Guillaume des Barres was saved out of the ring of enemies who had surrounded him 'the band which surrounded him opened'.[220] When the king, according to the *Philippis*, sent three thousand light cavalry against the mighty circular formation of Renaud de Dammartin's mercenaries:

> To put them into disorder and make them quit their position
> And open their interlaced crown.[221]

Can it be said after all this that William the Breton presents the battle as a series of single combats? Now for another problem – the general tactics on the battlefield.

Tactics and Leadership in the Battle of Bouvines

'Neither tactics nor leadership can be observed on either side', says Lot, even more definitely than Oman, who speaks of 'little manoeuvring on either side when the fight had once begun'.[222] This point also is worth considering.

It has been shown that for a long time Philip Augustus did not believe in the offensive intention of the enemy's approach and that in the end he was very late in taking the decision to give battle. This was the reason why the French foot were not in position by the time the French right wing had already begun to fight.

On this point too the sources are explicit. We know, of course, that the allies were quickly after their enemy, and the Anonymous of Béthune says that when they

---

218 *Ibid.*, vv. 82–4, p. 320.
219 *Chronicon*, c. 186, pp. 276–7; c. 188, p. 279; c. 189, pp. 280–1. *Philippis*, 1. XI, v. 176, p. 325; v. 234, p. 327; vv. 488–9, p. 338.
220 *Ibid.*, vv. 514–15, p. 339.
221 *Ibid.*, vv. 615–16, p. 343.
222 Lot, I, p. 235. Oman, I, p. 489.

advanced in battle array towards the enemy, they were not so well-ordered as the French.[223]

At this moment neither army was fully deployed: the French had of necessity to wait and see how broad the enemy front was going to be, for in the space between Cysoing in the south and Gruson in the north, a plain about two miles wide, they were in danger of flank and rear attacks and they had behind them the marshy banks of the Marcq, and the only bridge over it was at Bouvines. So Guérin matched the deployment of the allies with an equally broad disposition of the French cavalry. This made it impossible to keep a reserve, and once deploying of the troops had begun on this very broad front the allies had to follow the example of the French. Since the troops of Otto and Ferdinand came up in marching columns and no doubt needed a considerable time to take up their positions, it is worth noticing that bishop Guérin should have dared to begin the battle before all the French troops were in position, since he almost certainly could not know whether all the allied formations had arrived. The bishop took the initiative quite intentionally, hoping to make use of the fact that Otto's troops were not all there. As he had spread the French right wing out as far as possible so as not to be surprised from the rear or on the flank, he was able to start fighting and exploit the somewhat more powerful position of his own troops.

He made preparations for the general attack by using his light cavalry. Then he let the other formations of knights go into the attack in succession. There is also explicit proof that Ferdinand's troops were in looser formation and showed less discipline in their battle order, in the fact that the count of St Pol and the burgrave of Melun were able to breach the Flemish ranks in their first charge.

Meanwhile, Guérin let the centre and the left wing play a defensive part, since the French levies had not yet arrived. He therefore left the initiative in that quarter to the enemy. By the time the latter attacked, the French levies had come up and kept the allies in check. This can hardly be called 'manoeuvres', since the front was so spread out that neither side had a reserve. How could there be one on a two mile front with about 1,500 horsemen and about 5,000 men on both sides?

Oman starts here from false premises, from which he naturally reaches false conclusions. He has accepted exaggerated figures and thinks there were enough troops to make a reserve: 'It is curious indeed to notice that neither side fought with any real reserve whatever, though the numbers in the field were so great that it would have been easy to provide one. Otto should have told off some of his solid Flemish infantry for the purpose, properly placed, that would have enabled the knights to rally.'[224]

This shows how a wrong notion of the number involved leads to a false tactical judgment. We might add that Otto had the waggon with the imperial insignia, where he must certainly have left foot to make possible the regrouping of the front-line troops.

Actually there are manoeuvres perceptible in the battle. Thomas de St Valery

---

[223] *Op. cit.*, p. 768.
[224] Oman, I, pp. 473–4, 490.

started in the French centre and fought with the left wing thereafter, which shows that he had the chance to move about from one to the other through a lack of co-ordination in the allied camp. This leaves the final problem, which at the same time makes quite clear the reasons for the French victory.

The Causes of the Allied Defeat

It seems that the chief cause of the defeat of the allied army of Otto and Ferdinand was the hasty march to the battlefield. Their advance is described by the sources as a movement which took place without proper organization. Because the troops were tired they showed less discipline on the battlefield, which is confirmed by the chronicles. Finally it is clear that certain formations never took part in the battle at all. I have quoted the contingents from Brabant and Limbourg and the troops of Hugues de Boves, and the example of the men from Bruges. To them may be added the men of Ghent since it is stated that Renaud de Dammartin sent a message to Otto to go on fighting with the men from Ghent.[225] Is this not an indication that these too had taken little part in the fighting? Flemish foot are never mentioned in the battle by the most reliable source. We can only prove for certain that the mercenaries of Otto and Renaud fought as foot-soldiers. In the *Histoire de Guillaume le Maréchal* we find the echo of the over-hasty approach of the allies and its unfortunate result. Otto and Ferdinand are said to have had only a quarter of the forces the French had and it is indeed probable that the numerical superiority of the allies was not effective in the actual battle simply because their whole army did not take part.[226] It is certain that the numerical superiority of the allies in battle was very small in the end, if indeed there was any.

William the Breton, chaplain to the king, Philippe Mousket and the Anonymous of Béthune, give us in their chronicles an excellent tactical explanation for the allied defeat and for the victory of the French king.

THE BATTLE OF WORRINGEN, 5 JUNE 1288

General Outline

The battle of Worringen on the Rhine, north of Cologne, settled an armed dispute that had broken out early in 1283. Duchess Irmgard of Limbourg had died childless. Her lands stretched eastwards of the Meuse round the little town of Limbourg as far as Eupen and its environs. It was the question of the succession that started off a five years war. The territorial expansion which would follow the acquisition of Limbourg could change the whole balance of political power between the Meuse and the Rhine.

For Reinald of Guelders it was a splendid step towards the extension of his domain southwards. For duke John I of Brabant it would be the decisive factor in controlling the whole of the trade route between Bruges and Cologne, from Brabant to the Rhine. But this would make Brabant so powerful that it would constitute a serious threat to

---

225 William the Breton, *Chronicon*, c. 199, p. 291.
226 II, vv. 14743–8, p. 167; vv. 14787–800, pp. 168–9.

the archbishop of Cologne who till then, had been dominant in that part of the Rhineland. Reinald, as consort of Irmgard, held a life tenure of the inheritance from king Rudolf of Habsburg. But John bought the rights from the nearest relative of the late duchess, count Adolf of Berg, who was himself too weak to press his claim by force of arms.

There was trouble at once, for the count of Guelders was checked in his southward aspirations by the action of John of Brabant, while the latter had to do something in order not to be cut off from his connection with the Rhineland. The possibility of an expansion of Brabant forced the archbishop of Cologne, Siegfried of Westerburg, to come in to the quarrel, and to ally himself with Reinald. But the count of Guelders sold his rights to Limbourg in 1288 to the count of Luxembourg, who had also some claim. Walram of Valkenburg also joined Reinald. In 1286, he obtained the support of his father-in-law the count of Flanders Guy of Dampierre, whose son, John of Flanders, was the prince-bishop of Liège.

John I of Brabant was threatened on every side. He managed to avoid the strategic encirclement of his domain by adroit political manoeuvring. Against Reinald of Guelders he got the support of the counts of Cleves and Jülich and of Floris V of Holland, who in his turn could make difficulties for Guy of Dampierre. He made an alliance with the citizens of Cologne against their archbishop, and by wily concessions brought the bishop of Liège into his own camp.

The conflict was unresolved until 1288. When the citizens of Cologne rose against their archbishop, John I advanced to the Rhine, where he besieged the town of Worringen at the request of the rebels, who wanted to destroy the 'robber's castle' because ships passing were being forced to pay a crippling toll. The duke's army was reinforced by allies from the Rhineland. At that moment the Brabançons were deep in enemy territory, and archbishop Siegfried resolved to make use of this strategically promising situation, especially as John had laid siege to a castle, which was a tactical disadvantage. The prelate is said to have called on his allies in these words: 'A whale has got washed up on our land, and is already so close to the wall that we only need throw out a net to catch him. It will enrich the whole land, but it is a great fat creature which I cannot handle alone. Every man must hurry to stop our prey escaping'.[227]

Siegfried of Westerburg massed his army and that of his allies behind the Erft near Neuss. Then he took up a position between Worringen and the city of Cologne to cut off supplies to the duke's army and to make it raise the siege of the castle. On 4 June, he was at Brauweiler waiting for the arrival of the civic levies from Bonn, Andernach, and elsewhere. In a council of war, pressure by the count of Luxembourg led to a decision to attack on the following day. The archbishop objected to this, because this Saturday was especially dedicated to the Blessed Virgin.[228] After saying Mass on the morning of 5 June, he excommunicated the duke of Brabant and had the army drawn up in battle array. The Allies advanced in three great corps past Auweiler and Fuehlingen to the Rhine. First came the archbishop with his knights,

---

[227] Jan van Heelu, *Rijmkronijk*, vv. 4201–11, p. 159.
[228] *Ibid.*, vv. 4266–93, p. 161.

followed by the troops of the count of Luxembourg and the count of Guelders's contingent. Their formations were made up of noblemen from both principalities, reinforced with light cavalry. The whole army was strengthened with foot from the principality of Cologne and the county of Guelders.[229]

Before daybreak, John had the news from his spies and scouts. He ordered the trumpets to sound the call to arms at once. After Mass he moved off from the castle and crossed the Pletsch with his troops to an open plain, where knights could fight. Before he left, the trumpeters sounded the call to arms again.[230]

The duke took up a position in the centre of the Brabançon division. His armour was all decorated with his arms, 'sable, a lion or'. Unlike many princes of his day, who gave their insignia to one of their knights so as to escape recognition in battle, the duke wore his arms himself. Two horses were in readiness, so that he had a chance to mount a spare one during the battle.[231] His brother Godfrey was with him, and his two nephews de St Pol, with about ten French knights.[232] As there were so few of them, the duke had them accompanied by Rase of Gaver, lord of Liedekerke and Breda, with a company, and by the company of John Berthout, lord of Berlaar, including the knights banneret John of Schorisse and Wouter of Antoing and their followers. In the centre was the bailiff of Jodoigne with his followers and his banner.[233] As well as these two companies, the great Brabant division included the following:

3. The company of Wouter Berthout, lord of Malines, with his uncle Gillis Berthout and two knights banneret, each with their own banners, Geraard of Rotselaar and Arnoud of Walhain.[234]

4. Count Godfrey of Vianen with the banner of Asse.[235]

5. Arnoud of Diest with his son Geraard and his banner, which eventually replaced the standard of Brabant.[236]

6. The company of Geraard of Wezemaal.[237]

7. Arnoud of Wezemaal, marshal of Brabant, with his men.[238]

8. The provost of Nivelles had in his troop the banner of Gaasbeek which was carried by William Pipenpoi from Brussels.[239]

9. Thierry of Walcourt with his company.[240]

---

229 *Ibid.*, vv. 4329–46, 4350–4, 4366–71, pp. 163–5.
230 *Ibid.*, vv. 4381–4, p. 165; vv. 4439–57, p. 167.
231 *Ibid.*, vv. 4460–3, pp. 167–8; vv. 4485–6, p. 168; vv. 4497–4502, p. 169.
232 *Ibid.*, vv. 4516–17, p. 170. *Les grandes chroniques de France*, ed. J. Viard, SHF, Paris, 1933, VIII, p. 134: gives 11 companions for St. Pol. Cf. *Istore et Croniques*, I, pp. 189–90. Villani, *Historie Fiorentine*, pp. 330–1, speaks of a big retinue.
233 Heelu, vv. 4510–30, pp. 169–70, vv. 7620–9, p. 281, vv. 7642–7, p. 281.
234 See for these units: Heelu, vv. 4538–66, pp. 171–2, and for Berthout: vv. 7668–93, pp. 282–7.
235 *Ibid.*, vv. 7850–64, pp. 288–9.
236 *Ibid.*, vv. 7881–7904, pp. 289–90.
237 *Ibid.*, vv. 7982–7, p. 293.
238 *Ibid.*, vv. 8059–64, p. 295.
239 *Ibid.*, vv. 8077–83, 8120, pp. 296–7.
240 *Ibid.*, v. 8153, p. 298.

10. Although the lord of Adegem was not there, a large company had been entrusted to Steven of Itter, who was fighting under this banner.[241]
11. A great company under Renier of Wegeseten.[242]
12. The men of John, lord of Kuik, with two knights banneret, John of Arkel and John of Heusden.[243]
13. A company from Limbourg, comprising the Witthems, and the Mulrepas.[244]

The 'amman' of Brussels, the 'schout' of Antwerp and the 'mayor' of Tirlemont were also there, each with a banner and soldiers from his district.[245] They were probably included in the companies already mentioned. The companies of Witthems and Mulrepas had two banners, and according to Jan van Heelu included more than a hundred cavalrymen equipped with helmets, nine lords among them.[246]

The second division of duke John I's army consisted of the men of count Arnulf of Looz and count Walram of Jülich, with Frederick of Reifferscheid, Henry of Wildenburg, Gerard of Jülich, John Schevard of Rode, Gerlach of Dollendorf, Herman of Thomberg, John of Bedbur, the lord of Greifenstein, the count of Virneburg and the count of Weilnau.[247]

The third division was made up of the cavalry and foot-soldiers of the count of Berg, and the communal army from Cologne, who brought their own standard with them. There were four counts as leaders, Everhard of La Mark, Simon of Tecklenburg, Otto of Waldeck, and Gottfried of Ziegenhain. Henry of Windeck, brother of the count of Berg, was also there. The third division was stationed somewhat behind the others at first, close to the castle and along the banks of the Rhine.[248]

John dubbed about thirty noble squires knights before the battle. A few brothers of the Teutonic Order tried to bring about an agreement but met with no success.[249] Then the duke spoke to his Brabançons. He held up the example of their ancestors to them, praising their courage, and at the same time giving them various pieces of advice. He said he was going to fight in the foremost line himself, because he was better mounted than his subjects. Rich and poor, they were to stick to him with such courage and determination that nobody could attack him in the back or the flank. He would look after his own safety in front. If they saw him flee or surrender, they were to cut him down themselves.[250] He gave the standard of the duchy to Raas of Grez, who was to have two light cavalrymen as a guard. The duke himself had a body guard, Walter of Warfusee, lord of Momal, and Frank, bastard of Wezemaal. But no one was to hold the bridle of his horse, nor ride in front of him.[251]

241 *Ibid.*, vv. 8175–7, p. 299; vv. 8160–5, pp. 298–9.
242 *Ibid.*, vv. 8189–92, p. 299.
243 *Ibid.*, vv. 8229–33, p. 301.
244 *Ibid.*, vv. 7201–26, pp. 226–7.
245 *Ibid.*, vv. 4554–9, p. 171.
246 *Ibid.*, vv. 7201–26, especially 7215–26, pp. 266–7.
247 *Ibid.*, vv. 4570–85, pp. 172–3.
248 *Ibid.*, vv. 4594–4611, pp. 173–4.
249 *Ibid.*, vv. 4684–92, p. 177.
250 *Ibid.*, vv. 4716–22, p. 178.
251 *Ibid.*, vv. 4740–63, pp. 178–9.

Then he took up his position on a hill behind a marsh, waiting impatiently for the appearance of the enemy, who at that moment were out of sight, probably in the village of Fuehlingen. In front of the Brabant army was the Cologne–Worringen road. The enemy approached through a low-lying piece of flat land by the Rhine, the archbishop advancing against the third contingent of John's army, which was led by the count of Berg.[252] The Cologne–Worringen and Merkenich–Worringen roads made an angle in the battlefield. Both roads were edged with ditches. The battle took place in an angle formed between these two roads. At first the right wing of the duke's division did not seem to come as far as the Worringen–Cologne road, for they were easily outflanked by the troops from Guelders. But after the second body of knights had come up, the whole space between the two roads was filled with fighting men.

The Numbers Involved in the Battle

Before giving an account of the battle it will be best to investigate the numbers engaged, which present the most puzzling feature of the combat. There is nothing to tell us about the strength of the armies of Brabant, and before that year, 1288, we know just as little about their enemies.

According to Heelu, John I began his decisive campaign with '1,500 helmets', i.e. 1,500 knights, squires, and light cavalry or *sergeants*. In previous campaigns he had once had more than 1,000 cavalry at his disposal, on another occasion 1,200, and once a bit less than 2,000.[253] Each time the army was entirely made up of cavalry. Heelu says emphatically that for the Worringen campaign this means only men from Brabant, except for about 40 men, who included the followers of the St Pol brothers. However it has already been seen that the Limbourgers, Witthems and Mulrepas were there with about 100 horsemen. Did the chronicler not include them? The enemy would seem to have had 1,200 more horsemen than the whole of John's army, including the allies.[254] We do not accept the writer's assertion, because such numerical superiority would be apparent from the course of the battle itself. Can the 1,500 Brabant cavalrymen be accepted? It is possible that duke John may have collected as many, but it cannot be considered certain.

It has already been shown that Gilbert of Mons, chancellor of the count of Hainault, whose office made him well acquainted with the number of knights in Hainault, also gives reliable figures for Flanders and Brabant. There were 1,000 knights available for a great army in Flanders at the time, 700 knights in Hainault and as many in Brabant. We know that the number of knights dropped in the thirteenth century, but the squires who did not become knights went on serving in the army, so that the total number of mounted noblemen probably stayed at the same level as at the end of the twelfth century. In the second half of the thirteenth century the numerical strength of the armies was often given as the number of mounted men wearing metal armour. In Heelu's version horsemen are not necessarily noblemen any more, because he

---

252 *Ibid.*, vv. 4764–87, pp. 179–80.
253 *Ibid.*, v. 2139, p. 83: 1200; vv. 3674–5, p. 136: 1000; vv. 3790–1, p. 140, less than 2,000.
254 *Ibid.*, vv. 4312–13, p. 162. Elsewhere he speaks of 1,100 more horsemen in the enemy army: v. 5253, p. 196.

indicates them as the number of fighting men with helmets; he also talks about light cavalry or *sergeants*.

There were no civic levies from Brabant at the battle of Worringen.[225] It is therefore possible that the duke raised an army of 1,500 horsemen, thanks to the cities' financial support. But this seems rather doubtful since one of his successors, John III, in 1338 and 1339 had great difficulty in raising the 1,200 horsemen whom he had promised to king Edward III of England at the beginning of the Hundred Years' War. Indeed John III had to enlist mercenaries in 1338 and 1339 in order to have 1,289 of them on that occasion. But by then he had Limbourg as well, and many nobles who were on the enemy side in 1288 served with him then.[256]

There are some interesting facts about some of John I's allies in 1288 in an undated fragment that appears to come from 1297. In that year Guy of Dampierre had enlisted many of these lords as mercenaries with a certain number of their fighting men. The Rhineland nobles had then promised, or had already been paid for producing the following numbers:

The count of Jülich	100 heavy cavalry
The count of La Mark	120 heavy cavalry
The count of Dollendorf	10 heavy cavalry
The count of Virneburg	20 heavy cavalry
The count of Looz	100 heavy cavalry

This gives a total of 350 heavy cavalry for these lords.[257] Perhaps we can assume a total of 700 cavalry for the allies of John I in 1288, since they were so near home. With 1,300 or perhaps 1,500 horsemen from Brabant we get a figure of 2,000 to 2,200 cavalry for the duke's whole army.

His enemies had perhaps a slight superiority in numbers since the archbishop of Cologne was as powerful as the duke of Brabant or very nearly so. In the twelfth century he was certainly more powerful. Now he had good allies. The lord of Valkenburg had to send 100 heavy cavalry to Guy of Dampierre's army in 1297. The counts of Guelders and Luxembourg each had a good little army so that it is quite possible that these allies were rather stronger than John's army. Their number can perhaps be put at 2,200 to 2,400 cavalry. It is also possible that it was about the same as that of John's army.

These were great armies for their time, but we must remember that there were two coalitions at war. The fighting was to go on for a long time, which also goes to show

255 Cf. A. Wauters, *Le duc Jean Ier*, pp. 163, 332.
256 A. Wauters, 'La formation d'une armée brabançonne du temps du duc Jean III, de 1338 à 1339', *BCRH*, 5e série, 1891, I, pp. 192–205. Our calculation gives 989 cavalry. We add 300 horsemen which were promised by the count of Looz: L. Galesloot, ed., *Le livre des feudataires de Jean III, duc de Brabant*, CRH in 8°, Brussels, 1865, p. 259, n. 3. Probably they are the 1,200 horsemen which the duke had promised to send to Edward III: Jean le Bel, I, p. 159, but on p. 125 he says 1,000 heavy cavalry.
257 Verbruggen, *Het leger en de vloot*, pp. 53–4.
258 For the numbers: Wauters, *Jean Ier*, pp. 162–3. Villani, pp. 330–1 gives 1,500 horsemen for John I and 1,300 for his enemies.

that efficient fighting-machines were facing each other. It must also be remembered that a great deal of cavalry consisted of lightly armed horsemen who were not knights.

We have no reliable information for the foot. They probably amounted to 2,000 or perhaps 3,000 on each side.[258]

The Battle

When Siegfried of Westerburg's knights came into sight of the Brabant army, they were moving towards the Rhine; suddenly they turned left away from the river, between the Worringen–Merkenich road and the Rhine. Everything goes to show that the archbishop planned to attack the troops of the count of Berg who immediately sent a knight to John I to ask him to send help at once.[259]

The count of Virneburg had the post of 'overseer of the battle' or tactical commander of the duke's army. He advised the duke to stay where he was and to let the enemy advance, so that he could attack them just at the moment when they were engaged in crossing the road and the ditches, for in getting past these obstacles the archbishop's troops would naturally break rank and fall into confusion. If the duke were to attack at exactly the right moment with his well-ordered and well trained troops, he would derive a great advantage. But John decided he must hurry to the help of his ally, apparently setting no great store by the possibility of exploiting his advantageous position protected by a marsh, roads, and ditches. He wanted to achieve victory by force of armour, helmet and sword. He crossed the Cologne–Worringen road and advanced against the enemy who were coming up on a front stretching 'as far as the eye could see'.[260]

As soon as the archbishop saw that the Brabançons were advancing he left the actual bank of the Rhine and crossed the Merkenich–Worringen road and the ditches towards the duke. This moved the whole battle to convenient flat ground between the roads, where neither ditches nor streams hindered the troops. But as soon as the archbishop turned left with his troops, the lords of Limbourg and Luxembourg copied him so that these two and their troops were right in the middle of the field between the two roads.

The third body, led by the count of Guelders, came up behind to begin with, but soon after the others turned, they caught them up. So the three bodies of troops advanced together and practically formed a single mass which 'seemed so great and so mighty that they could gobble up anything that got in their way'.[261]

The armies moved slowly towards each other, riding as slowly as 'men who have a bride before them in the saddle'.[262] When the Brabançons noticed that the enemy were not advancing in such good order as before, the bastard of Wezemaal shouted joyfully: 'My lords, I can see full well that they know nothing about fighting. Let us attack, they are as good as beaten for their ranks have broken already.' Raas of Gaver

259 Heelu, vv. 4787–4805, p. 180.
260 *Ibid.*, vv. 4806–42, pp. 181–2.
261 *Ibid.*, vv. 4845–92, pp. 182–4.
262 *Ibid.*, vv. 4898–4903, p. 184.

was less optimistic: 'I can see that their line is both broad and long. They can surround us before we know it, let us thin out our ranks and lengthen our front before we meet them'.

Jan van Heelu comments that this is just how knights behave in the tournament. There they advance 'thin and wide' but this is no good in battle.[263] Raas of Gaver gave bad advice on this occasion, which was prompted by his fear of being surrounded. Liebrecht, lord of Dormaal, was indignant and shouted out:

> Thick and tight! Thick and tight!
> Let every man press up stoutly to his
> neighbour as close as he can.
> So we shall certainly win
> glory today!

Then rich and poor shouted together:

> Stick together, thick, thick!

And a *sergeant* gave the council to attack and kill the nobles first of all.

> As each man comes to any noble, let him
> not turn aside until he has slain him.
> For, were their army so great,
> that it stretched from here to Cologne,
> they will lose the battle if their nobles are killed.'[264]

Possibly some of the noblemen in the archbishop's army were disturbed by the disorderly marching of their troops. Jan van Heelu makes Herman of Haddemale say to the count of Luxembourg: 'I wish our troops were properly ordered in our units. Then we should be able to fight so as to do ourselves credit. For even if we finish off the Brabançons – the whole of the first division – as indeed we expect to do – there are still two more divisions ready anyway, and we have no defence against this, because our three divisions make up one great formation'. Lord Berroot of Halloy also complained about this negligence: 'How did we come to ride so that our divisions are disordered!'[265]

Skirmishing began at once. Franbach of Bingelen and Arnold of Yssche and the lay-brother Arnold, brother of the lord of Heusden, took part in it for the Brabant side. Members of the great family of Schavedries moved up in good order in a company including at least 110 horsemen, hoping to attack their hereditary enemies, the family of the Witthems and the Mulrepas, with whom they had a feud. But the Schavedries company could not pick out their enemy, so instead they attacked the troops of Godfrey of Brabant with tremendous force. The last distance between the armies was covered in a flash. Many of the enemy were shouting 'At the Duke! At the Duke!' and drove the Brabant troops back by the impetus of their charge. There

263 *Ibid.*, vv. 4906–30, pp. 184–5.
264 *Ibid.*, vv. 4938–61, pp. 185–6; quotations vv. 4947–51, 4854–61.
265 *Ibid.*, vv. 4987–5016, pp. 187–8.

were more of them than of John's knights, although some of them were slower in advancing, and the foot were still further behind.[266]

The press of hand-to-hand fighting was tremendous. The Brabant formations seem to have been particularly tightly packed, with knights and squires jammed knee to knee. The company of the knights banneret Kuik, Arkel, and Heusden was hard pressed and in danger. According to Heelu they were saved by other Brabant men dashing quickly to the rescue. The Brabant division fought with courage and skill, the wounded and exhausted falling back out of formation for a short time to let others move up from the rear. As soon as these riders had recovered a little from the breath-taking charge, they re-grouped themselves and returned to the battle.[267]

But the troops of the archbishop, the count of Luxembourg and Reinald of Guelders, made a single front, broader than that of the Brabant army, and they outflanked duke John's division, but luckily for the Brabançons, this did not cause much harm. Heelu ascribes this to the fact that the count of Guelders' outflanking troops got straight into the Brabant camp, plundered it ruthlessly, and then carried off the splendid loot to safety without returning to the battlefield. It seems that the second division attacked at this moment. Probably the count of Virneburg sent the troops of the counts of Looz and Jülich there, hoping to lengthen the Brabant front and so help them. The right wing of John's army at that moment probably stretched as far as the Cologne–Worringen road. The arrival of this second formation meant that only a few of Guelders' men were able to fall on the Brabant camp, robbing stores and tents. The loot was taken away under the command of Reinier de Ezel, but the Brabançons were so busy fighting, and kept their formation so well, that they took no notice of what was going on behind them.[268] They had been ordered not to break up their tactical units and to take no prisoners before the end of the battle, and they kept strictly to their instructions. The arrival of the second corps of their army restored the situation very quickly, and the battle became even more intense.

It was a bloody battle and a long one. The count of Luxembourg wanted to attack the duke of Brabant personally, but the press was so great that he could not get anywhere near him. Gerard of Wezemaal distinguished himself on the Brabant side. With William Pipenpoi and Gilles of Buzegem he penetrated the ranks of the family of the Oessenincs from the Ardennes, but his banner and his men could not get through after him. His horse was killed, and he only got back to the main body of Brabançons with the utmost difficulty.[269] The count of Luxembourg was driven back by Godfrey of Brabant, but then he took off his helmet to look round the battlefield, hoping to see his enemy the duke of Brabant. He went in the right direction, but there was no actual fighting between them, both being hustled away from each other in the press. Duke John was wounded in the arm by Walter of Wez, an enemy horseman who was later taken prisoner.[270] The count of Luxembourg's formation suffered heavily, which spurred him on to make a tremendous charge. One of his horsemen

266 *Ibid.*, v. 5088 ff, p. 191 ff.
267 *Ibid.*, vv. 5224–85, pp. 195–7.
268 *Ibid.*, vv. 5303–90, pp. 198–201.

269 *Ibid.*, vv. 7982–8039, pp. 293–5, and pp. 202–3.
270 *Ibid.*, pp. 203–8.

killed duke John's horse, and the horse of the standard-bearer of Brabant, Raas of Grez, went down at almost the same instant.

As the standard fell, the trumpeters of Brabant, who had been encouraging their side with trumpet calls throughout the attack, suddenly fell silent, fearing the worst. But one of the horsemen to whom the banner had been entrusted, Claas of Ouden, managed to raise the standard again, and then his stouthearted comrade, Walter of Capellen, took over. The agonizing moment was quickly over for Brabant, and the trumpets rang out again.[271]

Duke John now worked his way out of the struggling mass and managed to get on foot to the road, where Arnold van der Hofstat gave him his horse. The duke collected a group of 20 horsemen and returned to the fray. He made a determined charge straight across the field to the banner of Luxembourg and cut it down. Count Henry himself rushed up, but Meerbeke, one of duke John of Brabant's servants, wounded his horse. The count tried to wrest the duke out of his saddle, and to throw him to the ground. He stood up in his stirrups, but this movement left him partly unprotected by his armour. The knight Wouter van den Bisdomme attacked count Henry at this instant, and he fell dying from his horse.[272]

Meanwhile, the archbishop of Cologne had attacked the troops of the lord of Aarschot and the St Pol brothers, on the left wing of the Brabant army. A brave knight, Adolf of Nassau, who later became king of the Romans, bore his standard. The archbishop himself was putting up a very creditable fight in the front rank of his knights. This formation however was broken up after a long and tough battle,[273] when the Brabant troops under Godfrey had almost managed to break through. At about 3 o'clock the knights and peasants of the count of Berg came on to the scene with the civic levy from Cologne. Berg's peasants were wearing jackets and skullcaps and some of them had iron plates as protective armour. Most of them were armed with spiked clubs. The men of Cologne were better equipped: some of them had coats of mail, some hauberks and swords.

The peasants advanced shouting their war-cry: 'Hya, Berge romerike!' but at first they were not altogether clear who were friends or foe. When they reached the Worringen–Merkenich road they could still not tell their allies from their enemies. Then a Brabant horseman, called Battele, led them round behind the troops of the archbishop of Cologne.[274] Now the flank became the decisive sector. As soon as the archbishop saw these rough peasants appearing behind his troops, he would have given himself up at once to Godfrey of Brabant rather than fall into the hands of his own citizens. But the ground between them was so heaped with dead horses that the archbishop could not carry out his intention, and had to give himself up to his neighbour, Adolf of Berg, who immediately had him taken off to his castle at Monheim. However, he promised not to let the archbishop go without permission of the duke of Brabant.[275]

The archbishop's great standard was still flying over the battlefield, resplendent

[271] *Ibid.*, vv. 5668–5740, pp. 211–14.
[272] *Ibid.*, vv. 5745–5871, pp. 214–18.
[273] *Ibid.*, pp. 221–5.
[274] *Ibid.*, pp. 226–35.
[275] *Ibid.*, pp. 226–7.

on a tall staff above the turreted waggon, a wooden castle defended by his troops. This waggon had been brought up by several horses and then made fast with great posts in the ground. No one had managed to get the standard, nor pull it down. But the defenders were eventually exhausted, and finally resistance collapsed. Ordinary foot-soldiers without armour, who usually took no part in the battle, stormed this wooden castle with axes and swords, hoping to demolish this rallying point for the right wing. They were completely successful, while the peasants of Berg slew knights and horses without mercy. Enemies though they were, even Jan van Heelu thought it 'a terrible thing' that such brave knights should be stabbed in the back by low-born peasants.[276]

At the other end of the battlefield the count of Guelders was putting up a long and weary fight against the right wing, where duke John's allies were in action. But the ranks of Brabant's enemies were seriously thinned. At last the Brabançons made a fierce attack and brought down Reinald's standard so that resistance crumpled there too. The count of Guelders was taken prisoner, but the count of Looz got one of his pages to take off Reinald's coat of arms to prevent him being recognised and let him escape. The burgrave of Montenaken was ordered to lead him away from the field. Four Brabant knights took him prisoner again without realizing whom they had caught.[277] The lord of Valkenburg was fighting stoutly in the centre still. When he saw that the enemy pressure was getting too strong he began to fight as though in a tournament of the time. After fighting for some time in one spot, he withdrew a little to attack his foes in another, hoping to find weaker resistance.[278] He was able to go on fighting on this plan as long as the Brabant companies kept their formation tightly packed in their great division and did not come after him lest they broke their battle order. For that reason the men of Brabant still did not pursue their enemies.[279] When his banner fell, the lord of Valkenburg unfurled a new banner on a little hill opposite the Brabançons, and rallied some of the scattered knights.

Noblemen from Guelders who had lost their rallying point but who had no wish to leave the battlefield for fear of dishonour, gathered round him. As soon as he had a reasonable number, the lord of Valkenburg returned to the battle. But he kept clear of the Brabant formation and charged the troops of the count of Jülich, shouting the war-cry 'Montjoie, Montjoie!' He would not use his usual war-cry of 'Valkenburg' because he held the place in fee from the duke of Brabant. Both the count of Jülich and the lord of Valkenburg were wounded during the attack, but the latter was able to get away thanks to the lucky arrival of two of his kinsmen, the count of Looz and lord Arnold of Stein, and of friends who were fighting as followers of the count of Jülich. Men of the Schavedries family had been the first to go into action, and they were the last to break it off. They were overcome in the end by their old enemies the Mulrepas, leaving many dead.[280]

The battle was decisively won by the duke of Brabant's side, but his army was exhausted and they left it to their allies to pursue the fleeing enemy. It had been a

276 *Ibid.*, pp. 228–9, 236.
277 *Ibid.*, pp. 244–6.
278 *Ibid.*, vv. 6693–9, p. 247.

279 *Ibid.*, vv. 6744–55, p. 249.
280 *Ibid.*, pp. 249–53, 264–7.

long battle, from about 9 a.m. to 5 p.m. The duke stayed a while on the battlefield to satisfy himself that the enemy were not going to return again. At one moment it seemed probable: a large formation advanced with banners flying, and the men of Brabant did what they could to get their depleted ranks into order. Then they realized to their delight that it was their allies coming back from the pursuit bringing hordes of prisoners.[281]

The victorious army made for the camp which had been plundered ruthlessly. They had lost all the tents and wagons, and the duke had to rest in a mean little hovel.

It was a splendid victory. The archbishop of Cologne and the count of Guelders were among the prisoners, the count of Luxembourg was killed; hundreds of others lay dead on the field, hundreds more were captured. According to Heelu 1,100 of the enemy were dead and only 40 of Brabant's men.[282] The first figure is probably too high, the second ludicrously low. There are no reliable figures for the losses.

Late in the evening the trumpets sounded yet again:

> In such a fashion as to tell them
> that the meal was ready and that
> they were to come and eat.[283]

After that supper they could sleep well in the flush of victory, with neither sentries nor lookouts round the camp.[284]

Conclusion

The battle of Worringen is extremely significant for the study of the art of war in the thirteenth century because it is described in one of the best contemporary records. Heelu's detailed account takes up more than half the 8,948 lines of his *Yeeste*. He saw the battle himself and he knew the warfare of his time very well. The evidence of other writers can be virtually disregarded. But then the question arises, how far was even Heelu reliable? His account is, after all, a glorification of duke John and his Brabançons:

> 'The world has never held such good and brave men
> As were those Brabançons!
> . . .
> The best on earth, no doubt'.[285]

This means that the part played by his allies, such as the counts of Berg, Looz and Jülich is rather played down, although not entirely overlooked. He seems especially biased in his judgments of the part played by the second division, but is more just in his comments on the third.[286] This is how he describes the parts played by the various divisions:

---

281 *Ibid.*, pp. 272–3, 276–7.
282 *Ibid.*, vv. 7314–22, p. 270.
283 *Ibid.*, vv. 8856–75, p. 323; quote: vv. 8863–65.
284 *Ibid.*, vv. 8893–7, p. 324.
285 *Ibid.*, vv. 6140–3, p. 228, v. 7511, p. 277.
286 R. Jahn, 'Die Schlacht bei Worringen', Dissertation, Berlin, 1907, pp. 43–4.

> The large battle utterly
> Stuck with the duke, composed as it was
> Solely of the men of Brabant,
> Who, fighting in their units
> Pushed so hard against the enemy,
> – Although the struggle was unequal –
> That neither they nor their leader
> Were beaten into retreat.
> For they were so well-ordered
> That they remained together,
> However hard the enemy pushed them or charged at them.[287]

Then comes the second division:

> When the hard encounter was past,
> The other division advanced,
> The provost of Aachen and his followers.[288]

There are several references to the third division:

v. 6260   Before the third division came into action,
> The duke of Brabant fought
> Alone with his men.
> I dare not say what they would have done,
> These club-wielding footsoldiers,
> If the duke had been beaten,

> . . .

> Duke John had nearly achieved victory
v. 6955   For he had broken through the enemy

> . . .

> Then at last, there came up,
> His allies and their troops

> . . .

v. 6962   They found many men, facing defeat
> Who would not give up or flee

> . . .

> But they were hard pressed
> When these men came to help
> The duke, leading their peasants
v. 6970   To back them up;
> For they were being struck
> So murderously and mercilessly
> That there was no knight or sergeant,
> Who did not desire surrender,
> If he could have been taken for ransom
> With honour.

---

[287] Heelu, vv. 5235–46, p. 196.
[288] *Ibid.*, vv. 5937–9, p. 221.

. . .

        If the Brabançons had been left to
        Fight alone, sustaining the attack,
v. 7425   The struggle would have been too hard;
        But their allies joined the fight
        At that moment
        So that they could withdraw without wounds
        And without dying,
        Both peasants and lords alike,
        Brave and hardy,
        Nevertheless the Brabançons were very relieved.

. . .

        For although their allies
        Had not been present in the hard fighting before,
        They captured those men who did not dare advance
        Against the swords of the Brabançons,
v. 7440   Yet would not ride from the field
        Although they did not dare to fight.
        These enemy had grown in confidence
        And would have continued the fight,
        For now the Brabançons were tiring,
        But this was prevented
        By the arrival of the two rear divisions,
        Which easily took them prisoner.

In this account I have tried to avoid the probable exaggeration about the attack of the second division. There is a slight exaggeration in a reflection of Heelu on the breakthrough, but this is not in the account of the actual battle. Heelu's text can be taken as completely reliable.[289]

It should be mentioned at once how well-informed he is about the 30 squires who were dubbed knights, and how well he describes the splitting up into divisions and companies, each with the name of its commander, and often the names of the bannerets and the numbers of banners. In all probability he made a note of the name of the most important participants, and of the outstanding feats of arms at once, or almost immediately afterwards.[290]

Heelu says that he cannot tell everything he saw at the same time and that he has good knowledge of the things that he has not seen.[291] When he has finished the story of the battle he comes back again to the feats of arms of the companies, in order to add a few more details. At the same time he gives new facts about tactics which deserve mention.

We know that the chief tactical aim of the company commanders was to break through the enemy's lines, which they attempted with the commander himself, or

---

[289] R. Jahn, 'Die Schlacht bei Worringen', pp. 43–4.
[290] R. Jahn, 'Die Schlacht bei Worringen', p. 33.
[291] Heelu, vv. 4644–59, p. 175.

sometimes a standard-bearer, at their head. Of course, this is very difficult to do at the start of a battle, and it could happen that a leader broke through with only a few of his followers: this is what happened at Worringen. Wouter Berthout of Malines broke through the enemy ranks, but only one knight and two or three light horsemen got through with him. As soon as he had cut a way through, he was overwhelmed by a more powerful enemy group, and was seriously wounded, so that he died later in captivity.

> If at that instant hundred men had
> Broken through, as he did,
> The duke would have achieved victory
> Half a day earlier, or more,
> Than he did now.[292]

He praises the strong density of the Brabant companies, which the enemy could not break-up. This was what happened to John of Schorisse and Wouter of Antoing and their men:

> They stayed so pugnacious
> Always under their banners,
> That the enemy in no way
> Could break through their company.[293]

After Wouter Berthout had been taken prisoner, his uncle Giles Berthout, Gerard of Rotselaar and Arnold of Walhain raised the banner of the company again:

> So that both
> Banner and battle continued the fight,
> . . .
> Under his banner
> Lord Gerard of Rotselaar
> Maintened the fight
> Firmly and fiercely . . .
> (Lord Arnold) of Walhain
> Encouraged this battle so well
> By his brave feats
> That people saw clearly
> Where his banner was unfurled.[294]

There is also one more significant reference to the importance of the standards:

> The banner of Diest fell;
> But it was held up again
> So bravely and quickly,
> That it served then as the standard
> Of Brabant, and the combat

---

[292] *Ibid.*, vv. 7683–7, p. 283; vv. 7668–7735, pp. 282–5.
[293] *Ibid.*, vv. 7648–51, p. 282.
[294] *Ibid.*, vv. 7776–7, 7782–5, 7789–93, pp. 286-7.

Depended on it, during the time
That the duke was in difficulty.[295]

In short, Heelu did not only give a fine and detailed account of the battle of Worringen, but at the same time provided one of the best sources of the whole history of medieval warfare. It is valuable for general tactics, that is for the use of three divisions of knights. He emphasizes the great importance of the companies, of the tightly closed formations, and the standards as signals for a rallying-point for soldiers who had got scattered, and as a symbol of victory or defeat. He gives a good description of an approach march. There is also evidence for the depth of battle-array, in that he talks about the light horsemen who fought in front, in the middle and behind, which argues that there were three ranks.[296] This information gives an accurate picture of the companies.

Finally, he gives an impartial account of the part played by the duke of Brabant. For him, John was no tactician, judiciously ordering his three divisions to attack at carefully chosen points at vital moments. He shows him playing the part of an ordinary fighting knight, wearing his coat of arms and protected by a bodyguard, having his standard specially guarded as well. The real commander-in-chief seems to have been the count of Virneburg.

---

[295] *Ibid.*, vv. 7897–7904, p. 290.
[296] *Ibid.*, vv. 8678–92, p. 317.

V

STRATEGY

Medieval wars can be of two kinds. In the first kind the objective of the war is to *overthrow the enemy*, to render him politically helpless or militarily impotent. In the second kind the objective is *merely to occupy some castles, towns or a region* so that the conqueror can annex them or use them for bargaining at the peace negotiations. These two kinds of war can be studied through the ages. Clausewitz has made the distinction in his book *On War*.[1]

> Strategy is the use of the engagement for the purpose of the war. The strategist must . . . define an aim for the entire operational side of the war that will be in accordance with its purpose. . . . He will draft the plan of the war, and the aim will determine the series of actions intended to achieve it. He will . . shape the individual campaigns and, within these, decide on the individual engagements. . . . A prince or a commander can best demonstrate his genius by managing a campaign exactly to suit his objectives and his resources, doing neither too much nor too little.[2] Strategy decides the time when, the place where, and the forces with which the engagement is to be fought, and through this threefold activity exerts considerable influence on its outcome. Once the tactical encounter has taken place and the result – be it victory or defeat – is assured, strategy will use it to serve the object of the war.[3] In the strategy of overthrow the fighting forces of the enemy must be destroyed: that is, they must be put in such a condition that they can no longer carry on the fight. The country must be occupied; otherwise the enemy could raise fresh military forces. The enemy's will must be broken, the enemy government and its allies must be drive to ask for peace, or the population made to submit.[4]

Medieval wars present the same diversity as wars in other times. Commanders and learned chroniclers knew the various possibilities of strategy. They made plans for a crusade and several treatises on warfare.

Examples of the strategy of overthrow are the campaigns of Clodovech, conqueror of the kingdom of Syagrius in a single battle in 486, of that of the Alamanni in 496, and that of the Wisigoths in 507. The invasion of Spain in 711 is another example.

---

[1] Clausewitz, *On War* (eds and trans M. Howard and Peter Paret, Princeton, New Jersey, 1976). Note of 10 July 1827, p. 69.
[2] *Ibid.*, bk 2, c. 1; bk 3, c. 1; pp. 128, 177.
[3] *Ibid.*, bk 3, c. 8, p. 194.
[4] *Ibid.*, bk 1, c. 2, p. 90.

With an army of about 12,000 soldiers Tarik defeated the Wisigoths of Roderick in the battle of the Guadalete in July 711 and conquered a big part of Spain. The conquest was completed in 712 by Musa save for isolated regions in the Asturias mountains. In 1066 William the Conqueror defeated the English army of Harold at Hastings and won the whole kingdom.

Charles Martel used a remarkable strategy of overthrow. He always applied an offensive strategy with a rapid march against the enemy and an immediate attack. In March 716 he attacked Radbod and the Frisians but his army was too small; he lost many of his best men, and he had to retire. 'He sent envoys everywhere to order the men to come for the defense of the country', an order for the *lantweri*, before he attacked the army of the other adversary, Raganfred, at Ambléve. In 717, he took the offensive in Neustria and attacked the army of Raganfred and King Chilperic at Vinchy. The army of Chilperic and Raganfred was large but untrained. Charles had a smaller army with very competent warriors. He defeated his enemy and pursued him to Paris. He made the region submit to Austrasia. In 718, Charles invaded Saxony for the first time and reached the Weser. In 719, he renewed the offensive against Raganfred who was aided by Eudes, duke of Aquitaine. He defeated them at Soissons. After the death of Radbod, Charles invaded the south of Frisia in 719 and subdued the region. In 720, 722 and 724, he invaded Saxony. In 724, he went to Angers to impose his conditions on Raganfred. In 725, he invaded Alamannia and Bavaria and subdued both countries. He took the offensive against Eudes of Aquitaine, crossing the Loire and pursuing Eudes. In 732, he encountered Spanish Moslem forces at Poitiers, attacked and defeated them. In 733, he went to Burgundy, subdued the country and installed his *leudes* at the frontier and in the region. He then went to Orleans and took the possessions of his adversaries. In 733, he invaded the north of Frisia in Westergo. In 734, his fleet went from the Rhine to the North Sea, to the coast of Frisia; it sailed between the islands Westergo and Ostergo into the country and the Frankish warriors disembarked. The duke of the Frisians, Bubo, was defeated in the battle on the river Boorne. Bubo was killed, his army routed, and his country annexed to the kingdom of the Franks. While Charles was in Frisia he heard news of the death of duke Eudes of Aquitaine. He went with his army to Bordeaux and Blaye and occupied Aquitaine, before marching again to Burgundy to subdue the great men of the country and impose his authority in the territory in the south around Marseille: he installed his counts there. He sent Childebrand with an army to surround and attack Avignon, a little later he joined him with another part of his army. He attacked Avignon with battering rams and rope ladders and took the town. He then went to Narbonne and besieged it; a Moslem force came to aid the defenders. Charles attacked the Moslems on the Berre and defeated them. He then ravaged the region of Nîmes, Agde and Béziers, but an insurrection in Saxony obliged him to return to the north for a punitive expedition against the Saxons. In 737 Charles sent Childebrand with an army to Provence to subdue again the region of Avignon.

The Knowledge of Strategy

1. Moral Forces

'Moral forces are among the most important subjects in war. They form the spirit which permeates the whole being of war'.[5] Medieval commanders knew very well the importance of moral forces and used them on many occasions.

When the armies of Charlemagne were ready to invade the country of the Avars in 791, the soldiers fasted and prayed during three days, from 5 till 7 September. Everybody had to forsake wine and meat, except the sick, the old and the young warriors. The rich who wanted to drink wine had to pay one *solidus* a day. The poor had to pay according to their abilities but at least a penny a day. Everybody was encouraged to give alms. Every priest in good health had to sing a mass, and the clerics who knew psalms had to sing fifty a day, while they walked barefoot.[6] In 1066, William the Conqueror employed propaganda that was based on moral and ecclesiastical sentiments. The expedition to England was made to appear in the guise of a holy war under a papal banner.[7] Religious forces were used in the expeditions against the Moslems in southern Italy, in Sicily, in Spain, and in the crusades. A crusade was organized against the Albigensians. The Germans organized crusades against the pagan Slavs.[8]

In 1138 the defence of northern England organized by Archbishop Thurstan of York and some barons was in the nature of a holy war against the cruel behaviour of the Scots, 'more barbarous than any race of pagans'. Fasts and prayers prepared the warriors for the battle; the soldiers promised each other to fight bravely together and to win or die for their country; the parish priests led their soldiers; crosses and sacred banners were carried before them; the combat was given round a standard attached to a high mast put on a waggon on which was placed a pyx with the consecrated host and the banners of St Peter of York, St John of Beverley, and St Wilfred of Ripon.[9]

In 1234 the archbishop of Bremen preached a crusade in northern Germany and Flanders. An army of crusaders was assembled against the Stedinger and defeated them on 27 May 1234 at Altenesch. The Stedinger lived near Friesland and Saxony, surrounded by marshes and streams; they had been excommunicated for many years for their excesses and the non-payment of their tithes, and were found contemptuous of the church. They were warlike men who had attacked the neighbouring people,

---

5 *Ibid.*, Bk III, Ch. III.
6 Abel, Simson, and B. Simson, *Jahrbücher des fränkischen Reiches unter Karl den Groszen*, 2 vols, Leipzig, 1883–88, 2. pp. 21–2. Annales regni Francorum, anno 791, p. 88. Verbruggen, *L'armée et la stratégie de Charlemagne*, p. 430.
7 Douglas, 'William the Conqueror: Duke and King', in D. Whitelock, D.C. Douglas, C.H. Lemmon, F. Barlow, *The Norman Conquest: Its Setting and Impact*, pp. 62–3.
8 M. Bünding, *Das Imperium Christianum und die deutschen Ostkriege vom zehnten bis zum zwölften Jahrhundert*, Historische Studien herausgegeben von Dr Emil Ebering, Heft 366, Berlin, 1940, pp. 35 ff.
9 Poole, *From Domesday Book to Magna Carta*, p. 271. Beeler, *Warfare in England*, pp. 86–8. Hollister, *Military Organization of Norman England*, pp. 229–30. Delbrück, III, p. 419.

and had even waged war on the counts and the bishops several times; they were often victors, rarely defeated. For that reason, by authority of the pope, the Word of the Cross was preached against them in many dioceses. In that war about 2,000 of them were killed; the few survivors fled to the neighbouring Frisians.[10]

The medieval commanders tried to develop a corporate spirit in their army by establishing a sworn guild. The lords with their vassals, the wapentake, the brotherhoods, the communes stimulated comradeship in arms. Before battle they had their rites: fasting, prayers, mass, communion. On many occasions they promised the leaders and their commanders by oath to do their full duty in combat: at Lenzen in 929,[11] at the Lechfeld in 955,[12] at Northallerton in 1138.[13]

Louis VII of France admired the example of the Templars and imitated it. His crusaders constituted a brotherhood in which rich and poor promised by oath that they would not flee from the field and that they would execute all the orders of their master. They accepted Gilbert as master; Gilbert designated comrades, and each of them commanded 50 knights.[14]

In 1102, 80 mercenary knights at Bridgnorth showed professional pride and warlike corporate spirit. The three captains and the burgesses agreed to surrender the castle and town to Henry I. The mercenaries refused to collaborate and remained faithful to their master, Robert of Bellême. But the captains and burgesses admitted the royal forces. 'When the mercenaries came out through the crowds of besieging forces, they publicly lamented and bewailed the fact that they had been tricked by the fraud of their burgesses and captains; and before the whole army they laid bare the trickery of their associates, lest what had happened to them should bring other mercenaries into discredit.'[15]

The Norman knights were conscious of belonging to a nation of conquering warriors and were very proud of their successes: victors in every place, the pride of the world, victors over the English people, victors over the Sicilians, victors over the Greeks, of Capua and Apulia.[16] The national spirit was also very well developed in the armies of foot-soldiers when they had to fight against a foreign conqueror: the Scots, the Swiss, the Ditmarscher and the Flemings showed it very often. Class feeling also played a role when the townsfolk or the peasants had to fight against the noble knights.

The talents of the commander were also an important factor in medieval warfare. Charlemagne, William the Conqueror, Bohemond, Richard I, Edward III were all outstanding leaders. Charlemagne had magnanimity, prudence and discernment, constancy; the capacity to persist in his designs, becoming neither disheartened by setbacks nor intoxicated by success; and piety, which allowed him to use the moral

---

[10] *Chronica regia Coloniensis*, Cont. IV, anno 1234, p. 265.
[11] Widukind, 1. I, c. 36, p. 52.
[12] *Ibid.*, 1. III. c. 44, p. 124.
[13] Delbrück, III, p. 419.
[14] Odo of Deuil, pp. 71–2.
[15] J.O. Prestwich, *War and Finance in the Anglo-Norman State*, TRHS, 5th series, 4, 1954, p. 28. Orderic Vitalis, IV, pp. 173–5.
[16] Ralph of Caen, c. 79. William of Poitiers, c. 32, p. 228.

forces of religion against the Saxons, the Saracens, the Avars, the Slavs and the Danes. According to Einhard, he displayed magnanimity, constancy, prudence and patience in the war against the Saxons.[17] William the Conqueror had all the qualities, if we may believe his biographer, William of Poitiers: piety, wisdom, prudence, generosity, temperance, magnanimity, courage, boldness. Boldness and cautious foresight are among the noblest virtues of commanders according to Clausewitz. William showed both during the campaign of 1066.[18]

2. The Battle as the Means to Gain the End of the War

The medieval commanders knew that the battle was the most important means to gain the end of the war. When they expected that they had to give battle, they summoned the rest of their warriors for that purpose: *nomine prelii, ad pugnam, in nomine de bataia, nomine belli, pro bello nominato, ad bellum campale*, and so on.[19]

An excellent example of the ideas about a battle is found in the *Gesta consulum Andegavensium*.[20] When count Geoffrey Martel of Anjou was besieging Tours in 1044, and the enemy advanced to relieve the fortress, his seneschal Lisoius advised him: 'Leave the city which you are besieging. Summon your men from the fortifications, and you will be stronger to defend yourself. I shall hasten to you when you want to fight a battle. It is certainly better for us to fight together than to fight separately and get beaten. Battles are short, but the victor's prize is enormous. Sieges waste time, and the town is rarely taken. Battles overcome nations and fortified towns, and an enemy beaten in battle vanishes like smoke. Once the battle is over, and the enemy beaten, there is a great domain waiting for you around Tours.' In 1300, the royal advocate Pierre Dubois, at a time when it seemed to him that his master Philip the Fair was strong enough to lay hands on the rich lands round his own kingdom, wrote: 'Nowadays your Majesty's enemies no longer dare follow the old methods of warfare: they neither dare nor can risk a straightforward battle, fought out with sword, shield, and lance, in which they might well have been beaten by your ancestors. Now they are afraid of your army of knights, and fortify their positions on high hills, in towers and behind walls, rivers, marshes and moats, and with other defences and works against which your noble knights will be less effective than your quick-moving foot-soldiers. Against that sort of thing your splendid knights usually have to undertake long sieges'.[21] Pierre Dubois laments the enemy's avoidance of a quick decision in battle, because the proportionate strength of the fighting forces would be too much in the French king's favour. It is plain from the way he contrasts

---

17 *Vita Karoli*, c. 8. Ganshof, *The Carolingians and the Frankish Monarchy*, Studies in Carolingian History, tr. J. Sondheimer, London, 1971, p. 7.
18 William of Poitiers, pp. 148–50, 158, 170, 196, 210. Clausewitz, *On War*, Bk III, Ch. VI.
19 Guilhiermoz, *Essai sur l'origine de la noblesse en France*, pp. 290 ff.
20 *Chroniques des comtes d'Anjou et des seigneurs d'Amboise*, pp. 55–6.
21 Paris, Bibliothèque nationale, ms latin 6222 c, fo. 1v. Funck-Brentano, 'De exercituum commeatibus tercio decimo et quarto decimo saeculis post Christum natum', thesis, Paris, 1897, pp. 7–8. N. de Wailly, *Mémoire sur un opuscule*, Mémoires de l'Académie des inscriptions et Belles-Lettres 18, 2, pp. 436–47.

the old method and its quick results, thanks to battles, with the new method and its lengthy sieges, that it was recognized that a policy of total destruction brought the quickest and most decisive outcome.

When William the Conqueror landed in England in 1066, he did not immediately advance on London, but waited for the enemy near the coast. He kept his army well together, and his victory at Hastings overthrew the entire Anglo-Saxon kingdom. The learned men of his day fully understood his strategy. William of Poitiers wrote with justifiable pride: 'With his Norman troops and not much foreign help duke William overthrew all the cities of England in one day between nine o'clock and sunset.'[22] He also compares William the Conqueror's expedition with Julius Caesar's campaign in Britain. 'Julius Caesar twice made expeditions to England with 1,000 ships [actually 98 in the first and 800 in the second]. But the first time he did no great feat of arms, and did not venture from the coast, nor stay there for any length of time, although he had set up camps there, as was customary with the Romans. He crossed late in the summer and came back before the autumnal equinox. His legions were terrified when they realized that part of their fleet had been destroyed by currents and waves, and part was unusable through loss of equipment'. A few towns gave hostages, but only two sent hostages who were taken back to the continent. 'On the second expedition he took 100,000 foot-soldiers and Roman cavalrymen over [actually 5 legions and 2,000 cavalry, i.e. at least 17,500 legionaries and 2,000 cavalry] and many chiefs from the towns of Gaul came with their followers'. While the British horsemen had fought against Caesar in the flat country, the English waited for William's army on a hill. Caesar was attacked several times by the Britons. But William beat them in one day, and did it so thoroughly that they never dared fight again'.[23] The Roman general failed with larger forces, but William was successful. This comparison makes one think, although there was a great difference between the expeditions of Caesar and William. It also proves that the learned chroniclers of the Middle Ages knew that a battle could bring a quick and effective decision in a war.

'The fate of the kingdom of Jerusalem was decided by the . . . defeat at Hattîn' (1187).[24] The idea crops up elsewhere. During the crusade against the Albigensians the leader of the crusaders, Simon de Montfort, had enjoyed successes in 1209, 1210, and 1211. He conquered many castles and fortified towns, while the enemy carefully avoided battle, even during the winter season, when Simon stayed in the conquered district with a very small following. But late in 1211, count Raymond of Toulouse and his allies mounted a powerful counter-offensive. Simon sought the advice of his nobles in a council of war, for the situation seemed extremely critical. One of his faithful followers, Hugh de Lacy, advised him strongly not to defend a very strong fortress, Carcassonne or Fanjeaux, with his troops. He told the count to put his troops in the weakest castle, on the border, bring up his reinforcements there and fight a battle after concentrating his forces. Simon accepted this advice, and a battle very

---

22 William of Poitiers, c. 26, p. 208. [This can also be read as propaganda. William took from 1067–72 to completely conquer the kingdom.]
23 *Ibid.*, pp. 246–8. Caesar, *De bello gallico*, IV, 22, 3, 4; V, 8, 6.
24 Smail, *Crusading Warfare*, p. 16. Ernoul, *Chronique*, p. 159.

quickly followed when his enemies had hemmed him in at Castelnaudary and intercepted a supply column. Simon rushed to help his troops, for 'the result of the whole crusade depended on the outcome of this battle'.[25] Two years later he forced a battle again, after concentrating his troops – instead of defending the fortress of Muret he made a lightning sortie, and shattered his enemies in a tactically well thought-out and superbly executed attack. Simon's energetic way of leading the successful crusade was entirely consistent with his belief in battle as the best means of conquest.

In his plan for the conquest of the Holy Land, Henry II of Cyprus was the advocate of a strategy of overthrow. He aimed to defeat the enemy's main forces in Egypt, and so conquer the Holy Land. He therefore hoped to divide the enemy forces, by threatening them from Cyprus, then the sultan would have to keep one army in Syria and another in Egypt, having no idea where the attack would come.[26]

If the crusaders landed in Armenia and marched through Syria, they would have to waste time in besieging fortresses which were strong and well-situated. The sultan could come up out of Egypt with all his men to reinforce his Syrian army and to fight with well co-ordinated forces. If he did not come, and the crusaders then wanted to march out of the Holy Land to Cairo, they would have to pass through the desert, which would be dangerous and wearisome. The desert stretches for 8 days of a baggage-animal's march, but that means 16–20 days for an army. All supplies would have to be carried, and there was only a little brackish water in a few places. Therefore the troops would have to march through the desert in divisions of 3,000 to 4,000 men: but the sultan knew the desert much better, and could surprise these weak divisions with all his forces, and annihilate them separately. If the crusaders' army were to land in Egypt, the army which the sultan had left in Syria would have to stay there for fear of a Tartar attack overland, and of a sortie from Cyprus against the coastal regions. This would not happen if the crusaders were to land in Syria, for then the sultan would have little or nothing to fear in Egypt, and could move all his troops to Syria. But if the sultan were beaten in Egypt, the crusaders would find very little resistance left in Syria.

The results of defeat in a great battle were also very important. The failure of Charlemagne's campaign of 778 in Spain and the defeat during the retreat through the Pyrenees provoked a very serious crisis. The Saxons rebelled under Widukind, overran the 'march' and invaded the neighbouring Frankish counties. Revolts were possible in Gascony, Aquitaine, and Italy.[27] The defeat of Otto II at Capo Colonne by the Moslems in southern Italy was the end of the emperor's plan to establish his hegemony there. In the north, the Danes started an invasion in Germany. The Liutizes and the Abodrites revolted on the Elbe.[28]

---

25 William of Tudèle, *La chanson de la croisade albigeoise*, I, ed. E. Martin-Chabot, Paris, 1931, I, c. 91, pp. 212–14, c. 100, p. 228. *Petrus Vallium Sarnaii monachi, Historia Albigensis*, ed. P. Gruébin and E. Lyon, SHF, 3 vols, Paris, 1926–39, I, c. 271. Belperron, p. 230.
26 Mas Latrie, *Histoire de l'île de Chypre sous le règne des princes de la maison de Lusignan*, Paris, 1852, II, pp. 123–5.
27 Ganshof, *The Carolingians and the Frankish Monarchy*, p. 18.
28 Dhondt, 'Das frühe Mittelalter', in *Fischer Weltgeschichte*, Band 10, Frankfurt, 1968, p. 211.

The results of defeat in an important battle were well-known in the Middle Ages. In 1339 the army of Edward III of England and his allies was at Buironfosse, facing Philip V of France. The French leaders held a council of war and discussed whether it would be wise to fight. They decided against it, because the strategic situation favoured the enemy. 'If the French king's luck is out, and he gets beaten he will be killed or captured, and will lose his kingdom, but the king of England and the English leaders would lose neither land nor possessions if they were beaten'.[29] They were calculating that possibly a single battle could be decisive in a war only just begun.

3. *Superiority of Numbers*

'Superiority of numbers is in tactics, as well as in strategy, the most general principle of victory.' 'The superiority in numbers is the most important factor in the result of a combat, only it must be sufficiently great to be a counterpoise to all the other co-operating circumstances. The direct result of this is, that the greatest possible number of troops should be brought into action at the decisive point.'

'Whether the troops thus brought are sufficient or not, we have then done in this respect all that our means allowed. This is the first principle in strategy.'[30]

In most countries of western Europe, this principle was applied in the military service. The king could summon a *chevauchée*, a small force of vassals, a *host, expeditio, exercitus,* or army, the *host général, expeditio generalis, ost commune, ost bannie,* where still more warriors were summoned. When the prince expected a battle, he summoned every able-bodied man who was obliged to do military service. This was the *retrobannum* or *arrière ban.* All the vassals and the able-bodied freemen could be summoned. The terminology shows that the medieval prince tried to collect as big an army as possible. The commander could use also the general obligation for all freemen to defend their country in the case of an enemy invasion (*lantweri, defensio patriae*). In practice, it was very difficult to concentrate all warriors, and it was not always sensible to collect poorly equipped or inexperienced men.[31]

Many examples show that the invader has assembled a very big army, superior in numbers. Charlemagne's armies were bigger than those of his enemies and disposed of heavy cavalry of a better quality. The king invaded Lombardy with superior forces in 773, and stayed there till the enemy was completely subdued in 774. He had also much bigger armies in his campaign against Tassilo of Bavaria in 787. He sent superior forces against Brittany in 786, 799 and 811. During his wars in Saxony, he won a great victory at Detmold in 783. But his army seemed too small to continue the campaign and the king went back to Paderborn, where he waited for the reinforcements coming from his country. The Saxons had also reinforced their troops and waited for the Franks at the Haase. Charlemagne won a new victory, four weeks

---

[29] *Jean le Bel,* I, p. 163.
[30] Clausewitz, *On War,* Bk III, Ch. VIII.
[31] Guilhiermoz, pp. 290 ff. Hollister, *Military Organization of Norman England,* pp. 76–7. Verbruggen, 'De militaire dienst in het graafschap Vlaanderen', *Revue d'histoire du droit,* 1958, 26, pp. 453–4.

after the first, and exploited it with the utmost energy. The Frankish army destroyed the country, crossed the Weser and marched farther till they reached the Elbe.[32]

In 1066, William the Conqueror prepared the conquest of England very carefully. The enterprise was too big for Normandy's forces alone. The duke engaged mercenaries in the neighbouring principalities and formed a mighty army of knights, accompanied by foot-soldiers, archers and crossbowmen. While he was waiting for the enemy at Hastings, he received advice from Robert fitz Wymarc, that he should stay in his entrenchments and hold back for the moment from giving battle, because Harold had a very strong army. William answered that he was able to destroy Harold's army even if he had only 10,000 warriors of the 60,000 that he had transported there. The 10,000 warriors are perhaps near to the truth. William had enough soldiers of quality and could wait for his enemy.[33]

In a two-pronged invasion of Hainault in 1184 by Philip of Alsace and his troops, and the archbishop of Cologne, the duke of Brabant and their army, the invaders were much stronger than the count of Hainault and his warriors.[34] Philip Augustus had collected a bigger army than Philip of Alsace in 1185.[35] In 1213, the same king attacked again the county of Flanders with a very powerful army and Ferrand of Portugal was unable to put up a good defence.[36] Philip the Fair and his knights were so strong in 1297 that the count of Flanders and his troops reinforced by the army of Edward I did not dare to attack them.[37] In 1300, Philip the Fair's army conquered the rest of Flanders without a battle.[38]

Pierre Dubois understood this principle very well in 1300 when he wrote that the enemies of the king of France were afraid of his armies of knights. But the situation changed completely in 1302 when the Flemish townspeople and peasants raised larger armies than the king of France and defeated his knights. From Courtrai to Guinegatte (1479) the Flemish foot-soldiers frequently enjoyed numerical superiority against the French knights, and this was a major element in most of their victories.

When an absolute superiority of numbers is not attainable, a commander can produce a relative one at the decisive point, by making skilful use of the troops he has, and by surprising the enemy.

4. *The Surprise*

'The surprise of the enemy ... lies more or less at the foundation of all undertakings, for without it the preponderance at the decisive point is not properly conceivable. The surprise is, therefore, not only the means to the attainment of numerical

---

32 Annales regni Francorum, anno 783, pp. 64–7.

33 William of Poitiers, c. 10, p. 170.

34 Gilbert of Mons, *Chronicon Hanoniense*, pp. 171–4.

35 *Ibid.*, p. 181.

36 Verbruggen, *Het leger en de vloot*, p. 175.

37 *Ibid.*, p. 176.

38 *Ibid., loc. cit.*

superiority. It is also a substantive principle in itself, on account of its effect on morale.'[39]

In October 876 Charles the Bald and his army faced Louis of Saxony and his troops, which were on the other side of the Rhine near Cologne. Louis crossed the Rhine at Andernach and installed his camp there. He dispersed his warriors over a wide area to find fodder for the horses. Charles wanted to attack his adversary by surprise after a forced night march. But the archbishop of Cologne knew Charles' plan and sent a priest by a shorter way to Louis with the news that Charles' forces were on the march. During the night Charles' army marched over bad and difficult roads in the rain. The following day, when the battle started, Louis' troops were ready. The warriors and the horses of Charles were very tired by the long and difficult march and were defeated in the battle.[40]

In 892 king Odo of France assembled an army and gave the impression that he was advancing against the count of Flanders, Baldwin, in Arras. In reality he wished to invade Flanders. When Baldwin realized this, he left Arras and using a different route to that followed by the king, he went to Bruges where he arrived before the king and his army. Odos' surprise attack did not succeed.[41]

King Lothar of France made a successful surprise attack with his cavalry in 978 and took Aachen with the imperial palace, whence emperor Otto II escaped at the last moment. Lothar stayed in Aachen for three days. Otto II collected an army, followed Lothar and marched towards Paris. When the imperial army went back to Germany, it crossed the Aisne and made its camp. But the wagons with the supplies and the utensils necessary for the troops were still on the other side and suffered a surprise attack from the sons of Renier of Lorraine and the army of king Lothar. They killed many of the troops guarding the baggage and took all that they could carry away, inflicting great loss on the imperial army.[42]

On 14 September 1115 prince Roger of Antioch received information that his adversary Bursuq and a Moslem army were making their camp at a water point in the valley of Sarmin and were unaware of his presence with troops. Roger had been leading a defensive campaign during the whole season favourable for operations. Now he attacked immediately, surprising his enemy, and defeated him.[43]

On the night of March 20/21, 1304, Zealanders and Flemings from the army of Guy of Namur made a surprise attack on the camp of the Frisians and Hollanders on the island of Duiveland. They inflicted a heavy defeat on the army of William of Avesnes. After a series of unsuccessful attacks on the fortified town of Zierikzee, Guy of Namur and John of Renesse took possession of Holland, where only Haarlem

[39] Clausewitz, *On War*, Bk III, Ch. IX.
[40] Annales Fuldenses, anno 876, pp. 88–9. Annales Bertiniani, pp. 132–3. Regino of Prüm, *Chronicon*, ed. F. Kurze, MGH, SS, 1890, p. 112.
[41] *Annales Vedastini*, ed. B. von Simson, MGH, SS, 1909, anno 892, pp. 71–2.
[42] Richer, II, pp. 85–96. *Annales Altahenses maiores*, anno 978, ed. E.L.B. von Oefele, MGH, SS, 1891, pp. 13–14. Thietmar of Merseburg, *Chronicon*, ed. R. Holtzmann, MGH, SS, 9, Berlin, 1935, III, 8. Lampert of Hersfeld, *Annales*, ed. O. Holder-Egger, MGH, SS, 1894, p. 44. Delbrück, III, p. 340.
[43] Smail, *Crusading Warfare*, p. 147.

and Dordrecht held out. They also conquered Utrecht and its bishopric. Thus two principalities were almost completely overthrown in a brief campaign after a single night-attack. But then came another surprise. Witte van Haamstede raised a rebellion and chased the Flemings and Zealanders out just as quickly as they had come. After one month's occupation Holland was liberated. These few examples from widely differing areas and periods will serve to underline the importance of surprise in medieval strategy. Many more could be cited.[44]

5. Assembly of Forces

'The best strategy is always to be very strong, first generally then at the decisive point.' 'There is no more imperative and no simpler law for strategy than to keep the forces concentrated.' 'In strategy we can never employ too many forces.'[45]

In 1304, while Guy of Namur was besieging Zierikzee on the island of Schouwen by land and sea, Philip IV advanced towards the southern border of Flanders with a great army. A Franciscan friar from Ghent criticises Guy's strategy which led to an unfortunate division of the Flemish forces.[46] 'The prince was guilty of the sin of pride', he says. 'When he heard that Philip was advancing on Flanders, he ought to have arranged an armistice with William of Avesnes and the Dutch. Any great Christian prince in such circumstances could have left the besieged city and gone out with all his followers against the king without shame or disgrace, even with honour.' Guy ought to have advanced to the southern border of Flanders, which was the most important front. There his forces should have been massed against Philip, his most powerful enemy. Guy had also split up his forces in his own theatre of war, against the advice of his brother John and other experienced leaders, and had attacked his enemy by sea while he was besieging a powerful and well-defended town. This was very foolish, because he could easily have avoided a sea battle, while the enemy could only attack him with difficulty on land.

William Marshal also called attention to the importance of massing troops. In an address to his troops in 1217 he exulted over the enemy's division of his troops because it brought victory closer within reach: 'When their army is divided, we shall better defeat one part of their men than all together. This is right and reason, it seems to me.'[47]

In order to avoid splitting up his forces Saladin had the walls of almost all his fortresses pulled down after his defeat at Arsuf, during the Third Crusade, as he was afraid that these fortresses would fall into the hands of Richard I. This enabled him to reinforce his army in the field with men from the garrisons, and thus increased his chance of success if the king of England were successful in forcing a battle. But Saladin was so afraid of his enemy that he chose to avoid battle systematically. Even

44 Verbruggen, *Het leger en de vloot*, p. 181.
45 Clausewitz, *On War*, Bk III, Chs XI, XII.
46 *Annales Gandenses*, pp. 66–7.
47 *Histoire de Guillaume le Maréchal*, II, vv. 16177–80, p. 219.

so, he had strengthened his army in the field as a precaution.[48] Centuries before, the Ostrogoth Totila had done the same in Italy, and had reinforced his forces with the garrisons from the fortresses.[49]

Many commanders were blamed for not awaiting the arrival of all their forces: Baldwin I for his defeat at Ramla in 1102 and at al-Sannabra in 1113, prince Roger of Antioch for his defeat at the 'Field of Blood' in 1119, Raymond of Antioch for his defeat in 1149, and so on.[50]

Crusaders must never split their forces, but keep them well together, writes Fidenzio of Padua. The Tartars were beaten in Syria because their king split up his army after victory, thinking himself safe because he was a long way from Egypt, and the desert lay between him and his enemy. But the sultan of Egypt came up secretly, took the scattered Tartars by surprise, and utterly defeated them.[51]

On 23 June 1302, Guy of Namur summoned the forces of William of Jülich and Pieter de Coninc to Courtrai, to concentrate the Flemish rebel army for a decisive battle. This was done before the enemy's strength and intentions were known, and they massed in a very favourable position. Later, when Philip IV wanted to avenge his defeat at the battle of Courtrai and advanced with a great army, the defence of the country was proclaimed in Flanders. All available forces were massed in a suitable position facing the enemy, first on the Neuf-Fossé, then in the neighbourhood of Flines. Again in 1304 Philip of Chieti and William of Jülich massed their forces in the southern theatre of war.

There are other features of medieval warfare which show a contemporary awareness of strategy as well as the policy of the concentration of forces. The importance of the strategic approach, withdrawal, and pursuit were all understood, with their advantages and drawbacks.

In April 1104, Baldwin of Bourg summoned Bohemond and Tancred to help him against the Turks, who were advancing on Edessa. Baldwin himself was besieging the enemy city of Harran. Ralph of Caen describes his strategy thus: 'When the Turks heard that Bohemond was coming, they left Edessa and moved off. They wanted to fight, but disguised their intentions: first they pretended to flee, but it was just a trick to lead the pursuing Christians further astray. They wanted to reach a safe place by familiar tracks, while the pursuers faced fresh dangers in an unknown land, where they would starve, though the Turks could find food. While the retreating Moslems were collecting reinforcements the Christians were getting weaker and weaker. The Turks retreated for three days, till the Christians had crossed the river Khabour, and had the water behind them.'[52] Here, Ralph gives a very good description of the well-known advantages and disadvantages of a strategic march into enemy territory. His remarks show that the medieval commander knew them too.

---

[48] Lot, *Art militaire*, I, p. 160. Delbrück, III, p. 343.
[49] Delbrück, *loc. cit.*
[50] Smail, *Crusading Warfare*, pp. 125–6.
[51] Fidenzio of Padua, *Liber recuperationis Terrae Sanctae*, ed. G. Golubovich, Biblioteca Bio-Bibliografica della Terra Santa, 5 vols, Florence, 1906–27, II, pp. 34 ff.
[52] Ralph of Caen, *Gesta Tancredi*, p. 710.

After Richard's great victory at Arsuf, the Norman poet Ambroise lamented bitterly that the victory had not been strategically exploited by a relentless pursuit. 'If the army (of Saladin) had been more hotly pursued, chased and hunted, we should have conquered the land and it would be inhabited by Christians again.'[53]

These examples show that a knowledge of strategy was by no means lacking in the Middle Ages. A battle was recognized as the most efficient way of winning a war, and the leaders massed their troops in order to fight a decisive battle. They also knew how a victory could be exploited by strategic pursuit, and saw the advantages and disadvantages of strategic retreat and advance. Theoretical and practical knowledge of strategy is very clear in a whole series of plans for the conquest of the Holy Land, dating from the late thirteenth and early fourteenth centuries. They can be taken as treatises on the conduct of war, dealing with concrete examples. Some of them are truly remarkable, others too theoretical, but the important fact is that such treatises were written at all, creating a theoretical literature on the subject, and that the plans show so many points of agreement and continuity.

Plans for Wars

1. Plans for a Crusade

Some historians are convinced that there was no theoretical literature about tactics and strategy in the Middle Ages. A more careful and wide-ranging search would have shown that such a view is groundless. For tactics, and all kinds of problems concerning the order of the march, the Rule of the Knights Templar is very good. For the later Middle Ages, Jean de Bueil's *Le Jouvencel* is an excellent and original treatise dealing with all aspects of the art of war. Pierre Dubois' treatise on how to shorten wars is also interesting as a piece of theoretical literature.

Many historians have thought that battles and wars in the Middle Ages were unplanned. It has already been shown that this is untrue of individual battles and engagements: there are also interesting texts which show real planning for whole wars. Some are very modest in conception, and simply give the solution of a concrete situation with its little problems. Others are on a grander scale and discuss war by sea and land, and economic blockade. They often have some interesting ideas and some are based on an accurate knowledge of the theatre of war concerned.

After the fall of Acre in 1291, pope Nicholas IV made great efforts to get a new crusade going. He sought advice from several competent people about the possibilities. This gave rise to councils and plans at the end of the thirteenth century and early in the fourteenth, and at least eleven writers have developed interesting propositions which deserve to be discussed here.

53 Ambroise, vv. 6765–8, p. 181.

1. A plan of Charles II, king of Sicily, of about 1292[54]
2. A very detailed treatise by the Franciscan Fidenzio of Padua[55]
3. Pierre Dubois' *De Recuperatione Terre Sancte*, 1305–7, and a plan for setting up a kingdom of the East under Philip the Tall, written in 1308[56]
4. The ideas of Jacques de Molay, master of the Temple, 1307[57]
5. A treatise by the Armenian prince Hayton or Hethoum, 1307[58]
6. The plans of Raymund Lull, 1305 and 1309[59]
7. A plan for a war against Egypt, by king Henry II of Cyprus, 1311–12[60]
8. Guillaume Adam's *De modo extirpandi Sarracenos* (before 1318)[61]
9. The plan of Marino Sanudo, 1306 to 1321[62]
10. The *Directorium* of Burcard[63]
11. A study by the councillors of king Philip VI of France[64]

As well as the plans for a crusade or plans for the invasion of Egypt, three other documents should be considered. These are the proposal of the admiral Benedict Zaccaria to the French king for the sea war against England (1297), a comital ordinance for the conduct of the struggle against the Flemish rebels in 1325, and Pierre Dubois' proposals for shortening wars. In the eleven documents dealing with war with the Saracens, there is a very remarkable degree of accord on the outstanding problems. In order to avoid repetition it seems best to arrange them according to the most important idea in each, rather than to give each plan in turn, then the most interesting proposals for the solution of each problem can be discussed in more detail.

General principles

The most important points which are often mentioned are the necessity of peace between the Christian nations before a crusade can be undertaken, an alliance with the Tartars for a war against the Saracens, unification of the ecclesiastical military orders, the use of a fleet to blockade Egypt, to conduct economic warfare, and to

---

54 Paris, Bibl. Nat., ms français 6049, fo. 183v–190r. Delaville le Roulx, *La France en Orient au XIVe siècle*, 2 vols, Paris, 1885, I, pp. 16–19. Atiya, *The Crusade in the Later Middle Ages*, London, 1938, pp. 35–6.
55 Fidenzio of Padua, *Liber recuperationis Terrae Sanctae*, pp. 9–60. Delaville le Roulx, I, pp. 19–25. Atiya, pp. 36–43.
56 Pierre Dubois, *De recuperatione terre sancte. Traité de politique générale*, ed. V. Langlois, Paris, 1891. Delaville le Roulx, I, pp. 48–54. Atiya, pp. 49–52.
57 Paris, Arch, Nat., Trésor des chartes, J 456, no. 36, 1. F. Baluze, *Vitae Paparum Avenoniensium*, ed. G. Mollat, Paris, 1914–22, III, pp. 145 ff. Delaville le Roulx, I, pp. 55–7. Atiya, pp. 55–6.
58 *Flos Historiarum Terre Orientis*, RHC, Doc. arm; 1 pp. 469 ff. Delaville le Roulx, I, pp. 64–70. Atiya, pp. 62–4.
59 Delaville le Roulx, I, pp. 27–32. Atiya, pp. 74–94.
60 Mas Latrie, *Histoire de Chypre*, II, pp. 118–25. Delaville le Roulx, I, pp. 61–2. Atiya, pp. 58–60.
61 Guillaume Adam, *De modo extirpandi Sarracenos*, ed. C. Kohler, RHC, Doc. arm., II, pp. 521 ff. Delaville le Roulx, I, pp. 70–7. Atiya, pp. 65–7.
62 Marino Sanudi, *Liber secretorum fidelium crucis*, ed. Bongars, in *Gesta Dei per Francos*, II, Hannover, 1611, pp. 25–91. Delaville le Roulx, I, pp. 32–9. Atiya, pp. 116–27.
63 Ed. Reiffenberg, *Monuments pour servir à l'histoire des provinces de Namur, de Hainaut et de Luxembourg*, IV, pp. 227–312. Delaville le Roulx, I, pp. 90–7. Atiya, pp. 95–110.
64 Delaville le Roulx, II, pp. 7–11. Atiya, pp. 110–11.

make plundering raids, and finally the use of Cyprus and the Christian kingdom of Armenia as bases for the crusade.

The necessity of general peace among Christian nations is an old idea, which had already been expressed at the Council of Clermont before the first Crusade. It was taken up again by Charles II of Sicily, Pierre Dubois, who developed it best,[65] bishop Guillaume Durant, and Burcard.[66]

Most of these writers confidently reckon on armed help from the Tartars, who could intervene against the Saracens in Syria. They take no account of the fact that the Tartars might occupy the country, and are altogether very naive on this point. Even Hayton,[67] who would like to keep the crusaders and the Tartars well apart to avoid jealousy and quarrels, and would only let the Tartars come as far as Damascus, does not think they will want to stay in the Holy Land as it is too hot in summer.

The unification of the military Orders was also a fairly old idea. St Louis had thought of it. Pope Gregory X wanted to push it through at the Council of Lyon in 1274, at which Raymond Lull was also a convinced advocate of the plan.[68] Charles II of Sicily revived the plan again about 1291. The leader of the new Order was to be a king's son or a nobleman of very high rank, and should become king of the Holy Land after the capture of Jerusalem. He would have enormous wealth at his disposal, the tithes of all the churches in the world, alms, the rights of the Church in buying and selling, the money coming in from those who bought themselves out of going on a crusade, and that from the sale of the warhorses and equipment of dead princes, prelates, barons, knights and other warriors were to come to him.[69] Legacies and earlier gifts for the Holy Land should be looked into, and this money also collected. The new Order was to have a uniform on which the insignia of the Templars and Hospitallers were combined; a red cloak, instead of the Templars' red cross, with the white cross of the Hospitallers on it. King Charles II proposed a strength of 2,000 knights and 200 *sergeants*. Each knight was to have four mounts, a war-horse, a mule, and two ordinary horses. Two squires, preferably of noble birth, were to ride these latter. If the knight died, one of the squires could be dubbed knight and take his master's place. In the Holy Land they were to take care always to maintain these numbers. This army, the pilgrims who came to the Holy Land each year, and those Christians who had established themselves there permanently, were to look after the conquered territory.[70] Pierre Dubois also suggested the amalgamation of the military orders in 1308. The Order of the Templars, who were at that time held in custody, was to be abolished, and they were to have no part in the plan. He proposed that their possessions should be made over to the new Order, and used, among other purposes,

---

65 Paris, Bibl. Nat. ms fr. 6049, fo. 190r. For Dubois, see further Dubois, *De recuperatione . . .*
66 Delaville le Roulx, I, pp. 81–2, 90–1. Atiya, pp. 69, 100.
67 L. De Backer, *L'Extrême-Orient au moyen âge*, Paris, 1877, p. 245. Lot, *L'art militaire*, II, p. 352. Delaville le Roulx, I, p. 66.
68 Atiya, p. 36.
69 Paris, Bibl. Nat. ms fr. 6049, fo. 185v–186r ff.
70 *Ibid.*, fo. 187v–188r.

to maintain a fleet of a hundred or so galleys, which were to attack the coast of Egypt and wear it down before the crusade started.[71]

Through all these plans runs the idea of a fleet which is to attack the coast of Egypt. About 1266 Amaury de la Roche, commander of the Templars in France, advised the dispatch of a fleet of six galleys to the coast of Palestine. These ships were expected to bring in such rich plunder that they would pay for their own upkeep. At that time the king of Sicily had re-imposed the old prohibition against trading with the Moslems, but the Italian ports were not obeying it. Amaury de la Roche hoped also that the fleet would attack Alexandria and Damietta.[72] After the fall of Acre, pope Nicholas IV fitted out a fleet of twenty ships and sent them to Cyprus. King Henry II had equipped 15 vessels there. But an expedition against the coast of Asia Minor and Alexandria was unsuccessful.[73] Everyone was agreed, however, on the necessity of a fleet. Charles II of Sicily declared outright that the Moslems were far too powerful after 1291 to attack by land. They had chased the Christians out of the Holy Land and three times put the Tartars to flight. There was also no place at all where they would be safe after their landing. The Moslems were clever, and more adroit than the Christians in waging war. Even if they sometimes were unable to stop the Christians from landing on the coast, they could always withdraw and await their moment, and while the climate was taking its toll of the Christians, the Moslems could be preparing their counter-offensive. But the sultan's coast was very vulnerable, and full of rich towns and castles. Egypt's income came from trade:[74] iron, wood and slaves who were trained as Mamelukes, the best fighters the Moslems had, were all brought in by Christians. This trade had to be stopped, the revenue cut off, the coastal strip and Alexandria laid waste. Fidenzio of Padua, Jacques de Molay, Raymond Lull, Henry II of Cyprus, Pierre Dubois and Burcard all express the same idea. Guillaume Adam and Marino Sanudo go further still. Guillaume Adam proposed fitting out a small fleet into the Persian Gulf and the Indian Ocean, to cut off Egypt's trade with India and the Far East, and to make the Moslems use Armenian harbours. Marino Sanudo planned to divert the trade route along the Euphrates through Baghdad to Antioch in Syria. Fidenzio of Padua had already pointed out the possibility of importing spices into Armenia and from there exporting them again to the West. He was convinced that the Christians ought to attack by land and sea simultaneously. A fleet of at least 30 galleys, preferably 40 or 50, with the support of supply ships, offered these advantages:

1. The Moslems could not carry on any trade by sea while there was fighting in the Holy Land.
2. Christians living in the coastal strip of the Holy Land would be safe while the Moslems were blockaded and could not receive supplies.

---

[71] Dubois, *De recuperatione*, pp. 133–4.
[72] Paris, Arch. nat. J 456, no. 36, 3. Mas Latrie, II, pp. 71–2.
[73] Delaville le Roulx, I, p. 16. Atiya, p. 45.
[74] Paris, Bibl. nat., ms fr. 6049, fo. 184v–185r.

3. The sultan would lose the revenue he gained from trade. According to Fidenzio the sultan received the value of one ship for every three ships that anchored in a harbour, and according to Henry II of Cyprus, one out of four.[75]
4. Iron, tin, and other metals, wood, oil and honey could no longer be imported – none of these is found in Egypt.
5. The sultan would lose the income from trade with India. The Christians did not know that pepper and other spices could be brought into Armenia up the Persian Gulf. They could be brought to the West from there.
6. Egypt could no longer sell the products of its textile industry.
7. The sultan could not import any more slaves, who became the best warriors and admirals.
8. The fleet could lay waste the coastal strip of Egypt, which would be very difficult for the sultan to protect.
9. The sultan would have to leave troops in that area, thus weakening his forces in the Holy Land.
10. The fleet could bring reinforcements and stores to the crusaders in the Holy Land.
11. The fleet would patrol the sea and drive pirates away.[76]

Summary of the plans

Charles II of Sicily did not advise a general Crusade in 1291. He thought it possible to weaken the enemy by lightning attacks on the coast with a fleet of 50 galleys, 50 transport ships and 1,500 fighting-men. Later on, a large-scale expedition could be started after the amalgamation of the ecclesiastical military Orders. The fleet would have to support the army as long as it was advancing close to the coast of the Holy Land. On the journey, the crusaders were to anchor at Cyprus to give the troops a rest after their long and exhausting journey. Charles thought the landing should be at Acre or Tripoli, but suggested seeking the advice of a competent expert. After the conquest of the Holy Land, and the establishment of a military government with 2,000 knights and 200 *sergeants* in the area, colonization should be stimulated by all possible means so that Christians would settle there in considerable numbers.[77]

In 1307 Jacques de Molay opposed sending a small army, since this would be destroyed owing to the lack of any Christian stronghold in the Holy Land. Also nothing would be gained, he thought, by sending a small army to Christian Armenia. He thought 12–15,000 horsemen and 40–50,000 bowmen would be necessary. If 4,000 horsemen were sent, there would only be 500 left after a season in that arid and unhealthy land. The Armenians did not trust the Franks, and would not give them proper support in battle. Nothing but a massive crusade would do. This would mean fitting out a huge fleet, preferably with large ships, not with galleys which could not carry so many men. In order to give some idea of the numbers he thought necessary he repeated a saying of Baibars. This great sultan is supposed to have said

75 Mas Latrie, II, p. 121. Jacques de Molay: one ship out of three.
76 Fidenzio of Padua, pp. 46–50.
77 Ms fr. 6049, fo. 183v–190r. Delaville le Roulx, I, pp. 16–19. Atiya, pp. 35–6.

that he was prepared to take on 30,000 Tartars with his army or he would fight 15,000 Frankish horsemen, but if more Franks or more Tartars attacked him, he would not be able to hold out. Jacques de Molay concluded from this that 12 to 15,000 armoured cavalrymen and 50,000 foot-soldiers would be necessary. He advised the inclusion of 2,000 crossbowmen among the armoured horsemen.[78] Jacques de Molay also proposed a preliminary landing in Cyprus, from which base the invasion could be launched. A fleet of 10 galleys could prepare the way for their expedition from Cyprus. The leader of this fleet would have to be a man of some importance, not dependent on the great Italian seaports. It would be no good entrusting this to the Templars or Hospitallers, because the Italian seaports would take vengeance if their trade with Egypt was interrupted, and that would do great damage to both Orders.[79]

The Armenian prince Hayton (or Hethoum) took part in the defence of Armenia under King Hethoum against the plundering expeditions of the sultan's troops. After that, he returned to Cyprus and became a Praemonstratensian. In 1307 he settled in the West, and wrote the *Flos Historiarum Terre Orientis*. Like most of the other writers, he was reckoning on help from the Tartars. Like Marino Sanudo, but unlike Jacques de Molay, he supported the idea of a double expedition. A small preparatory crossing should be made by ten galleys carrying 1,000 knights and 3,000 foot-soldiers. Being himself an Armenian prince, Hayton naturally proposed a landing in Armenia, after a stay in Cyprus. The Tartars could attack the area around Aleppo, while the advance guard of the crusaders, with troops from Cyprus and Armenia could attack the enemy. If the sultan sent troops to Syria he would have to split his forces. If he did not, these Christian armies would conquer Tripoli and the province round it. After that the main crusade could start. He discusses the advantages of various approach routes. He did not know much about the way through North Africa and therefore said that the advice of well-informed persons must be sought. He discusses the overland route, through Europe to Byzantium and Asia Minor, and the sea route to Cyprus and the Holy Land, deciding in favour of the sea route to Cyprus. He suggested that the crusaders should wait until 29 September in order to avoid the heat of summer, and then land in Armenia or Antioch. The crusaders were to march from Armenia to Damascus, and then on to Jerusalem. The best thing would be for the Tartars to fight in the Aleppo area, and not to advance beyond Damascus.[80]

In his first treatise, the *Liber de fine* written in 1305, Raymond Lull expounded his plan. The leader of the crusade was to be a man of royal blood, and his followers kings' sons. The military Orders were to be united under this king. The new Order was to have all sorts of church revenues at its disposal, and the members were to wear a black habit with a red cross. Lull thought the overland route through Byzantium, Turkey and Armenia too long, too dangerous, and altogether too costly. He also discounted another possibility, the conquest of the island of Rosetta, off Alexandria. A crusade by sea to Cyprus and Armenia seemed to him too long, as well as needing both army and navy. Neither country could provision a great army.

---

[78] These numbers are exaggerated. Cf. the plan of Charles II of Sicily.
[79] *Vitae paparum*, III, pp. 145 ff. Delaville le Roulx, I, pp. 55–7. Atiya, pp. 55–6.
[80] Haytoum, *Flos historiarum*, pp. 469 ff. Delaville le Roulx, I, pp. 64–70. Atiya, pp. 63–4.

The approach route by Tunis, which St Louis had used, had already brought disaster.[81] He thought the best solution would be to attack Andalusia, which was surrounded by sea to the south and the kingdoms of Castile and Aragon to the north, so that the Moslems could not come to the rescue. After the systematic conquest of the kingdom of Andalusia the crusaders would have to take Ceuta in Africa. After that they could advance eastwards along the coast to Tunis. From Tunis he thought it possible to conquer the Holy Land or Egypt.

Lull also discussed the advantages the Christians would have over the Moslems by using this plan. These were military kingship and ecclesiastical order, while the Christian fleet dominated the sea and cut off Moslem help. The crossbow was better than the Turkish bow. The Christians would have better wood for lances at their disposal, and more iron for weapons, and have supplies in Spain. The Moslems would have three things in their favour, discipline, the Turkish bow, and the tactics of their light cavalry. So Lull suggested that the army should be divided into units of 10, 100, 1,000, 10,000 soldiers, and so on, each with its own leader. Strict discipline would have to be observed, and it would be best to become familiar with light cavalry tactics and make use of them.

A fleet commanded by an admiral was to transport 100 knights, 100 mounted crossbowmen, 50 crossbowmen, and 1,000 foot-soldiers, in galleys. These could attack the enemy coast, and would be able to take on 2,000 or more enemy horsemen. With one large ship and four galleys the admiral could take Rhodes and Malta, which were admirable bases for intercepting trade with the Saracens. He proposed excommunication with very heavy penalties and confiscation of the goods involved against those wicked Christians who traded with the enemy. He thought the sultan would be ruined by six years' blockade.[82]

In 1309, Lull developed his ideas further in the *Liber de acquisitione Terrae Sanctae*. One army was to take Ceuta, Morocco, Tunis, Bougie and Tlemcen in North Africa, and so reach the Egyptian border. Another was to conquer Constantinople and Syria, and get to the banks of the Nile through Arabia. In this way the Saracens would be threatened from two sides at once.[83]

Henry II of Cyprus propounded his plan at the Council of Vienne in 1311–12. In preparation for the great crusade the power of the sultan of Egypt would have to be weakened. A fleet was therefore to attack the coast of Egypt, Syria, and other Moslem lands. But this fleet was not to belong to Venice, Pisa, Genoa, or other great seaport, because its admiral would then allow his fellow countrymen to trade with the Saracens, while stopping the trade of other ports. He quoted an example of countermeasures taken by Genoa when the Hospitallers captured a Genoese ship which was trading with the enemy. After some years of preparation the sultan would be quite impoverished. Henry wanted 15 or 20 galleys, and proposed to add his own ships to them. The crusaders were to land in Cyprus first, and sail to Egypt from there. Henry opposed a landing in Armenia and a march through the Holy Land, because the

81 Atiya, pp. 78–80. Delaville le Roulx, pp. 27–32.
82 Atiya, pp. 81–2.
83 *Ibid.*, p. 85. Delaville le Roulx, pp. 30–1.

enemy would be able to concentrate his full strength against these armies, and because the march would anyhow be very difficult.[84] A landing in Egypt would split up the enemy force, because they would have to leave troops in the Holy Land. In addition, victory in Egypt would be decisive. Henry had heard it said that the enemy used to have 60,000 horsemen, a third of them were really good soldiers, a third mediocre, and another third poor. He advised the use of as many crossbowmen as possible in the crusade, as the Moslems were terrified of them.[85]

Guillaume Adam's *De modo Sarracenos extirpandi* was written before 1318. His idea was to prevent the Christians from trading with Egypt, by use of a fleet. After that, he wanted to divert trade from India along the Persian Gulf and the Euphrates to the Armenian ports by the use of a fleet. Trade from India could be intercepted by a Christian fleet in the Indian Ocean – three or four galleys would be enough. He would discourage pilgrimages to Jerusalem in order to cut off a source of enemy revenue – Christians after all had to pay their way. To prevent Byzantium exporting goods to Egypt it would be well to conquer that land. Adam therefore chose the overland route through Hungary and Bulgaria for the main crusade. After the conquest of Byzantium the Turks would have to be thrown out of Asia Minor. He proposed that the crusaders should use the island of Chios as a base. If the expedition were well prepared, Egypt would be so weakened that the large-scale offensive would be completely successful.[86]

The *Liber secretorum fidelium crucis* of the Venetian Marino Sanudo was written between 1306 and 1321. He wanted to strike first at the trade through Egypt by diverting to Syria the trade from India by way of Aden to Egypt, and preventing exports from Egypt. Spices would have to be brought from India to the Euphrates and by Baghdad to Antioch in Syria. A fleet of 10 galleys would be able to do a great deal of damage, and prepare for the general invasion. The admiral of the fleet would have to be chosen by the pope. He would have to be on good terms with Venice in order to get Venetian help. The fleet would also have to block the slave trade from the Crimea to Egypt. Two or three years of preparation would be enough for a general crusade. The crusaders would be able to reckon on help from the Christians in Nubia who would come up from the South, and on help from the Tartars, who would invade the Holy Land itself.

Marino Sanudo planned a minor crossing first with 300 knights and 15,000 foot-soldiers, since greater forces would be more costly and more difficult to keep supplied. These were to land in Egypt, as he did not believe in the land route through Asia Minor, nor in a landing in Armenia. Neither did he want a landing in Cyprus. The attack on the Egyptian coast was to follow the usual Venetian methods, first an occupation of the coastal area, then settlement. From April to October there would be a fleet of 20 galleys with 150 knights and 5,000 men to stop trade between Egypt and other Mediterranean countries. Finally the general crusading force was to come,

[84] See above.
[85] Mas Latrie, II, pp. 118–25. Delaville le Roulx, I, pp. 61–2. Atiya, pp. 58–60.
[86] *Documents arméniens*, II, pp. 521 ff. Delaville le Roulx, I, pp. 70–7. Atiya, pp. 65–7.

with 2,000 horsemen and 50,000 foot-soldiers. Victory in Egypt would bring the Moslems to their knees.[87]

Burcard dedicated his *Directorium* in 1332 to king Philip VI of France, who was about to set out on a crusade. He said that peace and concord must be restored among the Christian countries and the maritime powers. Enormous quantities of stores were to be bought in various countries, such as wheat, wine, oil, flour, vegetables, barley, cheese and salt meat. Weapons of every kind, and good equipment would also be needed. Genoa and Venice could supply the transport fleet. The Genoese, who had possessions on the Black Sea and near Constantinople, and the Venetians who had the Aegean Islands, could play a very important part.[88] A fleet of 10 or 12 galleys was to keep an eye on Syria's coastal waters and the sea round about, to stop forbidden trade. This fleet should be based in Cyprus. He regarded the North African route, proposed by Lull and also later by Philip de Mézières, as too long and too dangerous. It would mean taking strong castles and cities, and the Libyan desert was a difficult and dangerous obstacle. The sea journey via Cyprus was also long and dangerous. The Germans and French would be seasick, the horses would be weakened by the long journey. The army of St Louis had suffered great losses in Cyprus. Therefore Burcard would not consider this route. A third route lay through Italy, Dalmatia and Serbia, or from Brindisi through the Adriatic to Durazzo and thence to Constantinople. There was a fourth route through Germany, Hungary and Bulgaria to Constantinople. The king and the best part of the army should go by this route. A small army could accompany the galleys and the transport ships with the supplies through the Mediterranean. The contingents from southern France and Italy could take the third route. All the crusaders should be gathered together at Salonika. Burcard also advised taking Serbia and Byzantium, both inhabited by schismatic Christians. The Byzantines, he said, were not good fighters. The conquest of Serbia would be easy, and could be accomplished with 1,000 French knights and 5–6,000 foot-soldiers, for 15,000 Albanian horsemen[89] would support the crusaders, and the Serbian fortresses are not very strong, as Burcard himself had noticed.

After the conquest of Byzantium, the crusaders were to go on through Asia Minor. Burcard says that the Christians should not trust the Armenians. They would have therefore to cross the Bosphorus alone, and after that they would have no enemy at their back while they were marching through Asia Minor. The Turks could be conquered separately, for it would be very difficult to get help out of Egypt. The crusaders would have help from the Tartars and the support of the fleet. There would be great supplies from the conquered areas of Serbia, Byzantium and Asia Minor. He said that the Turks had no armour other than leather jerkins, and were only armed with bows. They could not wait for the impact of the armoured horsemen of the West,

---

[87] M. Sanudo, in *Gesta Dei per Francos*, II, pp. 25–39, 51, 81–91. Delaville le Roulx, I, p. 33. Atiya, pp. 120–2. The strength of the foot-soldiers is much exaggerated.
[88] Reiffenberg, *Monuments*, IV, pp. 248–50.
[89] These numbers are also exaggerated.

but had to evade battle, and use special light cavalry tactics. They were of little military value, just like the Byzantines and Egyptians.[90]

Plainly, Burcard underestimated the enemy strength. His plan is not as practical as many of the others: contrary to his views, the land route was very long and expensive, and extremely exhausting for both men and horses. The conquest of Byzantium and Serbia would also weaken the strength of the crusaders, and it is doubtful whether they would be in any state to go on.

Burcard's plan was very carefully studied at the court of Philip of Valois. The royal councillors decided that the land route was too long and too time-consuming, and the cost would be too great for the crusaders. Many horses would die on the journey, and the crusaders would quarrel about feeding and quartering. They thought that there would be perpetual difficulties with hostile princes, and the way lay through impoverished areas along poor roads. Apart from all that, the enemy would know at once the general direction of their approach, and start counter-measures, so that the element of surprise would be lost. This would not happen with a sea expedition. Noblemen might set out too late for an expedition over land, thinking they could catch up the royal army, but everyone had to sail at the same time for an expedition by sea. Philip's advisers sensibly opposed any attack on Serbia and Byzantium, and the proposed conquest of Asia Minor. They suggested going down the coast of Italy in order to avoid the dangers of the open sea, and massing the crusaders in Italy. By going down the Italian coast instead of marching through Italy they would not make the Italians think that the French king wanted to meddle with their affairs or had designs on their territory. At Naples the king could discuss the rest of the expedition with his uncle, king Robert of Anjou.[91] Burcard's plan was dropped completely.

There are two detailed treatises which deserve particular attention: those of Fidenzio of Padua and Pierre Dubois.

Fidenzio of Padua

Pope Gregory X had consulted Fidenzio at the Council of Lyons in 1274, and the latter had addressed himself to the problem from then onwards. He finished his treatise by 3 January 1291, in the pontificate of pope Nicholas IV, more than four months before the fall of Acre. It consisted of two parts, the first dealing with the history of the Holy Land, the second discussing how it could be conquered and held. It postulates three things – an efficient army, virtuous crusaders, and a really competent commander-in-chief.

The crusaders themselves, he wrote, must be plentiful in number, skilled in warfare, courageous and sensible. There were always plenty of Moslems, since the sultan ruled two kingdoms, Damascus and Egypt, and had more than 40,000 horsemen at his disposal, including many brave and experienced fighters. The Christians would therefore need to send 20,000, or, if possible, 30,000 horsemen, and a great many foot-soldiers as well.[92] The crusaders must be well-armed, and

[90] Reiffenberg, *Monuments*, IV, pp. 250–310. Delaville le Roulx, I, pp. 90–7. Atiya, pp. 95–110.
[91] Delaville le Roulx, II, pp. 7–11.
[92] Again exaggerated numbers.

skilled in archery – they must advance in disciplined order like the Moslems, whom Fidenzio himself had seen after the fall of Antioch in 1268, when he went into their camp to help Christian prisoners. The crusaders' army must advance in an orderly fashion, one in front of the other for their mutual protection in closely-packed formations. There must be large numbers of crossbowmen and archers posted among the knights to keep the Moslems at a distance. The latter often sent over showers of arrows, and the Christians would have to fight in the same way so that the Moslems could not approach close enough to attack. The crusaders' crossbowmen must continually harass the Moslems' horses, because they are unprotected, and the enemy are not so good at fighting on foot. This called for thousands of arrows, which Fidenzio thought could be taken into battle on carefully guarded pack-animals. These arrows would have to be shot at precisely the right moment, so that each could find its mark. The knights would have to learn about archery too. Moslems were afraid of the crusaders' lances, so they should bring plenty of good strong lances with them. If there were foot-soldiers to spare, possibly even too many of them for effective co-operation with the mounted troops, some formations of foot-soldiers would have to fight independently. Foot-soldiers with long lances could be closely massed with fixed weapons round the periphery of the forces, so that no enemy could penetrate their ranks. In these formations they would have to leave plenty of room so that the fighting men were not crowded together. There would have to be men with shields among the lancers, to defend them from enemy arrows – they would be a fortress wall protecting the others. Archers and crossbowmen would be there to kill the enemy's horses, or to keep them at a distance. All foot-soldiers would have to learn the use of the bow, and not go on a crusade without one. If possible they should wear body armour to protect them from enemy arrows.

The crusaders would have to be able to re-group their formations systematically. Whenever knights made a charge with couched lances, the Moslems broke up in disorder. But they regrouped at a trumpet signal, and attacked again. If the crusaders pursued the Moslems they could not easily catch them up because the enemy were lightly armed, and their horses unprotected. Moreover the crusaders' horses, being armoured, were more easily tired, and then the Moslems could attack them and their riders with arrows. According to Fidenzio, who knew less about Christian tactics than about the enemy's, the crusaders were not good at regrouping, and were even cowardly about it – which is not at all in agreement with the facts. But if the Christians could learn to keep on re-grouping, then the Moslems would have a more healthy respect for them and would cause less trouble. The crusaders must be brave men, and show no fear for they were fighting for a righteous cause. The shame of the enemy occupation of the Holy Land must be wiped out. A truly courageous bearing admits no capture, for it is not easy to get free again. Flight is as bad as death. The Christians would have to realise that the Moslems do not want to die, and quickly give in when they meet strong opposition, whereas the crusader wins eternal glory by death in battle, and forgiveness of all his sins.[93]

---

93 Fidenzio of Padua, pp. 28–30.

The crusaders' camp should not be too big, and should be pitched in the Moslem way, which Fidenzio had seen for himself, in a spot where there is plenty of food and water. It must be well guarded against a surprise attack, and fortified by a small ditch or other obstacle. Sentries must patrol the approaches day and night and probably the greater part of the army should always go armed, the rest having their weapons ready to hand, as the Tartars do in camp. The crusaders would have to take every castle, town and village, and disarm the inhabitants, so as to leave no enemies behind their backs.

Scouts would have to discover the Moslems' intentions, so that the crusaders could strike more effectively. Scouts help an army to avoid danger, and give a feeling of security and they make possible an attack on a weak enemy, because they make it possible to withdraw if the forces are insufficient. The better informed one is, the more confidently can one start an operation. The Moslem sultans make great use of scouts.[94] The crusaders must always move carefully and watchfully. They must never trust the enemy, never imagine themselves safe, never plunder or collect booty. The enemy had a habit of withdrawing, waiting to see what the crusaders were doing and then attacking. That was how conquering crusaders got beaten. It is much better to win a complete victory, and to chase the unbelievers, and only then to collect booty.

Crusaders must never split their forces, but keep them well together, as has been stated above. They must always think first, and then act with caution, as though they had eyes in their backs. Previous crusaders had often come to grief through their own folly.

A good knight needs all sorts of virtues; mercy strengthens a true Christian, and chastity preserves him from corruption, which flourishes in foreign parts, where there are wicked and perverted women. Humility makes a crusader willing to serve others, making him splendid, victorious and famous; charity and sympathy make Christians help each other as the Tartars do. Unity among Christians is supremely necessary among fighting men who are always in danger; moderation in food and drink – the Moslems take no wine with them on a campaign, and the Tartars use only milk and water – faithfulness, devotion to duty, and patience are all necessary; avarice and the desire for material wealth are forbidden. Christian soldiers must be God-fearing, and pray continuously, so that their prayers bring them victory as much as their battles. The Moslems pray a great deal.

An army cannot move without a commander-in-chief. He leads the expedition, and maintains unity and discipline. A good leader must first of all be a powerful man of outstanding character, so that he is respected and feared. A mighty leader can take many other Christians into his service, and pay them. Of course, it would be better if everyone fought at his own expense; many barons could really do this, but expect to be paid by the Church. The commander must lead a virtuous life. Through his own wisdom he can lead the army with care, and always choose the best solution to a problem, and he will collect wise men round him. He is a just man, and he must encourage others; this generosity allows the distribution of material goods to others.

[94] *Ibid.*, pp. 31–3.

This generosity must strike the mean between squandering and avarice. A good leader is a dedicated man and keeps watch over his Christian army. Gentleness in his own actions will encourage his followers to be peaceable men, so he must never be quick-tempered or quarrelsome. He must be a steadfast and strong personality who does not let himself be easily influenced.[95]

Then Fidenzio discusses how the various forces are to be employed. He foresees the army and a navy attacking the enemy simultaneously, and examines the navy's part first.

In all Christian maritime towns, he says, it must be absolutely forbidden to trade with Egypt or any of the sultan's possessions. The transgressors, however, do so very well out of it that they will never voluntarily give it up. Therefore a fleet must be fitted out. It must consist of 30, 40 or 50 well-equipped galleys and supply ships which can also fight the Moslems if necessary. (As has already been said, such a fleet has eleven great advantages).[96] The effect of such a fleet would be to force the Moslems to sue for peace or a truce with the Christians, or else see their land starve to death.

Christians in Egypt had told Fidenzio that their country would be ruined if trade with the Christians were stopped. He mentions several places which might serve as bases for such a fleet, but it would be best of course to have it as close to Egypt as possible. Cyprus, Acre, and the islands of Tortosa and Rhodes would all be suitable. The fleet would be manned by soldiers who had seafaring experience. They could carry out lightning attacks on the coast. The galley captains must be godly and true men, not covetous of earthly goods, careful, far-sighted and watchful in everything. An experienced admiral must be in charge. The captains must be free from Moslem influence, and impervious to corruption. They must beware of Greek fire, which nothing but vinegar or urine can quench. Therefore animals' skins must be laid out on the galleys. Probably the galleys would capture so much booty that they would pay for themselves.

The crusaders must wage war with justice. First, the inhabitants of an enemy town must be offered peace. If they surrender at once, they need only pay tribute-money, but if they refuse, they must be besieged. The crusaders would have to claim the whole of the Holy Land from the Euphrates to Egypt, and demand compensation for their expenses. If the enemy agreed there would be no fighting.[97] The fleet should cruise all the time off the Egyptian coast.

According to well-informed men, the fleet might by itself be enough to conquer the Holy Land. But it would still be necessary to reinforce Acre and the coastal strip with cavalry and foot-soldiers. The fleet must be kept there until victory is complete, and that could come about quickly.

Fidenzio then discusses routes. An approach by land through Constantinople and

[95] Ibid., p. 41.
[96] Ibid., pp. 46–50.
[97] Clausewitz points out that the aggressor is 'always peace loving', he would like to invade his neighbours peacefully unless there is organized resistance. On War, Bk VI, Ch. V. Fidenzio defends the same idea.

Armenia offers the advantages that the crusaders have their horses and pack-animals with them, can buy new ones on the way, and can pick up the necessary fodder in well-provided areas. They should ask local rulers for free and peaceful passage, and do no damage. In poor districts they will have to take food for several days with them. The crusaders would have to look after their safety, and will have to take workmen with them and cooking facilities on a small scale for their food and drink. Guides and interpreters will be necessary. A sea-passage by way of Venice, Genoa, or another port, would need a great many ships. A third way would be possible by crossing from Brindisi to Durazzo, where the crossing is short and would not need many ships. Then the crusaders could march to Constantinople. In any case, it is always useful to have a fleet to carry food supplies.[98]

The Christians could land in one of several places. A landing in Egypt could bring a decision immediately. The conquest of the island of Rasid would make it possible to starve Egypt out, but there are considerable difficulties about this. The crusaders have two armies, one on land, and one at sea as a navy. If the Saracens want to fight both, they must divide their forces and weaken themselves thereby. The further the two armies get from each other the weaker they become. On the other hand, the crusaders would not be spread over so great an area. Their fleet would be able to give support to the land army, without weakening the general strength. It would not therefore be advisable to attack Egypt simultaneously by land and sea. Egypt is very hot in summer, and plague could be an additional menace. The supply question is more difficult, and the enemy is stronger in Egypt than elsewhere. To offer a battle there is very dangerous. The Armenians and Tartars could give little or no help there.

It was also possible to land at Acre, which was still in Christian hands. There the crusaders could at once be helped by the military Orders – Templars, Hospitallers and the Teutonic knights and other noblemen. Merchants could provision the fleet and the crusaders would have the advantage of the advice of noblemen who were experienced in fighting against the Moslems. But Acre is by no means ideal for landing a large army. They would be surrounded on all sides by the Moslems, and they would have to use difficult passes which make provisioning awkward. Here again, it would be impossible to get help from the Armenians and Georgians.

Tripoli was also a good harbour, and although the town had been devastated it could be rebuilt, and the area round it is beautiful and healthy. The Christian population of Lebanon could help the crusaders. The narrow strip of land between the sea and the mountains would not permit the enemy to deploy a large army. The island of Tortosa has a harbour capable of sheltering many ships. It lies close to the mainland, but armies could not disembark thence. There is a broad open plain; but Margat and the Krak were close by, formerly Hospitallers' castles, but in Saracen hands by the time Fidenzio wrote and forming serious obstacles to an advance. The harbour of S. Simeon in the Gulf of Alexandretta offers anchorage for small ships at the mouth of the Orontes, and larger ones could use Portus Pallorum.[99]

Antioch was another good harbour, which Fidenzio could recommend. The

---

[98] Fidenzio of Padua, pp. 50–2.
[99] *Ibid.*, p. 56.

crusaders there would be at the northern extremity of the Holy Land, with no enemy close behind them, freely able to march southwards. It was healthy country, with beautiful valleys clothed with trees, well watered and amply stocked with food, wine, fish, fruit, etc. Acre lay not far off to the South. The friendly land of Armenia stretched northwards. Neither Cyprus nor Rhodes was very far away, and the enemy would have to come and fight a long way from Egypt, for they had few troops in Damascus. It would be best to land in Antioch in September or October. The crusaders would be able to rest in this temperate climate, and meanwhile summon the Christians in that area and send to the Tartars for help, unless the army was strong enough. They could get reinforcements from Armenia, and Georgia too. They could also meanwhile be strengthening Antioch, which was undefended, and from there they could march on to Aleppo, Damascus, and Jerusalem, while the fleet cruised off Egypt, draining off some of the enemy.[100]

For the actual fighting, Fidenzio recalls that the enemy are very much afraid of lances, and of attacks by knights. The Moslems have only a leather jerkin as armour, and leave their arms unprotected so as to have free movement for archery. Their legs are not protected. Their horses are not as powerful as those of the crusaders, and are not protected by armour. A good many of them are not very able fighting-men.

The Christians would have to keep a standing army in the Holy Land in order to hold it. They would have command of the sea as well with ten galleys. The cliffs of the coast near Jaffa, the hilltop of Montjoie, the range of hills between Jaffa and Jerusalem, and a few other places would have to be strongly fortified. The country would need a wise and rich governor, able to support knights himself, and to make his followers lead a life of Christian humility and wisdom. Finally, Fidenzio mentions the possibility of persuading the Mamelukes to leave the service of the sultan and come over to the Christians, and thus weaken the power of the enemy in Egypt.[101]

It will be seen from this summary that Fidenzio's treatise has given the whole question thorough consideration and that he was well acquainted with the Holy Land. But Fidenzio knew more about the Moslems' fighting technique than that of the Christians. His advice is eminently practical, and is the result of a remarkably careful study of warfare.

Pierre Dubois, De Recuperatione Terre Sancte

In this treatise Dubois sets out his plan for conquering the Holy Land. The land is thickly settled by Moslems, who can easily be reinforced by soldiers from neighbouring states. It will therefore take a really powerful army of crusaders to drive them out, and in order to form such a large army, the West must be at peace within itself. If there is war anywhere, crusaders will desert their fellows to go to the defence of their own country. The whole atmosphere will have to be so peaceful that there seems to be only one state, and that will have to be so much at unity in itself that divisions no longer exist. Now princes are all at odds with each other, he says, this

100 *Ibid.*, pp. 56–8.
101 *Ibid.*, pp. 58–60.

can only be solved by strengthening the defences of the Holy Land. As an example Dubois cites the Spaniards and the Germans, who are always so busy fighting among themselves that they can never find troops for the Holy Land. They only want to fight more and more at home.[102]

The first great problem is therefore the restoration of peace among Christians. Anyone who wants to fight will have to go to the Holy Land, and whoever will not conform will have to be punished. The prince and his followers will lose their possessions, as well as those who have provisioned these bloodthirsty men. They will have to be packed off to Palestine, and their families can follow them as soon as the land is conquered. If the latter do this voluntarily, or at once on receiving the order, their expenses and journey will be subsidized. They will not be excommunicated by the pope, for spiritual punishment brings the risk of incurring eternal punishment, which must be avoided, lest the number of devils be increased.[103]

It would naturally not suffice to forbid war in a Council, and the practical means of making these people go to the Holy Land must be thought out. Dubois therefore enlarges on the example of the rebellion of the count of Burgundy against the king of France. First of all, the count was sentenced by a council representative of all princes and the whole church. Then the king of France forbade the sending of supplies to Burgundy, meaning food and weapons as well as merchandise. Then the king marched in at harvest time and used that method of starvation and devastation which Dubois had expounded in detail in his treatise on the shortening of war. As soon as the rebels were forced to yield, they were punished with banishment to the Holy Land, where they were made to settle on the border, so that they would have to fight perpetually.[104]

The assets of a rebellious monarch, and any money owing to him must be seized and used for the expedition to the Holy Land. Anyone who does not conform to this law must be made to do so by the other princes and the pope, on pain of losing his own property. An international tribunal shall pronounce upon those monarchs and cities who acknowledge no higher authority.[105]

Once there is peace in Christendom, there will be enough fighting-men for a crusade. The city-republics of Genoa, Pisa and Venice, who have held up expeditions to the Holy Land until now by their own little wars, the cities of Tuscany and Lombardy and other cities, will then be able to live in peace, and can add their weight to the expedition.[106]

In Germany the emperor will no longer have to be elected, but the title will have to become hereditary, to avoid wars. The new ruler will have to pay the necessary annual subsidies for the Holy Land and send a great number of well-armed soldiers

---

[102] Dubois, *De recuperatione*, pp. 2–4.
[103] *Ibid.*, pp. 7–8. In c. 101, p. 82, the knights who do not promise by oath to keep the peace will be excommunicated.
[104] *Ibid.*, pp. 8–10, 17. See further the other treatise of Dubois.
[105] *Ibid.*, pp. 10–11.
[106] *Ibid.*, p. 10.

at his own expense. In Spain, the Moslems must first be driven out, in order to let the rulers go to the Holy Land.[107]

Huge sums of money must be collected, especially for the men who turn out to join the expedition on their own initiative. One important source of income will be the proceeds from the goods of the Templars, Hospitallers and other orders, established for the support and protection of the Holy Land. These possessions must be better managed in order to bring in more income.[108]

Ships are to be built with this money for the transport of impecunious soldiers, after which they can be used for the transport of reinforcements. They can bring useful merchandise from Palestine, and when they return from the West they can be laden with necessities for the colonists in the Middle East. These ships can also bring stores from the prosperous Mediterranean islands for the armies in the Holy Land.[109]

This annual income from the possessions of the military orders will bring such great wealth that it will be clear that the Templars and Hospitallers have been behaving treacherously towards the Holy Land up till now, and thus have sinned. This yearly sum will be supplemented by gifts from the faithful, and by the confiscated goods of those who go on making war despite the prohibition. Gifts from the faithful will be collected in the cathedral of each diocese and preferably used for the benefit of locally-recruited troops. The pope is to encourage the bishops to send soldiers. These must wear the same clothes – a uniform in fact – different for knights and foot-soldiers. The troops will also have with them the banner of the lord who sent them. The princes, or their representatives, must march with their own contingents, weapons and banners. All the subjects of a prince, whatever their rank, are to form one unit, if their number is sufficient. If there are not enough of them, then men of the same language must form a fighting unit. Even women and widows must help contribute enough weapons and clothes for their troops.

These crusading units will make a brave show when they 'march peaceably through towns, fortresses and villages, while the trumpets sound, or other instruments play, and they sing songs, as the troops march with gleaming weapons under splendidly waving banners. This will make a great impression, uplifting and warming the hearts of the beholders.' It would also help to make recruiting a success.[110]

The princes must promise that, even if they themselves return from the Holy Land, they will leave soldiers there with weapons and banners and the necessary money to maintain themselves. They must also promise to send the men's families to settle the land and reinforcements to settle the land. A brave and experienced knight must remain with every standard-bearer of a prince's banner.[111]

Every city and its surrounding district in the conquered land must come under the rule of a military governor. These will have *centuriones* under them, each commanding 8 cohorts of 12 men each, except the centurion's own, which shall consist of 15. This organisation will make for cohesion: 'the soldiers know each other and are used to each other, they protect and defend their comrades to the death'.[112] Experienced

---

107 *Ibid.*, pp. 12–13, 86–7.
108 *Ibid.*, p. 13.
109 *Ibid.*, p. 14.

110 *Ibid.*, pp. 14–15, c. 107, p. 91, pp. 15–16.
111 *Ibid.*, p. 16.
112 *Ibid.*, p. 17.

troops such as Spaniards should be posted to frontier districts whenever possible. Every city should know how many troops it must send. Every centurion must train his men in the use of weapons, according to their ability and the orders of the governors of the city.[113] Tactics must be adjusted to weather conditions, the terrain, the enemy, and the forces employed, as the commanders of the units think necessary.

Sea journeys are exhausting for men and beasts. There are not enough ships to transport them all at once, and everyone cannot go to the same port. But landings of small groups must be avoided, because they will be annihilated. For this reason a large part of the army must go by land, especially Germans, Hungarians, Greeks and the people from the North. The English, French, Spaniards, Lombards, Italians and islanders can go by sea, and anyone who is scared of the sea can go by land.[114]

Since it is best to attack the enemy in several places at once in order to make him split his forces, and thus beat him more easily, there should be four armies of which three should go by sea and one by land. Those who go by land must first ask the ruler through whose lands they are going for free access and unhindered passage and departure. These rulers should make arrangements for them at a reasonable price and the goods they need should be brought to the places through which the crusaders march.[115]

When the enemy realises that he is being attacked by these powerful forces it is possible that he will flee without fighting. If the fortresses, habitations, relics and sacred objects fall into Christian hands unharmed, and the Moslems surrender the land, they may be spared. But they must be threatened with total destruction if they try any tricks against the Christians.[116]

On the way home, Dubois suggests, one of the armies should put Charles of Valois, younger brother of the king of France, on the throne of Byzantium to which he has a claim. This king would then be close to the Holy Land and could send reinforcements. Thus the Mediterranean would be almost completely ruled by Christians, since they would be in possession of the north coast and the coast of the Holy Land. The Arabs and the Eastern nations would then be forced to trade with the Christians.[117]

It would not be enough to have peace among the temporal rulers only, but it would be necessary among the spiritual rulers as well. Dubois therefore proposes a whole series of reforms. Among other things he supports the abolition of the Papal States; the pope cannot simultaneously be a temporal and spiritual ruler nor should he be personally involved in war. Finally, Pierre Dubois advises king Philip the Fair of France not to take part personally in these wars, nor to expose his eldest son to such danger.[118]

---

113 *Ibid.*, c. 108, pp. 92–3, pp. 17–18.
114 *Ibid.*, pp. 18–19.
115 *Ibid.*, pp. 19, 88–9.

116 *Ibid.*, p. 89.
117 *Ibid.*, loc. cit.
118 *Ibid.*, pp. 33, 111–13, 114, n. 1.

2. *Other Plans for Wars*

The Strategic ideas of Pierre Dubois[119]

Dubois lamented that the enemies of Philip the Fair were unwilling to fight battles any more because the royal army was too strong, and castles and fortified towns made it impossible to finish a war quickly and successfully. Against such fortresses 'your army of splendid knights usually has to fight out a lengthy siege' he says.

> Your Majesty is bound to suffer, as your predecessors did, from these encircle-ments and long sieges, as experience, that teacher of all things, has shown. If your Majesty attacks the enemy's land with a small army it will soon be brought to bay. If you attack with a large army, and if you try to beat your enemy by besieging him, then you have to stay for a long time in the same place, which entails considerable loss of men and beasts, and shortages for the army, where the nobility have to bear very heavy expenses. A castle can hardly be taken within a year, and if it does fall, it means more expenses for the king's purse and for his subjects than the conquest is worth.

> Because of these lengthy, dangerous and arduous sieges, and because battle and assaults can be avoided, leaders are apt to come to agreements which are unfa-vourable to the stronger party. The besieger is on foreign ground, and is therefore bound to spend a disproportionately large amount in contrast with his enemy. He has to face greater dangers, and suffer greater losses. The enemy can call up men from neighbouring towns and fortresses and quietly await a favourable moment. In this way, with comparatively little trouble, loss, or expense, he can bring the invader to bay, because his men have only to come from their nearby homes.

> As well as this, it is difficult or even impossible for a large army to stay a long time in one place, because the nobility suffer. They are always rather dainty and sensitive on account of their upbringing and eating habits. They are not used to enduring the heat of summer and cannot do without luxurious food. They cannot stand the innumerable privations which they have met with even more than others in their long experience. The huge numbers of horses cannot be kept in one place and they lose condition through lack of fodder and fresh water, and suffer torture from the myriads of flies. Disease may break out owing to lack of care and cleanliness in the camp.

Dubois also mentions that a revolt by a duke or a count means that all his followers are guilty of lèse-majesté. But there is no point in condemning them all to death once the king has put down the rising: this would be useless cruelty. Yet if they go unpunished there will be no respect for law, and there is a danger of other rebellions against the king if there is no heavy penalty attached. It is an even more lamentable fact that the traditional methods of warfare mean the deaths of countless innocent people, who are not in a state of grace and will therefore go to hell when they die. Thus the number of devils is increased and that of the angels diminished, and this all happens without teaching the living, who live to fight another day. It is certainly best not to go to war at all, but as Aristotle says, war may be the only possible means

---

[119] 'Summaria brevis et compendiosa doctrina felicis expedicionis et abreviacionis guerrarum . . .', Paris, Bibl. Nat., MS lat. 6222 c.

of restoring peace or keeping it. So Dubois propounded a new method, which avoided the disadvantages of the older one. The king had had the chance to see the dangers of war for himself or had heard of them, after the French royal expeditions in Aragon, Flanders and Gascony.[120]

> If it is true, as they say, that the king has acquired sovereignty of the district of Arles, and the area this side of the Rhine, and of Lombardy, from the Mediterranean to the north, and wants to keep this land, he will have to realise that it consists of many duchies, counties, and provinces, whose inhabitants have always been ready to fight, and to whom war comes naturally through long experience. They have no fear of war, and the sons and nephews of the fallen will not be scared off by the death of their relatives. They will refuse to surrender, and constantly rebel, and not give in unless Your Majesty uses some much more drastic method, for they will always put their faith in their experience of war and their numerous fortresses, mountains, and passes.[121]

If the king tried to make these conquests by the usual methods, France would never have peace again. People would remember that this never happened under former kings, because it had been governed by the best rulers for the people and for the defence of the Church in the whole world. People would be so indignant that they would say that the king was only considering his own interests while their own blood was spilt and their possessions gambled away. People might even say harder things than that, so terrible that no right-minded person could bear to write them.[122]

In order to avoid this, and to make it possible for the king to look after his newly conquered territories, and add other conquests to his dominions, Dubois proposes a new method of warfare. He takes as an example a rebellion by the duke of Lorraine. First, efforts must be made to bring the duke round to a better frame of mind, and to get him to reaffirm his allegiance. After that, the greatest barons of the duchy should be told: if they continue to rebel, their possessions will be taken from them and they themselves will be punished. If that fails to work, then the royal army must attack.

> The king then sends his army with knights and foot-soldiers into the duke's land, just as the harvest begins to ripen. The troops appear outside towns and castles. If the garrisons refuse to open the gates, or to fight a battle, all the vines, fruit-trees, and plants must be destroyed throughout the area. The men of Lorraine are not to be killed, unless they are so bold as to attack the king's army and to force it to fight in self-defence. Those of the enemy who attack should only lose a hand or a foot, so that their souls do not go to hell. All fortresses situated near the Duchy should be stocked up with the grain, beasts, and fruit from the land which is laid waste. Enough soldiers should be left in these royal castles to guard all roads and small thoroughfares after the withdrawal of the French army, so that it will be impossible to provision the duchy. The duke and his people will soon starve like curs and not be able to survive. How can the duke raise an army when the whole year's hay, straw, and grain have been destroyed by fire? Furthermore, he cannot

---

[120] Summary of fo. 2v and 3. Cf. N. de Wailly, *Mémoire* . . ., p. 438.
[121] Fo. 3v. Cf. Dubois, *De recuperatione*, p. 120, n. 1. N. de Wailly, p. 439.
[122] Fo. 3v.

fight the king's armies who are encircling him in the winter. Under penalty of the same devastation, the surrounding lands must be forbidden to send food to the duchy, to let its inhabitants cross their borders or to let them pass through their lands.[123]

Starvation should bring the rebels to heel. This exemplary punishment may be expected to take away for ever any desire to rebel. Furthermore other people will be afraid and become an easy prey, 'so that his royal Majesty may graciously turn his attention to the subjection of other nations'.

This, with God's help, is certainly possible if the king bears in mind the following points.[124] First, the writer asks whether it is possible to crush a duchy without a battle, without determined resistance or without starting a general war. He thinks it is, for the king has so powerful an army that no one in his senses would dare sit and wait for such an army with the idea of fighting a set battle against it with iron and steel. How could any duke or count, acquainted with the royal army of France, dare do such a thing? If any such bold prince should make an appearance, prepared to defy the royal army, he will have to be punished, and that exceptionally severely, for trying to kill the king and defeat his army.[125] The king could also conquer north Italy. There too all food supplies could be destroyed and then a blockade be set up so that no neighbouring princes could feed the country. Thus the Lombards would be forced by terrible famine to yield their provinces to the king: 'the treasures of the world, which their wicked tricks have gained for them, will be given over to you, and they will obey you for ever as serfs. I do not believe that such a splendid conquest has been seen since the creation of the world.' If the Lombards could be subdued by this method of warfare, how could any other nation dare offer resistance? At this point the question may be raised, says Dubois, whether Lombardy is not so thickly populated, and has so many castles, that the emperors and kings of the Holy Roman Empire could never manage to subdue it in a short time. But innumerable unpaid soldiers would join the king of France on an expedition which is going to yield so much booty. It would also be possible to get the kings of Sicily and Germany to come in as allies. Finally Dubois points out that the king would be able to exploit the civil strife in the Lombard towns by allying himself with one of the factions, in order to crush the other and bring them all under his dominion.[126]

So much for the strategic ideas and plans of Pierre Dubois. His exaggerated estimate of the power of the French kingdom is evident in his conception of the strength of its fighting forces. He thinks that Philip the Fair could easily send off an army of 2,000 poor noblemen and 80,000 foot-soldiers without any hope of their return – indeed this would pass unnoticed by the French, since the king had such numberless fighting men at his disposal.[127] But Dubois did not retain this optimistic

---

[123] Fo. 4v–5. Funck-Brentano, *De exercitum*, pp. 11–12. Dubois, *De recuperatione*, p. 9, n. 1.

[124] Fo. 5. Funck-Brentano, *loc. cit.*

[125] Fo. 5v. N. de Wailly, p. 441.

[126] Fo. 8–8v. Funck-Brentano, *De exercituum*, pp. 12–13. Dubois, *De recuperatione*, p. 105, n. 1, 3, p. 111, n. 1.

[127] Fo. 9. Dubois, *De recuperatione*, p. 115, n. 1.

outlook for long: in 1300 he thought that Philip could overthrow the world,[128] but in 1305, just after the French defeat in the Flemish wars, he admitted: 'I do not think that nowadays anyone in his right mind can possibly think that a single monarch can rule the world, and that everyone would obey him. If anyone were to aspire to this, endless wars, revolutions and disputes would break out, which it would be impossible to control.'[129] Despite the fact that Philip the Fair was able to reckon on a powerful pro-French party among the nobles and upper classes in the towns, the royal fighting forces still seemed too weak to subjugate the Flemings once and for all.

A plan for warfare against the rebels in Flanders, 1325

Another strategic plan, dating from the first half of the fourteenth century, is couched in less general terms than the proposals of Dubois. It takes the form of a draft comital ordinance stating how the war was to be carried on from Ghent in 1325.[130]

The rebellion which had broken out in Bruges and maritime Flanders in 1323 suddenly increased in intensity in 1325. The count of Flanders, Louis of Nevers was forced to evacuate Ypres and was then captured at Courtrai and handed over to an army from Bruges. Zannekin, leader of the rebellion in maritime Flanders, took Ypres. The rebels then chose an uncle of the count, Robert of Cassel, as regent, while the army from Ghent recognised John of Namur as regent and remained faithful to the captured count. The rebels attacked Oudenaarde, then defeated the men of Ghent at Deinze on 15 July, but John of Namur defended Ghent successfully against them though he could rely only on Oudenaarde and the land of Alost. Grammont, Termonde, the Four Ambachten and the land of Waas sided with the rebels. It was in these circumstances that he or his councillors concocted a plan for the conduct of the war. Count John and the city of Ghent concluded a written agreement not to make any separate peace with the men of Bruges and the rebels. The economic blockade of the rebellious districts was announced, so that merchants could no longer travel from place to place with their goods. The people of Ghent were forbidden to have any dealings with the people of Bruges and Grammont, and these towns would be prevented from holding markets. This was certainly a counter-measure against the blockade that the rebels imposed on Ghent. The country round this city was still blockaded. In the north-west were the troops of Walter Rathgeer, who was at Eeklo and was able to rely on the support of the four Ambachten and the land of Waas. In the south-west, another band of rebels had taken up their position between Ghent and Oudenaarde. Ghent was also cut off from the sea by the district of Bruges, the four Ambachten and the land of Waas. The town of Termonde cut off the Scheldt in the east. Bruges and Ypres were not blockaded at all. Thus this measure of John's had no effect, but ambassadors from Ghent went to the king of France, who later forbade all trade with Flanders. This stop had some influence on the moderate section of the rebels.

The defence of Ghent was to be ensured by a close watch on the city gates with

---

[128] Fo. 6v. Dubois, *De recuperatione*, p. 129, n. 1.
[129] Dubois, *De recuperatione*, p. 54.
[130] Verbruggen, *Un projet d'ordonnance comtale sur la conduite de la guerre*, pp. 123–36.

troops from the count's army and the levies. Spies, messengers, and suspicious persons were to be kept out, but the count's soldiers were to have free passage at all times. Order was to be secured in the city itself, and assemblies were forbidden. It was also strictly forbidden to do any damage to the townspeople's possessions. Agreements were to be made for the care and feeding of the horses in order to avoid disputes between the city's ostlers and the count's knights, and the ostlers were not allowed to take a knight's armour or horse as a pledge at the moment when their owners had to go out to fight the enemy. The count's soldiers could move freely in the city by night, and if a quarrel started between the citizens and these nobles, it was to be settled at once.

A large part of the communal army was to remain in Ghent for the defence of the city: at the most, 200 crossbowmen and 3,000 levies were allowed to go out on warlike errands outside the city. The weavers of Ghent seemed rather untrustworthy, because they wanted to take part in the rising: weavers had already been banned from the city and those who worked there, about 2,192 in all, had to pay a special tax. In order to defend the tremendous perimeter of the city ramparts, and to keep the weavers under control, at least 4,000 levies were kept in the city.

The 200 crossbowmen and the 3,000 levies already mentioned could be used for offensive expeditions. Half of these had to be ready to go into action at any minute. It can be seen from these small numbers, which agree with the most reliable figures in the city records in Ghent, in what a difficult situation John of Namur and his Ghent followers found themselves. It is also clear that the men of Bruges and the rebels from maritime Flanders were able to raise much larger armies. But very strict discipline was maintained in all offensive expeditions. No one might break rank to go plundering without the marshal's permission, or to set fire to anything. All the booty which was captured had to be brought next day to the marshal to be sold. The takings were later divided between the armoured cavalry and the foot-soldiers, in just proportion.

John of Namur's plan and strict discipline had results. He and his followers won two victories during sorties, one at Nevele, in which 800 rebels were beaten, and another at Assenede. Many rebels went home at the onset of winter, and it seems from the forces employed in Nevele that they were less than the 100 crossbowmen and 1,500 levies who were standing at the ready in Ghent, while for an important expedition 200 crossbowmen and 3,000 ordinary foot-soldiers could be put into the field. John of Namur liberated the neighbourhood of Ghent, and on 3 and 4 December two Ghent aldermen entered the land of Waas to take oaths of allegiance from the inhabitants.[131]

John of Namur had originally wanted to recruit 200 foreign armoured cavalrymen as well, as they would be of more use than the levies. Also he would have liked to enrol the best of the foot-soldiers from the castellanies who were still on the count's side, but excluding the communes. These parts of the plan were scrapped, the first doubtless for want of money, the second probably because the countryside was not

131 J. Vuylsteke, *Gentse Stads- en Baljuwsrekeningen, 1280–1336*, Ghent, 1900, 2 vols, I, p. 435.

sufficiently safe and there were not enough convinced adherents of the count to be found.

The plan included a whole series of judicious measures which were entirely suited to the peculiar circumstances of the second half of the year 1325, and everything points to the fact that it was put into practice with some success.

The plan of Benedict Zaccaria for the war at sea against England

Between August and November 1297, Benedict Zaccaria, the admiral of Castile, was studying the state of the French fleet. He then made certain proposals to Philip the Fair for the war against England.[132] A fleet of transport ships and galleys was to be fitted out for the transport of knights and their horses, and foot-soldiers consisting of crossbowmen, lancers and spearmen. This would mean that they were fitted to fight the enemy in different ways:

1. In sea-battles.
2. By burning or capturing the enemy's ships in harbour, by attacking with the fleet or with soldiers who had been landed.
3. The fleet should land knights and other soldiers. These could undertake plundering raids, in which towns, villages and entire districts could be destroyed and burned. Only really well-fortified enemy towns could offer resistance to this sort of surprise attack. After its plundering the army would withdraw, re-embark and make another raid in another area. The enemy would not know where such an attack would come. It would be impossible for them to defend all parts of the country efficiently, and after a few such raids they would be worried and scared. If this army could take a town close to the coast, within easy reach of the fleet, it should then pretend to set about fortifying this town as if intending to occupy it. The enemy would have to raise an army to recapture the town, which would be both troublesome and expensive. As soon as the enemy had made a serious attempt to do this, the town should be set on fire, the army re-embark, and the fleet sail off to do the same elsewhere.
4. The enemy would have to spend a great deal of money. He would also become uneasy and be afraid that Scotland and Wales would help the French invaders.

Zaccaria was reckoning on 20 *huissiers* or transport ships, 4 galleys and 24 other ships. At the moment the king had 13: 7 were in harbour at Rouen, 5 at La Rochelle and La Réole, and the last at Calais. Zaccaria himself had 2. At La Rochelle, a big transport ship belonging to a merchant could be used on payment of a reasonable charge. Four of the royal galleys could be made higher, wider and longer aft, to turn them into transport ships. Each one could transport 20 men and their horses. 400 foot-soldiers or more would also be taken to help the knights. There would be 4,800 seamen in the fleet of 40 ships, so that there would be a total of 5,200 foot-soldiers and 400 knights.

---

[132] E. Boutaric, *Notices et extraits de documents inédits relatifs à l'histoire de France sous Philippe le Bel*, pp. 112–19. Ch. de la Roncière, *Histoire de la marine française*, I, Paris, 1899, p. 361. Atiya, p. 61, thinks that it is a plan for a Crusade.

Two of the four galleys of the fleet should always follow the transport to protect it, and give support to the knights while they were landing. The other galleys could regularly bring up supplies for the army and the horses, so that it always had what it needed, and would not have to search for provisions in enemy country, but could keep on attacking. If the knights and the foot-soldiers were well-supplied there would be enough of them to do a lot of damage to the enemy.

The knights' leader would have to be a man of experience, ready to stand up to great hardships and to play a very active part. His knights would have to be well-disciplined, skilled in the use of weapons, persevering and tough, because this sort of warfare makes tremendous demands physically. The best possible seamen must be recruited, 'paying efficient seamen brings good returns, paying inefficient ones is money thrown away'. Both knights and sailors were to be paid for four months. This would enable them to find good knights and sailors, and in the end the best is the cheapest. If they were well paid, they could bring their equipment and arms themselves, so that the king would not have to buy it for them. Also it would not be necessary to return to get the money for pay, for this means great loss of time, because during that time no one can be attacking, and the king would have to support the army for longer.

Then Zaccaria estimates the cost of these expeditions. The pay for 4,800 sailors cost 40 *sous tournois* per man. They can be had for 35 *sous*, but at 40 *sous* better men are available. To economise Zaccaria would only give them bread, water, beans and peas as food, while the men would have to provide their wine, meat and other foodstuffs. This would save a lot of work, and the king much expense, and the sailors would not be able to grumble about the food. These expenses would amount to 9,600 pounds *tournois* a month, i.e. 38,400 pounds for four months. The bread, beans and peas cost 15 *sous tournois* per month per man. Altogether this comes to 3,600 pounds *tournois*, or 14,400 for four months.[133] Fitting out the ships would cost 3,000 pounds: Zaccaria estimates the cost of masts, sails, ropes, caulking, and so on, at 5,000 pounds. Galleys would have to be brought from Gascony and Poitou in Rouen, which would cost another 3,000 pounds. His figure came to 63,800 pounds *tournois*.

In order to get this fleet ready immediately, someone would have to be chosen secretly to be in command of the knights. An advance of 20,000 pounds would be needed for fitting out the ships, and the same sum would be needed again in January to mass the ships at Rouen and recruit the men. The rest of the money would have to be on hand by the beginning of March: everything would have to be ready by April.

The king would have to forbid anyone from putting to sea from March to the end of June, to make it easy to recruit sailors without having to pay more than the normal rate.

Zaccaria's proposed attacks on England had much to offer. It was very difficult to intercept the invaders, as they would never stay anywhere long. Only the English fleet might react violently, but it was doubtful whether it was powerful enough and

---

133 Boutaric, p. 116, gives 2,300 and 14,600 pounds; both numbers are wrong.

could get there quickly enough to intercept the enemy. Of course, this possibility could not be excluded, but it did not alter the fact that this admiral, a man of considerable experience, had thought up a good plan. If the king of England were to organize the coastal defence of his whole country, it would cost an appalling sum. The Christian leaders hoped in the same way to inflict enormous damage and great losses on the sultan of Egypt. Before the French fleet was ready, in 1295, Philip the Fair protected the French coast with troops to prevent a landing by Edward I. This cost 600,000 pounds *tournois*.[134] The fitting out of a great fleet in 1295 cost a great deal more: 1,579,250 pounds *tournois*,[135] and brought no important result.

Offensive Strategy

The use of offensive strategy presupposes great strength and overall superiority compared with the enemy. If there is no numerical advantage, it is absolutely necessary that the quality of the troops should be higher. If a medieval ruler had the necessary means he was in a position to use a strategy of overthrow, and in this case the outcome of warfare depended on the enemy's reaction. If the enemy accepted battle, he could be destroyed in a great engagement, as the examples of king Harold in 1066 and king Guy de Lusignan in 1187 show.

Charlemagne used his superior strength to carry out concentric advances into enemy territory. In 773, the warriors of the Franks were assembled at Geneva. From there two armies set out against the weaker forces of the Lombards: one of them went over the Mont Cenis, the other over the Great St Bernard Pass. They marched across the plain of the Po towards Pavia, where the king of the Lombards resisted until June 774 and then yielded.[136] The Frankish army had kept up the siege during the winter. In the same year, Charlemagne sent four *scarae* to Saxony from Ingelheim. Three of them became involved in battle with the enemy, the fourth did not have to fight. It seems that they took different routes, otherwise the fourth would have had to fight too.[137]

In 778, the Frankish armies in Spain advanced towards the Moslems in two columns. One marched under Charlemagne to Pamplona, the other to Saragossa, where they finally met. But the expedition misfired, and ended in the surprise of the rearguard of the Franks by the Basques in the Pyrenees.[138] In 787, three armies were formed to overthrow duke Tassilo of Bavaria. The first came from Alamannia in the west, under Charlemagne, and marched to Augsburg. The second, which came from the north, was made up of Austrasians, Thuringians, and Saxons; they marched to the region of Pföring, on the Danube. The third army, led by Charlemagne's son

---

[134] Boutaric, *Mémoire anonyme sur la guerre contre l'Angleterre*, in *Notices et extraits*, p. 124.

[135] R. Fawtier, *L'Europe occidentale de 1270 à 1328, première partie. De 1270 à 1328*, in G. Glotz, *Histoire générale*, Histoire du moyen âge, 6, Paris, 1940, p. 193.

[136] *Annales regni Francorum*, anno 773, pp. 34–9.

[137] *Ibid.*, anno 774, p. 40.

[138] *Ibid.*, anno 778, pp. 50–1. R. Fawtier, *La chanson de Roland*, pp. 169–70.

Pepin, came from Italy by Trent to Bolzano. Tassilo found himself encircled, and surrendered.[139]

The Franks marched against the Avars in 791 with three armies. Franks, Saxons, Frisians and Thuringians marched along the left bank of the Danube through Bohemia. More Franks, Alamanni, and Bavarians went along the right bank under Charlemagne himself, both armies being supplied by boats on the river. Both crossed the Enns, which was the frontier between Bavaria and the land of the Avars, attacking many enemy fortifications on the way. The third army came up from Italy; it was a *scara* under Pepin, and had already won a victory. Charlemagne marched through the Wienerwald and on to the Raab, which he crossed, and followed it to the Danube. He laid the land of the Avars waste, but his army lost many horses through sickness.[140] In 795, with the help of the Croatian duke Woynimir, the army of Eric of Friuli broke through the 'ring', or circle of fortifications of the Avars, and plundered it. In 796, by a concentric advance with troops from Italy, Bavaria and Alamannia, Pepin dealt a mortal blow to the kingdom of Avars, already torn by internal strife, and drove them over the Theiss.[141]

This highly effective strategy of concentric advances was also used in 794 against the Saxons. Charlemagne led one army, and his son Charles marched with the other by way of Cologne. The Saxons were prepared at first to join battle south of Paderborn, but they abandoned that idea when they saw they were going to be attacked from both sides and gave in.[142]

In 805 the emperor's son Charles organised a campaign in Bohemia with three armies. He himself marched out of the west through eastern Francia and the Böhmerwald to Bohemia. Another army consisting of Saxons and Wends came from the north through the Erzgebirge. A third army, made up of Bavarians led by Adolf and Werner came from the southwest. They all joined forces at the Eger in the Bohemian plain. For forty days they devastated the enemy's territory, staying there till there was no longer food for the troops nor fodder for the horses. Duke Lecho of the Bohemians was killed during the attack, but the enemy avoided a major battle and withdrew into thickly wooded inaccessible areas of the country. Meanwhile a fourth army was creating a diversion. It arrived by ship in the Elbe and laid waste the region round Magdeburg.[143] This diversion was probably aimed at the Sorbs, who were attacked in 806. In the campaign of 806 the enemies were attacked on a broad front by three different kinds of troops: cavalry units of the *scara*, the army (*exercitus*), and a *manus*, which means a rather small force, probably also cavalry. The *manus* was probably made up of vassals from Bavaria, Alamannia and Burgundy, and was sent to Bohemia. It plundered the region and laid it waste. Charles sent his *scarae* over the Elbe and himself crossed the Saale with the army. Miliduoch,

---

139 *Annales regni Francorum*, anno 787, p. 78.
140 *Ibid.*, anno 791, p. 88. *Annales Laureshamenses, Alamannici, Guelferbytani et Nazariani*, ed. G. H. Pertz, MGH, SS, I, 2, 1826, 1829, I, p. 34.
141 *Annales regni Francorum*, anno 796, pp. 98–9. *Chronicon Moissiacense*, MGH, SS, I, p. 302.
142 *Annales regni Francorum*, anno 794, pp. 94–6.
143 *Ibid.*, anno 805, p. 120. *Annales Mettenses priores*, anno 805, pp. 93–4. *Chronicon Moissiacense*, ed. G.H. Pertz, MGH, SS, I, 2, 1826, 1829, II, p. 258.

duke of the Sorbs was killed and the whole region laid waste. After that the Franks built two castles, one on the bank of the Saale near Halle, and the other on the Elbe, upstream from Magdeburg.[144] In 812 there was again a concentric advance on the Wilzians by three *scarae*.[145]

Louis the Pious also used the same method of simultaneous attacks. In 820 three armies were formed with men from Saxony, eastern Francia, Alamannia, Bavaria and Italy. When the grass grew green in the spring the three corps marched into the land of Liudewit, duke of Croatia. The first army came from Italy via the Noric Alps; the second came through Carinthia, the third through Bavaria and Upper Pannonia. The first army marched on the right, and was slowed down by enemy resistance in the Alps. The third went on the left and had furthest to go. It had trouble in crossing the Drava. The central army went through Carinthia and three times met with strong enemy resistance, but managed to overcome it. After that it crossed the Drava and marched swiftly to the rendezvous appointed. While duke Liudewit resisted in a fortress on top of a hill the three armies devastated the countryside.[146] But the duke would not negotiate. After that, in 821, there was a new campaign with three armies, and again the countryside was laid waste. After a third campaign, with an army from Italy in 822, Liudewit had to flee, and was murdered.[147] In 824, Louis the Pious undertook a campaign with three armies against Brittany, who refused from time to time to recognise the dominion of the Franks. The expedition only started in the autumn, because there had been famine previously. The troops advanced from Rennes. Two armies were led by the emperor's sons, Pepin and Louis, the third was led by Louis the Pious himself. The land was devastated for days until the Bretons surrendered yet again.[148]

An interesting arrangement of armies was used in 800 at the siege of Barcelona. Louis the Pious had formed three armies.[149] One was besieging the city under Rotstagnus, count of Gerona; another was led by William, the future hero of the epic, and count Adhemar of Narbonne. This corps was stationed near the city to cover the besiegers against an attacking army. When the enemy was repulsed, William and Adhemar came back to Barcelona to take part in the siege. Louis stayed with the third army in Roussillon, from whence he could hasten to help the other two. Barcelona was taken.

In 809, Louis split his army into two. He went to Tortosa, with the larger part, meanwhile sending Isembard, Adhemar, Bera and Burellus with other troops to the interior. While the king was luring the enemy to Tortosa, these were to appear behind the latter's back, and attack him or else demoralise him by plunder and arson. These troops marched at night, and hid themselves by day in the woods. They marched for six days, crossing the Cinca and the Ebro on the seventh. After twenty days' march

[144] *Annales regni Francorum*, p. 122.
[145] *Chronicon Moissiacense*, p. 259.
[146] *Annales regni Francorum*, anno 820, pp. 152–3.
[147] *Ibid.*, anno 821, pp. 154–6; anno 822, p. 158.
[148] *Ibid.*, anno 824, p. 165.
[149] Astronomus, *Vita Hludovici imperatoris*, c. 13, pp. 612–13. *Chronicon Moissiacense*, MGH, SS, I, p. 307, places these operations in 803.

they reinforced the troops outside Tortosa, which did not however fall.[150] In 810, the main army marched on Tortosa again. A second army marched from Barcelona to the Ebro. They had neither baggage nor tents with them and lit no fire lest the smoke should betray them, and marched only at night. They had dismantled boats with them, each of the four parts of a boat were carried by two pack-animals. They crossed the Ebro with these boats after three days' march. But the surprise did not come off, and though they got to Tortosa and reinforced the main army, the city did not fall.[151]

Of course such concentric attacks with independent corps were only possible where a large army was available, which was certainly stronger than the enemy's. This was the case with Charlemagne and Louis the Pious. The main purpose was to assemble the various armies for battle. In each of these concentric attacks the various armies joined up before the enemy could defeat a single corps at a time. Such a strategy was perfectly suited to a situation where there was a small number of invasion routes into enemy country, as in the campaigns against the Lombards (778), the Bavarians (787), the Bohemians (805), and the Croats (820). The approach routes or passes were blocked or dominated by fortifications or needed only a small body to defend them. A single route was too risky because surprise was impossible. A concentric advance by two or three armies meant that the enemy had to split his forces to bar every entry. In that case the invader had a better chance of getting in at one place and outflanking the other garrisons of the other routes. A deep advance into enemy country might force the defender into a very rapid withdrawal. The invader had also a better chance to surprise the enemy with one or two corps, which by reason of their smaller size would be more mobile than a large army on a single route.

In 773, Charlemagne was held up in the Mont Cenis pass by the army of king Desiderius, king of the Lombards, who was defending the fortifications. But then the Frankish leader send his *scara* over the mountains to outflank Desiderius' men. The manoeuvre was successful and the king had to withdraw.[152] In 791, the Avars left their fortresses when they heard that Frankish troops were coming up on both banks of the Danube, and had a fleet on the water. In 820, the army advancing out of Italy were held up in the Alps. The central army had to overcome three bouts of enemy resistance.

The strategic method of the concentric approach and the simultaneous use of different routes of invasion were absolutely necessary to success in certain countries. This was very clear in the case of the attacks on Bohemia. There were only two important routes for attacking Bohemia; one was through the Erzgebirge, the Freiberger Mulde and the pass from Kulm to Brüx, used by the third army in 805, that is, the Saxons. This route was used by at least nine expeditions against Bohemia, namely in 805, 856, 892, 929, 1004, 1040, 1041, 1107 and 1126.[153] The second route

150 Astronomus, pp. 613–14.
151 *Ibid.*, pp. 614–15.
152 *Annales regni Francorum*, anno 773, pp. 34–9. *Annales Mettenses priores*, p. 60.
153 Schünemann, 'Deutsche Kriegführung im Osten während des Mittelalters', 1938, *Deutsches Archiv fur Geschichte des Mittelalters*, 2, p. 61.

lay through Regensburg to Cham then by the pass from Furth and Taus to Pilsen. This too was used nine times at least, in 805 by Charlemagne's eldest son, probably also in 929, 976, 1003, 1033, 1040, 1041, 1110 and in 1142.[154]

In several instances, however, the enemy systematically avoided battle against the powerful Frankish armies and their heavy cavalry and withdrew to the safety of his fortresses. When this happened, the fate of the campaign depended on the possibilities of supplying troops during a protracted siege. Often large-scale raids were enough to overcome his resistance.

Later rulers also used the strategy of multiple concentric attacks. King Henry I of France invaded Normandy with two armies in 1054. The king moved with the main army on the west bank of the Seine. The second army invaded Normandy from the east, under Odo, brother of the king. William the Conqueror and part of his forces opposed king Henry; count Robert of Eu stood against the French army of Odo. Robert of Eu attacked the dispersed forces by surprising Odo and defeated them. King Henry retreated when he heard the bad news.[155] Another two-pronged attack also met defeat. In 1214, king John attacked in the south-west of France, and emperor Otto and his allies attacked in the north. Both armies were defeated by the French forces. The example of the invasion of Hainault in 1184 by the army of Philip of Alsace from one side, and the army of the archbishop of Cologne and the duke of Brabant from the other side, has already been quoted. It was a successful punitive expedition. When Dubois, in his *De Recuperatione Terre Sancte*, was planning the collection of a really powerful army of crusaders he wrote that it was better to attack the enemy at different points in order to split his forces. He advised the arrival of one army by land and three by sea. At the same time such problems as the transport of troops could more easily be solved.[156]

In his proposal for the establishment of a Christian kingdom in the East for Philip the Tall, second son of Philip the Fair, in 1308, he proposed a diversion in the region of Acre, to draw off the Egyptian forces in that direction, and then to land in Egypt and conquer that.[157] Raymond Lull also advised the formation of two expeditionary corps, one to march through Morocco, Tunisia and Tripolitania, and the other by Constantinople and Syria.[158]

Charlemagne used a strategy of overthrow in his campaign against the Lombards in 773–74, and against duke Tassilo of Bavaria in 787. The decisive campaign in Saxony in 783 contains also the principal characteristics of the strategy of annihilation, with the battles at Detmold and on the Haase and the vigorous pursuit to the Elbe. William the Conqueror's strategy of overthrow was successful in 1066: he won England in a single battle. Saladin destroyed the army of king Guy de Lusignan at Hattin in 1187 and re-conquered the Holy Land.

---

154 *Ibid.*, *loc. cit.*
155 William of Jumiéges, *Gesta Normannorum ducum*, ed. J. Marx, Société d'histoire de la Normandie, Rouen, Paris, 1914, 1. VII, c. 10, pp. 128–30. William of Poitiers, c. 30, p. 70. Beeler, *Warfare in Feudal Europe*, pp. 45–6.
156 Dubois, pp. 18–19, 88–9.
157 *Ibid.*, p. 136.
158 Atiya, p. 85. Delaville le Roulx, pp. 30–1.

A would-be conqueror with a strong army had a preference for a strategy of annihilation: a single or two successful battles, a decisive pursuit and the submission of the country in a short campaign. The conqueror had to try to gain his aims quickly. The crusaders of the First Crusade elected to destroy the armies of their enemies in order to capture the holy places, and at Doryleum and Antioch they beat them each time in the open field. After a time of great weakness and privation they made a desperate sortie out of Antioch and crushed the enemy in battle, despite the fact that their army was very small. After the fall of Jerusalem they hastened towards the enemy army at Ascalon and defeated that too. Although their aims were originally in part religious, they were then able to establish states in the conquered territories, such as that of Edessa under Baldwin of Boulogne, and that round Antioch under Bohemond. Finally they established the kingdom of Jerusalem.

Two councils of war during their long campaign deserve special mention. In January 1099 they met to discuss the attack on Jerusalem under Raymond of St Gilles. Some noblemen proposed that Jabala should be taken first, and that an advance should then be made along the coast to capture one port after another. This strategy offered very easy provisioning by the fleet. But Tancred opposed the plan because the crusading army had only about 1,000 knights and 5,000 foot-soldiers, and was therefore too weak to take such well-defended ports in succession; in any case it would have taken a long time. A resolute march on Jerusalem, he said, would quickly lead to the conclusion of the crusade. The fall of the Holy City would make a great stir in the west, bringing new recruits to reinforce the army: capturing ports would not have the same effect. The arrival of these reinforcements would make the inhabitants of Jabala, Tripoli, Acre and Tyre leave their cities, which would fall into the crusaders' hands.[159]

This strategy called for a determined expedition to Jerusalem, to strike at the heart of the enemy's territory. The crusaders were ready on the march to destroy any armies who blocked their way.

A little later, there was another council of war at Ramla (3–6 June, 1099).[160] Since war had broken out with Egypt in the interval, some of the crusading leaders proposed attacking that country, in the hope of wiping out their army. Then they expected to be able to take Jerusalem without a struggle, and probably Alexandria and other Egyptian cities as well. They preferred this strategy of annihilation because they feared a disaster outside Jerusalem, where they would be fighting in tremendous heat without adequate food or water. Those opposed to this plan protested that the army numbered only 1,500 knights, and not many foot-soldiers, and that they would be going into an unfamiliar and remote land, with no hope of being able to stay there, and very little of getting away. They wanted to press on to Jerusalem, where the problems of supply would solve themselves. God would provide for his faithful servants, they said.

So at Ramla the more cautious plan was preferred to the adventurous expedition to Egypt, which is understandable since the crusaders were at last within sight of

---

159 Raymond of Aguilers, p. 273. Grousset, I, p. 129. Brandt, p. 205. Runciman, pp. 268–9.
160 Raymond of Aguilers, p. 292. Grousset, I, p. 151. Runciman, p. 277.

their goal. The small number of men in their army was bound to be an important factor in their plans too. Anyway it was impossible to set out to destroy the armies of all the rulers possessing a scrap of territory in the Holy Land. But there are unmistakable characteristics of a strategy of overthrow in their methods.

There are also a few remarkable strategic pursuits: after his victory on the river Haase in 783, Charlemagne pursued the Saxons over the Weser and reached the Elbe.[161] Otto I pursued the Hungarians for several days after their defeat at the Lechfeld in 955.[162] After the victory of the crusaders at Doryleum (1097), their pursuit coincided with their strategic advance.[163]

War on a grand scale was extremely difficult in the Middle Ages, owing to the small size of medieval states, the scarcity of the knights and the resultant small forces. Medieval leaders had to overcome numerous obstacles when they went to war: they were well aware that even with careful planning it would be impossible to destroy the enemy army since defence was much more stronger than attack, and they therefore tended to limit their aims. In most cases medieval wars had limited aims.

Medieval princes tried to conquer a castle, a town, a region, or a part of the principality. The conquest of a whole principality was already a big enterprise and took many years. The subjection of another kingdom did not happen often. In those conquests policy and strategy worked hand in hand to win new land and revenue.

Many wars had the appearance of a series of plundering raids and punitive expeditions in which the fields, houses and villages of the hostile inhabitants of the countryside suffered most terribly. This made considerable inroads on the economic resources of the enemy. Anything outside the walls or the fortress was burned or trampled and destroyed under the horses' hooves. But as long as the castle or the town was not taken the district was still the rightful owner's. These fortresses also hindered the exploitation of successes in the field. It was not possible to destroy the enemy completely, unless in isolated cases and for a short time, because protective armour spared the warrior's life. If the knights' high conception of honour did not mislead them, they found safe lodging in their castles. Then a new army was raised and they all waited for better days, when the equilibrium between the forces should be restored. In such a siege the attacker was sometimes so quickly exhausted that any advantage he might get was out of all proportion to the sacrifice involved.

Defensive Strategy

Defence is the stronger form of warfare. All means being equal on both sides, defence is easier than attack. Defence has the advantage of terrain, the theatre of war and its fortresses. It can unite its forces against the attacker who has to disperse his units to supply them. When the attacker invades the country with several armies, the defender

---

161 *Annales regni Francorum*, anno 783, pp. 64–7.
162 Cram, *Iudicium Belli. Zum Rechtscharakter des Krieges im deutschen Mittelalter*, Munster, Cologne, 1955, p. 155. Beeler, *Warfare in Feudal Europe*, p. 232.
163 Anonymous, *Gesta Francorum*, pp. 48, 54 [Hill, pp. 19–21]. Fulcher of Chartres, I, p. 336.

can operate on interior lines, concentrate superior forces on the decisive points, and overwhelm the enemy columns one after the other. The defender can also cut the communications of the enemy. He profits from time and all unexpected events, and from the wearing out of the invader. He gets political sympathy and the moral advantage which are derived from defending his own country; the other states, interested in the status quo can aid him.

1. *Defensive Systems of Medieval States*

In order to understand medieval strategy fully, and to see it in its proper perspective, it is necessary to consider briefly what sort of fortifications were built to strengthen the defences of various countries and how the lie of the land and natural obstacles could be exploited. Fortifications of every kind played an important part in the warfare of the time, and they largely explain why medieval defensive strategy was so much stronger than the offensive.

It would be very interesting to know the sums spent by medieval monarchs on fortifications in their countries. It is known that cities gave enormous sums for building walls and ramparts, and for digging moats. Unfortunately there is a total lack of information about costs for this period.

Even those principalities best protected by nature, and least accessible, were furnished with artificial defences. Mountain passes were blocked with palisades and stone walls, which like the *letzi* or *letzinen* of Switzerland sealed off these vital points of access to the invader.[164] These fortifications enabled the defender to hold up the enemy, and sometimes to stop him entering altogether. As they were checked in front, the enemy's flanks could be harassed by the defenders, who could cause great damage with large rocks, or could even make a bold attack. The Frankish defeats in the Pyrenean passes in 778 and 824 show the great dangers involved in advancing through mountain ranges. The Austrians were made to realise it to their shame and their cost at Morgarten in 1315. Mountains were the natural allies of the Scots and Welsh, who were able to withdraw into inaccessible places with their livestock and most valuable possessions, and wait for the invaders to retreat. In Ireland, the inhabitants not only exploited the peculiarities of the terrain in the mountains, but used the woods and bogs as defensive features. They blocked narrow roads through the woods with tree-trunks, or dug deep trenches and strengthened them with stout palisades. The paths between the bogs were similarly blocked. Light troops attacked the enemy in the flanks and rear, as did the Basques in the Pyrenees.[165] In Brittany, woods and rivers were also used against the enemy.[166] Later, castles or fortresses were built on steep cliffs and hills, and these were extremely difficult to take.

In Central Europe the Slavs fortified their country very early. In 791 the Avars had walls and ditches at the mouth of the Krems and in the Wienerwald.[167] By building

---

164 Durrer, pp. 74, 96. Delbrück, III, pp. 578–9.
165 Oman, I, pp. 402–3.
166 Ermoldus Nigellus, pp. 114, 123. *Annales regni Francorum*, anno 786, p. 72.
167 *Ibid.*, anno 791, p. 88.

fortresses, the Wends quickly blocked the natural route for an attack, the river Havel which Charlemagne used in 789, and which the Frisians used for shipping.[168] Bohemia enjoyed the protection of the wooded Erzgebirge, nearly forty miles wide. Fortresses were built at Taus in the west and Nachod in the east on the two invasion routes which flanked the forest.[169] These fortresses were manned at once whenever invasion threatened, and there were other fortresses in the interior. The Sudeten mountains protected Poland in the south-west, the Carpathians in the south, the border forest of Pomerania and Prussia in the north, and the Oder and the Bober in the west. Special fortresses were built wherever it was possible to cross the river. Poland was so strongly protected by nature and man-made fortifications that former kings or emperors had reached the Oder only with great difficulty, as Barbarossa wrote himself, and his chronicler Rahewin repeated it.[170] Hungary's borders were partly protected by the Carpathians, and in the south by the Danube, and the Drava, and by marshes and forests. On the dangerous western front facing the Germans, the river March flowed north of the Danube, then came the outlying spurs of the Little Carpathians, the fortress of Pressburg and the rivers Waag, Neutra and Gran.[171] South of the Danube the invasion route between the Neusiedler Lake and the river Rabnitz gets steadily narrower towards the interior of Hungary. The best line of defence was west of the Raab. The last section of the invasion route to the lower Rabnitz, close to the junction of the Raab and the Danube, could be flooded, and was defended with palisades. This fortress could only be taken in special cases of treachery or Hungarian disunity.[172]

Low-lying countries could be defended by an army with two special sorts of help – water, and fortresses, at first in the form of increasingly impregnable castles, later as fortified towns. But while the fortresses were easy to defend with small forces, and commanded a large area, as soon as the invader had to order a retreat at the end of the invasion season at the onset of the winter, the defence of a river involved tremendous problems. It needed a very large army to defend a stream or a river efficiently for any distance, besides, the attacker would always concentrate his efforts against a comparatively weak point in the defence, or make a weak spot for himself. If the invader had the necessary boats, it was always possible to force a crossing by adroit manoeuvres, or he could get across the obstacle in a surprise sortie at an undefended spot. But if the water ran through marshy ground, the problem was altogether different. Then it sufficed to occupy crossing-places constantly, or to fortify them considerably, and the water itself became a splendid line of defence, allowing the whole countryside, or a great part of it to be held by comparatively few troops. The defence of mountain ranges set similar problems.

A good fortress was the medieval ruler's best friend. The fear of the Northmen

[168] *Ibid.*, anno 789, pp. 84–5. Schünemann, pp. 58–9.
[169] Schünemann, p. 66.
[170] *Ibid.*, p. 68. Rahewinus, *Gesta Friderici. I, Imperatoris*, ed. G. Waitz and B. von Simson, MGH, SS, Hannover 1912, 1. III, c. 3, p. 168.
[171] Schünemann, pp. 70–1.
[172] *Ibid.*, pp. 71–2.

had taught this lesson, for castles were far the best weapon against the Vikings in England and western France, especially if they commanded a river. Castles were built in Germany as a defence against the Hungarian invasions.[173] Almost all feudal princes built lines of castles to protect the threatened border of their territories.[174] Baldwin II built a whole series of castles in Flanders on his most threatened side, the coast where 'castella ibi recens facta' – newly erected castles – prevented a plundering raid by the Vikings in 891.[175] In the south of the county of Flanders, Baldwin IV and to a greater extent Baldwin V set up a system of defence.[176] These important castles are regularly spaced:

St Omer to Aire	20 km
Aire to Béthune	24 km (Lillers is halfway between them)
Béthune to Lens	19 km
Lens to Douai	19 km (Hénin is between the two)

While Baldwin IV and Baldwin V were building a whole series of castles there, sources of that period mention the castle at Lille, further back in the country, and the Flemish castle at Tournai for the first time.[177] In 1030, the castle at Oudenaarde is mentioned for the first time just opposite the enemy fortress of Ename.[178] The Scheldt was defended by the castles of Ghent, Oudenaarde and Tournai. In the south, the great line of castles was continued by water defences, the Scarpe, the Deule, the Lys and the Aa, connected with each other by the Neuf-Fossé. According to a later tradition, Baldwin V had the Neuf-Fossé dug, and anywhere there was a gap open into Flanders, he is said to have built walls, ditches and palisades.[179] All these defences, together with the marshes along the Scarpe and the Neuf-Fossé, protected Flanders excellently to the south. The French chronicler William the Breton saw this for himself during the campaign of 1213. He writes about the land in the county: 'Many well stocked fishponds and many streams and ditches intersect the tracks so that there is scarcely a way through for an advancing army. Flanders is very well protected from the enemy, as long as there are no civil wars'.[180] Elsewhere he says

---

173 Lot, L'art militaire, I, p. 109.
174 R. Aubenas, 'Les Châteaux-forts des Xe et XIe siècles', Revue historique du droit français et étranger, 1938. G. Fleury, 'Recherches sur les fortifications du Maine', Revue historique et archéologique du Maine, 24, 29. P. Feuchère, Contribution à l'étude de l'origine des villes. Les castra et les noyaux pré-urbains en Artois du IXe au XIe siècles, Arras, 1949. A. Vermeersch, 'Les oppida en Brabant, 1123–1355', Anciens Pays et Assemblées d'Etats, 22, 1961. Beeler, Warfare in England, pp. 51–2, 208. R. Deprez, 'La politique castrale dans la principauté épiscopale de Liège du Xe au XIVe Siècle', MA 65, 1950.
175 Bovo Abbas, Relatio de inventione et elevatione S. Bertini, ed. O. Holder-Egger, MGH, SS, 15, 1, 1887, c. 6, p. 512.
176 Feuchère, Les castra et les noyaux pré-urbains en Artois, pp. 9–10, notes 55, 57.
177 Flandria generosa auctore monacho S. Bertini, cum continuationibus, ed. L.C. Bethmann, MGH, SS, IX, 1851, c. 9, p. 319. Gesta pontificum Cameracensium, ed. L.C. Bethmann, MGH, SS, VII, Gesta Lietberti, p. 493. Chronicon S. Andreae, pp. 534–5. Verbruggen, Note sur le sens des mots castrum, castellum, etc., RBPH, 28, 1950, pp. 147–9.
178 Ganshof, Les origines de la Flandre impériale, Annales de la Société Royale d'Archéologie de Bruxelles, 46, 1942–3, p. 24.
179 Flandria generosa, p. 320.
180 Philippis, II, 1. II, vv. 140–3, p. 46.

again that it is very difficult to take an army through Flanders.[181] The Franciscan of Ghent also wrote that the land was well protected by marshes which were very difficult to cross, and that it was very well fortified.[182] The castles were naturally built in the most favourable positions, where they commanded the whole country-side.

Even individual castles could be a thorn in the flesh of a powerful kingdom. During the reign of Philip I of France the castle at Montlhéry was famous because it caused so much trouble to the king and the local people. The king advised his son Louis VI to keep a good eye on this castle, for it had never let him enjoy any peace and quiet, and he had been prematurely aged by all the trouble and annoyance it caused. From Corbeil on the Seine and Châteaufort on the right side, the whole district of Paris, or the Parisis, was blockaded by Montlhéry which was situated between the two. The inhabitants of Paris and Orléans could never go from one town to the other without permission from the lord of the castle, unless they travelled with a strong armed escort.[183] That splendid castle, Château Gaillard, built by Richard I at Andelys, was the key to Normandy. The garrison held out for six months against siege and attacks by the army of Philip Augustus in 1203–4. This strong fortress had cost no less than 49,000 pounds sterling in 1197–8.[184] The castles were splendid bases for the little armies of the principalities. They played not only a defensive role, but also an important offensive one. Already in the times of the Northmen they made it possible to make a swift attack on little bands of these plunderers. Major attacks as well as local sorties could be mounted from these castles, and they were a perpetual thorn in the flesh for an invader who could not besiege them all at once. In 890, the lay abbot Rudolf of Friuli led just such sorties from St Vaast against the Northmen.[185]

Once the towns were fully developed, town-fortifications mostly took the place of the private castles of princes and nobles. We have seen how the kings of England and France encouraged the fortification of their towns. The granting of the status of a commune was not only intended to strengthen the army in the field with foot-soldiers, but often also to spur on the newly-founded town to set about making moats and ditches, and building walls. Sometimes the granting of the charter was a reward for services rendered in this way, as in the case of Mantes in 1158–59.[186] The communes which were set up in their French possessions by Henry II, Richard I and king John, who all used mercenaries, were certainly meant in the first instance to get the citizens to fortify their towns.[187]

The importance of the 'marches', or special frontier-administrations instituted by Charlemagne, must not be overlooked. On the threatened borders of his kingdom, or where an area was not completely conquered, several counties were put under the authority of a margrave, who was invested with special military powers as

---

181 *Ibid.*, 1. IX, vv. 478–9, p. 268.
182 *Annales Gandenses*, p. 41.
183 Suger, c. 8, p. 38.
184 Poole, *From Domesday Book to Magna Carta*, p. 373.
185 *Annales Vedastini*, p. 69.
186 Petit-Dutaillis, *Les communes françaises*, p. 116.
187 Poole, p. 370 and note 2.

commander of the troops in this area. He raised the army in the 'march', and was responsible for seeing that it was always ready to resist sudden enemy raids or invasions. He was also answerable for the defence of his area, protected by fortifications, and sometimes waste lands made the invasion more difficult. The fortifications were defended by garrisons of royal vassals, who had an important role in the defence of the 'march'. In case of invasion by the enemy, all the able-bodied freemen were called up for the defence of the country. The guard service and the construction of fortifications were done by the men who were too poor to do the complete military service.[188] In due course a large part of the frontier of the Frankish Empire was protected by 'marches'. In England the 'marcher lords' played a most important part in the defence of their land against raids by their neighbours, and in the subjection of south and central Wales. Against Scotland, the border lords and their followers were always having to turn out in order to intercept or foil the raids and attacks of the Scots, by going to the defence of their towns. After Bannockburn the defence of the northern border was almost entirely the responsibility of the nobles who defended the border castles for the king, together with their families and followers.

As will be seen from this very brief survey, the little medieval armies relied greatly in their defensive task on the castles and fortified towns, and they could always exploit natural obstacles. On the other hand, the invader had to besiege the fortresses and try to take them. Those princes who waged defensive war never stopped trying to make the fullest possible use of these fortresses, and of the watercourses, marshes, forests and mountain ranges. There is an excellent example of this in the case of the counts of Flanders in the defence of their domain against the emperor of the Roman Empire in the quarrel about the possession of Valenciennes in 1006–7, in 1049 and 1054, at the time of the struggle for imperial Flanders and the Mark of Antwerp, and from 1102 and 1107 in the fighting round Cambrai.[189]

The count's spies tried to find out where the enemy was approaching and where he was going to attack. After that they waited for the imperial army behind the Scheldt, in 1007 and in 1054, or in their fortresses in 1102 and 1007. The enemy's attacking strength was weakened by storming these fortresses, which usually caused many losses, and time was on the side of the defender. Sometimes the late season, as in 1102, or an unsuccessful attack, as in 1107, caused the invader to move off. The defenders rarely suffered serious losses: at most, when peace was signed, the count gave back all or part of the former conquered land. Thus in 1007 Valenciennes was lost, and the Mark of Antwerp in 1050, but apparently the count received Imperial Flanders in compensation. In 1056 he kept his conquests and in 1102 the emperor returned without having accomplished what he set out to do. In 1103 they reached agreement without loss on their side, while in 1107 the count received the viscounty of Cambrai and possession of the castle of Le Cateau-Cambrésis. Thus

188 Conrad, *Geschichte der deutschen Wehrverfassung*, Munich, 1939, I, p. 69. Dhondt, *Etudes sur la naissance des principautés territoriales en France*, Bruges, 1948, pp. 32–3.
189 Ganshof, *Les origines de la Flandre impériale*, pp. 108 ff. Verbruggen, *Het leger en de vloot van de graven van Vlaanderen*, pp. 171–4.

the defender ended up better off after the fighting than his enemy. 'To preserve is easier than to acquire' wrote Clausewitz.[190]

It has already been seen how in 1304 the Flemings made the king of France go to Tournai by a long roundabout route from Arras, in order to attack Flanders from there. Other invaders in small countries met with the same difficulties which the French king encountered in his campaigns against Flanders.

2. *Signals and Communications*

An efficient local signalling system among the defenders could greatly complicate the invader's task. When Charlemagne set up coastal defences against the Northmen he had the lighthouse at Boulogne repaired, and posted guards and garrisons along the coast. What communications were there between these posts? Were signals in use at that time? A casual mention by Nithard adds a little to the picture: during the defence of the Seine between Paris and Melun in 841 the various posts were in communication with each other by means of a signalling system such as ships use.

'By long tradition, from pre-Norman times, news of a hostile landing in England was to be spread over a wide area by means of a system of beacons on well known lofty sites.' In 1337 and 1338 the beacons were made ready in the coastal areas and on hilltops far from the sea. 'Empty wine tuns filled with sand were set one on another and on the top a man would sit keeping watch, looking across the sea.' 'Pitch was burnt to produce the light. It "showed better" and lasted longer than twigs. An additional means of spreading news appeared in November 1338 when sheriffs of south coast (and some other maritime) counties were instructed to arrange that at churches ordinarily only one bell should be rung. The ringing of all the bells was to signify a French attack.'[191]

In 1304, the Dutch used beacons to spread the news of the progress of the French-Dutch fleet commanded by Grimaldi, which was sailing to Zierikzee against the Flemish fleet and army of Guy of Namur.[192]

Signals were exchanged between lighthouses on the Mediterranean coast with fire and light signals by night, and with smoke signals by day. There was a sort of telegraph system, which quickly gave warning of an enemy approach in clear weather.[193] Along the coasts of Italy, Sardinia and Corsica the same warning system was used against the Moslems. They too had a similar signal-system on their stretch of Mediterranean coast between Alexandria and Tripoli, and they also sent out ships to collect information about the enemy fleet. Carrier pigeons released from these ships, brought reports back to land.[194] In 1088, the Moslems sent a report from the

---

[190] *On War*, Bk VI, Ch. I.

[191] H.J. Hewitt, *The Organization of War under Edward III*, Manchester, New York, 1966, pp. 4, 5, 9.

[192] Melis Stoke, *Rijmkroniek*, ed. W.J. Brill, Werken van het historisch Genootschap gevestigd te Utrecht, 2 vols, Utrecht, 1885, bk IX, vv. 633–9. J. Sabbe, *De vijandelijkheden tussen de Avesnes en de Dampierres*, p. 284.

[193] Ch. de la Roncière, *Histoire de la marine française*, I, pp. 77–8.

[194] *Ibid.*, p. 79.

island of Pantellaria to the emir of Africa in a letter fastened under a pigeon's wing.[195] Among the leaders of the first Crusade Godfrey of Bouillon was the first to hear of this practice of the Moslems. In September 1098 he made a treaty with Omar, governor of Azaz, who was in revolt against his overlord, Ridwan of Aleppo. Omar's ambassadors sent their master a carrier-pigeon with a letter reporting the negotiations, and urging him to stand firm until Godfrey could come to the rescue. The Moslems explained to the crusaders that this method of sending news was very quick and was also much the safest, since the ambassadors could not fall into enemy hands with the documents on them.[196]

A little later a carrier-pigeon fell into the hands of the crusaders between Acre and Caesarea, while they were marching to Jerusalem. It was taking a letter from the emir of Acre to the emir of Caesarea.[197] Fulcher of Chartres relates that the Moslems who lived in Palestine used to send letters from town to town with well-trained pigeons. They used them in Ascalon in 1125.[198] Wilbrand of Oldenburg, who visited the Holy Land, also mentioned this habit of the Moslems.[199] In 1249 the Saracens sent the news of the crusaders' invasion under St Louis three times to their sultan.[200]

The kings of the Holy Land also used pigeon-posts. During a plundering expedition in 1203 King Amalric II sent a pigeon to Acre. The bird had only a red thread round its neck, and no one in the city knew what it meant. But soon afterwards the king sent a second pigeon, with a letter reporting the success of his raid and his safe return.[201]

On 18 February 1282, Guy of Gibelet reported to the prince of Antioch that he had made three attempts to take Tripoli. Before the attack he was in communication with the commander of the Templars in Tripoli. They sent each other reports by pigeon, using a pre-arranged code, so that the enemy would not be able to understand their letters if the pigeons were intercepted.[202]

They also used another ancient method. As far back as 1182–83 it was the usual thing in the Holy Land to light a fire in a clearly visible spot as soon as the Moslems made an attack. More fires were lit in those towns and fortresses that saw the first, so that the whole area was quickly alerted and everyone could take the necessary steps.[203]

Robert the Frisian set a house on fire in Kapelle, north of what was later Sluis, as a signal of his arrival and for the rising in Flanders in 1071.[204] In 1237, Frederick II was warned by a smoke signal of the departure of the Lombard army before his attack

195 *Ibid.*, p. 80, n. 1.
196 Albert of Aix, pp. 437–8. Brandt, p. 194, Grousset, I, p. 118.
197 Raymond of Aguilers, p. 291. Brandt, p. 277, n. 43. Runciman, p. 276.
198 C. 67, anno 1125.
199 Peregrinatio, in *Peregrinatores medii aevi quatuor*, ed. J.M.C. Laurent, Leipzig, 1864, in 4°, p. 168.
200 Joinville, c. 35, p. 57.
201 Ernoul and Bernard le Trésorier, *Chronique*, p. 357.
202 Mas Latrie, *Histoire de Chypre*, III, pp. 665–6.
203 Ernoul and Bernard le Trésorier, p. 104.
204 Galbert, c. 69, p. 112.

at Cortenuova.[205] This method was often used in Italy: in Florence, look-out men had to light one, two or three fires, according to the strength of the enemy, and these fires were several times covered and uncovered according to pre-arranged signals. The fires were kept burning until the signal was passed on by another look-out post.[206] On the morning of 11 July 1302, the French garrison of the castle at Courtrai signalled to the French army with a burning torch and with swords.[207]

Such a signalling system could be used most effectively by a defender, who could take counter-measures to foil an enemy attack. Defence had still many other advantages.

3. *Advantages of Defence*

When the defender did not wish to accept battle, he could avoid it. 'No battle can take place unless by mutual consent.'[208] This sentence of Clausewitz is particularly true for the Middle Ages. Very often an invading army used a single route and the defender could avoid the enemy quite easily. In 1327 king Edward III and his army had to hunt for a long time to find the Scottish forces. Though both armies were willing to fight, the Scots chose so favourable a position that the English no longer dared attack them.[209] A really powerful invader such as Charlemagne or Louis the Pious could make his troops march in two or three corps so as to converge, each following a route of their own, and so pass through more of the enemy's territory. But the enemy could avoid any battle in the open field, by shutting himself up in strong fortresses, which could hold out until the end of the fighting season. Provisioning was more easily assured for the defenders than for the attackers, who had to bring supplies over long distances, or had to make their troops live off the land. Numerous fortresses made it possible to attack the invader's lines of communication, and seriously hinder the passage of his provision waggons. These castles increased steadily in number after the invasions of the Northmen, and were more stoutly constructed. As towns developed, their fortifications became increasingly important, and they were sometimes so extensive that the invader could not encircle the whole fortification. Small armies were powerless against them, and in large armies the besieger had tremendous difficulties in assuring supplies for weeks or even months. The season for such operations was quickly over. Normally they were started at the height of spring, when there was plenty of grass and fodder in the fields. When autumn came, or at the beginning of winter, they usually had to stop. It was exceptional for them to be carried on into the winter, and it could only be done if the attacker had enormous funds to pay his men, and could manage to keep them properly provided for.

In central Europe, the Germans had to reckon with unfavourable terrain, and

---

[205] Köhler, I, p. 220.

[206] *Ibid.*, III, 2. p. 347.

[207] Verbruggen, *De slag der gulden sporen*, p. 276.

[208] Clausewitz, *On War*, Bk IV, Ch. VIII.

[209] Jean le Bel, I, pp. 53–63, 64–73. Thomas Gray of Heton, pp. 154–5.

innumerable obstacles such as streams, rivers, marshes and thick forests. The enemy blocked the few possible routes for an enemy with fortresses. The scarcity of cultivated land made it impossible to provision the army.[210] It was impossible to give adequate protection to a long supply column, so in order to cut down the baggage-train, the army tried to live off the land. The campaign could not last longer than two to three months. As soon as the corn was ripe, about 1 August, the troops set off, and eight or ten weeks later they had to start back in order not to be overtaken by winter. The beginning of August to the middle of October was the usual time for campaigns to the east, and in that time the attackers had to press on as quickly as possible to the heart of the enemy territory. But the enemy avoided battle – he had mostly lighter troops than the heavy German cavalry, and so was better able to carry out reconnais-sance expeditions, and could more easily make his escape. Special light troops were entrusted with the defence of the border fortresses. The few roads were well guarded and that removed the possibility of surprise. The enemy knew the country better, and withdrew to the forests, marshes and mountains.[211]

Medieval commanders were so cautious in defence that they offered very few pitched battles. Einhard reports in his *Life of Charlemagne* that the emperor person-ally had to give battle only twice during the thirty years that he was at war with the Saxons.[212] Actually, there was more fighting, and the emperor took part in more than two battles. There were battles or combats in 774, in 775 on the Weser and near Lubbecke, in 778, in 779, and the Franks suffered a serious defeat in the Süntelge-birge in 782. There was a cavalry battle on the Lippe in 784.[213] However, this does not alter the fact that the really decisive battles were the two fought in 783 at Detmold and four weeks later on the Haase, and that these battles in fact broke the Saxon resistance.[214] That type of strategy was imposed by the reaction of the defenders. It is quite wrong to conclude, as Lot does 'the simple fact that it took thirty years to conquer Saxony, a small country, is the best proof that the Frankish armies were not worth much, and that their leader was in no way a great general'.[215] Delbrück is right when he compares Charlemagne's conquest of the Saxons with the attempts of the Romans to conquer the Germans.[216] Charlemagne was successful with a smaller army than the Romans.

The conquest of Wales and king Edward I's campaigns against Scotland saw few battles, because the defenders preferred not to risk defeat by a more powerful enemy. But like the Saxons in their great rebellion in 783, the Scots were willing to fight as soon as the rising became widespread, and their superiority in numbers allowed them to shake off the enemy yoke. This happened at Stirling Bridge in 1297 and at Falkirk in 1298. The insurgents also fought in 1306 and 1307, to chase the occupying forces from the land. There was another great battle in 1314 at Bannockburn, but here and

210 Schünemann, p. 56.
211 *Ibid.*, pp. 57–8.
212 C. 8, p. 26.
213 *Annales regni Francorum*, pp. 40–69, under the years quoted.
214 Delbrück, III, p. 67. Lot, *L'art militaire*, I, p. 104.
215 Lot, I, pp. 104–5.
216 Delbrück, III, pp. 59–62.

at Falkirk the Scots gave battle while they were besieging an enemy fortress, and they were largely obliged by the strategic situation to fight in the open field. On the other hand there were no proper battles in the campaigns of 1296, 1300, 1301–2, 1322 and 1327.

In Flanders there were battles of importance only at Cassel in 1071, Axpoel near Thielt in 1128, at Bouvines in 1214, Westkapelle in Zeeland in 1256, Furnes in 1297, Courtrai in 1302, Arques in 1303 and Mons-en-Pévèle in 1304, during the invasion of Zeeland in 1303, the attack on the enemy in Duiveland and the sea-battle of Zierikzee in 1304, and finally the battle of Cassel in 1328. At Cassel in 1071, Thielt in 1128, and Bouvines in 1214 the fighting was between the rival claimants to a throne, and they were bound to trust their luck and fight a battle to decide the issue. At Westkapelle the Flemish attackers were surprised during their landing in Zeeland, and the opportunity was too good for the defenders to let it slip. At Thielt, at Courtrai and at Zierikzee the fighting took place because one of the armies concerned was trying to relieve a castle besieged by the other. But in 1302 the Flemings were in revolt, and they acted in the same way as the Saxons and the Scots. They forced the battle at Mons-en-Pévèle themselves, which was also the result of a certain war-weariness following two years of unresolved conflict and fruitless negotiations. They attacked at Cassel in 1328, because they were in revolt and they hoped to surprise the enemy.

In general, battles were very few. The prudence of medieval commanders, when they had to give battle, confirms Clausewitz: 'It may sound strange, but for all who know war in this respect it is a fact beyond doubt, that much more strength of will is required to make an important decision in strategy than in tactics.' 'Boldness becomes of rarer occurrence the higher we ascend the scale of rank.'[217]

Apart from the few cases in which a battle was forced during the siege of an important fortress, battles were fought only when both sides wanted to, and thought they had a chance of winning. Most campaigns took place without any battles at all, as the examples of Saxony and Scotland show. Wales may be added to the list. It was also the case in Flanders during king Odo's campaign near Bruges in 892, during Baldwin V's struggle against the emperor in 1054, in the long conflict round Cambrai between the emperor and Robert II in 1102, 1103, and 1107, in the war between Philip of Alsace and Philip Augustus from 1181 to 1185, in the latter's campaign in Flanders in 1213, in Philip the Fair's expedition in September 1302 and in the various campaigns of the royal army after 1314.

If in general, medieval defensive strategy was based on avoiding, rather than offering, battle this was because the great number of castles and fortified towns allowed the defenders to shut themselves up and wait patiently to see what happened. Fortresses were nearly always strong enough to stand up to the attackers, whose siege engines were often inefficient. Putting them together on the spot wasted a lot of time, and they were often feeble or else were rendered ineffective by the defenders' counter-measures. As long as the fortresses themselves were in good condition and

[217] *On War*, Bk III, Ch. I, Ch. VI.

well provisioned, there was not much for a stout-hearted garrison to fear. The capture of a castle brought small advantage to an invader, who had to put into it a garrison who would be hard put to defend itself in a partly destroyed fortress. The defenders were nearer to sources of help and to their bases, and the invader was seldom strong enough to take all the fortresses in the area. Several campaigns by such powerful opponents as king Odo in Flanders in 892, Hugh the Great in 947,[218] the attack on Valenciennes by the coalition of the king of the Romans, the king of France and the duke of Normandy in 1006,[219] all failed completely. In other cases the invader managed to capture one fortress only, possibly Ghent in 1007,[220] Tournai in 1054,[221] where only a small body of knights had taken refuge after an unsuccessful combat. On that occasion, the great castle at Lille, where the count was leading the defence in person, was left unscathed. In 1102, the emperor wasted his time outside the mighty fortress at L'Ecluse until the onset of winter put an end to his campaign.[222] In 1107, an imperial attack on the town of Douai failed.[223] Bruges fought off all William Clito's attacks in 1128. The defence of Ghent in 1213 made the destruction of the French fleet in the Zwin at Damme possible and the campaign was unsuccessful despite a promising start.[224] At the time only Lille remained in the possession of the French king. The Flemings met with the same difficulties when they tried to take Zierikzee in their Zeeland offensive in 1303 and 1304.

In the east, German armies often found themselves powerless in the face of enemy fortresses. Already in the ninth century the Moravians and Croats had stout fortifications which successfully resisted all attacks. In 820, duke Liudewit held out in his castle till the Frankish armies had to give up. In 855, 864 and 869 campaigns against duke Rastizen, and in 872 and 892 against duke Zwentibald were unsuccessful.[225] In the first half of the tenth century it had already become more difficult to take the fortresses of the western Slavs, who had been easy enough to conquer in the previous century.[226] As soon as Bohemia and Poland became better organized as states, most sieges were unsuccessful until about the middle of the twelfth century. In 1011, the Germans bypassed Glogau and did not attack the fortress. In 1071, the emperor again avoided it, and set about conquering a small one, Nimptsch in Silesia. The castle was surrounded and stormed with wooden towers and ladders, but could not be taken. In

---

218 *Annales Vedastini*, anno 892, pp. 70–1. *Flodoard*, anno 947, 1881, p. 104.
219 Ganshof, *Origines de la Flandre impériale*, pp. 108–9.
220 *Annales Blandinienses*, anno 1007, p. 23. *Gesta episcoporum Cameracensium*, ed. L.C. Bethmann, MGH, SS, 7, 1846, 1. I, c. 115, p. 452, speaks of an attack, but not of the capture of the castle.
221 *Gesta Lietberti*, MGH, SS, VII, p. 494. *Chronicon S. Andreae, ibid.*, pp. 534–5. *Sigebertus Gemblacensis*, pp. 359–60. *Annales Blandinienses*, anno 1054, p. 26. *Annales Elmarenses*, 1054, p. 92. *Annales Elnonenses*, 1054, p. 157.
222 *Sigebertus Gemblacensis*, p. 368. *Chronicon S. Andreae*, p. 545.
223 'Gesta Galcheri', in *Gesta episcoporum Cameracensium continuata*, ed. G. Waitz, MGH, SS, 14, 1883, vv. 516–24, p. 206.
224 Galbert, c. 112, pp. 158–9. William the Breton, *Chronicon*, pp. 251–2.
225 *Annales Fuldenses*, annis 855, 864, 869, 872, 892, pp. 45–6, 62, 68–9, 75–6, 121. Schünemann, p. 75.
226 *Ibid.*, p. 75.

1029 Conrad II attacked Bautzen in vain. In 1109, Henry V's campaign failed at Beuthen and Glogau: he was less successful in the east than in Italy with his siege engines. In 1162–3, Henry the Lion, duke of Saxony, used the most modern machines in the east, such as had been used before at Crema and Milan in the Italian campaigns.[227] It will also be seen that many campaigns of the English kings were unsuccessful in Scotland and Wales.

Finally, there was a gigantic problem of supplies for the army. This was a really serious hindrance to medieval warfare.

4. *Supplies*

Charlemagne organized the supply of his army. The bishops, counts, abbots and the highest royal vassals were responsible for the convoys of food, equipment, weapons, siege material, clothes and an escort to protect them. In the capitulary of Aachen in 802–803 the emperor prescribed to carry flour, wine, bacon and abundant food. A supply of food for three months and clothes and weapons for six months were required. The bishops, counts, abbots and important royal vassals could furnish the weapons, the utensils and the clothes from their reserves. The royal and ecclesiastical domains could send the food.[228] In 806, the contingent of Abbot Fulrad was probably fed on the provisions the abbot had collected on the abbey farms. In 807, the poor soldiers received five solidi from those who stayed at home.[229] In practice it was only possible to carry enough food for a very short time, and after that it had to be bought locally. This led to trouble, for a sizeable army in transit immediately put up prices. The demand for commodities was very much greater than usual, and small supplies did not go far enough to give everyone his full share. As soon as prices rose, the military thought themselves cheated and became disgruntled. They were willing to pay for supplies, but at a fair price. Then the local inhabitants stopped supplies or else they were quickly exhausted, and the soldiers began to plunder.[230]

It was therefore necessary, if an army were to have a peaceful passage, to take the precaution of organizing markets attended by farmers and merchants from all over the country, so that the army was not simply eating its way through strictly local supplies. Later, sovereigns usually gave exemption from customs duties and rights of passage to those merchants who were prepared to supply their army.[231] Elsewhere provision was made for knights to take everything they would need for their horses and themselves, as in the truce of 1063 in the bishopric of Thérouanne.[232] As early as 876 there were merchants who provisioned the troops of Charles the Bald at the

---

[227] *Ibid.*, pp. 76–7.

[228] Capitulary of Aachen, *ais.* 802, 803, c. 10; letter to Fulrad, *ao.* 806; Memoratorium, *ao.* 807, c. 3; Capitulary of Boulogne, *ao.* 811, c. 10; Capitulare de villis, c. 30, 42, 64, 68; Capitularia, I, nos. 77, 75, 48, 74, 32. Ganshof, *Frankish Institutions*, pp. 67, 159–60.

[229] Memoratorium, *ao.* 807, c. 2. Capitularia, I, no. 48.

[230] An example in *Annales Fuldenses, anno 879*, pp. 92–3.

[231] Funck-Brentano, *De exercituum*, p. 43, n. 2; p. 64, n. 2; p. 65, n. 1.

[232] Sdralek, *Wolfenbüttler Fragmente*, in Knöpfler, Schrörs, Sdralek, Kirchengeschichtliche Studien, 1, 2, Munster, 1891, pp. 143–4.

time of the march to Andernach.[233] In an agreement made between the count of Hainault and the bishop of Liège, supplies were ensured by the establishment of local markets, while fodder for the horses could be taken in the open fields.[234] On the First Crusade, knights bought their food from merchants and the local inhabitants.[235] The cost was naturally very high for everyone; the ordinary soldiers had little money and were soon dependent on the moneybags of their lords, who in their turn soon found their expenses soaring and their resources dwindling. This all slowed down the Crusade. Some princes thought it best to make themselves masters of towns or even of whole areas to secure necessary supplies. Baldwin of Boulogne was the first to rule a conquered territory in this way. When the crusading army was in serious difficulties after the siege of Antioch, many of the knights went off to Edessa to get themselves on to the payroll of the generous new ruler.[236] Bohemond chose to hold Antioch, and Raymond of Toulouse, who disputed his claim to possession, wanted in his turn to conquer cities and establish a principality. Godfrey of Bouillon and Robert II of Flanders also felt themselves bound to besiege the town of Jabala in order to try to improve their finances. Finally, the less important crusaders grew so indignant, and so furious over the leaders' procrastination, that they destroyed the walls of the town of Marat an'Numan to prevent the Count of Toulouse from staying there.[237]

The crusaders' strategy was thus greatly hampered by having to provide for what was, for those days, a very numerous army. Other problems arose in connection with provisioning. The enormous booty which fell into the crusaders' hands after major battles or at the conquest of cities put a greatly increased amount of money into circulation, so that this also caused prices to rise. During the bad season merchants did not venture to put out to sea, while those who had plenty of stores preferred to hoard them till they could make tremendous profits at the right moment. Pirates from western Europe sailed along the coasts, such as the privateer Winimer with his Flemings, and men from Antwerp and Boulogne. Merchants of that sort knew exactly how to sell at the highest possible prices, and to get rich astonishingly quickly – an easy thing to do among fighting men leading a luxurious life amidst a host of dangers. In the Third Crusade, the army suffered terribly from the lack of wheat in the winter of 1190–91, from Christmas to Lent. The famine was so great that some Christians even deserted to the Moslems. The chronicler Ambroise, who lays special emphasis on the fact that he wrote from personal experience, relates that the arrival of a shipload of wheat in Acre forced the merchants to sell their hoarded grain. The price of wheat dropped suddenly from 100 to 4 bezants a measure.[238] Famine had weakened the crusaders and was followed by sickness, bad colds, swollen legs and the loss of teeth.[239]

233 *Annales Bertiniani, anno* 876, p. 133.
234 Gilbert of Mons, c. 9, p. 14.
235 Anonymous, *Gesta Francorum*, pp. 36, 64 [Hill, pp. 14, 26].
236 Brandt, pp. 190–1, 193.
237 *Ibid.*, pp. 199–200, 208–9.
238 Ambroise, vv. 4401–2, p. 118; p. 119; vv. 4495–6, p. 120; vv. 4215–19, p. 113.
239 *Ibid.*, vv. 4265–74, p. 114.

The problem of provisioning also played an important part in the Fourth Crusade as well. When the crusaders, hired by Venice, took the town of Zara, they received proposals from Alexius, son of Isaac II, to restore his father to the throne of Constantinople. This provoked sharp dissension among the crusaders. Some wanted to sail on to the Holy Land or to Egypt, others wanted to act on Alexius' suggestion. The great princes, the marquis of Montferrat, count Baldwin IX of Flanders and Hainault, and count Louis of Blois, were in favour of the diversion to Byzantium.[240] They maintained that the crusaders had neither the means nor the supplies to go in further for none of them could support a decent number of knights, or pay mercenaries or *sergeants* nor could they get siege-engines made. An ordinary knight, Robert de Clari, who was really a poor nobleman, confirmed that the crusaders had no more money or stores, as they had used them all up in their long delay in Venice and at Zara. Also, they had hired their ships for a year, half of which had already expired. If they went on with their journey to the Holy Land they would not be able to achieve anything useful, for lack of means to keep themselves and go on fighting.[241] The supporters of the plan to go to Constantinople hoped to get supplies from the emperor there, or to capture them. Finally they decided to sail for a month to Byzantium, and after accomplishing their task to set sail for Syria, unless the crusaders wanted to stay in Constantinople.[242] Their problem of supplies thus played a part in the change of direction in the Fourth Crusade, in which there were no great kings involved who could support large numbers. During the winter of 1203–4 the price of wine rose sharply, also of chickens and eggs: only biscuit remained cheap.[243]

Sickness broke also out in the crusading army which besieged Damietta in 1218. In the winter, writes Oliver of Paderborn, an eyewitness, the crusaders were afflicted with a sort of plague, for which the doctors found no cure. Sudden pains developed in the feet and shinbones, the gums and teeth were affected and they could not chew. The skin of the legs developed black and grey spots. Many died, others recovered in the spring of 1219.[244] There was famine this year. An enormously rich Syrian baron, Guy de Gibelet, did incalculable service to the crusaders by giving them the necessary money to buy food in Cyprus.[245]

St Louis had collected vast stores for his crusade to Egypt. Part of the victuals had been bought in advance two years earlier in Cyprus. Vats of wine were piled high, wheat and corn lay about in great heaps, looking like hills, for the rain had made the corn sprout on the surface of the mounds, so that they seemed to be covered with grass. When the grain was shipped for transport to Egypt, they threw away the outside layer, and the huge quantity that remained was quite fresh, just as though it were newly threshed.[246]

After the failure of the crusade in Egypt, St Louis stayed four years in the Holy

---

[240] Letter of the count of St Pol in *Chronica regia Coloniensis*, pp. 203–4.
[241] Robert de Clari, c. 16, p. 15; c. 33, p. 32.
[242] *Chronica regia Coloniensis, loc. cit.*
[243] Robert de Clari, c. 70, p. 60.
[244] *Chronica regia Coloniensis*, p. 331.
[245] Grousset, III, p. 221.
[246] Joinville, pp. 46–7.

Land. Then Joinville got in all his stores for the winter because they were so expensive in the bad season. He bought pigs, sheep, flour and maize for his followers, and habitually had twenty out of the fifty knights under his command sitting at his table.[247] In Egypt the crusaders had gone very hungry. The same disease broke out as in Damietta in 1218. The flesh dried up on their legs, and the skin was speckled with black and grey. Their gums began to rot, and they suffered from nose-bleeds.[248] In fact they probably had scurvy. Barbers used to cut away the dead flesh of their gums, naturally while the patients were fully conscious, and the sick men 'screamed like women in labour'.[249]

It was a welcome stroke of luck for the knights if they ever had a chance to hold out for any length of time on a campaign without prices rising enormously, and shortages becoming felt. Jean le Bel has given an interesting account of the story of some knights from the Low Countries in York in 1327. The army stayed more than six weeks in and around the town. During this time the price of a gallon of Gascon wine or Rhenish wine rose only by one penny. A fat capon cost only 3 or 4 pence, and two fat chickens cost three pence, and twelve fresh herrings cost one penny. Every day fodder, oats and straw for the horses were brought in to be sold cheaply, without the knight having to send a servant to fetch it. Such goods as kitchen utensils, pots and pans were also to be had cheaply.[250] During the campaign itself the king announced to the merchants and the local inhabitants that anyone who wanted to make a little money could bring bread, oats and other food, and he would be paid at once, and would have safe passage to the army when it stayed for some days in the same place.[251] But once the English were face to face with the Scots, they suffered hunger and thirst just as in other campaigns.[252] 'We stayed by the river a day and two nights', Jean le Bel writes, 'without bread, wine, or oats, indeed without provisions of any sort, and then for four days we had to buy badly baked bread, worth only one parisis, for 6 or 7 pence and a gallon of wine worth only 4 pence for 24 or 26. Everyone was so hungry that they snatched the goods out of the merchants' hands in order to get it before the others, and this caused a lot of trouble among the knights.'[253]

In the crusade against the Albigensians the crusaders had got control of the salt from the salt pits, and sold it during the siege of Carcassonne. Although they had been able to buy bread very cheaply, they had in the end to pay very large sums for it.[254] Food prices rose as time went on, because the local inhabitants fled with their stores, or hid or destroyed them, so that the cost of living rose continually for the crusaders.[255] A rich citizen of Cahors, Raimond de Salvanhic, and his brother Elie, set up as moneylenders to Simon de Montfort from 1209 onwards. These capitalists lent the count the required sums to keep his small standing army going. As security, Simon de Montfort gave the de Salvanhics all the booty from the captured town of

247 *Ibid.*, pp. 179–80.
248 *Ibid.*, c. 58, p. 103.
249 *Ibid.*, c. 60, p. 107.
250 Jean le Bel, I, pp. 47–8.
251 *Ibid.*, p. 59.

252 *Ibid.*, p. 58.
253 *Ibid.*, pp. 60, 70.
254 William of Tudèle, c. 25, p. 68.
255 *Ibid.*, p. 69, n. 4.

Lavour, clothes, wine, and grain.[256] He had already given them two seignories. But provisioning was always a serious problem, especially during a siege in which the garrison was playing an active part. Simon found this himself at Toulouse, where he broke camp on 29 July 1211, after twelve days' siege, because supplies were too precarious and too expensive.[257]

In the campaigns of the German kings in the east, the enemy did his utmost to prevent the invader from getting his supplies off the land. Cattle were removed or slaughtered, grain hidden or destroyed. If the expedition managed to penetrate deep into enemy territory the nagging problem arose of getting home again without starvation and heavy losses. The *Annales Regni Francorum* often find it worth reporting that the armies of Charlemagne or his sons returned without serious loss. This was more important than appeared at first sight. It is reported for example in 774, after the campaign in Saxony,[258] and in 791 after the campaign against the Avars.[259] In 820 the armies also came back safe and sound, except the third which had marched on the left flank. It had suffered severely from dysentery on the river Drava, where it had been held up by the rising of the river.[260] Often the journey had to be made by a different route because everything had been destroyed along the invasion route. But then they had to go through other passes or past enemy fortresses. In addition the enemy who had been driven out suddenly became the pursuer and could inflict heavy losses.

Supplies played a very important part there too. In 805, the young Charles started back as soon as his army's stores and the fodder for the horses were exhausted.[261] In 955, Otto the Great's army almost came to grief through starvation and sickness.[262] The emperor Henry II advanced to within two miles of his goal, Posen, in 1005, and then his army had to retreat. It was pursued by the Poles under Bolislav and suffered heavy losses while seeking food and supplies in the area. The king was forced to negotiate with his enemies and to make an unfavourable peace so that the army could return alive 'from their long expedition on which they had suffered so greatly from hunger.'[263] Ten years later part of the royal army which was guarding the baggage-train was completely destroyed by Polish archers.[264] In 1017, the king came back with his army through Bohemia, the territory of his ally, in order to seek food in a safe stretch of country. One of Conrad's Polish campaigns failed in 1029 for lack of food.[265] In 1030, shortage of supplies led to a heavy defeat during an invasion of Hungary; only the emperor and his followers escaped. The rest of the army surrendered in Vienna.[266] In 1051, the emperor Henry III had to abandon his supply ships

---

[256] *Ibid.*, c. 72, p. 174.
[257] *Ibid.*, p. 174, n. 1; c. 83, p. 198. Belperron, pp. 221, 226–7.
[258] *Annales regni Francorum*, anno 774, p. 40.
[259] *Ibid.*, anno 791, p. 89.
[260] *Ibid.*, anno 820, pp. 152–3.
[261] *Ibid.*, anno 805, p. 120.
[262] Widukind, c. 53–4, pp. 132–4. Schünemann, pp. 65–6.
[263] Thietmar, VI, 27, p. 306.
[264] Schünemann, p. 78.
[265] *Ibid.*, p. 79.
[266] *Annales Altahenses*, anno 1030, p. 18.

on the Danube, and his waggons, in order to advance with his knights and attack Hungary by another route. He devastated the whole area. His opponent, king Andrew I, had all provisions buried or destroyed in the district which Henry entered so that the German army had to endure 'indescribable pangs of starvation'.[267] The return to the Danube was terrible, but the army was saved by the courage of one part of it, which crossed the river in circumstances of the utmost danger. The following year, the army was faced with starvation again during the siege of Pressburg, and the campaign was a failure.[268] In 1074, the Hungarian king Geisa I also avoided a battle and hid all the grain and fodder.[269] The German army suffered terribly from hunger again. The Poles made use of the same strategy in 1109 against the emperor Henry V. King Lothar of Supplinburg's capitulation in 1126 was largely due to food shortage. In the first campaign of Frederick Barbarossa against the Poles, they destroyed their own fortresses, which they were afraid might fall into the hands of the enemy, and retreated in good order.[270]

Difficulties of supply in the east were so enormous that until the twelfth century it was quite exceptional for a powerful invading army to conquer them. Schünemann draws from this the 'paradoxical conclusion that the smaller the army was, the greater its chance of success'.[271] He quotes the success of Eric of Friuli and Pepin who had forced their way into the 'ring' of the Avars with a small army, but forgets that in so doing they were helped by internal strife among the Avars, and that Pepin was making his advance with more than one army.[272] In 1031 Conrad II won a victory in Poland when he had only the Saxons with him. The emperor Henry III won a striking victory in 1044 with soldiers from Bohemia and Bavaria, and his personal entourage. This example shows that small armies could be successful in favourable circumstances. Henry III had taken only a small army with him because he knew he would not find enough for a large one to eat.[273] Contrary to their usual custom, the Hungarians gave battle, certainly because they thought they could beat this little army. But they were beaten by the knights, and chased for six miles.[274] These examples from central Europe also show very clearly the enormous difficulties of securing supplies and their influence on the waging of war. The king had to face the terrible choice of risking starvation with a great army, or possible defeat with a smaller one. Their great armies were certainly not powerful enough to carry out a concentric approach, as was done in the time of Charlemagne and Louis the Pious; moreover, there were many more fortresses, and much stronger ones, in the enemy territory, and invasion routes were better defended. Other examples confirm Schünemann's paradox: Charlemagne conquered Saxony with smaller armies than the Romans who were not

267 Schünemann, *loc. cit.*
268 *Annales Altahenses*, anno 1052, p. 48.
269 Schünemann, p. 80.
270 Rahewinus, *Gesta Friderici*, 1. III, c. 3, p. 169.
271 Schünemann, p. 80.
272 See above.
273 *Annales Altahenses*, anno 1044, p. 35.
274 *Ibid.*, p. 36.

able to submit the Germans. William the Conqueror invaded England with less troops than the Romans. Heavy cavalry could conquer with smaller armies.

Many campaigns in the west also failed for lack of food. In 1167 Philip of Alsace rushed with a thousand knights to the help of the archbishop of Rheims in his own city. But he could only stay 24 hours, because the rebellious citizens had evacuated Rheims, and the count's army found no supplies there.[275] In 1174 the siege of Rouen was abandoned because the army of Louis VII and Philip of Alsace was running out of supplies.[276] An invasion of the county of Hainault by Philip of Alsace from one direction and the archbishop of Cologne and the duke of Brabant on the other, ended up as an exercise in plundering and destruction, cut short for lack of provisions.[277] At Acre in 1191, Philip of Alsace was well supplied with food from which he fed his starving fellow crusaders with kingly generosity.[278] The Flemish campaign of Philip Augustus failed in 1197 because his supply lines were cut.[279] In 1213 he sent a provision fleet to Damme. When these ships were destroyed by the enemy, he had to turn round and go home.[280]

In 1211, king John's invasion of Wales failed for lack of supplies.[281] In the campaign in 1265, undertaken by the future Edward I against Simon de Montfort, Simon's troops suffered severely from lack of their normal food, when they had to live off the land in Wales.[282] The same difficulties were experienced in feeding horses on whatever could be found locally. In September 1302 the French knights had to move their base, because the district's supplies of fodder were so quickly exhausted by this foraging.[283] This was one of the main reasons for the retreat of the royal army.

It was a great burden on the fighting men, and of course especially for the poorer ones, to have to provide their own supplies to participate in a long campaign. In August 1302 count John of Namur sent home the levies from Ghent and Ypres and the men from the surrounding districts, because they were plundering friend as well as foe in their necessity.[284] In the royal French army the leaders were up against the same problem, especially when there was delay in paying the men, which happened quite often. Philip the Fair made praiseworthy attempts to feed his army, and invited the merchants to bring along their goods free of customs duties, with full rights of passage and the promise of compensation for loss.[285] The Flemish leaders were more successful than the king in providing for their army. The levies from the Flemish towns always had a considerable number of waggons at their disposal with which

---

275 Joannes Saresbiriensis, *Epistolae*, ed. H.J.J. Brial, RHF, XVI, 1814, p. 568.
276 Godfrey of Bruil, *Chronica*, MGH, SS, XXVI, p. 20. Ralph of Diceto, *Opera historica*, ed. W. Stubbs, RS, 3 vols, London, 1875, I, p. 386.
277 Gilbert of Mons, c. 113, pp. 168–9.
278 *Sigeberti Continuatio Aquic.*, p. 427.
279 Ralph of Coggeshall, *Chronicon anglicanum*, ed. J. Stevenson, RS, London, 1875, pp. 77–8.
280 William the Breton, *Chronicon*, c. 170, pp. 251–2.
281 Poole, *From Domesday Book to Magna Carta*, p. 299.
282 Oman, I, p. 434.
283 *Annales Gandenses*, p. 40. Funck-Brentano, *De exercituum*, p. 14.
284 *Annales Gandenses*, p. 37.
285 *Chronique artésienne*, pp. 56, 72. Funck-Brentano, *De exercituum*, p. 43, n. 2; p. 64, n. 2; p. 65, n. 1.

they could transport supplies. Their weak point was the lack of money among the poor workmen of the guilds, as has just been mentioned.

Provisioning, as is always the case, had tremendous influence on discipline. In his *Mémoires*, General de Caulaincourt, Napoleon's close confidant, wrote: 'He didn't maintain discipline and closed his eyes to disorder. He didn't like others to speak of it if the disorders consisted only in drinking and eating. He was ready to grant that his system of warfare could not admit of severe discipline, as the troops were forced to subsist without any proper rationing.'[286]

In any army where the men were partly responsible for their own keep and arms, it is especially difficult to maintain discipline and to stop plundering. Gilbert of Mons writes very much to the point after the taking of the city of Namur by the knights, cavalry and foot of Hainault in 1188, that in such cases it is practically impossible to stop the men plundering the captured city. The count would have liked to prevent this, but was unable to do so.[287] When the royal French army sounded the retreat on 29 September, 1302, it was pursued by indomitable Flemings, who plundered the stores abandoned by the enemy against the orders of their leaders.[288]

Difficulty of supply was certainly one of the big problems in medieval warfare. Of course, the reason lies in the lack of economic resources in the districts where fighting was going on, and in the prince's lack of money. What was to be found on the spot could not possibly keep the armies supplied for long, and the larger stores and harvest were in castle-cellars, so that there was not enough in the open country for an invader.

5. *Defensive Manoeuvres*

The concentric approach of two or three armies meant the cutting of enemy lines of communication. He was then forced to fight, or else be shut up in one or more fortresses. But it was also possible to cut the enemies' lines and stop his supplies while defending a country. This could lead to the exhaustion of enemy forces, or even to their destruction. The Slavs used this strategy in the East.

In 955, the princes of the Abodrites, Stoinef and Nakon, let Otto the Great and his army advance as far as a broad marshy river. There they contested the crossing while they blocked the road behind their enemy with trees and brushwood, and left a detachment of troops there. Otto's men were surrounded for several days and suffered from hunger and sickness. The situation was impossible. Then, during the night, the margrave Gero managed to build three bridges a mile away, and cross the river. Otto followed with his army immediately. The Abodrites hastened to drive them back, but it was too late, and they were defeated by Otto and his men.[289] In this case, the defensive plan failed. Elsewhere it was more successful. In February 1126 king Lothar of Supplinburg made his way through the Kulm pass into Bohemia. But the enemy then occupied the pass in the rear of the Germans, while duke Sobieslav took

---

286 *Mémoires du général de Caulaincourt*, ed. J. Hanoteau, II, Paris, 1933, p. 378.
287 Gilbert of Mons, c. 143, pp. 219–20.
288 *Annales Gandenses*, p. 40.
289 Widukind, c. 53–4, pp. 132–4. Schünemann, pp. 65–6.

on King Lothar and his army in front. The king had to sue for peace.[290] This strategy usually led to the exhaustion of the enemy, as will be shown again.

In the Third Crusade, Richard I did not in the end dare to march on to Jerusalem. He was afraid of his army being cut off from the coast, which might have led to starvation or even to the extermination of the exhausted troops in a battle.[291]

In this connection it is worth glancing at the defence of the principality of Flanders by Count Baldwin IX against the invasion by king Philip Augustus of France in 1197. In July 1197 Baldwin had gone to war after making an alliance with Richard I. He quickly marched through the districts of Tournai and Cambrai, and took the castles.[292] Tournai itself fell quickly.[293] Then the count marched to Arras and laid siege to it along the eastern side.[294] But on the second day of the siege, Philip Augustus came up with a large army consisting of soldiers of several bishops, abbots and noblemen. On the eve of the Feast of the Assumption (14 August), the king appeared at Douai. On the advice of the monks of Anchin he went on to Aire, over the Lys and into Flanders, a move which was contrary to the advice of his counsellors, who tried to persuade their prince not to go into the dreaded county of Flanders. 'No king', wrote an English chronicler, 'had ever dared to go into that land because of the narrow lanes and roads, and because the great ditches one after another, were serious obstacles.' But the king was furious at his vassal's breach of faith and wanted to put an end to the trouble the Flemish counts caused him so he continued on through Bailleul to Ypres.[295] But Baldwin IX came up swiftly behind the king's army, which had moved on past him, and had every bridge destroyed so that the supply waggons could not reach the king's army. Most of the roads were also blocked, and there was nothing the French army could do except try to live off the land, which meant the dispersal of the army over a widespread area, in which it was perpetually being attacked by the fairly powerful Flemish. Ralph of Coggeshall relates that even the Flemish women were bold enough to attack French soldiers. After the king's troops had suffered severely from hunger for three days, Philip Augustus decided to parley and to humble himself before his rebellious vassal, saving his forces from certain destruction. Baldwin IX received his overlord very amicably and the nobility of his own nature led him to be hoodwinked by Philip Augustus, who promised to restore all the districts of Flanders he had taken, but failed to keep his promise. This example shows clearly that in certain cases the enemy's army can be destroyed even in defensive strategy.

Strategically speaking, the Flemish action against France between 1302–4 was of

---

[290] Schünemann, p. 68.

[291] Ambroise, vv. 10160–83, pp. 272–3.

[292] Rigord, *Gesta Philippi Augusti*, c. 115, p. 137. Roger of Hoveden, *Chronica*, IV, p. 19. Roger of Wendover, *Flores Historianum*, ed. G. Howlett, RS, 3 vols, London, 1886–1889, I, pp. 270–1. William of Newburgh, II, p. 495. Ralph of Coggeshall, *Chron. Anglic.*, pp. 77–8. Anonyme de Béthune, RHF, XXIV, p. 759. Ph. Mousket, II, p. 304.

[293] *Chartes de l'abbaye de Saint-Martin de Tournai*, ed. A. d'Herbornez, CRH in 4°, 2 vols, 1898–1902, I, no. 173, p. 177.

[294] *Sigeberti Cont. Aquic.*, *loc. cit.*

[295] Roger of Hoveden, *loc. cit.*, William of Newburgh, *loc. cit.*, Anonyme de Béthune, *loc. cit.*

a revolutionary character. The rebels did not avoid fighting in open country, nor did they shut themselves up in castles. True, they were not powerful enough to take the offensive themselves against the most mighty kingdom of the day, but they did not hesitate to come out against the enemy, and sometimes even were the first to offer battle. After their great victory in the battle of the Spurs at Courtrai on 11 July 1302, they found themselves again in September facing a royal army led by Philip the Fair. They drew up their troops successively at Vitry and Flines. In both cases they had chosen favourable spots, but the king made no attempt at all to drive them out of these good positions.[296] On 10 July 1303, the Flemings themselves offered battle. The constable of France did not dare fight it out with the rebels in the open field, and withdrew his army, despite the fact that the French had already beaten small bodies of Flemings, as for example at Arques on 4 April, 1303.[297]

Philip the Fair took the initiative again in the campaign of 1304. He left Arras, but did not get through the Pont-à-Vendin gap, which lay on the direct route to Flanders. An attempt to take the Pont-à-Raches gap failed. Then Philip made a great detour by way of Tournai, and tried to take the bridges over the Marcq at Bouvines and Pont-à-Tressin, but again he failed because the Flemish army came after him. However he managed to get from Tournai to Orchies without having to cross any water, and reached Faumont on 11 August. Then the Flemings blocked the way to Lille, having reached Pont-à-Marcq.[298] On 13 August the Flemings advanced half-way to the French camp. They chose such a strong position for themselves that the king, who came out to face them, did not dare attack.[299] There were parleys on 14, 15 and 16 August, but the king was in difficulties over supplies, and although the Flemish negotiators had assured him that their troops would fight, he decided to move off to open the gap of Pont-à-Vendin for his supply wagons.[300] Early on the morning of 17 August, the Flemings advanced again, this time to Mons-en-Pévèle and forced the king to stay where he was. On 18 August they moved towards the king's army again. Philip the Fair had to fight, south of the village of Mons-en-Pévèle.[301] When the Flemings had left the field, and so conceded victory to the king, they raised a new army which again marched towards the enemy at Lille, and was also ready to fight.[302]

The Flemings were not avoiding the enemy between 1302 and 1304, and it was not their choice that the conflict dragged on for so long. They could not impose a war of annihilation themselves, since their army was only strong in a defensive battle. But they always tried to finish the war quickly by a decisive battle. At Cassel in 1328

---

[296] *Annales Gandenses*, pp. 38–40. *Chronique artésienne*, pp. 55–6.

[297] Lot, *L'art militaire*, I, p. 267.

[298] *Chronique artésienne*, p. 83. Guiart, vv. 19927–30, pp. 285–6. *Chronographia regum Francorum*, I, p. 154.

[299] *Annales Gandenses*, p. 67. *Chronique artésienne*, p. 83. Guiart, vv. 19959–60, p. 286.

[300] *Annales Gandenses*, pp. 67–9. *Chronique artésienne*, p. 83. Guiart, vv. 19970–20010, p. 286. *Chronographia*, I, pp. 154–5.

[301] Guiart, vv. 20018–24, p. 286; vv. 20074–85, p. 287. *Chronique artésienne*, p. 84. *Annales Gandenses*, p. 69.

[302] *Annales Gandenses*, p. 82. Gilles le Muisit, pp. 77–8. *Chronographia*, I, p. 165.

and Westrozebeke in 1382 they were ready at once to stand up to the enemy attack. Here their strategy differs from that of the Scots under Robert Bruce after the battle of Bannockburn, where their leader purposely chose to avoid a major battle.[303] This revolutionary strategic attitude of the Flemings meant that the castles and rivers which had played so important a part in the defence of the country, from then onwards were of relatively minor importance. In their powerful citizen-armies the Flemings had a new fighting-force better able to replace the losses in battle, thanks to the high density of population, than were the smaller armies of knights, for whom noble birth was the sole qualification.

This attitude of the Flemings was the result of the increase in the population in the thirteenth century, of the growth of the towns, of the generally high standard of living, and of the feelings which inspired the troops. National feeling was sharply brought out in the fight against the French. The artisans were trying to improve their lot socially and thought that the great age of social equality had dawned. Politically, they took part in local government and even enjoyed a large majority on the magistrates' bench. Militarily, the victory at Courtrai had given them the necessary confidence in their own powers. They fought with unheard-of energy and in their youthful over-enthusiasm even started offensive action against the weaker allies of the king of France, Hainault and Holland.

Dithmarschen had only one invasion route. If the peasants knew that an enemy was ready to invade their land and if they had assembled their army, they could stop the enemy at the frontier. But the peasants preferred another solution. They abandoned the higher terrain, the *Geest*, and retreated with all their forces to the lower part of the land, the *Marsch*, along the North Sea. There the terrain was more favourable for the peasants who knew it better than the enemy, and were more mobile there than an army of knights which had to use the roads. On those roads the knights could be stopped by an entrenchment, and the land could be flooded by opening the sluices. At the most propitious moment, the peasant army attacked the immobile and paralysed enemy from all directions.

In the autumn of 1319, Gerard the Great, count of Holstein, invaded Dithmarschen with a powerful army and hoped to subjugate the country. He marched through the Geestland to Hemmingstedt and penetrated into the region of the Nordermarsch. After two fights the Ditmarscher peasants had to retreat to Oldenwöhrden. A peasant detachment retired into the church. The enemy set fire to the building and the peasants made a sortie. At the same time reinforcements for the peasants arrived from everywhere. They attacked the plundering enemy, put them to flight and cut their retreat in the difficult *Marsch* where they had erected obstacles. The enemy suffered heavy losses and had to flee.[304]

The medieval defender could also wait and see. When count Baldwin VII of Flanders challenged Henry I of England, who was then duke of Normandy, at Rouen, the latter took it calmly. He foresaw that the Fleming's resources would soon be

---

303 Oman, II, pp. 99–100. Delbrück, III, p. 458.
304 W. Lammers, *Die Schlacht bei Hemmingstedt*, p. 124. See also pp. 124–5, 131 ff.

exhausted and that he would have to turn back. He said: 'They can't take our land away with them.'[305]

In 1184, count Baldwin V of Hainault had to defend his principality against the count of Flanders who attacked on one side, and the archbishop of Cologne and the duke of Brabant who came on the other. He let the invader lay the countryside waste, while the army of Hainault garrisoned and held the castles and fortresses. Baldwin reassured his troops with the words attributed to Henry I: 'The enemy shall not take our country away with them.'[306] In 1185, in his war against Philip Augustus of France, count Philip of Alsace, who as a tactician and knight is regarded as one of the most gifted men of his time, decided to post garrisons in all border fortresses, to protect his own land and keep it in his possession. There were only about 400 knights left in his army, which normally numbered 1,000.[307]

Powerful kings of England had often tried to subdue the little land of Wales. They would naturally have liked very much to beat their enemy in a single battle and then to annex the country. But the Welsh princes withdrew into the mountains with their forces, or else escaped by fleeing to Ireland, whence they returned when there was a favourable opportunity.

There were innumerable wars between the Welsh and the English. A considerable part of the country was slowly subdued by the unceasing activity of the marcher lords, who lived on the doorstep. There is no need to give many examples here: a classic example of invasion by the king of England in 1211 will suffice. When king John set out to invade Wales in that year, his enemy Llewellyn used the normal strategy of the Welsh princelings. He withdrew into impenetrable mountains, where the inhabitants took their belongings and their cattle, so that the king's army found no food there and were afraid of starving. There was nothing for John to do but retreat.[308]

Similar invasions served to awaken the national spirit, or give it a powerful impetus. The Welsh quickly forgot the rivalries of their princelings. This happened for example when king John built a castle at Aberystwyth, which made it look as though he was intending to conquer the country. A revolt broke out; the castle was captured and destroyed. A general rebellion followed, and Llewellyn became leader of the national movement.[309]

Giraldus Cambrensis, writing a description of Wales at the end of the twelfth century, explained his method of subjugating the Welsh. The conqueror must be ready, he said, for a long campaign, a year at least, because the inhabitants would not come out and give battle but must be systematically worn down. He could lessen their power by stirring up quarrels among the princelings. He would have to use a fleet to cut their supply lines. Finally the conqueror would have to use light troops

[305] Herimannus Tornacensis, *Liber de restauratione S. Martini Tornacensis*, ed. G. Waitz, MGH, SS, XIV, 1883, c. 25, p. 284.
[306] Gilbert of Mons, c. 114, p. 174.
[307] *Ibid.*, c. 118, pp. 180–1.
[308] Poole, *From Domesday Book to Magna Carta*, p. 299.
[309] *Ibid.*, p. 300.

who could pursue and attack the enemy in the thickets and mountains where he had taken refuge.[310] Giraldus' suggestions proved to be excellent, for in general Edward I followed this plan in his conquest of the country a century later.

The conquest of Wales was achieved by a series of campaigns which were followed by rebellions of the conquered people. Edward's first campaign was very well prepared. It began in July 1277 and led to total submission in September. The king had a strong army and a fleet. The army was aided by woodcutters and labourers who made a road through the dense forests. The king stayed in north Wales, near the coast, marching from Chester to Flint, Rhuddlan and the Conway river. He built castles to subjugate the country. Llewellyn avoided battle and withdrew in the mountains. But the crops of the Welsh were taken in Anglesey and Llewellyn had to negotiate.[311]

The rebellion of 1282 was more dangerous and a long campaign was necessary from March 1282 to June 1283. The main royal army under Edward I advanced again from Chester along the coast to Flint and Rhuddlan. The earl of Gloucester commanded a separate army in the south, Roger Mortimer and his men were active at Montgomery, Roger l'Estrange and his warriors at Builth. A bridge of boats was constructed to cross to Anglesey. A fleet aided the armies. Llewellyn and his brother David avoided battle and retired in the mountains. But Llewellyn's army was surprised in his absence at Orewin Bridge in December 1282 and the prince was killed. David was captured in June 1283. A winter campaign had been necessary and a massive programme of castle building followed.[312]

There was a new rebellion in 1287, which was suppressed by two expeditions in that year, and in January 1288. The last rebellion started in 1294, both in south and north Wales. King Edward put it down by a campaign lasting six months. The king advanced again from Chester, the earl of Warwick commanded an army based at Montgomery, the earl of Pembroke had troops at Carmarthen, the earl of Hereford was with his forces in the south-east. The king left Chester with his army on 7 December 1294. This time he marched inland to Denbigh and from there he advanced to Conway where he arrived about Christmas. In the beginning of January he marched for the first time from Conway to Bangor. During the march the Welsh surprised and captured the whole of his baggage train. The king was forced to retire on Conway, where he was besieged and his army feared starvation. But in another part of the country English troops surprised the Welsh at Maes Moydog and defeated them (5 March 1295). Wales was finally beaten.[313]

Edward I had to use this strategy of attrition again when he wanted to conquer the Scots. The first campaign went off splendidly in 1296. In 21 weeks he had gone right through Scotland and brought it under his control, and it was annexed by England.

But in 1297 the Scots revolted. After William Wallace's victory over the English

---

[310] *Opera*, VI, pp. 218 ff. Poole, p. 292.
[311] Morris, *The Welsh Wars of Edward I*, pp. 129–36. M. Prestwich, *War, Politics and Finance under Edward I*, p. 28. M. Powicke, *The Thirteenth Century*, pp. 408 ff.
[312] Morris, pp. 153 ff. M. Prestwich, pp. 28–9. Powicke, pp. 421 ff.
[313] Morris, pp. 204–19; 240–67. M. Prestwich, pp. 29–30. Powicke, pp. 438–44.

at Stirling Bridge (11 September 1297) the Scots made raids in Northumberland and Cumberland. Edward I was in Flanders at the time, helping Guy de Dampierre against Philip the Fair, and could only make an expedition to Scotland in 1298. His great victory at Falkirk (22 July 1298) made it possible for him to provision his garrisons in the castles, but the Scots' rebellion was not ended.

The king started a fresh campaign on 24 June 1300. He besieged and took Caerlaverock in Galloway, and then went on to Wigtown. But this success was not enough, for the Scots withdrew and refused battle. In 1301 the king marched with one army from Berwick towards the Clyde, while another army advanced from Carlisle round the coast of Galloway. The Scots refused battle. The king stayed in Scotland during the winter.[314]

In May 1303, he undertook what appeared to be a decisive campaign. Scotland could offer no resistance: Stirling Castle alone held out for three months in 1304. For the second time the king wintered in Scotland. Then the country was annexed by England.[315]

But in 1306 a new rebellion broke out under Robert Bruce, who had himself crowned as king at Scone. He succeeded in driving the English out of Scotland. In 1314 he defeated a great English army under Edward II at Bannockburn.

Bruce's great contribution to the art of medieval warfare was that he mounted his fighting men on horses in order to make them mobile. This mounted foot was able to avoid battle more easily, and could harry and exhaust the English better when invading. The Scots themselves were able to attack with punitive expeditions, great raids thrusting deeply into northern England.[316]

The Scots king chose to fight a defensive war in which all the battles took place in well-chosen positions between mountains and marshes. He preferred to withdraw with his troops into the forests rather than into fortified castles, which were extremely difficult to get out of again. Bruce laid waste the countryside wherever the English attacked Scotland. He confined his own offensive actions to nocturnal raids and ambushes. For many years after Bannockburn the Scots kept their supremacy and the initiative, and sometimes even penetrated as far south as York. When a great English army advanced into Scotland in 1321, Bruce let it come as far as Edinburgh, so as to be able then to cut its lines of communication and force it to go back again through shortage of foodstuffs.[317]

The English kings were always faced with great difficulties in their Scottish expeditions; they were hindered partly by the difficult terrain through which the Scots could make a quick retreat, partly by the length of their lines of communication with their own country, and partly by the great distances they had to cover to reach the remote castles of Scotland. Moreover, the enemy was a rough and determined race, with its heart set on freedom and independence. Any rebellion in Scotland immediately brought out a larger army than the garrisons that the king of England could keep in their country. Scotland was not to be subdued.

314 M. Prestwich, pp. 34–6.   316 Morris, *Mounted Infantry*, p. 79.
315 M. Prestwich, pp. 36–7.   317 Oman, II, p. 99.

6. *Strategic Possibilities and the Theatre of War*

Schünemann says of central Europe that 'between Charlemagne's first campaign against the Slavs in 789, and Frederick Barbarossa's first Polish campaign in 1157, the head of state or his representatives undertook 175 campaigns against Germany's eastern neighbours'.[318] 'This does not include border skirmishes, nor the expeditions which the Saxons, from Henry IV onwards, started independently in the east and north. During this period the German kings did much more fighting in the east than in Italy, but with less result. About a third of the campaigns in the east accomplished more or less what they set out to do. A quarter of them were semi-successful, and the others failed: about 20 expeditions ended disastrously for the German army.'[319] The small measure of military success in the east is due to the greater problems that were involved: the difficulties of transport on the roads, which were few and very bad, the systematic building of defences along possible invasion routes and far into enemy territory, and the scanty sources of supply in the east which could not keep men and horses fed.

Elsewhere the same thing happened. William the Conqueror showed undoubted gifts as strategist and tactician in the conquest of the English, but after that, he could not produce any very striking results on the continent. He waged 'inconclusive wars, in which he never rose above the average generalship of his day.'[320] Richard I made use of strategy on a rather grander scale during the Third Crusade, at Acre, Arsuf and Jaffa, than he did in the west against Philip Augustus. It is surprising that the able general of 1190–91 actually scored fewer successes in 1194–99.[321] The same is true of Frederick Barbarossa, whose campaign in Asia Minor at the beginning of the Third Crusade is much more remarkable than his Italian expeditions.[322] Godfrey of Bouillon also led the crusaders with much more advanced strategy than he had ever been able to employ in his own country.

The more impressive results which the crusaders were able to achieve in the Holy Land were due to armies greater than those normally used in the west. In the east they found a wide expanse of land with few fortresses, so that their strategy was not so greatly hindered by many fortifications as it was in the west. This explains why the crusades had so little influence on strategy in western Europe. A comparison can be made, *mutatis mutandis*, with the First World War, 1914–18. In his profound and thoughtful book, *The Anatomy of Courage*, Lord Moran[323] regrets that the British army had no generals truly worthy of the name in this war. He also deplores the fact that that able strategist, Field-Marshal Lord Wavell, in his study *Generals and*

318 Schünemann, p. 56.
319 *Ibid., loc. cit.*
320 Stenton, *Anglo-Saxon England*, p. 601. [See, however, the views of J. Gillingham, 'William the Bastard at war', *Studies in Medieval History presented to R. Allen Brown*, ed. C. Harper-Bill, C. Holdsworth and J. Nelson, Woodbridge, 1989, pp. 141–158.
321 Oman, I, p. 355. [J. Gillingham has also revised views on Richard I's strategy: see *Richard the Lionheart*, pp. 245–74.]
322 *Ibid.*
323 London, 1945, pp. 192–3.

Generalship[324] gives no authoritative explanation of this. The generals in the First World War did not succeed in winning the war by skilful manoeuvres, but had to take refuge in an expensive strategy of attrition. Lord Wavell's answer to this was that the struggle in France from 1914–18 was siege-warfare on an enormous scale, and that this was the cause of the generals' failure.[325] General Allenby, who did not achieve much in France, showed himself a good strategist in Palestine: there he had superior forces, the front was less thickly manned in comparison with the west, and more space meant he was able to manoeuvre more freely. This explains the success in the east and the failure in the west, just as it did in the Middle Ages.

The Influence of the Church on Methods of Warfare

It may be asked whether the Church did not have a cramping effect on the warfare of the time, thereby encouraging the use of a strategy of attrition. The clergy made the most laudable efforts to curb small private wars through the Peace and the Truce of God in the tenth and eleventh centuries, but they were not successful. At the time of the First Crusade, and during the preparation of the subsequent crusades they did their best to make knights take part in these undertakings, instead of fighting out minor feuds among themselves or greater wars against their fellow-Christians. Many knights would have liked this too, for example at the time of Joinville in the thirteenth century,[326] and Dubois and other writers in their turn set out these ideas in the fourteenth century. Only really powerful princes, like the dukes of Normandy and the counts of Flanders, managed to limit the private wars of their nobles in their own lands, or virtually to stop them, like the kings of England. On the whole, wars between Christian monarchs were as fierce and frequent as before.

The Church forbade tournaments at many Councils, but were just as unsuccessful in this. The kings of England were comparatively successful, and so were the kings of France at various times. They acted not so much under papal influence as from a wish to have peace and good order within their realms, and not to waste their knights in pointless fighting. It was forbidden by some Councils to use crossbows against other Christians, but this did not prevent men from continuing to use and develop the crossbow.

The popes forbade the maintenance of bands of mercenaries, but this prohibition was as little observed as the others. If some monarchs did not use them, it was for financial reasons, or because the mercenaries were causing a lot of damage in their own country. As soon as fierce fighting broke out, such as that between Richard I and Philip Augustus, both rushed for help to these formidable bands. Both sides did the same during the crusades against the Albigensians.

Was there a powerful influence slowly at work in the world either in the character of warfare or its intensity? The ideology of knightly conventions and customs was

---

[324] Wavell, *The Good Soldier*, London, 1948, pp. 3–31.
[325] Lord Moran, *loc. cit.*
[326] Joinville, c. 55, p. 99.

indeed penetrated by Christian doctrine and this led to a more humane type of warfare. But this was also tempered by the scarcity of nobles, who were fighting against members of their own class, by the efficient protection given by their armour, and the understandable self-interest which encouraged the taking of prisoners. No one wanted to fight to the death, because it would only make the enemy more anxious to fight.

Naturally the Church exercised great influence in easing the lot of those who were taken prisoner in the fighting, and of the local inhabitants who were no longer sold into slavery as in former times, in securing protection of women and children, and in checking robbery and looting in enemy country. Knights were no longer chiefly fighting for what they could get as booty. But the facts show that the plundering of captured cities, such as Namur in 1118 and Liège in 1213, could not be prevented by some monarchs. It was usually the foot-soldiers who went in for plunder.

In the war against the enemies of the Faith, deep religious feeling led to fiercer and crueller fighting. This can be clearly seen in the First Crusade. In time the crusaders became less violent in their methods. This was not the result of a 'colonial policy', but it was an expression of a more general humane feeling. As the fighting went on, both sides developed considerable respect for each other, and came to see that inhumane behaviour was usually mutual, and brought with it serious disadvantages to both sides. After the departure of the crusaders there were only 200, or at the most 300 knights left with Godfrey of Bouillon. They had to be wary lest their methods amounted to suicide when they were fighting an enemy who had inexhaustible reserves close at hand, so prisoners were ransomed on both sides. But in the Third Crusade Richard I had the Moslem garrison of Acre slaughtered after their surrender.[327]

The war against the Albigensians was also fought with the utmost cruelty. Hundreds, perhaps thousands, of Albigensians were burned. Captured mercenaries were executed, on one occasion 300 *routiers* at the same time, and prisoners were mutilated.[328]

Once the passions were unleashed in medieval warfare no one remembered the normal laws of behaviour. Should one of the enemy break the rules his opponent reacted still more fiercely. Thus the war spread, and became fiercer and more cruel in character, and fighting was even more determined than before. That explains why monarchs turned to the use of mercenaries, despite the Church's bar, and the fact that they used such weapons as crossbows. It also led to the use of communal armies and ordinary archers, despite the fact that their knights often despised them, and would have preferred not to use them from social and military considerations, or from fear that these lowly subjects would upset the existing social order.

---

[327] Oman, I, p. 305.
[328] Belperron, pp. 165–8, 197, 203–4, 206–7, 220, 223, 241, 318, 334.

Conclusion

Medieval strategy displays great similarity to that of the sixteenth and seventeenth centuries, and more especially the eighteenth. Armies were small, and difficult to replace, therefore the leaders of the defence avoided battle, although it was one of the most effective means of gaining their ends. They often chose to manoeuvre, and the weaker of the contestants took refuge behind the defence of his many fortresses. This sort of strategy was dictated by social conditions, the equipment of armies, and the state and number of fortifications. This created a certain balance between the fighting nations, and this balance was not easily upset unless new methods were used. It is known that these methods were adopted at the end of the eighteenth century, and early in the nineteenth by the French Revolution. On a far smaller scale, but none the less visibly, this happened in Flanders in 1302 in the struggle against Philip the Fair.

Actually medieval monarchs could not fight in any other way, under pressure of all sorts of hindrances and obstacles which they could usually do nothing to remove. Sometimes it was possible through an alteration of the social composition of the armies to attain more definite results, but the fortresses of the enemy country still had to be put out of action. Changes in methods of recruiting armies were also extremely dangerous politically for the monarch who carried them out. Henry II and Richard I of England used mercenaries, and made comparatively less call on the normal military service of the knights, who had to pay scutage instead of doing military service. But this meant that English knights were no longer available for foreign military service, and it led to Magna Carta under king John. The monarch's power was limited by this, and at the same time lessened his capacity for future military operations. As has already been said, there was a similar change in the Holy Roman Empire after the reign of Frederick Barbarossa. But Philip Augustus succeeded, with the help of mercenaries and other troops, in extending his dominion so much that he afterwards had a much more powerful army of knights at his disposal, and had no more need to use mercenaries, while military service of the nobility was well-regulated.

But one must be extremely careful of hasty criticism of medieval commanders. On the whole, modern researchers are apt to lose sight of some of the difficulties with which they had to contend. Also we must not think that any failure was due to weak personality, or lack of insight and appreciation of the strategic position. If the Middle Ages produced no outstanding leaders, this is due to various obstacles and limiting factors, and to a complete lack of favourable opportunities for making use of their talents.

If we consult Clausewitz, we shall see that he lays down the following rules for wars with limited aims, such as were usually fought in the Middle Ages.

An aggressor starting a war of this kind: 1. Attempts to conquer an area or a district as far as this is possible without fighting a decisive battle. 2. Tries to capture an important supply centre. 3. Tries to capture a fortress. 4. Tries to fight a successful engagement having a particular significance.

The defender will react thus: 1. By defending his fortifications with his field-army. 2. By protecting his country by defending a broad front. 3. Where this is impossible, by defending the border by marches and sidewards movements of his army. 4. By avoiding fighting in unfavourable circumstances.[329]

From this review it appears that these methods were often employed, and that in certain cases they went for bigger targets and achieved them. In the Middle Ages, the land being attacked was defended by castles and fortified towns which were more numerous than the fortifications of the sixteenth to eighteenth centuries. The army could relieve the besieged spot or rush to its help, fight a battle if things looked promising or avoid it if the outlook were unfavourable. Clausewitz also mentions some aggressive methods by which the defender can make his strategy more effective:

1. Action against enemy lines of communication and store centres.
2. Diversions and raids in enemy territory.
3. Attacks on enemy units and posts in favourable circumstances, or threats of similar action.[330]

These methods were also employed in the Middle Ages. The action against lines of communication of Philip Augustus' army during his attack on Flanders in 1197 was most successful. In central Europe this strategy also brought notable victories. Raids into enemy territory were common occurrences in medieval wars, and the Scottish armies who moved about on horseback without baggage trains were very skilful at this. Attacks on units of the enemy army and night attacks in favourable circumstances also occurred frequently.

Mutatis mutandis, we can conclude that there was great similarity between medieval strategy and the eighteenth-century strategy of attrition, in which it was often thought better to avoid a bloody clash on the battlefield. Both arose from circumstances which made other methods of warfare impossible, or at least undesirable. The fact that medieval leaders acted as Clausewitz says in the beginning of the nineteenth century shows that their ideas were right, and that they could not normally have used any other method under the pressure of all sorts of inhibiting factors which they could not overcome. Their knowledge of strategy left nothing to be desired, but the practical means for large-scale operations were almost entirely lacking. Those commanders who had what they needed usually went in for a strategy of overthrow.

General Conclusion

Armoured cavalry dominated military life and the warfare of western Europe in the period under review. After the Franks had adopted heavy cavalry as their chief weapon, the Saxons and Thuringians copied their example. The Norman conquest of England by William I also introduced heavy cavalry to England.

[329] *On War*, Bk VI, Ch. 30.
[330] *Ibid.*, *loc. cit.*

The Frankish warriors fighting as heavy cavalry were vassals at first, then knights and finally nobles. They used original tactics, hoping that one powerful assault would start a breakthrough of the enemy lines. This western form of tactics differed completely from the age-old method of Oriental and Asiatic tactics of light cavalry. Up to the end of the Middle Ages there was a constant process of evolution in which armour, weapons and all equipment became increasingly heavy. They used tall, heavy, powerful horses as well. This led to perpetual competition between attacking weapons and defensive equipment. The nobles wanted the best possible protection for the life of their limited number of members. The knights adapted their tactics to their opponents, in the Holy Land against the Moslems, in the west against foot-soldiers.

This social class of knights remained the professional military class throughout the Middle Ages. But new social classes were rising by virtue of the development of trade and industry, and as time went on they too developed notable military qualities. Communal armies and peasants fought as foot-soldiers, whose value was constantly rising.

In the twelfth and early thirteenth centuries mercenaries were in action, who fought excellently on foot. In Italy, Flanders, Liège, Wales, Scotland, Switzerland and Dithmarschen levies and peasants were increasingly valuable as foot-soldiers from the eleventh to the fourteenth centuries, and their equipment improved greatly. In this sphere too, there was a lasting change. In Flanders and Scotland the foot had great successes which for a time threatened to upset the domination of the knights. English archers also won important victories with the help of their knights. The Swiss managed to establish the superiority of foot-soldiers over cavalry in this way.

In countries such as England, where both social classes produced good fighting men at the same time, tactical co-operation between both branches made great advances. Elsewhere, where such equilibrium was unknown, one of the two branches played a more important part than the other.

Strategically, the defences of states became increasingly strong. From the ninth century onwards castles were more and more solidly built: thereafter fortified towns became extremely important, and these fortifications were always being strengthened. Medieval monarchs contrived to fortify their lands very powerfully. The defence systems which they designed, or which developed in the course of centuries are a remarkable expression of their military ideas.

BIBLIOGRAPHY

Abbreviations

AA. SS.	*Acta Sanctorum quotquot orbe coluntur*, edited by the Bollandists, 65 vols in folio, 1643 ff.
Ac. roy. Belg., Cl. Lettres, Mém.	Académie royale de Belgique, Classe des Lettres, Mémoires.
AWLSK	Koninklijke Academie voor Wetenschappen, Letteren en Schone Kunsten van België. Klasse der Letteren, Brussels.
BCRH	*Bulletin (Compte rendu des séances) de la Commission royale d'histoire, Brussels.*
Bibl. Ec. Chartes	Bibliothèque de l'Ecole des Chartes.
BFPLUL	Bibliothèque de la Faculté de Philosophie et Lettres de l'Université de Liège.
Bibl. Soc. hist. droit	Bibliothèque de la société d'histoire du droit des pays flamands, picards et wallons.
CHM	Centre d'histoire militaire. Travaux, Musée royal de l'armée, Brussels.
Coll. Picard	Collection de textes pour servir à l'étude et à l'enseignement de l'histoire, Picard, Paris.
CFMA	Les classiques français du moyen âge.
CHFMA	Les classiques de l'histoire de France au moyen âge.
CRH	Publications de la Commission royale d'histoire.
EHR	*English Historical Review*
MGH, AA	Monumenta Germaniae Historica, Auctores Antiquissimi, 15 vols in 4º, Hannover, 1877–1919.
MGH, SS	Monumenta Germaniae Historica, Scriptores, Hannover, 34 vols, 1826–1934, 32 vols in folio, 2 in 4º.
MGH, SRM	Monumenta Germaniae Historica, Scriptores rerum merovingicarum, 7 vols, in 4º, 1884–1920.
MGH, SS in usum scholarum	Scriptores rerum germanicarum in usum scholarum ex Monumentis Germaniae Historicis separatim editi, in 8º.
PL	J.P. Migne, *Patrologia latina*, 221 vols, Paris, 1844–1855.
RBHM	*Revue belge d'histoire militaire.*
RBPH	*Revue belge de philologie et d'histoire.*
RHC	Recueil des historiens des croisades, edited by the Académie des Inscriptions et Belles-Lettres, 16 vols, in fº, Paris, 1841–1906.
RHC, Hist. occ.	Recueil des historiens des croisades. Historiens occidentaux.

RHC, Hist.   *ibid.*, Historiens orientaux.
or.
RHC,   *ibid.*, Documents arméniens.
Doc. arm.
RHF   Recueil des historiens des Gaules et de la France, ed. M. Bouquet, and, from
              t. XIV, the Académie des Inscriptions et Belles-Lettres, 24 vols, in fº.
RIHM   *Revue Internationale d'Histoire Militaire.*
RS: Rolls   Rerum Britannicarum Medii Aevi Scriptores, 224 vols, in 8º, London,
Series   1858–1896.
SHF   Société de l'histoire de France.
SSCI   Settimane di Studio del Centro Italiano di Studi sull'alto medioevo.
TRHS   *Transactions of the Royal Historical Society.*

Manuscript Sources

Bruges. Archives of the City (Stadsarchief): Stadsrekeningen (City Accounts), years
    1303 and 1304. Special accounts: year 1316 and 1321–1322.
Ghent. Archives of the State (Rijksarchief): Fonds St-Genois, nº 1098. Supplement
    Verbaere, nº 33 bis.
Lille. Archives départementales: Cartulaire de Namur, pièce 29, f º 17 bis, vº.
Paris. Archives Nationales: Trésor des chartes, J. 456, nº 36, J. 543, nº 17.
Paris. Bibliothèque Nationale:
Ms français 6049, fº 183 vº ff. (Plan of Charles II of Sicily).
Ms latin 6222 c: Pierre Dubois, Summaria brevis et compendiosa doctrina felicis
    expeditionis et abreviationis guerrarum ac litium regni Francorum.
Ms latin 7242: Fidentius de Padua, Liber recuperationis, f º 85–126.

Printed Sources

Actes des comtes de Flandre (1071–1128), ed. F. Vercauteren, CRH in 4º, Brussels, 1938.
Ademar of Chabannes, Chronicon, ed. J. Chavanon, Coll. Picard, Paris, 1897.
Albert of Aix, *Liber christianae expeditionis pro ereptione, emundatione, et restitutione
    sanctae Hierosolymitanae ecclesiae*, RHC, Hist. occ., 4.
Ambroise, *L'estoire de la guerre sainte*, ed. G. Paris, Coll. de documents inédits sur
    l'histoire de France, Paris, 1897.
Anciennes Chroniques de Flandre, ed. N. de Wailly and L. Delisle, RHF, 22.
Andreas Marchianensis, *Historia regum Francorum. Continuatio (excerpta)*, ed. G.
    Waitz, MGH, SS, 26, 1882.
Anna Comnena, *The Alexiad*, ed. B. Leib, Coll. byzantine, Association G. Budé, Paris,
    3 vols, 1937–1945.
Annales Altahenses maiores, ed. E.L.B. von Oefele, MGH, SS in usum scholarum, 1891.
Annales Anglorum antiqui (excerpta), ed. R. Pauli, MGH, SS, 13, 1881.
Annales Bertiniani, ed. G. Waitz, MGH, SS in usum scholarum, 1883.
Annales Blandinienses, see *Annales de Saint-Pierre de Gand*, etc.
Annales Egmundenses, ed. O. Oppermann, in Fontes Egmundenses, Werken uitgegeven
    door het Historisch Genootschap gevestigd te Utrecht, 3rd series, nº 61, Utrecht, 1935.
*Annales Elmarenses, Annales Elnonenses, Annales Formoselenses, see Annales de
    Saint-Pierre de Gand*, etc.

Annales Fuldenses, ed. F. Kurze, MGH, SS in usum scholarum, 1891.

Annales Gandenses, ed. F. Funck-Brentano, Coll. Picard, Paris, 1896.

Annales Gandenses, ed. H. Johnstone, Medieval Classics, London, 1951.

Annales Hildesheimenses, ed. G. Waitz, MGH, SS in usum scholarum, 1878.

Annales Laureshamenses, Alamannici, Guelferbytani et Nazariani, ed. G.H. Pertz, MGH, SS, 1, 2, 1826, 1829.

Annales Mettenses priores, ed. B. von Simson, MGH, SS in usum scholarum, 1905.

Annales necrologici Prumienses, ed. G. Waitz, MGH, SS, 13, 1881.

Annales regni Francorum, ed. F. Kurze, MGH, SS in usum scholarum, 1895.

Annales Sancti Amandi, Annales Tiliani, Annales Laubacenses, Annales Petaviani, ed. G.H. Pertz, MGH, SS, 1, 1826.

Annales Sangallenses maiores, ed. G.H. Pertz, MGH, SS, 1, 1826.

'Annales S. Petri Erphesfurtenses maiores', ed. O. Holder-Egger, in *Monumenta Erphesfurtensia*, MGH, SS in usum scholarum, 1899.

Les Annales de Saint-Pierre de Gand et de Saint-Amand: Annales Blandinienses, Annales Elmarenses, Annales Formoselenses, Annales Elnonenses, ed. Ph. Grierson, CRH in 8º, Brussels, 1937.

Annales Vedastini, ed. B. von Simson, MGH, SS in usum scholarum, 1909.

Annalista Saxo, ed. G. Waitz, MGH, SS, 6, 1844.

Anonyme de Béthune, Chronique française des rois de France, ed. L. Delisle, RHF, 24, 1904.

Anonymous, Gesta Francorum et aliorum Hierosolimitanorum, ed. L. Bréhier, CHFMA, Paris, 1924.

Anonymus, Regum Franciae chronicon, RHF, 22.

Anonymus Laudunensis, Chronicon universale (excerpta), ed. G. Waitz, MGH, SS, 26, 1882.

Anonymus Remensis, Historiae (excerpta), ed. O. Holder-Egger, MGH, SS, 26, 1882.

Anselmus, *Gesta pontificum Trajectensium et Leodiensium*, ed. R. Koepke, MGH, SS, 7, 1846.

Astronomus, *Vita Hludovici imperatoris*, ed. G.H. Pertz, MGH, SS, 2, 1829.

Balduinus Avennensis, *Chronicon Hanoniense, quod dicitur Balduini Avennensis*, ed. J. Heller, MGH, SS, 25, 1880.

Balduinus Ninovensis, *Chronicon*, ed. O. Holder-Egger, MGH, SS, 25, 1880.

Baudouin d'Avesnes, *Chroniques abrégées, continuation*, ed. Kervyn de Lettenhove, in: Istore et Croniques de Flandre, 1, Brussels, 1879.

Bayeux Tapestry, The, ed. D.M. Wilson, London, 1985.

Bayeux Tapestry, The, ed. E. MacLagan, in The King Penguin Books, London, 1945.

Bec, P., *Petite anthologie de la lyrique occitane du moyen âge*, Avignon, 1954.

Beha ed-Din, *Anecdotes et beaux traits de la vie du Sultan Youssof (Salah ed-Din)*, RHC, Hist. or., 3.

Bernard of Clairvaux, *see* St Bernard.

Bernard le Trésorier, *see* Ernoul.

Boutaric, E., 'Notices et extraits de documents inédits relatifs à l'histoire de France sous Philippe le Bel', in *Notices et extraits des manuscrits de la Bibliothèque impériale*, 20, 2, Paris, 1862, pp. 83–237.

Bovo abbas, Relatio de inventione et elevatione S. Bertini, ed. O. Holder-Egger, MGH, SS, 15, 1, 1887.

Bretel, *see* Jacques Bretel.

Breton, *see* William the Breton.

Bueil, *see* Jean de Bueil.

Buntinx, W., 'Het Transport van Vlaanderen, 1305–1517'. Unpublished dissertation, Ghent University, 1965.

Burcard, Directorium, ed. Reiffenberg, Monuments pour servir à l'histoire des provinces de Namur, de Hainaut et de Luxembourg, 4.

Cantatorium sive Chronicon Sancti Huberti, ed. K. Hanquet, CRH in 4º, Brussels, 1906.

Capitularia regum Francorum, ed. A. Boretius and V. Krause, MGH, Leges, in 4º, 2 vols, 1883–1897.

Chançun de Willame, La, ed. E. Stearns Tyler, New York, 1919.

Chanson d'Antioche, ed. P. Paris, 2 vols, Paris, 1848.

Chanson d'Aspremont, ed. L. Brandin, CFMA, 19, 25, Paris, 1919–1921.

Chanson de Roland, ed. J. Bédier, Paris, 1922.

Chartes de l'abbaye de Saint-Martin de Tournai, ed. A. D'Herbomez, CRH in 4º, 2 vols, 1898–1902.

Chrétien de Troyes, Der Percevalroman, ed. Wendelin Foerster, 5, 2nd edn by Alfons Hilka, Halle (Saale), 1932.

Chronica regia Coloniensis, cum continuationibus, ed. G. Waitz, MGH, SS in usum scholarum, 1880.

Chronicon comitum Flandrensium, ed. J.J. De Smet, Corpus Chronicorum Flandriae, CRH in 4º, 1, Brussels, 1837.

Chronicon Moissiacense, ed. G.H. Pertz, MGH, SS, 1, 2, 1826, 1829.

Chronicon S. Andreae castri Cameracesii, ed. L.C. Bethmann, MGH, SS, 7, 1846.

Chronicon S. Martini Turonense (excerpta), ed. O. Holder Egger, MGH, SS, 26, 1882.

Chronique artésienne et chronique tournaisienne, ed. F. Funck-Brentano, Coll. Picard, Paris, 1899.

Chronique normande du XIVe Siècle, ed. A. and E. Molinier, SHF, Paris, 1882.

Chroniques des comtes d'Anjou et des seigneurs d'Amboise, ed. L. Halphen and R. Poupardin, Coll. Picard, Paris, 1913.

Chroniques liégeoises, ed. S. Balau and E. Fairon, 2, CRH in 4º, Brussels, 1931.

Chroniques de Saint-Denis, ed. Daunou and Naudet, RHF, 20, 1840.

Chronographia regum Francorum, ed. H. Moranvillé, SHF, 3 vols, Paris, 1891–1897.

Clari, *see* Robert de Clari.

Codagnellus, *see* Johannes Codagnellus.

Colens, J., 'Le compte communal de la ville de Bruges. Mai 1302 à février 1303', *Annales de la Société d'Emulation de Bruges*, 35, Bruges, 1886.

Couronnement de Louis, Le, ed. E. Langlois, CFMA, 22, Paris, 1920.

Dehaisnes, Abbé, and Finot, J., 'Inventaire sommaire des archives départementales. Nord'. *Archives civiles*. Série B, 1, 2, Lille, 1906.

Dubois, *see* Pierre Dubois.

Ducasse, A., *La guerre raconteé par les combattants*, Paris, 2 vols, 1932.

Dudo of St-Quentin, De moribus et actis primorum Normanniae ducum, ed. J. Lair, Caen, 1865, in 4º.

Einhard, Vita Karoli Magni imperatoris, ed. L. Halphen, CHFMA, 4th edn, Paris, 1967.

Ekkehardus, Chronicon universale, ed. G. Waitz, MGH, SS, 6, 1844.

'Epistulae et chartae ad historiam primi belli sacri spectantes', ed. H. Hagenmeyer, *Die Kreuzzugsbriefe aus den Jahren 1088–1100, Innsbrück*, 1901.

Ermoldus Nigellus, Carmen, ed. E. Faral, CHFMA, Paris, 1932.

Ernoul, Chronique d'Ernoul et de Bernard le Trésorier, ed. L. de Mas Latrie, SHF, Paris, 1871.

Eudes de Saint-Maur, Vie de Bouchard le Vénérable, comte de Vendôme, de Corbeil, de Melun et de Paris (Xe et XIe siècles), ed. Ch. de la Roncière, Coll. Picard, Paris, 1892.

Fidenzio of Padua, Liber recuperationis Terrae Sanctae, ed. G. Golubovich, Biblioteca Bio-Bibliografica della Terra Santa, 5 vols, Florence, 2, 1906–1927.

Flandria generosa auctore monacho S. Bertini, cum continuationibus, ed. L.C. Bethmann, MGH, SS, 9, 1851.

Flodoard, Annales, ed. Ph. Lauer, Coll. Picard, Paris, 1905.

Flodoard, Historia Remensis ecclesiae, ed. J. Heller and G. Waitz, MGH, SS, 13, 1881.

Florence of Worcester, Chronicon ex Chronicis, ed. B. Thorpe, 2 vols, London, 1848–1849; (*excerpta*) ed. R. Pauli, MGH, SS, 13, 1881.

Folcuinus, Gesta abbatum S. Bertini Sithiensium (649–962), ed. O. Holder-Egger, MGH, SS, 13, 1881.

Fredegar, Chronicarum libri IV, ed. B. Krusch, MGH, SRM, 2, 1888.

Fulcher of Chartres, *Gesta Francorum Hierusalem expugnantium*, RHC, Hist. occ., 3.

Funck-Brentano, F., 'Additions au Codex diplomaticus Flandriae', Bibl. Ec. Chartes, 57, 1896, pp. 373–417 and 529–72.

Galbert of Bruges, De multro, traditione et occisione gloriosi Karoli comitis Flandriarum, ed. H. Pirenne, Coll. Picard, Paris, 1891.

Genealogia comitum Flandriae Bertiniana cum continuationibus, ed. L.C. Bethmann, MGH, SS, 9, 1851.

Geoffroy de Paris, Chronique rimée, ed. N. de Wailly and L. Delisle, RHF, 22.

Gervase of Canterbury, The Chronicle of the reigns of Stephen, Henry II and Richard I, ed. W. Stubbs, RS, 2 vols, London, 1879–1880.

Gesta abbatum Lobbiensium, ed. W. Arndt, MGH, SS, 21, 1869.

Gesta episcoporum Cameracensium, ed. L.C. Bethmann, MGH, SS, 7, 1846.

Gesta episcoporum Cameracensium continuata, ed. G. Waitz, MGH, SS, 14, 1883. (Gesta Galcheri episcopi. Gesta Buchardi episcopi).

Gesta Federici I. imperatoris in Lombardia (Annales Mediolanenses maiores), ed. O. Holder-Egger, MGH, SS in usum scholarum, 1892.

Gesta pontificum Cameracensium, ed. L.C. Bethmann, MGH, SS, 7, 1846 (Gesta Lietberti episcopi).

Gesta regis Henrici II Benedicti Abbatis, ed. W. Stubbs, RS, 2 vols, 1867.

Gilbert of Mons, Chronicon Hanoniense, ed. L. Vanderkindere, CRH in 8°, Brussels, 1904.

Gilles le Muisit, Chronique et annales, ed. H. Lemaître, SHF, Paris, 1905.

Gilliodts-Van Severen, L., *Inventaire des archives de la ville de Bruges*, 1, Bruges, 1871.

Giovanni Villani, see Villani.

Giraldus Cambrensis, *De rebus a se gestis, libri III*, ed. J.S. Brewer, RS, London, 1861.

Giraldus Cambrensis, *Expugnatio Hibernica*, ed. J.F. Dimock, Opera, 5, RS, London, 1867.

Giraldus Cambrensis, *Itinerarium Kambriae*, ed. J.F. Dimock, Opera, 6, RS, London, 1868.

Godfrey of Bruil, *Chronica*, RHF, 12, (excerpta), ed. O. Holder-Egger, MGH, SS, 26, 1882.

Grandes chroniques de France, 8, ed. J. Viard, SHF, Paris, 1933.

Gray of Heton, Sir Thomas, *Scalachronica*, ed. J. Stevenson, Maitland Club, 40, Edinburgh, 1836.

La guerre de Metz en 1324, ed. E. De Bouteiller, Paris, 1875.

Guillaume Adam, *De modo extirpandi Sarracenos*, ed. Ch. Kohler, RHC, Doc. arm., 2.

Guillaume Guiart, *La branche des royaus lingnages*, ed. N. de Wailly and L. Delisle, RHF, 22.

Guillaume de Pouille, *La geste de Robert Guiscard*, ed. M. Mathieu, Istituto Siciliano di Studi Bizantini e Neoellenici, Testi e Monumenti, Testi 4, Palermo, 1961.

Guillelmus de Nangiaco, *Chronicon*, ed. Daunou and Naudet, RHF, 20. Continuatio, *ibid.*

Guy, bishop of Amiens, *Carmen de Hastingae Proelio*, ed. C. Morton and H. Muntz, Oxford Medieval Texts, Oxford, 1972.

Hariulf, Chronicon Centulense, ed. F. Lot, Coll. Picard, Paris, 1894.

Hariulf, *Vita S. Arnulfi episcopi Suessionis*, ed. O. Holder-Egger, MGH, SS, 15, 2, 1888.

Hayton (Hethoum), *Flos historiarum Terre Orientis*, RHC, Doc. arm., 1.

Henry of Huntingdon, *Historia Anglorum*, ed. Th. Arnold, RS, London, 1879.

Henry of Valenciennes, *Histoire de l'empereur Henri de Constantinople*, ed. J. Longnon, Documents relatifs a l'histoire des croisades, Paris, 1948.

Herimannus Tornacensis, *Liber de restauratione S. Martini Tornacensis*, ed. G. Waitz, MGH, SS, 14, 1883, pp. 282–84.

Histoire de Guillaume le Maréchal, comte de Striguil et de Pembroke et régent d'Angleterre, ed. P. Meyer, SHF, 3 vols, Paris, 1891–1901.

Historia ducum Normanniae et regum Angliae, ed. O. Holder-Egger, MGH, SS, 26, 1882.

Historia episcoporum Autissiodorensium, RHF, 18.

Humbertus de Romanis, *De eruditione religiosorum praedicatorum*, in Maxima Bibliotheca veterum patrum, Editio Lugdunensis, 25, Lyons, 1677.

Ibn al-Athir, *Kamel-Altevarykl* (extrait), RHC, Hist. or., 1.

Isidore of Seville, *Historia Gothorum, Wandalorum, Sueborum*, ad a. DCXXIV, ed. T. Mommsen, MGH, AA, 11.

Istore et croniques de Flandre, ed. Kervyn de Lettenhove, CRH in 4°, 2 vols, Brussels, 1879–1880.

'Itinerarium peregrinorum et Gesta Ricardi regis', ed. W. Stubbs, in *Chronicles and Memorials of the Reign of Richard I*, RS, 1, 1884.

Jacques Bretel, *Le tournoi de Chauvency*, ed. M. Delbouille, BFPLUL, 49, Liège, Paris, 1932.

Jacques de Hemricourt, *Le Miroir des Nobles de la Hesbaye*, ed. C. de Borman and A. Bayot, in Oeuvres de Jacques de H., CRH in 4°, 1, Brussels, 1910.

Jan Van Heelu, *Rijmkronijk*, ed. J.F. Willems, CRH in 4°, Brussels, 1836.

Jean de Bueil, *LeJouvencel*, ed. C. Favre and L. Lecestre, SHF, 2 vols, Paris, 1887–1889.

Jean le Bel, *Chronique*, ed. J. Viard and E. Déprez, SHF, 2 vols, Paris, 1904–1905.

Joannes Saresbiriensis, *Epistolae*, ed. H.J.J. Brial, RHF, 16, 1814.

Johannes Codagnellus, *Annales Placentini*, ed. O. Holder-Egger, MGH, SS in usum scholarum, 1901.

John of Hocsem, *Chronicon*, ed. G. Kurth, CRH in 8°, Brussels, 1927.

John of Winterthur, *Chronicon*, ed. F. Baethgen, MGH, in 8°, nova series, 3, 1924.

Johnen, J. 'Philipp von Elsass', BCRH, 79, 1910, pp. 341–469.

Joinville, Jean de, *Histoire de saint Louis*, ed. N. de Wailly, SHF, Paris, 1868.

Journaux du Trésor de Philippe IV le Bel, ed. J. Viard, Collection de documents inédits sur l'histoire de France, Paris, 1940.

Lambertus Ardensis, *Historia comitum Ghisnensium*, ed. J. Heller, MGH, SS, 24, 1879.

Lambertus de Wattrelos, *Annales Cameracenses*, ed. G.H. Pertz, MGH, SS, 16, 1859.

Lampert of Hersfeld, *Annales*, ed. O. Holder-Egger, MGH, SS in usum scholarum, 1894.

Langlois, Ch. V., 'Un Mémoire inédit de Pierre du Bois, 1313: De Torneamentis et Justis', *Revue historique*, 41, 1889, pp. 84–91.

Limburg-Stirum, Th. de, *Codex diplomaticus Flandriae, 1296–1325*, 2 vols, Bruges, 1878–1889, in 4°.

Liudprand, *Antapodosis*, in *Opera*, ed. J. Becker, MGH, SS in usum scholarum, 1915.

Livre des feudataires de Jean III, duc de Brabant, Le, ed. L. Galesloot, CRH in 8°, Brussels, 1865.

Livre Roisin, Le, ed. R. Monier, Bibl. Soc. hist. droit, 2, Paris, Lille, 1932.

Lodewijk Van Velthem, *Spiegel Historiael (1248–1316)*, ed. H. Vander Linden, W. de Vreese, P. De Keyser, A. Van Loey, CRH in 4°, 3 vols, Brussels, 1906–1938.

Lois, enquêtes et jugements des Pairs du Castel de Lille, Les, ed. R. Monier, Bibl. Soc. hist, droit, 3 Lille, 1937.

Mansi, J., *Sacrorum conciliorum nova et amplissima collectio*, 21, 22, Venice, 1776–1778, in f°.

Marino Sanudo, *Liber secretorum fidelium crucis*, ed. Bongars, in Gesta Dei per Francos, 2, Hannover, 1611.

Mauricii Strategicon, ed. G.T. Dennis, Corpus Fontium Historiae Byzantinae, 17, Vienna, 1981.

Melis Stoke, *Rijmkroniek*, ed. W.G. Brill, Werken van het Historisch Genootschap gevestigd te Utrecht, 2 vols, Utrecht, 1885.

Miracula S. Rictrudis, AA. SS. Mai 3.

Miracula S. Ursmari in itinere per Flandriam facta, ed. O. Holder-Egger, MGH, SS, 15, 2, 1888.

Moran, *The anatomy of Courage*, London, 1945.

Nabholz, H., *Geschichte der Schweiz*, Zurich, 1932.

Nithard, *Historiarum libri IIII*, ed. Ph. Lauer, CHFMA, Paris, 1926.

Notae historicae Sangallenses, ed. G.H. Pertz, MGH, SS, 1, 1826.

Odo of Deuil, *De via Sancti Sepulchri a Ludovico Francorum rege inita*, ed. H. Waquet, Documents relatifs à l'histoire des croisades, Paris, 1949.

Ordericus Vitalis, *Historiae ecclesiasticae libri XIII*, ed. A. le Prevost and L. Delisle, SHF, 5 vols, Paris, 1838–1855.

Ordonnances des rois de France de la troisième race, 4, Paris, 1734.

Otto of St Blasien, *Chronica*, ed. A. Hofmeister, MGH, SS in usum scholarum, 1912.

Petrus Vallium Sarnaii monachi, *Hystoria albigensis*, ed. P. Guébin and E. Lyon, SHF, 3 vols, Paris, 1926–1939.

Philippe Mousket, *Chronique rimée*, ed. de Reiffenberg, CRH in 4°, 2 vols, Brussels, 1836–1838.

Pierre Dubois, *De recuperatione terre sancte. Traité de politique générale*, ed. Ch. V. Langlois, Coll. Picard, Paris, 1891.

De pugna Boviniensi. I. Relatio Marchianensis, ed. G. Waitz. *II. Catalogus captivorum*, ed. A. Molinier, MGH, SS, 26, 1882.

Rabanus Maurus, *De procinctu romanae militiae*, ed. Dummler, Zeitschrift für deutsches Altertum, 15, 1872.

Rahewinus, *Gesta Friderici I. Imperatoris*, ed. G. Waitz and B. von Simson, MGH, SS in usum scholarum, Hannover, 1912.

Ralph of Caen, *Gesta Tancredi in expeditione Hierosolymitana*, RHC, Hist. occ., 3.
Ralph of Coggeshall, *Chronicon anglicanum*, ed. J. Stevenson, RS, London, 1875.
Ralph de Diceto, *Opera historica*, ed. W. Stubbs, RS, 3 vols, London, 1876.
Ralph Glaber, *Historiarum libri V*, ed. M. Prou, Coll. Picard, Paris, 1886.
Raoul de Cambrai, *Chanson de geste*, ed. P. Meyer and A. Longnon, Société des anciens textes français, Paris, 1882.
Raymond of Aguilers, *Historia Francorum qui ceperunt Jherusalem*, RHC, Hist. occ., 3.
Regino of Prüm, *Chronicon*, ed. F. Kurze, MGH, SS in usum scholarum, 1890.
La règle du Temple, ed. H. de Curzon, SHF, Paris, 1886.
Reinerus, *Annales S. Jacobi Leodiensis*, ed. G.H. Pertz, MGH, SS, 16, 1859.
Richer, *Historia*, ed. R. Latouche, CHFMA, 2 vols, Paris, 1930–1937.
Rigord, *Gesta Philippi Augusti*, ed. H.F. Delaborde, SHF, 1, Paris, 1882.
Robert de Clari, *La conquête de Constantinople*, ed. Ph. Lauer, CFMA, Paris, 1924.
Robert of Auxerre, *Chronicon*, cum continuationibus, ed. O. Holder-Egger, MGH, SS, 26, 1882.
Robert of Torigni, *Chronicle*, ed. R. Howlett, RS, London, 1889.
Robert the Monk, *Historia Hierosolymitana*, RHC, Hist. occ., 3.
Roger of Hoveden, *Chronica*, ed. W. Stubbs, RS, 4 vols, London, 1868–1871.
Roger of Wendover, *Flores Historiarum*, ed. G. Hewlett, RS, 3 vols, London, 1886–1889.
*H. de Romanis, *De eruditione religiosorum praedicatorum*, Maxima bibliotheca veterum patrum 25, Lyons, 1677.
St-Genois, J. de, *Inventaire analytique des chartes des comtes de Flandre*, Ghent, 1843–1846.
S. Bernardus, *De laude novae militiae*, PL, 182.
S. Bernardus, *Epistolae*, ed. L. Delisle, RHF, 15, 1878.
Sarrasin, *Le Roman du Hem*, ed. A Henry, Travaux de la faculté de philosophie et lettres de l'Université de Bruxelles, 9, Brussels, 1939.
Scripta de feodis ad regem spectantibus, RHF, 23, p. 693, c. 23.
Sdralek, M., 'Wolfenbüttler Fragmente', in Knöpfler, Schrörs, Sdralek, *Kirchengeschichtliche Studien*, 1, 2, Munster, 1891.
Select Charters, ed. W. Stubbs, 9th edn, Oxford, 1913.
Le siège de Barbastre, ed. J.L. Perrier, CFMA, Paris, 1926.
Sigebertus Gemblacensis, *Chronica, cum continuationibus; Auctarium Affligemense; Auctarium Hasnoniense*, ed. L.C. Bethmann, MGH, SS, 6, 1944.
Sigebertus Gemblacensis Chronographiae Auctarium Affligemense, ed. P. Gorissen, AWLSK, Verhandelingen, 15, 1952.
Simon, *Gesta abbatum S. Bertini Sithiensium (1021–1145)*, ed. O. Holder-Egger, MGH, SS, 13, 1881.
Stenton, D.M., *English Society in the Early Middle Ages (1066–1307)*, Harmondsworth, 1951.
Strategikon, in *Arriani Tactica et Mauricii Ars Militaris libri duodecim*, ed. J. Scheffer, Upsala, 1664.
Suger, *Historia gloriosi regis Ludovici*, ed. A. Molinier, Coll, Picard, Paris, 1887.
Suger, *Vita Ludovici grossi regis*, ed. H. Waquet, CHFMA, Paris, 1929.
Tacitus, *Germania*, ed. J. Perret, Coll. Budé, Paris, 1949.
Teulet, A., *Layettes du trésor des chartes*, 1, Paris, 1863.

Thietmar of Merseburg, *Chronicon*, ed. R. Holtzmann, MGH, SS, nova series, 9, Berlin, 1935.

Thomas Gray of Heton, *see* Gray of Heton.

Vegetius: Flavius Vegetius Renatus, *Epitoma rei militaris*, ed. C. Lang, Stuttgart, 1967.

Verbruggen, J.F., 'Un projet d'ordonnance comtale sur la conduite de la guerre, pendant le soulèvement de la Flandre maritime', *BCRH*, 118, 1953, pp. 115–36.

Villani, Giovanni, *Historie Fiorentine*, ed. L.A. Muratori, *Rerum Italicarum Scriptores*, 13.

Villehardouin, *La conquête de Constantinople*, ed. E. Faral, CHFMA, 2 vols, Paris, 1938–1939.

Vita Heinrici IV imperatoris, ed. W. Eberhard, MGH, SS in usum scholarum, 1899.

Vita Odiliae (De triumpho S. Lamberti in Steppes), ed. J. Heller, MGH, SS, 25, 1880.

Vitae Paparum Avenoniensium, ed. G. Mollat, 4 vols, Paris, 1914–1922.

Wace, *Roman de Rou et des ducs de Normandie*, ed. H. Andresen, 2 vols, Heilbronn, 1878–1879.

Wailly, N. de, *Mémoire sur un opuscule, intitulé: Summaria brevis et compendiosa doctrina felicis expeditionis et abbreviationis guerrarum ac litium regni Francorum*, Mémoires de l'Académie des Inscriptions et Belles-Lettres, 18, 2, pp. 435–94.

Walter Map, *Liber de nugis curialium*, ed. R. Pauli, MGH, SS, 27, 1885.

Walterus Tervacensis, *Vita Caroli boni comitis Flandriae*, ed. R. Köpke, MGH, SS, 12, 1856.

Wartmann, H., *Urkundenbuch der Abtei St Gallen*, 1, Zurich, 1863.

Wavell, *The Good Soldier*, London, 1948.

Widukind of Corvey, *Rerum gestarum Saxonicarum libri tres*, ed. H.E. Lohmann and P. Hirsch, MGH, SS in usum scholarum, 1935.

Wilbrand of Oldenburg, *Peregrinatio*, ed. J.M.C. Laurent, in *Peregrinatores Medii Aevi quatuor*, Leipzig, 1864, in 4°.

Wilhelmus Andrensis, *Chronica Andrensis*, ed. J. Heller, MGH, SS, 24, 1879.

William of Jumièges, *Gesta Normannorum ducum*, ed. J. Marx, Société d'histoire de la Normandie, Rouen, Paris, 1914.

William of Malmesbury, *De gestis regum Anglorum, libri V: Historiae novellae libri III*, ed. W. Stubbs, RS, 2 vols, London, 1887–1889.

William of Newburgh, *Historia rerum anglicarum*, ed. R. Howlett, RS, 2 vols, London, 1884–1885.

William of Poitiers, *Gesta Guillelmi ducis Normannorum et regis Anglorum*, ed. R. Foreville, CHFMA, Paris, 1952.

William of Tudèle, *La chanson de la croisade albigeoise*, 1, ed. E. Martin-Chabot, CHFMA, Paris, 1931.

William of Tyre, *Historia rerum in partibus transmarinis gestarum*, RHC, Hist. occ., 1, 2 vols.

William the Breton, *I. Chronicon. II. Philippis*, in *Oeuvres de Rigord et Guillaume le Breton*, ed. R.F. Delaborde, SHF, 2 vols, Paris, 1882–1885.

Secondary Works

Abel, S., and Simson, B. von, *Jahrbücher des fränkischen Reiches unter Karl den Groszen*, 2 vols, Leipzig, 1883–1888.

Atiya, A.S., *The Crusade in the later Middle Ages*, London, 1938.

Aubenas, R., 'Les châteaux-forts des Xe et XIe siècles', *Revue historique du droit français et étranger*, 4th series, 17, 1938, pp. 548–586.

Bachrach, B.S., 'The Alans in Gaul', *Traditio*, 23, 1967, pp. 476–89.

Bachrach, B.S., 'The Origin of Armorican Chivalry', *Technology and Culture*, 10, 1969, pp. 166–71.

Bachrach, B.S., 'Charles Martel, Mounted Shock Combat, the Stirrup, and Feudalism', *Studies in Medieval and Renaissance History*, 7, 1970, pp. 49–75.

Bachrach, B.S., 'The Feigned Retreat at Hastings', *Mediaeval Studies*, 33, 1971, pp. 344–7.

Bachrach, B.S., *Merovingian Military Organization, 481–751*, Minneapolis, 1972.

Bachrach, B.S., 'Early Medieval Fortifications in the "West" of France: A Revised Technical Vocabulary', *Technology and Culture*, 16, 1975, pp. 531–69.

Bachrach, B.S., 'Fortifications and Military Tactics: Fulk Nerra's Strongholds circa 1000', *Technology and Culture*, 20, 1979, pp. 531–49.

Bachrach, B.S., 'Charlemagne's Cavalry: Myth and Reality', *Military Affairs*, 47, 1983, pp. 181–7.

Bachrach, B.S., 'The Angevin Strategy of Castle Building in the Reign of Fulk Nerra, 987–1040', *The American Historical Review*, 88, 1983, pp. 533–60.

Bachrach, B.S., 'Some Observations on the Military Administration of the Norman Conquest', *Proceedings of the Battle Conference on Anglo-Norman Studies*, 8, 1985, pp. 1–25.

Bachrach, B.S., 'On the Origins of William the Conqueror's Horse Transports', *Technology and Culture*, 26, 1985, pp. 505–31.

Bachrach, B.S., 'Animals and Warfare in Early Medieval Europe', SSCI, 31, Spoleto, 1985, pp. 707–64.

Bachrach, B.S., '*Caballus et Caballarius* in Medieval Warfare', in *The Study of Chivalry*, ed. H. Chickering, Kalamazoo, MI, 1986, pp. 173–211.

Backer, L. De, *L'Extrême-Orient au moyen âge*, Paris, 1877.

Balon, J., 'L'organisation militaire des Namurois au XIVe siècle', *Annales de la Société archéologique de Namur*, 40, 1932, pp. 1–86.

Bédier, J., *Les légendes épiques. Recherches sur la formation des chansons de geste*, 3rd edn, 4 vols, Paris, 1926–1929.

Beeler, J., *Warfare in England, 1066–1189*, Ithaca, New York, 1966.

Beeler, J., *Warfare in Feudal Europe, 730–1200*, Ithaca, London, 1971.

Belperron, P., *La croisade contre les Albigeois et l'union du Languedoc à la France (1209–1249)*, Paris, 1942.

Blair, C., *European Armour*, Batsford, 1958.

Bloch, M., *La société féodale. La formation des liens de dépendance* and *La société féodale. Les classes et le gouvernement des hommes*, in *L'évolution de l'humanité*, 34, 34bis, 2 vols, Paris, 1949.

Boudet, J., ed., *The Ancient Art of Warfare*, 2 vols, London, n.d.

Boussard, J., *Les mercenaires au XIIe siècle. Henri II Plantagenêt et les origines de l'armée de métier*, Bibl. Ec. Chartes, 106, 1945–1946, pp. 189–224.

Boussard, J., 'Services féodaux, milices et mercenaires dans les armées, en France, aux Xe et XIe siècles', SSCI, 15, 1, Spoleto, 1968, pp. 131–68.

Boutaric, E., *Institutions militaires de la France avant les armées permanentes*, Paris, 1863.

Bradbury, J., *The Medieval Archer*, Woodbridge, 1985.

Bradbury, J., *The Medieval Siege*, Woodbridge, 1992.

Brandt, C.D.J., *Kruisvaarders naar Jeruzalem*, Utrecht, 1950.

Brooks, F.W., *The Battle of Stamford Bridge*, York, 1956.

Brown, R. Allen, 'The Battle of Hastings', *Proceedings of the Battle Conference on Anglo-Norman Studies*, 3, 1980, pp. 1–21, 197–201.

Brown, R. Allen, 'The Norman Conquest', *TRHS*, Fifth Series, 17, London, 1967, pp. 109–30.

Bünding, M., 'Das Imperium Christianum und die deutschen Ostkriege vom zehnten bis zum zwölften Jahrhundert', *Historische Studien herausgegeben von Dr Emil Ebering*, Heft 366, Berlin, 1940.

Bullough, D.A., '*Europae Pater*: Charlemagne and his achievement in the light of recent scholarship', *EHR*, 75, 1970, pp. 84–90.

Buttin, F., 'La lance et l'arrêt de cuirasse', *Archaeologia*, 99, 1965, pp. 77–178.

Calmette, J., *Le monde féodal*, Coll. Clio, Paris, 1937.

Calmette, J., *La société féodale*, Paris, 1942.

Cartellieri, A., *Philipp II. August, König von Frankreich*, 5 vols, Leipzig, 1899–1922.

Chibnall, M., 'Military Service in Normandy before 1066', *Proceedings of the Battle Conference on Anglo-Norman Studies*, 5, 1982, pp. 65–77.

Clausewitz, Carl von, *Vom Kriege*, 16th edn, by W. Hahlweg, Bonn, 1952.

Clausewitz, Carl von, *On War*, ed. and transl. M. Howard and Peter Paret, Princeton, New Jersey, 1976.

Cohen, G., *Histoire de la chevalerie en France au moyen âge*, Paris, 1949.

Conrad, H., *Geschichte der deutschen Wehrverfassung*, 1, Munich, 1939.

Contamine, P., *Guerre, Etat et société à la fin du moyen âge. Etudes sur les armées des rois de France, 1337–1494*, Paris, The Hague, 1972.

Contamine, P., *La guerre au moyen âge*, Paris, 1980.

Coville, A., 'L'Europe occidentale de 1270 à 1380. II. 1328 à 1380', in G. Glotz, Histoire générale. Histoire du moyen âge, 6, Paris, 1941.

Cram, K.-G., *Iudicium Belli. Zum Rechtscharakter des Krieges im deutschen Mittelalter*, Munster, Cologne, 1955.

Crosland, J., *William the Marshal*, London, 1962.

Cru, J.N., *Du témoignage*, Paris, 1930.

Cru, J.N., *Témoins. Essai d'analyse et de critique des souvenirs de combattants édités en français de 1915 à 1928*, Paris, 1930.

Curry, A. & Hughes, M., eds, *Arms, Armies and Fortifications in the Hundred Years War*, Woodbridge, 1994.

Daniels, E., *Geschichte des Kriegswesens. II. Das mittelalterliche Kriegswesen*, Sammlung Göschen, 498, 2nd edn, Berlin, Leipzig, 1927.

Delaville le Roulx, J., *La France en Orient au XIVe siècle*, 2 vols, Paris, 1885.

Delbrück, H., *Geschichte der Kriegskunst im Rahmen der politischen Geschichte*, 3, Berlin, 2nd edn, 1923.

Delpech, H., *La tactique au XIIIe siècle*, 2 vols, Paris, 1886.

Denholm-Young, N., 'The Tournament in the Thirteenth Century', in *Studies in medieval History presented to F.M. Powicke*, Oxford, 1948, pp. 240–68.

Deprez, R., 'La politique castrale dans la principauté épiscopale de Liège du Xe au XIVe siècle', *Le Moyen Age*, 65, 1959, pp. 501–38.

Douglas, D.C., 'William the Conqueror: Duke and King', in D. Whitelock, D.C. Douglas,

C.H. Lemmon, F. Barlow, *The Norman Conquest. Its Setting and Impact*, London, 1966, pp. 45–76.

Drummond, J.D., 'Studien zur Kriegsgeschichte Englands im 12. Jahrhundert', Berliner Dissertation, 1905.

Duby, G., *Le dimanche de Bouvines*, Paris, 1973.

Duby, G., *Guerriers et paysans. VIIe–XIIe siècle*, Paris, 1973.

Duby, G., *Guillaume le Maréchal*, Paris, 1984.

Duby, G., *La société chevaleresque*, Paris, 1979.

Dunan, M.E., 'Les châteaux-forts du comté de Luxembourg et les progrès dans leur défense sous Jean l'Aveugle. 1309–1346', *Publications de la Section historique de l'Institut Grand-Ducal de Luxembourg*, 70, Luxembourg, 1950.

Durrer, R., 'Premiers combats de la Suisse primitive pour la liberté', in M. Feldmann and H.G. Wirz, eds, *Histoire militaire de la Suisse*, 1er Cahier, Berne, 1915.

Duyse, H. Van, 'Le goedendag, arme flamande. Sa légende et son histoire', *Annales du Cercle historique et archéologique de Gand*, 2, 1896, pp. 1–65.

Erben, W., 'Kriegsgeschichte des Mittelalters', *Historische Zeitschrift*, Beiheft 16, Berlin, 1929.

Erdmann, C., 'Die Burgenordnung Heinrichs I', *Deutsches Archiv*, 6, 1943, pp. 59–101.

Espinas, G., *Une guerre sociale interurbaine dans la Flandre wallonne au XIIIe siècle. Douai et Lille, 1284–1285*, Bibl. Soc. hist. droit, Paris, Lille, 1930.

Fawtier, R., *La chanson de Roland. Etude historique*, Paris, 1933.

Fawtier, R., *L'Europe occidentale de 1270 à 1380. Première partie. De 1270 à 1328*, in G. Glotz, Histoire générale. Histoire du moyen âge, 6, Paris, 1940.

Feuchère, P., *Contribution à l'étude de l'origine des villes. Les castra et les noyaux pré-urbains en Artois du IXe au XIe siècle*, Arras, 1949.

Finó, J.-F., *Forteresses de la France médiévale. Construction, attaque, défense*, Paris, 3rd edn, 1977.

France, J., 'La guerre dans la France féodale à la fin du IXe et au Xe siècles', *RBHM*, 23, 1979, pp. 177–98.

France, J., 'The military history of the Carolingian period', *RBHM*, 26, 1985, pp. 81–100.

Frauenholz, E. von, *Entwicklungsgeschichte des deutschen Heerwesens*, Munich, 2 t. in 3 vols, 1935–1937. *I. Das Heerwesen der germanischen Frühzeit, das Frankenreiches und das ritterlichen Zeitalters*.

Fris, V., 'Blavotins et Ingherkins. Une guerre privée dans la Flandre maritime au XIIe siècle', *Bull. de la société d'histoire et d'archéologie de Gand*, 14, 1906, pp. 133–85.

Fris, V., *De slag bij Kortrijk*, Kon. Vlaamse Academie, Ghent, 1902.

Funck-Brentano, F., 'De exercituum commeatibus tercio decimo et quarto decimo saeculis post Christum natum', Thesis, Paris, 1897.

Funck-Brentano, F., *Féodalité et chevalerie*, Paris, 1946.

Funck-Brentano, F., 'Mémoire sur la bataille de Courtrai (1302, 11 juillet) et les chroniqueurs qui en ont traité pour servir à l'historiographie du règne de Philippe le Bel', Mémoires de l'Académie des Inscriptions et Belles-Lettres (Savants étrangers), 1re série, 10, 1, 1894, pp. 235–326.

Funck-Brentano, F., *Philippe le Bel en Flandre*, Paris, 1897.

Gaier, C., *Art et organisation militaires dans la principauté de Liège et dans le comté de Looz au Moyen Age*, Ac. roy. Belg., Cl. Lettres, Mém., in 8º, 59, Brussels, 1968.

Gaier, C., *Les armes*, Typologie des sources du moyen âge occidental, 34, Turnhout, 1979.

Gaier, C., 'La cavalerie en Europe occidentale du XIIe au XIVe siècle: un problème de mentalité', *RIHM*, 1971, pp. 385–96.

Gaier, C., *L'Industrie et le Commerce des Armes dans les Anciennes Principautés belges du XIIIe à la fin du XVème siècle*, BFPLUL, 202, Liège, Paris, 1973.

Ganshof, F.L., 'L'armée sous les Carolingiens', SSCI, 15, 1, Spoleto, 1968, pp. 109–30.

Ganshof, F.L., 'La cavalerie dans les armées de Charlemagne', Académie des Inscriptions et Belles-Lettres. Comptes rendus, 1952, pp. 531–6.

Ganshof, F.L., *The Carolingians and the Frankish Monarchy. Studies in Carolingian History*, transl. J. Sondheimer, London, 1971.

Ganshof, F.L., *Les destinées de l'Empire en Occident de 395 à 888*, in G. Glotz, Histoire générale. Histoire du moyen âge, 1, 2, 2nd edn, Paris, 1941.

Ganshof, F.L., *Qu'est-ce que la Féodalité?* 2nd edn, Brussels, 1947.

Ganshof, F.L., *Frankish Institutions under Charlemagne*, ed. and transl. Bryce and Mary Lyon, Providence, R.I., 1968.

Gautier, L., *La chevalerie*, 3rd edn, Paris, 1895, in 4°.

Géraud, H., 'Les routiers au XIIe siècle', Bibl. Ec. Chart., 3, 1841–1842, pp. 125–47.

Géraud, H., 'Mercadier. Les routiers au XIIIe siècle', ibid., pp. 417–47.

Glover, R., 'English Warfare in 1066', *EHR*, 67, 1952, pp. 1–18.

Gorissen, P., 'De Karweien der Brabantsche Kloosterhoeven in de XIVe eeuw', *BCRH*, 110, 1945, pp. 1–50.

Grousset, R., *Histoire des croisades*, 3 vols, Paris, 1935–1936.

Grundmann, H., 'Rotten and Brabanzonen, Söldnerheeren im 12. Jahrhundert', *Deutsches Archiv für Geschichte des Mittelalters*, 5, 1942, pp. 419–92.

Guilhiermoz, P., *Essai sur l'origine de la noblesse en France au moyen âge*, Paris, 1902.

Halkin, L.E., 'Pour une histoire de l'honneur', Annales, Economies, Sociétés, Civilisations, 4, 1949, pp. 433–44.

Hardy, E., *Les origines de la tactique française*, 2 vols, Paris, 1879.

Hay, D., 'The Division of the Spoils of War in XIVth Century England', *TRHS*, 5th Series, 4, 1954, pp. 91–109.

Heermann, O., 'Die Gefechtsführung abendländischer Heere im Orient in der Epoche des ersten Kreuzzuges', Dissertation, Marburg, 1887.

Hefele, C.J. von, *Conciliengeschichte*, 5, Freiburg, 1886.

Hemelrijck, M. Van, *De Vlaamse Krijgsbouwkunde*, Tielt, 1950.

Henrard, P., 'Les mercenaires dits Brabançons au moyen âge', *Annales de l'Académie d'Archéologie de Belgique*, 22, 2e série, 2, 1866, pp. 416–35.

Hewitt, H.J., *The Organization of War under Edward III*, Manchester, New York, 1966.

Hollister, C.W., *Anglo-Saxon Military Institutions*, Oxford, 1962.

Hollister, C.W., *The Military Organization of Norman England*, Oxford, 1965.

Huizinga, J., *The Waning of the Middle Ages*, London, 1924.

Jähns, M., *Handbuch einer Geschichte des Kriegswesens von der Urzeit bis zur Renaissance*, 1, Leipzig, 1880.

Jahn, R., 'Die Schlacht bei Worringen', Berliner Dissertation, 1907.

Joris, A., 'Remarques sur les clauses militaires des privilèges urbains liégeois', *RBPH*, 37, 1959, pp. 297–316.

Koch, H.W., *Medieval Warfare*, London, 1978.

Koechlin, H., *Chapelle de la Leugemeete à Gand. Peintures murales. Restitution*, Ghent, 1936.

Köhler, G., *Die Entwickelung des Kriegswesens und der Kriegführung in der Ritterzeit von Mitte des 11. Jahrhunderts bis zu den Hussitenkriegen*, 3 t. in 5 vols, Breslau, 1886–1889; *Ergänzungsheft, die Schlachten von Tagliacozzo und Courtrai betreffend*, Breslau, 1893.

Kurth, G., *La cité de Liège au moyen âge*, 1, 2, Liège, Brussels, 1910.

Labande, E.-R., *Rinaldo Orsini, comte de Tagliacozzo*, Monaco, Paris, 1939.

Lachauvelaye, J., *Guerres des Français et des Anglais du XIe au XVe siècle*, 2 vols, Paris, 1875.

Lammers, W., *Die Schlacht bei Hemmingstedt. Freies Bauerntum und Fürstenmacht im Nordseeraum*, Quellen und Forschungen zur Geschichte Schleswig-Holsteins, 28, Neumünster, Heide in Holstein, 1954.

Langlois, Ch. V., 'Le service militaire en vertu de l'obligation féodale', in *L'armée à travers les âges*, 3 t., Paris, 1899–1902, t. I, pp. 63–86.

Lecoy de la Marche, A., *La chaire française au moyen âge*, Paris, 1868.

Lefebvre des Noëttes, *L'attelage. Le cheval de selle à travers les âges*, 2 vols, Paris, 1931.

Lemmon, C.H., 'The Campaign of 1066', in D. Whitelock, D.C. Douglas, C.H. Lemmon, F. Barlow, *The Norman Conquest. Its Setting and Impact*, London, 1966, pp. 79–122.

Lemmon, C.H., *The Field of Hastings*, St Leonards-on-Sea, 4th edn, 1970.

Lewis, N.B., 'The English Forces in Flanders, August–November 1297', in *Studies in medieval History presented to F.M. Powicke*, Oxford, 1948, pp. 310–18.

Lewis, N.B., 'The Organisation of indentured Retinues in fourteenth-century England', *TRHS*, 4th Series, 27, 1945, pp. 29–39.

Lot, F., *L'art militaire et les armées au moyen âge en Europe et dans le Proche-Orient*, 2 vols, Paris, 1946.

Lot, F., *Les destinées de l'Empire en Occident de 395 à 888*. 1, in: G. Glotz, Histoire générale. Histoire du Moyen Age, Paris, 1940.

Lot, F., *La France des origines à la guerre de Cent ans*, Paris, 1941.

Lot, F., *La Gaule*, Paris, 1947.

Lot, F., 'La langue du commandement dans les armées romaines et le cri de guerre français au moyen âge', *Mélanges Félix Grat*, 1, Paris, 1946, pp. 203–09.

Lot, F., *Les invasions germaniques. La pénétration mutuelle du monde barbare et du monde romain*, Paris, 3rd edn, 1945.

Luchaire, A., *Les communes françaises à l'époque des Capétiens directs*, Paris, 1890.

Lyon, B., 'The dividends from war in the Low Countries (1338–1340)', in *Peasants & Townsmen in medieval Europe. Studia in honorem Adriaan Verhulst*, ed. J.M. Duvosquel, E. Thoen, Ghent, 1995, pp. 693–705.

Lyon, B., 'The role of cavalry in medieval warfare: horses, horses all around and not a one to use', in *Mededelingen AWLSK, Academiae Analecta*, 49, 1987, pp. 77–90.

Maere d'Aertrycke, M. de, *De la Colme au Boulenrieu*, Namur, 1935.

Mas Latrie, L. de, *Histoire de l'île de Chypre sous le règne des princes de la maison de Lusignan*, 2, Paris, 1852.

Mens, A., 'De "Brabanciones" of bloeddorstige en plunderzieke avonturiers', *Miscellanea historica in honorem A. de Meyer*, 1, Louvain, Brussels, 1946, pp. 558–70.

Meyer, H., *Die Militärpolitik Friedrich Barbarossas im Zusammenhang mit seiner Italienpolitik*, Historische Studien herausgegeben von Dr Emil Ebering, Heft 200, Berlin, 1930.

Morris, J.E., 'Mounted Infantry in medieval Warfare', *TRHS*, Third Series, 8, 1914, pp. 77–102.

Morris, J.E., *The Welsh Wars of Edward I*, Oxford, 1901.

Norgate, K., 'William of Ypres', in *The Dictionary of National Biography*, 21, London, 1937–1938.

Oman, Sir Charles, *A History of the Art of War in the Middle Ages*, 2nd edn, 2 vols, London, 1924.

Painter, S., *French Chivalry*, Baltimore, 1940.

Painter, S., *William Marshal, Knight-Errant, Baron, and Regent of England*, Baltimore, 1933.

Palmer, J.J.N., ed., *Froissart: Historian*, Woodbridge, 1981.

Perroy, E., *The Hundred Years War*, New York, 1951.

Petit-Dutaillis, C., 'Les communes françaises. Caractères et évolution des origines au XVIIIe siècle', in *L'évolution de l'humanité*, 44, Paris, 1947.

Pieri, P., 'Alcune quistioni sopre la Fanteria in Italia nel periodo comunale', Rivista storica Italiana, series 4, 4, 1933, pp. 561–614.

Pieri, P., *Il Rinascimento e la crisi militare italiana*, Milan, 1952.

Pirenne, H., *Histoire de Belgique*, illustrated edition, 1, Brussels, 1948, in f °.

Pirenne, H., *Le soulèvement de la Flandre maritime de 1323–1328*, CRH in 8°, Brussels, 1900.

Poole, A.L., 'From Domesday Book to Magna Carta, 1087–1216', in *The Oxford History of England*, Oxford, 1951.

Powicke, M., *The Thirteenth Century, ibid.*, Oxford, 1953.

Prestwich, J.O., 'War and Finance in the Anglo-Norman State', *TRHS*, 5th Series, 4, 1954, pp. 19–43.

Prestwich, M., *War, Politics and Finance under Edward I*, London, 1972.

Prinz, F., *Klerus und Krieg im früheren Mittelalter. Untersuchungen zur Rolle der Kirche beim Aufbau der Königsherrschaft*, Stuttgart, 1971.

Riché, P., *La vie quotidienne dans l'empire carolingien*, Paris, 1973.

Rolland, P., *Tournai 'Noble Cité'*, Brussels, 1944.

Roncière, Ch. de la, *Histoire de la marine française*, 1, Paris, 1899.

Round, J.H., *Geoffrey de Mandeville. A Study of the Anarchy*, London, 1892.

Rousseau, F., 'La Meuse et le pays mosan en Belgique. Leur importance historique avant le XIIIe siècle', Annales de la Société archéologique de Namur, 39, Namur, 1930.

Rousset, P., *Les origines et les caractères de la première croisade*, Neuchâtel, 1945.

Roy, J.-H., Deviosse, J., *La Bataille de Poitiers, 733*, Paris, 1966.

Runciman, S., *A History of the Crusades*, 3 vols, Cambridge, 1951–1954.

Sandberger, D., *Studien über das Rittertum in England vornehmlich während des 14. Jahrhunderts*, Historische Studien herausgegeben von Dr Emil Ebering, Heft 310, Berlin, 1937.

Sander, E., 'Der Belagerungskrieg im Mittelalter', *Historische Zeitschrift*, 165, 1941–1942, pp. 99–110.

Sanders, I.J., *Feudal Military service in England*, Oxford, 1956.

Schaufelberger, W., *Der Alte Schweizer und sein Krieg. Studien zur Kriegführung vornehmlich im 15. Jahrhundert*, Zurich, 1952.

Schmithenner, P., *Krieg und Kriegführung im Wandel der Weltgeschichte*, Potsdam, 1930.

Schmithenner, P., *Freien Söldnertum des abendländischen Imperiums des Mittelalters*, Münchener Historische Abhandlungen. II. Reihe, Heft 4, Munich, 1934.

Schneider, H., 'Die Neugestaltung der Waffenhalle im Schweizerischen Landesmuseum in Zürich', *RIHM*, 9, 1950, pp. 351–6.

Schünemann, K., 'Deutsche Kriegführung im Osten während des Mittelalters', *Deutsches Archiv fur Geschichte des Mittelalters*, 2, 1938, pp. 54–84.

Sivéry, G., 'L'enquête de 1247 et les dommages de guerre en Tournaisis, en Flandre gallicante et en Artois', *Revue du Nord*, 59, 1977, pp. 7–17.

Six, G., 'La bataille de Mons-en-Pévèle', *Annales de l'Est et du Nord*, 1, 1905, pp. 210–33.

Slicher van Bath, B.H., *Boerenvrijheid*, Groningen, 1948.

Smail, R.C. 'Art of War', in *Medieval England*, ed. by A.L. Poole, 1, Oxford, 1958, pp. 128–67.

Smail, R.C., *Crusading Warfare (1097–1193)*, Cambridge, 1956.

Smets, G., *Henri Ier, duc de Brabant (1190–1235)*, Brussels, 1908.

Spatz, W., *Die Schlacht von Hastings*, Berlin, 1896.

Sproemberg, H., 'Die feudale Kriegskunst', in *Beiträge zur Belgisch-Niederländischen Geschichte, Forschungen zur Mittelalterlichen Geschichte*, 3, Berlin, 1959, pp. 30–55.

Stein, H., *Archers d'autrefois, archers d'aujourd'hui*, Paris, 1925, in 4°.

Stenton, F.M., 'Anglo-Saxon England', in *The Oxford History of England*, 2nd edn, Oxford, 1947.

Stenton, F.M., *The first Century of English Feudalism, 1066–1166*, Oxford, 1932.

Strickland, M., ed., *Anglo-Norman Warfare. Studies in Late Anglo-Saxon and Anglo-Norman Military Organization and Warfare*, Woodbridge, 1992.

Thordemann, B., Nörlund, P., Ingelmark, B.E., *Armour from the Battle of Wisby, 1361*, 2 vols, in 4°, Stockholm, 1939.

Tourneur-Aumont, J.M., *La bataille de Poitiers (1356) et la construction de la France*, Poitiers, 1940.

Tout, T.F., 'Some neglected Fights between Crécy and Poitiers', *The Collected Papers of T.F. Tout*, II, Manchester, 1934, pp. 227–31.

Tout, T.F., 'The Tactics of the Battles of Boroughbridge and Morlaix', *ibid.*, pp. 221–5.

Tout, T.F., *The Place of the Reign of Edward II in English History*, Manchester, 1914.

Vanderkindere, L., *Le siècle des Artevelde. Etudes sur la civilisation morale et politique de la Flandre et du Brabant*, Brussels, 1879.

Verbruggen, J.F., 'La tactique militaire des armées de chevaliers', *Revue du Nord*, 29, 1947, pp. 161–80.

Verbruggen, J.F., 'De Gentse minderbroeder der Annales Gandenses en de krijgskunst in de periode 1302–1304', *Handelingen Maatschappij voor Geschiedenis en Oudheidkunde te Gent. Nieuwe reeks*, 4, 1949, pp. 3–19.

Verbruggen, J.F., 'Le problème des effectifs et de la tactique à la bataille de Bouvines en 1214', *Revue du Nord*, 31, 1949, pp. 181–93.

Verbruggen, J.F., *De slag der gulden sporen. Bijdrage tot de geschiedenis van Vlaanderens vrijheidsoorlog, 1297–1305*, Antwerp, Amsterdam, 1952.

Verbruggen, J.F., 'L'art militaire en Europe occidentale du IXe au XIVe siècle', *RIHM*, 16, 1955, pp. 486–96.

Verbruggen, J.F., 'De militaire dienst in het graafschap Vlaanderen', *Revue d'histoire du droit*, 26, 1958, pp. 437–65.

Verbruggen, J.F., *Het leger en de vloot van de graven van Vlaanderen vanaf het ontstaan tot in 1305*, AWLSK, Verhandelingen, 38, 1960.

Verbruggen, J.F., 'La tactique de la chevalerie française de 1340 à 1415', *Publications de l'Université de l'Etat à Elisabethville*, 1, 1961, pp. 39–48.

Verbruggen, J.F., *Het gemeenteleger van Brugge van 1338 tot 1340 en de Namen van de weerbare mannen*, CRH in 8º, Brussels, 1962.

Verbruggen, J.F., 'L'armée et la stratégie de Charlemagne', in *Karl der Grosse*, ed. W. Braunfels, 1, Dusseldorf, 1965, pp. 420–36.

Verbruggen, J.F., 'L'art militaire dans l'empire carolingien (714–1000)', *RBHM*, 23, 1979, 1980, pp. 289–310, 393–412.

Verbruggen, J.F., 'De getalsterkte van de ambachten in het Brugse gemeenteleger (1297–1340)', *RBHM*, 25, 1984, pp. 461–80.

Verbruggen, J.F., '*1302 in Vlaanderen. De Guldensporenslag*', CHM. Travaux, 13, Brussels, 1977.

Verbruggen, J.F., *Vlaanderen na de Guldensporenslag. De vrijheidsstrijd van het graafschap Vlaanderen, 1303–1305*, Bruges, 1991.

Verbruggen, J.F., 'De slag bij de Pevelenberg (18 aug. 1304)', *Bijdragen voor de geschiedenis der Nederlanden*, 6, 1952, pp. 169–98, and *Het Leger. De Natie*, 7, Brussels, 1952, pp. 258–62, pp. 338–42.

Verbruggen, J.F., *De slag bij Guinegate, 7 augustus 1479*, CHM. Travaux, 27, Brussels, 1993.

Verbruggen, J.F., 'De rol van de ruiterij in de middeleeuwse oorlogvoering', *RBHM*, 30, 1994, pp. 389–418.

Vercauteren, F., 'Comment s'est-on défendu, au IXe siècle dans l'empire franc contre les invasions normandes?', *Annales du XXXe Congrès de la Fédération archéologique et historique de Belgique*, 2, Brussels, 1936, pp. 117–32.

Vercauteren, F., *Luttes sociales à Liège*, Brussels, 1943.

Verlinden, Ch., *Robert Ier le Frison, comte de Flandre*, Univ. Gent. Werken uitgegeven door de Faculteit van Wijsbegeerte en Letteren, 72, Antwerp, Paris, The Hague, 1935.

Vermeersch, A., 'Les oppida en Brabant, 1123–1355', *Anciens Pays et Assemblées d'Etats*, 22, 1961, pp. 31–46.

Verriest, L., *Les luttes sociales et le contrat d'apprentissage à Tournai jusqu'en 1424*, Brussels, 1912.

Vigne, F., de, *Recherches historiques sur les costumes civils et militaires des gildes et des corporations de métiers*, Ghent, 1847.

Wauters, A., *Le duc Jean Ier et le Brabant sous le règne de ce prince (1267–1294)*, Ac. roy. Belg., Mém., 13, Brussels, Liège, 1862.

Wauters, A., 'La formation d'une armée brabançonne du temps du duc Jean III, de 1338 à 1339', *BCRH*, 5th series, 1891, pp. 192–205.

Werner, K.F., 'Heeresorganisation und Kriegführung im deutschen Königreich des 10. und 11. Jahrhunderts', SSCI, 15, 2, Spoleto, 1968, pp. 791–843.

Werveke, A. Van, *Het Godshuis van Sint-Jan en Sint-Pauwel te Gent*, Maatschappij der Vlaamse Bibliophilen, 4th series, 15, Ghent, 1909, and a vol. of plates.

Werveke, H. Van, *Gand. Esquisse d'histoire sociale*, Brussels, 1946.

White, Lynn, Jr, *Medieval Technology and Social Change*, Oxford, 1962.

Willems L., 'Notes sur la querelle des Blauvoets et des Isengrins', *Bull. de la Société d'histoire et d'archéologie de Gand*, 14, 6, 1906, pp. 253–90.

Wise, T., *Medieval Warfare*, London, 1976.

Wise, T., *The Wars of the Crusades. 1096–1291*, London, 1978.

Wodsak, F., 'Die Schlacht bei Kortrijk', Berliner Dissertation, 1905.
Wyffels, C., *De oorsprong der ambachten in Vlaanderen en Brabant*, AWLSKB, Verhandelingen, 13, 1951.

INDEX

Printed and bound by CPI Group (UK) Ltd, Croydon, CR0 4YY

13/04/2025

14656522-0004